P9-ARC-945

Countries of the World

The Caribbean

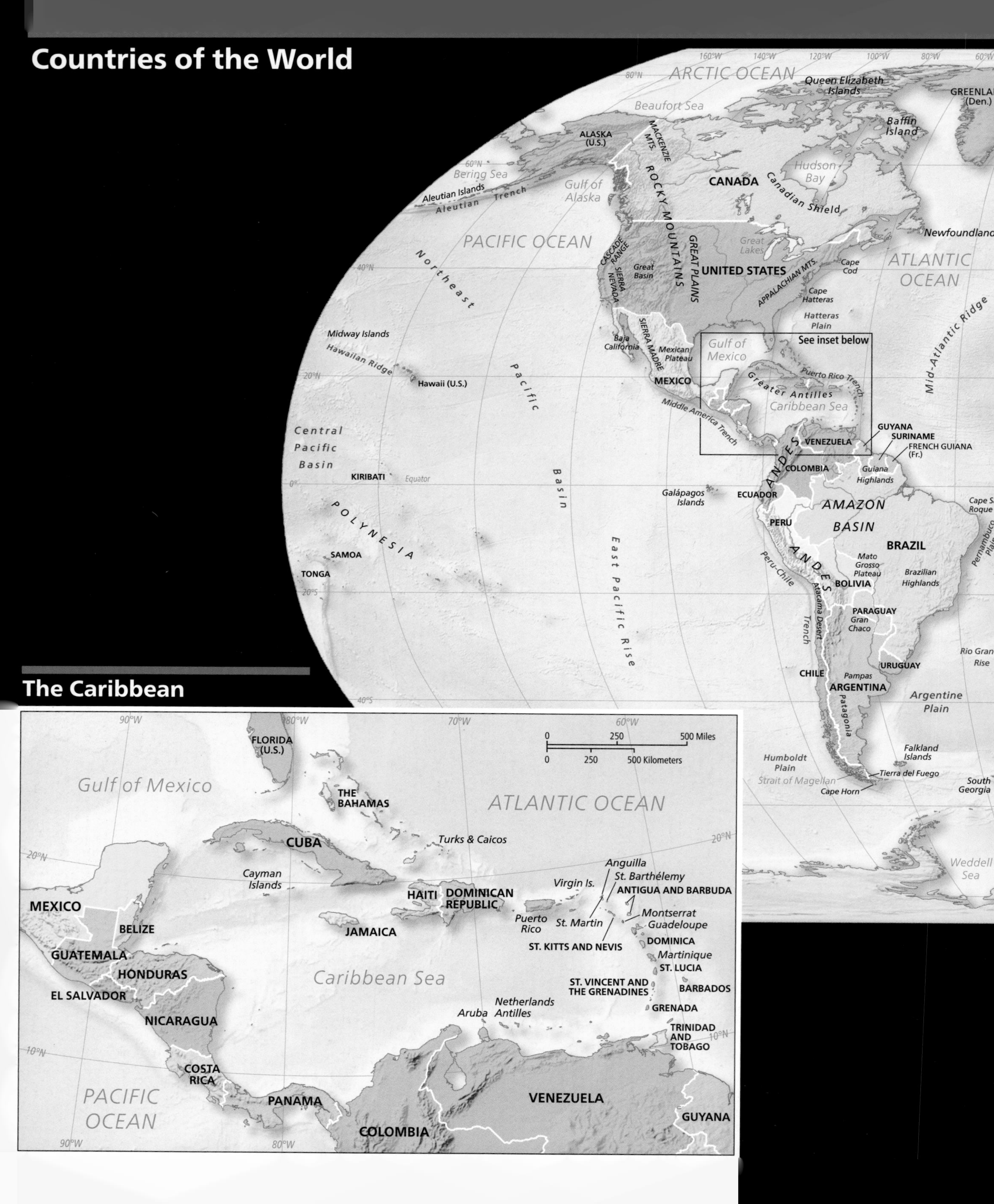

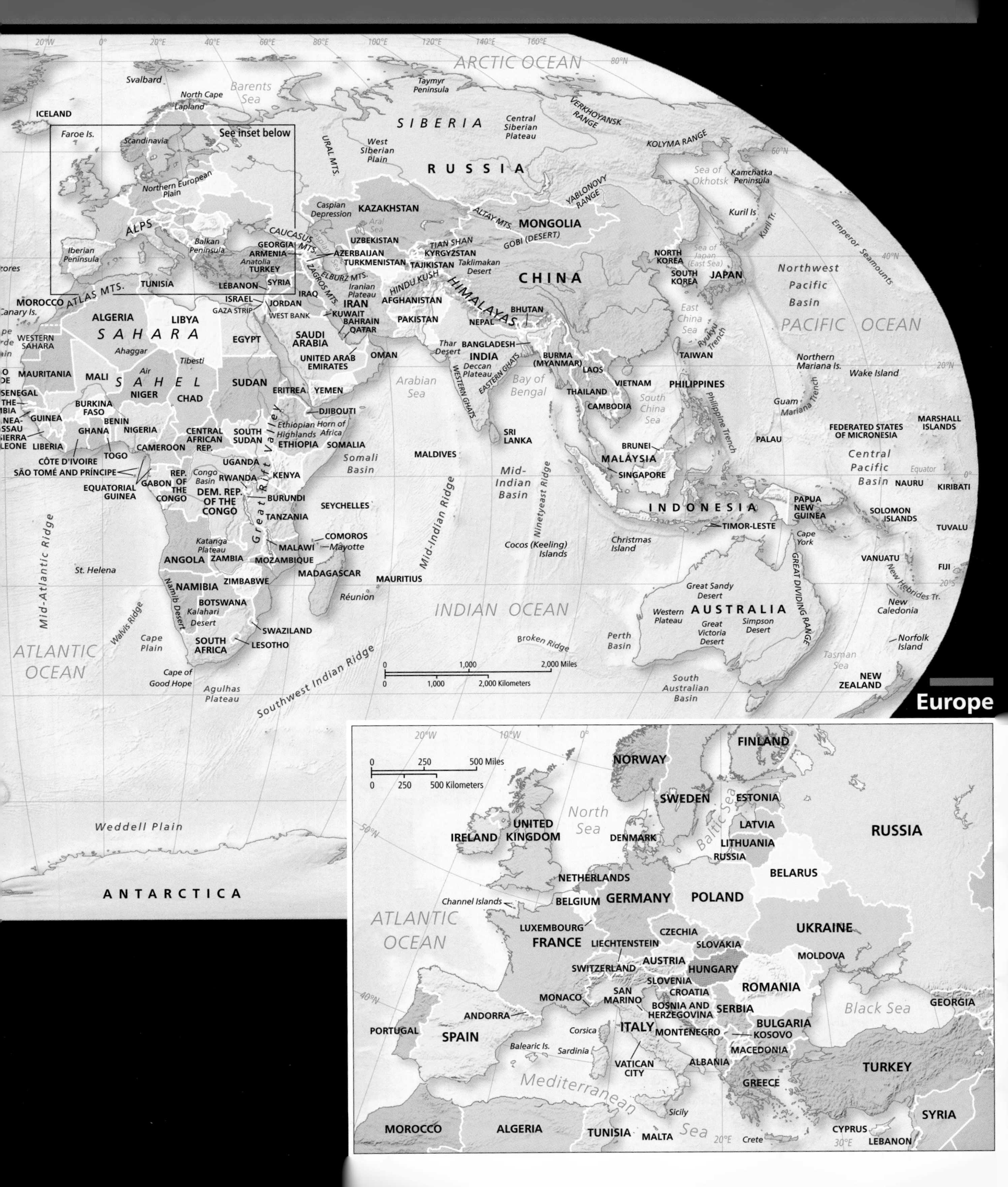

ARCTIC OCEAN
Svalbard
Barents Sea
North Cape
Lapland
ICELAND
Faroe Is.
Scandinavia
See inset below
Northern European Plain
ALPS
Iberian Peninsula
Balkan Peninsula
Anatolia
Taymyr Peninsula
SIBERIA
Central Siberian Plateau
VERKHOYANSK RANGE
KOLYMA RANGE
URAL MTS.
West Siberian Plain
RUSSIA
Sea of Okhotsk
Kamchatka Peninsula
YABLONOVY RANGE
Kuril Is.
Kuril Tr.
Emperor Seamounts
Caspian Depression
KAZAKHSTAN
Aral Sea
ALTAY MTS.
MONGOLIA
GOBI (DESERT)
CAUCASUS MTS.
Caspian Sea
UZBEKISTAN
TIAN SHAN
KYRGYZSTAN
GEORGIA
ARMENIA
AZERBAIJAN
TURKMENISTAN
TAJIKISTAN
Taklimakan Desert
TURKEY
ELBURZ MTS.
ZAGROS MTS.
HINDU KUSH
HIMALAYAS
NORTH KOREA
Sea of Japan (East Sea)
SOUTH KOREA
JAPAN
Northwest Pacific Basin
CHINA
MOROCCO
ATLAS MTS.
TUNISIA
LEBANON
SYRIA
IRAQ
Iranian Plateau
IRAN
AFGHANISTAN
Canary Is.
ISRAEL
JORDAN
GAZA STRIP
WEST BANK
KUWAIT
BAHRAIN
QATAR
PAKISTAN
NEPAL
BHUTAN
East China Sea
Ryukyu Trench
PACIFIC OCEAN
ALGERIA
LIBYA
SAHARA
EGYPT
SAUDI ARABIA
WESTERN SAHARA
Ahaggar
Tibesti
UNITED ARAB EMIRATES
OMAN
Thar Desert
BANGLADESH
INDIA
Deccan Plateau
BURMA (MYANMAR)
TAIWAN
Northern Mariana Is.
MAURITANIA
MALI
Air
SAHEL
NIGER
CHAD
SUDAN
ERITREA
YEMEN
Arabian Sea
WESTERN GHATS
EASTERN GHATS
Bay of Bengal
LAOS
VIETNAM
PHILIPPINES
Wake Island
SENEGAL
GUINEA
BURKINA FASO
BENIN
GHANA
NIGERIA
TOGO
LIBERIA
CÔTE D'IVOIRE
CAMEROON
CENTRAL AFRICAN REP.
SOUTH SUDAN
DJIBOUTI
Ethiopian Highlands
Horn of Africa
ETHIOPIA
SOMALIA
THAILAND
CAMBODIA
South China Sea
Philippine Trench
Guam
Mariana Trench
MARSHALL ISLANDS
FEDERATED STATES OF MICRONESIA
SRI LANKA
MALDIVES
PALAU
BRUNEI
MALAYSIA
SINGAPORE
Central Pacific Basin
Equator
NAURU
KIRIBATI
SÃO TOMÉ AND PRÍNCIPE
EQUATORIAL GUINEA
GABON
REP. OF THE CONGO
Congo Basin
RWANDA
DEM. REP. OF THE CONGO
UGANDA
KENYA
BURUNDI
TANZANIA
Great Rift Valley
Somali Basin
Mid-Indian Basin
Mid-Indian Ridge
Ninetyeast Ridge
SEYCHELLES
INDONESIA
PAPUA NEW GUINEA
TIMOR-LESTE
SOLOMON ISLANDS
TUVALU
Mid-Atlantic Ridge
Katanga Plateau
ANGOLA
ZAMBIA
MALAWI
COMOROS
Mayotte
MOZAMBIQUE
Cocos (Keeling) Islands
Christmas Island
Cape York
VANUATU
FIJI
St. Helena
MADAGASCAR
MAURITIUS
ZIMBABWE
NAMIBIA
Namib Desert
BOTSWANA
Kalahari Desert
Réunion
INDIAN OCEAN
Great Sandy Desert
Western Plateau
AUSTRALIA
Great Victoria Desert
Simpson Desert
GREAT DIVIDING RANGE
New Hebrides Tr.
New Caledonia
Norfolk Island
Walvis Ridge
ATLANTIC OCEAN
Cape Plain
SOUTH AFRICA
SWAZILAND
LESOTHO
Broken Ridge
Perth Basin
Tasman Sea
NEW ZEALAND
Cape of Good Hope
Agulhas Plateau
Southwest Indian Ridge
0 1,000 2,000 Miles
0 1,000 2,000 Kilometers
South Australian Basin
Weddell Plain
ANTARCTICA
Europe
FINLAND
NORWAY
0 250 500 Miles
0 250 500 Kilometers
SWEDEN
ESTONIA
North Sea
LATVIA
UNITED KINGDOM
IRELAND
DENMARK
Baltic Sea
LITHUANIA
RUSSIA
NETHERLANDS
BELARUS
Channel Islands
BELGIUM
GERMANY
POLAND
ATLANTIC OCEAN
LUXEMBOURG
CZECHIA
UKRAINE
FRANCE
LIECHTENSTEIN
SLOVAKIA
MOLDOVA
SWITZERLAND
AUSTRIA
HUNGARY
SLOVENIA
ROMANIA
CROATIA
MONACO
SAN MARINO
BOSNIA AND HERZEGOVINA
SERBIA
GEORGIA
Black Sea
ANDORRA
BULGARIA
PORTUGAL
SPAIN
Corsica
ITALY
MONTENEGRO
KOSOVO
Balearic Is.
Sardinia
MACEDONIA
VATICAN CITY
ALBANIA
TURKEY
GREECE
Mediterranean Sea
Sicily
SYRIA
MOROCCO
ALGERIA
TUNISIA
MALTA
Crete
CYPRUS
LEBANON

What's *Your* Map to Human Geography?

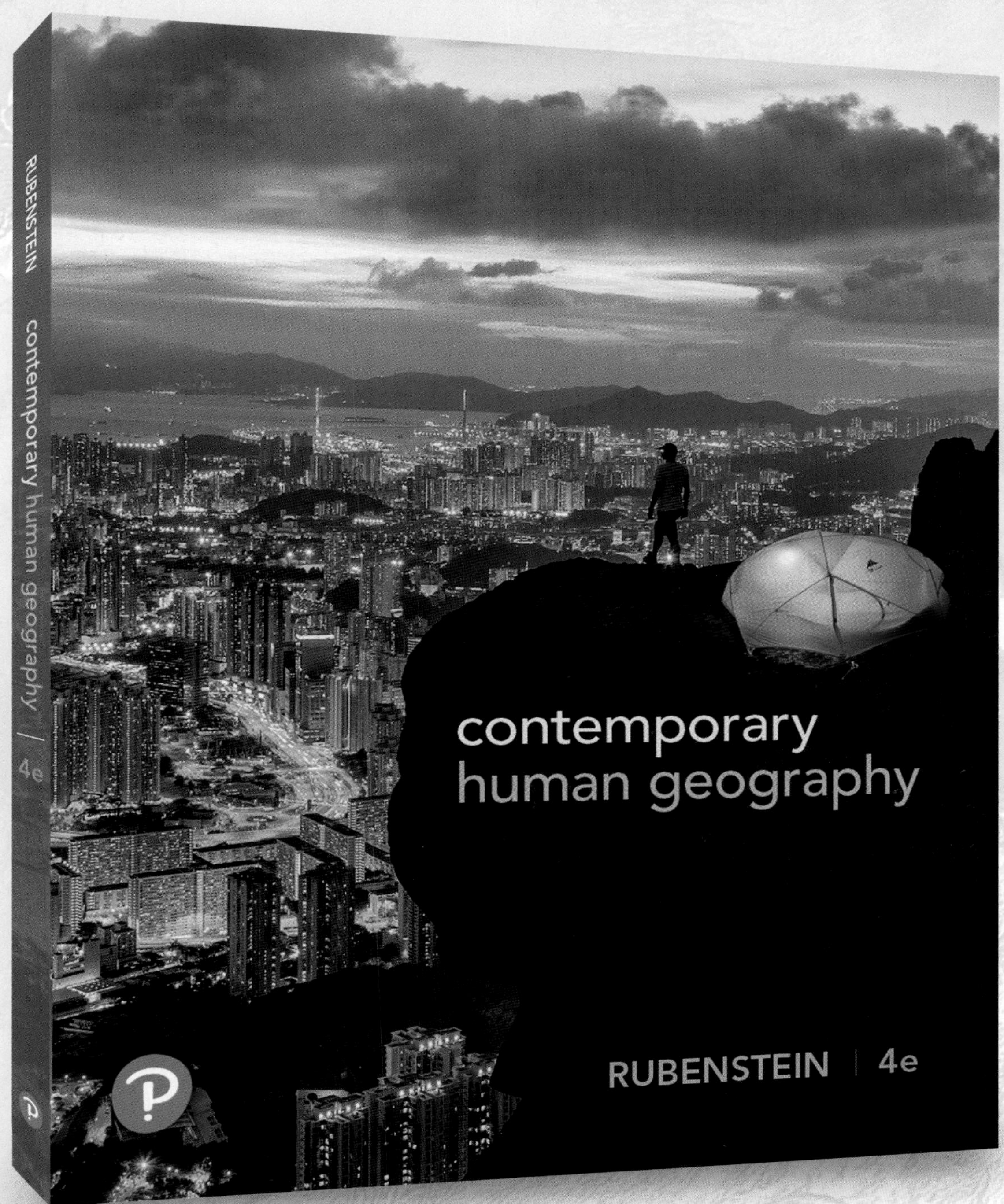

Contemporary Human Geography **is a modular springboard into essential human and cultural geography concepts. Designed for the modern student, this innovative text explores the key issues of contemporary human geography in a bold, visual style. Topics are organized into self-contained, two-page spreads, supported by cutting-edge cartography and a rich array of media and assessment, including videos and MapMaster 2.0™ in Mastering™ Geography.**

A Brief, Visual Introduction

HALLMARK! The highly-visual modular approach of this text consists of chapters made up of self-contained two-page spreads—a reliable presentation that gives instructors flexibility when assigning material to students.

2.1 KEY ISSUE 1 **Where are people distributed?**

Population Concentrations

- Explain reasons for the distribution of the world's peoples.

Human beings are not distributed uniformly across Earth's surface (Figure 2.1.1). World maps depict this distribution in several ways.

▲ 2.1.1 **POPULATION CONCENTRATION, SOUTHEAST ASIA** Housing in Jakarta, Indonesia.

Population Portions

The world can be divided into seven portions, each containing approximately 1 billion people (Figure 2.1.2). The small size of the Asia portions shows the large number of the world's inhabitants living there.

► 2.1.2 **POPULATION PORTIONS** Each of the seven portions contains approximately 1 billion inhabitants.

Population Cartogram

A cartogram depicts the size of countries according to population rather than land area, as is the case with most maps (Figure 2.1.3).

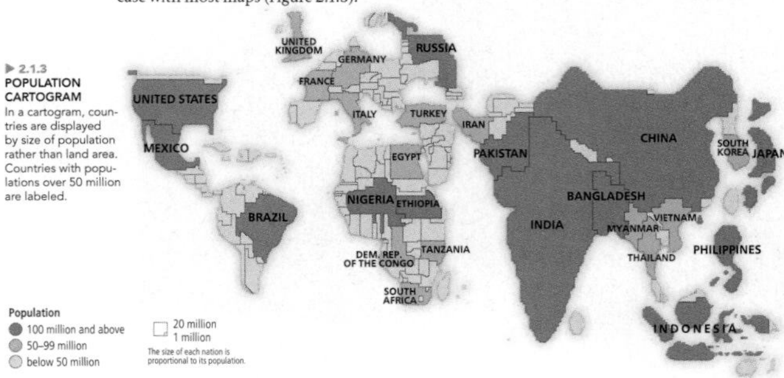

► 2.1.3 **POPULATION CARTOGRAM** In a cartogram, countries are displayed by size of population rather than land area. Countries with populations over 50 million are labeled.

Population Clusters

Two-thirds of the world's inhabitants live in four regions—East Asia, South Asia, Southeast Asia, and Europe (Figure 2.1.4). The four population concentrations occupy generally low-lying areas, with temperate climate and soil suitable for agriculture. Physical environments that are too dry, too cold, too wet, or too mountainous have relatively few inhabitants (Figure 2.1.5).

The areas of Earth that humans consider too harsh for occupancy have diminished over time, whereas the portion of Earth's surface occupied by permanent human settlement—called the **ecumene**—has increased.

SPARSELY POPULATED COLD LANDS Much of the land near the North and South poles is perpetually covered with ice or the ground is permanently frozen (permafrost).

EUROPE CLUSTER Europe includes four dozen countries, ranging from Monaco, with 1 square kilometer (0.7 square miles) and a population of 38,000, to Russia, the world's largest country in land area when its Asian part is included. Three-fourths of Europe's inhabitants live in cities, and fewer than 10 percent are farmers.

EAST ASIA CLUSTER Nearly one-fourth of the world's people live in East Asia, primarily in China, the world's most populous country. China's population is clustered near the Pacific Coast and in several fertile river valleys that extend inland, though much of China's interior is sparsely inhabited mountains and deserts.

SPARSELY POPULATED HIGH LANDS The highest mountains in the world are steep, snow covered, and sparsely settled.

► 2.1.4 **POPULATION DISTRIBUTION**

Persons per square kilometer
- 1,000 and above
- 250–999
- 25–249
- 5–24
- 1–4
- below 1

ARCTIC OCEAN
ATLANTIC OCEAN
PACIFIC OCEAN
INDIAN OCEAN
TROPIC OF CANCER
EQUATOR
TROPIC OF CAPRICORN

0 1,500 3,000 Miles
0 1,500 3,000 Kilometers

SPARSELY POPULATED WET LANDS Located primarily near the equator, the combination of rain and heat rapidly depletes nutrients from the soil and thus hinders agriculture.

SPARSELY POPULATED DRY LANDS Areas too dry for farming cover approximately 20 percent of Earth's land surface. Unless irrigated, deserts lack sufficient water to grow crops that could feed a large population, although some people survive there by raising animals, such as camels.

SOUTH ASIA CLUSTER Nearly one-fourth of the world's people live in South Asia, which includes India, Pakistan, Bangladesh, and Sri Lanka. The largest concentration of people within South Asia lives along a 1,500-kilometer (900-mile) corridor from Lahore, Pakistan, through India and Bangladesh to the Bay of Bengal.

SOUTHEAST ASIA CLUSTER More than 600 million people live in Southeast Asia. The largest population concentration is on Indonesia's island of Java, inhabited by more than 100 million people.

▼ 2.1.5 **SPARSELY POPULATED COLD LANDS** Angmagssalik, Greenland.

Applied Human Geography

NEW What's Your Geography? activities ask students to apply the skills and techniques of geographers to their personal experiences and local environments, helping to connect the relevance of human geography with everyday life.

WHAT'S YOUR POLITICAL GEOGRAPHY?

Check out the shape of your state's legislative districts.

1. In your search engine, ***enter*** *[your state] congressional district map.* If you live in a state with only one state-wide at large Representative (Alaska, Delaware, Montana, North Dakota, South Dakota, Vermont, and Wyoming), enter another state.
2. Are the districts compact and geometrically shaped, or are they irregularly shaped? If irregularly shaped, can you see a geographical reason for the shape, perhaps a natural feature such as a body of water, or a cultural boundary such as between ethnicities?
3. A gerrymander score has been calculated for each Congressional district (Figure 8.9.5). Use your Internet browser to ***search*** for *gerrymander score*. Or ***search*** *How gerrymandered is your Congressional district?* at **www.washingtonpost.com**. The higher the score, the more severe the gerrymandering. What is the gerrymander score for your Congressional district? Did you expect your district to have a higher score or a lower score? Why?

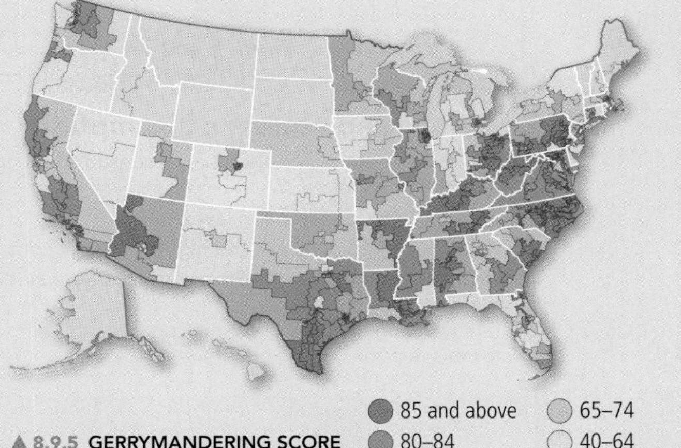

▲ 8.9.5 **GERRYMANDERING SCORE**

85 and above
80–84
75–79
65–74
40–64
none

DEBATE IT!
Should countries restrict immigration?

Immigration has become a controversial issue in many developed countries, including the United States and much of Europe.

CONTROL THE NUMBER OF IMMIGRANTS

- Immigrants compete for jobs with people already in the country and make it harder for citizens to find jobs.
- Immigrants place strains on services designed for citizens, such as schools and hospitals.
- Immigrants lack understanding and support for the host country's cultural traditions.

▲ 3.10.2 **ANTI-IMMIGRANT RALLY**
Cambridgeshire, United Kingdom.

WELCOME IMMIGRANTS

- Immigrants fill low-paying jobs that citizens don't want, such as in food services and agriculture.
- Immigrants place limited demands on public services.
- The different cultural heritage of immigrants enriches the life of the host country.

▲ 3.10.3 **PRO-IMMIGRANT RALLY**
London, United Kingdom.

UPDATED Debate It! features present two sides of a complex human geography topic, encouraging students to engage in active debate and decision-making. Readers may find that they agree with one side of the debate, or they may find merits in both perspectives.

Analyzing Earth's Dynamic Geography

NEW Geospatial Analysis activities leverage GIS-inspired MapMaster 2.0 in Mastering Geography, allowing students to layer various thematic maps to analyze spatial patterns and data at regional and global scales. The interactive maps are fully mobile, with enhanced analysis tools, such as split screen, bivariate mapping, data probing, map styling, and data filtering. Students can geolocate themselves in the data and upload their own data for advanced mapmaking. This tool includes zoom and annotation functionality, with hundreds of map layers integrating recent data from authoritative sources such as the PRB, the World Bank, NOAA, NASA, USGS, United Nations, the CIA, and more.

Geospatial Analysis

Log in to the Mastering Geography Study Area to access MapMaster 2.0

Emissions and energy consumption

Carbon dioxide emissions and energy consumption have both increased. At the national scale, are the two related?

Add the *Energy Consumption* layer.

1. What world regions have the highest energy consumption per capita?
2. ***Add*** the *Carbon Dioxide Emissions* layer and ***select*** *Join with data layer*. Probe the map. Are countries with high carbon dioxide emissions per capita those with relatively high energy consumption per capita or relatively low? What might account for this relationship?

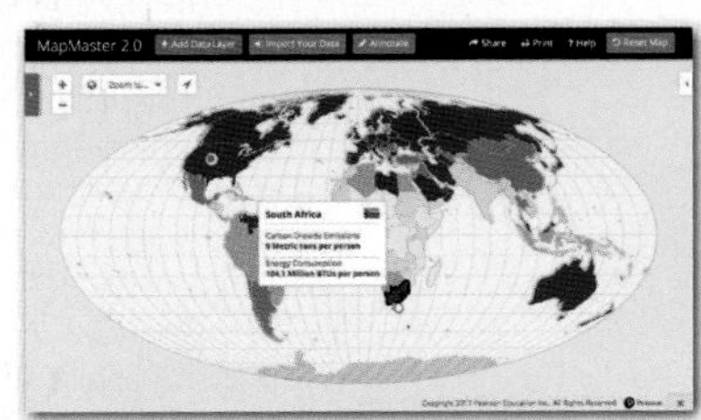

▲ **14.CR.7 ENERGY CONSUMPTION & CARBON DIOXIDE EMISSIONS**

NEW Research & Analyze activities have students explore data from authoritative and up-to-date online sources, responding to critical thinking questions based on the data.

Surging Seas
https://goo.gl/Cj4osb.

RESEARCH & ANALYZE

Rising sea level

Climate change has raised the global sea level about 8 inches since 1880, and by nearly 2 feet along the U.S. East Coast. The interactive map at **SurgingSeas.org** shows different amounts of flooding, depending on the level of sea level rise.

At **SurgingSeas.org**, ***click*** *Maps & Tools*, then *Risk Zone* map. At *Enter a Global Coastal Place*, ***type*** *Miami*.

1. What are some of the features in Miami Beach that would be underwater if the sea level rises 5 feet?
2. ***Click*** *Property*. Are properties in Miami Beach at risk of sea level rise mostly of high value or low value? Why might that be?

▶ **1.13.6 IMPACT OF RISING SEA LEVEL ON MIAMI**

Review, Analyze, & Apply

NEW Review, Analyze, & Apply. The final two-page spread of each chapter reviews the main points of the chapter, organized around the four Key Issues. The end-of-chapter material also includes *Key Terms* as well as numerous activities, including *Thinking Geographically*, *GeoVideos*, *Geospatial Analysis*, and *Explore* activities.

CHAPTER 3

Review, Analyze, & Apply

KEY ISSUE 1 Where Are Migrants Distributed?

Emigration is migration from a location, immigration is migration to a location, and net migration is the difference between the two. The largest numbers of migrants are from Asia and Latin America to North America and from Asia to Europe. The principal sources of immigrants to the United States have changed over time.

▲ 3.CR.1 NATURALIZATION CEREMONY

1. In recent years, has your community seen net in-migration or net out-migration? What factors might explain your community's net migration?

KEY ISSUE 2 Where Do People Migrate Within Countries?

Two main types of internal migration are interregional (between regions of a country) and intraregional (within a region). Large countries, including the United States and Canada, have had important patterns of interregional migration. Two intraregional migration patterns are from rural to urban areas (especially in developing countries) and from urban to suburban areas (especially in developed countries).

THINKING GEOGRAPHICALLY

▲ 3.CR.2 LOS ANGELES SUBURBS

2. Have you personally experienced (a) international migration, (b) interregional migration, or (c) intraregional migration? If so, why did your family migrate? Was the experience easy or difficult? Why?

KEY ISSUE 3 Why Do People Migrate?

People migrate for a combination of push and pull factors. Most people migrate for economic reasons, pushed from areas with limited economic prospects and pulled to areas of relative prosperity. Some migration is caused by environmental factors, as well as political and other cultural factors.

THINKING GEOGRAPHICALLY

▲ 3.CR.3 TODAY'S GRADUATES, TOMORROW'S MIGRANTS?

3. When you graduate from your school, do you expect to undertake international, interregional, or intraregional migration? Why?

KEY ISSUE 4 What Challenges Do Migrants Face?

Many countries, including the United States, limit the number of immigrants. For many developed countries, the demand for legal residency from international migrants significantly exceeds the number of slots set by the government. Hostility to immigrants is common, including among some Europeans.

THINKING GEOGRAPHICALLY

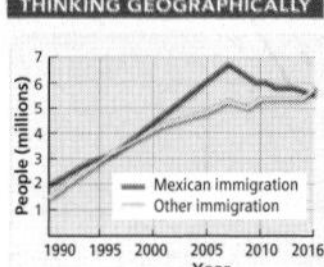

▲ 3.CR.4 UNAUTHORIZED IMMIGRANTS IN U.S.

4. The number of unauthorized immigrants from Mexico to the United States has been declining since 2007. Given the push and pull factors underlying people's reasons for migrating, what might account for this decline?

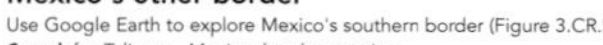

Mexico's other border

Use Google Earth to explore Mexico's southern border (Figure 3.CR.5).

Search for *Talisman, Mexico, border crossing.*

1. Use *Street View* for a ground-level view of the border crossing. Which if any of Mexico's border crossings with the United States in Figure 3.9 does the Talisman one resemble? Why?
2. ***Click*** the X in the upper left to return to aerial view. ***Zoom*** out to around 3 km.
3. What is the country bordering Mexico? The border mostly follows a river. What is the river's name?
4. Follow the river to the south. Do you see any other official border crossings? Does the border look easy to cross or difficult? Why?

▲ 3.CR.5 MEXICO'S SOUTHERN BORDER

CHAPTER 3 MIGRATION

Key Terms

Asylum seeker (p. 73) Someone who has migrated to another country in the hope of being recognized as a refugee.

Brain drain (p. 78) Large-scale emigration by talented people.

Chain migration (p. 78) Migration of people to a specific location because relatives or members of the same nationality previously migrated there.

Counterurbanization (p. 71) Net migration from urban to rural areas in developed countries.

Emigration (p. 64) Migration from a location.

Floodplain (p. 74) The area subject to flooding during a given number of years, according to historical trends.

Guest worker (p. 82) A term once used for a worker who migrated to the developed countries of Northern and Western Europe, usually from Southern and Eastern Europe or from North Africa, in search of a higher-paying job.

Immigration (p. 64) Migration to a new location.

Internal migration (p. 65) Permanent movement within a particular country.

Internally displaced person (IDP) (p. 73) Someone who has been forced to migrate for similar political reasons as a refugee but has not migrated across an international border.

International migration (p. 65) Permanent movement from one country to another.

Interregional migration (p. 65) Permanent movement from one region of a country to another.

Intervening obstacle (p. 72) An environmental or cultural feature of the landscape that hinders migration.

Intraregional migration (p. 65) Permanent movement within one region of a country.

Migration (p. 64) A form of relocation diffusion involving a permanent move to a new location.

Migration transition (p. 64) A change in the migration pattern in a society that results from industrialization, population growth, and other social and economic changes that also produce the demographic transition.

Net migration (p. 64) The difference between the level of immigration and the level of emigration.

Pull factor (p. 72) A factor that induces people to move to a new location.

Push factor (p. 72) A factor that induces people to leave old residences.

Quota (p. 79) In reference to migration, a law that places maximum limits on the number of people who can immigrate to a country each year.

Refugees (p. 73) People who are forced to migrate from their home country and cannot return for fear of persecution because of their race, religion, nationality, membership in a social group, or political opinion.

Remittance (p. 75) Transfer of money by workers to people in the country from which they emigrated.

Unauthorized immigrant (p. 80) A person who enters a country without proper documents to do so.

GeoVideo

Log in to the Mastering Geography Study Area to view this video.

Title: Xenophobia in Lampedusa

Thousands of unauthorized migrants from Tunisia arrived in small boats on Lampedusa, an island in the Mediterranean Sea with 6,000 inhabitants that is part of Italy.

1. What push and pull factors motivated the Tunisians to migrate to Lampedusa?
2. How have most of the 6,000 inhabitants of Lampedusa reacted to the arrival of Tunisians?
3. Explain why Tunisians have been migrating to Lampedusa, by consulting a map showing the location of the island.

Mastering Geography

Looking for additional review and test prep materials? Visit the Study Area in Mastering Geography to enhance your geographic literacy, spatial reasoning skills, and understanding of this chapter's content. Access MapMaster™ interactive maps, video case studies, *In the News* current articles, flashcards, self-study quizzes, an eText of *Contemporary Human Geography*, and more. **pearson.com/mastering/geography**

Geospatial Analysis

Log in to the Mastering Geography Study Area to access MapMaster 2.0.

Europe's immigrants and emigrants

Substantial immigration is occurring within Europe. Let's see where people are coming and going.

Add the *Net Migration* data layer. ***Select*** the *Settings* icon from the *Legend*, and ***select*** *Show Political Labels*. ***Add*** the *Gross National Income per capita* layer and ***select*** *Split Map Window*. ***Zoom*** to Europe.

1. Europe can be divided between east and west. Which of the two has net outmigration, and which has net inmigration?
2. Which half of Europe has higher gross national income per capita?
3. In what way do you think the patterns on the two maps are associated with each other?

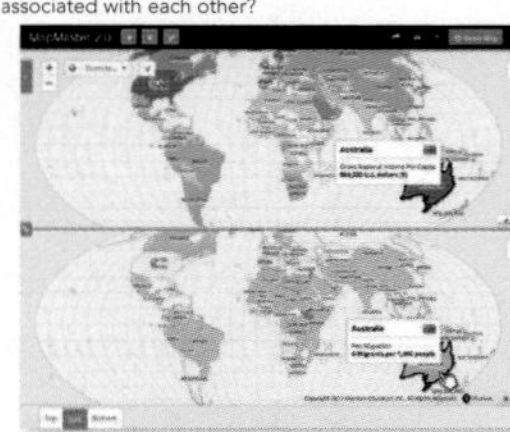

▲ 3.CR.7 NET MIGRATION AND GROSS NATIONAL INCOME PER CAPITA EUROPE

Continuous Learning
Before, During, and After Class

Mobile Media and Reading Assignments Ensure Students Come to Class Prepared.

Pearson eText in Mastering Geography gives students access to the text whenever and wherever they can access the internet. eText features include:

- Available on smartphones, tablets, and computers.
- Seamlessly integrated videos and other rich media.
- Fully accessible (screen-reader ready).
- Configurable reading settings, including resizable type and night reading mode.
- Instructor and student note-taking, highlighting, bookmarking, and search.

Pre-Lecture Reading Quizzes are easy to customize & assign

Reading Questions ensure that students complete the assigned reading before class and stay on track with reading assignments. Reading Questions are 100% mobile ready and can be completed by students on mobile devices.

with Mastering™ Geography

Learning Catalytics and Engaging Media

What has Professors and Students excited? Learning Catalytics, a 'bring your own device' student engagement, assessment, and classroom intelligence system, allows students to use their smartphone, tablet, or laptop to respond to questions in class. With Learning Catalytics, you can:

- Assess students in real-time using open ended question formats to uncover student misconceptions and adjust lecture accordingly.
- Automatically create groups for peer instruction based on student response patterns, to optimize discussion productivity.

> *"My students are so busy and engaged answering Learning Catalytics questions during lecture that they don't have time for Facebook."*
>
> Declan De Paor, *Old Dominion University*

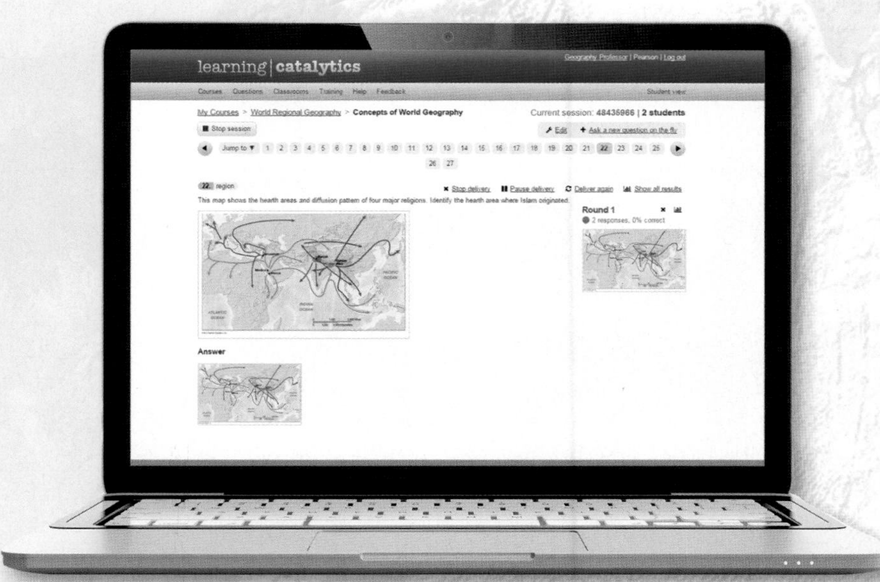

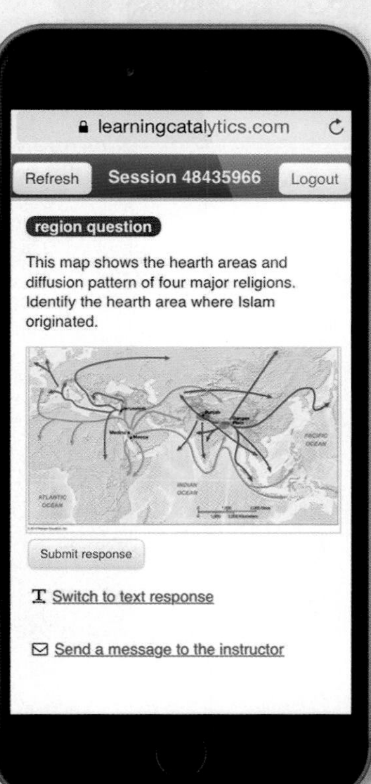

Enrich Lecture with Dynamic Media

Teachers can incorporate dynamic media into lecture, such as Videos, MapMaster 2.0 Interactive Maps, Google Earth Virtual Tour Videos, and Geoscience Animations.

Mastering Geography

Mastering Geography delivers engaging, dynamic learning opportunities—focusing on course objectives and responsive to each student's progress—that are proven to help students absorb human geography course material and understand challenging geography processes and concepts. Visit **www.pearson.com/mastering/geography**.

Easy to Assign, Customizable, Media-Rich, and Automatically Graded Assignments

UPDATED! Over 240 Geography Videos from sources such as the BBC, The Financial Times, and Television for the Environment's *Life* and *Earth Report* series. Available for student self study or for assignment with quizzes.

Drag the appropriate labels to their respective targets. Note that "transitional" is used twice.

Hints

birth rate
total population
industrial
transitional
preindustrial
death rate
postindustrial

Births and deaths (per thousand per year)
40
30
20
10
Stage 1:
Stage 2:
Stage 3:
Stage 4:
Stage 5:
Time

Reset Help

Submit My Answers Give Up

HALLMARK! Thinking Spatially & Data Analysis activities coach students through spatial reasoning and real world data analysis activities related to core geography concepts.

21st Century Technology & Tools for Today's Students

NEW! MapMaster 2.0 Interactive Map Activities are inspired by GIS, allowing students to analyze spatial patterns and data at regional and global scales by combining multiple thematic maps. The maps are now fully mobile, with enhanced analysis tools, such as split screen, allowing students to geolocate themselves in the data and upload their own data for advanced mapmaking. This tool includes zoom and annotation functionality, with hundreds of map layers leveraging recent data from authoritative sources such as the PRB, the World Bank, NOAA, NASA, USGS, United Nations, the CIA, and more.

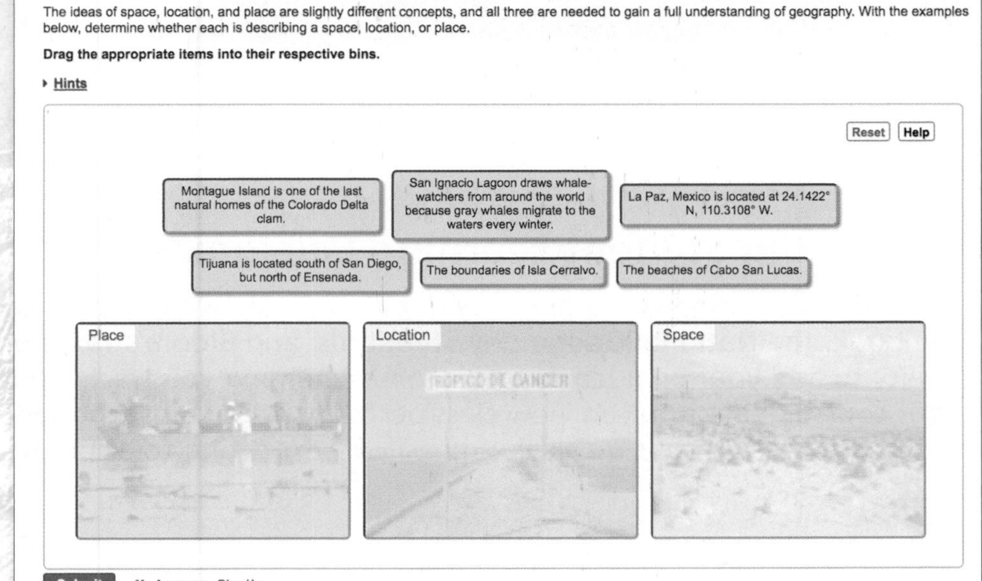

UPDATED! GeoTutor Activities help students master even the most challenging geography concepts with highly visual, kinesthetic, and data-rich activities focused on critical thinking and the application of core geoscience concepts.

Resources for YOU, the Instructor

Mastering Geography provides you with everything you need to prep for your course and deliver a dynamic lecture, in one convenient place. Resources include:

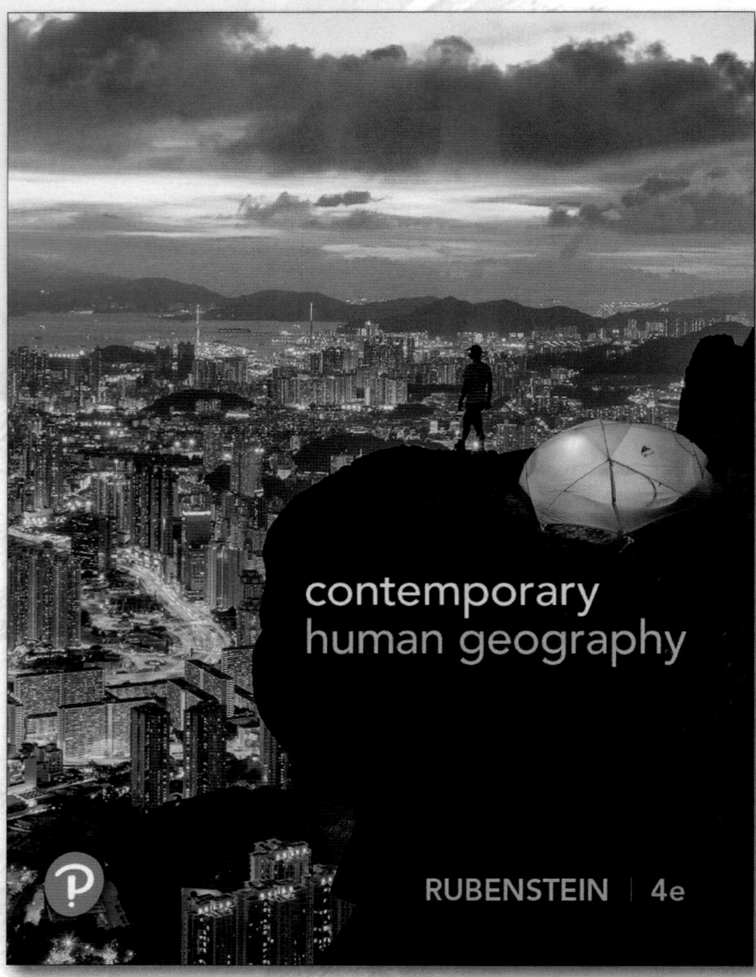

LECTURE PRESENTATION ASSETS FOR EACH CHAPTER

- PowerPoint Lecture Outlines
- PowerPoint Clicker Questions
- Files for all illustrations, tables, and photos from the text

TEST BANK

- The *Test Bank* in Microsoft Word formats
- TestGen Computerized *Test Bank*, which includes all the questions from the test bank in a format that allows you to easily and intuitively build exams and quizzes

TEACHING RESOURCES

- *Instructor Resource Manual* in Microsoft Word and PDF formats
- Pearson Community Website **www.communities.pearson.com/northamerica/s/**
- Goode's *World Atlas*, 23rd Edition
- Mann/Kump, *Dire Predictions: Understanding Climate Change*, 2nd Edition

Measuring Student Learning Outcomes

All of the Mastering Geography assignable content is tagged to key learning concepts from the book, the National Geography Standards, and Bloom's Taxonomy. You also have the ability to add your own learning outcomes, helping you track student performance against your course goals. You can view class performance against the specified learning outcomes and share those results quickly and easily by exporting to a spreadsheet.

Contemporary Human Geography

Fourth Edition

James M. Rubenstein

MIAMI UNIVERSITY, OXFORD, OHIO

Executive Editor, Geosciences Courseware: Christian Botting
Director, Courseware Portfolio Management: Beth Wilbur
Content Producer: Brett Coker
Managing Producer: Michael Early
Product Marketing Manager: Alysun Burns
Executive Field Marketing Manager: Mary Salzman
Courseware Portfolio Management Specialist, Content Development: Jonathan Cheney
Courseware Director, Content Development: Ginnie Simione Jutson
Courseware Editorial Assistant: Sherry Wang
Rich Media Content Producer: Mia Sullivan
Full-Service Vendor: SPi Global
Full-Service Project Manager: Julie Kidd
Copyeditor: Hope Madden
Illustrations: International Mapping
Art Coordinator: Kevin Lear
Design Manager: Mark Ong
Cover and Interior Designer: Elise Lansdon
Design Layout & Photo Researcher: Stuart Jackman
Rights & Permissions Project Manager: Erica Gordon
Rights & Permissions Specialist: Joseph Ian G. Panday
Rights & Permissions Management: Eric Schrader
Manufacturing Buyer: Stacey J. Weinberger
Cover Photo Credit: Chan Srithaweeporn/Getty Images

Library of Congress Cataloging-in-Publication Data

Names: Rubenstein, James M., author.
Title: Contemporary human geography / James M. Rubenstein, Miami University, Oxford, Ohio.
Description: Fourth edition. | New York, NY : Pearson Education, [2019]
Identifiers: LCCN 2017053151 | ISBN 9780134746227
Subjects: LCSH: Human geography—Textbooks.
Classification: LCC GF41 .R8 2019 | DDC 304.2—dc23
LC record available at https://lccn.loc.gov/2017053151

1 18

www.pearson.com

ISBN 10: 0-134-74622-8; ISBN 13: 978-0-134-74622-7 (Student edition)
ISBN 10: 0-134-77243-1; ISBN 13: 978-0-134-77243-1 (Books à la Carte edition)

Brief Contents

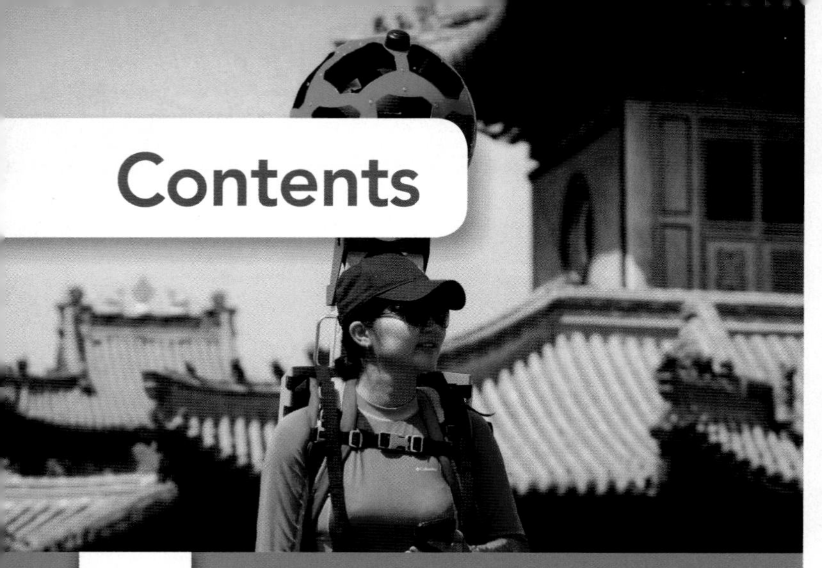

Contents

1 This is Geography

2 Population & Health

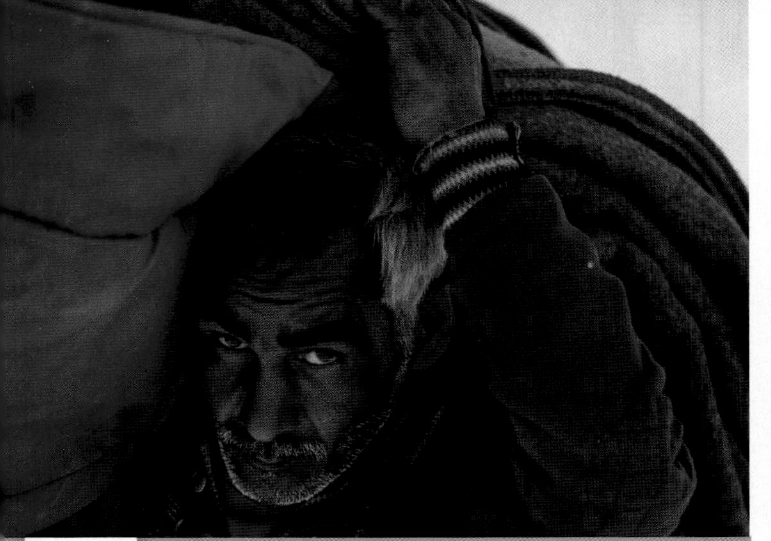

3 Migration

4 Folk & Popular Culture

5 Languages

6 Religions

7 Ethnicities

8 Political Geography

9 Food & Agriculture

10 Development

11 Industry

12 Services

Mont-Royal
Montréal-Trust
Complexe Les Ailes
CENTRE
EATON
MONTRÉAL
La Baie
AYLMER
MAYOR
SAINTE-CATHERINE
SAINT-ALEXANDRE
DE BLEURY
Sheraton
STANLEY
250 Lévesque
Château Champlain
CARMICHAEL
DOWD
ANDERSON
Édifice Gare Windsor

Preface

Welcome to a truly contemporary geography textbook! We live in a visual age, and geography is a highly visual discipline, so Pearson—the world's leading publisher of geography textbooks—invites you to study human geography as a visual subject.

The fourth edition of *Contemporary Human Geography* builds on the strengths of the first three editions, while responding to user feedback to make important changes and improvements, and incorporating innovative features, current data, and new information.

NEW & ENHANCED FEATURES

This edition brings substantial changes in both organization and content, as well as updated information and data. Especially important is the consideration of digital as well as paper versions of the book. This book has been designed to be legible—and attractive—in either paper or electronic format. Several features integrated into the text enhance student understanding and analytic skills.

New & Updated in the 4th Edition

- **NEW *What's Your Geography?*** features ask students to apply the skills and techniques of geographers to their real-world experiences and environments. *What's Your Geography?* helps students connect the relevance of human geography to their everyday lives.
- **NEW *Geospatial Analysis*** activities leverage GIS-inspired MapMaster 2.0 in Mastering Geography, allowing students to analyze spatial patterns and data at regional and global scales through overlaying multiple maps. The fully-mobile interactive maps have enhanced analysis tools, such as split screen, bivariate mapping, data probing, map styling, and data filtering. Students can geolocate themselves in the data and upload their own data for advanced mapmaking. MapMaster 2.0 includes zoom and annotation functionality, with hundreds of map layers leveraging recent data from sources such as the PRB, the World Bank, NOAA, NASA, USGS, United Nations, the CIA, and more.
- **NEW *Research & Analyze*** activities help students examine data from authoritative and up-to-date online sources and to respond to critical thinking questions based on the data.
- **UPDATED *Debate It!*** features present two sides of a complex human geography topic and encourages students to engage in active debate and decision-making. Readers may find that they agree with one side of the debate, or they may find merits in both perspectives.
- **UPDATED Word clouds,** on the first page of each chapter visually depict the most important concepts and terms to be addressed in the chapter.
- **UPDATED Location maps** present a spatial overview of each chapter, identifying select places explored in each chapter's applications and case studies.
- **UPDATED *Explore*** features have students use Google Earth™ to investigate in more detail a concept or place discussed in the chapter and answer questions based on their observations.
- **UPDATED *GeoVideo*** features integrate videos related to core subjects of each chapter. Students are encouraged to log into Mastering Geography to view videos that explore contemporary applications of chapter topics.
- **UPDATED *Thinking Geographically*** questions consist of several visual and thought-provoking "essay-style" questions at the end of each chapter, suggesting directions for further reflection, based on concepts and themes developed in the chapter.

NEW & ENHANCED ORGANIZATION

This book has a clear, easy-to-use organization and outline.

- **Opening spread.** Each chapter opens with an outline of the four Key Issues that will be addressed in the chapter, and introduces key terms and places found in the chapter.
- **Key Issues.** Each chapter follows an outline based on four Key Issues that outline the main topics and big questions in human geography covered in the chapter.
- **Self-contained spreads.** Each two-page spread is titled and numbered to enhance the clarity of the outline.
- **Learning Objectives.** Each two-page spread (or "module") begins with a Learning Objective that frames the main concept of that spread for students.

- **Self-contained pages.** Each page within the two-page spreads is also self-contained. As a result, maps and photos appear next to where they are discussed in the text. No more going through a chapter to find a figure that has been referenced on one page but actually appears on another page. This approach is especially critical for reading the eText on a tablet or computer.
- **Review, Analyze, & Apply.** The final two-page spread of each chapter (four pages for Chapter 1) reviews the main points of the chapter, organized around the four Key Issues. The end-of-chapter material also includes Key Terms as well as the activity features described above, including Thinking Geographically, GeoVideos, Geospatial Analysis, and Explore activities.

NEW & ENHANCED CONTENT

Human geography is a dynamic subject. Topics that were central to the discipline a generation ago have faded in importance, while new ones take their place. Each chapter naturally provides updates of the most recently available data. Below are examples of entirely new material included in each chapter.

What basic concepts do geographers use? The first portion of the book welcomes students to the study of human geography and introduces basic concepts that geographers use. Geographers employ several concepts to describe the distribution of people and activities across Earth, to explain reasons underlying the observed distribution, and to understand the significance of the arrangements.

Chapter 1 provides an introduction to ways that geographers think about the world. New topics include volunteered geographic information (VGI), citizen science, participatory GIS, and mashups. Geography's five most basic concepts (place, region, scale, space, connection) are introduced through the example of Timor-Leste, one of the world's newest and least-familiar countries. The discussion of sustainability includes new information on the drought in the U.S. West.

Where are people located in the world? Why do some places on Earth contain large numbers of people or attract newcomers whereas other places are sparsely inhabited? Chapters 2 and 3 examine the distribution and growth of the world's population, as well as the movement of people from one place to another.

Chapter 2 (Population & Health) includes an expanded discussion of gender- and age-related health issues, as well as the continuing debate over health care in the United States. As the rate of population growth declines from its peak during the second half of the twentieth century, population geography is increasingly concerned with the health of humans, not just their fertility and mortality.

Chapter 3 (Migration) includes recent controversies concerning U.S. borders and the surge of migration into Europe from Africa and Asia. The *What's Your Geography?* feature helps students consider their own family's migration stories.

How are different cultural groups distributed? Geographers look for similarities and differences in the cultural features at different places, the reasons for their distribution, and the importance of these differences for world peace. Chapters 4 through 8 analyze the distribution of different cultural traits and beliefs and the political challenges that result from those spatial patterns.

Chapter 4 (Folk & Popular Culture) includes new material on differences in popular culture within and between countries. The chapter also expanded coverage of the diffusion of various forms of social media, as well as limitations on accessing them.

Chapter 5 (Languages) uses the leading authority *Ethnologue*'s latest 5-point classification of languages as institutional, developing, vigorous, in trouble, and dying. A new *Debate It!* feature focuses on the need for learning foreign languages.

Chapter 6 (Religions) has been substantially reorganized and rewritten, and includes input from some of the nation's leading authorities on the geography of religions. A new section has been added concerning the contemporary diffusion of religions.

Chapter 7 (Ethnicities) includes new material on ethnic enclaves in large cities, including London, Paris, and New York. A new *Debate It!* feature considers recent independence movements among ethnicities.

Chapter 8 (Political Geography) addresses current conflicts and terrorist organizations. The chapter also includes a new *Debate It!* feature on "Brexit" (Britain's withdrawal from the European Union) and updated information on gerrymandering.

How do people earn a living in different parts of the world? Human survival depends on acquiring an adequate food supply. One of the most significant distinctions among people globally is whether they produce their food directly from the land or buy it with money earned by performing other types of work. Chapters 9 through 12 look at the three main ways of earning a living: agriculture, manufacturing, and services. Chapter 13 discusses cities, where the world's economic and cultural activities are increasingly centered.

Chapter 9 (Food & Agriculture) now precedes the chapter on development, in accordance with the order suggested by the Advanced Placement™ Human Geography course syllabus. Key Issue 4 includes expanded information on trade, productivity, biotechnology, and sustainability.

Chapter 10 (Development) reflects recent changes in United Nations development indices and the organization's sustainable development goals.

The chapter includes an expanded discussion of gender-related development, including inequality and empowerment. The chapter also addresses current challenges to the international trade development path.

Chapter 11 (Industry) has been reorganized, though still maintaining the geographic distinction between site and situation factors. Readers are asked to identify the national origin of their t-shirts and their car.

Chapter 12 (Services) includes expanded discussion of the new sharing economy, such as Uber™ and Airbnb™. New features include an interactive study of food deserts.

Chapter 13 (Urban Patterns) includes updated census definitions of "urban." A new case study illustrates the CBD (Central Business District) of Mobile, Alabama. The chapter also contains new material on transportation epochs and bicycles in urban areas.

What issues result from using Earth's resources? Geographers recognize that cultural problems result from the depletion, destruction, and inefficient use of the world's natural resources. Chapter 14 is devoted to a study of issues related to the use of Earth's natural resources. Readers are asked about their use of plastic bottles, a major cause of solid waste pollution.

CONTEMPORARY PERSPECTIVES

The main purpose of this book is to introduce you to the study of geography as a social science by emphasizing the relevance of geographic concepts to human problems. It is intended for use in college-level introductory human or cultural geography courses. The book is written for students who have not previously taken a college-level geography course.

Titling this book "contemporary" is a bold claim. All credible geography books—including this one—contain up-to-date statistics, recent world events, and current geographic concepts. This book claims to be more contemporary—not merely up-to-date—for three reasons.

1. **We live in an electronic age.** This book has been designed to be equally usable—and attractive—in both paper or digital formats. Most books are still composed in pages designed for paper—as in the past—and converted to electronic format after printing of the paper version. As a result, the conversion to electronic format is frequently awkward. For example, maps and photos are often placed in the paper version in positions that don't work well in electronic format.

   This is the best-looking human geography textbook available anywhere in paper—and it is also the best-designed book for electronic reading. Furthermore, within the book, some of the learning will take place through accessing information online. Quick Response codes (QRs), URLs, online searches—these are the tools of contemporary teaching.

2. **We live in a visual age.** This book has been composed in the reverse order of traditional textbooks. A traditional book has the text written first and the graphic material is added later almost as an afterthought. Instead of beginning with an author's complete manuscript, this book starts with an outline and a visual concept for each two-page module in the book. What would be the most important geographic idea presented on the spread, and what would be the most effective visual way to portray that idea? The maps, graphs, and photos are placed on the page first, and the text is written around the graphics. The production of this book does not have a traditional manuscript; from the outset, the text is written to complement the graphics.

3. **We live in a sound bite age.** This book replaces the narrative style of traditional books. Each page of this book is self-contained. Material doesn't carry over to the next page. This places more of a premium on clear, concise outlining as an important pedagogical feature. The text introduces maps, graphs, and photos so that captions can be as brief as possible.

CONTEMPORARY RELEVANCE

Many speculated that geography would be irrelevant in the twenty-first century. Geography's future was thought to be grim because the diffusion of electronic communications and social media would make it easier for human activities to be conducted remotely. If any piece of information could be accessed from any place in the world (at least where electronic devices work), why live, shop, work, or establish a business in a crowded city or a harsh climate?

In reality, geography has become more, not less, important in people's lives and the conduct of business. Here are several ways that location matters more now than in the past, because of—not despite—the diffusion of electronic devices:

1. Smartphones and other electronic devices match specific demand to supply in a particular locality. For example: Restaurant apps match hungry people to empty seats in a locality's restaurants. Real estate apps help people find housing for sale or for rent in a locality. Social apps let people know where their friends in a particular locality are hanging out that night. Transportation apps match vehicles with available seats to people trying to get to specific locations.

   These sorts of apps generate data on people's preferences in space, which in turn helps even more location-based business get started and grow. Instead of looking for restaurants in printed "Yellow Pages," we find places to eat that are mapped on our device and in our locations. No wonder that geography apps, in the form of maps (including navigation) and travel (including transportation), rank as two of the five most frequently used services on smartphones.

2. Electronic devices are essential to the smooth movement of people and goods. For example: Turn-by-turn information can prevent you from getting lost or steer you back if you do get lost. Traffic jams on overcrowded roads can be avoided or minimized. Vehicles in the future will be driverless, so you can spend driving time working, learning, or social networking. Instead of turning on a radio to hear traffic information, we look at the red and green traffic flow patterns on an electronic map.
3. The people who make all of these new location-based apps are themselves highly clustered in a handful of places in the world, such as the San Francisco Bay Area. Ideas—both brilliant and far-fetched—are still easier to communicate face-to-face than across long distances. Living and working in places like Silicon Valley, despite high expenses and choking traffic jams, put people next to other like-minded innovators in the electronic-based geography of the twenty-first century.
4. Electronic devices also impact the changing geography of cultural diversity. What if you searched for an available restaurant table in a foreign language? Would you find the same places? What if you conducted an Internet search in a foreign country? Would you find the same information?

LOCAL DIVERSITY VS. GLOBALIZATION

A central theme in this book explores the tension between two important themes—cultural diversity and globalization. In many respects, we are living in a more unified world economically, culturally, and environmentally. Geography's spatial perspectives help to relate economic change to the distributions of cultural features such as languages and religions, demographic patterns such as population growth and migration, and natural resources such as energy, water quality, and food supply.

This book argues, though, that after a period when globalization of the economy and culture has been a paramount concern in geographic analysis, local diversity now demands equal time. People are taking deliberate steps to retain distinctive cultural identities. They are preserving little-used languages, fighting fiercely to protect their religions, and questioning free trade agreements. Local diversity even extends to addressing issues, such as climate change, that at first glance are considered global. For example, the "greenest" cars for motorists to drive in Oregon are different than the "greenest" cars for Ohio.

Since 2013, I have written a weekly column for our local newspaper on behalf of our local cooperatively owned grocery store. The column has come to extol the virtues of "local" here in Midwestern USA: the local food, the local farmers, the local seasons, and the locally owned co-op. I admire the farmers and the agriculture from far away, but our local food is more nutritious, consumes less energy, and tastes better. In a world where we feel anger and helplessness at the plight of people in other places, it is at the local scale that we all can make a difference.

THE PUBLISHING TEAM

The steps involved in creating most traditional textbooks haven't changed much. The book passes from one to another like a baton in a relay race. The author writes a manuscript, which then passes in turn through development, editing, and production specialists on the way to the printing press. The preface typically includes a perfunctory litany of acknowledgments for the many fine people who contribute to the development, editing, and production of the book.

In contrast, this book starts as a genuine partnership among the key development, editorial, and production teams. For this truly contemporary book, collaborative partnership better describes its creation. The traditional separation of development, editorial, and production personnel does not occur, and in fact the lines among these functions are deliberately blurred.

Christian Botting, Executive Editor for Geosciences at Pearson Education, is the captain of this team. He has now been the leader on seven of my book projects. Because Pearson is the dominant publisher of college geography textbooks, the person in charge of geography wields considerable influence in shaping what is taught in the nation's geography curriculum. Christian knows when to lead the market and when to listen to users, when to innovate and when to stick with success, when to let the team do its job and when to step in and make a tough decision. His instincts are infallible.

Corey Brincks, Research Assistant, first came to my attention as a sophomore at Miami University. Although the only sophomore in a class of 22 seniors, he was the strongest student in the class. He has since co-authored with me a couple of papers on the auto industry. Corey has embarked on a career at nonprofit organizations concerned with international development in Asia, including stints in Timor-Leste and Vietnam. His imprint appears in this book from the very first feature on Timor-Leste to the very last feature on cars of the future.

Stuart Jackman is the creative genius responsible for the spectacular graphics. He deserves the lion's share of the credit for giving this book the best graphics in geography. Stuart honed his craft as longtime Design Director at DK Education. DK is well-known for producing the best travel guides. The DK "style" is immediately recognizable as distinctive from traditional geography books. You can tell that the graphics are the central element of the book, not an afterthought.

Kevin Lear, Senior Project Manager at International Mapping, and his team produce the outstanding maps for this book. Back in the 1980s, Kevin was the first cartographer to figure out how to produce computer-generated full-color maps that are more accurate and more attractive than hand-drawn ones.

Jonathan Cheney, Portfolio Management Specialist at Pearson Education, plays a key role at the start of the project by reviewing and collating the many reviews and sorting out what needs to be preserved and what needs to be improved. Jonathan reviews the rough drafts of each spread of each chapter that Stuart and I prepare, and helps develop many of the special features.

Brett Coker, Content Producer at SPi Global, serves as ringmaster. Brett oversees the unusually complex task of managing this book's extremely nontraditional work flow.

Julie Kidd, Project Manager at SPi Global, smoothly manages the flow of copyediting and other production tasks for this project.

Carole Katz, Research Consultant, ably assisted with development of material, especially languages and environment.

REVIEWERS

I would like to extend a special thanks to my colleagues who served as reviewers on the first four editions, as well as on overlapping material from *Introduction to Contemporary Geography*:

Roger Balm, Rutgers University
Joby Bass, University of Southern Mississippi
Steve Bass, Mesa Community College
David C. Burton, Southmoore High School
Michelle Calvarese, California State University, Fresno
Craig S. Campbell, Youngstown State University
Edward Carr, University of South Carolina
Carolyn Coulter, Atlantic Cape Community College
Ronald Davidson, California State Univ., Northridge
Kathryn Davis, San Jose State University
Stephen Davis, University of Illinois, Chicago
Owen Dwyer, Indiana University-Purdue Univ., Indianapolis
Anthony Dzik, Shawnee State University
Leslie Edwards, Georgia State University
Caitie Finlayson, University of Florida
Barbara E. Fredrich, San Diego State University
Kurt Fuellhart, Shippensburg University
Doug Gamble, University of North Carolina Wilmington
Piper Gaubatz, University of Massachusetts, Amherst
Daniel Hammel, University of Toledo
James Harris, Metropolitan State College of Denver
Leila Harris, University of Wisconsin
Susan Hartley, Lake Superior College
Marc Healy, Elgin Community College
Scot Hoiland, Butte College
Georgeanne Hribar, Old Dominion University
Wilbur Hugli, University of West Florida
Anthony Ijomah, Harrisburg Area Community College
Karen Johnson-Webb, Bowling Green State University
Melinda Kashuba, Shasta College
Oren Katz, California State University, Los Angeles
Marti Klein, Saddleback College
John Kostelnick, Illinois State University
Olaf Kuhlke, University of Minnesota, Duluth
Peter Landreth, Westmont High School
Jose López-Jiménez, Minnesota State Univ., Mankato
Claudia Lowe, Fullerton College
Ken Lowrey, Wright State University
Lawrence Mastroni, SW Oklahoma State Univ.
Jerry Mitchell, University of South Carolina
Brian Molyneaux, University of South Dakota
Eric C. Neubauer, Columbus State Community College
Stephen O'Connell, University of Central Arkansas
Ray Oman, University of the District of Columbia
Lynn Patterson, Kennesaw State University
Lashale Pugh, Youngstown State University
Timothy Scharks, Green River Community College
Justin Scheidt, Delta College
Debra Sharkey, Cosumnes River College
Wendy Shaw, Southern Illinois University, Edwardsville
Laurel Smith, University of Oklahoma
James Tyner, Kent State University
Richard Tyre, Florida State University
Mark VanderVen, Western Washington University
Daniel Vara, College Board Advanced Placement Human Geography Consultant
Timothy Vowles, University of Northern Colorado
Anne Will, Skagit Valley College
Lei Xu, California State University, Fullerton
Daisaku Yamamoto, Central Michigan University
Robert C. Ziegenfus, Kutztown University of Pennsylvania

Digital & Print Resources

FOR STUDENTS & TEACHERS:

This edition provides a complete human geography program for students and teachers.

Mastering Geography with Pearson eText for *Contemporary Human Geography*

The Mastering platform is the most widely used and effective online homework, tutorial, and assessment system for the sciences. It delivers self-paced coaching activities that provide individualized coaching, focus on course objectives, and are responsive to each student's progress. The Mastering system helps teachers maximize class time with customizable, easy-to-assign, and automatically graded assessments that motivate students to learn outside of class and arrive prepared for lecture. Mastering Geography offers:

- Assignable activities that include GIS-inspired MapMaster 2.0™ interactive maps, *Encounter Human Geography* Google Earth™ Explorations, GeoVideos, GeoTutors, Thinking Spatially & Data Analysis activities, end-of-chapter questions, reading quizzes, Test Bank questions, map labeling activities, and more.
- Student study area with GIS-inspired MapMaster 2.0 interactive maps, Geoscience Animations, web links, geography videos, glossary flash cards, "In the News" current articles, reference maps, an optional Pearson eText and more.

www.pearson.com/mastering/geography

FOR TEACHERS

Instructor Resource Manual (Download Only) (0134791835)

Updated for the fourth edition, the *Instructor Resource Manual* is intended as a resource for both new and experienced instructors. It includes lecture outlines, additional source materials, teaching tips, advice about how to integrate online media, and various other ideas for the classroom.
www.pearson.com/mastering/geography

TestGen® Computerized Test Bank (Download Only) (0134767780)

TestGen is a computerized test generator that lets instructors view and edit *Test Bank* questions, transfer questions to tests, and print the test in a variety of customized formats. This *Test Bank* includes over 1,000 multiple choice and short answer/ essay questions. Questions are correlated to the revised U.S. National Geography Standards and Bloom's Taxonomy to help instructors better map the assessments against both broad and specific teaching and learning objectives. The questions are also tagged to chapter specific learning outcomes. The Test Bank is available in Microsoft Word, and is importable into Blackboard.
www.pearson.com/mastering/geography

Instructor Resource Materials (Download Only) (0134791843)

The *Instructor Resource Materials* provides high-quality electronic versions of photos and illustrations from the book in JPEG, pdf, and PowerPoint formats, as well as customizable PowerPoint lecture presentations, Classroom Response System questions in PowerPoint, and the *Instructor Resource Manual* and *Test Bank* in MS. Word and TestGen formats. For easy reference and identification, all resources are organized by chapter.

FOR STUDENTS

Teaching College Geography: A Practical Guide for Graduate Students and Early Career Faculty (0136054471)

This two-part resource provides a starting point for becoming an effective geography teacher from the very first day of class. Divided in two parts, Part One addresses "nuts-and-bolts" teaching issues. Part Two explores being an effective teacher in the field, supporting critical thinking with GIS and mapping technologies, engaging learners in large geography classes, and promoting awareness of international perspectives and geographic issues.

Aspiring Academics: A Resource Book for Graduate Students and Early Career Faculty (0136048919)

Drawing on several years of research, this set of essays is designed to help graduate students and early career faculty start their careers in geography and related social and environmental sciences. *Aspiring Academics* stresses the interdependence of teaching, research, and service—and the importance of achieving a healthy balance of professional and personal life—while doing faculty work. Each chapter provides accessible, forward-looking advice on topics that often cause the most stress in the first years of a college or university appointment.

Practicing Geography: Careers for Enhancing Society and the Environment (0321811151)

This book examines career opportunities for geographers and geospatial professionals in business, government, nonprofit, and educational sectors. A diverse group of academic and industry professionals share insights on career planning, networking, transitioning between employment sectors, and balancing work and home life. The book illustrates the value of geographic expertise and technologies through engaging profiles and case studies of geographers at work.

Goode's World Atlas, 23rd Edition (0133864642)

Goode's World Atlas has been the world's premier educational atlas since 1923, and for good reason. It features over 250 pages of maps, from definitive physical and political maps to important thematic maps that illustrate the spatial aspects of many important topics. The 23rd edition includes digitally produced reference maps, as well as new thematic maps on demography, global climate change, sea level rise, CO_2 emissions, polar ice fluctuations, deforestation, extreme weather events, infectious diseases, water resources, and energy production.

The atlas is also available in Pearson Collections and in various eText formats, including an upgrade option from Mastering Geography courses.

Encounter Human Geogrtaphy Workbook & Website by Jess C. Porter (0321682203)

For classes that do not use Mastering Geography, *Encounter Human Geography* provides rich, interactive explorations of human geography concepts through Google Earth. Students explore the globe through themes such as population, sexuality and gender, political geography, ethnicity, urban geography, migration, human health, and language. All chapter explorations are available in print format as well as online quizzes, accommodating different classroom needs. All worksheets are accompanied with corresponding Google Earth KMZ media files, available for download for those who do not use Mastering Geography, from www.mygeoscienceplace.com

Dire Predictions: Understanding Climate Change, 2nd edition, by Michael Mann and Lee R. Kump (0133909778)

Periodic reports from the Intergovernmental Panel on Climate Change (IPCC) evaluate the risk of climate change brought on by humans. But the sheer volume of scientific data remains inscrutable to the general public, particularly to those who may still question the validity of climate change. In just over 200 pages, this practical text presents and expands upon the essential findings of the IPCC's 5th Assessment Report in a visually stunning and undeniably powerful way to the lay reader. Scientific findings that provide validity to the implications of climate change are presented in clear-cut graphic elements, striking images, and understandable analogies.

The **Second Edition** covers the latest climate change data and scientific consensus from the IPCC Fifth Assessment Report and integrates links to online media. The text is also available in various eText formats, including an upgrade option from Mastering Geography courses.

Television for the Environment *Earth Report* Geography Videos on DVD (0321662989)

This three-DVD set is designed to help students visualize how human decisions and behavior have affected the environment and how individuals are taking steps toward recovery. With topics ranging from the poor land management promoting the devastation of river systems in Central America to the struggles for electricity in China and Africa, these 13 videos from Television for the Environment's global *Earth Report* series recognize the efforts of individuals around the world to unite and protect the planet.

About the Author

Dr. James M. Rubenstein received his B.A. from the University of Chicago in 1970, M.Sc. from the London School of Economics and Political Science in 1971, and Ph.D. from Johns Hopkins University in 1975. He was Professor of Geography at Miami University for 37 years, where he taught urban and human geography. Dr. Rubenstein is now a full-time writer. In addition to this book, Dr. Rubenstein is the author of *The Cultural Landscape,* the bestselling textbook for college and high school human geography, as well as co-author of *Introduction to Contemporary Geography*, both published by Pearson Education. He also conducts research in the automotive industry and has published four books on the subject—*The Changing U.S. Auto Industry: A Geographical Analysis* (Routledge); *Making and Selling Cars: Innovation and Change in the U.S. Auto Industry* (The Johns Hopkins University Press); *A Profile of the Automobile and Motor Vehicle Industry: Innovation, Transformation, Globalization* (Business Expert Press); and *Who Really Made Your Car? Restructuring and Geographic Change in the Auto Industry*(W.E. Upjohn Institute, with Thomas Klier). He also writes a weekly column about local food for *The Oxford Press*. Winston, a lab-husky mix with one brown eye and one blue eye, takes Dr. Rubenstein for long walks in the woods every day.

This book is dedicated to my wife
Bernadette Unger, the love of my life,
and my companion through life.

About our Sustainability Initiatives

Pearson recognizes the environmental challenges facing this planet, as well as acknowledges our responsibility in making a difference. This book is carefully crafted to minimize environmental impact. The binding, cover, and paper come from facilities that minimize waste, energy consumption, and the use of harmful chemicals. Pearson closes the loop by recycling every out-of-date text returned to our warehouse.

Along with developing and exploring digital solutions to our market's needs, Pearson has a strong commitment to achieving carbon-neutrality. As of 2009, Pearson became the first carbon- and climate-neutral publishing company, having reduced our absolute carbon footprint by 22% since then. Pearson has protected over 1,000 hectares of land in Columbia, Costa Rica, the United States, the UK and Canada.

In 2015, Pearson formally adopted *The Global Goals for Sustainable Development,* sponsoring an event at the United Nations General Assembly and other ongoing initiatives. Pearson sources 100% of the electricity we use from green power and invests in renewable energy resources in multiple cities where we have operations, helping make them more sustainable and limiting our environmental impact for local communities.

The future holds great promise for reducing our impact on Earth's environment, and Pearson is proud to be leading the way. We strive to publish the best books with the most up-to-date and accurate content, and to do so in ways that minimize our impact on Earth. To learn more about our initiatives, please visit **https://www.pearson.com/corporate/sustainability.html**

http://goo.gl/y8GvK6

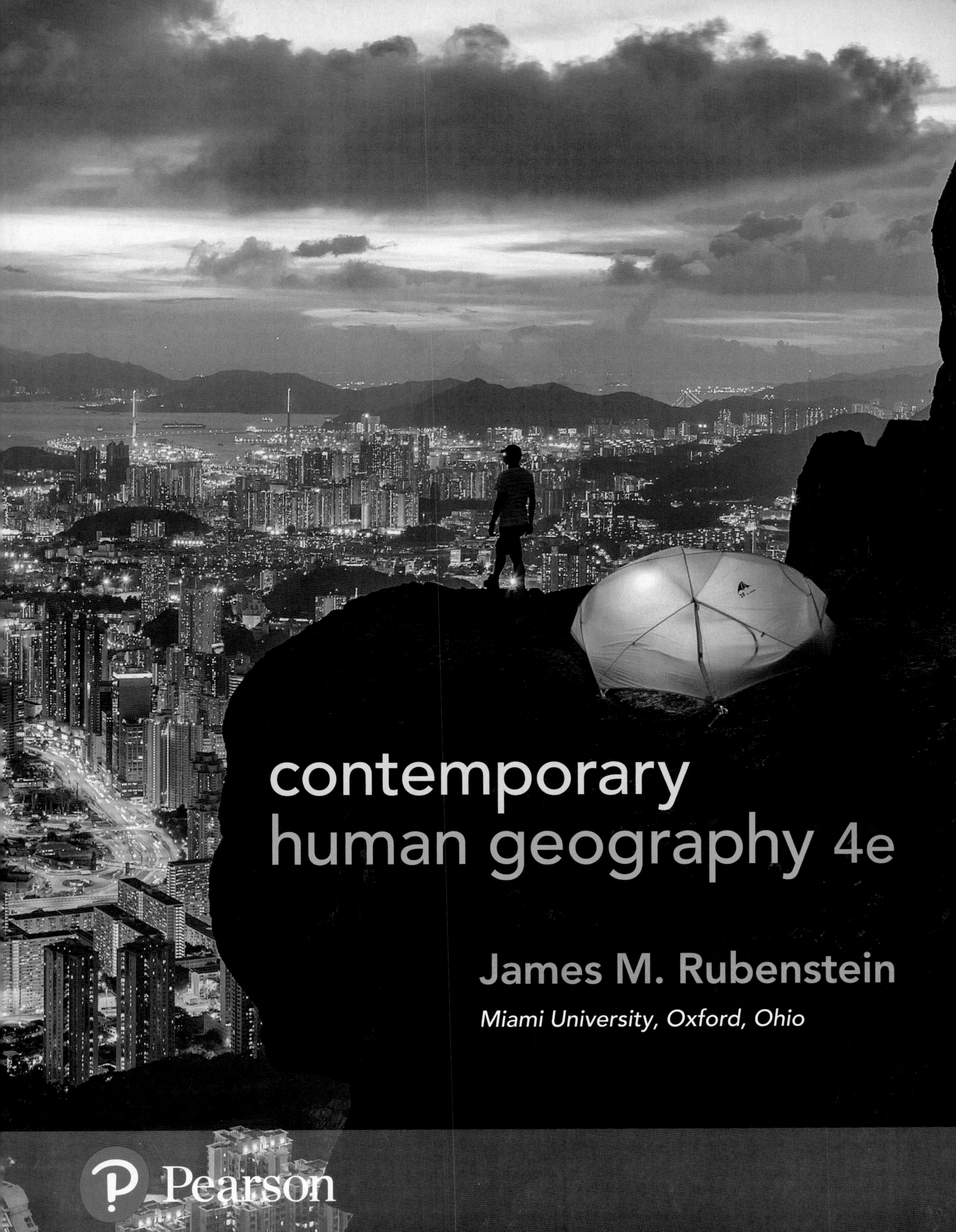
contemporary
human geography 4e
James M. Rubenstein
Miami University, Oxford, Ohio
Pearson

CHAPTER 1

This is Geography

Contemporary geography is the scientific study of where people and activities are found across Earth's surface and the reasons why they are found there. Geography is distinctive because it encompasses both social science and natural science. This book focuses on geography as a social science (human geography).

◀ Google Street View camera documenting Ulan Bator, Mongolia.

KEY ISSUES

1 Why Is Geography a Science?

Geography's most distinctive tool is the map. Prehistoric humans were the first people to make maps. Contemporary tools enable cartographers—and anyone else who has access to electronic devices—to make precise maps and to interpret their meaning.

2 Why Is Every Place Unique?

Geographers understand that each location on Earth is in some ways unique. Each specific place or larger region on Earth possesses a unique combination of features.

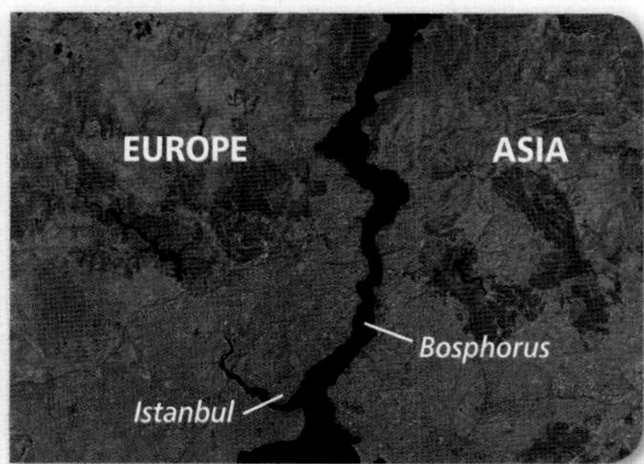

3 Why Are Different Places Similar?

Many features are organized in a regular manner across space. Some regularities are global in scale, whereas others have distinctive local character.

4 Why Are Places Connected?

Distinctive to geography is the importance given to connections between human activities and the physical environment. Some human activities are sustainable, but others are not.

LOCATIONS IN THIS CHAPTER

New York City, p. 8
Boston, p. 15
The Netherlands, p. 28
Venice, p. 8
Çatalhöyük, p. 6
Chicago, p. 17
Nevada, p. 8
California, p. 29
Los Angeles, p. 22
Sun City, p. 10
Florida, p. 17
Everglades, p. 26
Baltimore, p. 19
Washington D.C., p. 9
Miami, p. 29
Istanbul, p. 15
Kenya, p. 12
World's longest name, p. 14
Ulan Bator, p. 2
China, p. 24
India, p. 85
Timor-Leste, pp. 4,5

spatial interaction · place · pattern · GPS · science · GIS · gender & ethnicity · latitude & longitude · diffusion · sustainability · geographic grid · density · projection · region · cartography · unequal access · globalization · connection · site & situation · space · scale · where & why · concentration · maps · ecosystem

▲ 1.1.1
TIMOR-LESTE
A market in Dili, the capital of Timor-Leste. Timor-Leste is one of the world's poorest countries.

Welcome to Geography

- **Summarize geography's five most basic concepts.**

The word geography, invented by the ancient Greek scholar Eratosthenes (ca. 276-ca. 194 B.C.), is based on two Greek words. Geo mans "Earth" and graphy means "to write." Human geographers ask two questions: Where are people and activities found on Earth? Why are they there?

Geography and History

In his framework of all scientific knowledge, the German philosopher Immanuel Kant (1724-1804) compared geography and history:

GEOGRAPHERS . . .	HISTORIANS . . .
identify the location of important places.	identify the dates of important events.
explain why one human activity is found near another.	explain why one human activity follows another chronologically.
ask where and why.	ask when and why.
organize material spatially.	organize material chronologically.
recognize that an action at one point on Earth can result from actions at another point, which can consequently affect conditions elsewhere.	recognize that an action at one point in time can result from past actions and can in turn affect future ones.

History and geography differ in one especially important manner. A geographer can take a plane or car to another place on Earth (Figures 1.1.1 and 1.1.2), but a historian cannot travel back to another time in the past. This ability to reach other places lends excitement to the discipline of geography.

▼ 1.1.2 **CAPE FATUCAMA, TIMOR-LESTE**
A massive statue called Cristo Rei [Christ the King] towers over the coast of Timor-Leste.

Geographers Explain *Where* and *Why*

This chapter introduces basic concepts that geographers employ to address their "where" and "why" questions. To explain where things are, one of geography's most important tools is a map. Maps are discussed in the next several pages.

Geographers employ several basic concepts to explain why every place on Earth is in some ways unique and in other ways related to other locations. To explain why every place is unique, geographers have two basic concepts:

- A **place** is a specific point on Earth distinguished by a particular characteristic. Every place occupies a unique location, or position, on Earth's surface.
- A **region** is an area of Earth defined by one or more distinctive characteristics.

To explain why different places are interrelated geographers have three basic concepts:

- **Scale** is the relationship between the portion of Earth being studied and Earth as a whole. Geographers are increasingly concerned with the global scale.
- **Space** refers to the physical gap or interval between two objects. Geographers observe that many objects are distributed across space in a regular manner, for discernible reasons.
- **Connection** refers to relationships among people and objects across the barrier of space. Geographers are concerned with the various means by which connections occur. They are especially interested in connections between human activities and the physical environment.

Timor-Leste (East Timor), one of the world's newest countries, illustrates geography's five basic concepts: Place (Figure 1.1.3), region (Figure 1.1.4), scale (Figure 1.1.5), space (Figure 1.1.6), and connection (Figure 1.1.7).

▲ 1.1.3 PLACE
The Democratic Republic of Timor-Leste is an independent country situated on the eastern half of the island of Timor. The western portion of the island is mostly part of Indonesia.

▲ 1.1.4 REGION
Timor-Leste is located in Southeast Asia, one of the major areas of the world that geographers identify.

▲ 1.1.5 SCALE
At a local scale, in Timor-Leste's rural villages, such as Aituto, people trade and purchase locally-produced food and goods at a village market. At a global scale, the capital city Dili has supermarkets selling food imported from Indonesia, China, Australia, New Zealand, Portugal, and Brazil.

▲ 1.1.6 SPACE
The gap between places can be minimal or substantial. The distance between the capital Dili and Mount Ramelau, the country's highest elevation (2,986 meters, 9,797 feet), is only 70 kilometers (43 miles). In reality, the gap is substantial, because travel from Dili to Mount Ramelau requires a 5 hour drive followed by a 5 hour hike.

▲ 1.1.7 CONNECTION
Aeroporto Internacional Presidente Nicolau Lobato connects Timor-Leste with Australia, Indonesia, and Singapore.

Ancient & Medieval Maps

- **Summarize the development of the science of cartography.**

Geography's most important tool for thinking spatially about the distribution of features across Earth is a **map**. A map is a two-dimensional or flat-scale model of Earth's surface, or a portion of it. For centuries, geographers have worked to perfect the science of mapmaking, called **cartography**.

Geography in the Ancient World

The science of geography has prehistoric roots (Figure 1.2.1). Major contributors to geographic thought in the ancient eastern Mediterranean included:

- Thales of Miletus (ca. 624–ca. 546 B.C.), who applied principles of geometry to measuring land area.

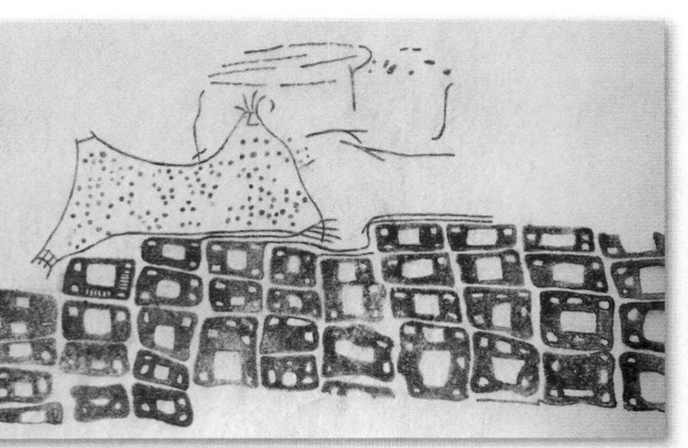

▲ 1.2.1 **ONE OF THE EARLIEST SURVIVING MAPS** This map, dating from 6200 B.C., depicts the town of Çatalhöyük, in present-day Turkey and the eruption of the Hasan Dağ (Mount Hasan) twin-peaks volcano, which is actually located around 140 km northeast of the town. Archaeological evidence indicates that the volcano did erupt around the time that the map was made. The map is now in Turkey's Konya Archaeological Museum.

- Anaximander (610–ca. 546 B.C.), a student of Thales, who made a world map based on information from sailors and argued that the world was shaped like a cylinder.
- Pythagoras (ca. 570–ca. 495 B.C.), who may have been the first to propose a spherical world and argued that the sphere was the most perfect form.
- Hecateus (ca. 550–ca. 476 B.C.), who may have produced the first geography book, called Ges Periodos ("Travels Around the Earth").
- Aristotle (384–322 B.C.), who was the first to demonstrate that Earth was spherical on the basis of evidence.
- Eratosthenes (ca. 276–ca. 195 B.C.), the inventor of the word geography, who accepted that Earth was round (as few others did in his day), calculated its circumference within 0.5 percent accuracy, divided Earth into five climatic regions, and described the known world in one of the first geography books.
- Strabo (ca. 63 B.C.–ca. A.D. 24), who described the known world in a 17-volume work titled Geography.
- Ptolemy (ca. A.D. 100–ca. 170), who wrote the eight-volume Guide to Geography, codified basic principles of mapmaking, and prepared numerous maps that were not improved upon for more than 1,000 years (Figure 1.2.2).

China was another center of early geographic thought. Ancient Chinese geographic contributions included:

- "Yu Gong" ("Tribute of Yu"), a chapter in a book called Shu Jing ("Classic of History"), which was the earliest surviving Chinese geographical writing, by an unknown author from the fifth century B.C., described the economic resources of the country's different provinces.
- Pei Xiu, the "father of Chinese cartography," who produced an elaborate map of the country in A.D. 267.

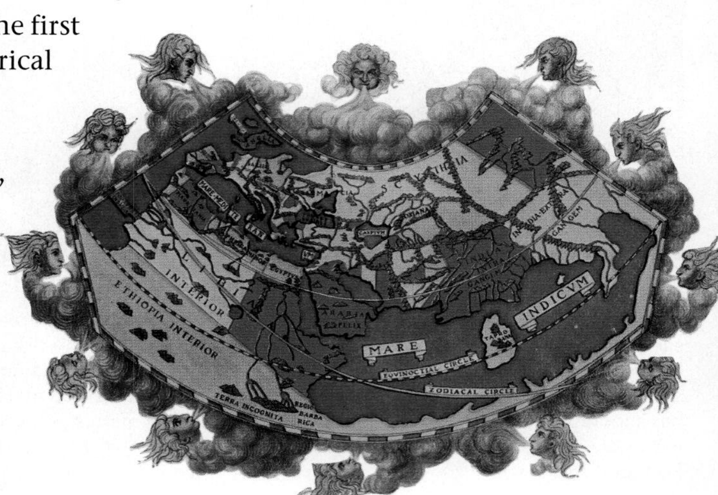

▶ 1.2.2 **WORLD MAP BY PTOLEMY, CA. A.D. 150** The map shows the known world at the height of the Roman Empire, surrounding the Mediterranean Sea and Indian Ocean.

Geography's Revival

After Ptolemy, little progress in mapmaking or geographic thought was made in Europe for several hundred years. Maps became less mathematical and more fanciful, showing Earth as a flat disk surrounded by fierce animals and monsters.

Geographic inquiry continued, though, outside Europe. Contributors outside of Europe included:

- Muhammad al-Idrisi (1100–ca. 1165), a Muslim geographer who prepared a world map and geography text in 1154, building on Ptolemy's long-neglected work (Figure 1.2.3).
- Abu Abdullah Muhammad Ibn-Battuta (1304–ca. 1368), a Moroccan scholar, who wrote Rihla ("Travels") based on three decades of journeys covering more than 120,000 kilometers (75,000 miles) through the Muslim world of northern Africa, southern Europe, and much of Asia.

Making maps as reference tools revived during the Age of Exploration and Discovery. Columbus, Magellan, and other explorers who sailed across the oceans in search of trade routes and resources in the fifteenth and sixteenth centuries required accurate maps to reach desired destinations without wrecking their ships. In turn, cartographers used information collected by the explorers to create more accurate maps.

Influential European cartographers included:

- Martin Waldseemüller (ca. 1470–ca. 1521), a German cartographer who was credited with producing the first map to use the label "America"; he wrote on the map (translated from Latin) "from Amerigo the discoverer . . . as if it were the land of Americus, thus America (Figure 1.2.4)."
- Abraham Ortelius (1527–1598), a Flemish cartographer, who created the first modern atlas and was the first to hypothesize that the continents were once joined together before drifting apart.
- Bernhardus Varenius (1622–1650), who produced Geographia Generalis, which stood for more than a century as the standard treatise on systematic geography.

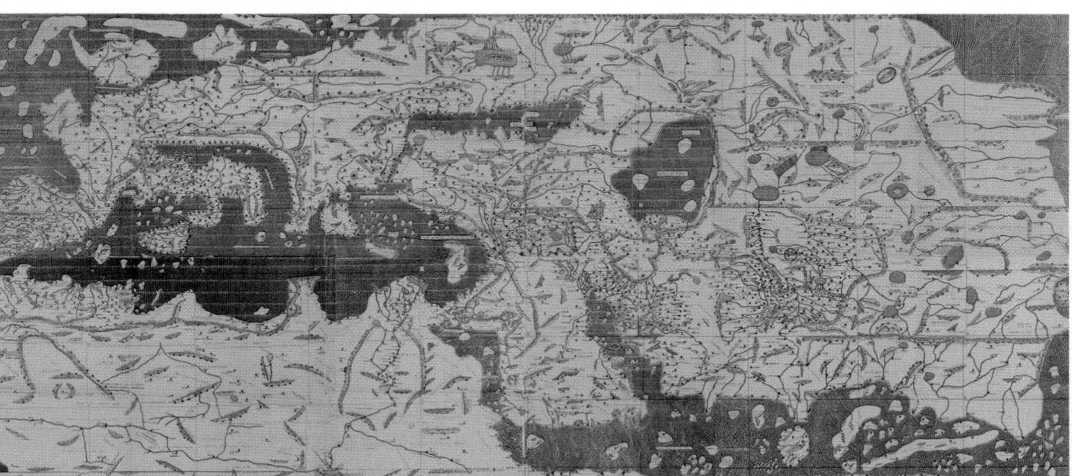

◀ **1.2.3 WORLD MAP BY AL-IDRISI, 1154**
Al-Idrisi built on Ptolemy's map, which had been neglected for nearly a millenium.

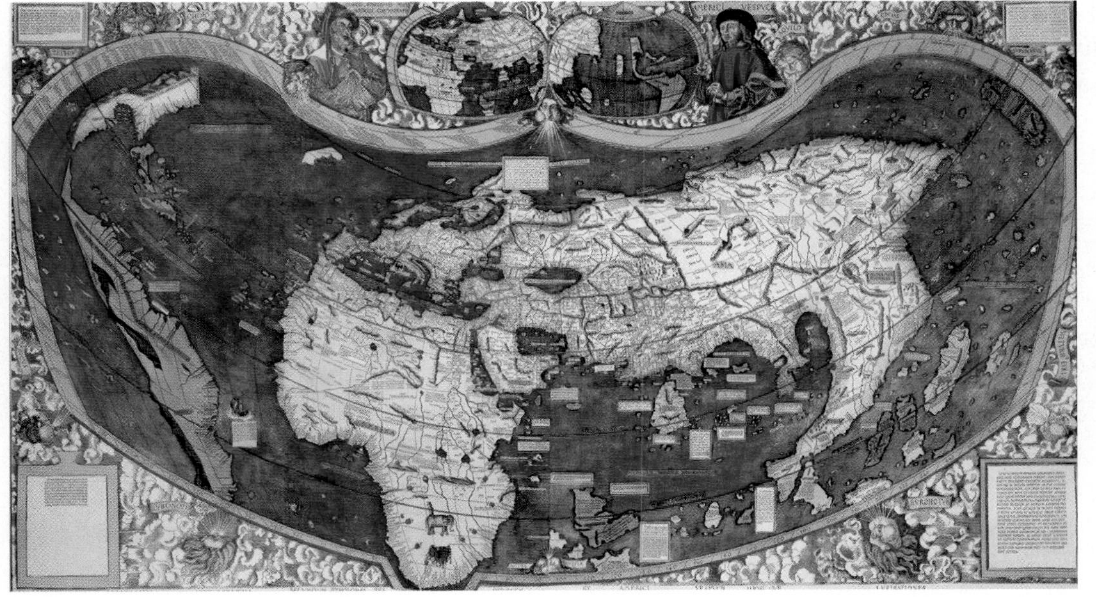

◀ **1.2.4 WORLD MAP BY WALDSEEMÜLLER, 1508**
The name "America" appears in very small print on the map.

Contemporary Geographic Tools

- Explain geography's contemporary analytic mapping tools.

Maps are not just paper documents in textbooks. They have become an essential tool for contemporary delivery of online services through smart phones, tablets, and computers.

GIScience: Analyzing Data

Geographic information science (GIScience) is analysis of data about Earth acquired through satellite and other electronic information technologies. A **geographic information system (GIS)** captures, stores, queries, and displays the geographic data. GIS produces maps (including those in this book) that are more accurate and attractive than those drawn by hand. Each type of information is stored in a layer.

The science of taking measurements of Earth's surface from photographs is called **photogrammetry**. The acquisition of data about Earth's surface from a satellite orbiting Earth or from other long-distance methods is **remote sensing**. At any moment, an aerial sensor attached to a satellite, airplane, or drone may be recording the image of a tiny area on Earth's surface (Figure 1.3.1).

Corporations and government agencies use photogrammetry and remote sensing to create high-quality 3D virtual representations of portions of Earth. These maps can depict the distribution of a wide variety of urban and rural features (Figure 1.3.2).

GIScience helps geographers create more accurate and complex maps and measure changes over time in the characteristics of places. Layers of information acquired through remote sensing and produced through GIS can be described and analyzed. GIScience enables geographers to calculate whether relationships between objects on a map are significant or merely coincidental.

GPS: Pinpointing Locations

Our smart phones, tablets, and computers are equipped with **Global Positioning System (GPS)**, which is a system that determines the precise position of something on Earth. The GPS in use in the United States includes two dozen satellites placed in predetermined orbits; a series of tracking stations to monitor and control the satellites; and receivers that compute position, velocity, and time from the satellite signals.

GPS is most commonly used for navigation. Pilots of aircraft and ships stay on course with GPS. On land, GPS detects a vehicle's current position, the motorist programs the desired destination into a GPS device, and the device provides instructions on how to reach the destination.

Thanks to GPS, our electronic devices provide us with a wealth of information about the specific place on Earth we currently occupy. The locations of all the information we gather and photos we take with our electronic devices are recorded through **geotagging**, which is identification and storage of a piece of information by its precise latitude and longitude coordinates. Geotagging has led to concerns about privacy (refer ahead to Debate It! feature on page 25).

▲ 1.3.1 **PHOTOGRAMMETRY**
A drone flies a test course in Nevada to determine the precision of its mapping capabilities.

▲ 1.3.2 **3D VIRTUAL REPRESENTATION**
A 3D Google Earth image of Venice, Italy, is projected on a large screen at the Whitney Museum of American Art in New York.

VGI: Collecting and Sharing Data

Most of the maps fed into our electronic devices are provided by a handful of companies (Figure 1.3.3). However, smart phones, tablets, and computers enable individuals to make maps and share them with others. **Volunteered geographic information (VGI)** is the creation and dissemination of geographic data contributed voluntarily and for free by individuals. VGI is part of the broader trend of **citizen science**, which is scientific research by amateur scientists, and **participatory GIS (PGIS)**, which is community-based mapping. Citizen science and PGIS collect and disseminate local knowledge and information through electronic devices.

After Hurricane Maria devastated Puerto Rico in September 2017, geographers at Miami University mapped a southeastern section of the island. Using software from the Humanitarian OpenStreetMap Team, the geographers placed on the map outlines of buildings from satellite imagery taken before the hurricane. The Red Cross requested the map to help identify where to respond first (Figure 1.3.4).

A **mashup** is a map that overlays data from one source on top of a map provided by a mapping service, such as Google Maps or Google Earth. The term mashup refers to the practice of overlaying data from one source on top of one of the mapping services; the term comes from the hip hop practice of mixing two or more songs.

▲ 1.3.3 GOOGLE STREET MAPPING

Individuals can create mashups on their personal computers because mapping services provide access to the application programming interface (API), which is the language that links a database such as an address list with software such as mapping software (see What's Your Geography?).

◀ 1.3.4 PARTICIPATORY GIS Miami University geographers help Red Cross map devastation in Puerto Rico from Hurricane Maria.

WHAT'S YOUR GEOGRAPHY?

Mental Maps

A **mental map** is a personal representation of a portion of Earth's surface. A mental map depicts what an individual knows about a place, and it contains personal impressions of what is in the place and where the place is located.

1. Draw on paper a mental map depicting your route between two familiar places, such as between home and geography class. Show the paths (roads or walkways) and landmarks along the route, such as buildings or shops.
2. Compare your mental map to those made by others in your class. How detailed is your depiction of paths and landmarks compared to those of others? At school, for example, a senior is likely to have a more detailed map than a newcomer.
3. Compare your mental map to a map of the same area from Google Maps or Bing Maps. How accurate is your map? Did you forget something important or put something in the wrong place?
4. At **OpenStreetMap.org**, see if your route has been mapped. ***Click*** the arrow icon to the right of *Go*. ***Enter*** your starting and ending addresses. ***Choose*** car, bicycle, or foot. ***Press*** *Go*. Is this your preferred route? Why or why not (Figure 1.3.5)? Do what you consider important landmarks appear on the map? Why or why not?

▲ 1.3.5 OPENSTREETMAP, WASHINGTON, D.C. The path by foot from the Association of American Geographers office (green pin) to the National Geographic office (red pin) passes several landmarks, including three churches.

Interpreting Maps

▲ 1.4.1
USING A MAP
Electronic maps have not completely replaced paper ones.

- **Understand the concepts of map scale and projection.**

To make a map, a cartographer must make two decisions:

- How much of Earth's surface to depict on the map (map scale).
- How to transfer a spherical Earth to a flat map (projection).

Map Scale

Should a map show the entire globe, or a country, or a city (Figure 1.4.1)? To make a scale model of the entire world, many details must be omitted because of lack of space. Conversely, a map showing only a small portion of Earth's surface can provide a wealth of detail about a particular place.

The level of detail and the amount of area covered on a map depend on its **map scale**, which is the relationship of a feature's size on a map to its actual size on Earth. Map scale is presented in three ways (Figure 1.4.2):

- A ratio or fraction shows the numerical ratio between distances on the map and Earth's surface. A scale of 1:1,000,000 means that 1 unit (for example, inch, centimeter, foot, finger length) on the map represents 1 million of the same unit on the ground. The 1 on the left side of the ratio always refers to a unit of distance on the map, and the number on the right always refers to the same unit of distance on Earth's surface.
- A written scale describes the relationship between map and Earth distances in words. For example, in the statement "1 centimeter equals 10 kilometers," the first number refers to map distance and the second to distance on Earth's surface.
- A graphic scale usually consists of a bar line marked to show distance on Earth's surface. To use a bar line, first determine with a ruler the distance on the map in inches or centimeters. Then hold the ruler against the bar line and read the number on the bar line opposite the map distance on the ruler. The number on the bar line is the equivalent distance on Earth's surface.

▼ 1.4.2
MAP SCALE,
Sun City, Arizona.

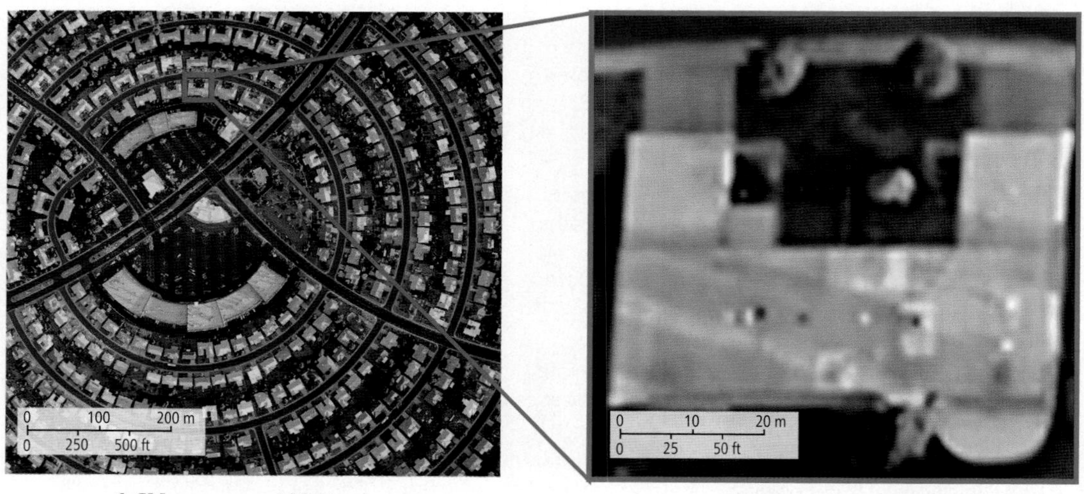

1 CM on map = 100M
1 :10,000

1 CM on map = 10M
1 :1,000

Projection

Earth is very nearly a sphere and is therefore accurately represented with a globe. However, a globe is an extremely limited tool with which to communicate information about Earth's surface. A small globe does not have enough space to display detailed information, whereas a large globe is too bulky and cumbersome to use. And a globe is difficult to photocopy, display on a computer screen, or carry in a car. Consequently, most maps, including those in this book, are flat.

Earth's spherical shape poses a challenge for cartographers because drawing Earth on a flat piece of paper unavoidably produces some distortion. Cartographers have invented hundreds of clever methods of producing flat maps, but none produces perfect results (Figures 1.4.3, 1.4.4, 1.4.5, and 1.4.6). The scientific method of transferring locations on Earth's surface to a flat map is called **projection**.

The problem of distortion is especially severe for maps depicting the entire world. Four types of distortion can result:

1. The ***shape*** of an area can be distorted, so that it appears more elongated or squat than in reality.
2. The ***distance*** between two points may become increased or decreased.
3. The ***relative size*** of different areas may be altered, so that one area may appear larger than another on a map but is in reality smaller.
4. The ***direction*** from one place to another can be distorted.

Animation: Map Projections
https://goo.gl/Sfk5GG

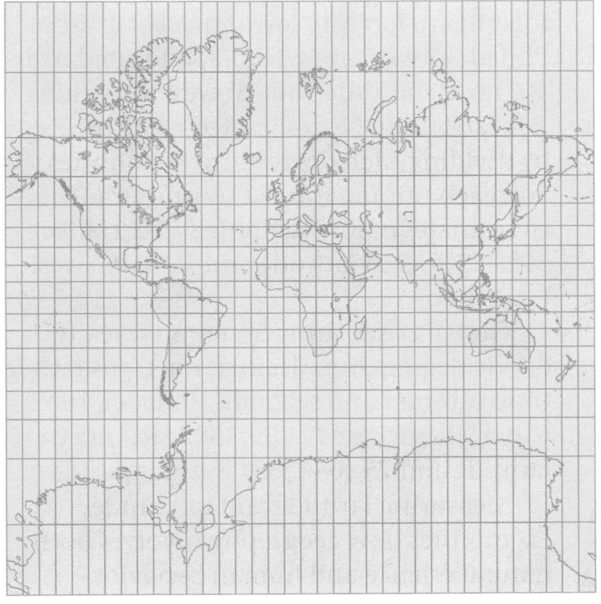

▲ 1.4.3 **MERCATOR PROJECTION**
This has little distortion of shape and direction. Its greatest disadvantage is that relative size is grossly distorted, making high-latitude places near the North and South poles look much larger than they actually are.

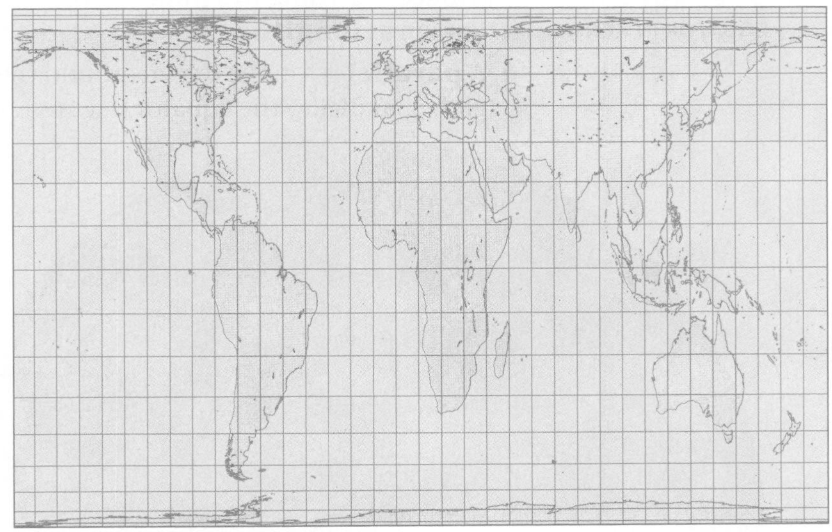

▲ 1.4.4 **GALL-PETERS PROJECTION**
In contrast with the Mercator projection, does not distort relative size but does distort shape.

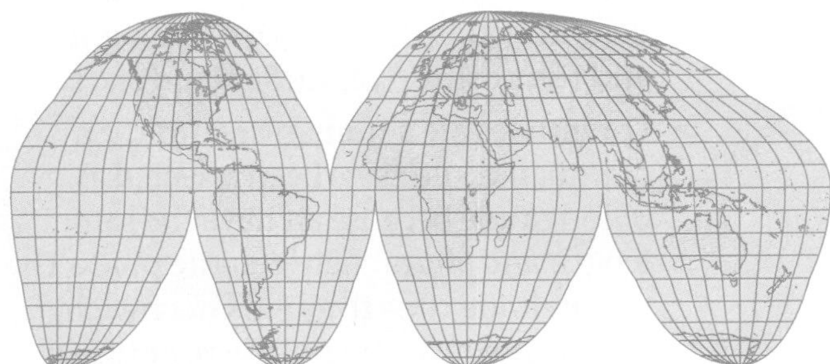

▲ 1.4.5 **GOODE HOMOLOSINE PROJECTION**
This separates the Eastern and Western hemispheres into two pieces, a characteristic known as interruption. The meridians (the vertical lines), which in reality converge at the North and South poles, do not converge at all on the map. Also, they do not form right angles with the parallels (the horizontal lines).

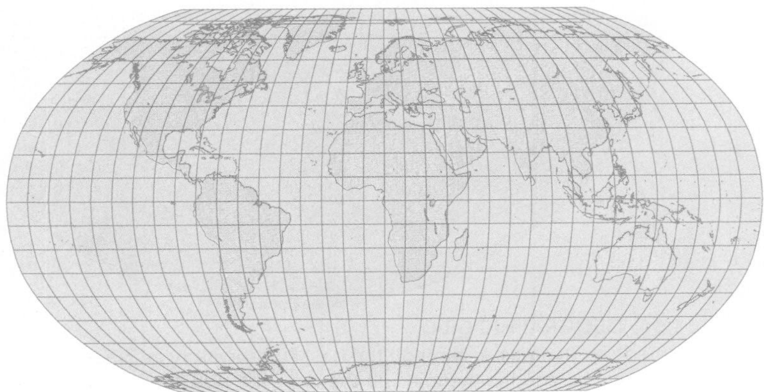

▲ 1.4.6 **ROBINSON PROJECTION**
This is useful for displaying information across the oceans. Its major disadvantage is that by allocating space to the oceans, the land areas are smaller than on interrupted maps of the same size.

▲ 1.5.1 THE EQUATOR IN KENYA

The Geographic Grid

- Explain how the geographic grid determines location and time of day.

The geographic grid is a system of imaginary arcs drawn in a grid pattern on Earth's surface. The geographic grid plays an important role in telling time.

Latitude and Longitude

The location of any place on Earth's surface can be described by these human-created arcs, known as meridians and parallels, two sets of imaginary arcs drawn in a grid pattern on Earth's surface:

- A **meridian** is an arc drawn between the North and South poles. The location of each meridian is identified on Earth's surface according to a numbering system known as **longitude**.
- A **parallel** is a circle drawn around the globe parallel to the equator (Figure 1.5.1) and at right angles to the meridians. The numbering system to indicate the location of a parallel is called **latitude**.

Since Earth is roughly spherical, distances on the geographic grid are expressed in degrees of longitude and latitude based on the 360 degrees in a circle (Figure 1.5.2).

Latitude and longitude are used together to identify locations. For example, Philadelphia, Pennsylvania, is located near 40° north latitude and 75° west longitude. A location can be designated more precisely by dividing each degree into 60 minutes (') and each minute into 60 seconds ("). The coordinates of Philadelphia's City Hall are 39°57'8" north latitude and 75°9'49" west longitude.

Global Positioning Systems typically divide degrees into decimal fractions rather than minutes and seconds. Philadelphia's City Hall is located at 39.9523882° north latitude and 75.1640233° west longitude.

Measuring latitude and longitude exemplifies how geography involves both natural science and human behavior.

- Latitudes are scientifically derived by Earth's shape and its rotation around the Sun. The equator (0° latitude) is the parallel with the largest circumference, where every day has 12 hours of daylight. Even in ancient times, latitude could be determined by the length of daylight and the position of the Sun and stars.
- Longitudes are a human creation. Any meridian could have been selected as 0° longitude because all have the same length and all run between the poles. The 0° longitude runs through Greenwich, and is known as the **prime meridian**, because England was the world's most powerful country when longitude was first accurately measured and the international agreement was made.

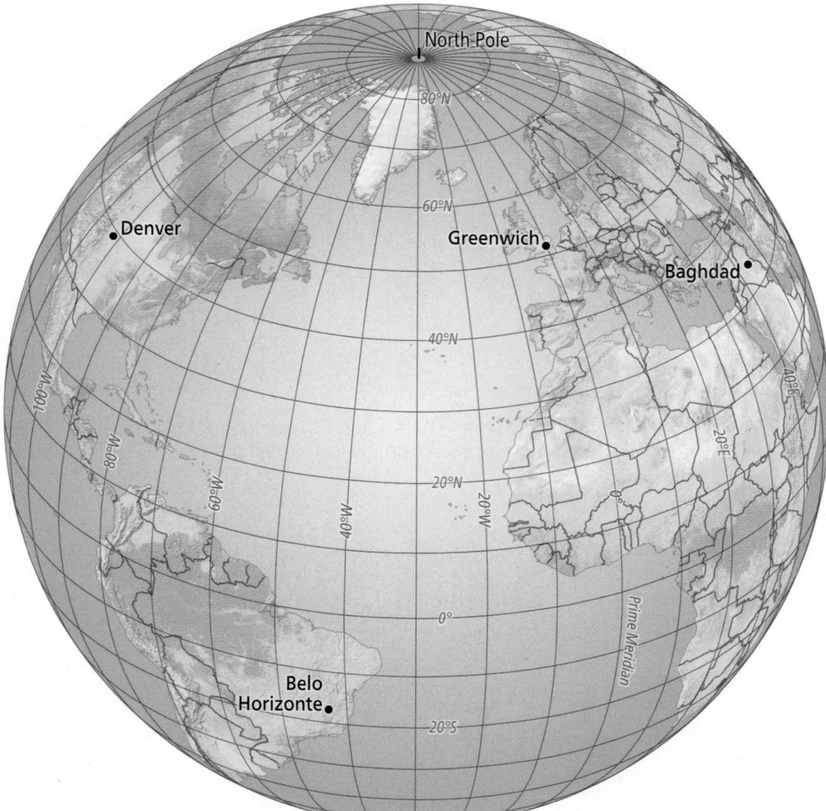

▲ 1.5.2 GEOGRAPHIC GRID
The meridian that passes through the Royal Observatory at Greenwich, England, is 0° longitude, and the meridian on the opposite side of the globe from 0° is 180° longitude. A meridian is numbered between 0°and 180° east or west longitude, depending on whether it is east or west of 0°. The equator is 0° latitude, the North Pole 90° north latitude, and the South Pole 90° south latitude. A parallel is numbered between 0°and 90° north or south latitude, depending on whether it is north or south of the equator.

Telling Time

Longitude is the basis for calculating time. Recall that Earth as a sphere is divided into 360° of longitude (the degrees from 0° to 180° west longitude plus the degrees from 0° to 180° east longitude).

As Earth rotates daily, these 360 imaginary lines of longitude pass beneath the cascading sunshine. If we let every fifteenth degree of longitude represent one time zone, and divide the 360° by 15°, we get 24 time zones, or one for each hour of the day. By international agreement, **Coordinated Universal Time (UTC)**, known informally as **Greenwich Mean Time (GMT)**, which is the time at the prime meridian (0° longitude), is the master reference time for all points on Earth.

Each 15° band of longitude is assigned to a standard time zone (Figure 1.5.3). The western United States, which is near 120° west longitude, is therefore 8 hours earlier than UTC (the 120° difference between the prime meridian and 120° west longitude, divided by 15° per hour, equals 8 hours). Thus when the time in Nevada in the winter is 10:32 A.M., it is 6:32 P.M. (or 18:32 hours, using a 24-hour clock) UTC. During the summer, many places in the world, including most of North America, move the clocks ahead one hour; so in the summer when it is 6:32 P.M. UTC, the time in Nevada is 11:32 A.M.

The **International Date Line** is an arc that for the most part follows 180° longitude, although it deviates in several places to avoid dividing land areas. When the International Date Line is crossed heading east (toward America), the clock moves back 24 hours, or one entire day. When it is crossed heading west (toward Asia), the calendar moves ahead one day.

Inability to measure longitude was the greatest obstacle to exploration and discovery for many centuries. Ships ran aground or were lost at sea because no one on board could pinpoint longitude. In 1714, the British Parliament enacted the Longitude Act, which offered a prize equivalent to several million in today's dollars to the person who could first measure longitude accurately.

Most eighteenth-century scientists were convinced that longitude could be determined only by the position of the stars. English clockmaker John Harrison won the prize by connecting longitude and time. He invented the first portable clock that could keep accurate time on a ship—because it did not have a pendulum (Figure 1.5.4). When the Sun was directly overhead of the ship—noon local time—Harrison's portable clock set to Greenwich time could say it was 2 P.M. in Greenwich, for example, so the ship would be at 30° west longitude because each hour of difference was equivalent to traveling 15° longitude.

▲ 1.5.4 **HARRISON'S CLOCK**
This clock helped people in the eighteenth century calculate longitude.

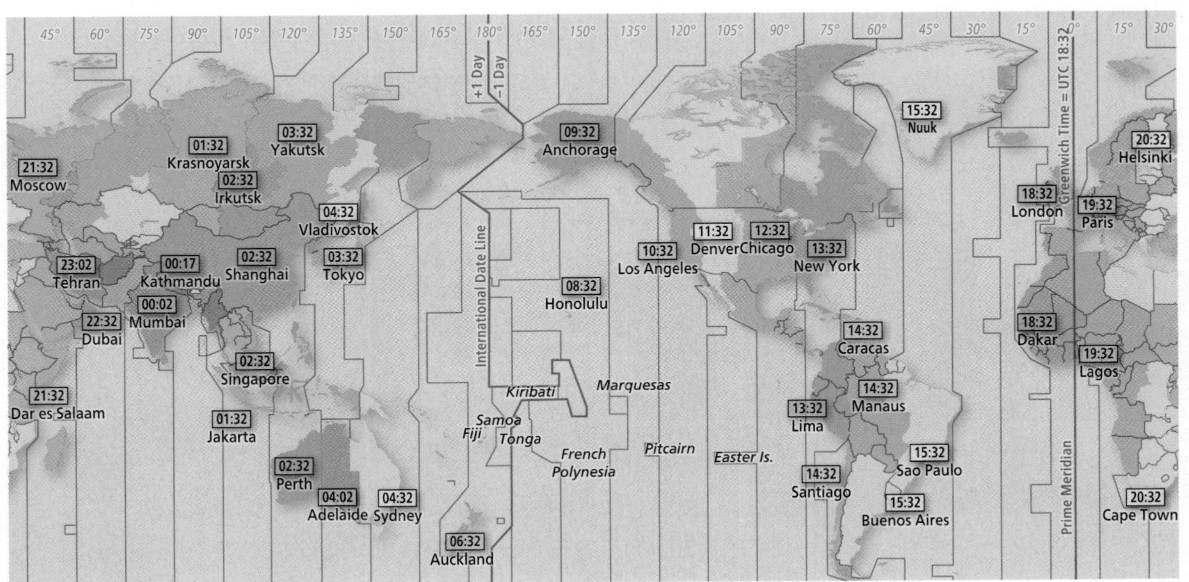

▲ 1.5.3 **TIME ZONES**
The United States and Canada share four standard time zones: Eastern (5 hours earlier than UTC, near 75° west), Central (6 hours earlier than UTC, near 90° west), Mountain (7 hours earlier than UTC, near 105° west), and Pacific (8 hours earlier than UTC, near 120° west). The United States has two additional standard time zones: Alaska (9 hours earlier than UTC, near 135° west) and Hawaii-Aleutian (10 hours earlier than UTC, near 150° west). Canada has two additional standard time zones: Atlantic (4 hours earlier than UTC, near 60° west) and Newfoundland (3 1/2 hours earlier than UTC). The residents of Newfoundland assert that their island, which lies between 53° and 59° west longitude, would face dark winter afternoons if it were in the Atlantic Time Zone and dark winter mornings if it were 3 hours earlier than UTC.

Place: A Unique Location

- Summarize the distinctive features of a place.

Humans possess a strong sense of place—that is, a feeling for the features that contribute to the distinctiveness of a particular spot on Earth—perhaps a hometown, vacation destination, or college. Describing the features of a place is an essential building block for geographers to explain similarities, differences, and changes across Earth. Geographers analyze where particular places are located and the combination of features that make each place on Earth distinct.

Geographers describe a feature's place on Earth by identifying its **location**, which is the position that something occupies on Earth's surface. In doing so, they consider three ways to identify location: place name, site, and situation.

Place Names

Because all inhabited places on Earth's surface—and many uninhabited places—have been named, the most straightforward way to describe a particular location is often by referring to its place name. A **toponym** is the name given to a place on Earth (Figure 1.6.1).

A place may be named for a person, perhaps its founder or a famous person with no connection to the community, such as George Washington. Some settlers selected place names associated with religion, such as St. Louis and St. Paul, whereas other names derive from ancient history, such as Athens, Attica, and Rome, or from earlier occupants of the place.

The Board of Geographical Names, operated by the U.S. Geological Survey, was established in the late nineteenth century to be the final arbiter of names on U.S. maps. In recent years the board has been especially concerned with removing offensive place names, such as those with racial or ethnic connotations.

Names can be controversial. This book utilizes the name Czechia rather than Czech Republic in accordance with recent Czech government preferences. However, a 2013 poll found 73 percent of people in that country disliked the name Czechia.

▲ 1.6.1 **WORLD'S LONGEST PLACE NAME**
This place in New Zealand is recognized as the world's longest one-word place name. It translates from the Maori language as "The summit where Tamatea, the man with the big knees, the climber of mountains, the land-swallower who travelled about, played his nose flute to his loved one."

Site

The second way that geographers describe the location of a place is **site**, which is the physical character of a place. Important site characteristics include climate, water sources, topography, soil, vegetation, latitude, and elevation. The combination of physical features gives each place a distinctive character.

Site factors have always been essential in selecting locations for settlements, although people have disagreed on the attributes of a good site, depending on cultural values. Some have preferred a hilltop site for easy defense from attack. Others have located settlements near convenient river-crossing points to facilitate communication with people in other places. Humans have the ability to modify the characteristics of a site. Central Boston is more than twice as large today as it was during colonial times (Figure 1.6.2).

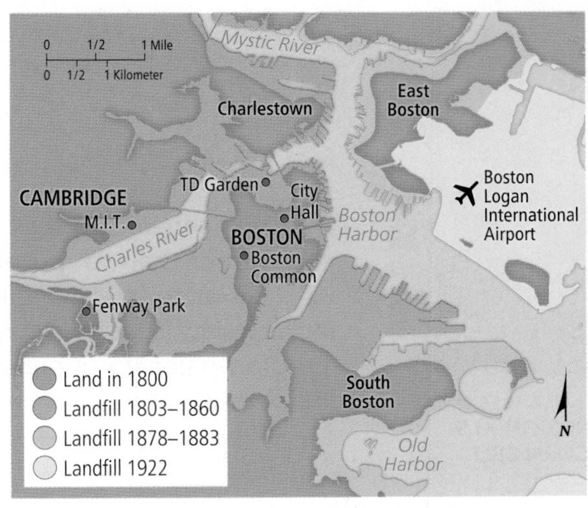

▲ 1.6.2 **CHANGING SITE OF BOSTON**
The site of Boston has been altered by filling in much of Boston Harbor. Colonial Boston was a peninsula connected to the mainland by a very narrow neck. During the nineteenth century, a dozen major projects filled in most of the bays, coves, and marshes. A major twentieth-century landfill project created Logan Airport. Several landfill projects continue into the twenty-first century.

Situation

Situation is the location of a place relative to other places. Situation is a valuable way to indicate location, for two reasons:

- Situation helps us find an unfamiliar place by comparing its location with a familiar one. We give directions to people by referring to the situation of a place: "It's down past the courthouse, beside the large elm tree."
- Situation helps us understand the importance of a location. Many places are important because they are accessible to other places. For example, because of its situation, Istanbul has become a center for the trading of goods and culture between Europe and Asia (Figure 1.6.3).

▼ ▶1.6.3 **SITUATION OF ISTANBUL**
Istanbul is situated along the Bosphorus, a waterway between the Black and Mediterranean seas. Europe lies to the west and Asia to the east. (a) Satellite image of Istanbul; (b) Photograph of Istanbul.

▲ 1.7.1 FORMAL REGION: U.S. CORN BELT

Region: A Unique Area

- Identify three types of regions.

The "sense of place" that humans possess may apply to a larger area of Earth rather than to a specific point. An area of Earth defined by one or more distinctive characteristics is a region. People, activities, and environment display similarities and regularities within a region and differ in some way from those of other regions. A region gains uniqueness from possessing not a single human or environmental characteristic but a combination of them.

Cultural Landscape

The designation region can be applied to any area larger than a point and smaller than the entire planet. Geographers most often apply the concept at one of two scales:

- Several neighboring countries that share important features, such as those in Latin America.
- Many localities within a country, such as those in southern California.

A region derives its unified character through the **cultural landscape**, which is a combination of cultural features such as language and religion, economic features such as agriculture and industry, and physical features such as climate and vegetation. The southern California region can be distinguished from the northern California region, for example.

Formal Region

Geographers identify three types of regions—formal, functional, and vernacular.

A **formal region**, also called a **uniform region**, is an area within which most people share one or more distinctive characteristics. The shared feature could be a cultural value such as a common language, an economic activity such as production of a particular crop, or an environmental property such as climate (Figure 1.7.1). In a formal region, the selected characteristic is present throughout.

Some formal regions are easy to identify, such as countries or local government units. Montana is an example of a formal region, characterized with equal intensity throughout the state by a government that passes laws, collects taxes, and issues license plates. The formal region of Montana has precise and legally recognized boundaries, and everyone living within them shares the status of being subject to a common set of laws.

In other kinds of formal regions, a characteristic may be predominant rather than universal. For example, the North American winter wheat belt is a formal region in which wheat is the most commonly grown crop, but other crops are grown there as well. And the winter wheat belt can be distinguished from the corn belt, which is a region where corn is the most commonly grown crop (Figure 1.7.2).

In identifying a formal region, it is important to recognize the diversity of cultural, economic, and environmental factors, even while making a generalization. A minority of people in a region may speak a language, practice a a religion, or possess resources different from those of the majority. People in a region may play distinctive roles in the economy and hold different positions in society based on their gender or ethnicity.

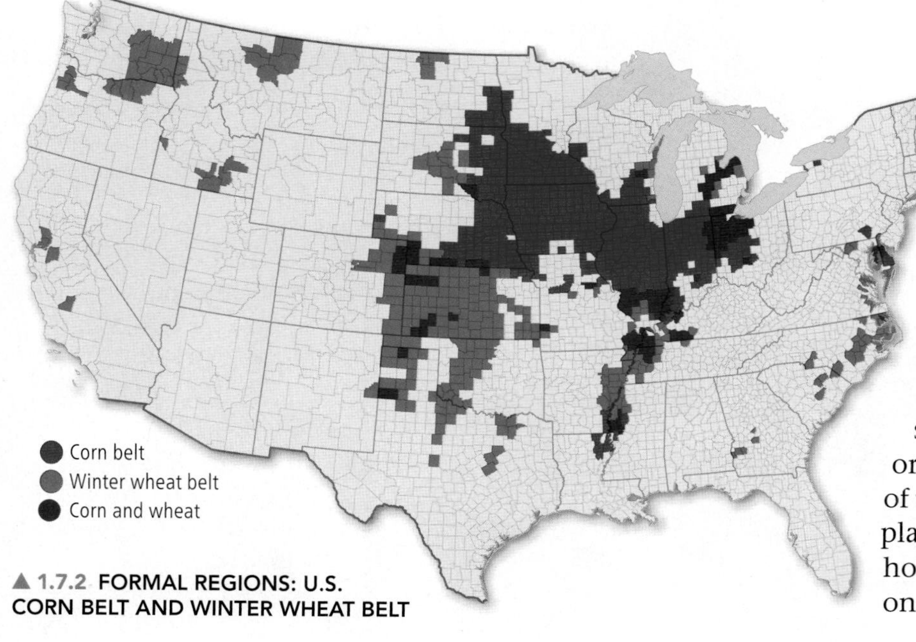

▲ 1.7.2 FORMAL REGIONS: U.S. CORN BELT AND WINTER WHEAT BELT

Functional Region

A **functional region**, also called a **nodal region**, is an area organized around a node or focal point. The characteristic chosen to define a functional region dominates at a central focus or node and diminishes in importance outward. The region is tied to the central point by transportation or communications systems or by economic or functional associations.

Geographers often use functional regions to display information about economic areas. A region's node may be a shop or service, with the boundaries of the region marking the limits of the trading area of the activity. People and activities may be attracted to the node, and information may flow from the node to the surrounding area.

An example of a functional region is the reception area of a TV station (Figure 1.7.3). At the center of its service area, a TV station's over-the-air signal is strongest, and the percentage of cable and satellite dish receivers tuned to that station is highest. At some distance from the center, more people are watching a station originating in another city (Figure 1.7.4). That place is the boundary between the nodal regions of the two TV market areas.

Social media offer numerous examples of functional regions. Although social media can be used to interact equally with someone nearby and someone far away, in reality most interaction is with people nearby and fewer with people far away. Nonetheless, new technology can break down some traditional functional regions. Through the Internet, customers can shop at distant stores, and newspapers composed in one place are delivered to customers elsewhere.

▲ 1.7.3 FUNCTIONAL REGION: TV STATION
Miami, Florida.

ALABAMA
GEORGIA
Mobile
Pensacola
Panama City
Thomasville
Tallahassee
Jacksonville
Gainesville
Orlando
Tampa
St. Petersburg
West Palm Beach
Ft. Myers
Naples
Miami

▲ 1.7.4 FUNCTIONAL REGIONS: FLORIDA TV MARKETS
Designated market areas (DMAs) within Florida are examples of functional regions. In the case of westernmost Florida, the node—the TV station—is in an adjacent state (Mobile, Alabama). The state of Florida is an example of formal region.

Vernacular Region

A **vernacular region**, or **perceptual region**, is an area that people believe exists as part of their cultural identity. Such regions emerge from people's informal sense of place rather than from scientific models developed through geographic thought. An example of a vernacular region is the U.S. Midwest (Figure 1.7.5). However, the actual location of the Midwest depends on the feature being mapped (Figure 1.7.6). A useful way to identify a perceptual region is to get someone to draw a mental map.

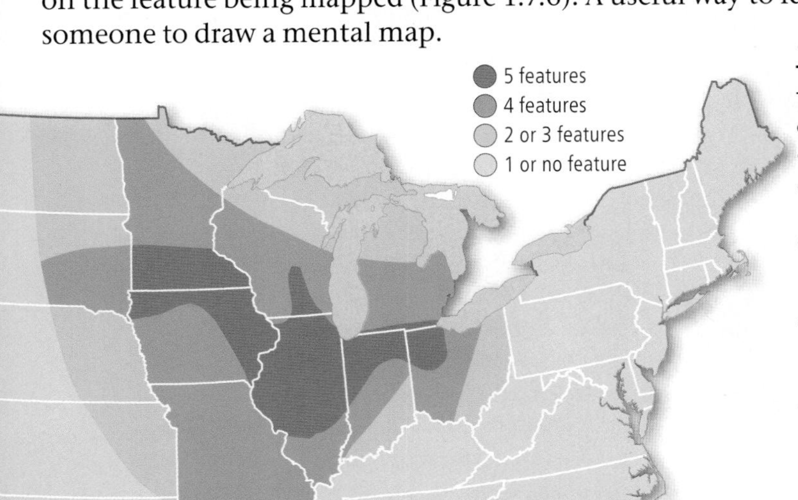

◀ 1.7.5 VERNACULAR REGION: THE MIDWEST
The Midwest is a vernacular region that can be defined in a number of ways:

- U.S.Census definition
- At least 50% self-identify as a Midwesterner
- Eastern Broadleaf forest or Prairie parkland ecosystem
- At least 60% "like" a team in the MLB A.L. or N.L. Central Division
- 75% of the nation's corn production

▼ 1.7.6 FUNCTIONAL REGION: CHICAGOLAND
Chicago, the largest city in the Midwest, is an example of the node of a functional region.

▲ 1.8.1 GLOBAL CULTURE: JEANS AND MCDONALD'S

Scale: From Global to Local

- Compare local and global scales in economy and culture.

Scale is the relationship between the portion of Earth being studied and Earth as a whole. Geographers think about scale at many levels, from local to global.

Although geographers study every scale from the individual to the entire Earth, increasingly they are concerned with global-scale patterns and processes. **Globalization** refers to actions or processes that involve the entire world and result in making something worldwide in scope. Geographers observe processes fostering globalization of the economy and globalization of culture (Figure 1.8.1).

Globalization of the Economy

A few people living in very remote regions of the world may be able to provide all of their daily necessities. But most economic activities undertaken in one region are influenced by interaction with decision makers located elsewhere.

Globalization of the economy has been led primarily by transnational corporations, sometimes called multinational corporations (Figure 1.8.2). A **transnational corporation** conducts research, operates factories, and sells products in many countries, not just where its headquarters and principal shareholders are located.

Every place in the world is part of the global economy, but globalization has led to more specialization at the local level. Each place plays a distinctive role, based on its local assets, as assessed by transnational corporations. A locality may be especially suitable for a transnational corporation to conduct research, to develop new engineering systems, to extract raw materials, to produce parts, to store finished products, to sell them, or to manage operations. In a global economy, transnational corporations remain competitive by correctly identifying the optimal location for each of these activities. Factories are closed in some locations and opened in others.

Geographers divide the world into regions of developed countries and regions of developing countries. Various shared features—such as per capita income, level of education, and life expectancy—distinguish developed regions and developing regions. Possession of wealth and material goods is higher in developed countries. These differences are discussed in more detail in Chapter 10.

Globalization of Culture

Geographers observe that increasingly uniform cultural preferences produce uniform "global" landscapes of material artifacts and of cultural values. Fast-food restaurants, service stations, and retail chains deliberately create a visual appearance that varies among locations as little as possible. That way, customers know what to expect, regardless of where in the world they happen to be.

As more people become aware of elements of global culture and aspire to possess them, local cultural beliefs, forms, and traits are threatened with extinction. The survival of a local culture's distinctive beliefs, forms, and traits may be threatened by interaction with such social customs as wearing jeans and Nike shoes, consuming Coca-Cola and McDonald's hamburgers, and communicating using cell phones and computers.

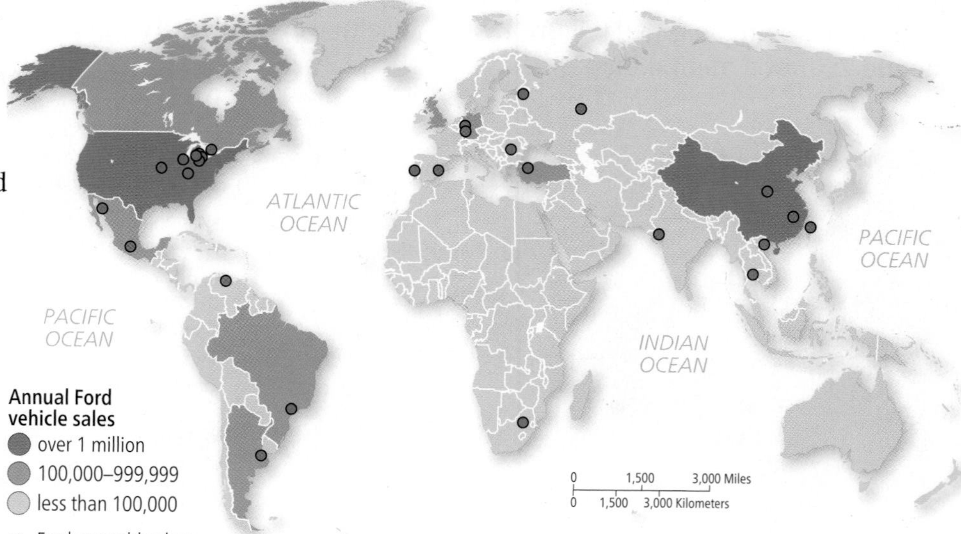

▶ 1.8.2 GLOBAL ECONOMY: FORD MOTOR COMPANY SALES AND VEHICLE ASSEMBLY PLANTS

Local Diversity

Globalization has not destroyed the uniqueness of an individual place's culture and economy. Human geographers understand that many contemporary social problems result from a tension between forces promoting global culture and economy on the one hand and preservation of local economic autonomy and cultural traditions on the other hand. Strong adverse reaction to globalization by many people in both developed and developing countries has inspired efforts to restore local cultural traditions and sever economic relations with others places. Countries and regions within countries have disagreed sharply on the appropriate policies to improve economic conditions.

Cultural differences among places not only persist but actually flourish in many places. The communications revolution that promotes globalization of culture also permits preservation of cultural diversity. TV, for example, was once limited to a handful of channels displaying one set of cultural values. With the distribution of programming through cable, satellite, Internet, and streaming services, people now can choose from an infinite number of programs in many languages.

With the globalization of communications, people in two distant places can watch the same TV program. At the same time, with the fragmentation of the broadcasting market, two people in the same house can watch different programs. Groups of people on every continent may aspire to wear jeans, but they might live with someone who prefers skirts. In a global culture, companies can target groups of consumers with similar tastes in different parts of the world.

Spatial Association

A region gains meaning through its unique combination of features. The presence of some of these features may be coincidental, but others are related to each other. **Spatial association** occurs within a region if the distribution of one feature is related to the distribution of another feature. Spatial association is strong if two features have very similar distributions, and spatial association is weak if two features have very different distributions.

Figure 1.8.3 displays the distribution of three features in Baltimore City—income, life expectancy at birth, and nonconforming liquor stores—that display a close spatial association. East and West Baltimore have (a) the lowest incomes, (b) the lowest life expectancy (as explained in Chapter 2, the number of years a baby born this year is expected to live), and (c) the most nonconforming liquor stores (liquor stores that do not conform to current law but were legal when opened). The presence of a large number of nonconforming liquor stores indicates that a neighborhood has more liquor stores than considered appropriate. The maps show that the areas with the lowest income and lowest life expectancy have the most nonconforming liquor stores.

▼ 1.8.3 **SPATIAL ASSOCIATION IN BALTIMORE CITY**
(a) Income
(b) Life expectancy at birth
(c) Nonconforming liquor stores

(a)

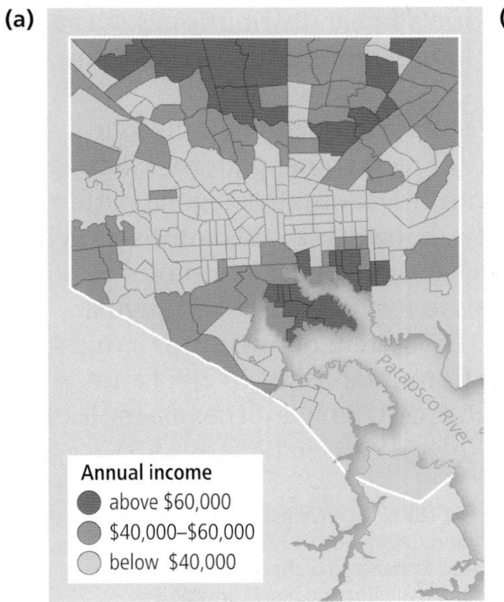

(b)

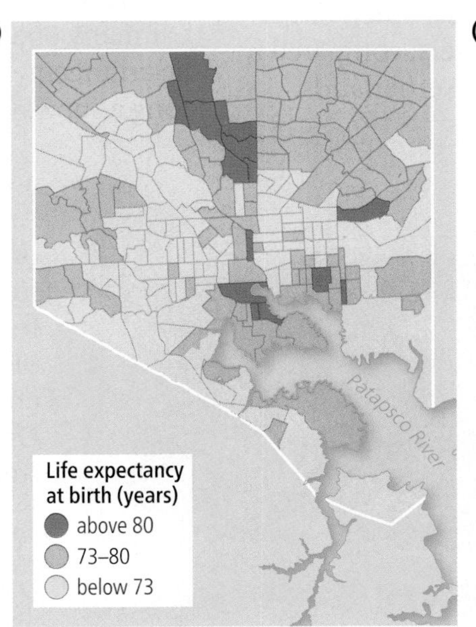

(c)

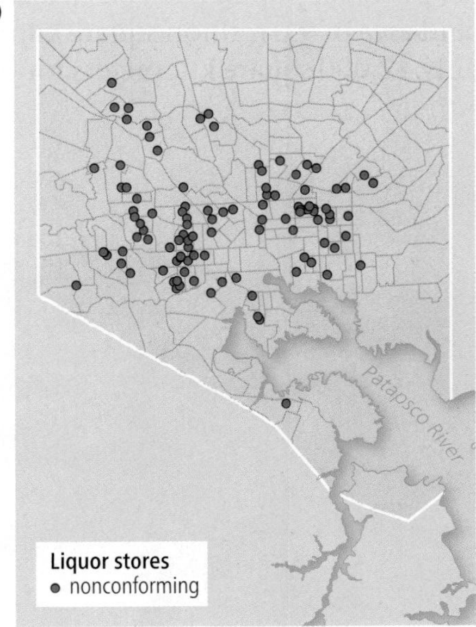

Space: Distribution of Features

- **Explain three properties of distribution.**

Space refers to the physical gap or interval between two objects. Geographers observe that many objects are distributed across space in a regular manner, for discernible reasons. Geographers think about the arrangement of people and activities found in space and try to understand why those people and activities are distributed across space as they are.

Distribution Properties: Density

Geographers explain how features such as buildings and communities are arranged across Earth. On Earth as a whole, or within an area of Earth, features may be numerous or scarce, close together or far apart. The arrangement of a feature in space is known as its **distribution**. Geographers identify three main properties of distribution across Earth—density, concentration, and pattern.

Density is the frequency with which something occurs in space. The feature being measured could be people, houses, cars, trees, or anything else. The area could be measured in square kilometers, square miles, hectares, acres, or any other unit of area.

Remember that a large number of a feature does not necessarily lead to a high density. Density involves two measures—the number of a feature and the land area. China is the country with the largest number of people—approximately 1.4 billion—but it does not have the world's highest density. The Netherlands, for example, has only 17 million people, but its density of 505 persons per square kilometer is much higher than China's 144 persons per square kilometer. China may have a larger population, but it also has a much larger land area of 9.6 million square kilometers, compared to only 42,000 square kilometers for the Netherlands.

Distribution Properties: Concentration

The extent of a feature's spread over space is its **concentration**. If the objects in an area are close together, they are clustered; if relatively far apart, they are dispersed. To compare the level of concentration most clearly, two areas need to have the same number of objects and the same size area.

Geographers use concentration to describe changes in distribution. For example, the distribution of people across the United States is increasingly dispersed. The total number of people living in the United States is growing slowly—less than 1 percent per year—and the land area is essentially unchanged. But the population distribution is changing from relatively clustered in the Northeast to more evenly dispersed across the country.

Distribution Properties: Pattern

The third property of distribution is **pattern**, which is the geometric arrangement of objects in space. Some features are organized in a geometric pattern, whereas others are distributed irregularly. Geographers observe that many objects form a linear distribution, such as the arrangement of houses along a street or stations along a subway line.

Objects are frequently arranged in a square or rectangular pattern. Many American cities contain a regular pattern of streets, known as a grid pattern, which intersect at right angles at uniform intervals to form square or rectangular blocks. The system of townships, ranges, and sections established by the Land Ordinance of 1785 is another example of a square or grid pattern (Figure 1.9.1).

◀ 1.9.1 **PATTERN: TOWNSHIP AND RANGE**
The U.S. Land Ordinance of 1785 divided much of the United States into a checkerboard pattern, which is still visible in agricultural areas.

Distribution Properties: Your Space

Look around your classroom. How many people are in the room? That number divided by the size of the room is the density. Are the people spread evenly through the classroom, or are they bunched together in one part of the room? That's the concentration—either clustered or dispersed. Are the desks lined up in rows or distributed randomly around the room? That's the pattern.

Concentration is not the same as density. Two neighborhoods could have the same density of housing but different concentrations. In a dispersed neighborhood, each house has a large private yard, whereas in a clustered neighborhood, the houses are close together and the open space is shared as a community park (Figure 1.9.2).

The distribution of major-league baseball teams illustrates the difference between density and concentration (Figure 1.9.3). After remaining unchanged during the first half of the twentieth century, the distribution of major-league baseball teams changed during the second half of the twentieth century.

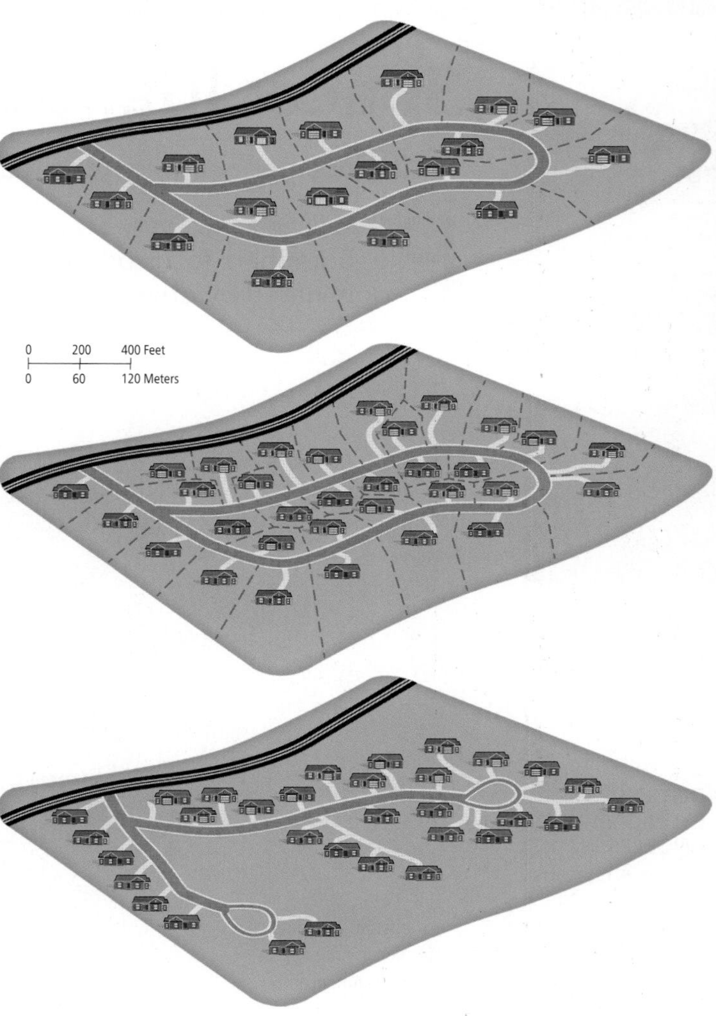

▶ 1.9.2 **DISTRIBUTION OF HOUSES**
The top plan for a residential area has a lower density than the middle plan (18 houses compared to 32 houses on the same area of land), but both have dispersed concentrations. The middle and lower plans have the same density (same number of houses and same area of land), but the distribution of houses is more clustered in the lower plan. The lower plan has shared open space in the center of the development, whereas the middle plan provides a larger, private yard surrounding each house.

◀ 1.9.3 **DISTRIBUTION OF BASEBALL TEAMS**
The changing distribution of North American baseball teams illustrates the difference between density and concentration. As a result of these relocations and additions, the density of teams increased, and the distribution became more dispersed.

These 6 teams moved to other cities during the 1950s and 1960s:

- **Braves**—Boston to Milwaukee in 1953, then to Atlanta in 1966
- **Browns**—St. Louis to Baltimore (Orioles) in 1954
- **Athletics**—Philadelphia to Kansas City in 1955, then to Oakland in 1968
- **Dodgers**—Brooklyn to Los Angeles in 1958
- **Giants**—New York to San Francisco in 1958
- **Senators**—Washington to Minneapolis (Minnesota Twins) in 1961

These 14 teams were added between the 1960s and 1990s:

- **Angels**—Los Angeles in 1961, then to Anaheim (California) in 1965
- **Senators**—Washington in 1961, then to Dallas (Texas Rangers) in 1971
- **Mets**—New York in 1962
- **Astros**—Houston (originally Colt .45s) in 1962
- **Royals**—Kansas City in 1969
- **Padres**—San Diego in 1969
- **Expos**—Montreal in 1969, then to Washington (Nationals) in 2005
- **Pilots**—Seattle in 1969, then to Milwaukee (Brewers) in 1970
- **Blue Jays**—Toronto in 1977
- **Mariners**—Seattle in 1977
- **Marlins**—Miami (originally Florida) in 1993
- **Rockies**—Denver (Colorado) in 1993
- **Rays**—Tampa Bay (originally Devil Rays) in 1998
- **Diamondbacks**—Phoenix (Arizona) in 1998

Space: Identity & Inequality

- **Discuss geographic approaches to cultural identity.**

Patterns in space vary according to gender, ethnicity, and sexuality. Some human geographers focus on the needs and interests of cultural groups that are dominated by other groups.

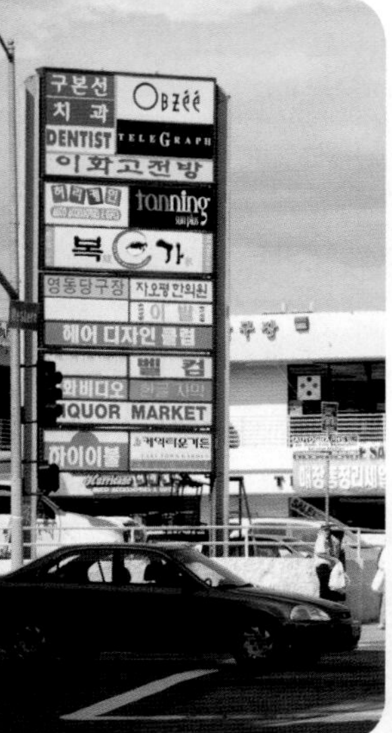

▲ 1.10.1 **DISTRIBUTION BY ETHNICITY: KOREATOWN** Los Angeles.

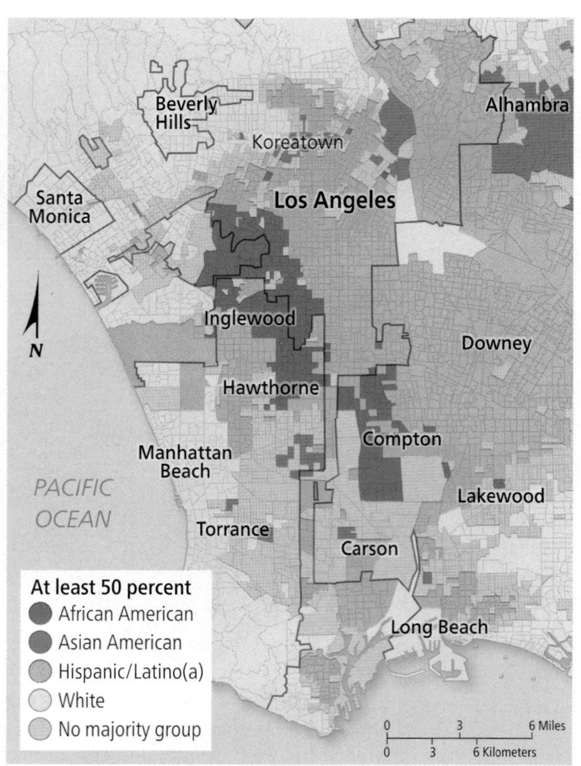

▶ 1.10.2 **DISTRIBUTION BY ETHNICITY: LOS ANGELES** African Americans are clustered to the south of downtown Los Angeles and Hispanics to the east. Asian American neighborhoods are contiguous to the African and Hispanic areas.

Distribution by Ethnicity

The distribution of ethnicities in the United States varies considerably at all scales, as discussed in detail in Chapter 7. Ethnicities are also highly clustered in distinctive areas within cities, as discussed in detail in Chapters 7 and 13 (Figures 1.10.1 and 1.10.2)

Distribution by Sexual Orientation

Lesbian, gay, bisexual, transgender, and queer (LGBTQ) people may be attracted to some locations to reinforce spatial interaction with other LGBTQ people. At the international scale, some countries protect LGBTQ people, whereas other countries criminalize the practice (Figure 1.10.3).

▼ 1.10.3 **DISTRIBUTION OF SEXUAL ORIENTATION** The International Lesbian, Gay, Bisexual, Trans and Intersex Association maps the distribution of laws that discriminate or protect based on sexual orientation or gender identity.

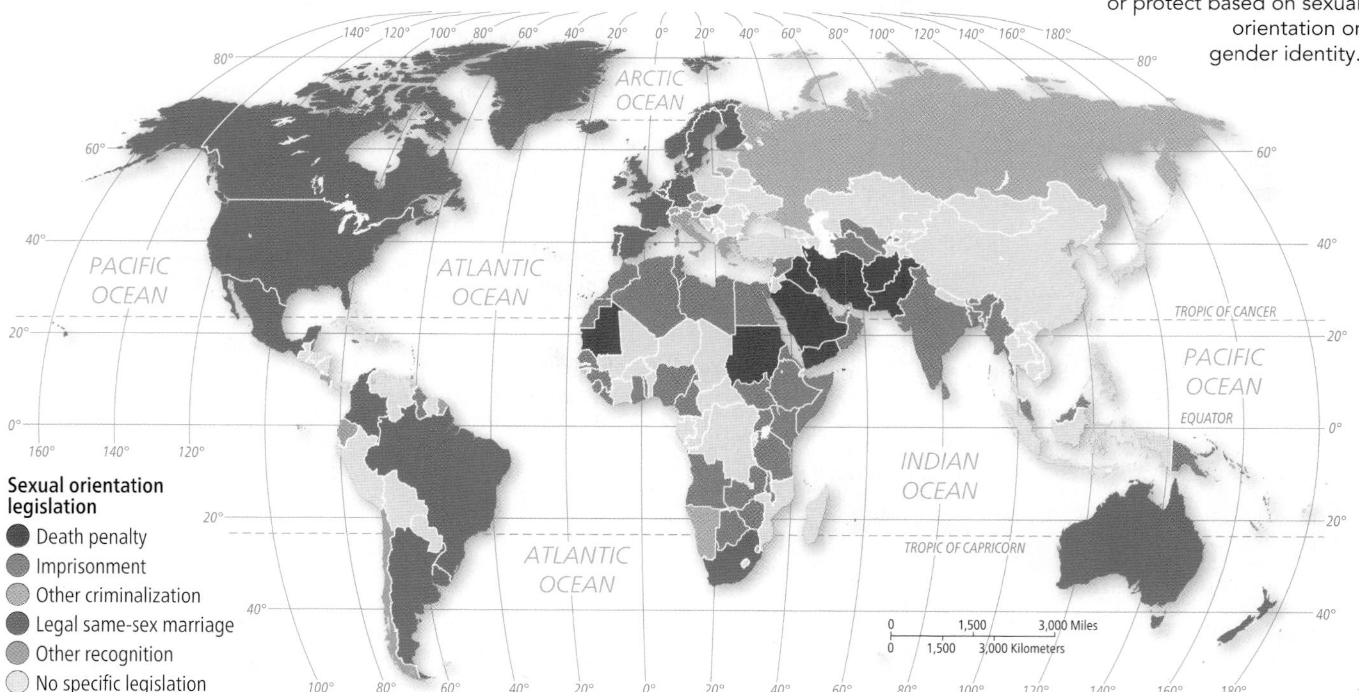

Distribution by Gender

The United Nations has not found a single country in the world where the average income earned by women exceeds that earned by men (discussed in more detail in Chapter 10). Worldwide, the average income of women is around 55 percent that of men (Figure 1.10.4). At best, women in a handful of countries have achieved near-equality with men.

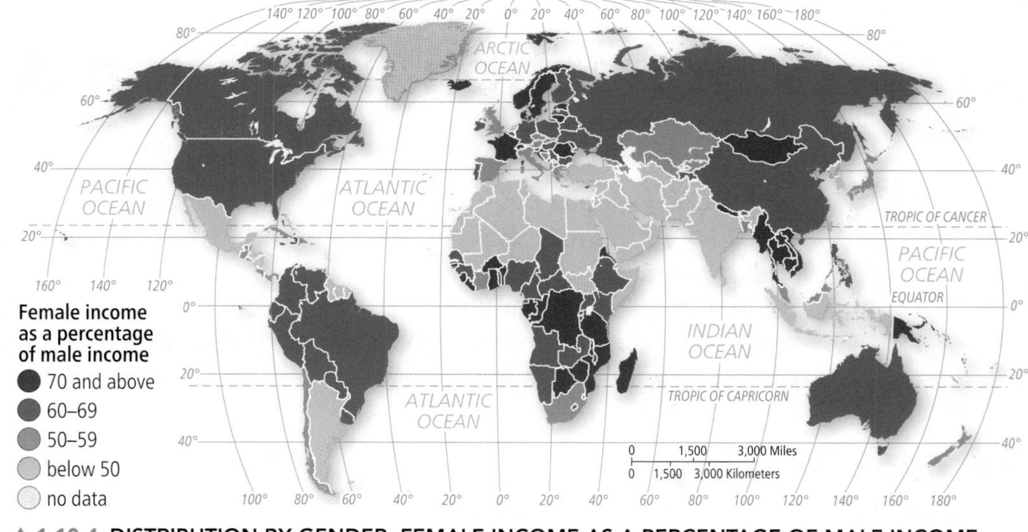

▲ **1.10.4 DISTRIBUTION BY GENDER: FEMALE INCOME AS A PERCENTAGE OF MALE INCOME**
According to the United Nations, the average income earned by women is less than that of men in every country in the world.

Unequal Access

Electronic communication was once viewed as the "death" of geography because the ease of communications between distant places removed barriers to interaction. In reality, because of unequal access, geography matters even more than before.

People have unequal access to interaction in part because the quality of electronic service varies among places. Internet access depends on availability of electricity to power the computer and a service provider. Seconds count. Broadband service requires proximity to a digital subscriber line (DSL), a cable line, or other services. Most importantly, a person must be able to afford to pay for the communications equipment and service.

Countries in Africa, Asia, and Latin America contain 85 percent of the world's population and nearly all of its population growth. However, these countries find themselves on a periphery, or outer edge, with respect to the wealthier core regions of North America, Europe, and Japan. People in peripheral regions, who once toiled in isolated farm fields to produce food for their families, now produce crops for sale in core regions or have given up farm life altogether and migrated to cities in search of jobs in factories and offices. As a result, the global economy has produced greater disparities than in the past between the levels of wealth and well-being enjoyed by people in the core and in the periphery. The increasing gap in economic conditions between regions in the core and periphery that results from the globalization of the economy is known as **uneven development** (Figure 1.10.5). Economic inequality has also increased within countries (Figure 1.10.6).

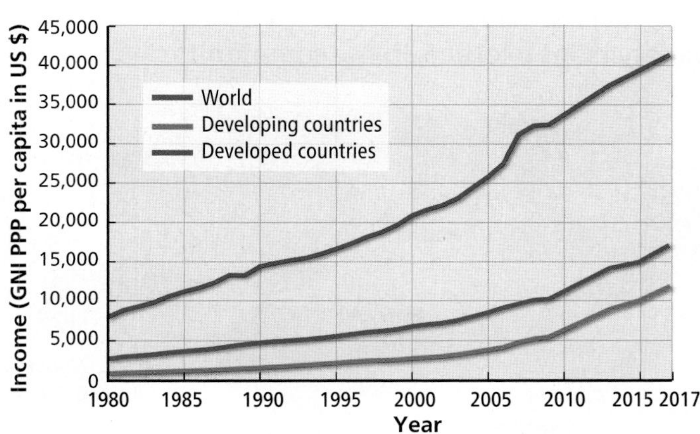

▲ **1.10.5 INEQUALITY: INCOME GAP BETWEEN RICH AND POOR COUNTRIES**
Income has increased much more rapidly in developed countries than in developing ones. Chapter 10 discusses specific ways to measure income, including GNI PPP.

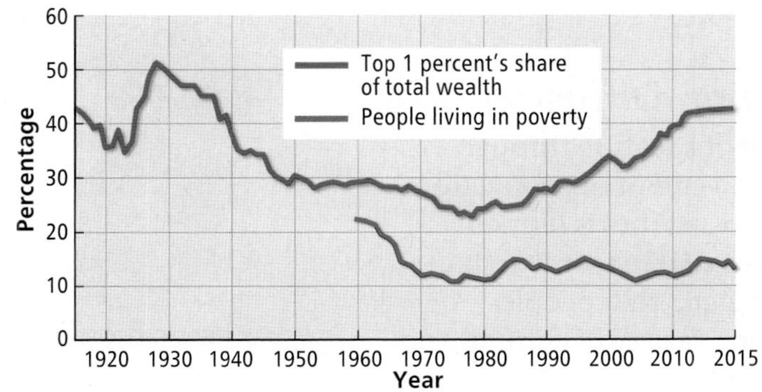

▲ **1.10.6 INEQUALITY: U.S. WEALTH AND POVERTY**
The share of U,S. wealth held by the wealthiest 1 percent declined from the 1930s through the 1970s and began rising again in the 1980s. The percentage of people living in poverty declined during the 1960s but has remained relatively unchanged since then.

Connection: Diffusion & Interaction

- Describe how features spread through diffusion.

Connection refers to relationships among people and objects across the barrier of space. Geographers are concerned with the various means by which connections occur.

An innovation originates at a node, known as a hearth, and spreads across space from one place to another through a process of **diffusion**. Geographers document the location of nodes of innovation and the processes by which diffusion carries things elsewhere.

Expansion Diffusion

The spread of a feature from one place to another in an additive process is **expansion diffusion**. This expansion may result from one of three processes:

- **Hierarchical diffusion** is the spread of an idea from persons or nodes of authority or power to other persons or places (Figure 1.11.1). Hierarchical diffusion may result from the spread of ideas from political leaders, socially elite people, or other important persons to others in the community.
- **Contagious diffusion** is the rapid, widespread diffusion of a characteristic throughout the population it occurs when something goes viral. For example, new music or an idea goes viral because web surfers throughout the world have access to the same material simultaneously (Figure 1.11.2).
- **Stimulus diffusion** is the spread of an underlying principle. For example, innovative features of Apple's iPhone and iPad have been adopted by competitors.

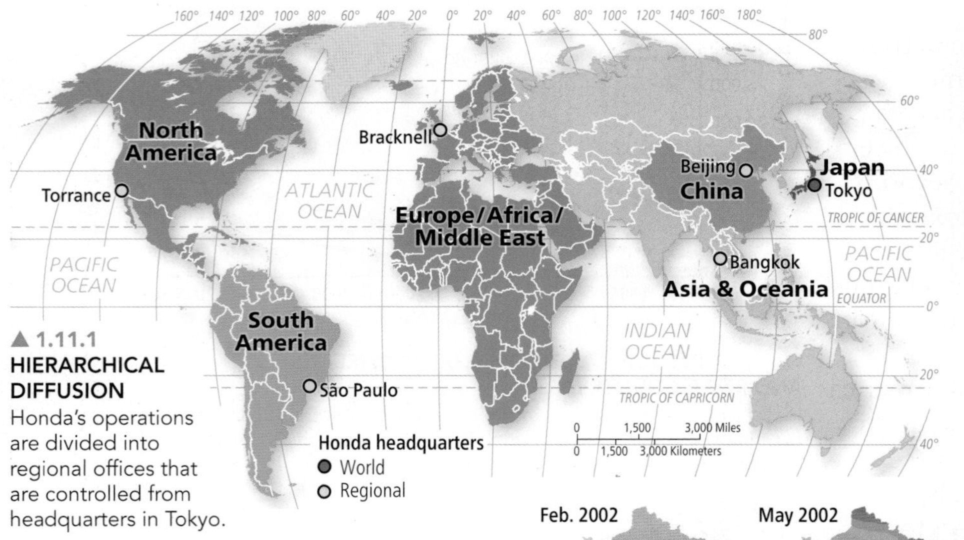

▲ 1.11.1 HIERARCHICAL DIFFUSION
Honda's operations are divided into regional offices that are controlled from headquarters in Tokyo.

▲ 1.11.2 CONTAGIOUS DIFFUSION
The hoverboard was invented in China and quickly diffused to other places.

Relocation Diffusion

The spread of a feature through physical movement of people from one place to another is termed **relocation diffusion**. We shall see in Chapter 3 that people migrate for a variety of cultural and environmental reasons. As discussed in chapters 4 through 7, when people move they carry with them their culture, including language, religion, and ethnicity (Figure 1.11.3)

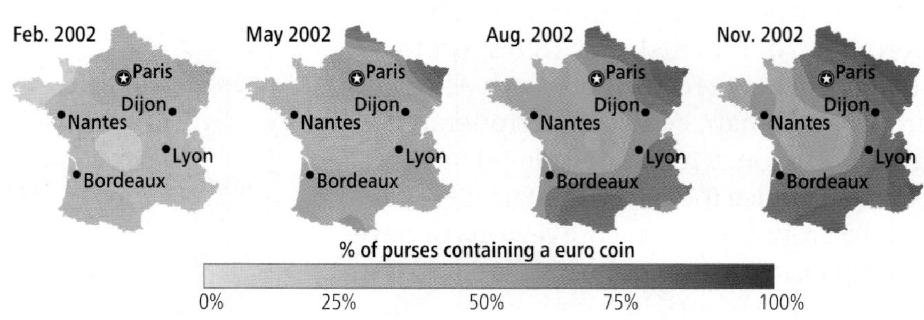

▲ 1.11.3 RELOCATION DIFFUSION
Introduction of a common currency, the euro, in 12 European countries in 2002 gave scientists an unusual opportunity to measure relocation diffusion from hearths. Each of the 12 countries minted its own coins in proportion to its share of the region's economy. A country's coins were initially distributed only inside its borders, although the coins could also be used in the other 11 countries. Scientists in France took month-to-month samples to monitor the proportion of coins from each of the other 11 countries. The percentage of coins from a particular country is a measure of the level of relocation diffusion to and from France.

Spatial Interaction

Connections between cultural groups can have several results:

- **Assimilation** is the process by which a group's cultural features are altered to resemble those of another group. The cultural features of one group may come to dominate the culture of the assimilated group.
- **Acculturation** is the process of changes in culture that result from the meeting of two groups. Changes may be experienced by both of the interacting cultural groups, but the two groups retain two distinct culture features.
- **Syncretism** is the combination of elements of two groups into a new cultural feature. The two cultural groups come together to form a new culture.

Interaction takes place through a **network**, which is a chain of communication that connects places. Some airlines, for example, have networks known as hub-and-spokes (Figure 1.11.4).

The farther away someone is from another, the less likely the two are to make connections. The diminishing in importance and eventual disappearance of a phenomenon with increasing distance from its origin is called **distance decay**.

Distance decay is much less severe than in the past because connections are more rapid. The reduction in the time it takes to diffuse something to a distant place is **space-time compression** (Figure 1.11.5).

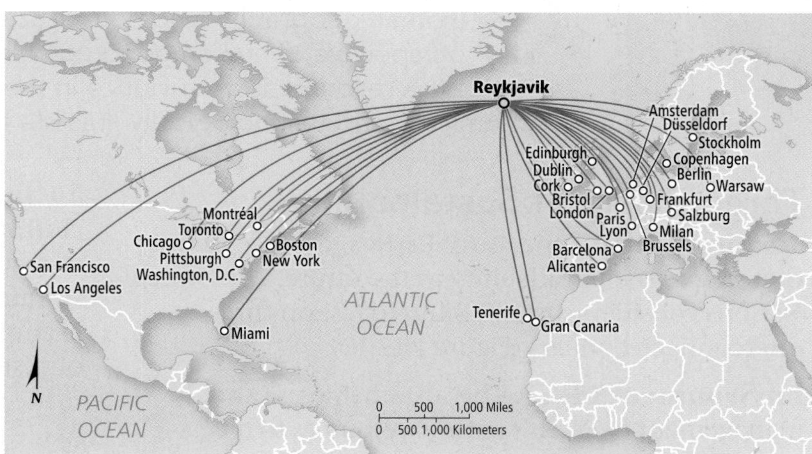

▲ 1.11.4 **SPATIAL INTERACTION: AIRLINE HUB-AND-SPOKE NETWORK**
WOW Air flies planes from a large number of places into a hub airport at Reykjavik, Iceland, and a short time later sends the planes to another set of places.

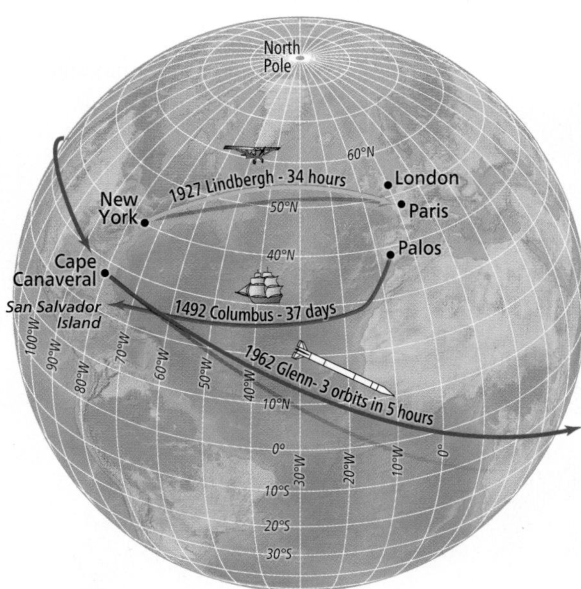

▲ 1.11.5 **SPACE-TIME COMPRESSION**
Transportation improvements have shrunk the world. In 1492, Christopher Columbus took nearly 900 hours (37 days) to sail across the Atlantic Ocean. In 1927, Charles Lindbergh was the first to fly nonstop across the Atlantic, taking 33.5 hours. In 1962, John Glenn, the first American to orbit in space, crossed above the Atlantic in about 1/2 hour and circled the globe three times in 5 hours.

DEBATE IT!
GPS on or off?

Most of our cell phones have a GPS tracking device that can pinpoint our precise location. By default, most phones have this geotagging feature turned on. Should you leave location service on or turn it off (Figures 1.11.6 and 1.11.7)?

CRIMINAL ACTIVITY SHOULD BE TRACKED

- Knowledge of a phone's movements helps law enforcement agencies identify, find, and prosecute criminals.
- Criminal activities, such as drug sales, are often done by cell phone.
- Criminal behavior is not an activity that should be protected by privacy laws.

▲ 1.11.6 **GPS TRACKING WITH LOCATION SERVICES ON**

EVERYONE IS ENTITLED TO PRIVACY

- Protecting individual privacy is part of the service promised by phone companies.
- Once accessible to one agency, phone information may be more easily hacked by others.
- Embarrassing information irrelevant to a criminal case may become public.

▲ 1.11.7 **LOCATION SERVICES OFF**

Connection: Sustainability

- **Explain connections among the three pillars of sustainability and among Earth's physical systems.**

Geography is distinctive because it studies connections between social science (human geography) and natural science (physical geography). From the perspective of human geography, nature offers humans a large menu of resources. A **resource** is a substance in the environment that is useful to people, economically and technologically feasible to access, and socially acceptable to use.

Three Pillars of Sustainability

Sustainability is the use of Earth's resources in ways that ensure their availability in the future. The United Nations considers sustainability to rest on three interconnected pillars (Figure 1.12.1):

Environment Pillar. The sustainable use and management of Earth's natural resources to meet human needs such as food, medicine, and recreation is **conservation**. Resources such as trees and wildlife are conserved if they are consumed at a less rapid rate than they can be replaced (Figure 1.12.2).

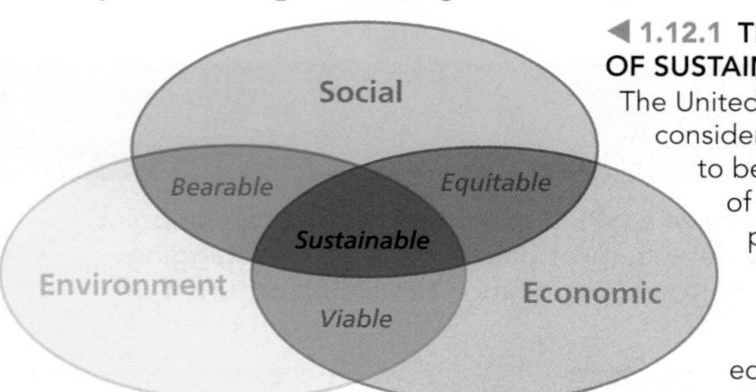

1.12.1 THREE PILLARS OF SUSTAINABILITY
The United Nations considers sustainability to be a combination of environmental protection, economic development, and social equity.

Social Pillar. Humans need shelter, food, and clothing to survive, so they make use of resources to meet these needs. Consumer choices can support sustainability when people embrace it as a value. For example, consumers might prefer clothing made of sustainable resources such as cotton, or clothing made of unsustainable resources such as polyester made from petroleum. They can also choose products that benefit people living in a particular place (Figure 1.12.3).

Economic Pillar. Natural resources acquire a monetary value through exchange in a marketplace (Figure 1.12.4). The price of a resource depends on the value placed on it by people, and on people's technological ability to obtain it. The greater the supply of a resource, the lower the price; the greater the demand for it by people, the higher the price.

1.12.3 SOCIAL PILLAR: SUGARCANE FARMERS
The U.S. Army Corps of Engineers built levees and canals in the Everglades. These modifications opened up land for growing sugarcane and protected the growing South Florida population from flooding. However, the modifications also had unintended consequences, including polluted water and threats to native vegetation and animals.

1.12.2 ENVIRONMENTAL PILLAR: EVERGLADES
The Everglades was once a very wide and shallow freshwater river, slowly flowing south from Lake Okeechobee to the Gulf of Mexico. A sensitive ecosystem of plants and animals once thrived in this distinctive landscape, but much of it was destroyed by human actions to promote the economy.

1.12.4 ECONOMIC PILLAR: TOURISM
Everglades National Park, established in 1947, attracts around 1 million visitors a year. The National Park Service tries to provide an enjoyable visit while protecting the area's fragile environment.

Earth's Connected Physical Systems

Geographers classify natural resources as part of four interconnected systems. These four physical systems are classified as either biotic or abiotic. A **biotic** system is composed of living organisms. An **abiotic** system is composed of nonliving or inorganic matter. Three of Earth's four systems are abiotic:

- The **atmosphere:** a thin layer of gases surrounding Earth (Figure 1.12.5a).
- The **hydrosphere:** all of the water on and near Earth's surface (Figure 1.12.5b).
- The **lithosphere:** Earth's crust and a portion of upper mantle directly below the crust (Figure 1.12.5c).

One of the four systems is biotic:

- The **biosphere:** all living organisms on Earth, including plants and animals, as well as microorganisms (Figure 1.12.5d).

The names of the four spheres are derived from the Greek words for stone (litho), air (atmo), water (hydro), and life (bio).

A group of living organisms and the abiotic spheres with which they interact is an **ecosystem** (Figure 1.12.6). The scientific study of ecosystems is **ecology**. Ecologists study interrelationships between living organisms and the three abiotic environments, as well as interrelationships among the various living organisms in the biosphere.

▼ 1.12.5 FOUR PHYSICAL SYSTEMS

1.12.5a ATMOSPHERE
A thin layer of gases surrounds Earth at an altitude up to 480 kilometers (300 miles). As atmospheric gases are held to Earth by gravity, pressure is created. Variations in air pressure from one location to another are responsible for producing such weather features as wind blowing, storms brewing, and rain falling.

1.12.5d BIOSPHERE
The biosphere encompasses all of Earth's living organisms.

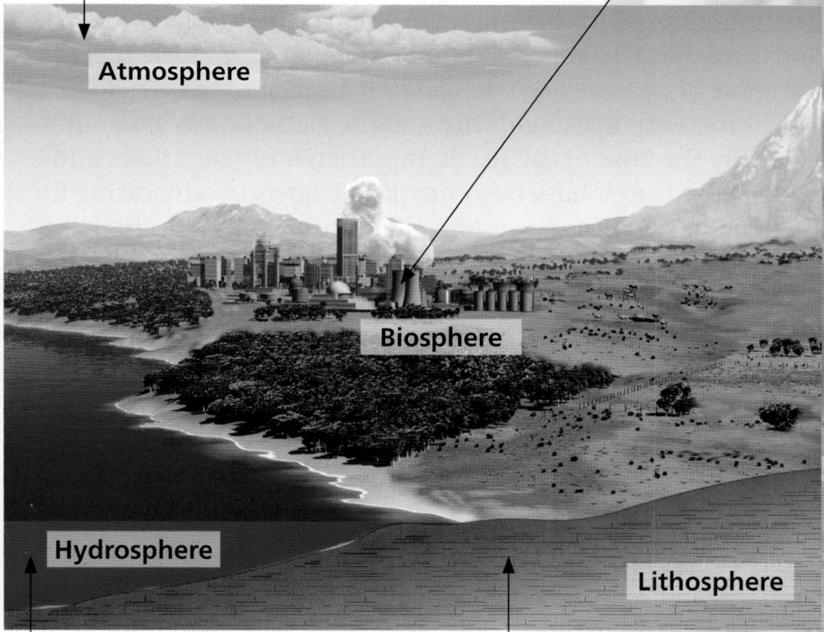

1.12.5b HYDROSPHERE
Water exists in liquid form in the oceans, lakes, and rivers, as well as groundwater in soil and rock. It can also exist as water vapor in the atmosphere, and as ice in glaciers. Over 97 percent of the world's water is in the oceans. The oceans supply the atmosphere with water vapor, which returns to Earth's surface as precipitation, the most important source of freshwater.

1.12.5c LITHOSPHERE
Earth is composed of concentric spheres made of different materials. The core is a dense, metallic sphere about 3,500 kilometers (2,200 miles) in radius. Surrounding the core is a mantle about 2,900 kilometers (1,800 miles) thick. The mantle is mostly solid rock, but it is pliable and can flow slowly. The crust is a thin, brittle outer shell 8 to 40 kilometers (5 to 25 miles) thick. The lithosphere encompasses the crust and a portion of the mantle extending down to about 70 kilometers (45 miles). Powerful forces deep within Earth shape the crust to form mountains, continents, and ocean basins.

▲ 1.12.6
ECOSYSTEM
Black howler monkey in Brazil's tropical rainforest.

Humans & Their Environment

- Compare and contrast sustainable and unsustainable ecosystems.

The geographic study of human–environment relationships is known as **cultural ecology**. Geographers are interested in two main types of human–environment interaction: how people adjust to their environment, and how they modify it.

Adjusting to the Environment

Nineteenth-century geographers argued that the physical environment *caused* social development, an approach called **environmental determinism**. To explain connections between human activities and the physical environment, modern geographers embrace possibilism. According to **possibilism**, the physical environment may limit some human actions, but people have the ability to adjust to their environment. People can choose a course of action from many alternatives in the physical environment (Figure 1.13.1).

▶ ▼ 1.13.1
POSSIBILISM: ALTERNATIVE BEHAVIORS
(a) Some humans prefer to mow their lawns, whereas others (b) prefer to let wildflowers grow.

Sustainable Ecosystem: The Netherlands

The Dutch have modified their environment with two distinctive types of construction projects—polders and dikes (Figure 1.13.2). A **polder** is a piece of land that is created by draining water from an area. All together, the Netherlands has 6,500 square kilometers (2,600 square miles) of polders, comprising 16 percent of the country's land area. The Dutch government has reserved most of the polders for agriculture to reduce the country's dependence on imported food.

The Dutch have also constructed massive dikes to prevent the North Sea, an arm of the Atlantic Ocean, from flooding much of the country. The Zuider Zee project in the north converted a saltwater sea to a freshwater lake called Lake IJssel. Some of the lake has been drained to create polders. The Delta Plan in the southwest closed off several rivers with dams after a devastating flood killed nearly 2,000 people in 1953.

With these two massive projects completed, attitudes toward modifying the ecosystem have changed in the Netherlands. Plans have been scrapped to build more polders in Lake IJssel, and some dikes have been deliberately broken to flood fields. Still, climate change could threaten the Netherlands' coast line by raising the level of the sea. Rather than build new dikes and polders, the Dutch have become world leaders in advocating for the reduction in human actions that result in climate change.

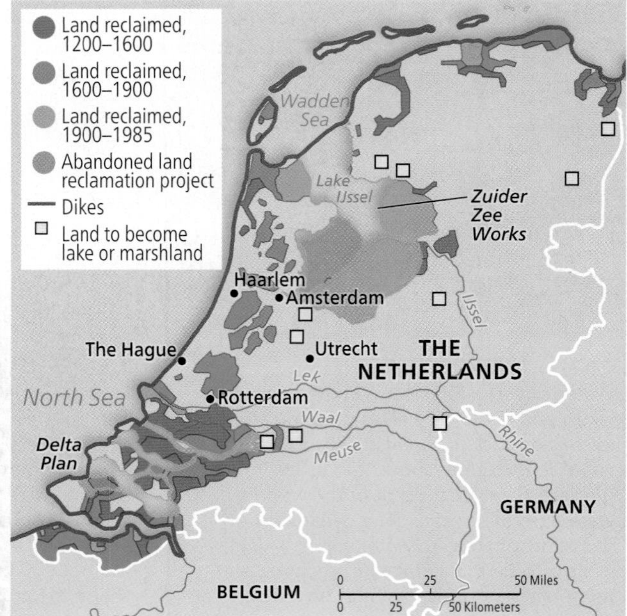

▶ 1.13.2
SUSTAINABLE ECOSYSTEM: THE NETHERLANDS
The Dutch have considerably altered the site of the Netherlands through creation of polders and dikes.

Unsustainable Ecosystem: California

California and neighboring states in the U.S. Southwest have grown rapidly and prospered despite limited supplies of water. An extended drought in recent years, followed by flooding, has called into question the region's ability to sustain its residents' current lifestyles (Figures 1.13.3 and 1.13.4).

In normal times, California gets around 70 percent of its water from surface water sources, such as melting snow from mountains. Aqueducts and pipes carry water from the Colorado River to cities and farmland hundreds of kilometers away. A 1922 agreement determines how much of the Colorado River is allocated to California, Arizona, and Nevada. The other 30 percent of California's water comes from groundwater sources, which are underground. In recent years, the level of precipitation has been extremely low, so less water has been available from surface sources. As a result, groundwater consumption has been supplying more than 60 percent of California's water demand. Groundwater is being removed more rapidly than it is being replenished.

Residents and businesses use only 20 percent of California's water. The other 80 percent goes to agriculture. The biggest challenge posed to the sustainability of California's ecosystems by the drought is for agriculture. Much of the land used for agriculture in California does not get enough rainfall even in normal times to grow crops.

▶ 1.13.3 **CALIFORNIA DROUGHT**
Cachuma Lake, Santa Barbara County, California, in 2015, after four years of drought. The lake is the primary source of drinking water for one-quarter million people in California.

▲ 1.13.4 **CALIFORNIA FLOOD**
Oroville Dam, California, 2017, damaged spillway.

▲ 1.13.5 **UNSUSTAINABLE ECOSYSTEM: CALIFORNIA**
Water usage by hydrological region. Urban areas use much less water per capita than do agricultural areas.

The counties with the highest per capita use of water are the major agricultural counties (Figure 1.13.5); the fields are irrigated with water brought in from elsewhere.

Surging Seas
https://goo.gl/Cj4osb.

RESEARCH & ANALYZE
Rising sea level

Climate change has raised the global sea level about 8 inches since 1880, and by nearly 2 feet along the U.S. East Coast. The interactive map at **SurgingSeas.org** shows different amounts of flooding, depending on the level of sea level rise.

At **SurgingSeas.org**, ***click*** *Maps & Tools*, then *Risk Zone* map. At *Enter a Global Coastal Place*, ***type*** *Miami*.

1. What are some of the features in Miami Beach that would be underwater if the sea level rises 5 feet?
2. ***Click*** *Property*. Are properties in Miami Beach at risk of sea level rise mostly of high value or low value? Why might that be?

▶ 1.13.6 **IMPACT OF RISING SEA LEVEL ON MIAMI**

CHAPTER 1

Review, Analyze, & Apply

KEY ISSUE 1 Why Is Geography a Science?

Geography is most fundamentally a spatial science. Geographers use maps to display the location of objects and to extract information about places. Early geographers drew maps of Earth's surface based on exploration and observation. Contemporary GIScience, including remote sensing, GPS, VGI, geotagging, and GIS, assist geographers in understanding reasons for observed regularities across Earth.

THINKING GEOGRAPHICALLY

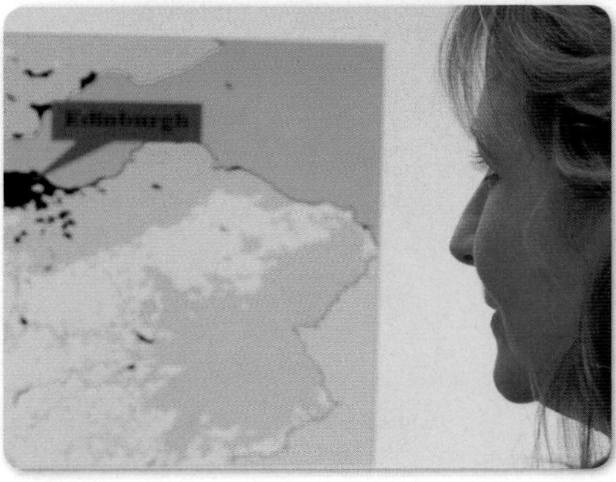

◀ 1.CR.1 **GIS** The SoilFit project uses GIS to provide police investigations with forensic evidence from soil.

1. Geography plays an important role on our electronic devices. What was the most recent geographic item that you consulted on your electronic device? Describe how this item illustrated each of geography's five basic concepts of place, region, scale, space, and connection.

KEY ISSUE 2 Why Is Each Point on Earth Unique?

Geographers identity unique places (specific points) and regions (areas) distinguished by distinctive combinations of cultural as well as economic and environmental features.

THINKING GEOGRAPHICALLY

◀ 1.CR.2 **BIG SUR, CALIFORNIA** The Pacific coast of California is a distinctive vernacular region.

2. The South and the West are commonly cited vernacular regions in the United States. What are some features that you would expect to distinguish one of these regions?

KEY ISSUE 3 Why Are Different Places Similar?

Geographers work at all scales, from local to global. The global scale is increasingly important because few places in the contemporary world are totally isolated. Because places are connected to each other, they display similarities. Geographers study the interactions of groups of people and human activities across space, and they identify processes by which people and ideas diffuse from one location to another over time.

THINKING GEOGRAPHICALLY

◀ 1.CR.3 **VISITING GRANDMA?**

3. Identify a place other than your hometown where you have a connection. What is the nature of the interaction that you have with that place? Explain how the interaction illustrates one or more types of diffusion.

KEY ISSUE 4 Why Are Some Actions Not Sustainable?

Sustainability is the use of Earth's resources in ways that ensure their availability in the future. Sustainability is based on three interrelated pillars: environmental, economic, and social action. An ecosystem comprises a group of living organism in the biosphere and their interaction with the atmosphere, lithosphere, and biosphere. The sustainability of some of Earth's resources is being damaged by humans.

THINKING GEOGRAPHICALLY

◀ 1.CR.4 **YELLOWSTONE PARK** Visitors cluster in Lower Geyser Basin.

4. Name a park (national, state, or local) that is familiar to you. Describe the ways that your experiences in the park illustrate each of the three pillars of sustainability.

GeoVideo

Log in to the Mastering Geography Study Area to view this video.

How GPS Works

A Global Positioning System (GPS) determines the precise position of something on Earth through a series of satellites, tracking stations, and receivers.

1. Describe the infrastructure that supports GPS devices.
2. According to the video, how accurate is the current GPS system? What are the limits of GPS technology?
3. Based on what you learned in the video, why do you think the U.S. Navy has decided to reinstate celestial navigation? Explain.

▲ 1.CR.5 HOW GPS WORKS

Geospatial Analysis

Log in to the Mastering Geography Study Area to access MapMaster 2.0.

Environmental Challenges for the Dutch

Add the *World Elevations* layer. ***Click*** the *Settings* icon in the *Legend* and ***select*** *Show Political Labels.*

Zoom in as far as possible to center the map on the Netherlands (northwestern Europe between Belgium and United Kingdom). ***Add*** the *Population Density* layer and ***select*** *Split map window.*

1. ***Hover*** over the Netherlands. What is the elevation of this area?
2. Compare the elevation map to the population density map. Describe the distribution of population within the Netherlands (density, concentration, and pattern).
3. What environmental challenges do people living in the Netherlands face? How are the Dutch addressing these challenges? Are these challenges likely to become more severe or less severe in the coming years? Explain your answer.

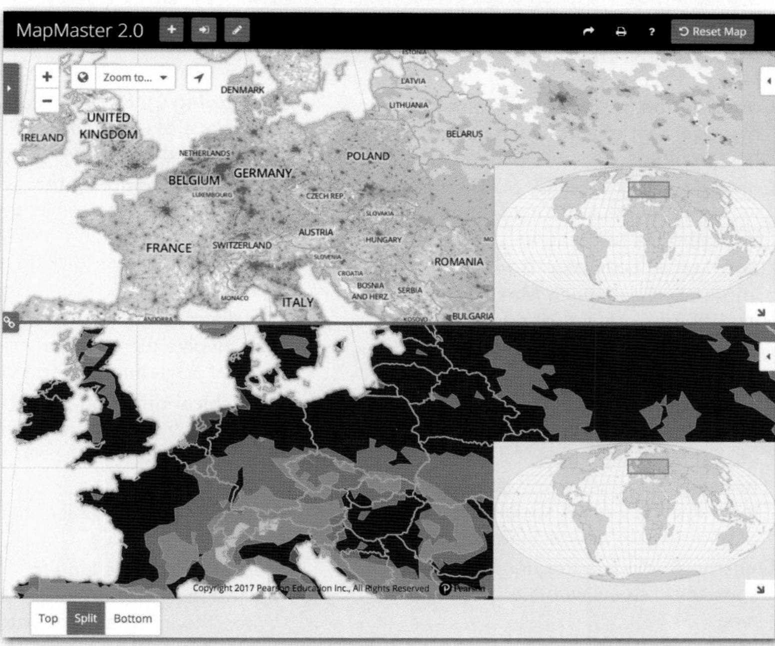

▲ 1.CR.6 ELEVATION OF THE NETHERLANDS

Mastering Geography

Looking for additional review and test prep materials? Visit the Study Area in Mastering Geography to enhance your geographic literacy, spatial reasoning skills, and understanding of this chapter's content. Access MapMaster™ interactive maps, video case studies, *In the News* current articles, flashcards, self-study quizzes, an eText of *Contemporary Human Geography*, and more.

pearson.com/mastering/geography

Key Terms

Abiotic (p. 27) Composed of nonliving or inorganic matter.

Acculturation (p. 25) The process of changes in culture that result from the meeting of two groups, each of which retains distinct cultural features.

Assimilation (p. 25) The process by which a group's cultural features are altered to resemble those of another group.

Atmosphere (p. 27) The thin layer of gases surrounding Earth.

Biosphere (p. 27) All living organisms on Earth, including plants and animals, as well as microorganisms.

Biotic (p. 27) Composed of living organisms.

Cartography (p. 6) The science of making maps.

Citizen science (p. 9) Scientific research by amateur scientists.

Concentration (p. 20) The spread of something over a given area.

Connection (p. 5) The relationships among people and objects across the barrier of space.

Conservation (p. 26) The sustainable management of a natural resource to meet human needs.

Contagious diffusion (p. 24) The rapid, widespread diffusion of a feature or trend throughout a population.

Coordinated Universal Time (UTC) informally **Greenwich Mean Time, (GMT)** (p. 13) The time in the zone encompassing the prime meridian, or 0° longitude.

Cultural ecology (p. 28) A geographic approach that emphasizes human-environment relationships.

Cultural landscape (p. 16) An approach to geography that emphasizes the relationships among social and physical phenomena in a particular study area.

Density (p. 20) The frequency with which something exists within a given unit of area.

Diffusion (p. 24) The process of spread of a feature or trend from one place to another over time.

Distance decay (p. 25) The diminished importance and eventual disappearance of a phenomenon with increasing distance from its origin.

Distribution (p. 20) The arrangement of something across Earth's surface.

Ecology (p. 27) The scientific study of ecosystems.

Ecosystem (p. 27) A group of living organisms and the abiotic spheres with which they interact.

Environmental determinism (p. 28) A nineteenth- and early twentieth-century approach to the study of geography which argued that the general laws sought by human geographers could be found in the physical sciences. Geography was therefore the study of how the physical environment caused human activities.

Expansion diffusion (p. 24) The spread of a feature or trend among people from one area to another in an additive process.

Formal region (or **uniform region)** (p. 16) An area in which most people share in one or more distinctive characteristics.

Functional region (or **nodal region)** (p. 17) An area organized around a node or focal point.

Geographic information science (GIScience) (p. 8) Analysis of data about Earth acquired through satellite and other electronic information technologies.

Geographic information system (GIS) (p. 8) A computer system that captures, stores, queries, and displays geographic data.

Geotagging (p. 8) Identification and storage of a piece of information by its precise latitude and longitude coordinates.

Global Positioning System (GPS) (p. 8) A system that determines the precise position of something on Earth through a series of satellites, tracking stations, and receivers.

Globalization (p. 18) Actions or processes that involve the entire world and result in making something worldwide in scope.

Hierarchical diffusion (p. 24) The spread of a feature or trend from one key person or node of authority or power to other persons or places.

Hydrosphere (p. 27) All of the water on and near Earth's surface.

International Date Line (p. 13) An arc that for the most part follows 180° longitude. When the International Date Line is crossed heading east (toward America), the clock moves back 24 hours, or one entire day. When it is crossed heading west (toward Asia), the calendar moves ahead one day.

Latitude (p. 12) The numbering system used to indicate the location of parallels drawn on a globe and measuring distance north and south of the equator (0°).

Lithosphere (p. 27) Earth's crust and a portion of upper mantle directly below the crust.

Location (p. 14) The position of anything on Earth's surface.

Longitude (p. 12) The numbering system used to indicate the location of meridians drawn on a globe and measuring distance east and west of the prime meridian (0°).

Map (p. 6) A two-dimensional, or flat, representation of Earth's surface or a portion of it.

Map scale (p. 10) The relationship between the size of an object on a map and the size of the actual feature on Earth's surface.

Mashup (p. 9) A map that overlays data from one source on top of a map provided by a mapping service.

Mental map (p. 9) A representation of a portion of Earth's surface based on what an individual knows about a place that contains personal impressions of what is in the place and where the place is located.

Meridian (p. 12) An arc drawn on a map between the North and South poles.

Network (p. 25) A chain of communication that connects places.

Parallel (p. 12) A circle drawn around the globe parallel to the equator and at right angles to the meridians.

Participatory GIS (PGIS) (p. 9) Community-based mapping, representing local knowledge and information.

Pattern (p. 20) The geometric or regular arrangement of something in a particular area.

Photogrammetry (p. 8) The science of taking measurements of Earth's surface from photographs.

Place (p. 5) A specific point on Earth, distinguished by a particular characteristic.

Polder (p. 28) Land that the Dutch have created by draining water from an area.

Possibilism (p. 28) The theory that the physical environment may set limits on human actions, but people have the ability to adjust to the physical environment and choose a course of action from many alternatives.

Prime meridian (p. 12) The meridian, designated as 0° longitude, that passes through the Royal Observatory at Greenwich, England.

Projection (p. 11) A system used to transfer locations from Earth's surface to a flat map.

Region (p. 5) An area distinguished by one or more distinctive characteristics.

Relocation diffusion (p. 24) The spread of a feature or trend through bodily movement of people from one place to another.

Remote sensing (p. 8) The acquisition of data about Earth's surface from a satellite orbiting the planet or from other long-distance methods.

Resource (p. 26) A substance in the environment that is useful to people, is economically and technologically feasible to access, and is socially acceptable to use.

Scale (p. 5) The relationship between the portion of Earth being studied and Earth as a whole.

Site (p. 15) The physical character of a place.

Situation (p. 15) The location of a place relative to another place.

Space (p. 5) The physical gap or interval between two objects.

Space-time compression (p. 25) The reduction in the time it takes to diffuse something to a distant place as a result of improved communications and transportation systems.

Spatial association (p. 19) The relationship between the distribution of one feature and the distribution of another feature.

Stimulus diffusion (p. 24) The spread of an underlying principle.

Sustainability (p. 26) The use of Earth's renewable and nonrenewable natural resources in ways that do not constrain resource use in the future.

Syncretism (p. 25) The combining of elements of two groups into a new cultural feature.

Toponym (p. 14) The name given to a portion of Earth's surface.

Transnational corporation (p. 18) A company that conducts research, operates factories, and sells products in many countries, not just where its headquarters or shareholders are located.

Uneven development (p. 23) The increasing gap in economic conditions between core and peripheral regions as a result of the globalization of the economy.

Vernacular region (or **perceptual region**) (p. 17) An area that people believe exists as part of their cultural identity.

Volunteered geographic information (VGI) (p. 9) Creation and dissemination of geographic data contributed voluntarily and for free by individuals.

Explore

Dili

Use Google Earth to explore Dili, capital of Timor-Leste, one of the world's newest and poorest countries, featured at the beginning of this chapter.

Fly to *Dili, Timor-Leste.*

Click the *Street View* icon. ***Select*** one of the blue dots along the waterfront.

1. What do you see on the water side of the street? Is there an attractive beach? Are people swimming in the water? Does this look attractive to you? Why or why not?
2. What activities are taking place on the land side? Is the area attractive? Why or why not?
3. Take a look at the road nearest the water. Is it busy with traffic or quiet? Why might that be?

▲ 1.CR.7 **DILI, TIMOR-LESTE**

▼ 1.CR.8 **WATERFRONT, DILI, TIMOR-LESTE**

CHAPTER

2 Population & Health

More people are alive at this time than at any other point in Earth's history, and most of the growth is concentrated in less developed countries. Can Earth sustain nearly 8 billion people now, let alone the added billions in the future? Geographers have unique perspectives on the ability of people to live on Earth. India, shown in this image, will soon be the world's most populous country, so its future population growth will have a major impact on the future population of the world as a whole.

◀ Filling containers with water supplied by a truck, New Delhi, India.

KEY ISSUES

1 Where Are People Distributed?

Humans are not distributed uniformly across Earth. They are highly clustered in particular places, whereas places like Greenland are sparsely populated.

2 Why Is Population Increasing?

Population is growing at different rates in different regions. Every country is at some stage in a process known as the demographic transition.

3 How Does Health Vary by Region?

Patterns of health and provision of medical care vary across space. Health and medical care have improved in the world as a whole, but less so in places like Zimbabwe.

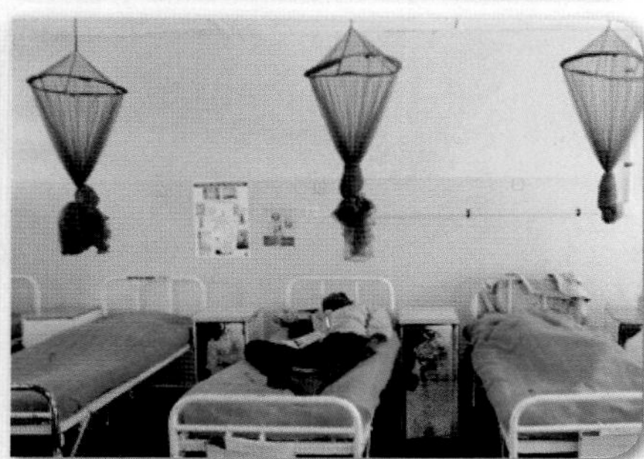

4 How Might Population Change In the Future?

Geographers see strong connections between the size and growth of population and the adequacy of resources in some places, such as Cambodia and India.

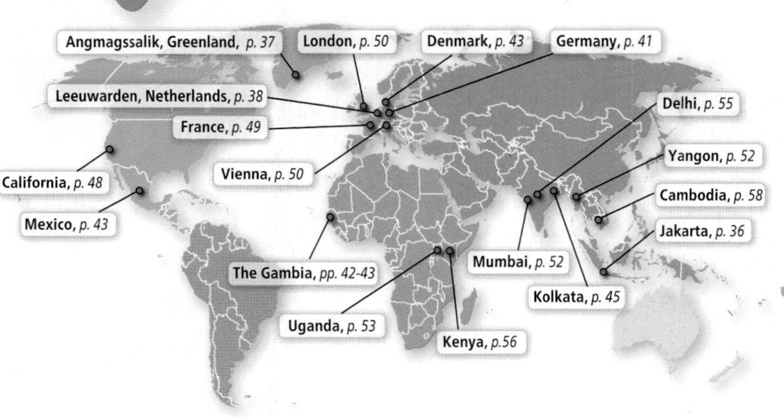

cartogram
medical services
distribution
overpopulation
life expectancy
pandemic
concentration
epidemiologic transition
zero population growth
maternal mortality
infectious diseases
population pyramid
density
total fertility rate
crude birth rate
demographic transition
crude death rate
infant mortality rate
sex ratio
natural increase
dependency ratio
malthus
potential support ratio
HIV/AIDS

Population Concentrations

- **Explain reasons for the distribution of the world's peoples.**

Human beings are not distributed uniformly across Earth's surface (Figure 2.1.1). World maps depict this distribution in several ways.

▲ 2.1.1
POPULATION CONCENTRATION, SOUTHEAST ASIA
Housing in Jakarta, Indonesia.

Population Portions

The world can be divided into seven portions, each containing approximately 1 billion people (Figure 2.1.2). The small size of the Asia portions shows the large number of the world's inhabitants living there.

▶ 2.1.2
POPULATION PORTIONS
Each of the seven portions contains approximately 1 billion inhabitants.

Population Cartogram

A cartogram depicts the size of countries according to population rather than land area, as is the case with most maps (Figure 2.1.3).

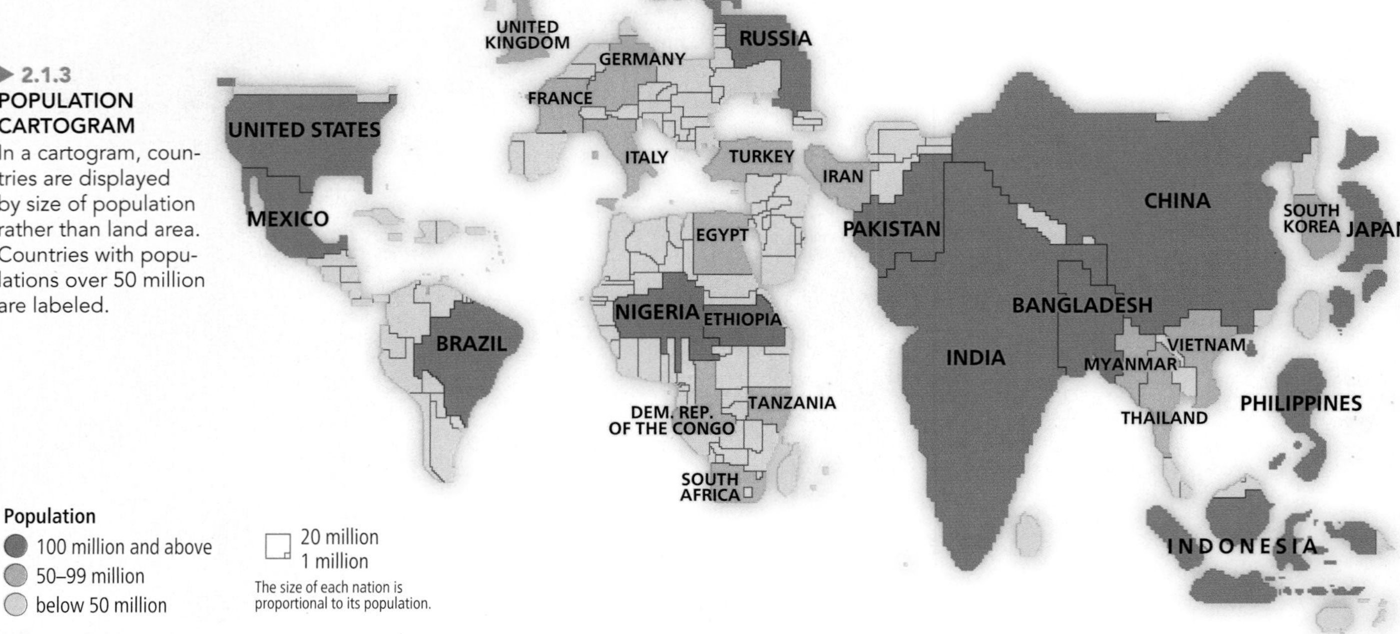

▶ 2.1.3
POPULATION CARTOGRAM
In a cartogram, countries are displayed by size of population rather than land area. Countries with populations over 50 million are labeled.

Population Clusters

Two-thirds of the world's inhabitants live in four regions—East Asia, South Asia, Southeast Asia, and Europe (Figure 2.1.4). The four population concentrations occupy generally low-lying areas, with temperate climate and soil suitable for agriculture. Physical environments that are too dry, too cold, too wet, or too mountainous have relatively few inhabitants (Figure 2.1.5).

The areas of Earth that humans consider too harsh for occupancy have diminished over time, whereas the portion of Earth's surface occupied by permanent human settlement—called the **ecumene**—has increased.

EAST ASIA CLUSTER

Nearly one-fourth of the world's people live in East Asia, primarily in China, the world's most populous country. China's population is clustered near the Pacific Coast and in several fertile river valleys that extend inland, though much of China's interior is sparsely inhabited mountains and deserts.

EUROPE CLUSTER

Europe includes four dozen countries, ranging from Monaco, with 1 square kilometer (0.7 square miles) and a population of 38,000, to Russia, the world's largest country in land area when its Asian part is included. Three-fourths of Europe's inhabitants live in cities, and fewer than 10 percent are farmers.

SPARSELY POPULATED COLD LANDS

Much of the land near the North and South poles is perpetually covered with ice or the ground is permanently frozen (permafrost).

SPARSELY POPULATED HIGH LANDS

The highest mountains in the world are steep, snow covered, and sparsely settled.

▶ **2.1.4 POPULATION DISTRIBUTION**

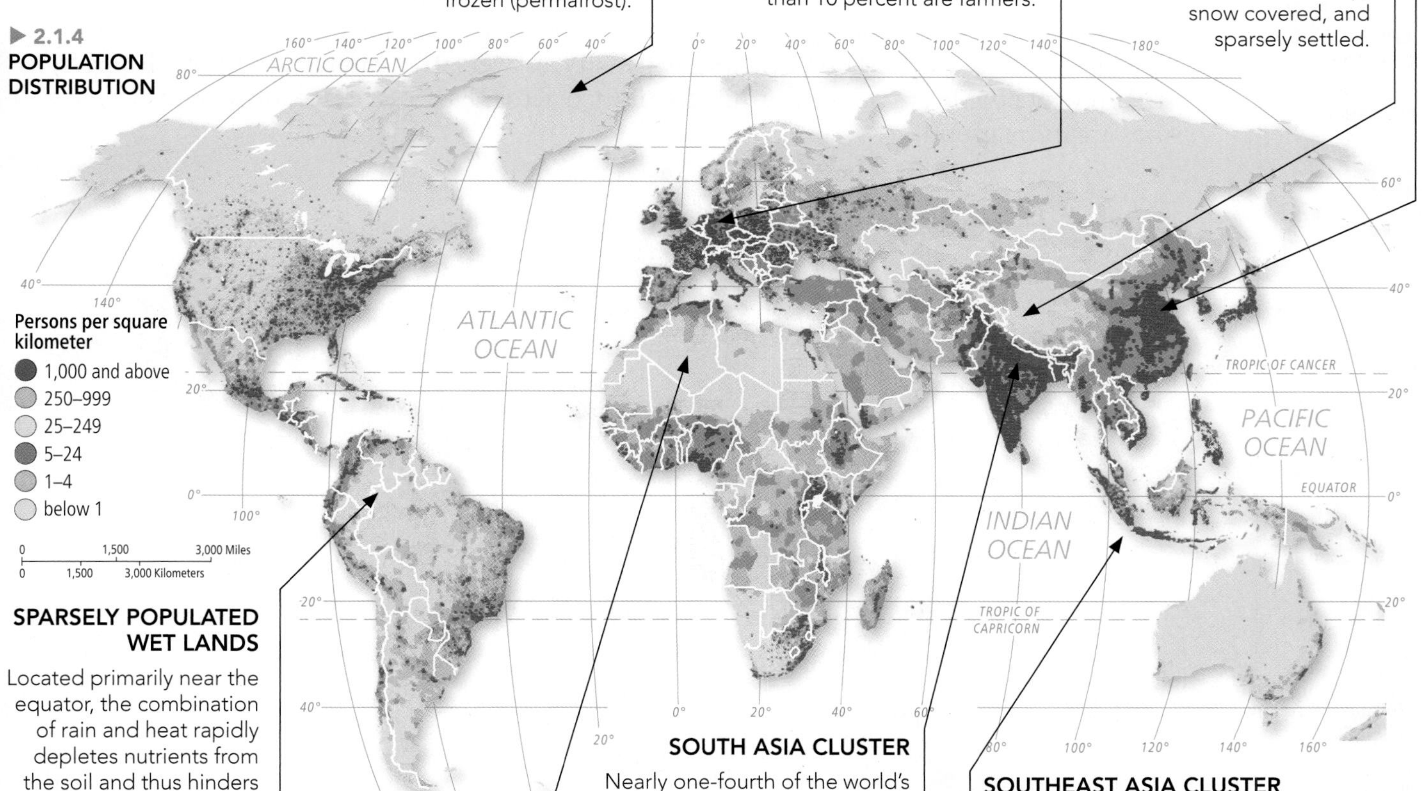

SPARSELY POPULATED WET LANDS

Located primarily near the equator, the combination of rain and heat rapidly depletes nutrients from the soil and thus hinders agriculture.

SPARSELY POPULATED DRY LANDS

Areas too dry for farming cover approximately 20 percent of Earth's land surface. Unless irrigated, deserts lack sufficient water to grow crops that could feed a large population, although some people survive there by raising animals, such as camels.

SOUTH ASIA CLUSTER

Nearly one-fourth of the world's people live in South Asia, which includes India, Pakistan, Bangladesh, and Sri Lanka. The largest concentration of people within South Asia lives along a 1,500-kilometer (900-mile) corridor from Lahore, Pakistan, through India and Bangladesh to the Bay of Bengal.

SOUTHEAST ASIA CLUSTER

More than 600 million people live in Southeast Asia. The largest population concentration is on Indonesia's island of Java, inhabited by more than 100 million people.

▼ **2.1.5 SPARSELY POPULATED COLD LANDS**
Angmagssalik, Greenland.

▲ 2.2.1 **HIGH ARITHMETIC DENSITY** Leeuwarden, The Netherlands.

Population Density

- **Define three types of density used in population geography.**

Density was defined in Chapter 1 as the frequency with which something exists within a given unit of area. Population density is the number of humans living within an area such as the Netherlands (Figure 2.2.1). Here are three examples of population density frequently used by geographers.

Arithmetic Density

Geographers most frequently use **arithmetic density**, which is the total number of objects in an area (Figure 2.2.2). In population geography, arithmetic density refers to the total number of people divided by total land area. To compute the arithmetic density, divide the population by the land area. Figure 2.2.3 shows several examples.

Arithmetic density enables geographers to compare the number of people living in different regions of the world. Thus, arithmetic density answers the "where" question. However, to explain why people are not uniformly distributed across Earth's surface, other density measures are more useful.

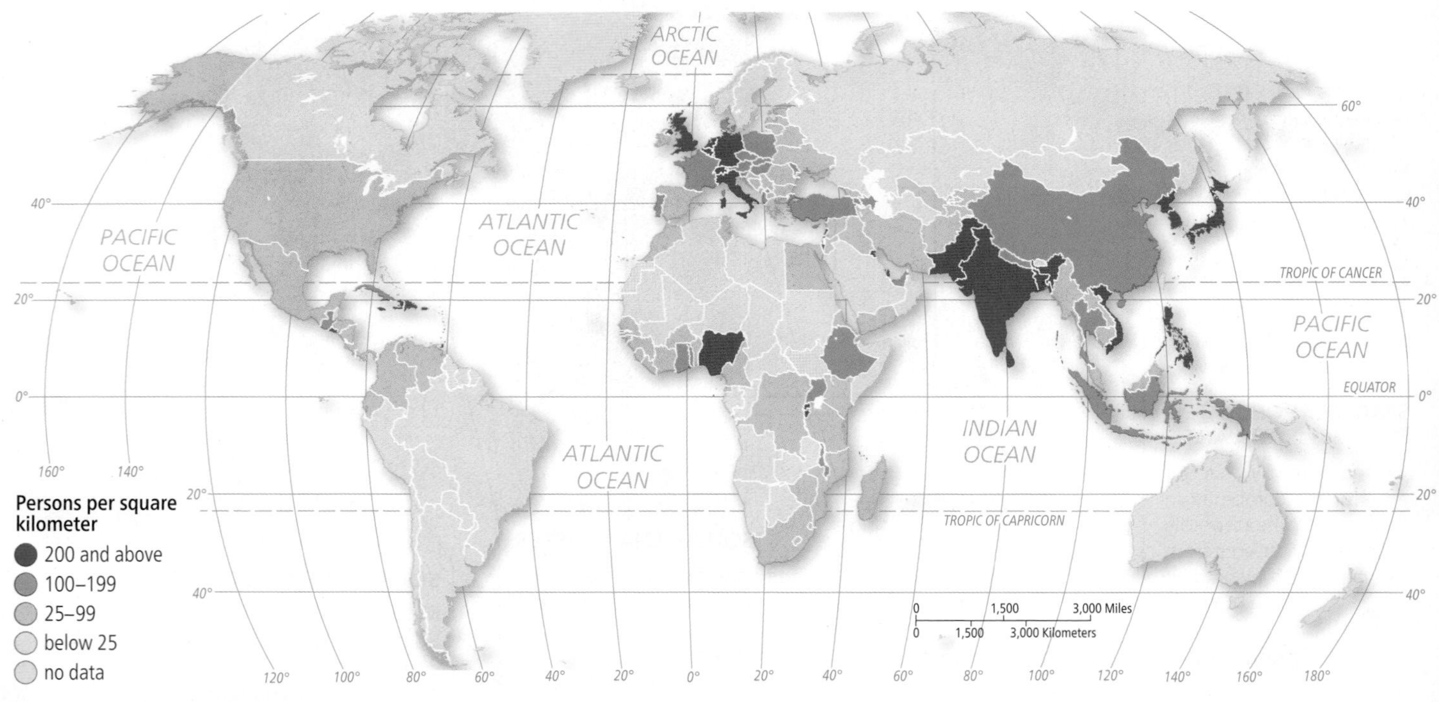

▲ 2.2.2 **ARITHMETIC DENSITY**

▶ 2.2.3 **DENSITIES OF FOUR COUNTRIES** Density figures are in persons per square kilometer.

Country	Arithmetic Density	Physiological Density	Agricultural Density	Percentage Farmers	Percentage Arable Land
Egypt	221	2,497	221	28	4
United States	35	79	1	2	45
The Netherlands	505	924	10	2	55
Canada	4	83	1	2	5

Physiological Density

Looking at the number of people per area of a certain type of land in a region provides a more meaningful population measure than arithmetic density. Land suited for agriculture is called **arable land**. The number of people per unit area of arable land is called the **physiological density** (Figure 2.2.4).

Comparing physiological and arithmetic densities helps geographers understand the capacity of the land to yield enough food for the needs of the people. In Egypt, for example, the large difference between the physiological density and arithmetic density, as shown in Figure 2.2.3, indicates that most of the country's land is unsuitable for intensive agriculture. In fact, all but 5 percent of Egyptians live in the Nile River valley and delta because it is the only area in the country that receives enough moisture (by irrigation from the river) to allow intensive cultivation of crops.

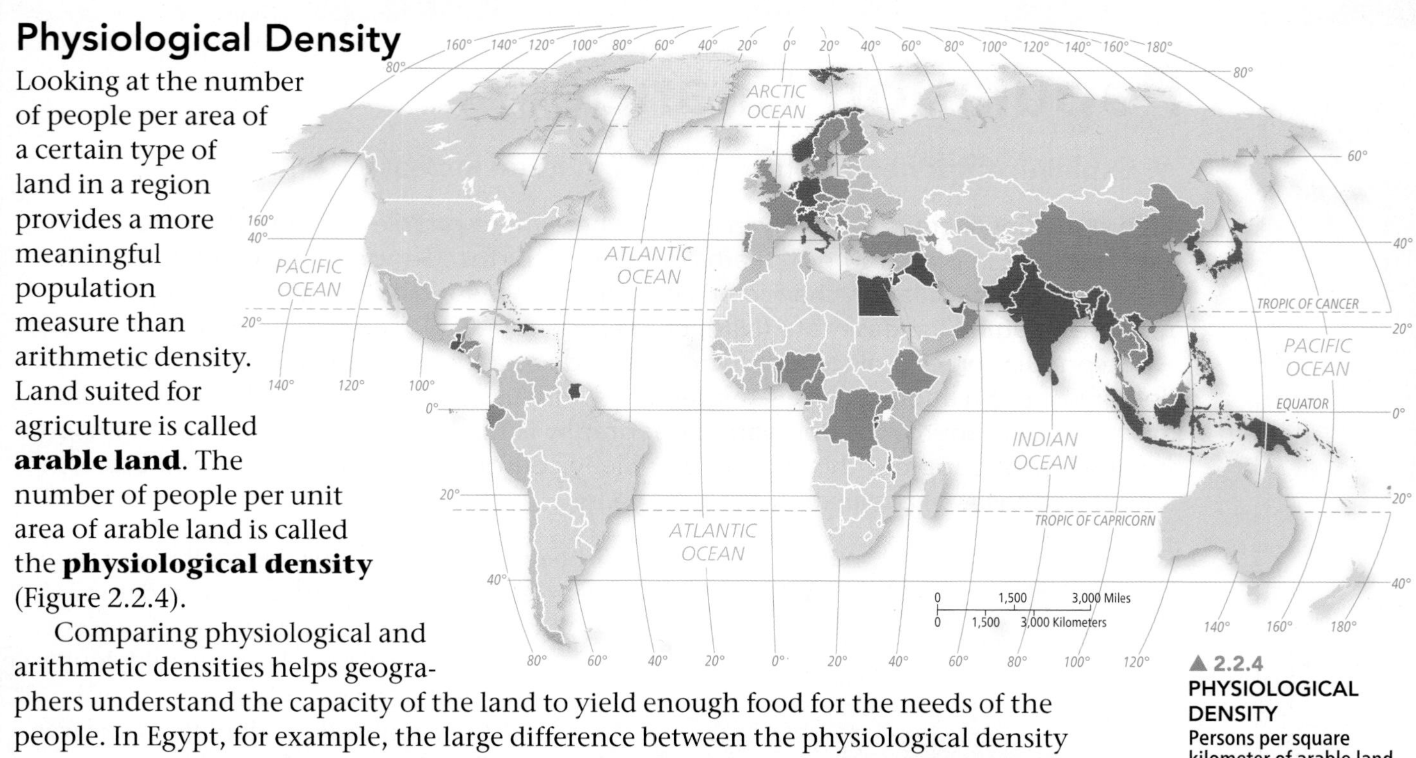

▲ 2.2.4
PHYSIOLOGICAL DENSITY
Persons per square kilometer of arable land
- 400 and above
- 200–399
- 100–199
- below 100
- no data

Agricultural Density

Agricultural density is the ratio of the number of farmers to the amount of arable land (Figure 2.2.5). Figure 2.2.3 shows several examples.

Two countries can have similar physiological densities but produce significantly different amounts of food. Countries in higher stages of economic development are able to access more sophisticated technology, enabling them to produce higher crop yields with fewer people.

To understand relationships between population and resources in a country, geographers examine a country's physiological and agricultural densities together. For example, the physiological densities of both Egypt and the Netherlands are high, but the Dutch have a much lower agricultural density than the Egyptians. Geographers conclude that both the Dutch and Egyptians put heavy pressure on the land to produce food, but the more efficient Dutch agricultural system requires fewer farmers than does the Egyptian system.

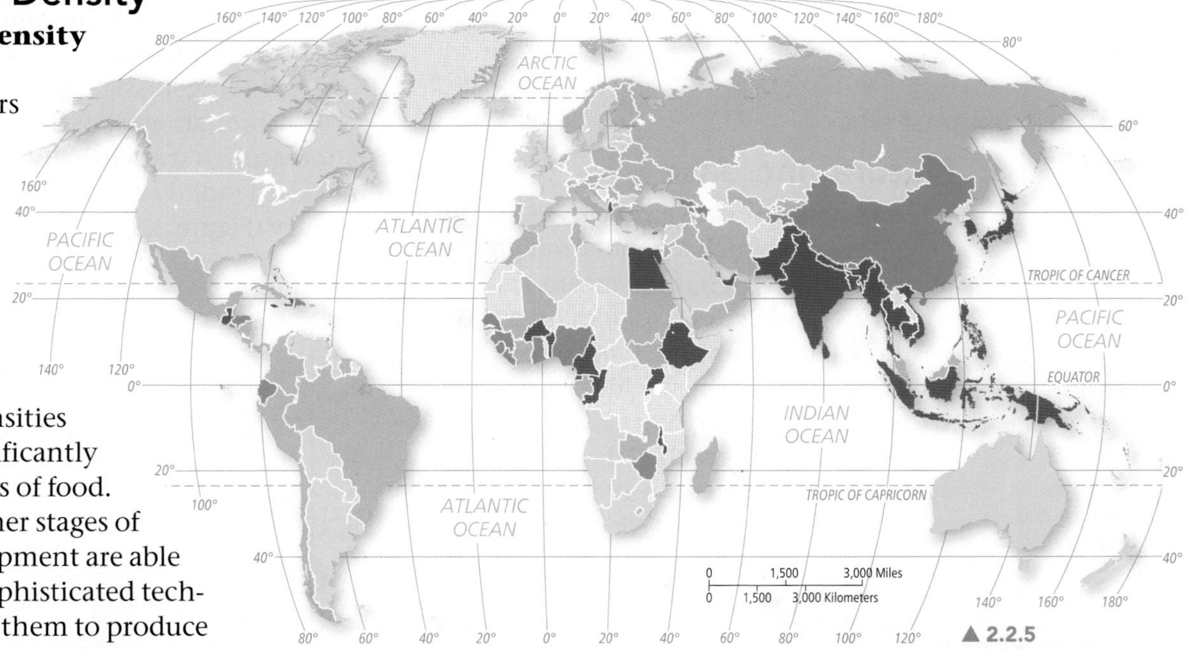

▲ 2.2.5
AGRICULTURAL DENSITY
Farmers per square kilometer of arable land
- 50 and above
- 25–49
- 5–24
- below 5
- no data

Population Change

- **Explain components contributing to natural increase.**

Population increases rapidly in places where more people are born than die, and it declines in places where deaths outnumber births. Geographers most frequently measure population change in a country or the world as a whole by using three measures: natural increase rate (NIR), crude birth rate (CBR), and crude death rate (CDR).

The population of a place also increases or decreases as people move in or out. This element of population change—migration—is discussed in Chapter 3. The single most important data source for population geography is the **census**, in which a country counts the number of people within its borders. Many countries, including the United States, conduct a census of population every 10 years.

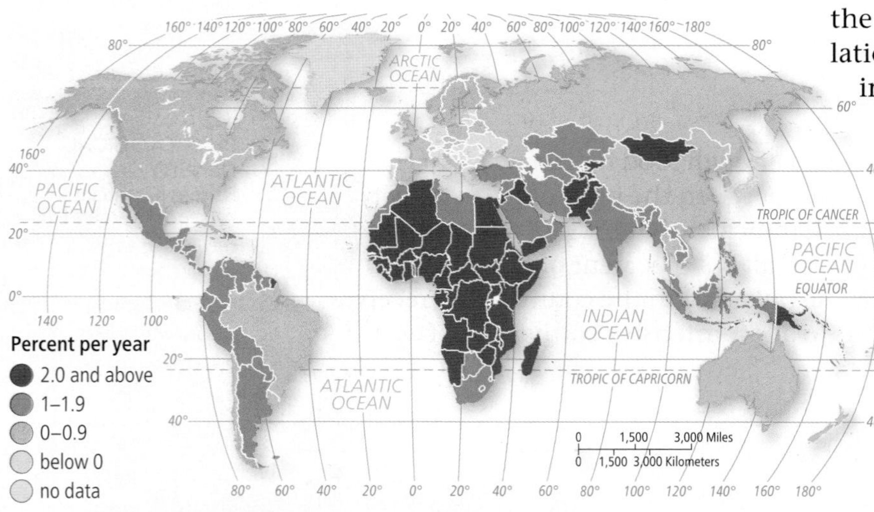

▲ 2.3.1 NATURAL INCREASE RATE

Natural Increase

The **natural increase rate (NIR)** is the percentage by which a population grows in a year. The term natural means that a country's growth rate excludes migration. World NIR is currently 1.1, meaning that the population of the world is growing by 1.1 percent per year (Figure 2.3.1).

The world NIR reached its all-time peak of 2.1 percent in 1968, and it has declined every year since 1987.

Since the 1970s, the world has been adding 1 billion people every 12 years. As the base continues to grow in the twenty-first century, a change of only one-tenth of 1 percent can produce very large swings in population growth.

The rate of natural increase affects the **doubling time**, which is the number of years needed to double a population, assuming a constant rate of natural increase. At the current rate of 1.1 percent per year, world population would double in about 62 years. When the NIR was 2.1 percent in 1968, doubling time was 33 years.

Developing countries have accounted for nearly all of the world's NIR since 1980. Since 1980, 66 percent of the world's population growth has been in Asia, 20 percent in Africa, 9 percent in Latin America, 4 percent in North America, and 1 percent in Europe, including Russia (Figure 2.3.2).

Through most of human history, population growth was virtually nil. Population increased rapidly beginning in the eighteenth century (Figure 2.3.3).

▼ 2.3.2 REGIONAL DISTRIBUTION OF POPULATION GROWTH

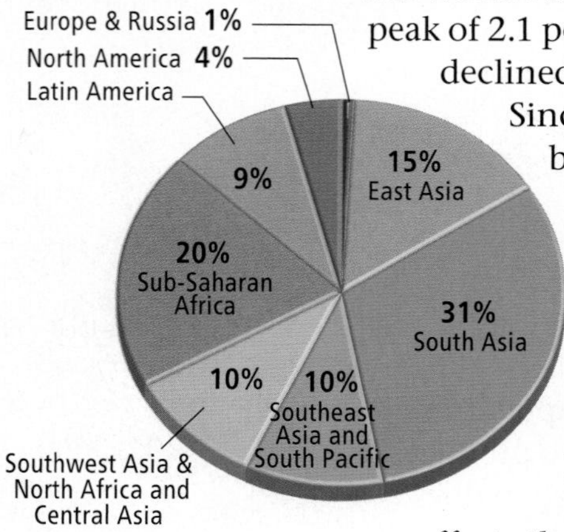

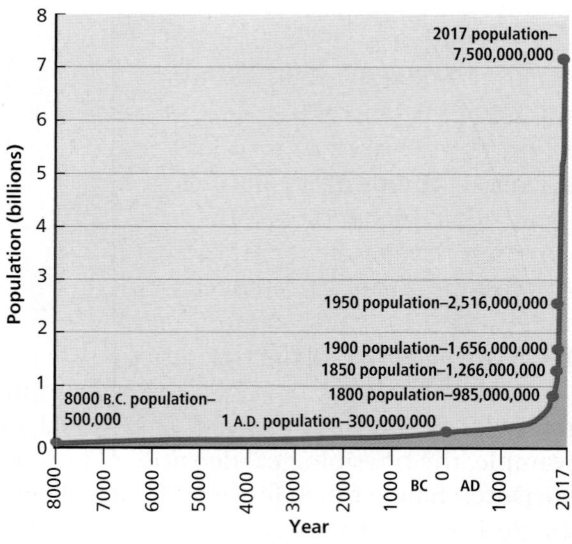

▲ 2.3.3 WORLD POPULATION GROWTH THROUGH THE PAST 10,000 YEARS

Fertility

The **crude birth rate (CBR)** is the total number of live births in a year for every 1,000 people alive in the society. The current world CBR of 20 means that for every 1,000 people alive, 20 babies are born over a one-year period.

The world map of CBRs mirrors the distribution of NIRs. As was the case with NIRs, the highest CBRs are in sub-Saharan Africa, and the lowest are in Europe (Figure 2.3.4). Many sub-Saharan African countries have a CBR over 40, whereas many European countries have a CBR below 10.

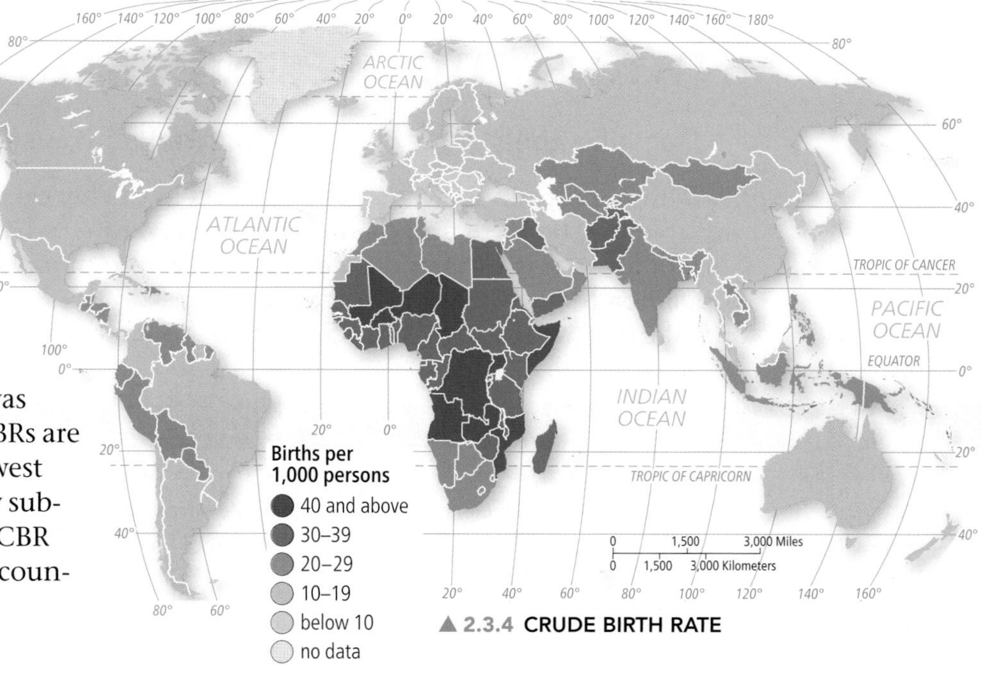

▲ 2.3.4 CRUDE BIRTH RATE

Mortality

The **crude death rate (CDR)** is the total number of deaths in a year for every 1,000 people alive in the society. Comparable to the CBR, the CDR is expressed as the annual number of deaths per 1,000 population.

The CDR does not follow the same regional pattern as the NIR and CBR (Figure 2.3.5). The combined CDR for all developing countries is actually lower than the combined rate for all developed countries. Furthermore, the variation among CDRs is much less extreme than the variation among CBRs. The CDR is 8 in developing countries and 10 in developed countries, whereas the CBR is 21 in developing countries and 11 in developed countries.

Deaths per 1,000 persons
14 and above
10–13
6–9
below 6
no data

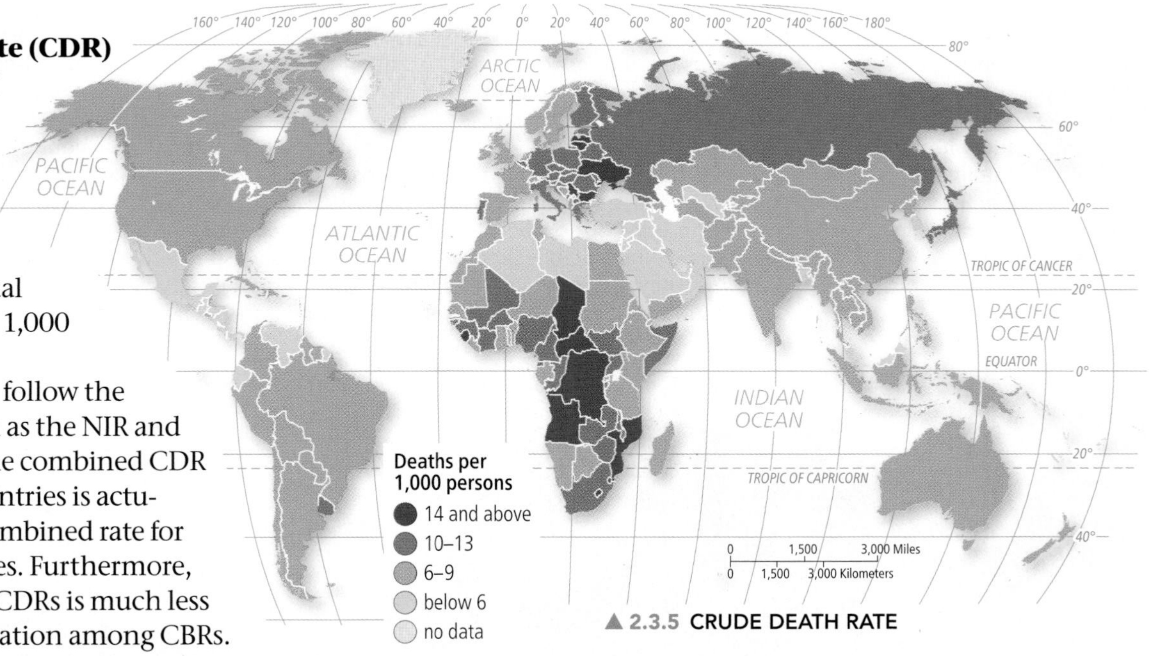

▲ 2.3.5 CRUDE DEATH RATE

Why does Denmark, one of the world's wealthiest countries, have a higher CDR than The Gambia, one of the poorest? Why does Germany, one of the world's wealthiest countries, with one of the world's best health-care systems, have one of the world's highest CDRs (Figure 2.3.6)? The answer is that the populations of different countries are at various stages in an important process known as the demographic transition, discussed on the next page.

▶ 2.3.6 AGING POPULATION
Germany.

The Demographic Transition

- **Describe the stages of the demographic transition.**

The **demographic transition** is a process of change in a society's population from high crude birth and death rates and low rate of natural increase to a condition of low crude birth and death rates, low rate of natural increase, and higher total population (Figure 2.4.1). The process consists of four stages, and every country is in one of them. A possible Stage 5 is discussed later in this chapter.

STAGE 1	STAGE 2	STAGE 3	STAGE 4
• Very high CBR • Very high CDR • Very low NIR	• Still high CBR • Rapidly declining CDR • Very high NIR	• Rapidly declining CBR • Moderately declining CDR • Moderate NIR	• Very low CBR • Low, slightly increasing CDR • 0 or negative NIR
The stage for most of human history, because of unpredictable food supply, as well as war and disease. During most of stage 1, people depended on hunting and gathering for food. A region's population increased when food was easily obtained and declined when it was not. No country remains in stage 1 today.	In developed countries 200 years ago, because the **Industrial Revolution** generated wealth and technology, some of which was used to make communities healthier places to live. In many developing countries during mid-20th century, because the **medical revolution** transferred penicillin, vaccines, insecticides, and other medicines from developed countries (Figure 2.4.2).	In developed countries 100 years ago. People chose to have fewer children, in part a delayed reaction to the decline in mortality in stage 2, and in part a recognition that a large family was no longer an economic asset after migration from farms to cities. Many developing countries have moved into stage 3 in recent years, especially where government policies strongly discourage large families.	In some developed countries in recent years. With increasing numbers of women working in the labor force outside the home, and fewer women as full-time homemakers, women are less likely to be available for full-time care of young children. Families also choose to have fewer children because of increased access to family-planning information and birth-control methods.

Stage 1 Stage 2 Stage 3 Stage 4

Crude birth and death rates (per 1,000): 0, 10, 20, 30, 40, 50, 60

Natural increase rate (%): 0, 1, 2, 3

Natural increase

Birth

Death

Low growth High growth Decreasing growth Low growth

Time →

▲ 2.4.1 DEMOGRAPHIC TRANSITION MODEL

◀ 2.4.2 STAGE 2: THE GAMBIA

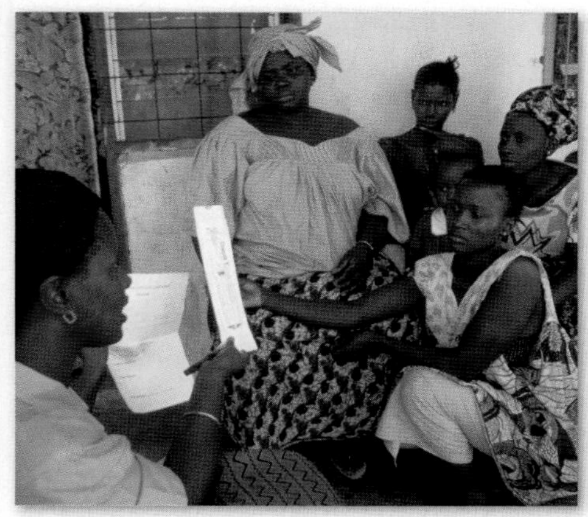

▲ 2.4.3 THE GAMBIA: FAMILY PLANNING

▲ 2.4.4 MEXICO: LARGE FAMILY

▲ 2.4.5 DENMARK: AGING POPULATION

Stage 2 (High Growth): The Gambia

The Gambia is the smallest country in Africa, and one of the poorest. As a colony of the United Kingdom until 1965, The Gambia was in Stage 1 of the demographic transition. The death rate declined rapidly beginning in the 1970s, when the World Health Organization launched a program to immunize children in a number of countries, including The Gambia. This program helped to reduce the CDR in The Gambia, transitioning the country from stage 1 to stage 2, where it is now.

The Gambian government first adopted a policy to reduce births during the 1990s. However, fewer than 10 percent of women of reproductive age practice family planning (Figure 2.4.3). Contraceptive use is not provided to women under age 21, and unmarried mothers must obtain parental consent in order to receive family planning services.

Stage 3 (Moderate Growth): Mexico

Colonial Mexico was in stage 1 of the demographic transition. Periods of population increase alternated with infectious diseases that brought sharp population decline.

Mexico entered stage 2 of the demographic transition during the twentieth century, through a combination of lower death rates as well as higher birth rates. The government of Mexico believed that higher birth rates would be good for the country's economic growth (Figure 2.4.4).

A dramatic decline in birth rates came after 1974, when a Constitutional amendment guaranteed families the legal right to decide on the number and spacing of children, and a National Population Council was established to promote family planning through education. Forty percent of Mexico's married women have sterilizations.

Stage 4 (Low Growth): Denmark

Denmark, like most European countries, has reached stage 4 of the demographic transition. The country entered stage 2 of the demographic transition in the nineteenth century, when the CDR began its permanent decline. The CBR then dropped in the late nineteenth century, and the country moved on to stage 3.

Since the 1970s, Denmark has been in stage 4, with roughly equal CBR and CDR. The CDR is unlikely to decline unless another medical revolution, such as a cure for cancer, keeps older elderly people alive much longer (Figure 2.4.5). Denmark may have entered a possible Stage 5, with a declining NIR (see Section 2.10). As a result of differences in CBR, CDR, and NIR, The Gambia, Mexico, and Denmark have very different demographic transition graphs (Figure 2.4.6).

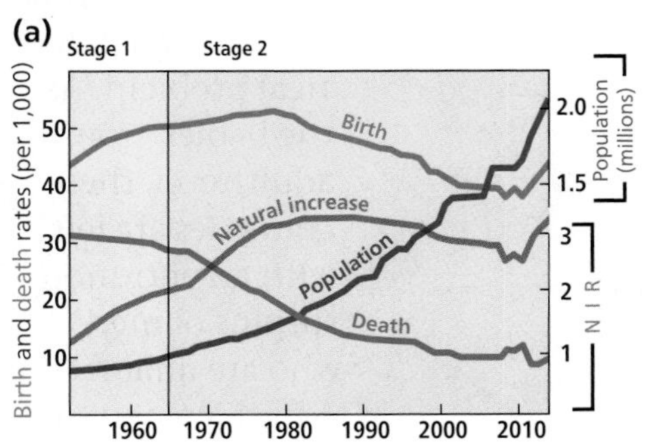

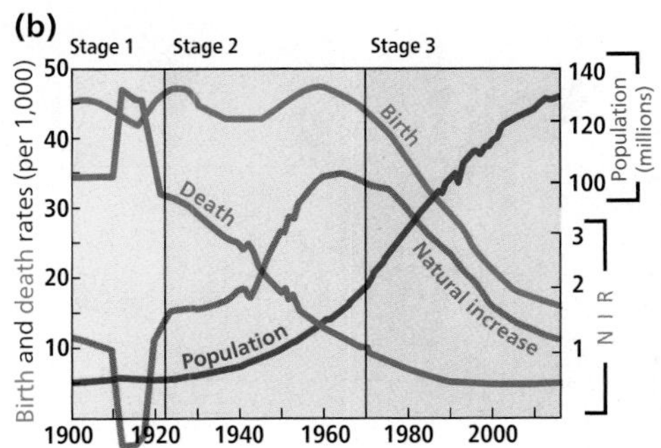

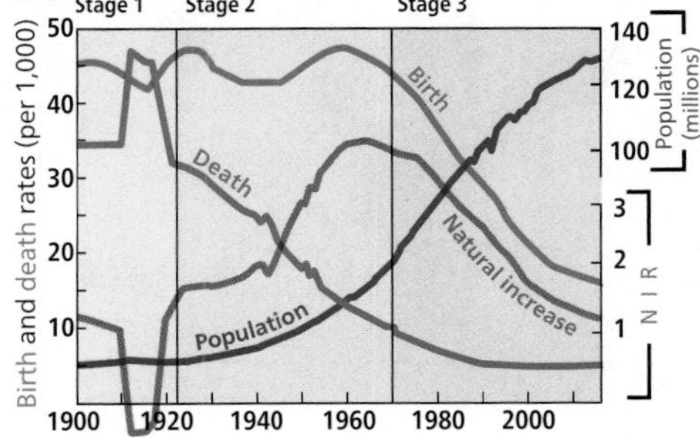

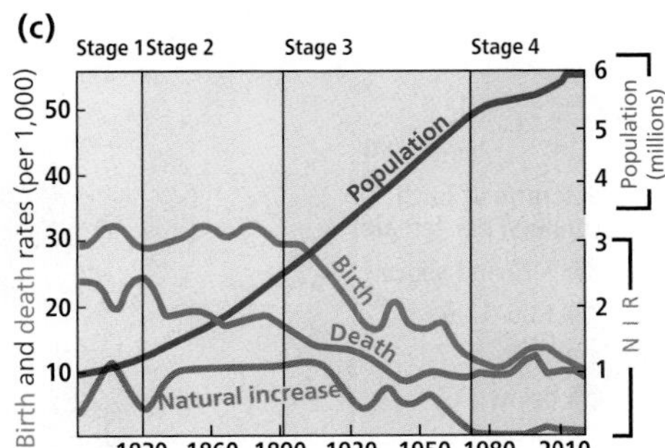

▲ 2.4.6 DEMOGRAPHIC TRANSITION FOR (a) THE GAMBIA, (b) MEXICO, AND (c) DENMARK

▲ 2.5.1 **CHINA'S UNBALANCED SEX RATIO**
116 boys for every 100 girls at birth.

Health & Gender

- **Explain health risks faced by baby girls and mothers.**

As world NIR slows and more countries move into stage 3 or 4 of the demographic transition, geographers increasingly turn their attention to the health of the record number of people who are alive. Females face especially challenging health risks at childbirth. Both the mother and the baby girl are at risk.

Baby Girls at Risk

Around 700,000 female babies are "missing" every year in China and India, as a result of gender-based sex selection. The United Nations Population Fund estimates that overall 117 million females have gone "missing" throughout Asia over the past several decades. The females are "missing" either because the fetus was aborted before birth, the female baby was killed in infancy, or the newborn female is being raised somewhere remote and not reported to census and health officials.

We know about the large number of "missing" females because of the **sex ratio**, which is the number of males per 100 females in the population. The standard biological level for humans at birth is around 105 male babies for every 100 female babies. Scientists are not sure why a few more males than females are born.

The standard biological ratio is characteristic of the developed regions of North America and Europe, as well as in the developing regions of Latin America and sub-Saharan Africa. However, the sex ratio at birth is 116:100 in China and 109:100 in India (Figure 2.5.1). The percentage of newborn females in the world's two most populous countries is much too low to be random (Figure 2.5.2).

The extremely low percentage of female babies in China and India results from cultural preference on the part of parents to have sons rather than daughters. Sons are regarded as more likely than girls to help the family economically. Government policies in these two countries to promote smaller families have resulted in parents bringing into life more male babies than female babies.

Efforts to ban gender-based sex selection have been ineffective because people instead seek out unregulated providers of these services. The United Nations concludes that the "root cause" of sex selection is gender inequality. Many Chinese and Indians have decided that if they are going to have a small number of children, they want them to be boys.

Aside from ethical questions about the devaluation of female lives, the widespread practice of sex selection in China and India is creating a practical problem. As the babies grow to adulthood, these countries are left with an enormous surplus of men who are unable to find women to marry.

▼ 2.5.2 **SEX RATIO AT BIRTH**

Sex ratio at birth (male(s) per female)
- 1.10 and above
- 1.06–1.09
- 1.05
- below 1.05
- no data

Mothers at Risk

The **maternal mortality rate** is the annual number of female deaths per 100,000 live births from any cause related to or aggravated by pregnancy or its management (excluding accidental or incidental causes). The worldwide maternal mortality rate in 2015 was 216, amounting to more than 300,000 women. The rate exceeds 500 deaths per 100,000 live births in sub-Saharan Africa, compared to 8 in Europe (Figure 2.5.3). Nonetheless, the world has made progress: the world maternal mortality rate was 385 in 1990.

▲ 2.5.3 **MATERNAL MORTALITY RATE**

Maternal mortality rate (per 100,000 live births)
- 300 and above
- 100–299
- 20–99
- below 20
- no data

According to the United Nations, the most common cause of maternal death in poor countries is heavy bleeding ("obstetrical hemorrhage"), followed by high blood pressure ("hypertensive disorders of pregnancy"). Developed countries have medical facilities, advanced technologies, and trained personnel to limit the incidence of life-threatening conditions during childbirth.

The maternal mortality rate in the United States (14) is higher than in other developed countries. In addition, the United States is one of only a dozen countries where the rate has increased since 1990, and the only developed country. The higher rate is attributable to difficulties faced by people with low incomes in the United States in gaining access to health care.

▼ 2.5.4 **GIVING BIRTH, KOLKATA, INDIA**
Training midwifes at Kolkata Nursing College.

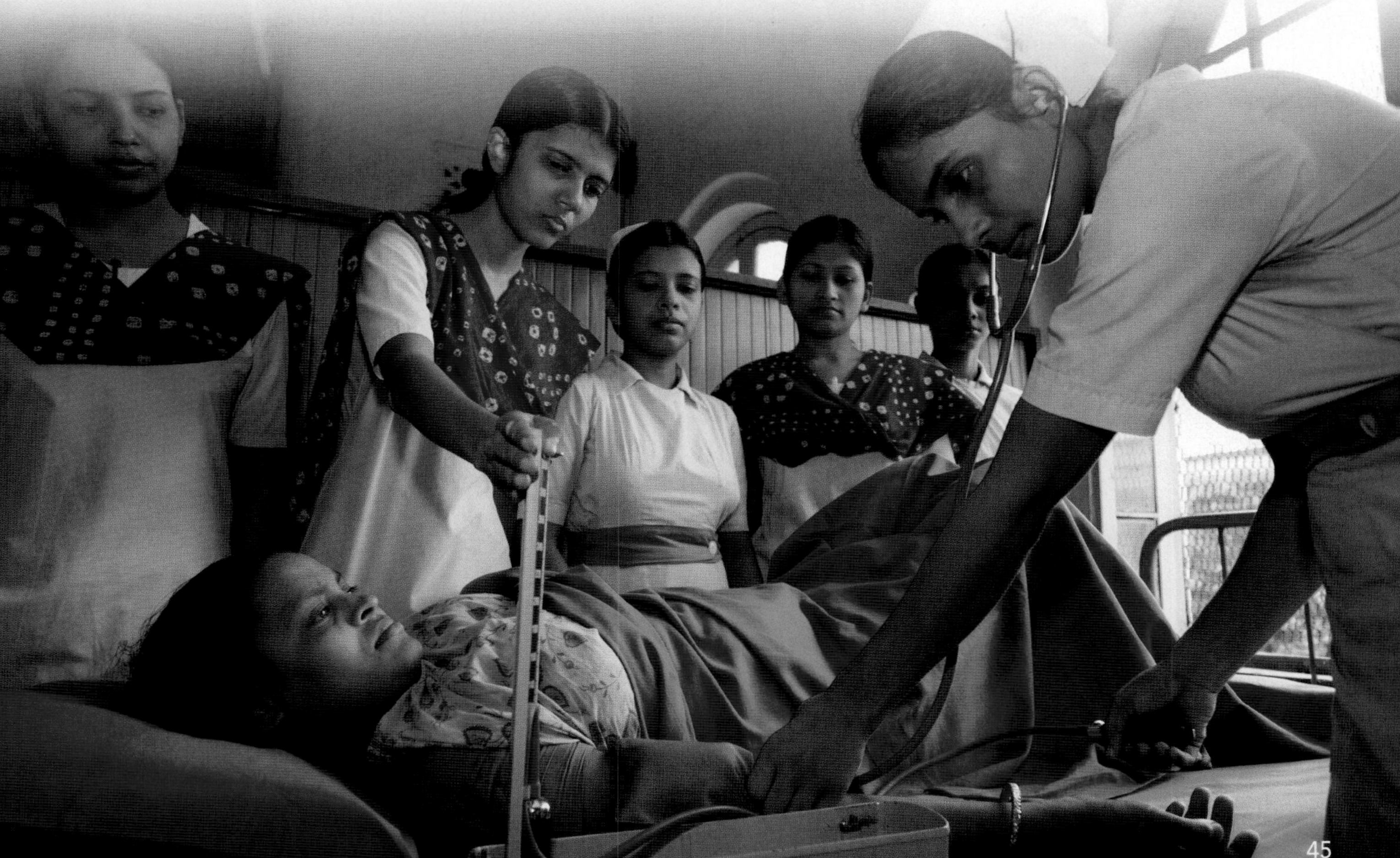

Aging & Health

- **Compare regional differences in percentages of young and old.**

A country's stage of the demographic transition determines the percentage of people in different age groups. A country in stage 2 of the demographic transition typically has a relatively high percentage of young people, whereas a country in stage 4 has a relatively high percentage of elderly people. The percentage of different age groups helps to explain a country's distinctive health challenges.

Caring for Younger People

The **infant mortality rate (IMR)** is the annual number of deaths of infants under 1 year of age, compared with total live births (Figure 2.6.1). As is the case with the CBR and CDR, the IMR is usually expressed as the number of deaths among infants per 1,000 births rather than as a percentage (per 100). In general, the IMR reflects a country's health-care system.

The global distribution of IMRs follows a clear pattern: Lower IMRs are found in countries with well-trained doctors and nurses, modern hospitals, and large supplies of medicine. The IMR is 4 in European countries in stage 4, compared with an IMR of 56 in sub-Saharan Africa.

Despite relatively high IMRs, developing countries have much higher percentages of young people. In sub-Saharan Africa, 43 percent of the population is under age 15, whereas only 16 percent are under age 15 in Europe (Figure 2.6.2).

Caring for Older People

As countries progress through the demographic transition, they face increasing percentages of older people who need adequate levels of income and medical care after they retire from their jobs. The "graying" of the population places a burden on governments in developed countries to meet these needs. The **potential support ratio** (also known as the **elderly support ratio**) is the number of working-age people (ages 15 to 64) divided by the number of persons 65 and older (Figure 2.6.3).

The world's potential support ratio is currently around 9, meaning that there are 9 people of working age for every elderly person. In 2050, the ratio is expected to decline to around 4, meaning that there will be only 4 people of working age available to support elderly people who have retired from work. Thus, as the ratio gets smaller, fewer workers are available to contribute to pensions, health care, and other support that older people need.

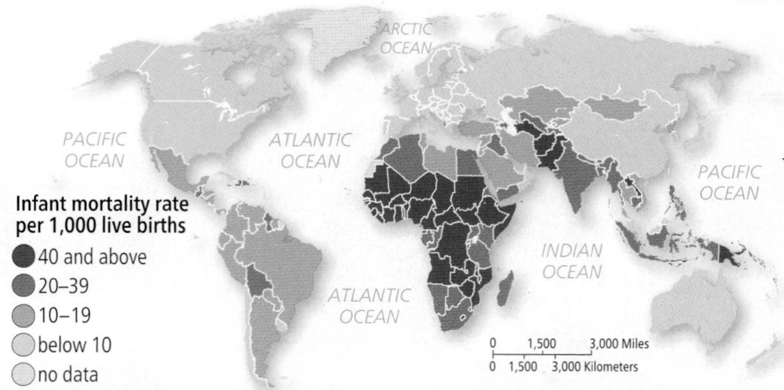

▲ 2.6.1 INFANT MORTALITY RATE

ARCTIC OCEAN
PACIFIC OCEAN
ATLANTIC OCEAN
PACIFIC OCEAN
INDIAN OCEAN
ATLANTIC OCEAN
Percent persons under age 15
40 and above
30–39
20–29
below 20
no data
0 1,500 3,000 Miles
0 1,500 3,000 Kilometers

▲ 2.6.2 POPULATION UNDER AGE 15

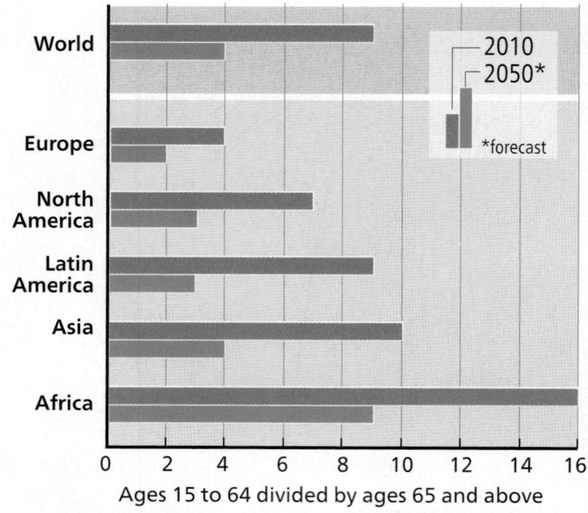

▲ 2.6.3 POTENTIAL (ELDERLY) SUPPORT RATIO

Comparing Young and Old

Life expectancy is the average number of years an individual can be expected to live, given current social, economic, and medical conditions. Life expectancy at birth measures the average number of years a newborn infant can expect to live at current mortality levels (Figures 2.6.4). People on average in wealthy countries live much longer than in poorer ones. Babies born today can expect to live to 81 in Europe, but to only 60 in sub-Saharan Africa.

The **dependency ratio** is the number of people who are too young or too old to work, compared to the number of people in their productive years. Dependents are normally classified as people under age 15 and over age 65. The larger the dependency ratio, the greater the financial burden on those who are working to support those who do not. The dependency ratio is 52 percent in Europe, compared to 85 percent in sub-Saharan Africa.

A **population pyramid** is a bar graph that displays the percentage of a place's population for each age and gender. A country that is in stage 2 of the demographic transition, such as The Gambia, has a pyramid with a broader base than that of a country in stage 4, such as Denmark, indicating a higher percentage of young people. In contrast to The Gambia's more evenly tapering pyramid, the highest levels of Denmark's pyramid are wider on the right because in Denmark women live longer than men (Figure 2.6.5).

The large percentage of children in sub-Saharan Africa strains the ability of these relatively poor countries to provide needed services such as schools, hospitals, and day-care centers. On the other hand, the "graying" of the population places a burden on developed countries to meet their needs for income and medical care after they retire from jobs.

▶ 2.6.4 LIFE EXPECTANCY AT BIRTH

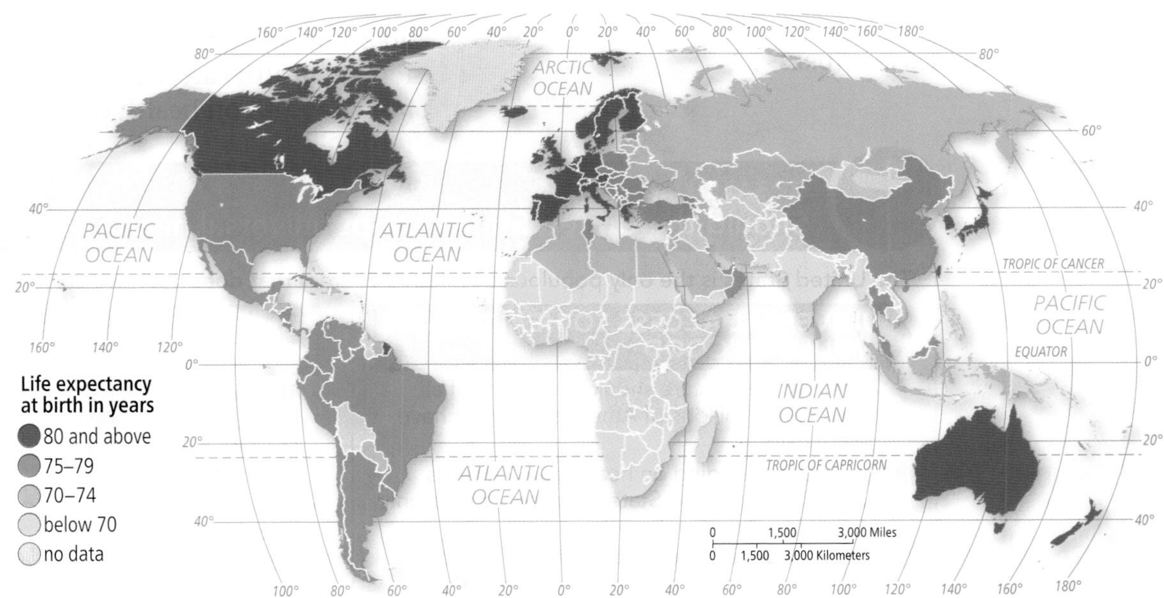

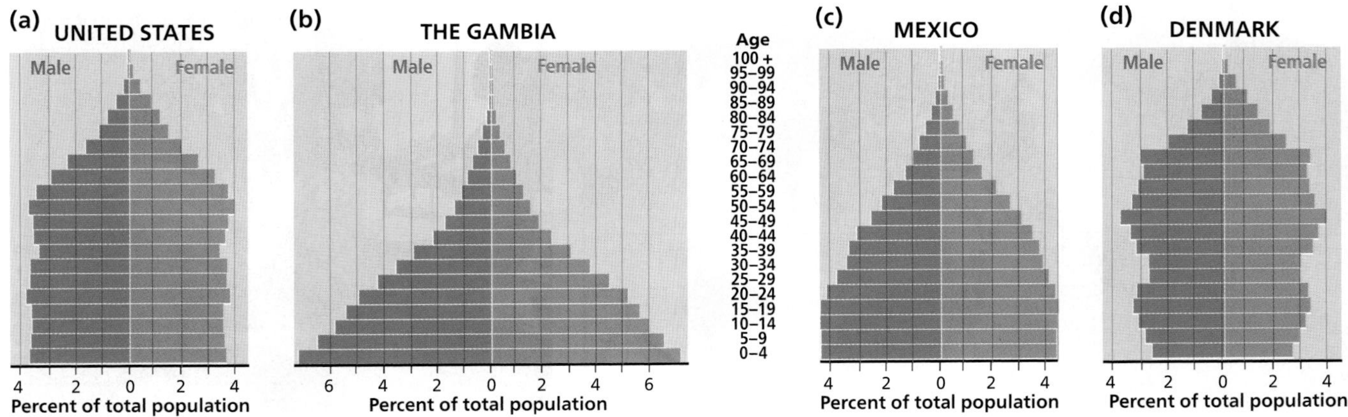

▲ 2.6.5 POPULATION PYRAMIDS

The length of the bar is the percentage of the total population in each 5-year age group. Males are on the left in blue and females on the right in red.

▲ 2.8.1 **STAGE 1: BLACK PLAGUE** Monument to the Black Plague, Vienna, Austria.

Epidemiologic Transition

- **Summarize the four stages of the epidemiologic transition.**

Epidemiology is the branch of medical science concerned with the incidence, distribution, and control of diseases that are prevalent among a population at a particular time and are produced by some special causes not generally present in the affected place.

The **epidemiologic transition** focuses on distinctive health threats in each stage of the demographic transition. Epidemiologists rely heavily on geographic concepts such as scale and connection because measures to control and prevent an epidemic derive from understanding its distinctive distribution and method of diffusion. The concept was originally formulated by epidemiologist Abdel Omran in 1971.

Stage 1: Pestilence & Famine (High CDR)

Infectious diseases are a principal causes of human deaths. History's most violent stage 1 epidemic was the Black Plague (bubonic plague), which was probably transmitted to humans by fleas from migrating infected rats. About 50 million Europeans—60 percent of the region's population—died between 1347 and 1350 (Figure 2.8.1).

Stage 2: Receding Pandemics

A **pandemic** is disease that occurs over a wide geographic area and affects a very high proportion of the population.

Cholera, contracted primarily from exposure to contaminated water, has been a troubling pandemic during the early years of stage 2. Poor people crowding into rapidly growing industrial cities face high risk of cholera until safe water and sewer systems can be constructed.

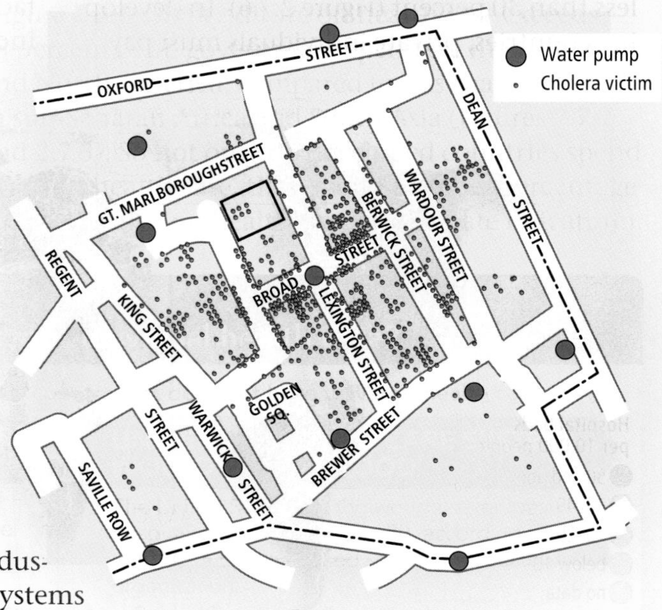

▲ 2.8.2 **SIR JOHN SNOW'S CHOLERA MAP**

British physician Dr. John Snow (1813–1858) fought one of the worst nineteenth century pandemics, cholera, with a handmade map that anticipates GIS by more than a century (Figure 2.8.2). On a map of London's Soho neighborhood, Snow overlaid two maps, one showing the addresses of cholera victims and the other, the location of water pumps where the poor residents of Soho obtained their drinking water. The overlay map showed that cholera victims were not distributed uniformly through Soho, but that a large percentage of cholera victims were clustered around one pump, on Broad Street. Tests at the Broad Street pump later proved that the water there was contaminated.

Cholera persists today in places still in stage 2 of the demographic transition, where many people lack access to clean drinking water, especially sub-Saharan Africa and South and Southeast Asia (Figure 2.8.3).

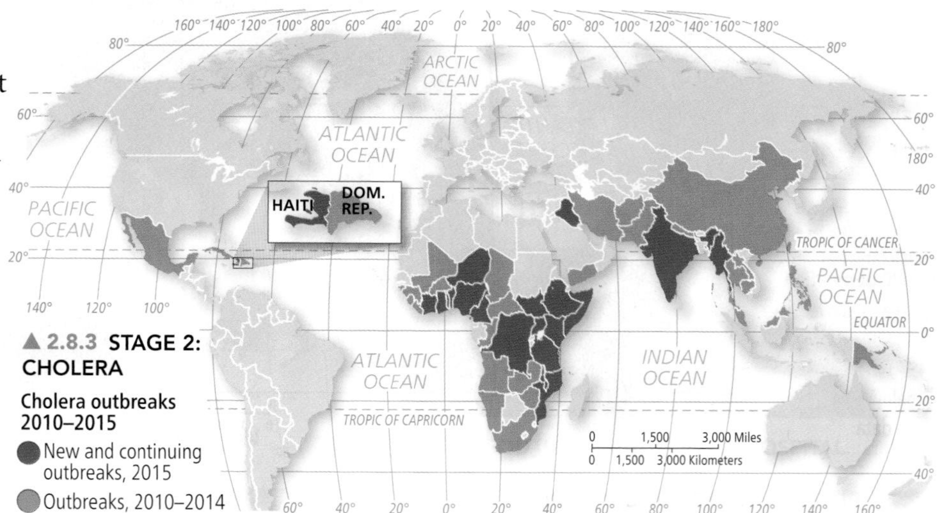

▲ 2.8.3 **STAGE 2: CHOLERA**

Stage 3: Degenerative Diseases

Stage 3 of the epidemiologic transition, the stage of degenerative and human-created diseases, is characterized by a decrease in deaths from infectious diseases and an increase in chronic disorders associated with aging. The two especially important chronic disorders in stage 3 are cardiovascular diseases, such as heart attacks, and various forms of cancer (Figure 2.8.4). The global pattern of cancer is the opposite of that for stage 2 diseases; sub-Saharan Africa and South Asia have the lowest incidence of cancer, primarily because of the relatively low life expectancy in those regions.

Stage 4: Delayed Degenerative Diseases

The epidemiologic transition was extended by S. Jay Olshansky and Brian Ault to stage 4. The major degenerative causes of death—cardiovascular diseases and cancers—linger, but the life expectancy of older people is extended through medical advances. Through medicine, cancers spread more slowly or are removed altogether. Operations such as bypasses repair deficiencies in the cardiovascular system. On the other hand, consumption of non-nutritious food and sedentary behavior have resulted in an increase in obesity in stage 4 countries (Figure 2.8.5).

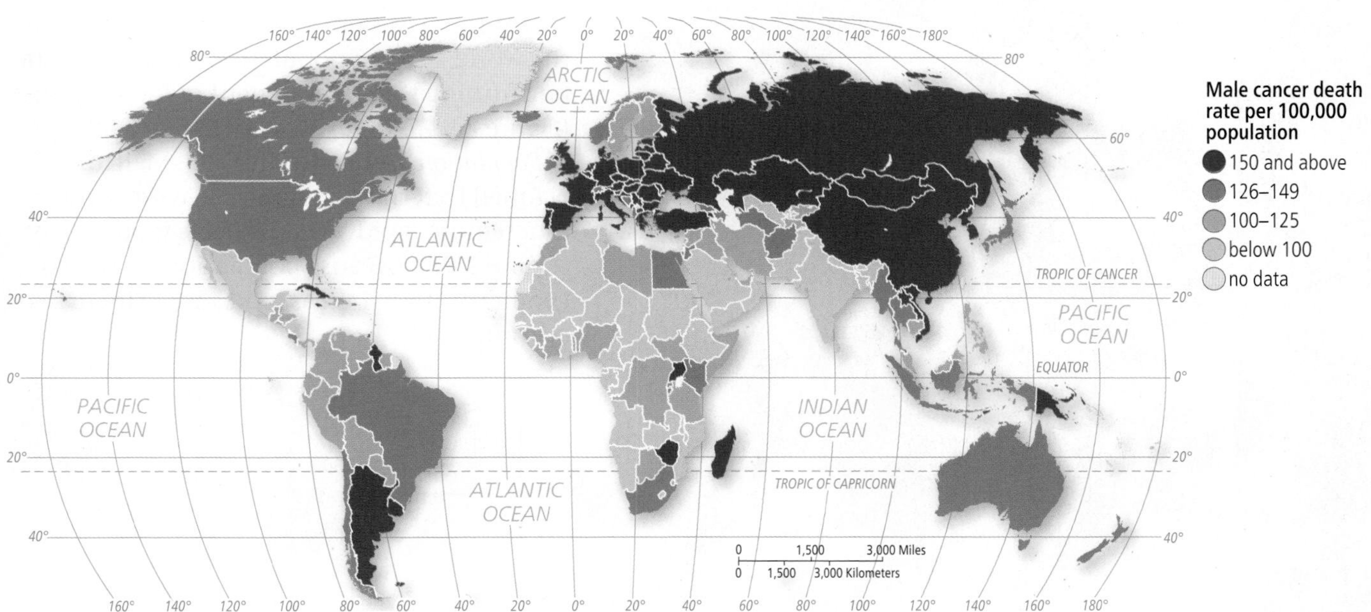

▲ 2.8.4 STAGE 3: MALE CANCER

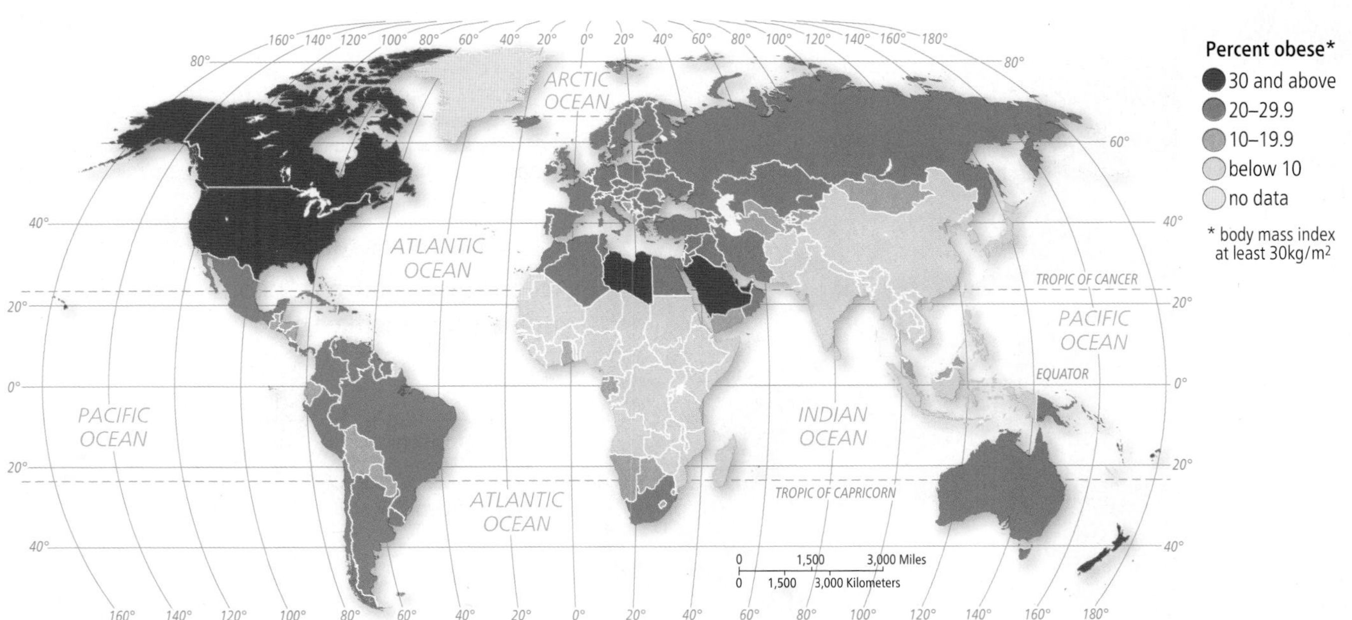

▲ 2.8.5 STAGE 4: OBESITY

Population & Resources

- Summarize arguments supporting and opposing Malthus's theory.

Geographic concepts offer insights into future population and health trends. In view of the current size of Earth's population and the NIR, will there soon be too many of us? Or will Earth's total population stabilize and even decline in the future?

Overpopulation is a condition in which the number of people in an area exceeds the capacity of the environment to support life at a decent standard of living (Figure 2.9.1). English economist Thomas Malthus (1766–1834) was one of the first to argue that the world's rate of population increase was far outrunning the development of food supplies (Figure 2.9.2). In *An Essay on the Principle of Population*, published in 1798, Malthus claimed that the population was growing much more rapidly than Earth's food supply (Figure 2.9.3) because population increased geometrically, whereas food supply increased arithmetically.

▲ 2.9.1 **POPULATION OUTSTRIPS RESOURCES** Women in line to collect their daily requirement of water, Mumbai, India.

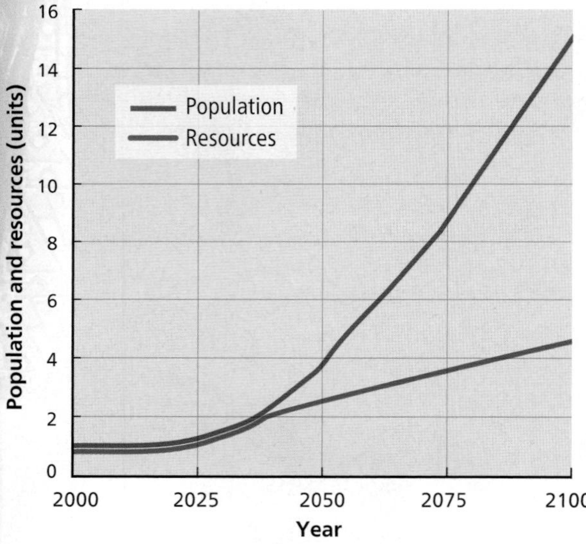

▲ 2.9.2 **MALTHUS'S THEORY**

According to Malthus, people and food supply increase like this:

Today	1 person, 1 unit of food
25 years from now	2 persons, 2 units of food
50 years from now	4 persons, 3 units of food
75 years from now	8 persons 4 units of food
100 years from now	16 persons, 5 units of food

▶ 2.9.3 **EXPANDING RESOURCES** Market, Yangon, Myanmar

Population and Resources: The Current Picture

Malthus's views remain influential today. Contemporary geographers and other analysts are taking another look at Malthus's views, because of Earth's unprecedented rate of natural increase during the twentieth century. Neo-Malthusians argue that characteristics of recent population growth make Malthus's thesis more frightening than when it was first proposed more than 200 years ago.

In Malthus's time, only a few relatively wealthy countries had entered stage 2 of the demographic transition. Now, relatively poor countries are in stage 2. As a result, the gap between population growth and resources is wider in some countries than even Malthus anticipated.

World population growth is outstripping a wide variety of resources, not just food production. The world faces a frightening future in which billions of people are engaged in a desperate search for food, water, and energy (Figure 2.9.4).

▲ 2.9.4 **NEO-MALTHUSIAN FEARS**
Lining up for food aid in Uganda.

Malthus's Critics

Criticism has been leveled at both the population growth and resource depletion sides of Malthus's equation. Many geographers consider Malthusian beliefs unrealistically pessimistic because they are based on a belief that the world's supply of resources is fixed rather than expanding.

Critics also argue that population growth is not a problem. To the contrary, a larger population could stimulate economic growth and therefore production of more food. Marxist critics argue that poverty and hunger are a result of an unjust society and economic inequality, not population growth. The world possesses sufficient resources to eliminate hunger and poverty, if only these resources are shared equally.

Malthus's Theory and Reality

Evidence from the past half-century lends support to both Neo-Malthusians and their critics. Malthus was fairly close to the mark on resources but much too pessimistic on population growth. Overall food production has increased during the last half-century somewhat more rapidly than Malthus predicted in countries such as China and India (Figures 2.9.5). Better growing techniques, higher-yielding seeds, and cultivation of more land have contributed to the expansion in the food supply (see Chapter 9). On the other hand, the food supply has barely kept up with population growth in Africa (Figures 2.9.6).

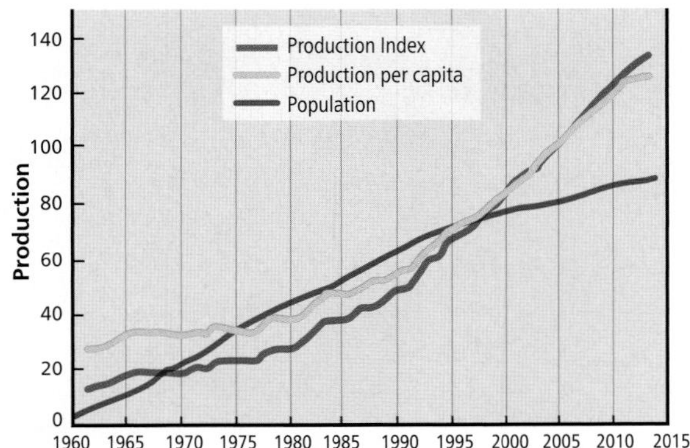

▲ 2.9.5 **MALTHUS'S THEORY APPLIED TO CHINA**
Food production has increased much more rapidly than population.

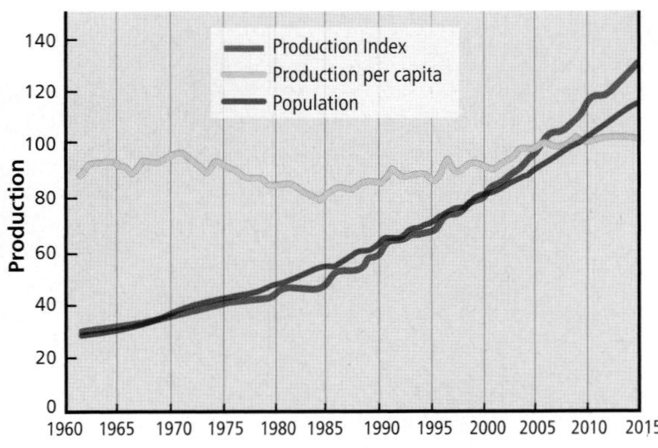

▲ 2.9.6 **MALTHUS'S THEORY APPLIED TO AFRICA**
Food production is barely keeping up with population growth.

Population Futures

- **Describe a possible stage 5 of the demographic transition.**

A possible stage 5 of the demographic transition is predicted by demographers for some developed countries. Stage 5 would be characterized by a very low CBR, an increasing CDR, and therefore a negative NIR (Figure 2.10.1). After several decades of very low birth rates, a stage 5 country would have relatively few young women aging into childbearing years. As members of the smaller pool of women choose to have fewer children, birth rates would continue to fall even more dramatically than in stage 4.

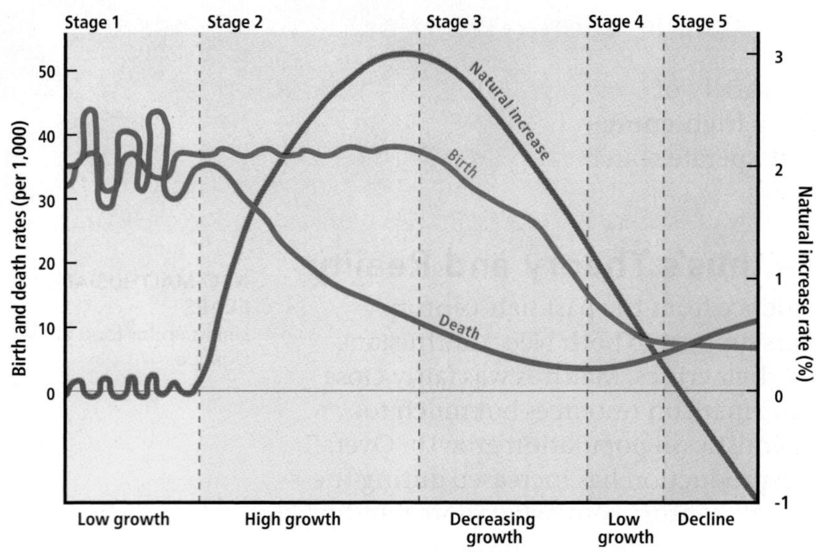

▲ 2.10.1 THE DEMOGRAPHIC TRANSITION INCLUDING STAGE 5
Stage 5 would have a negative NIR, because the CDR would increase to be higher than the CBR.

Total Fertility Rate

The United Nations estimates that world population will be around 10 billion in 2100. The estimate is based on the **total fertility rate (TFR)**, which is the average number of children a woman will have throughout her childbearing years, roughly ages 15 through 49 (see What's Your Geography feature). The TFR for the world as a whole is 2.5, and varies between 5.0 in sub-Saharan Africa and 1.6 in Europe (Figure 2.10.2).

Zero population growth (ZPG) is a TFR in which the population neither grows nor declines, in other words an NIR of zero. A TFR below approximately 2.1 over a period of time produces ZPG. Europe has had ZPG for several decades, and the region's population is growing only because of migration, as discussed in the next chapter.

▶ 2.10.2 TOTAL FERTILITY RATE

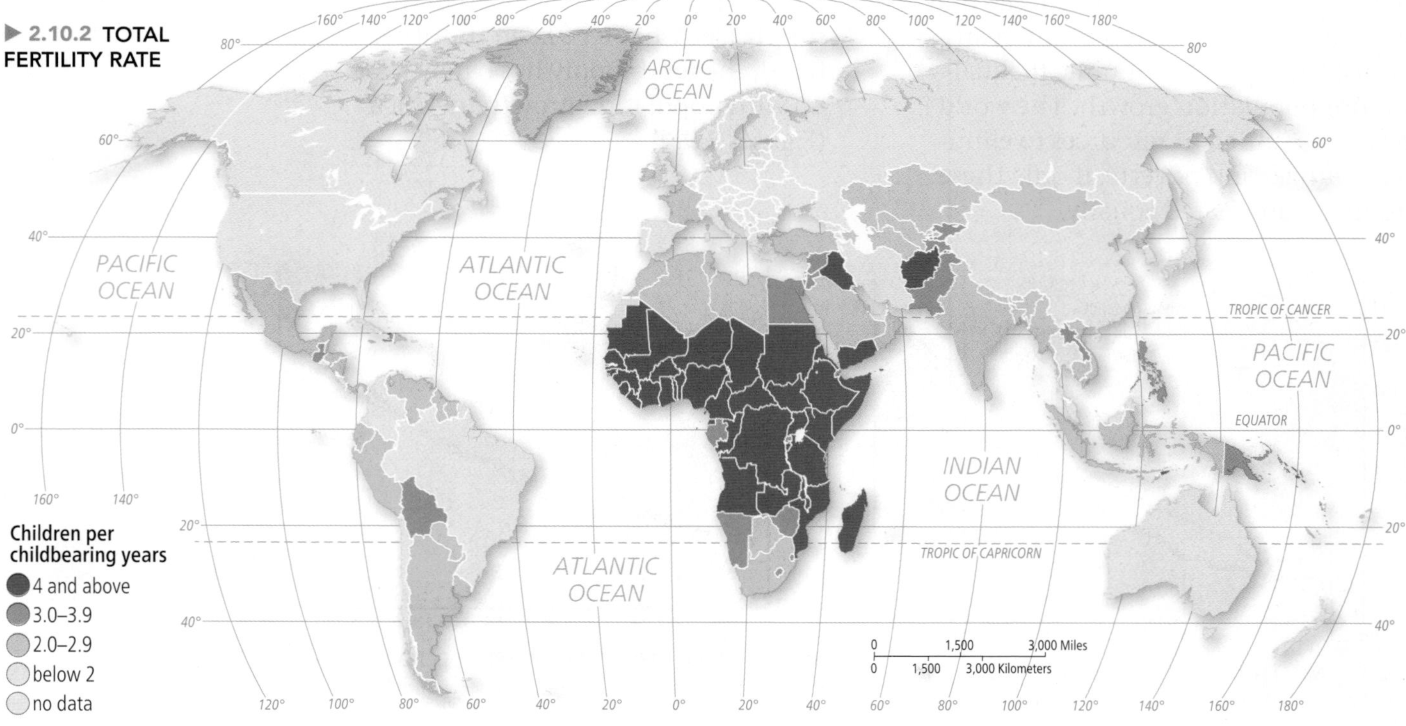

Population Futures in Asia

Populous countries in Asia, including China, India, and Japan, will heavily influence future world population.

CHINA'S FUTURE POPULATION

The core of the Chinese government's family-planning program has been the One Child Policy, which enabled the country to make substantial progress in reducing its NIR.

Under the One Child Policy, a couple needed a permit to have a child. Couples received financial subsidies, a long maternity leave, better housing, and (in rural areas) more land if they agreed to have just one child. People also received free contraceptives, abortions, and sterilizations.

With the UN forecasting China to lose population by 2100, the government has abandoned the One Child Policy. But after decades of intensive education and coercion, most Chinese have accepted the benefits of family planning and small families.

▲ 2.10.3 PROMOTING FAMILY PLANNING, DELHI, INDIA

INDIA'S FUTURE POPULATION

India has had a national family planning program since 1952. Most controversially, during the 1970s India set up camps to perform sterilizations—surgical procedures in which people were made incapable of reproduction. Widespread opposition to the sterilization program grew in the country, because people feared that they would be forcibly sterilized, and it increased distrust of other family-planning measures as well.

Government-sponsored family-planning programs in India have emphasized education. Still, the now dominant form of birth control continues to be sterilization of women (Figure 2.10.3).

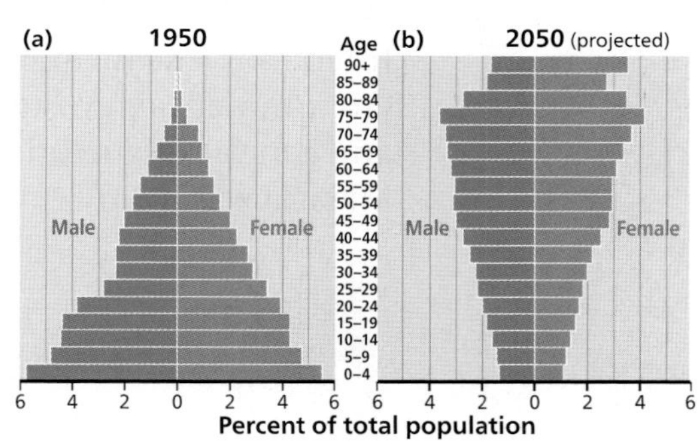

▲ 2.10.4 JAPAN'S CHANGING POPULATION PYRAMIDS

JAPAN'S FUTURE POPULATION

If the demographic transition is to include a stage 5, Japan will be one of the world's first countries to reach it. The UN forecasts Japan's population to decline by one-third by 2100. With the population decline will come an increasing percentage of elderly people (Figure 2.10.4).

Japan faces a severe shortage of workers. Rather than combine work with child rearing, Japanese women are expected to make a stark choice: either marry and raise children or remain single and work. According to Japan's most recent census, the majority has chosen to work.

WHAT'S YOUR **POPULATION** GEOGRAPHY?

Population and Fertility

The size of the world's future population (Figure 2.10.5) ultimately depends on decisions made by people of childbearing age concerning the number of children they will have.

1. What is the TFR of your mother? How does that figure compare with those for your grandmothers?
2. How many children do you expect to have? Is that number more, less, or the same as your mother? How confident are you in your answer? What factors make you feel confident or unsure of your answer?
3. Compare your answers with others in your class or with your friends. Calculate the mean response for your group by totaling all the individual answers and dividing by the number of respondents. Compute the TFR separately for the men and the women. Do the figures differ? If so, what might account for the difference?
4. Demographers explain that a TFR of 2.1 is needed to maintain the same size of population. A TFR of 1.9, as in the United States, means that the number of births is not sufficient to maintain the current size of the U.S. population. Yet the U.S. population is actually increasing by 0.4 percent per year. What accounts for the increasing population, if not the number of births?

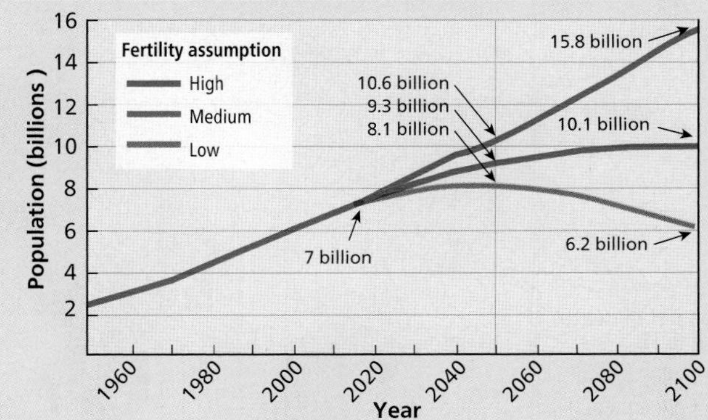

▲ 2.10.5 U.N. FUTURE POPULATION ESTIMATES

Epidemiological Futures

- **List reasons for a possible stage 5 of the epidemiologic transition.**

Recall that in the possible stage 5 of the demographic transition, CDR rises because more of the population is elderly. Some medical analysts argue that the world is moving into stage 5 of the epidemiologic transition, brought about by a reemergence of infectious and parasitic diseases. Infectious diseases thought to have been eradicated or controlled have returned, and new ones have emerged. Other epidemiologists dismiss recent trends as a temporary setback in a long process of controlling infectious diseases.

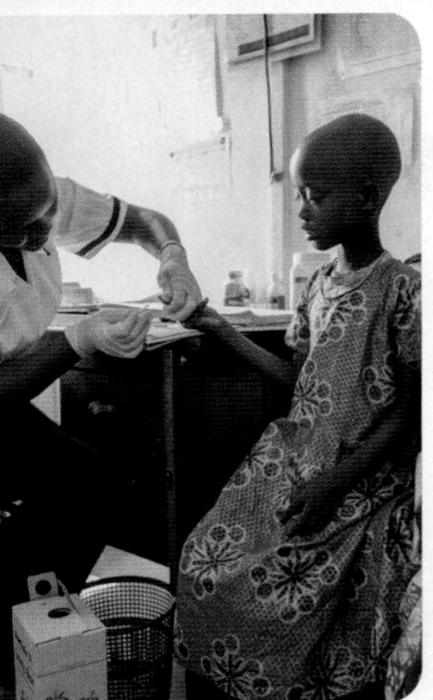

▲ 2.11.1 **MALARIA**
Testing for malaria in Kenya.

Three reasons help to explain the possible emergence of a stage 5 of the epidemiologic transition: evolution, poverty, and diffusion.

Reason for Possible Stage 5: Evolution

Infectious disease microbes have continuously evolved and changed in response to environmental pressures by developing resistance to drugs and insecticides. Antibiotics and genetic engineering contribute to the emergence of new strains of viruses and bacteria. Malaria was nearly eradicated in the mid-twentieth century by spraying DDT in areas infested with the mosquito that carried the parasite. However, malaria now causes around one-half million deaths worldwide annually, nearly all in sub-Saharan Africa (Figures 2.11.1 and 2.11.2). A major reason is the evolution of DDT-resistant mosquitoes.

Number of deaths due to malaria
- 1,000 and above
- 100–999
- 1–99
- none reported
- no data

▲ 2.11.2 **MALARIA DEATHS**
Malaria is found primarily in tropical regions of developing countries.

Reason for Possible Stage 5: Poverty

Infectious diseases are more prevalent in poor areas than other places because unsanitary conditions may persist, and most people can't afford the drugs needed for treatment. Tuberculosis (TB) is an example of an infectious disease that has been largely controlled in developed countries but remains a major cause of death in developing countries (Figure 2.11.3). An airborne disease that damages the lungs, TB (often called "consumption") spreads principally through coughing and sneezing. TB is more prevalent in poor areas because the long, expensive treatment poses a significant economic burden.

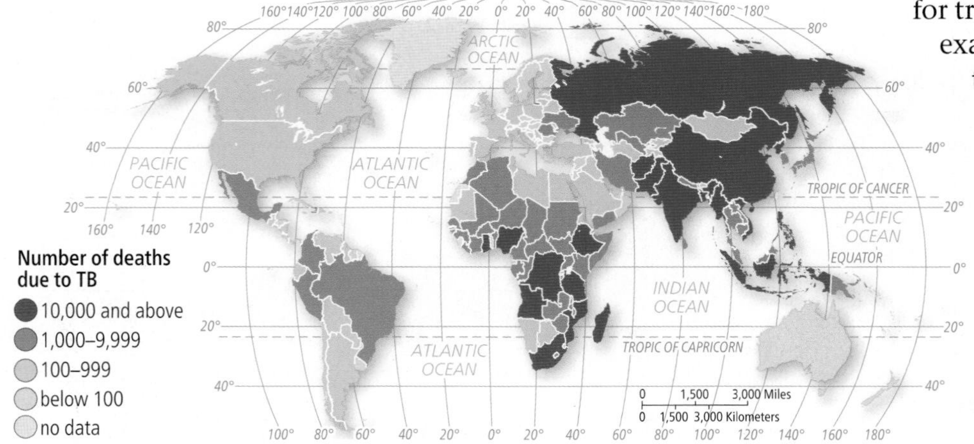

▲ 2.11.3 **TUBERCULOSIS (TB) DEATHS**
Deaths from TB are found primarily in developing countries unable to pay for the expensive treatment.

Reason for Possible Stage 5: Increased Connections

Pandemics have spread in recent decades through the process of relocation diffusion, discussed in Chapter 1. As they travel, people carry diseases with them and are exposed to the diseases of others.

The most lethal pandemic in recent years has been AIDS (acquired immunodeficiency syndrome). Worldwide, 35 million people died of AIDS from the beginning of the epidemic through 2016, and 37 million were living with HIV (human immunodeficiency virus, the cause of AIDS). The impact of AIDS has been felt most strongly in sub-Saharan Africa, home to 26 million of the world's 37 million HIV-positive people (Figure 2.11.4).

AIDS diffused from sub-Saharan Africa through relocation diffusion, both by Africans and by visitors to Africa returning to their home countries. AIDS entered the United States during the early 1980s through New York, California, and Florida. Not by coincidence, the three leading U.S. airports for international arrivals are in these three states (Figure 2.11.5). Though AIDS diffused to every state during the 1980s, these three states, plus Texas (a major port of entry by motor vehicle), accounted for half of the country's new AIDS cases in the peak year of 1993.

The number of new AIDS cases has dropped sharply because of the rapid diffusion of preventive methods and medicines such as AZT. The rapid spread of these innovations is an example of expansion diffusion rather than relocation diffusion.

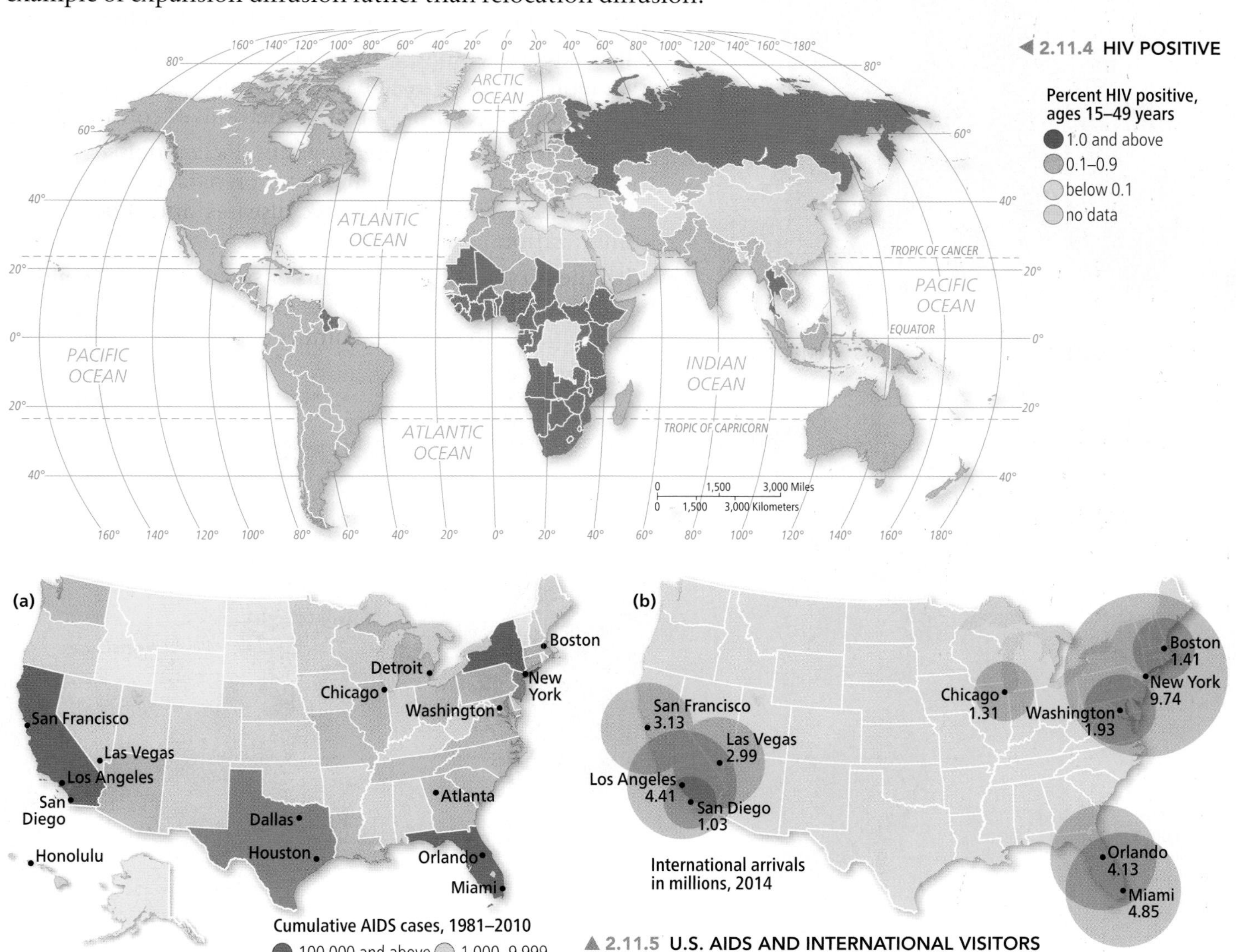

2.11.4 HIV POSITIVE

▲ 2.11.5 U.S. AIDS AND INTERNATIONAL VISITORS
Because AIDS arrived in the United States primarily through air travelers, the pattern of diffusion of AIDS closely matches the distribution of visitors from overseas.

Family Futures

- **Evaluate reasons for declining birth rates.**

The CBR has declined rapidly since 1990, from 27 to 20 in the world as a whole and from 31 to 21 in developing countries (Figures 2.12.1 and 2.12.2). Two strategies have been successful in reducing birth rates.

▲ 2.12.1 REPRODUCTIVE HEALTH CLINIC, CAMBODIA

Lowering CBR through Education and Health Care

One approach to lowering birth rates emphasizes the importance of improving local economic conditions. A wealthier community has more money to spend on education and health-care programs that promote lower birth rates. According to this approach:

- With more women able to attend school and to remain in school longer, they would be more likely to learn employment skills and gain more economic control over their lives.
- With better education, women would better understand their reproductive rights, make more informed reproductive choices, and select more effective methods of contraception.
- With improved health-care programs, IMRs would decline through such programs as improved prenatal care, counseling about sexually transmitted diseases, and child immunization.
- With the survival of more infants ensured, women would be more likely to choose to make more effective use of contraceptives to limit the number of children.

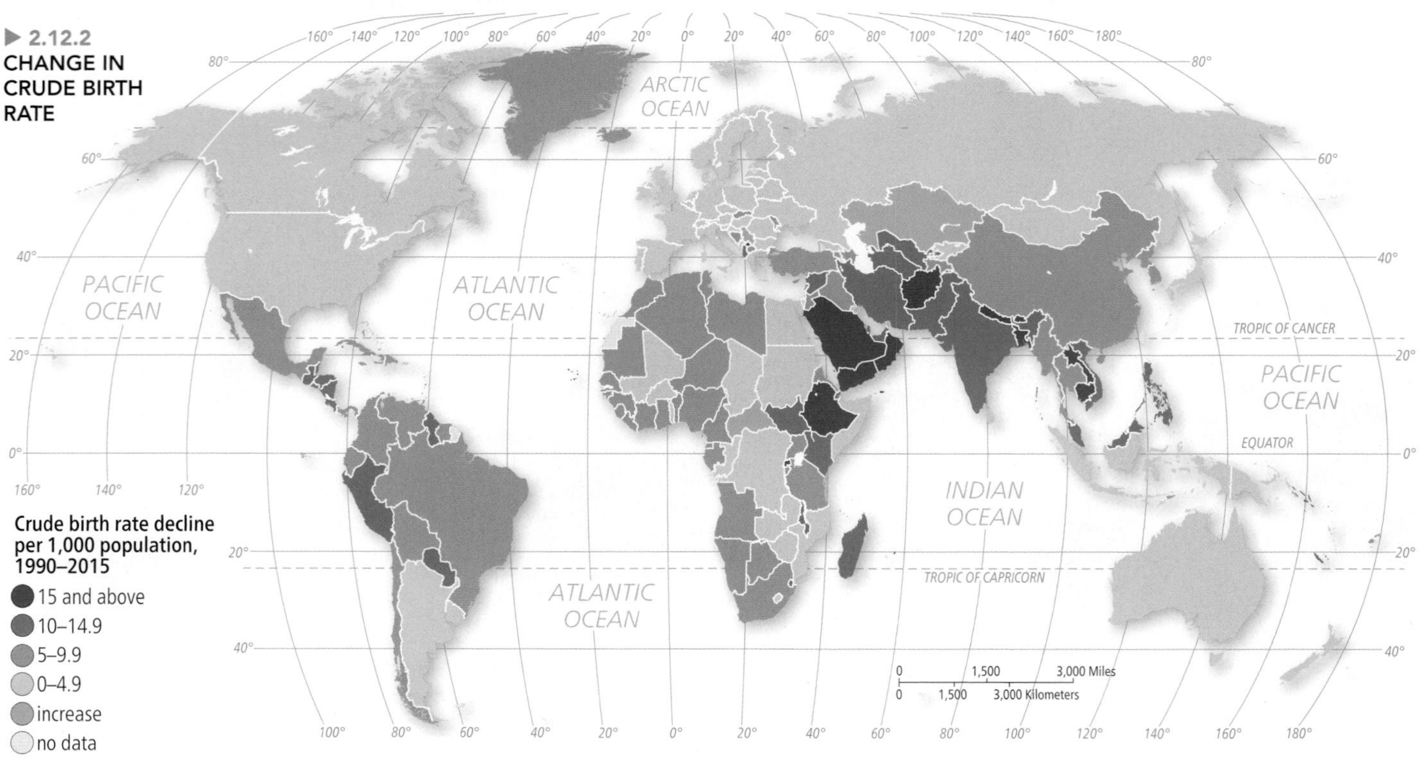

▶ 2.12.2 CHANGE IN CRUDE BIRTH RATE

Lowering CBR through Contraception

The other approach to lowering birth rates emphasizes the importance of rapidly diffusing modern contraceptive methods (Figure 2.12.3). Economic development may promote lower birth rates in the long run, but the world cannot wait around for that alternative to take effect. Putting resources into family-planning programs can reduce birth rates much more rapidly. In developing countries, demand for contraceptive devices is greater than the available supply. Therefore, the most effective way to increase their use is to distribute more of them cheaply and quickly. According to this approach, contraceptives are the best method for lowering the birth rate.

Rapid growth in the acceptance of family planning in a number of developing countries is evidence that in the modern world, ideas can diffuse rapidly, even to places where people have limited access to education and modern communications (see Research & Analyze feature). The percentage of women using contraceptives is especially low in sub-Saharan Africa, so the alternative of distributing contraceptives could have an especially strong impact there.

Many oppose birth-control programs for religious and political reasons (Figure 2.12.4). Adherents of several religions have convictions that prevent them from using some or all birth-control methods. Opposition is especially strong in some countries to terminating pregnancy by abortion.

▼ 2.12.3 WOMEN USING FAMILY PLANNING

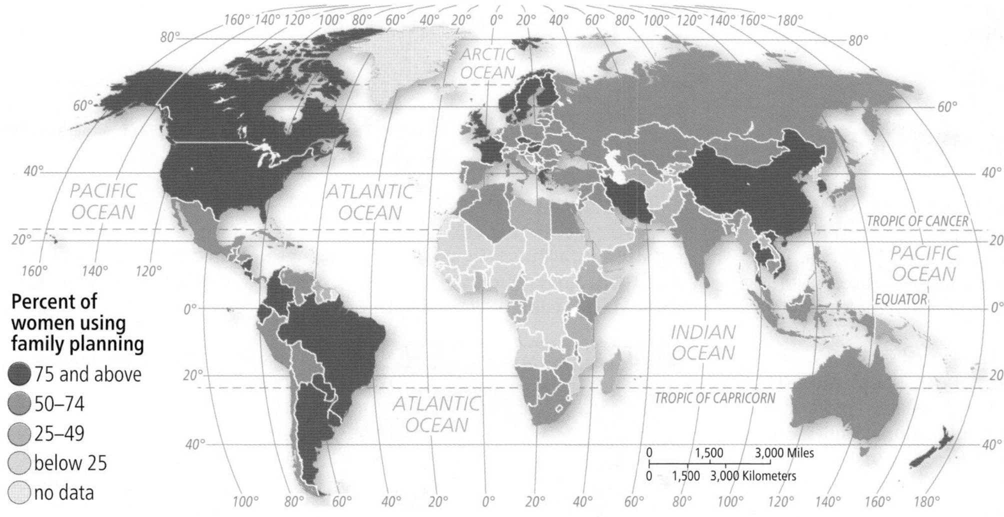

▼ 2.12.4 ABORTION OPPONENTS, IRELAND

RESEARCH & ANALYZE
Comparing family planning

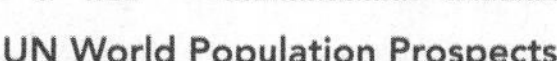
UN World Population Prospects

https://goo.gl/ATTDPG

Bangladesh has had little improvement in wealth and literacy, but it has seen changes in the use of contraception.

In your search engine, ***enter*** *UN Contraceptive Prevalence* or go to **esa.un.org** and ***search*** *World Contraceptive Use 2015*. Under *Data*, ***click*** *Contraceptive prevalence* and ***open*** the spreadsheet. ***Scroll down*** to the rows for *Bangladesh*.

1. For the earliest year (1975–76), what percentage of people age 10–49 were using any form of contraception? For the most recent date?.
2. What are the top two methods of contraception in Bangladesh at the most recent date?
3. Compare the prevalence and type of contraception in Bangladesh with those in Figure 2.12.5. What might account for the similarities and differences?

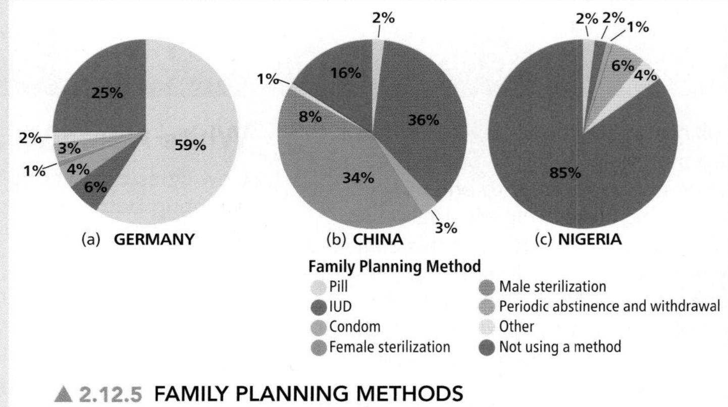

▲ 2.12.5 FAMILY PLANNING METHODS

CHAPTER 2

Review, Analyze, & Apply

KEY ISSUE 1 Where Are People Distributed?

Two-thirds of the world's inhabitants are clustered in four regions. Human beings tend to avoid parts of Earth's surface that they consider to be too wet, too dry, too cold, or too mountainous. Several measures of density are used to describe where people live in the world, and the relationship between people and natural resources.

THINKING GEOGRAPHICALLY

▲ 2.CR.1 HONG KONG, CHINA

1. Scientists disagree about the effects of high density on human behavior. Some laboratory tests have shown that rats display evidence of increased aggressiveness, competition, and violence when very large numbers of them are placed in a box. Does living in very high density places, such as Hong Kong, cause humans to behave especially aggressively or violently? Why or why not?

KEY ISSUE 2 Why Is Population Increasing?

The demographic transition helps to explain why regions have varying rates of population growth. Virtually all the world's natural increase is concentrated in the developing countries of Africa, Asia, and Latin America. The difference in natural increase between developed countries and developing countries results from differences in birth rates rather than in death rates.

THINKING GEOGRAPHICALLY

▲ 2.CR.2 BOOMERS AND GEN Z

2. Compared with previous generations, boomers (born 1946–64) received more education, and women were more likely to work outside the home. Boomers married later (if at all), and were more likely to cohabit. They had fewer children and more children while unmarried. In what ways do you think the Gen Z generation (born after 1995) might display similar or different demographic characteristics than Boomers? Why?

KEY ISSUE 3 How Does Health Vary by Region?

Countries have distinctive patterns of gender and age, depending on the stage of the demographic transition, and they display different health conditions and medical services. Health care varies widely around the world because developing countries generally lack resources to provide the same level of health care as developed countries.

THINKING GEOGRAPHICALLY

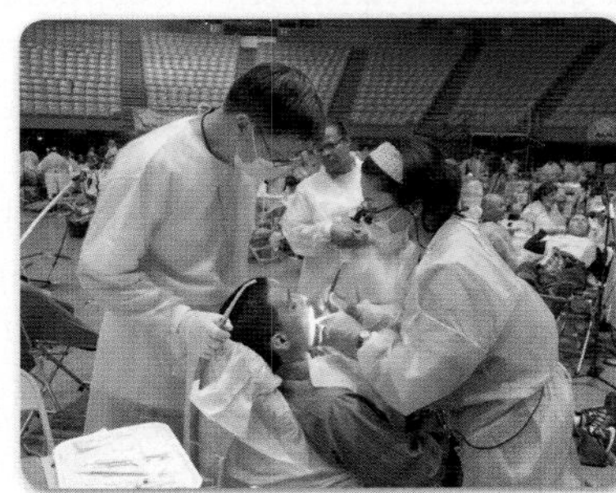

3. Health care indicators for the United States do not always match those of other developed countries. What reasons might explain these differences? Why might a need exist for a medical clinic in a sports arena, such as in Los Angeles?

◀ 2.CR.3 FREE DENTAL CLINIC, LOS ANGELES

KEY ISSUE 4 How Might Population Change In the Future?

Malthus argued in 1798 that population would grow more rapidly than resources. Recent experience shows that population has not grown as rapidly as Malthus forecast. Birth rates have declined in some places primarily through education and health care, and in other places primarily through diffusion of contraception.

THINKING GEOGRAPHICALLY

▲ 2.CR.4 JAPAN: POSSIBLE STAGE 5

4. Some geographers believe that the demographic transition now has a fifth stage in places such as Japan, but the leading international demographic organizations, such as the Population Reference Bureau (PRB) and the UN Population Fund, are sticking with four stages. What sort of evidence might help to determine the existence of a possible stage 5?

Mastering Geography

Looking for additional review and test prep materials? Visit the Study Area in Mastering Geography to enhance your geographic literacy, spatial reasoning skills, and understanding of this chapter's content. Access MapMaster™ interactive maps, video case studies, *In the News* current articles, flashcards, self-study quizzes, an eText of *Contemporary Human Geography*, and more.
pearson.com/mastering/geography

GeoVideo

Log in to the Mastering Geography™ Study Area to view this video.

White Horse Village Urbanization

New cities being constructed in rural China will bring better jobs and living conditions to millions of farmers and their families, but also end an ancient way of life.

1. In general, would the village farmers prefer to work in a new factory or remain on their land? Explain.
2. Do village residents have a choice about whether their land becomes a new industrial city? Explain.
3. In the view of China's economic planners, why is urbanization of the countryside essential?

Key Terms

Agricultural density (p. 39) The ratio of the number of farmers to the total amount of arable land (land suitable for agriculture).

Arable land (p. 39) Land suited for agriculture.

Arithmetic density (p. 38) The total number of people divided by the total land area.

Census (p. 40) A complete enumeration of a population.

Crude birth rate (CBR) (p. 41) The total number of live births in a year for every 1,000 people alive in the society.

Crude death rate (CDR) (p. 41) The total number of deaths in a year for every 1,000 people alive in the society.

Demographic transition (p. 42) The process of change in a society's population from a condition of high crude birth and death rates and low rate of natural increase to a condition of low crude birth and death rates, low rate of natural increase, and higher total population.

Dependency ratio (p. 47) The number of people under age 15 and over age 64 compared to the number of people active in the labor force.

Doubling time (p. 40) The number of years needed to double a population, assuming a constant rate of natural increase.

Ecumene (p. 37) The portion of Earth's surface occupied by permanent human settlement.

Epidemiologic transition (p. 50) The process of change in the distinctive causes of death in each stage of the demographic transition.

Epidemiology (p. 50) The branch of medical science concerned with the incidence, distribution, and control of diseases that are prevalent among a population at a special time and are produced by some special causes not generally present in the affected locality.

Industrial Revolution (p. 42) A series of improvements in industrial technology that transformed the process of manufacturing goods.

Infant mortality rate (IMR) (p. 46) The total number of deaths in a year among infants under 1 year of age for every 1,000 live births in a society.

Life expectancy (p. 47) The average number of years an individual can be expected to live, given current social, economic, and medical conditions. Life expectancy at birth is the average number of years a newborn infant can expect to live.

Maternal mortality rate (p. 45) The annual number of female deaths per 100,000 live births from any cause related to or aggravated by pregnancy or its management (excluding accidental or incidental causes).

Medical revolution (p. 42) Medical technology invented in Europe and North America that has diffused to the poorer countries in Latin America, Asia, and Africa. Improved medical practices have eliminated many of the traditional causes of death in poorer countries and enabled more people to live longer and healthier lives.

Natural increase rate (NIR) (p. 40) The percentage growth of a population in a year, computed as the crude birth rate minus the crude death rate.

Overpopulation (p. 52) A situation in which the number of people in an area exceeds the capacity of the environment to support life at a decent standard of living.

Pandemic (p. 50) Disease that occurs over a wide geographic area and affects a very high proportion of the population.

Physiological density (p. 39) The number of people per unit area of arable land, which is land suitable for agriculture.

Population pyramid (p. 47) A bar graph that represents the distribution of population by age and sex.

Potential support ratio (or elderly support ratio) (p. 46) The number of working-age people (ages 15 to 64) divided by the number of persons 65 and older.

Sex ratio (p. 44) The number of males per 100 females in the population.

Total fertility rate (TFR) (p. 54) The average number of children a woman will have throughout her childbearing years.

Zero population growth (ZPG) (p. 54) A decline of the total fertility rate to the point where the natural increase rate equals zero.

Geospatial Analysis

Log in to the Mastering Geography Study Area to access MapMaster 2.0.

Obesity and Income

Chapter 1 defined spatial association. Let's investigate possible spatial association among demography and health features.

Add *Gross National Income per capita*. In the *Legend*, ***deselect*** all income classes below $20,000. Only $20,000–$49,999 and $50,000–$103,630 are to be displayed.

Add the *Adult Obesity Rate* layer and ***select*** *Join with data layer*. In the *Legend*, ***deselect*** the two lowest classes for *Gross National Income per capita*.

1. ***Hover*** over the United States. What are the figures for income and obesity for the United States?
2. Is the obesity rate in the United States relatively high or low compared with other countries with relatively high incomes? What might account for this?

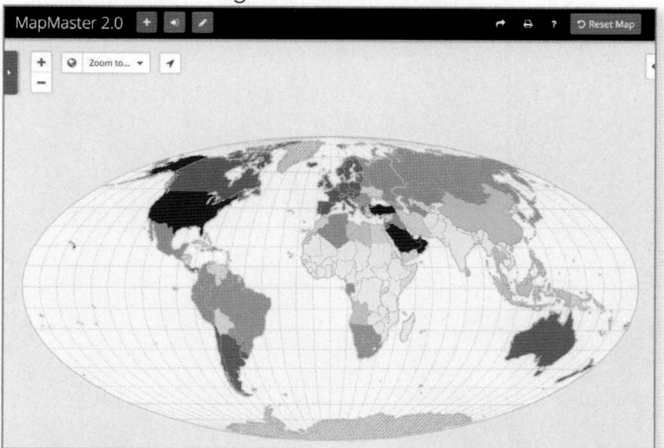

▲ 2.CR.5 **OBESITY AND GROSS NATIONAL INCOME PER CAPITA**

Explore

Nagel-Gulab, Egypt

Use Google Earth to explore Nagel-Gulab, a small town in Egypt along the banks of the Nile River.

Search for *Nagel-Gulab, Egypt*.

1. What color is most of the land immediately to the west of the town? Does this indicate that the land is used for agriculture, or is it desert?
2. How wide is the green strip? Why is the green strip closer to the river and the tan area further away?

▲ 2.CR.6 **NILE RIVER NEAR NAGEL-GULAB, EGYPT**

CHAPTER

3 Migration

Migration is the permanent move to a new location. Geographers study migration in part because it is increasingly important in explaining changes in population in various places and regions. Migration is also important because when people migrate, they take with them to their new home cultural values and economic practices. At the same time, they become connected with the cultural and economic patterns of their new place of residence.

◀ Iraqi refugee displaced from his home by fighting carries bedding on his shoulders.

KEY ISSUES

1 Where Are Migrants Distributed?

People emigrate from some places and immigrate to other places. The United States has long been an especially important destination for migrants.

2 Where Do People Migrate Within Countries?

Large countries may have extensive migration between regions. Migration is also important within regions of countries, especially from rural areas into urban areas.

3 Why Do People Migrate?

People migrate for cultural, environmental, and economic reasons. Women and children comprise increasing shares of migrants.

4 What Challenges Do Migrants Face?

People often face legal restrictions on their ability to immigrate into another country. In some places, they also face hostility from people already residing there.

LOCATIONS IN THIS CHAPTER

net migration
immigration
chain migration
border
refugee
brain drain
migrant worker
intraregional migration
push and pull factors
emigration
interregional migration
asylum seeker
unauthorized immigrants
intervening obstacle
guest worker
migration transition
internally displaced person

Global Migration Patterns

- **Describe the types of migration and the principal flows of migration.**

▲ 3.1.1
EMIGRATION
Emigrants from the United Kingdom to Australia in the 1940s, at the end of World War II.

A permanent move to a new location is called **migration**. It is a form of relocation diffusion, which was defined in Chapter 1 as the spread of a characteristic through the bodily movement of people from one place to another.

Emigration (or out-migration) is migration from a location (Figure 3.1.1); **immigration** (or in-migration) is migration to a location. The difference between the number of immigrants and the number of emigrants is the **net migration**.

Geography has no comprehensive theory of migration, although an outline of migration "laws" written by nineteenth-century geographer E. G. Ravenstein is the basis for contemporary geographic migration studies. To understand where and why migration occurs, Ravenstein's "laws" can be organized into three groups:

- The distance that migrants typically move (discussed in Sections 3.1 through 3.4).
- The reasons migrants move (discussed in Sections 3.5 and 3.6).
- The characteristics of migrants (discussed in Section 3.7 through 3.10).

Migration Transition

Geographer Wilbur Zelinsky identified a **migration transition**, which consists of changes in a society comparable to those in the demographic transition (Figure 3.1.2). The migration transition is a change in the migration pattern in a society that results from the social and economic changes that also produce the demographic transition. According to the migration transition, international migration is primarily a phenomenon of countries in stage 2 of the demographic transition (Figure 3.1.3), whereas internal migration is more important in stages 3 and 4.

▶ 3.1.2
MIGRATION TRANSITION AND DEMOGRAPHIC TRANSITION COMPARED

Stage	Demographic Transition	Migration Transition
1	Low NIR, high CBR, high CDR	High daily or seasonal mobility in search of food
2	High NIR, high CBR, rapidly declining CDR	High international emigration and interregional migration from rural to urban
3	Declining NIR, rapidly declining CBR, declining CDR	High international immigration and intraregional migration from cities to suburbs
4	Low NIR, low CBR, low CDR	Same as stage 3

▼ 3.1.3 **IMMIGRATING TO THE UNITED STATES**
Mexican immigrants in Tohono O'odham Nation land, Arizona, 2011. After illegally crossing the U.S.-Mexico border, the immigrants were lost in the Sonoran Desert for a week. Exhausted, they requested the U.S. Border Patrol to take them back to Mexico. They were trying to reach Phoenix, Arizona, to find work.

Distance of Migration

Ravenstein's "laws" for the distance that migrants travel to their new homes:

- Most migrants relocate a short distance and remain within the same country.
- Long-distance migrants to other countries head for major centers of economic activity.

Migration can be divided into international migration and internal migration (Figure 3.1.4). **International migration** is a permanent move from one country to another. **Internal migration** is a permanent move within the same country. Internal migration can be divided into **interregional migration** (movement from one region of a country to another) and **intraregional migration** (movement within one region).

About 3 percent of the world's people are international migrants—that is, they currently live in countries other than the ones in which they were born. On a global scale, the three largest flows of migrants are (Figure 3.1.5):

- From Asia to Europe.
- From Asia to North America.
- From Latin America to North America.

◀ 3.1.4 **MEXICO'S INTERNATIONAL AND INTERNAL MIGRATION**

The global pattern in Figure 3.1.5 reflects the importance of migration from developing countries in stage 2 of the demographic transition to developed countries. Asia, Latin America, and Africa have net out-migration, and North America, Europe, and South Pacific have net in-migration. Migrants from countries with relatively low incomes and high natural increase rates head for relatively wealthy countries, where job prospects are brighter.

ARCTIC OCEAN
ATLANTIC OCEAN
ATLANTIC OCEAN
PACIFIC OCEAN
INDIAN OCEAN
0 1,000 2,000 Miles
0 1,000 2,000 Kilometers

Net migration
- gain 1 million and above
- gain less than 1 million
- loss less than 1 million
- loss 1 million and above
- no data

Number of migrants
- 3 million and above
- 1–3 million

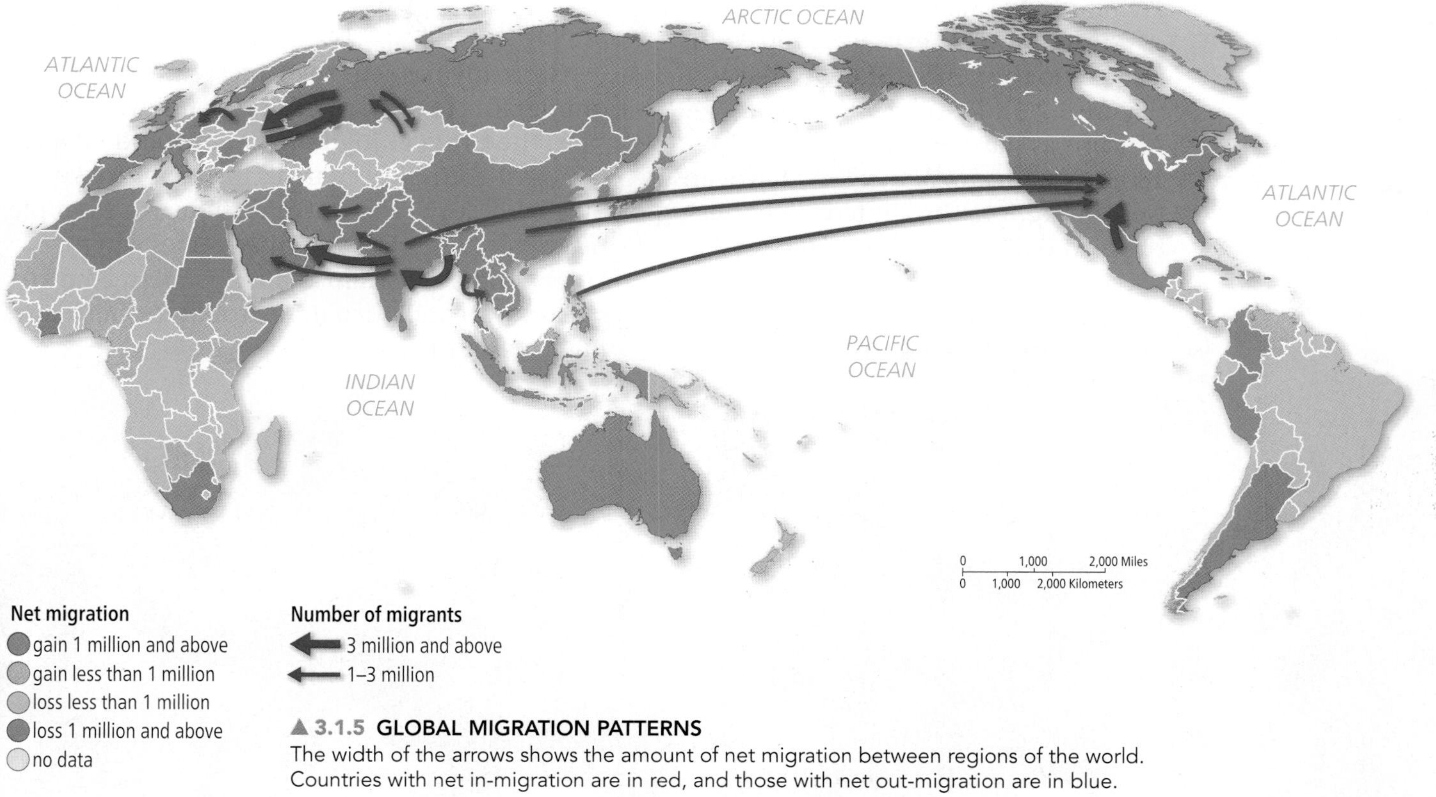

▲ 3.1.5 **GLOBAL MIGRATION PATTERNS**
The width of the arrows shows the amount of net migration between regions of the world. Countries with net in-migration are in red, and those with net out-migration are in blue.

▲ 3.2.1 **COLONIAL IMMIGRATION** Most African Americans are decended from Africans forced to migrate as slaves during the eighteenth century.

Changing U.S. Immigration

- Describe the different sources of immigrants during the three main eras of U.S. immigration.

The United States plays a special role in the study of international migration. The world's third–most-populous country is inhabited overwhelmingly by direct descendants of immigrants. The United States has had three main eras of immigration:

- Colonial settlement in the seventeenth and eighteenth centuries.
- Mass European immigration in the late nineteenth and early twentieth centuries.
- Asian and Latin American immigration in the late twentieth and early twenty-first centuries.

U.S. Immigration at Independence

Immigration to the American colonies and the newly independent United States came from two principal places: 62 percent from Europe and 38 percent from sub-Saharan Africa. Half of the European immigrants came from the modern-day United Kingdom and Republic of Ireland. British immigrants established colonies along the Atlantic Coast, beginning with Jamestown, Virginia, in 1607, and Plymouth, Massachusetts, in 1620.

Most of the Africans were forced to migrate to the United States as slaves (Figure 3.2.1). The importation of Africans as slaves was made illegal in 1808, though another 250,000 Africans were brought to the United States during the next half-century (see Chapter 7).

Nineteenth-Century Immigration

Nearly 90 percent of nineteenth-century U.S. immigrants came from Europe. Migration from Europe to the United States peaked at several points:

- 1840s and 1850s: Primarily from Ireland and Germany.
- 1880s and 1890s: Primarily from northern and western Europe, including Norway and Sweden, as well as Germany and Ireland.
- 1900–1910s: Primarily from southern and eastern Europe, including Italy and Russia (Figure 3.2.2).

Germany has sent the largest number of immigrants to the United States, followed by Italy, the United Kingdom, Ireland, and Russia. Frequent boundary changes in Europe make precise national counts impossible. For example, most Poles came to the United States when Poland did not exist as an independent country, so they were included in the totals for Germany, Russia, or Austria.

▼ 3.2.2 **EMIGRANTS FROM ITALY AWAIT ENTRY INTO THE UNITED STATES AT ELLIS ISLAND, APPROXIMATELY 1910**

Current U.S. Immigration

More than three-fourths of recent U.S. immigrants have emigrated from two regions: Latin America and Asia (Figure 3.2.3). Officially, Mexico passed Germany in 2006 as the country that has sent to the United States the most immigrants ever, although because of the large number of undocumented immigrants Mexico probably became the leading source during the 1980s (see Section 3.9). The four leading sources of U.S. immigrants from Asia are China (including Hong Kong), the Philippines, India, and Vietnam. One-half of immigrants arrive in California, New York, or Florida (Figure 3.2.4).

Although the source of immigrants to the United States has changed from predominantly Europe to Asia and Latin America, the principal reason for immigration remains the same: rapid population growth associated with stage 2 of the demographic transition limited prospects for economic advancement at home. With poor conditions at home, immigrants were lured by economic opportunity and social advancement in the United States (Figure 3.2.5).

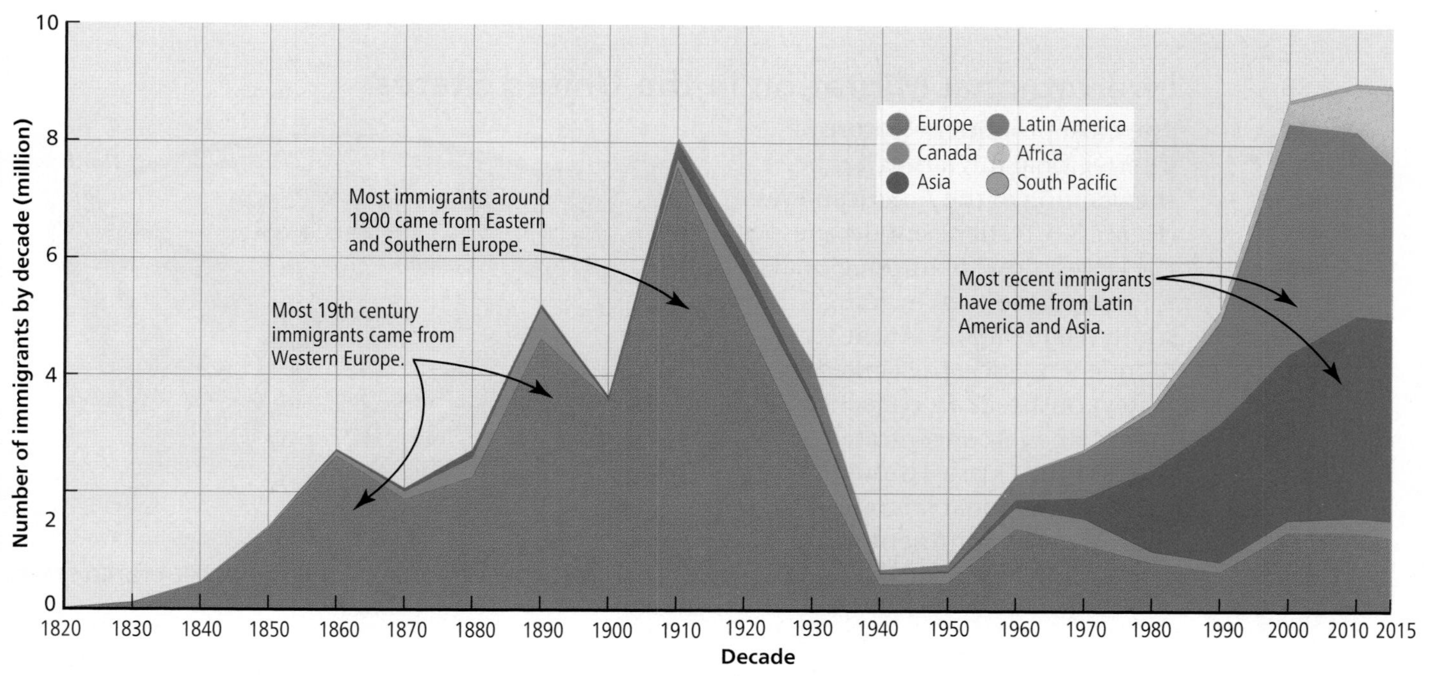

▲ 3.2.3 TWO CENTURIES OF IMMIGRATION TO THE UNITED STATES

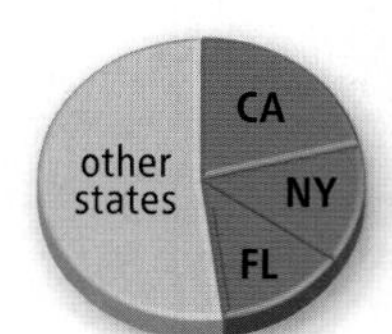

▲ 3.2.4 DESTINATION OF IMMIGRANTS BY U.S. STATES

◀ 3.2.5 POSTER INVITING IMMIGRANTS TO THE UNITED STATES, 1919

Migration Between Regions

- Compare the principal patterns of migration between regions within large countries.

▲ 3.3.1 PIONEERS HEADING TO AMERICAN WEST

In the past, people migrated from one region of a country to another in search of better farmland. Lack of farmland pushed many people from the more densely settled regions of the country and lured them to the frontier, where land was abundant. Today, the principal type of interregional migration is from rural to urban areas. Most jobs, especially in the service sector, are clustered in urban areas (see Chapter 12).

The world's five largest countries in land area—Russia, Canada, the United States, China, and Brazil—have all experienced interregional migration characterized by a large number of people moving long distances.

Interregional Migration in the United States

The most prominent feature of interregional migration has been the opening of the American West (Figure 3.3.1). In recent decades, the largest flows of interregional migrants have been heading south (Figure 3.3.2). At the time of independence, the United States consisted of a collection of settlements concentrated on the Atlantic Coast. Through mass interregional migration, the rest of the continent was settled and developed (Figure 3.3.3).

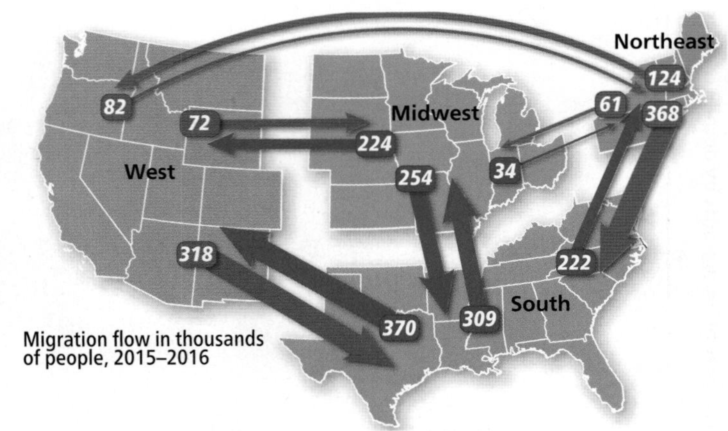

▲ 3.3.2 INTERREGIONAL MIGRATION IN THE UNITED STATES

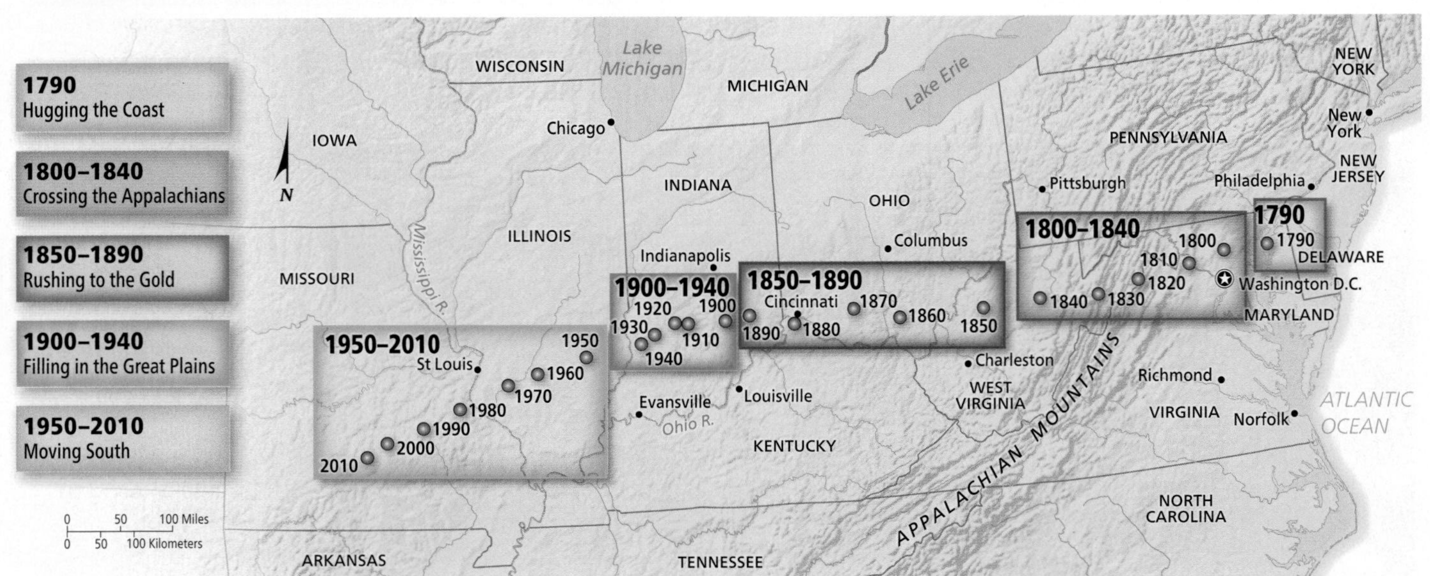

▲ 3.3.3 CHANGING CENTER OF U.S. POPULATION

The U.S. Census Bureau computes the country's population center at the time of each census. If the United States were a flat plane placed on top of a pin, and each individual weighed the same, the population center would be the point where the population distribution causes the flat plane to balance on the pin. The changing location of the center of the U.S. population graphically demonstrates the interregional migration of the American people to the West, and more recently to the South.

Interregional Migration in Russia

The population of Russia is highly clustered in the western, or European, portion of the country. Interregional migration was an important tool to open up the sparsely inhabited Asian portion, especially during the Soviet Union period. Soviet policy encouraged factory construction near remote raw materials rather than near existing population concentrations (see Chapter 11). To build up an adequate labor force, the Soviet government forced people to undertake interregional migration. In recent years, interregional migration has reversed, with net in-migration toward Europe, where the largest cities and job opportunities are clustered (Figure 3.3.4).

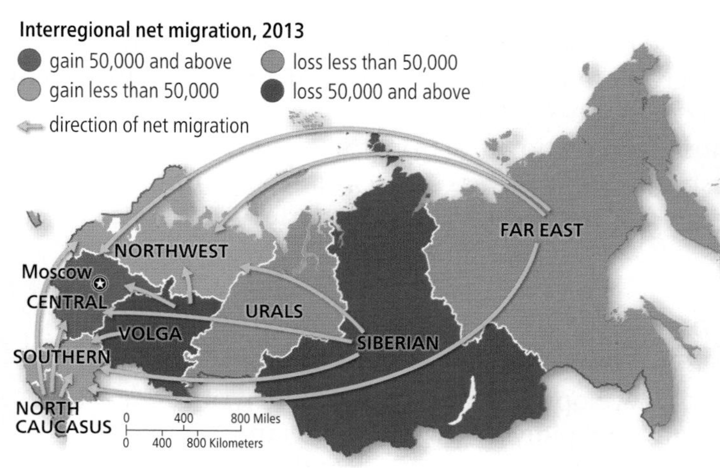

▲ 3.3.4 RUSSIA INTERREGIONAL MIGRATION

Interregional Migration in Canada

Canada, like the United States, has had interregional migration primarily from east to west for nearly two centuries. Since 2011, British Columbia has had most of Canada's net in-migration (Figure 3.3.5).

Interregional Migration in Brazil

Most Brazilians live in a string of large cities near the Atlantic Coast, whereas the tropical interior has been sparsely inhabited. To increase the attractiveness of the interior, the government moved its capital in 1960 from Rio to a newly built city called Brasília. Development of Brasília has stimulated net in-migration to the interior (Figure 3.3.6).

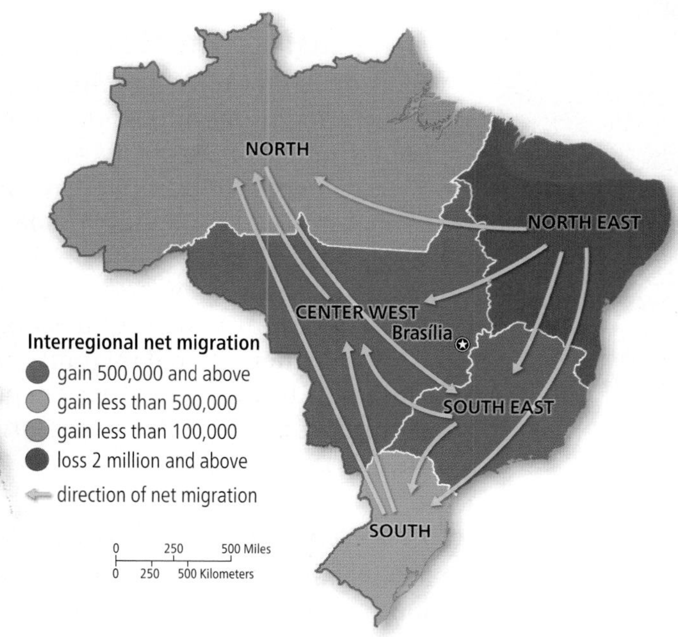

▲ 3.3.6 BRAZIL INTERREGIONAL MIGRATION

Interregional Migration in China

More than 150 million Chinese have migrated in recent decades from rural areas in the interior of the country to urban areas in the east, where jobs are most plentiful (Figure 3.3.7). The government once severely limited the ability of Chinese people to make interregional moves, but restrictions have been lifted in recent years.

▼ 3.3.7 MIGRANTS ARRIVE IN BEJING, CHINA

▲ 3.3.5 CANADA INTERREGIONAL MIGRATION

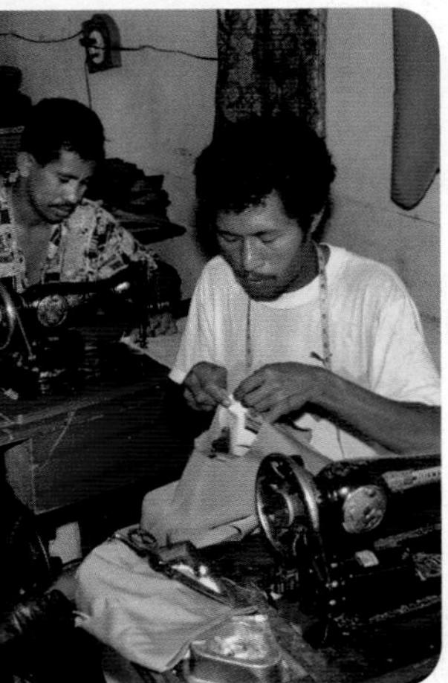

▲ 3.4.1 **INTRAREGIONAL MIGRATION: ECONOMIC ADVANCEMENT**
Migrating from rural areas in Timor-Leste to the capital Dili to work in a clothing factory.

Migration Within a Region

- Describe three types of migration that take place within a region.

Intraregional migration is much more common than interregional or international migration. Most intraregional migration is from rural to urban areas in developing countries and from cities to suburbs in developed countries.

Migration from Rural to Urban Areas

Migration from rural (or nonmetropolitan) areas to urban (or metropolitan) areas began in the 1800s in Europe and North America as part of the Industrial Revolution (see Chapter 11). The percentage of people living in urban areas in the United States, for example, increased from 5 percent in 1800 to 50 percent in 1920 and 81 percent in 2016.

In recent years, urbanization has diffused to developing countries of Asia, Latin America, and Africa (Figures 3.4.1 and 3.4.2). Between 1950 and 2016, the percentage living in urban areas increased from 40 percent to 80 percent in Latin America, from 15 percent to 49 percent in Asia, and from 10 percent to 41 percent in sub-Saharan Africa.

As with interregional migrants, most people who move from rural to urban areas seek economic advancement. They are pushed from rural areas by declining opportunities in agriculture and are pulled to the cities by the prospect of work in factories or in service industries.

Migration from Urban to Suburban Areas

Most intraregional migration in developed countries is from cities out to surrounding suburbs. The population of most cities in developed countries has declined since the mid-twentieth century, while suburbs have grown rapidly. Nearly twice as many Americans migrate from cities to suburbs each year as migrate from suburbs to cities (Figure 3.4.3). Comparable patterns are found in Canada and Europe.

The major reason for the large-scale migration to the suburbs is not related to employment, as is the case with other forms of migration. Instead, people are pulled by a suburban lifestyle. Suburbs offer the opportunity to live in a detached house rather than an apartment, surrounded by a private yard where children can play safely. A garage or driveway on the property guarantees space to park cars at no extra charge. Suburban schools tend to be more modern, better equipped, and safer than those in cities.

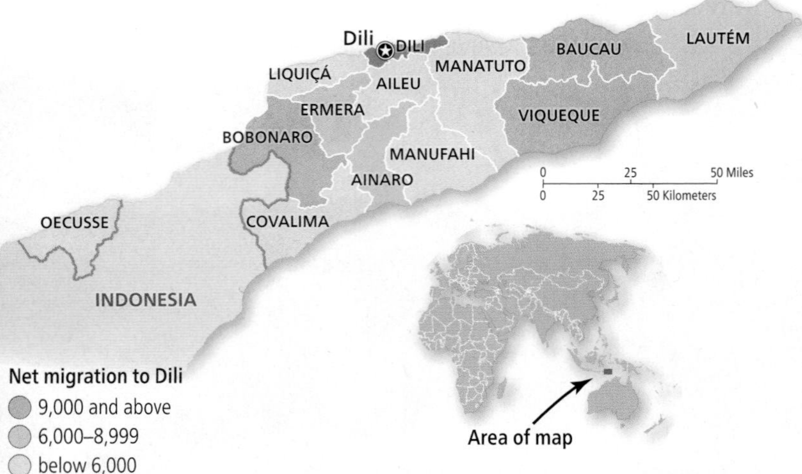

▲ 3.4.2 **INTRAREGIONAL MIGRATION: TIMOR-LESTE**
Intraregional migration has been from rural areas into Dili, the capital and largest city. All of the country's municipalities (named on the map) have net outmigration to Dili.

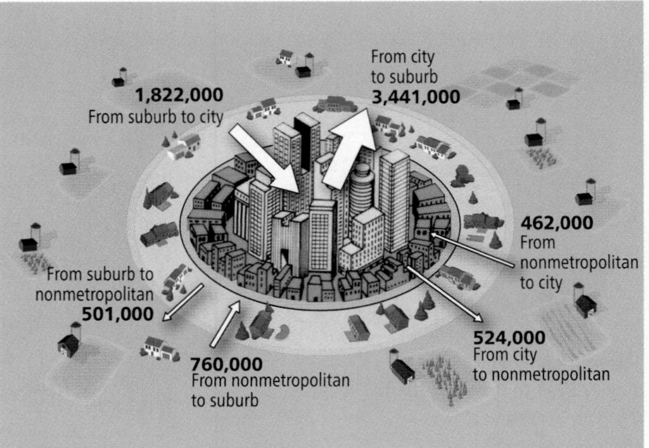

▲ 3.4.3 **INTRAREGIONAL MIGRATION: UNITED STATES**
Intraregional migration is primarily from cities to suburbs. Figures are total U.S. intraregional migrants in 2015.

Migration from Urban to Rural Areas

Developed countries witnessed a new migration trend during the late twentieth century. For the first time, more people immigrated into rural areas than emigrated out of them. Net migration from urban to rural areas is called **counterurbanization**.

The boundary where suburbs end and the countryside begins isn't precisely defined. Counterurbanization results in part from very rapid expansion of outer suburbs. But most counterurbanization represents migration from cities and suburbs to small towns and rural communities (Figure 3.4.4).

▲ 3.4.4 COUNTER-URBANIZATION: IDAHO

As with suburbanization, people move from urban to rural areas for lifestyle reasons. Some are lured to rural areas by the prospect of swapping the frantic pace of urban life for the opportunity to live where they can own horses or grow vegetables. Others move to farms but work in nearby factories, small-town shops, or other services. In the United States, evidence of counterurbanization can be seen primarily in rural counties in states such as Colorado, Idaho, and Montana (Figure 3.4.5).

With modern communications and transportation systems, no location in a developed country is truly isolated, either economically or socially (Figure 3.4.6). We can buy most products online and have them delivered quickly. We can follow the fortunes of our favorite teams, thanks to cable, satellite dishes, and webcasts.

Intraregional migration in the United States has slowed considerably since the 1980s (Figure 3.4.7). Counterurbanization is not a phenomenon every year. Most intraregional migration in the United States continues to be between cities and suburbs. However, cities have become more attractive especially to younger people (see Chapter 13).

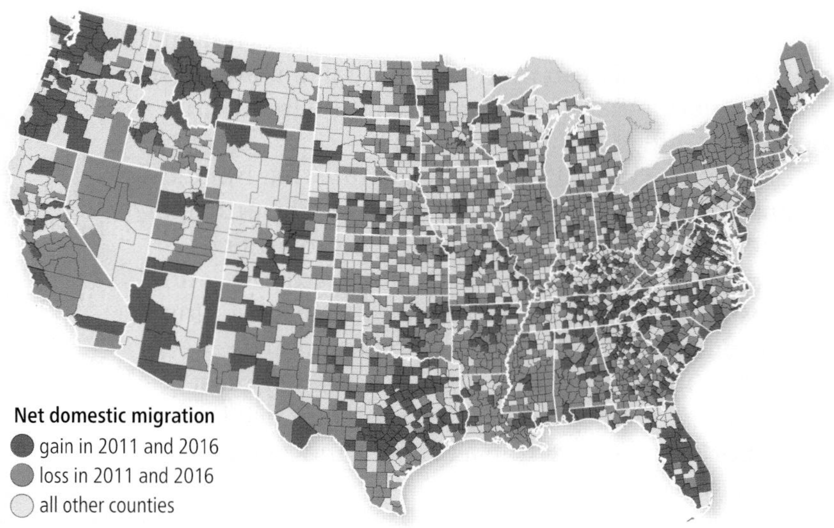

▲ 3.4.5 **NET MIGRATION BY COUNTY IN 2011 AND IN 2016.** Most counties that had net in-migration in both 2006 and 2014 are in rural areas, such as Colorado, Idaho, Montana, North Dakota, and West Texas.

▼ 3.4.6 COUNTERURBANIZATION: COLORADO

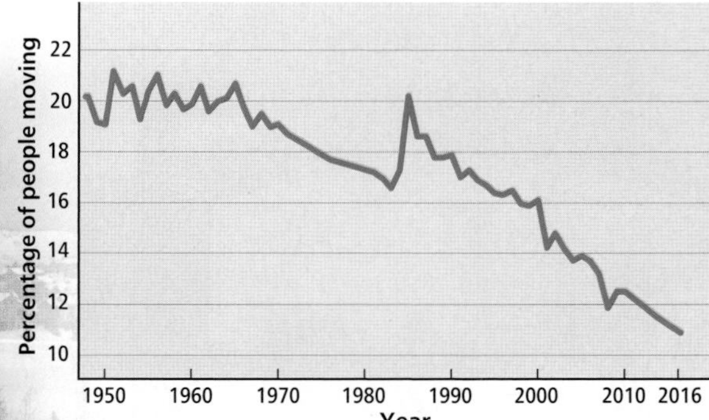

▲ 3.4.7 PERCENTAGE OF AMERICANS MOVING IN A YEAR

▲ 3.5.1 TRAIL OF TEARS NATIONAL HISTORIC TRAIL

Cultural & Forced Migration

- Explain cultural reasons for migration.

People migrate because of push factors and pull factors:

- A **push factor** induces people to move out of their present location.
- A **pull factor** induces people to move into a new location.

As migration for most people is a major step not taken lightly, both push and pull factors typically play a role. To migrate, people view their current place of residence so negatively that they feel pushed away, and they view another place so attractively that they feel pulled toward it.

Ravenstein's Reasons for Migrating

Ravenstein's "laws" suggest three reasons why people might migrate: cultural (discussed in this section), environmental, and economic (see Section 3.6). Migration may involve a combination of these reasons, and ranking their relative importance may be difficult and even controversial. Personal reasons, such as family status and schools, can motivate cultural migration. At the international scale, cultural migration frequently occurs because of political conflict.

An environmental or political feature that hinders migration is an **intervening obstacle**. The principal obstacle traditionally faced by migrants to other countries was environmental: the long, arduous, and expensive passage over land or by sea. Transportation improvements have diminished environmental obstacles. Today, the major obstacles faced by most immigrants are political. Legally, a migrant needs a passport to emigrate from a country and a visa to immigrate to a new country.

Trail of Tears

Cultural migration is sometimes involuntary. For example, within North America, Native Americans migrated west in the nineteenth century. But their migration was forced rather than voluntary. This inequality was written in law, when the Indian Removal Act of 1830 authorized the U.S. Army to remove five Indian tribes from their land in the southeastern United States and move them to Indian Territory (now the state of Oklahoma).

The five removals opened up land for whites to settle, but relocated the tribes to places that were too dry to sustain their traditional ways of obtaining food. An estimated 46,000 Native Americans were uprooted, and many of them died in the long trek to the west. The route became known as the Trail of Tears; parts of it are preserved as a National Historic Trail (Figures 3.5.1, 3.5.2, and 3.5.3).

▼ 3.5.2 TRAIL OF TEARS
The Memorial Passage sculpture in Chattanooga, Tennessee, marks the beginning of the forced journey of Cherokee Tribes west to Oklahoma.

▼ 3.5.3 TRAIL OF TEARS ROUTES

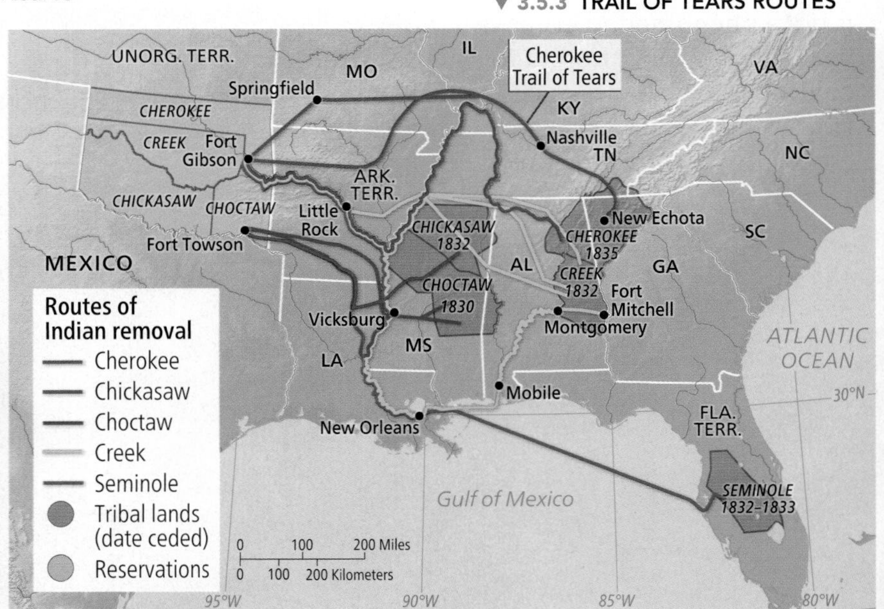

▲ 3.5.4 CULTURAL MIGRATION: REFUGEES

Forced Political Migration

International cultural migration is also sometimes involuntary. The United Nations High Commission for Refugees (UNHCR) recognizes three groups of people who are forced to migrate for political reasons:

- A **refugee** has been forced to migrate to another country to avoid the effects of armed conflict, situations of generalized violence, violations of human rights, or other disasters and cannot return for fear of persecution because of race, religion, nationality, membership in a social group, or political opinion.
- An **asylum seeker** is someone who has migrated to another country in the hope of being recognized as a refugee.
- An **internally displaced person (IDP)** has been forced to migrate for similar political reasons as a refugee but has not migrated across an international border.

The United Nations counted 22.5 million refugees, 40.3 million IDPs, and 2.8 million asylum seekers in 2016 (Figure 3.5.4). The largest numbers of refugees in 2016 were forced to migrate from Afghanistan, Syria, Myanmar, and South Sudan because of continuing civil wars in those countries (Figures 3.5.5 and 3.5.6). Neighboring countries received the most refugees—Pakistan and Iran from Afghanistan, Lebanon and Turkey from Syria, Uganda and Ethiopia from South Sudan, and Bangladesh from Myanmar.

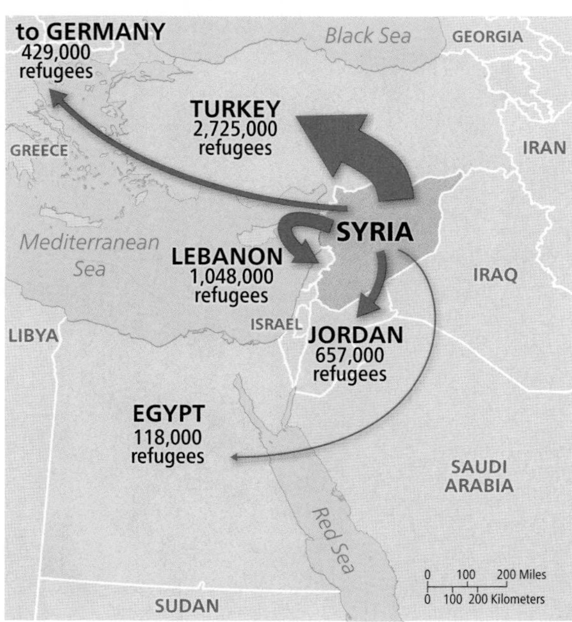

▲ 3.5.5 DISTRIBUTION OF REFUGEES FROM SYRIA

▼ 3.5.6 REFUGEES FROM SYRIA
Arriving in Greece.

Economic & Environmental Reasons to Migrate

- Explain economic and environmental reasons for migration.

People sometimes migrate for environmental reasons, pulled toward physically attractive regions and pushed from hazardous ones. People often emigrate from places that have few job opportunities and immigrate to places where jobs seem to be available.

Environmental Reasons for Migrating

In this age of improved communications and transportation systems, people can live in environmentally attractive areas that are relatively remote and still not feel too isolated from employment, shopping, and entertainment opportunities. Attractive environments for migrants include mountains, seasides, and warm climates.

Migrants are also pushed from their homes by adverse physical conditions. Water—either too much or too little—poses the most common environmental threat. Many people are forced to move by water-related disasters because they live in a vulnerable area, such as a floodplain (Figure 3.6.1). The **floodplain** of a river is the area subject to flooding during a specific number of years, based on historical trends. People living in the "100-year floodplain," for example, can expect flooding on average once every century. Many people are unaware that they live in a floodplain, and even people who do know often choose to live there anyway.

A lack of water pushes others from their land (Figure 3.6.2). Hundreds of thousands have been forced to move from the Sahel region of northern Africa because of drought conditions. The people of the Sahel have traditionally been pastoral nomads, a form of agriculture adapted to dry lands but effective only at low population densities (see Chapter 9).

The capacity of the Sahel to sustain human life—never very high—has declined recently because of population growth and several years of unusually low rainfall. Consequently, many of these nomads have been forced to move into cities and rural camps, where they survive on food donated by the government and international relief organizations (Figure 3.6.3).

▲ 3.6.1 **FLOODING**
Hanoi, Vietnam.

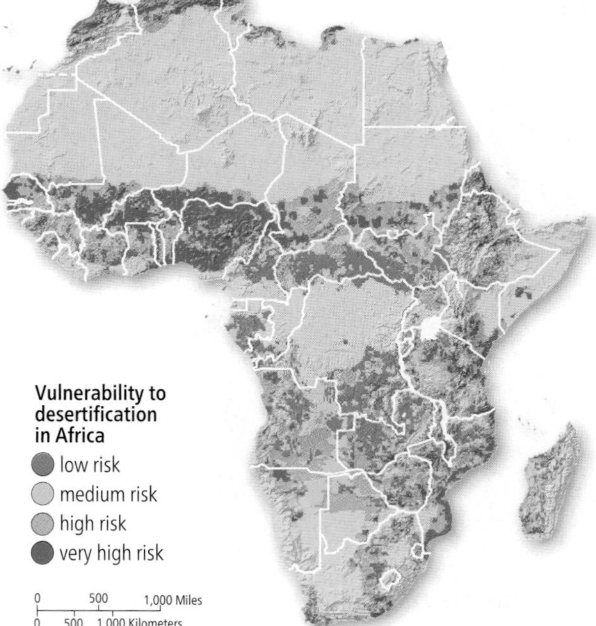

▼ 3.6.2 **DESERTIFICATION (SEMIARID LAND DEGRADATION) IN AFRICA**

◀ 3.6.3 **SAHEL**
People digging for something edible.

Economic Reasons

The United States and Canada have been especially prominent destinations for economic migrants. Many European immigrants to North America in the nineteenth century truly expected to find streets paved with gold. While not literally so gilded, the United States and Canada did offer Europeans prospects for economic advancement. This same perception of economic plenty now lures people to the United States and Canada from Latin America and Asia.

The relative attractiveness of a region can shift with economic change. Ireland was a place of net out-migration through most of the nineteenth and twentieth centuries. Dire economic conditions produced net out-migration in excess of 200,000 a year during the 1850s. The pattern reversed during the 1990s, as economic prosperity made Ireland a destination for immigrants, especially from Eastern Europe. However, the temporary collapse of Ireland's economy as part of the severe global recession starting in 2008 brought a return to net out-migration for several years (Figure 3.6.4).

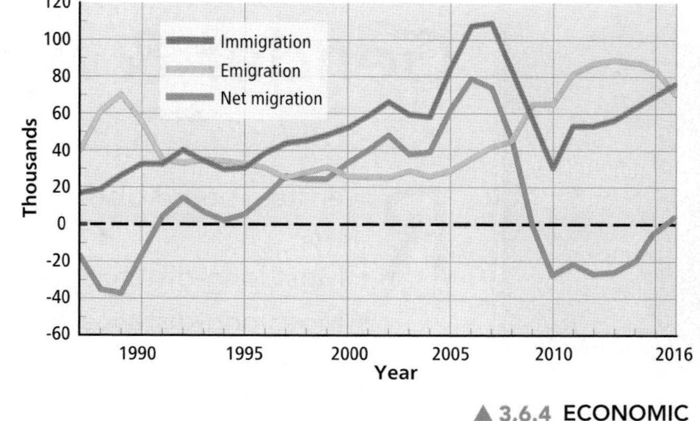

▲ **3.6.4 ECONOMIC MIGRATION: IRELAND**
With few job prospects, Ireland historically had net out-migration until the 1990s. The severe recession of the early twenty-first century brought net out-migration back to Ireland for several years.

Remittances

Migrants who find work in another country frequently send a portion of the wages they have earned to relatives back home. The transfer of money by workers to people in the country from which they emigrated is a **remittance**.

The total amount of remittances worldwide was $582 billion in 2015. The figure has been increasing by nearly 10 percent annually. Remittances are increasingly important source of wealth for people in developing countries, especially with cutbacks in official assistance from foreign governments and international aid agencies.

People in India received the most remittances in 2015 ($69 billion), followed by people in China ($64 billion). The United States was the leading source of remittances in 2015 ($134 billion), followed by Saudi Arabia ($46 billion) (Figure 3.6.5).

The cost of transferring money is high in many places. Banks and firms such as Western Union that specialize in money transfers charge high fees for the service, an average of 9 percent worldwide. To transfer $200 from the United States, it costs an average of $6 to Mexico and $12 to Haiti; it costs around $20 to transfer $200 between many African countries.

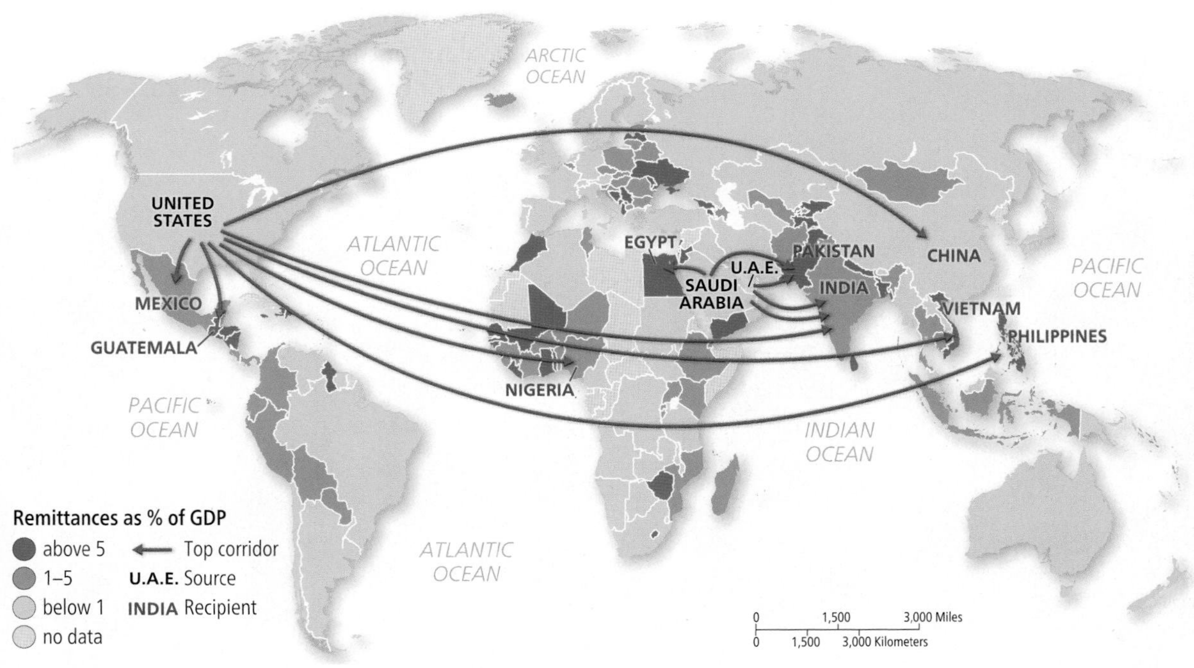

◀ **3.6.5 REMITTANCES**
The United States and Saudi Arabia are the leading sources of remittances. Corridors with at least $5 billion in remittances are named.

Gender & Age of Migrants

- Describe the demographic characteristics of international migrants.

▲ 3.7.1 YOUNG ADULT MIGRANTS, TRIPOLI, LIBYA

Ravenstein noted distinctive gender and family-status patterns in his migration "laws":

- Most long-distance migrants are male.
- Most long-distance migrants are adult individuals rather than families with children.

Adult males may have constituted a large majority in the past (Figure 3.7.1), but that pattern has changed. Globally, males still outnumber females, but the percentage of migrants who are women has been increasing.

Age of Migrants

Ravenstein theorized that most long-distance migrants were young adults seeking work, rather than children or elderly people. Recent migration patterns in the United States match the theory in some respects but not in others:

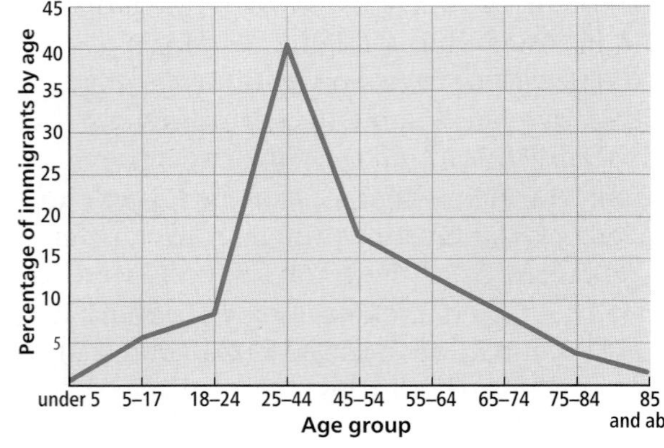

▶ 3.7.2 AGE OF IMMIGRANTS TO THE UNITED STATES

- A relatively high share of U.S. immigrants are young adults, as Ravenstein expected. People between the ages of 20 and 39 comprise 49 percent of recent immigrants, compared to only 27 percent of the entire U.S. population (Figure 3.7.2).
- Immigrants are, as expected, less likely to be elderly people. Only 5 percent of recent U.S. immigrants are over age 65, compared to 15 percent of the entire U.S. population. However, in developing countries, immigrants are more likely to be elderly—only 6 percent of the total population but 8 percent of immigrants.
- Children under age 20 comprise 21 percent of immigrants, only slightly lower than the 27 percent share in the total U.S. population. In developing countries, immigrants are much less likely to be children; people under age 20 comprise 35 percent of the total population but only 23 percent of the migrants (Figure 3.7.3).

▼ 3.7.3 TEENAGE IMMIGRANTS These teenagers trying to reach the United States were intercepted as they attempted to cross into Guatemala.

Gender of Migrants

Ravenstein theorized that males were more likely than females to migrate long distances to other countries because searching for work was the main reason for international migration, and males were much more likely than females to be employed. This held true for U.S. immigrants during the nineteenth and much of the twentieth centuries, when about 55 percent were male. But female immigrants to the United States began to outnumber male immigrants around 1970, and they now comprise 55 percent of the total. Female immigrants also outnumber males in other developed countries (Figure 3.7.4).

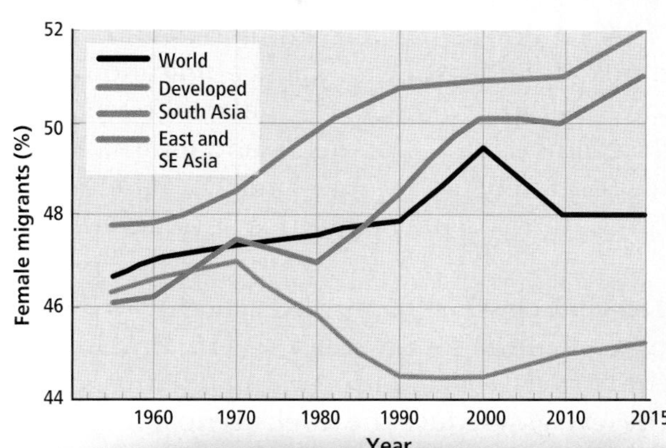

◀ **3.7.4 PERCENT FEMALE IMMIGRANTS** Female immigrants outnumber males in developed countries.

▼ **3.7.5 FEMALE IMMIGRANTS** Taking the oath to become U.S. citizens.

The gender mix of Mexicans who come to the United States without authorized immigration documents—currently the largest group of U.S. immigrants—has changed sharply. In the 1980s, males constituted 85 percent of the Mexican migrants arriving in the United States without proper documents, according to U.S. census and immigration service estimates. But since the 1990s, women have accounted for about half of the unauthorized immigrants from Mexico (Figure 3.7.5).

In developing countries, male immigrants still outnumber female ones. The situation varies widely among regions, however. Approximately one-half of emigrants from East and Southeast Asia are women, compared to only 44 percent from South Asia.

Two factors contribute to the larger share of females migrating to developed countries than theorized by Ravenstein:

- Because most people migrate to developed countries for job opportunities, the high percentage of women in the labor force in these countries logically attracts a high percentage of female immigrants.
- Some developed countries have made it possible for wives to join husbands who have already immigrated.

The increased female migration to the United States partly reflects the changing role of women in Mexican society. In the past, rural Mexican women were obliged to marry at a young age and to remain in the village to care for children. Now some Mexican women are migrating to the United States to join husbands or brothers already in the United States, but most are seeking jobs. At the same time, women feel increased pressure to get jobs in the United States because of poor economic conditions in Mexico.

▲ 3.8.1
IMMIGRATION CONTROL
People in the United Kingdom wait for visas to go to India.

Government Immigration Policies

- Describe government policies that restrict immigration.

Most countries, including the United States, have adopted selective immigration policies that admit some types of immigrants but not others (Figure 3.8.1). Policies toward immigrants and refugees are influenced by a number of factors: public opinion (for or against admitting migrants), economic (positive and negative impacts of newcomers on the local economy), resources (ability of the country to accommodate newcomers), and international relations (perception of humanitarian responsibility among the family of nations). The weight given to each of these factors can determine how countries address immigration.

The U.N. classifies countries according to four types of immigration policies: (1) maintain the current level of immigration, (2) increase the level, (3) reduce the level, (4) no policy. Similarly, emigration policies are identified by the same four classes.

According to the U.N., 21 countries seek more immigrants, 32 want fewer immigrants, 116 wish to maintain the current level, and 25 do not have a policy. Ten of the 21 countries with policies to encourage more immigration are in Europe, including most of the former Communist countries of Central and Eastern Europe. The 32 countries with policies to reduce immigration include 10 in Southwest Asia & North Africa and 8 in sub-Saharan Africa (Figure 3.8.2).

The distribution of emigration policies is different. The U.N. found policies to increase emigration in 18 countries, to decrease emigration in 46 countries, to maintain the current level in 43 countries, and 88 with no policy. The 18 countries wishing to increase emigration include 5 each in South Asia, Southeast Asia, and the South Pacific. Sub-Saharan Africa had the most countries seeking to lower emigration.

Many countries have immigration policies that contribute to a **brain drain**, which is a large-scale emigration by talented people. Scientists, researchers, doctors, and other professionals migrate where they can make better use of their abilities.

Asians have made especially good use of the priorities set by the U.S. immigration laws. Many well-educated Asians enter the United States under the preference for skilled workers. Once admitted, they can bring in relatives under the family reunification preference. Eventually, these immigrants can bring in a wider range of other relatives from Asia, through a process of **chain migration**, which is the migration of people to a specific location because relatives or members of the same nationality previously migrated there.

▼ 3.8.2
IMMIGRATION POLICIES

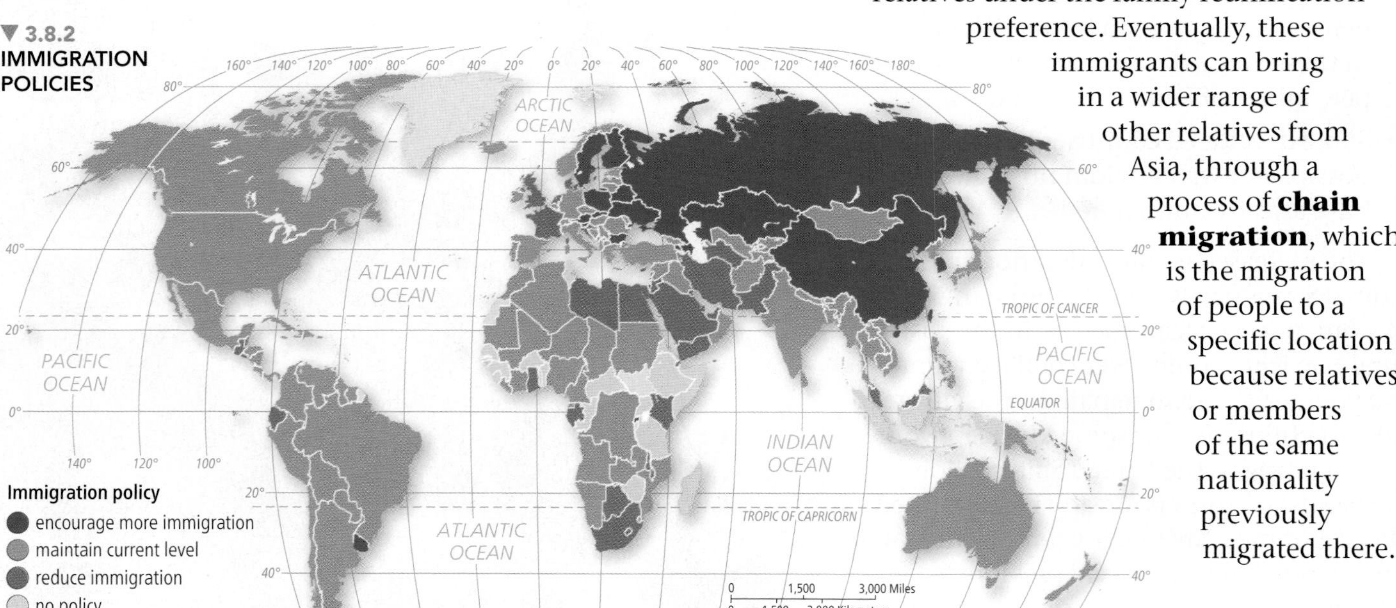

U.S. Quota Laws

The era of unrestricted immigration to the United States ended when Congress passed the Quota Act in 1921 and the National Origins Act in 1924. These laws established a **quota**, which is a maximum limit on the number of people who could immigrate to the United States during a one-year period.

The 1924 Act specified that for each country with native-born persons already living in the United States, 2 percent of their number (based on the 1910 census) could immigrate each year. This ensured that most immigrants would come from Europe. Quotas have evolved to limit the total annual intake of immigrants to 700,000 globally, and 20,000 from any single country.

Because the number of applicants for admission to the United States far exceeds the quotas, Congress has set preferences:

- Family reunification. Approximately three-fourths of immigrants are admitted to reunify families, primarily spouses or unmarried children of people already living in the United States. The typical wait for a spouse to gain entry is currently about five years.
- Skilled workers. Exceptionally talented professionals receive most of the remainder of the quota.
- Diversity. A few immigrants are admitted by lottery under a diversity category for people from countries that historically sent few people to the United States.

The quota does not apply to refugees (Figure 3.8.3). Also admitted without limit are spouses, children, and parents of U.S. citizens. The number of immigrants can vary sharply from year to year, primarily because numbers in these two groups are unpredictable.

▼ 3.8.3 **U.S. IMMIGRATION** Immigrants receive U.S. citizenship papers, Tucson, Arizona.

WHAT'S YOUR MIGRATION GEOGRAPHY?

Family Mapping

Families often display immigration records on a family tree. Geographers instead can display records on a family map.

1. On a sheet of paper or in an electronic spreadsheet, record an interregional or international migration taken by each of your family members. If the individual moved many times, record the one that seems most significant to your family, such as the one that brought two of your ancestors together.
2. On a blank base map of the world or only the portion of it that you need for your family geography, draw an arrow that connects where (if anywhere) you immigrated from to reach your current home. Was your family geography map complex or difficult to depict? Why?
3. Did any member of your family arrive in the United States through Ellis Island (Figure 3.8.4)? If so, are you able to find their records on line at libertyellisfoundation.org?

▲ 3.8.4 **ELLIS ISLAND**

U.S.–Mexico Immigration Issues

- Summarize the diversity of conditions along the U.S.–Mexico border.

The number of people allowed to immigrate into the United States is at a historically high level, but the number who wish to come is even higher (Figure 3.9.1). Many who cannot legally enter the United States immigrate illegally. Those who do so are entering without proper documents and thus are called **unauthorized immigrants**. The principal reason for unauthorized immigration to the United States is to seek a job.

▲ 3.9.1
U.S.–MEXICO BORDER WALL
Family members separated by the border wall between Sunland, New Mexico, and Ciudad Juarez, Mexico, are reunited for 3 minutes at an event organized by the Border Network for Human Rights on International Human Rights Day, 2017.

Characteristics of Unauthorized Immigrants

The Pew Hispanic Center estimated that 11.0 million unauthorized immigrants lived in the United States in 2015. The number increased rapidly between 1990 and 2005 (Figure 3.9.2). After hitting a peak of 12.2 million in 2007, the number declined because of reduced job opportunities in the United States during the severe recession that started in 2008. The number of unauthorized immigrants entering the United States is now less than the number leaving.

Other information about unauthorized immigrants, according to Pew Hispanic Center:

- **Source country.** Around 5.9 million of the 11 million unauthorized immigrants came from Mexico. The remainder are about evenly divided between other Latin American countries and other regions of the world.
- **Children.** The 11 million unauthorized immigrants included 1 million children. In addition, while living in the United States, unauthorized immigrants have given birth to approximately 4.5 million babies, who are legal citizens of the United States.

According to Pew, 66 percent of unauthorized immigrants had been in the United States for 10 years or more as of 2014, and only 14 percent for less than 5 years.

▲ 3.9.2
UNAUTHORIZED IMMIGRANTS IN THE UNITED STATES

Mexico's Border with the United States

The U.S.–Mexico border is 3,141 kilometers (1,951 miles) long (see Research & Analyze feature and Figure 3.9.3). A joint U.S.–Mexican International Boundary and Water Commission is responsible for keeping official maps, on the basis of a series of nineteenth-century treaties. The commission is also responsible for marking the border by maintaining 276 six-foot-tall iron monuments erected in the late nineteenth century, as well as 440 fifteen-inch-tall markers added in the 1970s. The United States has constructed a barrier covering approximately one-fourth of the border. Actually locating the border is difficult in some remote areas.

Americans are divided concerning whether unauthorized migration helps or hurts the country. This ambivalence extends to specific elements of immigration law.

Americans would like more effective border patrols so that fewer unauthorized immigrants can get into the country, but a majority say that they do not want money spent to build more barriers along the border.

Most Americans support a work-related program to make unauthorized immigrants legal, and they oppose raids on workplaces in attempts to round up unauthorized immigrants. Most Americans support a path to U.S. citizenship for unauthorized immigrants.

Most Americans support the right of children of unauthorized immigrants to remain in the United States. Some Americans, however, see children as having violated immigration laws if they were born in the United States to unauthorized immigrants or brought to the United States at a young age.

RESEARCH & ANALYZE
U.S.–Mexico border crossings

Border crossings between the United States and Mexico look very different depending on where one is trying to cross (Figure 3.9.3). Go to **http://www.bts.dot.gov** and ***search*** *border crossing entry data*. Compare the pedestrian and vehicle data for different U.S–Mexico incoming border crossings.

1. Driving across the border in urban areas, such as between San Diego and Tijuana, can have heavy traffic (Figure 3.9.4). What are some of the attractions and challenges in trying to cross the border here?
2. Crossing the border on foot legally is possible in several places, such as between Progresso, Texas, and Nuevo Progresso, Mexico (Figure 3.9.5). What are some of the attractions and challenges in trying to cross the border here?
3. In some places, the border runs through sparsely inhabited regions, such as Sasabe, Arizona (Figure 3.9.6). What are some of the attractions and challenges in trying to cross the border here?
4. Some crossings are in small towns, such as between Columbus, New Mexico, and Palomas, Mexico (Figure 3.9.7). What are some of the attractions and challenges in trying to cross the border here?

▲ 3.9.4 U.S.–MEXICO BORDER: SAN DIEGO AND TIJUANA

▲ 3.9.5 U.S.–MEXICO BORDER: PROGRESSO AND NUEVO PROGRESSO

▼ 3.9.3 U.S.–MEXICO BORDER

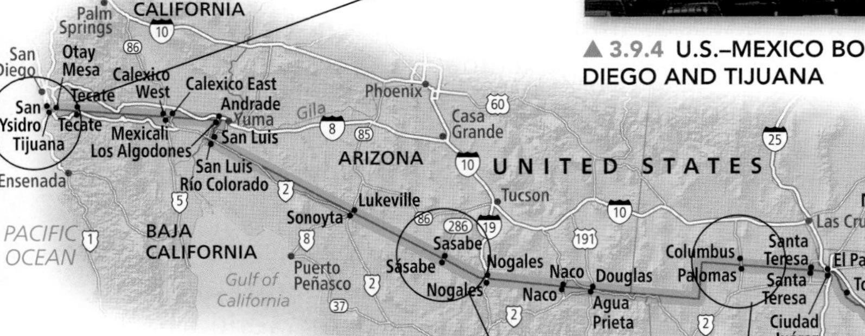

▲ 3.9.6 U.S.–MEXICO BORDER: NEAR SASABE, ARIZONA AND MEXICO

▲ 3.9.7 U.S.–MEXICO BORDER: COLUMBUS AND PUERTO PALOMAS

Border Crossing Entry Data

https://goo.gl/kU7514

Europe Immigration Issues

- Understand attitudes toward immigrants in Europe.

Migration issues have been especially troubling for Europeans in recent years. The level of immigration has been increasing between European countries and into Europe from elsewhere in the world. The ease with which people are able to cross borders into Europe and among countries within Europe has been controversial.

Guest Workers

Until recently, immigrants were regarded as useful additions to the labor force in Europe. With most European countries in stage 4 or 5 of the demographic transition, characterized by stagnant or declining population, immigrants took low-status and low-skill jobs that local residents didn't want to do. In cities such as Berlin, Brussels, Paris, and Zurich, immigrants provide essential services, such as driving buses, collecting garbage, repairing streets, and washing dishes.

In the 1960s and 1970s, Germany and other wealthy European countries operated **guest worker** programs, in which people from poorer countries were allowed to immigrate temporarily to obtain jobs. Guest workers were expected to return to their countries of origin once their work was done.

However, many immigrants who arrived originally under the guest worker program have remained permanently in Europe. They, along with their children and grandchildren, have become citizens of the host country.

Although relatively low paid by European standards, immigrants could earn far more than they would at home. By letting their people work elsewhere, poorer countries reduce their own unemployment problems. Immigrants also help their native countries by sending remittances back home to their families.

Migration Patterns in Europe

Europe (including Russia) is home to 76 million of the world's 244 million immigrants as of 2015. Otherwise stated, Europe has less than 10 percent of the world's total population but more than 30 percent of the world's migrants. Germany and Russia each have 12 million immigrants, the United Kingdom has 9 million, France has 8 million, and Spain and Italy have 6 million each.

Overall, around 10 percent of Europe's population consists of immigrants. The foreign-born population is 41 percent in Luxembourg and 29 percent in Switzerland. Germany, the most populous country in Europe (other than Russia), not only has the largest number of immigrants, it also has one of the largest percentages of immigrants.

Europe's 76 million immigrants include 46 million originating in another European country and 30 million from other regions of the world. The general pattern of movement of migrants, both within Europe and into Europe from other regions of the world, is from south and east to north and west.

Russia is the country of origin in Europe for the largest number of immigrants, 6 million, followed by 5 million from Ukraine, 4 million each from Kazakhstan and Poland, and 3 million each from Morocco, Romania, and Turkey (Figure 3.10.1).

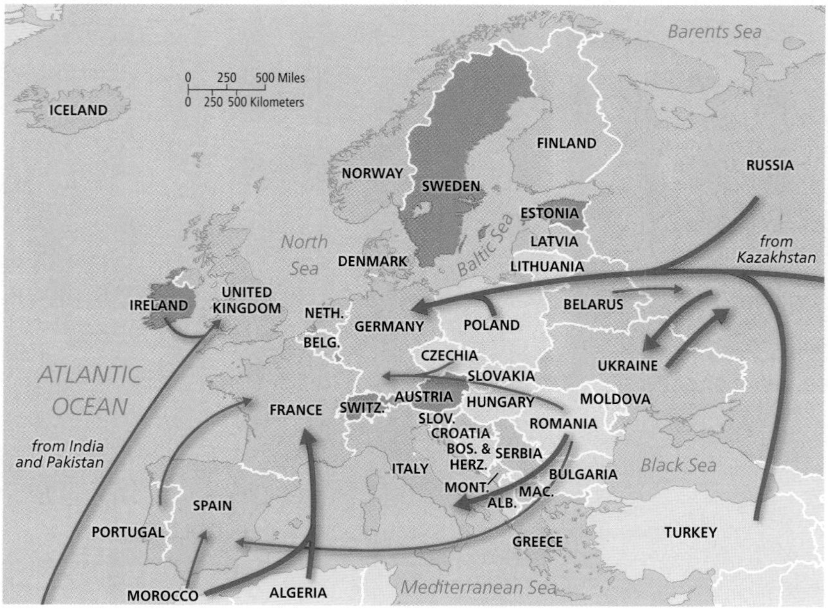

Percent foreign born
15 and above
5–15
below 5
Migration flows
More than 1,000,000
500,000–1,000,000

3.10.1 IMMIGRATION IN EUROPE

Attitudes toward Immigrants

Hostility to immigrants has become a central plank in the platform of political parties in many European countries. These parties blame immigrants for crime, unemployment, and high welfare costs. Above all, the anti-immigration parties fear that long-standing cultural traditions of the host country are threatened by immigrants who adhere to different religions, speak different languages, and practice different food and other cultural habits. From the standpoint of these parties, immigrants represent a threat to the centuries-old cultural traditions of the host country (Figure 3.10.2).

Anti-immigrant attitudes in Europe were heightened with the arrival of more than 1 million refugees from Asia beginning in 2015. Around half of these refugees came from Syria, and Afghanistan and Iraq were the states of origin of most of the remainder. These refugees faced murder, rape, torture, and loss of property in their home countries. Most arrived in Europe without authorization after travelling across the Mediterranean Sea in flimsy boats or walking overland through Southeast Europe. Compounding the tensions, the vast majority of the unauthorized immigrants were Muslims arriving in predominantly Christian Europe during the same time as a series of terrorist attacks in Europe were carried out by supporters of radical Muslim organizations (see Chapters 6 and 8).

Immigration has been an especially important issue in elections in a number of European countries. Many voters have favored reducing the level of immigration (Figure 3.10.3).

DEBATE IT!

Should countries restrict immigration?

Immigration has become a controversial issue in many developed countries, including the United States and much of Europe.

CONTROL THE NUMBER OF IMMIGRANTS

- Immigrants compete for jobs with people already in the country and make it harder for citizens to find jobs.
- Immigrants place strains on services designed for citizens, such as schools and hospitals.
- Immigrants lack understanding and support for the host country's cultural traditions.

WELCOME IMMIGRANTS

- Immigrants fill low-paying jobs that citizens don't want, such as in food services and agriculture.
- Immigrants place limited demands on public services.
- The different cultural heritage of immigrants enriches the life of the host country.

▲ **3.10.2 ANTI-IMMIGRANT RALLY**
Cambridgeshire, United Kingdom.

▲ **3.10.3 PRO-IMMIGRANT RALLY**
London, United Kingdom.

CHAPTER 3 Review, Analyze, & Apply

KEY ISSUE 1 Where Are Migrants Distributed?

Emigration is migration from a location, immigration is migration to a location, and net migration is the difference between the two. The largest numbers of migrants are from Asia and Latin America to North America and from Asia to Europe. The principal sources of immigrants to the United States have changed over time.

THINKING GEOGRAPHICALLY

1. In recent years, has your community seen net in-migration or net out-migration? What factors might explain your community's net migration?

▲ 3.CR.1 NATURALIZATION CEREMONY

KEY ISSUE 2 Where Do People Migrate Within Countries?

Two main types of internal migration are interregional (between regions of a country) and intraregional (within a region). Large countries, including the United States and Canada, have had important patterns of interregional migration. Two intraregional migration patterns are from rural to urban areas (especially in developing countries) and from urban to suburban areas (especially in developed countries).

THINKING GEOGRAPHICALLY

2. Have you personally experienced (a) international migration, (b) interregional migration, or (c) intraregional migration? If so, why did your family migrate? Was the experience easy or difficult? Why?

▲ 3.CR.2 LOS ANGELES SUBURBS

KEY ISSUE 3 Why Do People Migrate?

People migrate for a combination of push and pull factors. Most people migrate for economic reasons, pushed from areas with limited economic prospects and pulled to areas of relative prosperity. Some migration is caused by environmental factors, as well as political and other cultural factors.

THINKING GEOGRAPHICALLY

3. When you graduate from your school, do you expect to undertake international, interregional, or intraregional migration? Why?

▲ 3.CR.3 TODAY'S GRADUATES, TOMORROW'S MIGRANTS?

KEY ISSUE 4 What Challenges Do Migrants Face?

Many countries, including the United States, limit the number of immigrants. For many developed countries, the demand for legal residency from international migrants significantly exceeds the number of slots set by the government. Hostility to immigrants is common, including among some Europeans.

THINKING GEOGRAPHICALLY

4. The number of unauthorized immigrants from Mexico to the United States has been declining since 2007. Given the push and pull factors underlying people's reasons for migrating, what might account for this decline?

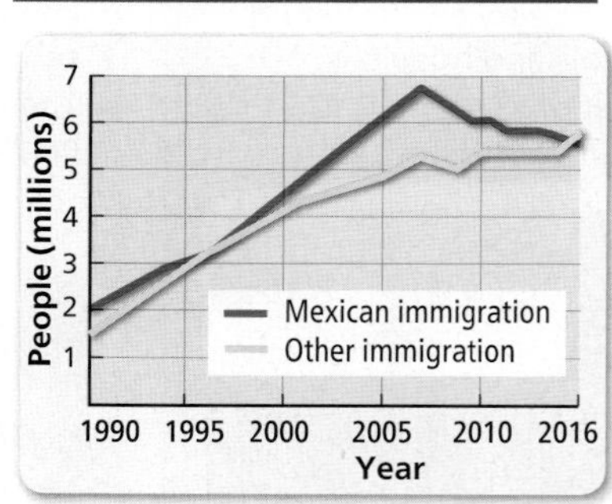

▲ 3.CR.4 UNAUTHORIZED IMMIGRANTS IN U.S.

Explore

Mexico's other border

Use Google Earth to explore Mexico's southern border (Figure 3.CR.5).

Search for *Talisman, Mexico, border crossing*.

1. Use *Street View* for a ground-level view of the border crossing. Which if any of Mexico's border crossings with the United States in Figure 3.9 does the Talisman one resemble? Why?
2. ***Click*** the X in the upper left to return to aerial view. ***Zoom*** out to around 3 km.
3. What is the country bordering Mexico? The border mostly follows a river. What is the river's name?
4. Follow the river to the south. Do you see any other official border crossings? Does the border look easy to cross or difficult? Why?

▲ 3.CR.5 MEXICO'S SOUTHERN BORDER

Key Terms

Asylum seeker (p. 73) Someone who has migrated to another country in the hope of being recognized as a refugee.

Brain drain (p. 78) Large-scale emigration by talented people.

Chain migration (p. 78) Migration of people to a specific location because relatives or members of the same nationality previously migrated there.

Counterurbanization (p. 71) Net migration from urban to rural areas in developed countries.

Emigration (p. 64) Migration from a location.

Floodplain (p. 74) The area subject to flooding during a given number of years, according to historical trends.

Guest worker (p. 82) A term once used for a worker who migrated to the developed countries of Northern and Western Europe, usually from Southern and Eastern Europe or from North Africa, in search of a higher-paying job.

Immigration (p. 64) Migration to a new location.

Internal migration (p. 65) Permanent movement within a particular country.

Internally displaced person (IDP) (p. 73) Someone who has been forced to migrate for similar political reasons as a refugee but has not migrated across an international border.

International migration (p. 65) Permanent movement from one country to another.

Interregional migration (p. 65) Permanent movement from one region of a country to another.

Intervening obstacle (p. 72) An environmental or cultural feature of the landscape that hinders migration.

Intraregional migration (p. 65) Permanent movement within one region of a country.

Migration (p. 64) A form of relocation diffusion involving a permanent move to a new location.

Migration transition (p. 64) A change in the migration pattern in a society that results from industrialization, population growth, and other social and economic changes that also produce the demographic transition.

Net migration (p. 64) The difference between the level of immigration and the level of emigration.

Pull factor (p. 72) A factor that induces people to move to a new location.

Push factor (p. 72) A factor that induces people to leave old residences.

Quota (p. 79) In reference to migration, a law that places maximum limits on the number of people who can immigrate to a country each year.

Refugees (p. 73) People who are forced to migrate from their home country and cannot return for fear of persecution because of their race, religion, nationality, membership in a social group, or political opinion.

Remittance (p. 75) Transfer of money by workers to people in the country from which they emigrated.

Unauthorized immigrant (p. 80) A person who enters a country without proper documents to do so.

GeoVideo

Log in to the Mastering Geography Study Area to view this video.

Title: Xenophobia in Lampedusa

Thousands of unauthorized migrants from Tunisia arrived in small boats on Lampedusa, an island in the Mediterranean Sea with 6,000 inhabitants that is part of Italy.

1. What push and pull factors motivated the Tunisians to migrate to Lampedusa?
2. How have most of the 6,000 inhabitants of Lampedusa reacted to the arrival of Tunisians?
3. Explain why Tunisians have been migrating to Lampedusa, by consulting a map showing the location of the island.

Mastering Geography

Looking for additional review and test prep materials? Visit the Study Area in Mastering Geography to enhance your geographic literacy, spatial reasoning skills, and understanding of this chapter's content. Access MapMaster™ interactive maps, video case studies, *In the News* current articles, flashcards, self-study quizzes, an eText of *Contemporary Human Geography*, and more. **pearson.com/mastering/geography**

Geospatial Analysis

Log in to the Mastering Geography Study Area to access MapMaster 2.0.

Europe's immigrants and emigrants

Substantial immigration is occurring within Europe. Let's see where people are coming and going.

Add the *Net Migration* data layer. ***Select*** the *Settings* icon from the *Legend*, and ***select*** *Show Political Labels*. ***Add*** the *Gross National Income per capita* layer and ***select*** *Split Map Window*. ***Zoom*** to Europe.

1. Europe can be divided between east and west. Which of the two has net outmigration, and which has net inmigration?
2. Which half of Europe has higher gross national income per capita?
3. In what way do you think the patterns on the two maps are associated with each other?

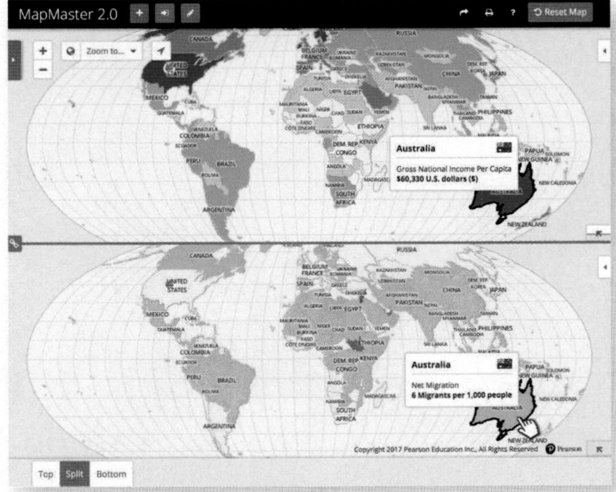

▲ 3.CR.7 NET MIGRATION AND GROSS NATIONAL INCOME PER CAPITA EUROPE

CHAPTER

4 Folk & Popular Culture

Culture is the body of material traits, customary beliefs, and social forms that together constitute the distinct tradition of a group of people. Chapter 4 focuses on the first part of this definition (material traits)—the visible elements that a group possesses and leaves behind for the future. A consideration of culture follows logically from the discussion of migration in Chapter 3. Two locations have similar cultural beliefs, objects, and institutions because people bring along their culture when they migrate. Differences emerge when two groups have limited interaction.

◀ Baseball practice, Gaza City.

KEY ISSUES

1 How Are Leisure Activities Distributed?

Compared to folk culture, popular culture activities, including leisure and recreation, are more likely to originate at a specific time and place and to diffuse over a wider region.

2 How Is Material Culture Distributed?

Material folk culture, including food, shelter, and clothing, is more likely to vary between places, whereas popular culture is more likely to vary between points in time.

3 Why Is Access to Culture Unequal?

Popular culture is increasingly likely to diffuse through electronic media. People in some regions lack access to electronic media.

4 What Challenges Do Folk and Popular Culture Face?

Although popular culture tends to produce uniform landscapes, differences in cultural preferences persist among people in different regions.

LOCATIONS IN THIS CHAPTER

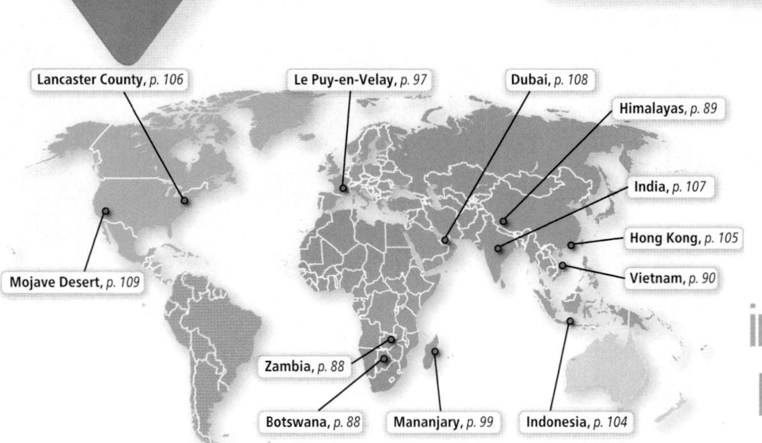

popular culture
custom
social media
housing
face cover
hearth
instagram
sustainability
leisure
interconnectivity
habit
internet freedom
terroir
folk culture
TV
reggae
time use
cultural identity
material culture
soccer
taboo
media access
dress code
cultural homogenization

Elements of Folk & Popular Culture

- Identify geographic differences between folk and popular culture.

Geographers define **culture** as the body of material traits, customary beliefs, and social forms that together constitute the distinct tradition of a group of people. This chapter focuses on the first part of this definition (material traits)—the visible elements that a group possesses and leaves behind for the future.

▲ 4.1.1 **HABIT AND CUSTOM**
It's a custom for male executives and politicians to wear business suits, but as CEO of Fiat Chrysler, Sergio Marchionne had a habit of wearing a black sweater, even when meeting with President Donald Trump.

Culture falls into two basic categories that differ according to scale:

- **Folk culture** is traditionally practiced primarily by small, homogeneous groups living in relative isolation from other groups.
- **Popular culture** is found in large, heterogeneous societies that share certain customs (such as wearing jeans) despite differences in other personal characteristics.

Culture can be distinguished from a habit or a custom. A **habit** is a repetitive act that a particular individual performs, such as wearing jeans to class every day. A **custom** is a repetitive act of a group, performed to the extent that it becomes characteristic of the group, such as many students typically wearing jeans to class (Figure 4.1.1).

Two types of customs are emphasized in this chapter:

- Material culture: Food, clothing, and shelter. All people must consume food, wear clothing, and find shelter, but different cultural groups do so in distinctive ways (Figure 4.1.2).
- Leisure activities: Arts and recreation. Each cultural group has its own definition of meaningful art and stimulating recreation (Figure 4.1.3).

Each social custom has a unique origin, pattern of diffusion, and spatial distribution.

▲ 4.1.2 **MATERIAL CULTURE**
Cooking roots, Botswana.

◀ 4.1.3 **LEISURE ACTIVITIES**
Playing soccer, Zambia.

Origin

Culture originates at a **hearth**, a center of innovation.

- Folk culture often has anonymous hearths, originating from anonymous sources, at unknown dates, through unidentified originators. It may also have multiple hearths, originating independently in isolated locations.
- Popular culture is typically traceable to a specific person or corporation in a particular place. The originator may incorporate elements of folk culture into a product that appeals to a wider audience in multiple locations. It is most often a product of developed countries, especially in North America and Europe.

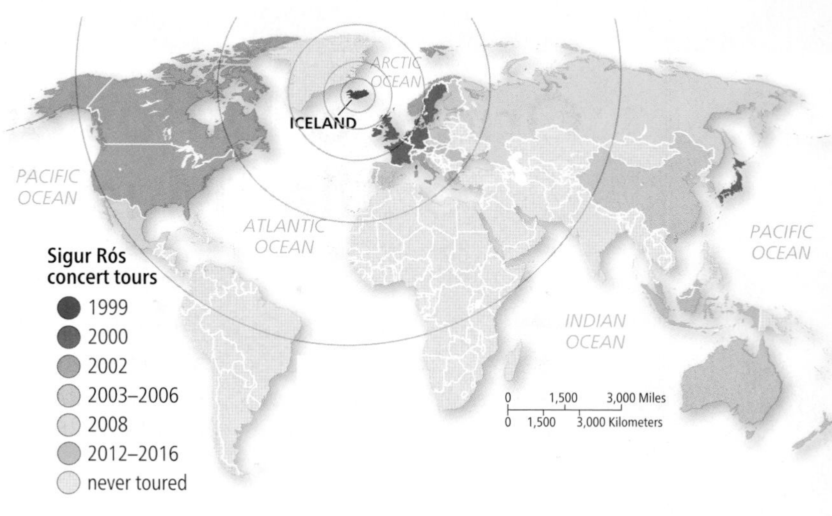

▲ 4.1.4 DIFFUSION OF POPULAR CULTURE
Sigur Rós concert tours.

Diffusion

Folk and popular cultures have different processes of diffusion:

- Folk culture is transmitted from one location to another relatively slowly and on a small scale, primarily through relocation diffusion (migration).
- Popular culture typically spreads through a process of hierarchical diffusion, diffusing rapidly and extensively from hearths or nodes of innovation with the help of modern communications. For example, the music group Sigur Rós performed first in their home country of Iceland. As their popularity increased, the group performed elsewhere in Europe, then in other regions of the world (Figure 4.1.4).

Distribution

Folk and popular cultures have different distributions:

- Folk culture has a distinctive distribution influenced by a combination of local physical and cultural factors. For example, in a study of artistic customs in the Himalaya Mountains, geographers P. Karan and Cotton Mather revealed that distinctive views of the physical environment emerge among neighboring cultural groups that are isolated (Figure 4.1.5).
- Popular culture is distributed widely across many countries, with little regard for physical factors. The distribution is influenced by the ability of people to access the material. The principal obstacle to access is lack of income to purchase the material.

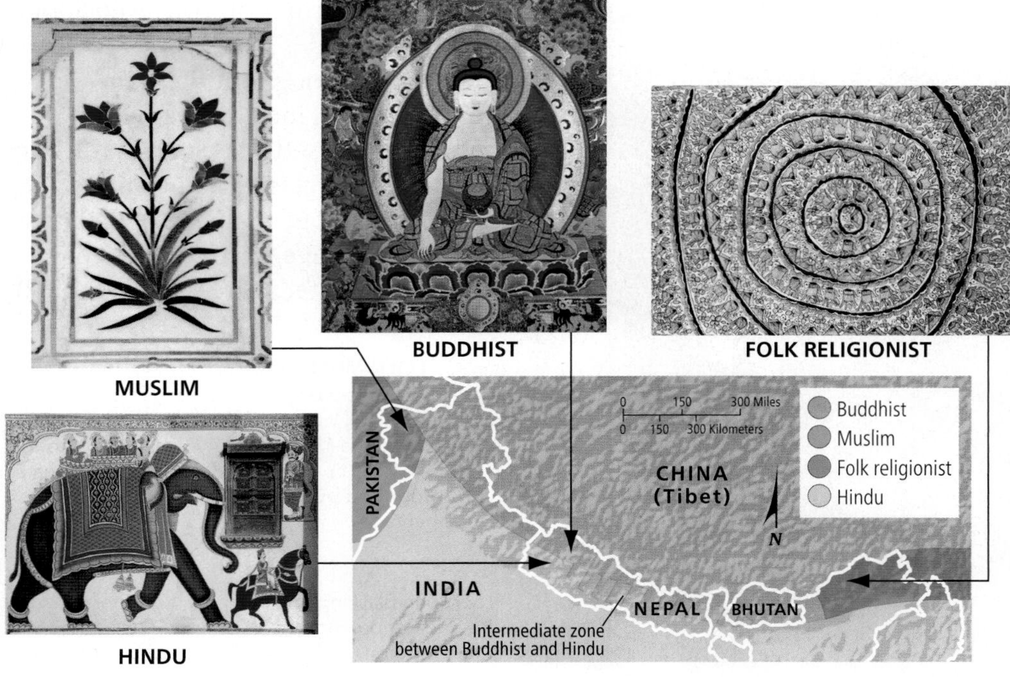

◀ 4.1.5 DISTRIBUTION OF FOLK CULTURE: ART IN THE HIMALAYAS
Buddhists. Buddhists paint idealized divine figures, such as monks and saints, often set in the local environment.
Hindus. Hindus create scenes from everyday life and familiar local scenes. Their paintings sometimes include a deity in a domestic scene.
Muslims. Islamic folk art is inspired by the area's beautiful plants and flowers. In contrast with the paintings from the Buddhist and Hindu regions, these paintings do not typically include human figures.
Folk religionists. Animists from Myanmar (Burma) and elsewhere in Southeast Asia, who have migrated to the eastern region of the study area, paint symbols and designs that derive from their religion rather than from the local environment.

Origin & Diffusion of Folk & Popular Music

- Explain differences in origin and the diffusion of folk and popular music.

Every culture in human history has had some tradition of music, argues music researcher Daniel Levitan. As music is a part of both folk and popular culture traditions, it can be used to illustrate the differences in the origin, diffusion, and distribution of folk and popular culture.

▲ 4.2.1 **FOLK MUSIC: CHINA** Chinese dancers perform in Confolens, France, headquarters for the International Council of Organizations of Folklore Festivals and Folk Arts, which aims to preserve traditional art and organize folk festivals for dance, music, and other social customs.

Folk Music

According to a Chinese legend, folk music was invented in 2697 B.C., when the Emperor Huangdi sent Ling Lun to cut bamboo poles that would produce a sound matching the call of the phoenix bird. In reality, folk songs usually originate anonymously and are transmitted orally. As people migrate, folk music travels with them as part of the diffusion of folk culture.

Folk songs may tell a story or convey information about life-cycle events, such as birth, death, and marriage, or environmental features, such as agriculture and climate (Figure 4.2.1). A song may be modified from one generation to the next as conditions change, but the content is most often derived from events in daily life that are familiar to the majority of the people.

For example, in Vietnam, where many people are subsistence farmers, information about agricultural technology was traditionally conveyed through folk songs. The following folk song provides advice about the difference between seeds planted in summer and seeds planted in winter:

Ma chiêm ba tháng không già
Ma mùa tháng ruôi át la'không mong[1]

This song can be translated as follows:

While seedlings for the summer crop are not old when they are three months of age,
Seedlings for the winter crop are certainly not young when they are one-and-a-half months old.

The song hardly sounds lyrical to a Western ear. But when English-language folk songs appear in cold print, similar themes emerge, even if the specific information conveyed about the environment differs.

Festivals throughout Vietnam feature music in locally meaningful environmental settings, such as hillsides or on water. Singers in traditional clothes sing about elements of daily life in the local village, such as the trees, flowers, and water sources (Figure 4.2.2).

◀ 4.2.2 **FOLK MUSIC: QUAN HO, VIETNAM** Vietnamese singers perform Quan Ho folk songs as part of the annual Lim Festival, which is held annually on the 13th to the 15th day of the first lunar month. Quan Ho folk music dates back more than 500 years and is recognized by UNESCO as part of humanity's cultural heritage.

[1]From John Blacking and Joann W. Kealiinohomoku, eds., *The Performing Arts: Music and Dance* (The Hague: Mouton, 1979), 144. Reprinted by permission.

Popular Music

In contrast to folk music, popular music is written by specific individuals for the purpose of being sold to or performed in front of a large number of people. It frequently displays a high degree of technical skill through manipulation of sophisticated electronic equipment.

As with other elements of popular culture, popular musicians have more connections with performers of similar styles, regardless of where in the world they happen to live, than they do with performers of different styles who happen to live in the same community.

In the United States, New York and Los Angeles attract the largest number of musicians so they can be near sources of employment and cultural activities that attract a wide variety of artists, not just performers of a specific type of music. Nashville is also a leading center for musicians, especially those performing country and gospel. Compared with New York and Los Angeles, Nashville has the highest concentration of musicians, as a percentage of its much smaller population. (Figure 4.2.3).

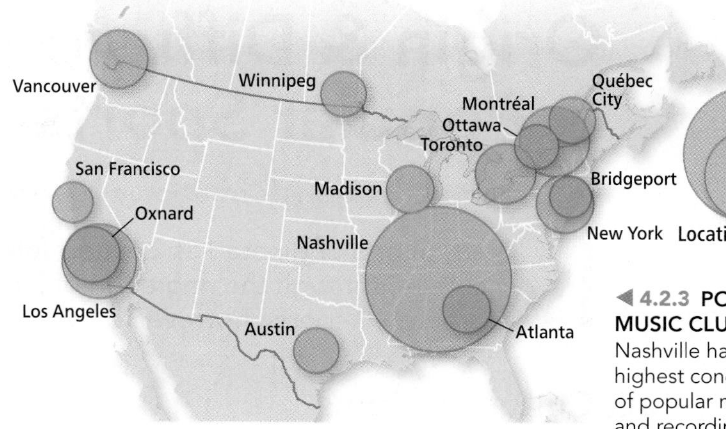

◀ 4.2.3 **POPULAR MUSIC CLUSTERS** Nashville has by far the highest concentration of popular musicians and recording studios in North America. Three Canadian cities also rank among the top five.

In the past, according to Richard Florida, Charlotta Mellander, and Kevin Stolarick, musicians clustered in particular communities according to shared interest in specific styles, such as Tin Pan Alley in New York, Dixieland jazz in New Orleans, country in Nashville, and Motown in Detroit. Now with the globalization of popular music, musicians are less tied to the culture of particular places and instead increasingly cluster in communities where other creative artists reside, regardless of the particular style (see Research & Analyze feature and Figure 4.2.4).

RESEARCH & ANALYZE

Diffusion of reggae's revival

Reggae music originated as an element of folk culture in Jamaica during the 1960s and enjoyed a revival in the twenty-first century as an element of popular culture. Google News Lab has documented searches for the term "reggae" by location between 2004 and 2015.

1. View reggae around the world map by typing into your web browser *Vogue reggae by the number* or go to **Vogue.com** and search for *reggae by the numbers.* At the world scale, what three world regions appear to be the hearths for the revival of reggae?
2. How does the number of searches for *reggae* change beginning during 2013? What might account for this change?
3. Stop the animation at the earliest date (01/2004). ***Zoom*** in on North America. What two cities in North America are the hearths for the revival of reggae?
4. While zoomed in on North America, ***turn on*** the animation. Describe the pattern of searches for *reggae* during the 10-year period covered by the animation.

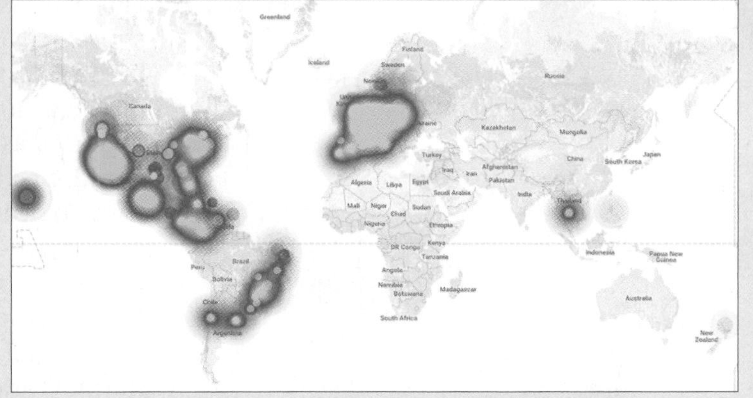

▲ 4.2.4 **DIFFUSION OF GOOGLE SEARCHES FOR REGGAE**

Google News Lab

https://goo.gl/4eg6MD

Origin & Diffusion of Folk & Popular Sports

- Describe the transformation of sports from folk to popular culture.

Many sports originated as isolated folk customs and were diffused like other folk culture, through the migration of individuals. The contemporary diffusion of organized sports, however, displays the characteristics of popular culture.

Soccer's Folk Culture Origins

Soccer, the world's most popular sport—known in most of the world as football—originated as a folk custom in England during the eleventh century. It was transformed into a part of global popular culture beginning in the nineteenth century.

Early football games resembled uncontrolled mob scenes. A large number of people from two villages would gather to kick the ball. The winning side was the one that kicked the ball into the center of the rival village. Because football disrupted village life, English kings issued several bans between the fourteenth and seventeenth centuries. At this point, football was an English folk custom rather than a global popular custom.

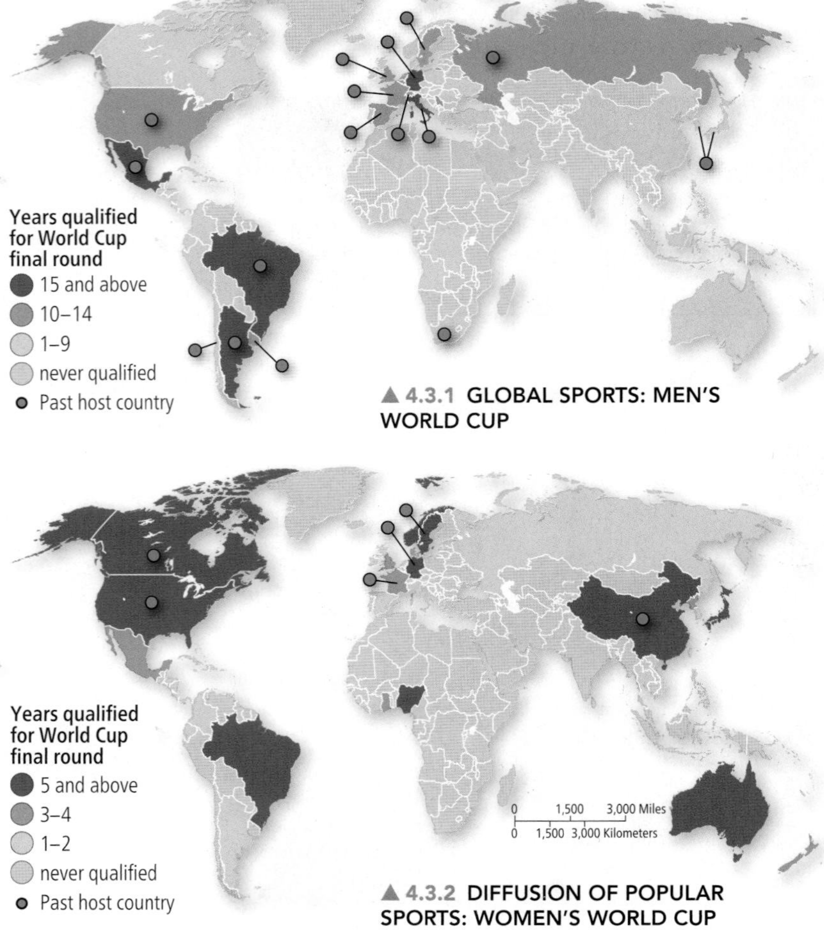

▲ 4.3.1 GLOBAL SPORTS: MEN'S WORLD CUP

▲ 4.3.2 DIFFUSION OF POPULAR SPORTS: WOMEN'S WORLD CUP

Soccer as Popular Culture

The transformation of football from an English folk custom to global popular culture began in the 1800s. Football and other recreation clubs were founded in the United Kingdom, frequently by churches, to provide factory workers with organized recreation during leisure hours. Sport became a subject that was taught in school.

Increasing leisure time permitted people not only to participate in sporting events but also to view them. With more disposable income, spectators paid to see first-class events. To meet public demand, football clubs began to hire professional players. Several British football clubs formed an association in 1863 to standardize the rules and to organize professional leagues. Organization of the sport into a formal structure in the United Kingdom marks the transition of football from folk to popular culture.

The word soccer originated after 1863, when supporters of the game formed the Football Association. "Association" was shortened to "assoc", which ultimately became twisted around into the word soccer.

Beginning in the late 1800s, the British exported association football around the world, first to continental Europe and then to other countries. In the twentieth century, soccer, like other sports, was further diffused by new communication systems, especially radio and TV.

The global popularity of soccer is seen in the World Cup, in which national soccer teams compete every four years, including in Russia in 2018 for men (Figure 4.3.1) and in France in 2019 for women (Figure 4.3.2). Thanks to TV, each men's final breaks the record for the most spectators of any event in world history.

Olympic Sports

To be included in the Summer Olympics, a sport must be widely practiced in at least 75 countries and on four continents (50 countries for women). The 2020 Summer Olympics features competition in 33 sports (Figure 4.3.3). The two leading team sports in the United States—American football and baseball—are not included.

Regionally Distinctive Sports

Most other sports have diffused less than soccer. Cultural groups still have their own preferred sports, which are often unintelligible to people elsewhere. Consider the following:

- Cricket is popular primarily in the United Kingdom and former British colonies, especially in South Asia, the South Pacific, and Caribbean islands.
- Ice hockey prevails, logically, in colder climates, especially in Canada, the northern United States, northern Europe, and Russia.
- Wushu, martial arts that combine forms such as kicking and jumping with combat such as striking and wrestling, are China's most popular sports.
- Baseball, once confined to North America, became popular in Japan after it was introduced by American soldiers who occupied the country after World War II (Figure 4.3.4).
- Australia rules football is a sport distinct from soccer and the football played in North America. Distinctive forms of football developed in Australia, as well as the United States and Canada, as a result of lack of interaction among sporting nations during the nineteenth century.
- Lacrosse was traditionally played by the Iroquois, who called it guhchigwaha, which means "bump hips." European colonists in Canada picked up the game from the Iroquois and diffused it to a handful of U.S. communities, especially in Maryland, upstate New York, and Long Island. In recent years, lacrosse has fostered cultural identity among the Iroquois Confederation of Six Nations (Cayugas, Mohawks, Oneidas, Onondagas, Senecas, and Tuscaroras), because they have been invited by the International Lacrosse Federation to participate in the Lacrosse World Championships, along with teams from sovereign states, such as Australia, Canada, and the United States (Figure 4.3.5).

Despite the diversity in distribution of sports across Earth's surface and the anonymous origin of some games, organized spectator sports today are part of popular culture. The common element in professional sports is the willingness of people throughout the world to pay for the privilege of viewing, in person or on TV or the Internet, events played by professional athletes.

◀ 4.3.3 **POPULAR SPORTS: OLYMPICS**
800 meter event.

▼ 4.3.4 **REGIONS OF BASEBALL FANS**
The area of support for a baseball team is an example of a functional region, with most intense support near where the team plays, and weaker support on the periphery.

▲ 4.3.5 **IROQUOIS NATIONALS LACROSSE**
Gewas Schnidler, a member of the Onondaga Nation, has played lacrosse for the Iroquois Nationals, the only team composed entirely of Native American (First Nations) members sanctioned to compete in international sports. Schnidler is holding his passport, which is issued by the Iroquois (known in the Nation's language as Haudenosaunee Confederacy). The Iroquois Nationals were unable to travel to the 2010 World Lacrosse Championship in the United Kingdom, because U.K. immigration officials would not accept their Haudenosaunee Confederacy passports.

(a)

Distribution of Folk & Popular Clothing

- Compare reasons for distribution of clothing styles in folk and popular culture.

Material culture includes the three most important necessities of life: clothing, food, and shelter. Popular clothing, food, and shelter vary more in time than in place. They originate through the invention of a particular person or corporation, and they diffuse rapidly across Earth to locations with a variety of physical conditions. Access depends on an individual having a sufficiently high level of income to acquire the material possessions associated with popular culture.

▲▶ 4.4.1 FOLK CLOTHING: RELIGION
Some Jewish men (a) and Muslim women (b) wear modest black clothes including head coverings.

(b)

▲ 4.4.2 FOLK CLOTHING: ENVIRONMENTAL FACTORS
Some Dutch people wear wooden shoes to keep their feet dry on ice and water.

IRAN
SAUDI ARABIA
SUDAN
PACIFIC OCEAN
INDIAN OCEAN
ATLANTIC OCEAN

0 1,000 2,000 Miles
0 1,000 2,000 Kilometers

- No pressure to veil or not wear a veil
- Modesty by custom; veiling rare
- Dress code may be required; veiling uncommon
- Dress code required, veiling may be common
- Dress code enforced with violence or legal prosecution
- Minor to strong pressure against veiling

▲ 4.4.3 FOLK CLOTHING: WOMEN'S DRESS CODES

Folk Clothing Preferences

People living in folk cultures have traditionally worn clothing in part in response to distinctive agricultural practices and climatic conditions. Cultural factors, such as religious beliefs, can also influence clothing preferences (Figure 4.4.1). In popular culture, clothing preferences generally reflect occupations rather than particular environments.

People wear distinctive folk clothing for a variety of environmental and cultural reasons. The folk custom in the Netherlands of wearing wooden shoes may appear quaint, but it still has practical uses in a wet area (Figure 4.4.2).

Increased travel and the diffusion of media have exposed North Americans and Europeans to other forms of dress, just as people in other parts of the world have come into contact with Western dress. The poncho from South America, the dashiki of the Yoruba people of Nigeria, and the Aleut parka have been adopted by people elsewhere in the world. The continued use of folk costumes in some parts of the globe may persist not because of distinctive environmental conditions or traditional cultural values but to preserve past memories or to attract tourists.

Wearing traditional clothing in countries dominated by popular culture can be controversial, and conversely so can wearing popular clothing in countries dominated by folk-style clothing. Especially difficult has been the coexistence of the loose-fitting combination body covering, head covering, and veil traditionally worn by women in Southwest Asia & North Africa with casual Western-style popular women's clothing, such as open-necked blouses, tight-fitting slacks, and revealing skirts (see Debate It! feature and Figure 4.4.3).

Popular Clothing Preferences

Contemporary fashion and popular clothing takes place in an interconnected world. Fashionable clothes, which constantly feature new styles, are among the most globally-distributed products available to consumers today. Individual clothing habits reveal that popular culture can be distributed across the landscape with little regard for distinctive physical features.

Instead, popular clothing habits are more likely to reflect occupation and income. A lawyer or business executive, for example, tends to wear a dark suit, light shirt or blouse, and necktie or scarf, whereas a factory worker wears jeans and a work shirt. A lawyer in New York is more likely to dress like a lawyer in Mexico than like a factory worker in New York.

Women's clothes, in particular, change in fashion from one year to the next. The color, shape, and design of dresses change to imitate pieces created by clothing designers. For social purposes, people with sufficient income may update their wardrobe frequently with the latest fashions.

Improved communications have permitted the rapid diffusion of clothing styles from one region of Earth to another. Original designs for women's dresses, created in Paris, Milan, London, or New York, are reproduced in large quantities at factories in Asia and sold for relatively low prices in North American and European chain stores. Speed is essential in manufacturing copies of designer dresses because fashion tastes change quickly.

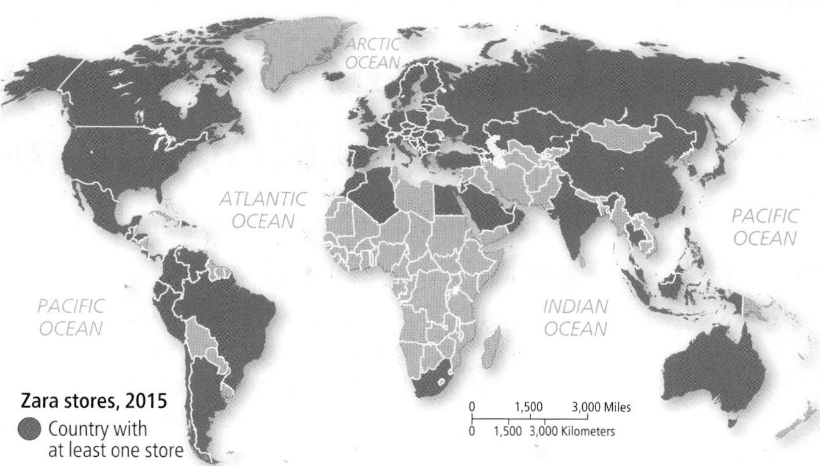

▲ 4.4.4 POPULAR CLOTHING: COUNTRIES WITH ZARA STORES

In the past, years could elapse from the time an original dress was displayed to the time that inexpensive reproductions were available in the stores. Now the time lag is only a few weeks because of the diffusion of electronic communications.

Most people wear clothing that fits the cultural traditions where they live. But the diffusion of popular clothing is eroding local variations. A shopper who wants to buy a trendy international retail brand of clothing like Zara can find the same jeans at identical-looking Zara stores in Indonesia and Spain (Figure 4.4.4). And the clothing itself may have been made in another region of the world (see Chapter 11). However, consumers in two places who choose the same brand of jeans will wear them in different cultural contexts. Clothing considered commonplace and traditional in one part of the world may be viewed as bold and controversial in another.

DEBATE IT!
Wearing face covers in Europe

Garments that cover the face are typically worn by women who adhere to traditional folk customs in Southwest Asia & North Africa (refer to Figures 4.4.1b and 4.4.3). The niqaab is a veil that covers the bottom half of the face. The burqa covers the entire face and body, leaving a mesh screen to see through. European countries, including France and Belgium, prohibit women from wearing them in public. (Figures 4.4.5 and 4.4.6).

PROHIBIT BURQA AND NIQAAB IN PUBLIC

- The coverings obliterate personal identity and treat women like second-class citizens.
- The ban protects gender equality and the dignity of women.
- Complete covering of the face poses a security risk by preventing identification of an individual.

▶ 4.4.5 POSTER SUPPORTING THE BAN

PERMIT BURQA AND NIQAAB IN PUBLIC

- Governments have no business determining clothing preferences.
- The ban shows lack of understanding and intolerance of Muslim cultural traditions.
- The ban infringes on a woman's religious, free speech, and privacy rights.

▶ 4.4.6 PROTESTER AGAINST THE BAN

Distribution of Folk & Popular Food & Housing

- Describe regional variations in folk and popular food and housing.

Folk food and housing habits are products both of environmental conditions and cultural traditions. Inhabitants of a region must consider the soil, climate, terrain, vegetation, and other characteristics of the environment in the production of their food and shelter. In the popular culture of the twenty-first century, food preferences in particular seem far removed from folk traditions

Folk Housing

All humans need a place to live. Distinctive environmental and cultural features influence the provision of housing in folk cultures.

The type of building materials used to construct folk houses is influenced partly by the resources available in the environment. Stone, grass, sod, and skins may be used, but the two most common building materials in the world are wood and brick.

Older houses in the United States display local folk culture traditions. In contrast, housing built in the United States since the 1940s demonstrates how popular customs vary more in time than in place.

Geographer Fred Kniffen identified three major hearths, or nodes, of folk house forms in the United States (Figure 4.5.1). When families migrated westward in the 1700s and 1800s, they cut trees to clear fields for planting and used the wood to build houses, barns, and fences. The style of pioneer homes reflected whatever style was prevailing at the place on the East Coast from which they migrated.

Popular Housing

Houses built in the United States since the mid-twentieth century display popular culture influences. The degree of regional distinctiveness in housing style has diminished because rapid communication and transportation systems provide people throughout the country with knowledge of alternative styles. Furthermore, most people do not build the houses in which they live. Instead, houses are usually mass-produced by construction companies.

Houses show the influence of shapes, materials, detailing, and other features of architectural style in vogue at any one point in time. In the years immediately after World War II, which ended in 1945, most U.S. houses were built in a modern style. Since the 1960s, styles that architects call neo-eclectic have predominated.

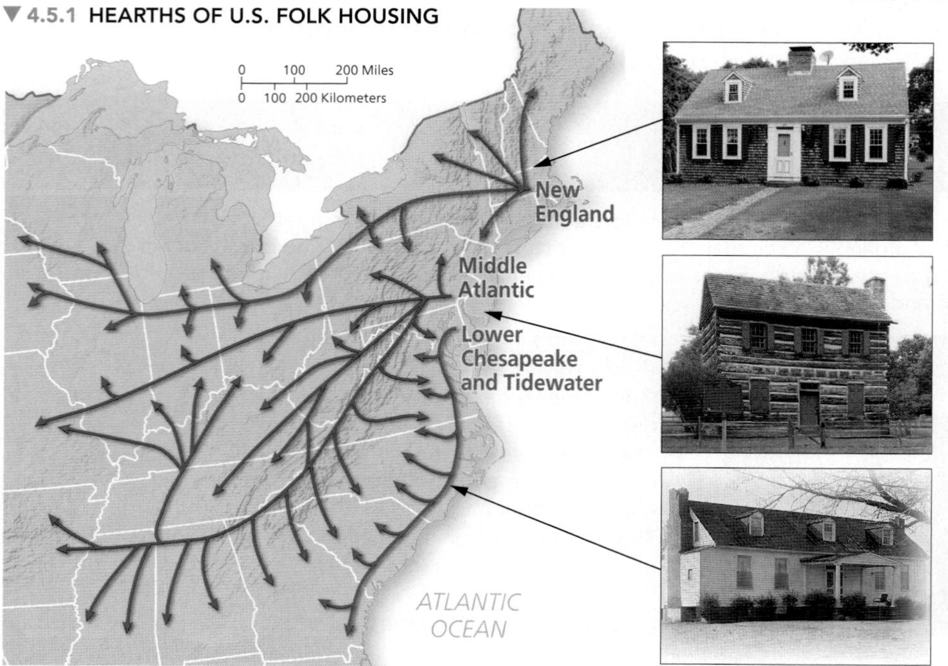

▼ 4.5.1 HEARTHS OF U.S. FOLK HOUSING

New England. The distinctive style was box shaped with a central hall. The New England house types can be found throughout the Great Lakes region as far west as Wisconsin because this area was settled primarily by migrants from New England.

Middle Atlantic. The principal house type was known as the I-house, typically two full stories in height, one room deep and at least two rooms wide. Middle Atlantic migrants carried their house type westward across the Ohio Valley and southwestward along the Appalachian trails.

Lower Chesapeake/Tidewater. The style typically comprised one story, with a steep roof and chimneys at either end. Migrants spread these houses from the Chesapeake Bay and Tidewater, Virginia, area along the Southeast Coast. In wet areas, houses in the coastal southeast were often raised on piers or on brick foundations.

Folk Food Customs

The characteristics of particular environments influence folk food preferences. The French term *terroir* denotes the contribution of a location's distinctive physical features to the way food tastes. **Terroir** is the sum of the effects on a particular food item of soil, climate, and other features of the local environment. For example, a special type of lentil is grown only around the village of Le Puy-en-Velay, France (Figure 4.5.2). The lentil has a distinctive flavor because of the area's volcanic soil and dry growing season.

According to many folk customs, everything in nature carries a signature, or distinctive characteristic, based on its appearance and natural properties. Consequently, people may desire or avoid certain foods in response to perceived beneficial or harmful natural traits.

In folk cultures, certain foods are eaten because their natural properties are perceived to enhance qualities considered desirable by the society. For example, the Abipone people in Paraguay eat jaguars, stags, and bulls to make them strong, brave, and swift.

A restriction on behavior imposed by social custom is a **taboo**. Other social customs, such as sexual practices, carry prohibitions, but taboos are especially strong in the area of food. For example, the Abipone people believe that consuming hens or tortoises will make them cowardly. The Ainu people in Japan avoid eating otters because they are believed to be forgetful animals, and consuming them could cause loss of memory.

▲ 4.5.2 **FOLK FOOD CUSTOMS: TERROIR**
The village of Le Puy-en-Velay, France, is the home of a type of lentil that is the first vegetable to be registered and protected by the French government and the European Union.

Popular Food Culture

Cultural values are a stronger influence on popular food preferences than are environmental features. Still, some regional variations can be observed, and environmental factors influence some popular food choices.

Why do Coca-Cola and Pepsi have different sales patterns (Figure 4.5.3)? Coca-Cola is the sales leader in most of the Western Hemisphere except in Canada's French-speaking province of Québec. Pepsi won over the Québécois with advertising that tied Pepsi to elements of uniquely French Canadian culture. The major indoor arena in Québec City is named the Colisée Pepsi (Pepsi Coliseum).

In Southwest Asia, religion influences cola preferences. At one time, the region's predominantly Muslim countries boycotted products that were sold in predominantly Jewish Israel. Because Coke but not Pepsi was sold in Israel, in most of Israel's predominantly Muslim neighbors preferred Pepsi.

In Russia, politics have influenced cola preferences. Under communism, government officials made a deal with Pepsi to allow that cola to be sold in the Soviet Union. With the breakup of the Soviet Union and the end of communism, Russians quickly switched their preference to Coke because Pepsi was associated with the discredited Communist government.

◀ 4.5.3 **POPULAR FOOD PREFERENCES: COKE VERSUS PEPSI**
Coca-Cola leads in sales in the United States, Latin America, Europe, and Russia. Pepsi leads in Canada and South and Southwest Asia.

Percent market share held by leading soft drink
Pepsi Coke
75 and above
50–74
25–49
below 25
no data

0 1,500 3,000 Miles
0 1,500 3,000 Kilometers

4.6 KEY ISSUE 3 **Why is access to culture unequal?**

Electronic Diffusion of Culture

- **Explain how TV and the Internet have altered diffusion of popular culture.**

Culture diffuses rapidly around the world, primarily through electronic media. The latest fashions in material culture and leisure activities can be viewed by anyone with access to electronic media. Thanks to electronic media, people participating in folk culture have greater awareness of popular culture, and at the same time people participating in the world's popular culture scene gain increased access to folk culture.

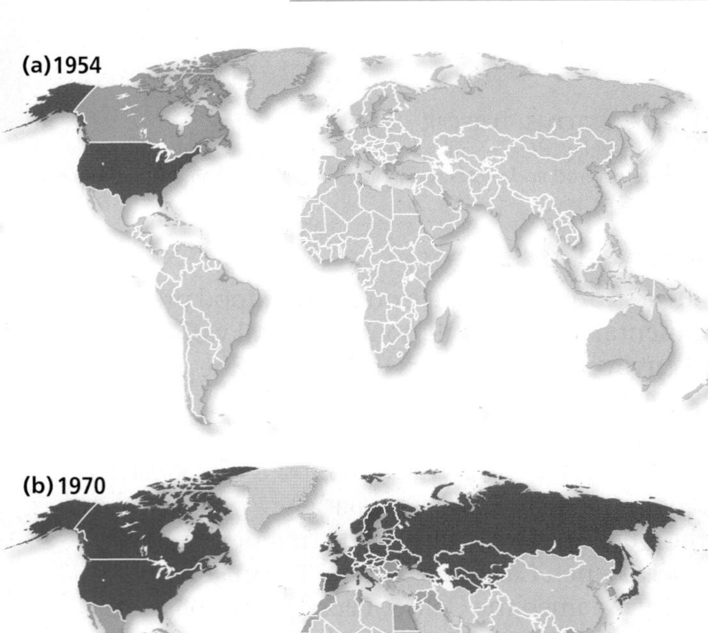

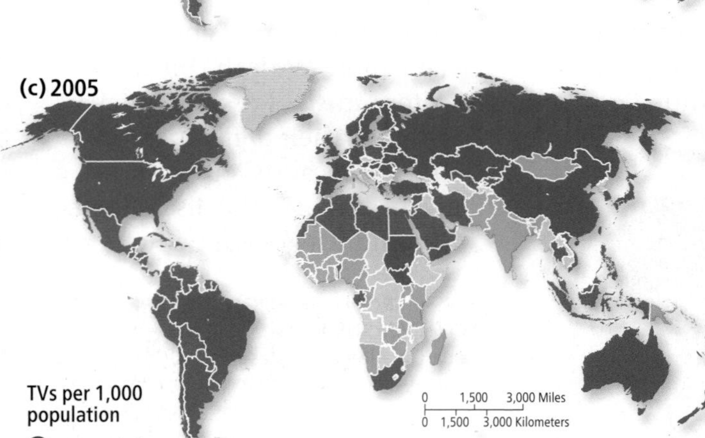

▲ 4.6.1 **DIFFUSION OF TV**
TVs per 1,000 inhabitants in (a) 1954, (b) 1970, and (c) 2005.

Diffusion of TV: Mid-Twentieth Century

The principal obstacle to diffusion of popular culture is lack of access to electronic media. Access is limited primarily by lack of income. In some developing countries access is also limited by lack of electricity and phone service.

The world's most important electronic media format by far is TV. During the twentieth century, TV supplanted other formats, notably radio and telegraph, and diffused from the United States to Europe and other developed countries and then to developing countries (Figure 4.6.1).

Into the twenty-first century, other formats have become popular, but they have not yet supplanted TV worldwide. TV remains especially important for popular culture for two reasons:

- Watching TV is the most popular leisure activity in the world. The average human watched 3.1 hours of TV per day in 2015, and the average American watched 4.6 hours.
- TV is the most important mechanism by which popular culture, such as professional sports, rapidly diffuses across Earth.

Figure 4.6.2 shows changes in the distribution and diffusion of TVs in the United States. The density of TVs in the United States has increased, as TV diffused through the U.S. population. At the same time, TV has diffused to the rest of the world, leaving the United States with an ever-decreasing concentration of the world's TV sets.

	1954	1970	2005
Density: ***Number of U.S. TVs (millions)***	32	82	219
U.S. diffusion: ***TVs per 1,000 population***	196	395	882
Global diffusion: ***U.S. share of world's TVs (%)***	86	25	16

▲ 4.6.2 **CHANGING DISTRIBUTION AND DIFFUSION OF TV**

Diffusion of the Internet: Late Twentieth Century

The average human spent 2 hours per day on the internet in 2016. The diffusion of Internet service follows the pattern established by television a generation earlier, but at a more rapid pace (Figure 4.6.3):

	1995	2000	2017
Density: ***Number of U.S. internet users (millions)***	25	124	287
U.S. diffusion: ***internet users per 1,000 population***	94	441	886
Global diffusion: ***U.S. share of world's internet users (%)***	63	35	7

▲ 4.6.3 CHANGING DISTRIBUTION AND DIFFUSION OF THE INTERNET

- In 1995, most countries did not have Internet service, and the United States had two-thirds of the world's users (Figure 4.6.4).
- Between 1995 and 2000, Internet usage increased rapidly in the United States, but the worldwide increase was much greater. As Internet usage diffused rapidly, the share of the world's Internet users clustered in the United States declined from two-thirds to one-third.
- Between 2000 and 2017, Internet usage continued to increase rapidly in the United States, to more than three-fourths of the population. Again, the U.S. increase was more modest than in the rest of the world, and the share of the world's Internet users found in the United States continued to decline, to 7 percent in 2017.

Note that all six maps in Figures 4.6.1 and 4.6.4 use the same intervals. For example, the highest class in all maps is 300 or more per 1,000. What is different is the time interval period. The diffusion of TV from the United States to the rest of the world took a half-century, whereas the diffusion of the Internet took only a decade. Given the history of TV, the Internet is likely to diffuse further in the years ahead at a rapid rate and challenge TV as the most frequently consumed media format (Figure 4.6.5).

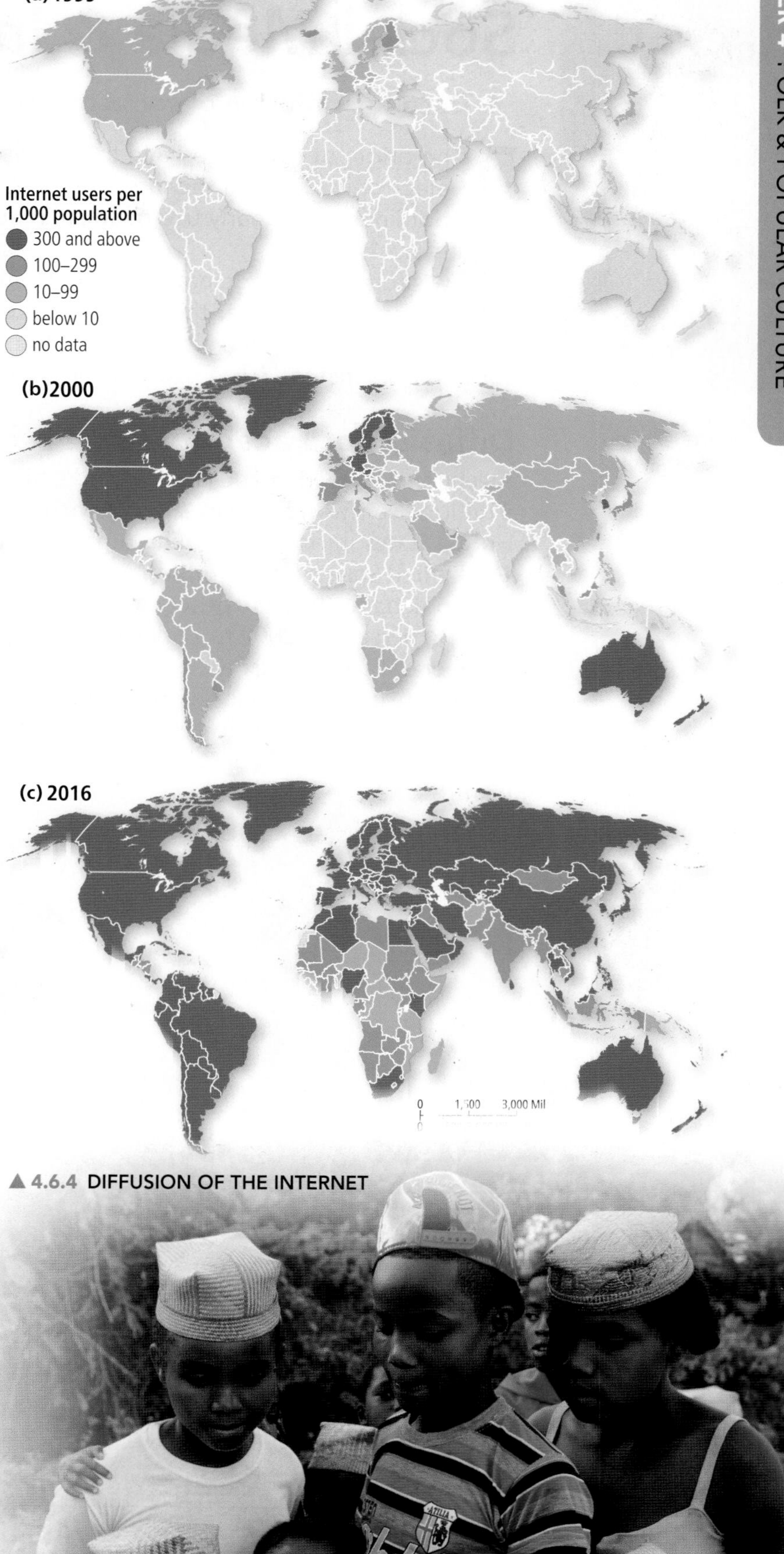

▲ 4.6.4 DIFFUSION OF THE INTERNET

▶ 4.6.5 DIFFUSION OF SMARTPHONES
Mananjary, Madagascar.

Social Media & Interconnectivity

- Trace the diffusion of social media.

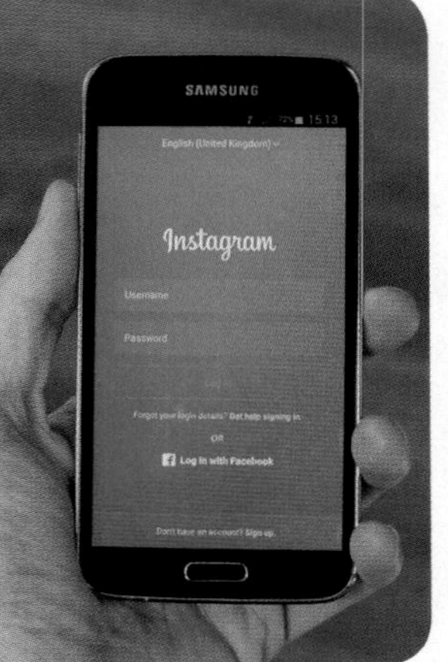

▲ 4.7.1 **INSTAGRAM** Fastest-growing social media platform.

The origin of social media in the twenty-first century has followed the pattern of electronic media in the late twentieth century. People based in the United States dominated the early use of social media such as Facebook, Twitter, and Instagram (Figure 4.7.1).

Now social media originating in the United States are diffusing to the rest of the world. However, whether the rate and extent of diffusion continue remains to be seen. Will U.S. dominance diminish as people elsewhere in the world embrace other forms of social media instead? The evidence is mixed.

Diffusion of Facebook

Facebook, founded in 2004 by Harvard University students, has diffused rapidly, to around 2 billion users worldwide in 2017. As with the first few years of TV and the Internet, the United States started out with far more Facebook users than any other country (Figure 4.7.2). The United States had 55 million Facebook users in 2009 and 219 million users in 2017. But as Facebook has diffused to other countries, the share of users in the United States has declined, from 34 percent in 2009 to 12 percent in 2017. In 2018, India is set to have the world's largest number of Facebook users.

Despite diffusion of social media and communications systems, more electronic information is available in developed countries. For example, Google Maps has extensive Street View coverage in developed countries but remains spotty in developing countries (Figure 4.7.3).

▼ 4.7.2 DIFFUSION OF FACEBOOK

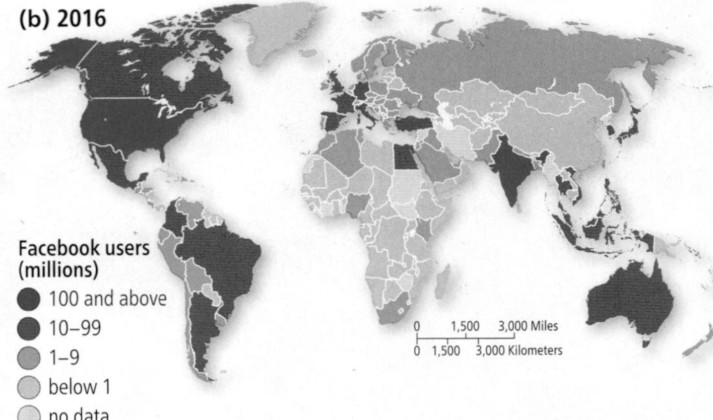

▼ 4.7.3 AVAILABILITY OF GOOGLE STREET VIEW

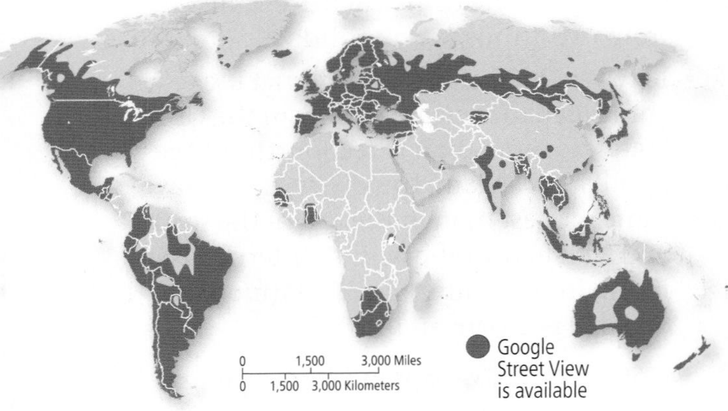

Diffusion of Smartphones

Smartphone ownership is also diffusing rapidly. The percentage of Americans owning smartphones increased from 35 percent in 2011 to 77 percent in 2016. More than 90 percent of Americans between 18 and 29 years old have smartphones, but ownership is also increasing rapidly among older Americans. Internationally, the rate of ownership of smartphones remains higher among developed countries than among developing ones, but the gap is narrowing.

Diffusion of Twitter and Instagram

The United States was the source of one-third of all Twitter messages in 2014. Another one-third originated in six other countries—India, Japan, Germany, the United Kingdom, Brazil, and Canada (Figure 4.7.4). In the case of Twitter, the second leading Twitter country is one of the world's poorest, India. This may be a preview of future trends, in which electronic communications advances diffuse rapidly to developing countries, not just to other developed countries (Figure 4.7.5).

Americans dominate the most popular Instagram accounts by followers. Eight of the ten Instagram users with the largest number of followers in 2017 were American entertainers (Selena Gomez, Ariana Grande, Beyoncé, Taylor Swift, Kim Kardashian, Kylie Jenner, Dwane Johnson, and Kendall Jenner). The two non-Americans were the soccer player Cristiano Ronaldo (from Portugal), and the singer Justin Bieber (from Canada).

Instagram is following a similar pattern to other social media. In 2017, 17 percent of Instagram users were in the United States. However, the United States was only the third most frequently photographed country on Instagram. Italy was first and Japan second.

Notably absent from the list of leading Facebook, Instagram, and Twitter users is the world's most populous state, China (Figure 4.7.6). China's government has limited the ability of the Chinese people to use these social media. QZone and Weibo are distinctively Chinese systems permitted by the government (Figure 4.7.7).

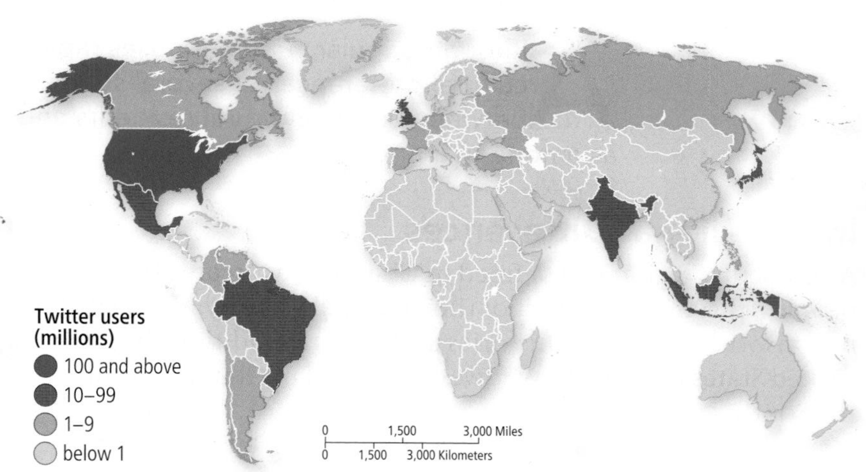

▲ 4.7.4 DISTRIBUTION OF TWITTER

	Twitter		Facebook		Instagram	
	2009	2017	2009	2017	2009	2017
Density: *Number of U.S. users (millions)*	7	70	55	219	0	120
U.S. diffusion: *users per 1,000 population*	22	123	179	621	0	375
Global diffusion: *U.S. share of world's users (%)*	51	21	34	12	0	17

▲ 4.7.5 CHANGING DISTRIBUTION AND DIFFUSION OF FACEBOOK, TWITTER, AND INSTAGRAM

▲ 4.7.6 WEIBO, ONE OF CHINA'S MOST POPULAR SOCIAL MEDIA SITES

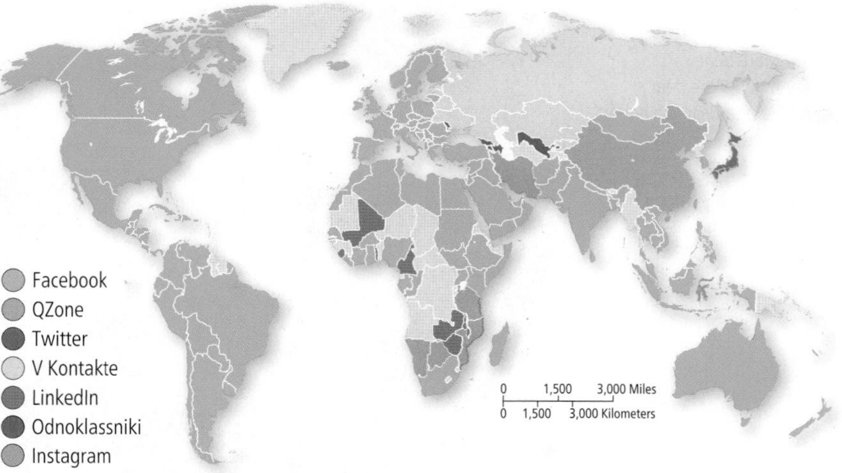

▲ 4.7.7 MOST POPULAR SOCIAL NETWORK

Facebook is most popular except in countries where the government limits people's access to it.

Geographic Differences in Popular Culture

- **Describe how popular culture varies by region.**

Although popular culture diffuses rapidly to many places, differences persist in cultural preferences at several scales. Examples can be found of differences between urban and rural residents and between regions within a country, as well as among countries.

Interregional Differences

A vernacular region was defined in Chapter 1 as an area that people believe exists as part of their cultural identity. Vernacular regions with distinctive histories and cultural traditions in the United States include the Midwest (depicted in Chapter 1) and the South.

Traditional cultural differences among vernacular regions can be reinforced by contemporary social media. For example, Twitter users in the South tweet the word "church" more frequently than the word "beer," whereas the opposite is the case in the Northeast (Figure 4.8.1).

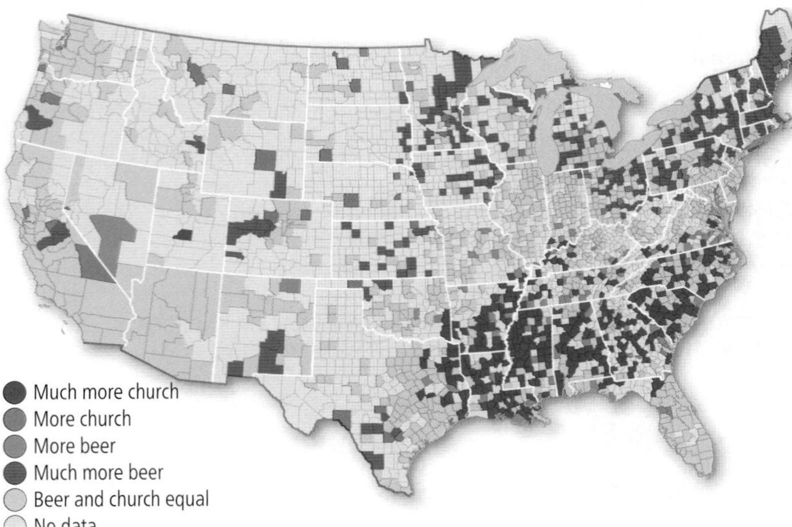

▲ 4.8.1 BEER OR CHURCH TWEETS

▶ 4.8.2 POSTER IN CHINA FOR AMERICAN-MADE KUNG FU PANDA 3

International Cultural Differences

Despite global diffusion, many elements of popular culture can vary significantly among countries. The cultural traditions of a group of people can affect the specific elements of popular culture that are appreciated. Elements of popular culture produced in one place may be regarded as controversial in another place.

An example is the 2017 Disney remake of the film Beauty and the Beast, which included a scene with two male characters kissing. The prospect of two men kissing on screen generated a controversy in Russia, where polls have shown most people opposed to same-sex marriage. The film was eventually released in Russia, but only adults were allowed to view it.

At the same time, elements of popular culture originating in one place are increasingly adopted by people elsewhere, especially young people who may be especially open to unfamiliar ideas and cultural values. To seek wider audiences, producers of popular culture try to create products that are designed to appeal to wider audiences. Hollywood producers increasingly tailor movies to appeal to people in many countries, not just Americans. For example, during the production of the first Kung Fu Panda, one of the highest grossing films in Chinese box-office history, the production team travelled to China and studied Chinese art and philosophy. The success transformed the film into a continuing series (Figure 4.8.2).

Urban-Rural Differences

TV remains the most important medium of popular culture, but Americans on average are watching fewer live TV programs emanating from over-the-air broadcast stations. Instead, they are increasingly likely to stream programs through computers, tablets, and smartphones (Figure 4.8.3).

Rural spaces, whose economies tend to focus more heavily on agriculture and manufacturing, tend to value more traditional forms of popular culture. Urban spaces, characterized by concentrations of wealth, migration, and diverse ethnic groups, may value more progressive forms of popular culture.

Urban and rural residents of the United States prefer different TV shows. Crime shows depicting values of law and order are more popular in rural areas, whereas satirical comedies challenging accepted norms are relatively popular in urban areas (Figures 4.8.4, 4.8.5, and 4.8.6).

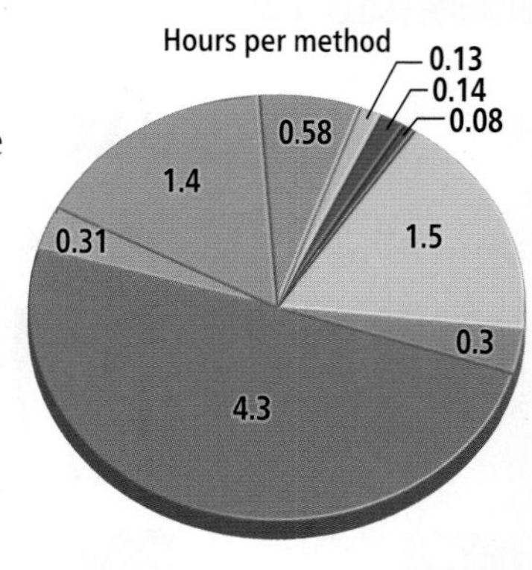

▲ **4.8.3 METHODS FOR OBTAINING PROGRAMMING**

Live TV
DVR
Radio
DVD
Game console
Multi Media device
Internet on PC
App on smart phone
App on tablet

◀ **4.8.4 TV SHOWS PREFERRED IN URBAN AREAS**

These were the shows that urban residents were more likely than rural residents to "like" in Facebook:

Adventure Time
American Horror Story
Family Guy
Game of Thrones
It's Always Sunny in Philadelphia
Modern Family
MythBusters
Once Upon a Time
Orange is the New Black
Saturday Night Live
So You Think You Can Dance
The Big Bang Theory
The Daily Show
The Simpsons
The Tonight Show
Tosh.0

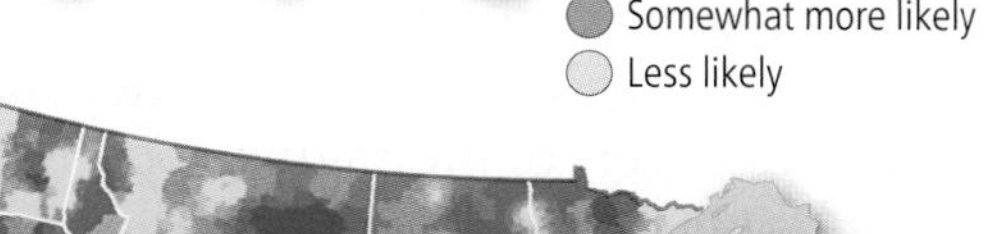

◀ **4.8.5 TV SHOWS PREFERRED IN RURAL AREAS**

These were the shows that rural residents were more likely than urban residents to "like" in Facebook:

16 and Pregnant
American Dad
America's Funniest Home Videos
Bones
Cake Boss
Criminal Minds
Dancing With the Stars
Deadliest Catch
Duck Dynasty
Fast n'Loud
Grey's Anatomy
NCIS
Pawn Stars
Pretty Little Liars
Ridiculousness
Rob Dyrdek's Fantasy Factory
Supernatural
Teen Mom
The Vampire Diaries
The Voice
The Walking Dead
Wipeout

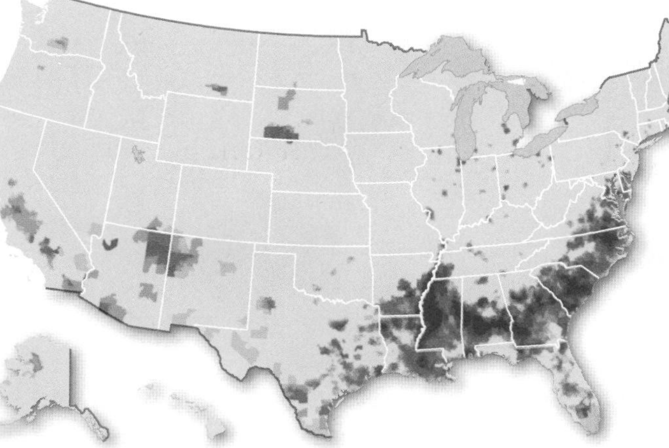

◀ **4.8.6 TV SHOWS PREFERRED IN THE SOUTHEAST**

106 & Park
Bad Girls Club
Empire
Keeping Up With the Kardashians
Law & Order: SVU
Love & Hip Hop
Real Housewives of Atlanta
Scandal
SpongeBob SquarePants
The First 48
The Tom and Jerry Show

Accessing Media

- **Explain challenges to accessing social media.**

Most Americans take for granted their unfettered access to information and communications through the Internet and cell phones. This free access, largely unrestricted by government, is not found in many other countries (Figure 4.9.1).

▲ **4.9.1 LIMITED FREEDOM TO MEDIA**
Indonesian journalists demonstrate for access to information.

Limiting Access to Media

The organization Freedom on the Net measures the level of Internet and digital media freedom in 65 countries. Only 19 of the 65 countries surveyed by Freedom on the Net were classified as "free," 31 were "partly free," and 15 were "not free" (Figure 4.9.2). China, Syria, Iran, and Ethiopia had the worst scores in 2016.

Two-thirds of all Internet users live in countries where criticism of the government, military, or ruling family are subject to censorship, according to Freedom on the Net. Furthermore, Internet freedom around the world has been declining every year that Freedom on the Net has been measuring it.

Social media users face increasing penalties, and governments are increasingly going after users of messaging apps. Because the Internet can diffuse information directly from one citizen to large groups of others, governments feel threatened by increasing citizen awareness.

▼ **4.9.2 INTERNET FREEDOM**
Excluded are countries with limited Internet connectivity (mostly in Africa) and countries with connectivity but insufficient evidence (mostly in Europe). Each of the 65 countries received a numerical score from 0 (the most free) to 100 (the least free). Countries were classified "free" if they had a score of 30 or below, "partly free" if they had a score between 31 and 60, and "not free" if they had a score above 60.

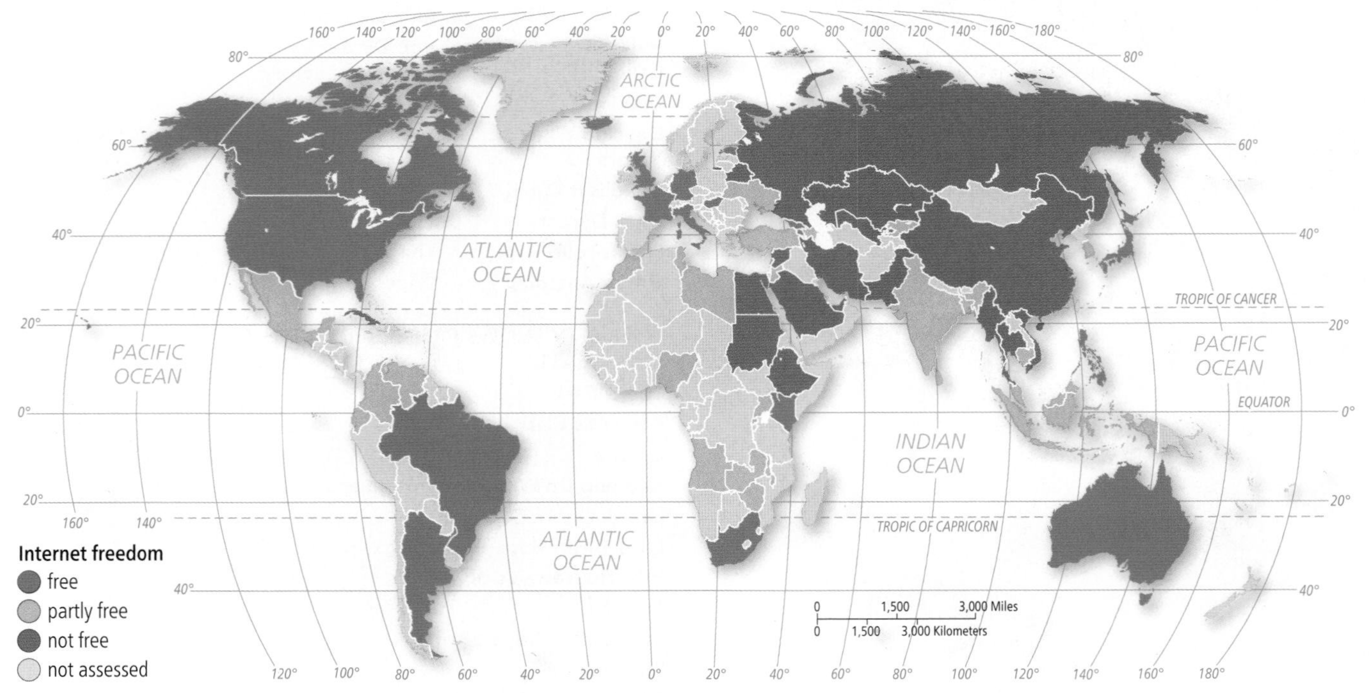

Internet Restrictions

Freedom on the Net identifies three categories of restrictions on the free use of the Internet: banned technology, blocked content, and violated user rights.

Banned technology. Governments can effectively prevent unwanted electronic technology by regulating the underlying technology platforms that are supported by the infrastructure in the country. Some governments prohibit the sale of certain models of phones, tablets, and computers. Devices that are permitted must be configured to exclude certain applications and technologies.

China is especially aggressive at restricting foreign applications. The small number of Facebook and Twitter users in China, displayed in Figures 4.7.2, 4.7.4, and 4.7.7, is evidence of those restrictions.

Blocked content. Some websites are censored or prevented altogether from being seen on devices in a particular country. Blocking Internet content continues a widespread practice with TV.

OpenNet Initiative has identified three types of Internet content that are routinely censored in other countries:

- Political content that expresses views in opposition to those of the current government or that is related to human rights, freedom of expression, minority rights, and religious movements (Figure 4.9.3). Sites through which people can sign petitions or calls for protest are increasingly censored.
- Social content related to sexuality, gambling, and illegal drugs and alcohol.
- Security content related to armed conflicts, border disputes, separatist movements, and militant groups.

Violated user rights. Governments are finding it increasingly difficult to stop the diffusion of technology. Their citizens are finding ways to circumvent government restrictions on ownership of hardware, use of software, and viewing of online content.

Instead, according to Freedom on the Net, governments are turning to harassing their citizens through physical attacks and imprisonment because of their Internet activity. Users are increasingly jailed for "liking" material considered offensive by the government.

Freedom on the Net has also determined that women and the LGBTQ community have been targeted in a number of countries for their online activities. Content and websites dealing with this content are increasingly blocked.

A number of countries require transnational corporations to maintain a local server in order to do business there. The government has the right to access the data that is stored on the local server.

◀ 4.9.3 **SOCIAL MEDIA AND POLITICAL PROTEST**
A policeman confronts a woman and tries to stop her from filming other officers as they restrain a pro-democracy protester in Hong Kong, China.

WHAT'S YOUR CULTURAL GEOGRAPHY?

Cultural geographers are especially interested in variations in the use of leisure time. The U.S. Department of Labor Bureau of Labor Statistics periodically conducts the American Time Use Survey to determine how people spend their day. Distinctive patterns can be observed, depending on age, gender, ethnicity, and place of residence (Figure 4.9.4).

1. For a typical weekday, record the amount of time you spend on the following activities: sports & exercising, socializing & communicating with others, watching TV, reading, relaxing & thinking, using the computer for games & leisure, and other.
2. In your search engine, enter bls *atus table 11*, or go to **www.bls.gov/** and search *atus table 11*.
3. Compare the amount of time you spend on each of the activities in step 1 with the average for another family member. For which activities are your times much higher or lower? Why might that be?
4. Compare the amount of time you spend on each activity with the average for all Americans in your age group. For which activities are your times much higher or lower than average? Why might that be?
5. Compare the amount of time you spend on each activity with the average for all Americans of your sex. For which activities are your times much higher or lower than average? Why might that be?

(a) **Age 20-24 years**

(b) **Age 65-74 years**

Sports and Exercise
Socializing
TV
Reading
Relaxing
Computer games
Other

▲ 4.9.4 **TYPICAL WEEKDAY LEISURE TIME ACTIVITIES FOR AMERICANS**
(a) age 20–24, (b) age 65–74

Sustainability Challenges for Folk Culture

- **Summarize the challenges facing folk culture.**

Elements of folk and popular culture face challenges in maintaining identities that are sustainable into the future. For folk culture, the challenges are to maintain unique local landscapes in an age of globalization.

Many fear the loss of folk culture, especially because rising incomes can fuel demand for the possessions typical of popular culture. When people turn from folk to popular culture, they may also turn away from the society's traditional values.

▲ 4.10.1 **AMISH** Amish children use scooters to get to school, Lancaster County, Pennsylvania.

Amish Migration: Preserving Cultural Identity

For folk culture, increased connection with popular culture can make it difficult to maintain centuries-old practices. Shunning mechanical and electrical power, the Amish still travel by horse and buggy and continue to use hand tools for farming. The Amish have distinctive clothing, farming, religious practices, and other customs (Figure 4.10.1).

Although the Amish number only about one-quarter million, their folk culture remains visible on the landscape in at least 19 U.S. states (Figure 4.10.2). The distribution of Amish folk culture across a major portion of the U.S. landscape is explained by examining the diffusion of their culture through migration.

Several hundred Amish families migrated to North America in two waves. The first group, primarily from Bern, Switzerland, and the Palatinate region of southwestern Germany, settled in Pennsylvania in the early 1700s, enticed by William Penn's offer of low-priced land. Because of lower land prices, the second group, from Alsace, in northeastern France, settled in Ohio, Illinois, and Iowa in the United States and Ontario, Canada, in the early 1800s. From these core areas, groups of Amish migrated to other locations where inexpensive land was available.

According to Amish tradition, every son is given a farm when he is an adult, but land suitable for farming is expensive and hard to find in Lancaster County because of its proximity to growing metropolitan areas. With the average price of farmland in southwestern Kentucky less than one-fifth that in Lancaster County, an Amish family can sell its farm in Pennsylvania and acquire enough land in Kentucky to provide adequate farmland for all the sons. Amish families are also migrating from Lancaster County to escape the influx of tourists who come from the nearby metropolitan areas to gawk at the distinctive folk culture. This geographic diffusion of Amish communities across multiple states has increased the difficulty of maintaining distinctive cultural identities.

▼ 4.10.2 **DISTRIBUTION OF AMISH**

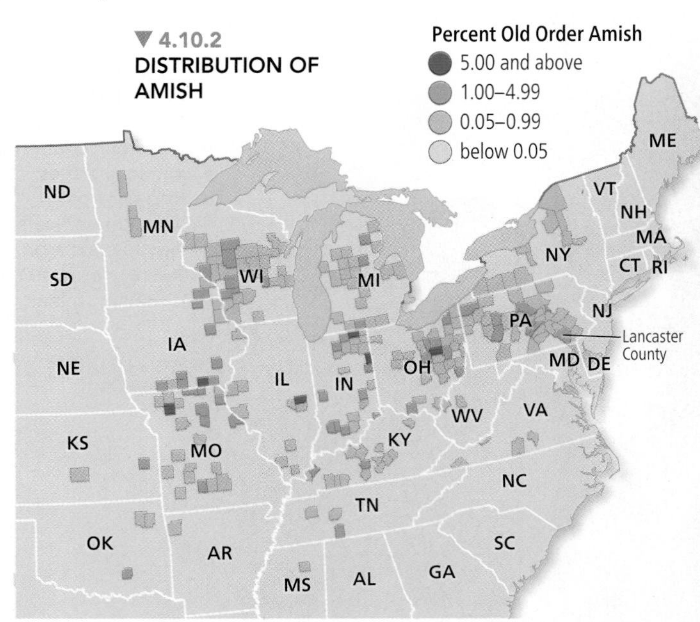

Marriage in India: Challenging Cultural Values

Rapid changes in long-established cultural values can lead to instability, and even violence, in a society. This threatens not just the institutions of folk culture but the sustainability of the society as a whole.

The global diffusion of popular culture has challenged the subservience of women to men that is embedded in some folk customs. Women may have been traditionally relegated to performing household chores, such as cooking and cleaning, and to bearing and raising large numbers of children. Those women who worked outside the home were likely to perform agricultural work or trade handicrafts.

Global diffusion of popular social customs has had an unintended negative impact for women in India: an increase in demand for dowries. Traditionally, a dowry was a "gift" from one family to another, as a sign of respect. In the past, the local custom in much of India was for the groom to provide a small dowry to the bride's family. In the twentieth century, the custom reversed, and the family of a bride was expected to provide a substantial dowry to the husband's family (Figure 4.10.3).

The government of India enacted anti-dowry laws in 1961, but the ban is widely ignored. In fact, dowries have become much larger in modern India and an important source of income for the groom's family. A dowry can take the form of either cash or expensive consumer goods, such as cars, electronics, and household appliances.

The government has tried to ban dowries because of the adverse impact on women. Resentment felt by Indian women was captured in a comedic video game, Angry Brides (Figure 4.10.4). If the bride's family is unable to pay a promised dowry or installments, the groom's family may cast the bride out on the street, and her family may refuse to take her back. Husbands and in-laws angry over the small size of dowry payments kill around 8,000 women annually in India, and disputes over dowries lead to 90,000 cases of torture and cruelty toward women by men.

▲ 4.10.3 PROTESTING DOWRY IN INDIA

▲ 4.10.4 PROTESTING DOWRY IN INDIA: ANGRY BRIDES

The Future of Folk Culture

Folk cultural traditions are increasingly subject to influences from the outside world as people migrate for economic opportunities, and opt for less expensive and more appealing alternatives increasingly available worldwide. Movie watchers are drawn to the flashiness and high production quality of Western films. Jeans and t-shirts can be less expensive, and sometimes more durable than traditional clothing alternatives. These popular culture elements are altering folk culture, even in remote locations.

Historically, the variety of folk cultures was a key ingredient ensuring diverse identities and opinions. Folk culture is challenged to preserve the vibrancy and diversity that existed before global economic and communication systems came into being.

Sustainability Challenges for Popular Culture

- Identify stresses that popular culture can place on the local environment.

For popular culture, challenges derive from the sustainability of practices designed to promote uniform landscapes and experiences. Popular culture can significantly modify or control the environment. It may be imposed on the environment rather than spring forth from it, as with many folk customs.

▲ 4.11.1 **SKI DUBAI** The temperature in the United Arab Emirates exceeds 100°F much of the year, but people can snow ski year-round indoors in this building.

In order to enjoy some popular customs, the environment must be modified in order to enable participation in a leisure activity, sometimes dramatically. Even if the resulting built environment may be difficult to visually differentiate from its "natural," equivalent, it is actually the deliberate creation of people in pursuit of popular social customs.

The spread of popular culture results in the loss of distinctive features of folk culture, and a convergence of cultural preferences across larger spaces. The process of reduction in cultural diversity through the diffusion of popular culture is known as **cultural homogenization**. Developed countries in North America and Europe have been most successful in diffusing elements of their popular culture, resulting in dominance of their material culture and social values in the rest of the world.

The diffusion of some popular customs can adversely impact environmental quality and cultural diversity in multiple ways:

- Pollution of the landscape.
- Depletion of scarce natural resources.

▼ 4.11.2 **SKIING IN THE DESERT** Indoor skiing, United Arab Emirates.

Uniform Physical Landscapes

Popular culture can pollute the landscape by modifying it with little regard for local environmental conditions, such as climate and soil (Figure 4.11.1 and 4.11.2). To create a uniform landscape, hills may be flattened and valleys filled in. The same building and landscaping materials may be employed regardless of location. Features such as golf courses consume large quantities of land and water; nonnative grass species are planted, and fertilizers and pesticides are laid on the grass to ensure an appearance considered suitable for the game.

The distribution of popular culture around the world tends to produce more uniform landscapes. The spatial expression of a popular custom in one location will be similar to another. In fact, promoters of popular culture want a uniform appearance to generate "product recognition" and greater consumption.

Uniform Cultural Experiences

Over time, the uniform landscapes of popular culture replace folk landscapes and offer a different set of cultural experiences to inhabitants. The diffusion of fast-food restaurants is a good example of such uniformity. A fast-food restaurant is usually organized as a **franchise**, which is an agreement between a corporation and businesspeople to market that corporation's products in a local area. The franchise agreement lets the local outlet use the company's name, symbols, trademarks, methods, and architectural styles. A uniform sign is prominently displayed.

The success of fast-food restaurants depends on large-scale mobility: People who travel or move to another city immediately recognize a familiar place. To both local residents and travelers, the local franchise is immediately recognizable as part of a national or multinational company. Newcomers can be confident that the restaurant will reflect familiar values of international popular culture rather than strange and potentially uncomfortable local customs.

Uniformity in the appearance of the landscape is promoted by a wide variety of other popular structures in North America, such as gas stations, supermarkets, and motels. These structures are designed so that both local residents and visitors immediately recognize the purpose of the building.

Physical expression of uniformity in popular culture has diffused from North America to other parts of the world. American motels and fast-food chains have opened in other countries. These establishments appeal to North American travelers, yet most customers are local residents who wish to sample American customs they have seen on television.

Golf

Golf courses, because of their large size (80 hectares, or 200 acres), provide a prominent example of imposing popular culture on the environment (Figure 4.11.3). A surge in U.S. golf popularity spawned construction of several hundred courses during the late twentieth century. Geographer John Rooney attributed this to increased income and leisure time, especially among recently retired older people and younger people with flexible working hours. This trend slowed into the twenty-first century because of the severe recession.

▲ 4.11.3 **PRIMM VALLEY GOLF COURSE**
Mojave Desert, Nipton, California.

The distribution of golf courses is not uniform across the United States. Although golf is perceived as a warm-weather sport, the number of golf courses per person is actually greatest in north-central states (Figure 4.11.4). People in these regions have a long tradition of playing golf, and social clubs with golf courses are important institutions in the fabric of the regions' popular customs.

Golf courses are designed partially in response to local physical conditions. Grass species are selected to thrive in the local climate and still be suitable for the needs of greens, fairways, and roughs. Existing trees and native vegetation are retained if possible. Yet, as with other popular customs, golf courses remake the environment—creating or flattening hills, cutting grass or letting it grow tall, carting in or digging up sand for traps, and draining or expanding bodies of water to create hazards and maintain the course.

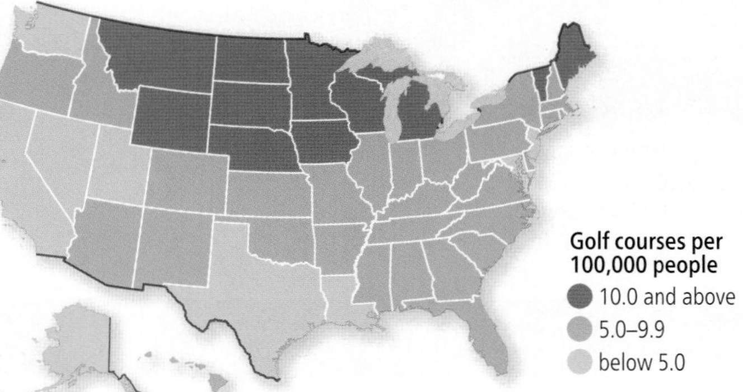

▲ 4.11.4 **U.S. GOLF COURSES**
The highest concentration of golf courses is in the upper Midwest.

CHAPTER 4

Review, Analyze, & Apply

KEY ISSUE 1 How Are Leisure Activities Distributed?

Folk culture is traditionally practiced primarily by small, homogeneous groups living in relative isolation from other groups. Popular culture is found in large, heterogeneous societies that share certain customs. Popular culture is typically traceable to a specific person or corporation in a particular place, primarily in developed countries. Folk culture often has anonymous hearths, originating from anonymous sources, at unknown dates, through unidentified originators.

THINKING GEOGRAPHICALLY

▲ 4.CR.1 **FOOTBALL** Calcio Fiorentino soccer, Florence, Italy.

1. Calcio Fiorentino is a form of soccer originating in Italy 500 years ago. Based on this photo, what are some differences between Calcio Fiorentino and modern soccer? What geographic processes of origin, diffusion, and distribution might help to explain why Calcio Fiorentino is not the predominant form of modern soccer? Do you, your friends, or classmates participate in a sport that differs from the most popular national and international sports? If so, how has your atypical sport originated and diffused?

KEY ISSUE 2 How Is Material Culture Distributed?

Folk customs derive from environmental conditions and cultural traditions. Popular clothing, food, and shelter vary more in time than in space.

THINKING GEOGRAPHICALLY

▲ 4.CR.2 **PHILIPPINES HIGH SCHOOL STUDENTS** Mansalay Catholic High School.

2. Think of a time when you or someone you know was expected or required to wear a specific outfit or type of clothing. What individual or organization was responsible for setting this expectation or requirement? What cultural values were the clothing requirement created to support?

KEY ISSUE 3 Why Is Access to Culture Unequal?

Popular culture diffuses rapidly through electronic and social media. TV, Facebook, and social media users were originally clustered in the United States, but high rates of usage then diffused to other countries. Access to social media is inhibited in some countries by lack of income or government restrictions.

THINKING GEOGRAPHICALLY

▲ 4.CR.3 **ACCESS DENIED**

3. Consider the social media platforms that are most significant to you. How might the organization of your social life and consumption of media change if you and your friends were not able to access these platforms? What challenges would you encounter if you suddenly lost access to these platforms in an emergency situation?

KEY ISSUE 4 What Challenges Do Folk and Popular Cultures Face?

Folk culture is challenged to maintain unique local traditions despite globalization. Popular culture is challenged to maintain diverse landscapes and sustainable practices.

THINKING GEOGRAPHICALLY

▲ 4.CR.4 **ZARA STORE, CHINA**

4. Zara sells clothing in many countries through stores and online. Go to the company's website, zara.com. Review the clothing currently featured on the website for U.S. shoppers. Now select a country in Africa or Asia. Is Zara featuring the same clothing as in the United States or different? Why do you think Zara has made this choice? How—if at all—does the clothing offered in the African or Asian country reflect distinctive folk customs?

Mastering Geography

Looking for additional review and test prep materials? Visit the Study Area in Mastering Geography to enhance your geographic literacy, spatial reasoning skills, and understanding of this chapter's content. Access MapMaster™ interactive maps, video case studies, *In the News* current articles, flashcards, self-study quizzes, an eText of *Contemporary Human Geography*, and more. **pearson.com/mastering/geography**

Key Terms

Cultural homogenization (p. 108) The process of reduction in cultural diversity through the diffusion of popular culture.

Culture (p. 88) The body of customary beliefs, social forms, and material traits that together constitute a group's distinct tradition.

Custom (p. 88) The frequent repetition of an act, to the extent that it becomes characteristic of the group of people performing the act.

Folk culture (p. 88) Culture traditionally practiced by a small, homogeneous, rural group living in relative isolation from other groups.

Franchise (p. 109) An agreement between a corporation and businesspeople to market that corporation's products in a local area.

Habit (p. 88) A repetitive act performed by a particular individual.

Hearth (p. 89) A center of innovation.

Popular culture (p. 88) Culture found in a large, heterogeneous society that shares certain habits despite differences in other personal characteristics.

Taboo (p. 97) A restriction on behavior imposed by social custom.

Terroir (p. 97) The contribution of a location's distinctive physical features to the way food tastes.

Explore

Ski Dubai

Pictures of skiing in the desert are on page 108. Let's see what else is in the vicinity of the desert ski resort.

Search for *Ski Dubai.*

1. What is housed in the structure immediately adjacent to Ski Dubai?
2. What places to eat are located in the Ski Dubai structure? Why might these restaurants wish to locate here?
3. Use Street View to enter inside Ski Dubai. Check out the skiing. How challenging does the course appear?
4. How are the women dressed, and what are they doing in Ski Dubai? How might this differ from a ski area in the United States?

▲ 4.CR.5 **SKI DUBAI SNOW PARK**

Geospatial Analysis

Log in to the Mastering Geography Study Area to access MapMaster 2.0

Connectivity in Sub-Saharan Africa

Sub-Saharan Africa has relatively poor mobile phone coverage and relatively low Internet usage. But there are exceptions.

Add the *Internet Users* layer. ***Select*** the *Settings* icon from the *Legend*, and ***select*** *Show Political Labels.* ***Add*** the *Cellular Phones* layer and ***select*** *Split Map Window.* ***Zoom*** to Sub-Saharan Africa.

1. What are the only four countries in sub-Saharan Africa that have at least 400 Internet users per 1,000 population?
2. How many of the four countries with relatively high Internet users have relatively extensive cellular phone subscriptions (at least 800 subscriptions per 1,000 inhabitants)?
3. How might people stay connected in the countries with high Internet usage but low cellular phone subscriptons.
4. How might people stay connected in the countries with high cellular phone subscriptions but low Internet usage?

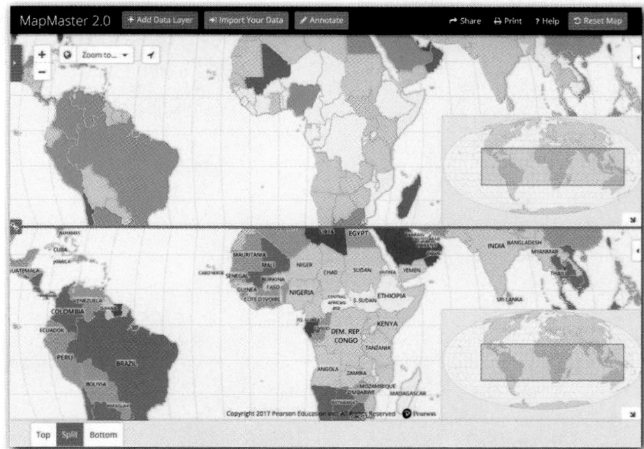

▲ 4.CR.6 **INTERNET AND CELLULAR PHONE COVERAGE**

GeoVideo

Log in to the Mastering Geography™ Study Area to view this video.

Bhutan

A small kingdom in the Himalaya mountains between India and China, Bhutan is known for its distinctive folk culture.

1. How is the fact that mountain climbing is forbidden in Bhutan a reflection of the country's folk culture?
2. Based on the video, how prevalent is global, popular culture in Bhutan? Explain.
3. List and discuss at least three reasons for the survival of folk culture in Bhutan.

CHAPTER 5 Languages

Language is an important part of culture. It is the means through which other cultural values are communicated. People are trying to preserve local languages as one of the basic elements of cultural identity. At the same time, people around the world are learning English to participate in a global economy and culture. In Europe, for example, 94 percent of high school students learn English. In contrast, only 20 percent of students in the United States take a foreign language.

◀ Learning to write Chinese characters in school, Guilin, China.

KEY ISSUES

1 How Are Languages Distributed?

Languages can be classified as belonging to a family. Individual languages and families display distinctive distributions.

2 How Do Languages Spread?

Like other cultural features, the contemporary distribution of languages results from processes of origin and diffusion.

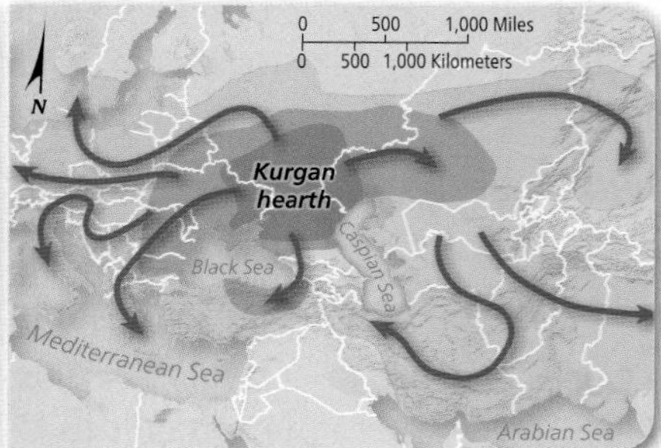

3 How Do Languages Vary Among Places?

Geographers observe variations within languages. In some countries, multiple languages are used.

4 Why Do Languages Survive or Perish?

The list of world languages is in constant flux. Some lesser-used languages are disappearing, whereas others are being preserved and invented.

LOCATIONS IN THIS CHAPTER

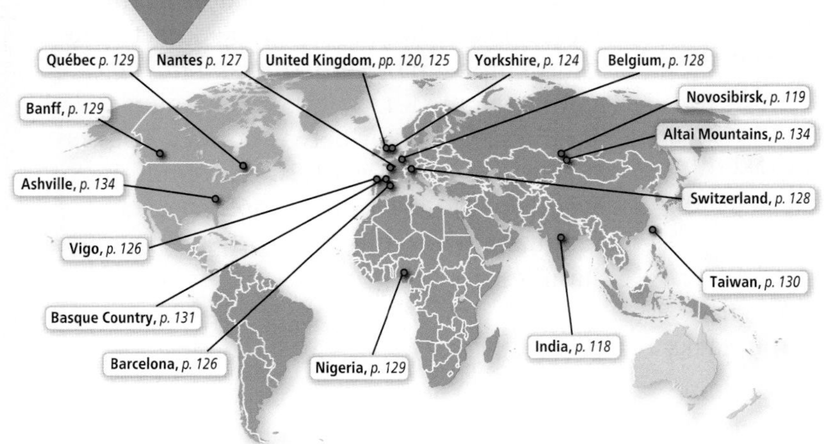

language branch
sedentary farmer theory
developing language
bilingual & multilingual
threatened language
ebonics
isolated language
vigorous language
isogloss
lingua franca
endangered language
language family
official language
extinct language
creole
dialect
pidgin
logogram
writing system
institutional language
literary tradition
language group
nomadic warrior theory
dying language

▲ 5.1.1 **TWO LARGEST LANGUAGE FAMILIES**
Indo-European (which includes English) and Sino-Tibetan (which includes the Chinese languages) are the two most widely spoken language families.

Classifying Languages

- Describe how languages are classified.

Language is a system of communication through speech, a collection of sounds that a group of people understands to have the same meaning. Earth's collection of languages is one of our most obvious examples of cultural diversity. The study of languages follows logically from migration because the contemporary distribution of these many languages around the world is largely a result of the migrations of people.

Ethnologue, one of the most authoritative sources of languages (see www.ethnologue.com), estimates that the world has 7,099 currently spoken languages, including 90 spoken by at least 10 million people, 307 by between 1 million and 10 million people, and 6,702 by less than 1 million people. *Ethnologue* classifies the status of the 7,099 languages into 576 institutional, 1,601 developing, 2,455 vigorous, 1,547 threatened, and 920 dying.

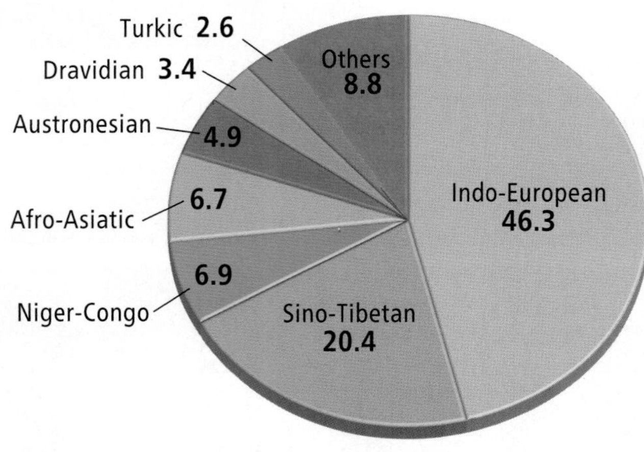

▲ 5.1.2 **LANGUAGE FAMILIES**
The chart shows the percentage of people who speak a language from each major family.

- An **institutional language** is used in education, work, mass media, and government. It has a **literary tradition**, which means it is written as well as spoken.
- A **developing language** is spoken in daily use by people of all ages, from children to elderly individuals, and has a literary tradition.
- A **vigorous language** is spoken in daily use by people of all ages, but lacks a literary tradition.
- A **threatened language** is used for face-to-face communication, but is losing users.
- A **dying language** is still used by older people, but is not being transmitted to children.

The world's languages can be organized into families, branches, and groups:

- A **language family** is a collection of languages related through a common ancestral language that existed long before recorded history.
- A **language branch** is a collection of languages within a family related through a common ancestral language that existed several thousand years ago; differences are not as extensive or as old as between language families, and archaeological evidence can confirm that the branches derived from the same family.
- A **language group** is a collection of languages within a branch that share a common origin in the relatively recent past and display many similarities in grammar and vocabulary.

Ethnologue identifies 141 language families. Two-thirds of the people in the world speak a language that belongs to the Indo-European or Sino-Tibetan language family (Figure 5.1.1). Five other language families are used by between 2 and 7 percent of the world (Figure 5.1.2). The remaining 9 percent of the world's people speak a language belonging to the other 134 smaller families.

Language Families

Figure 5.1.3 depicts individual languages as leaves, the major language families as tree trunks, and language branches and groups as branches.

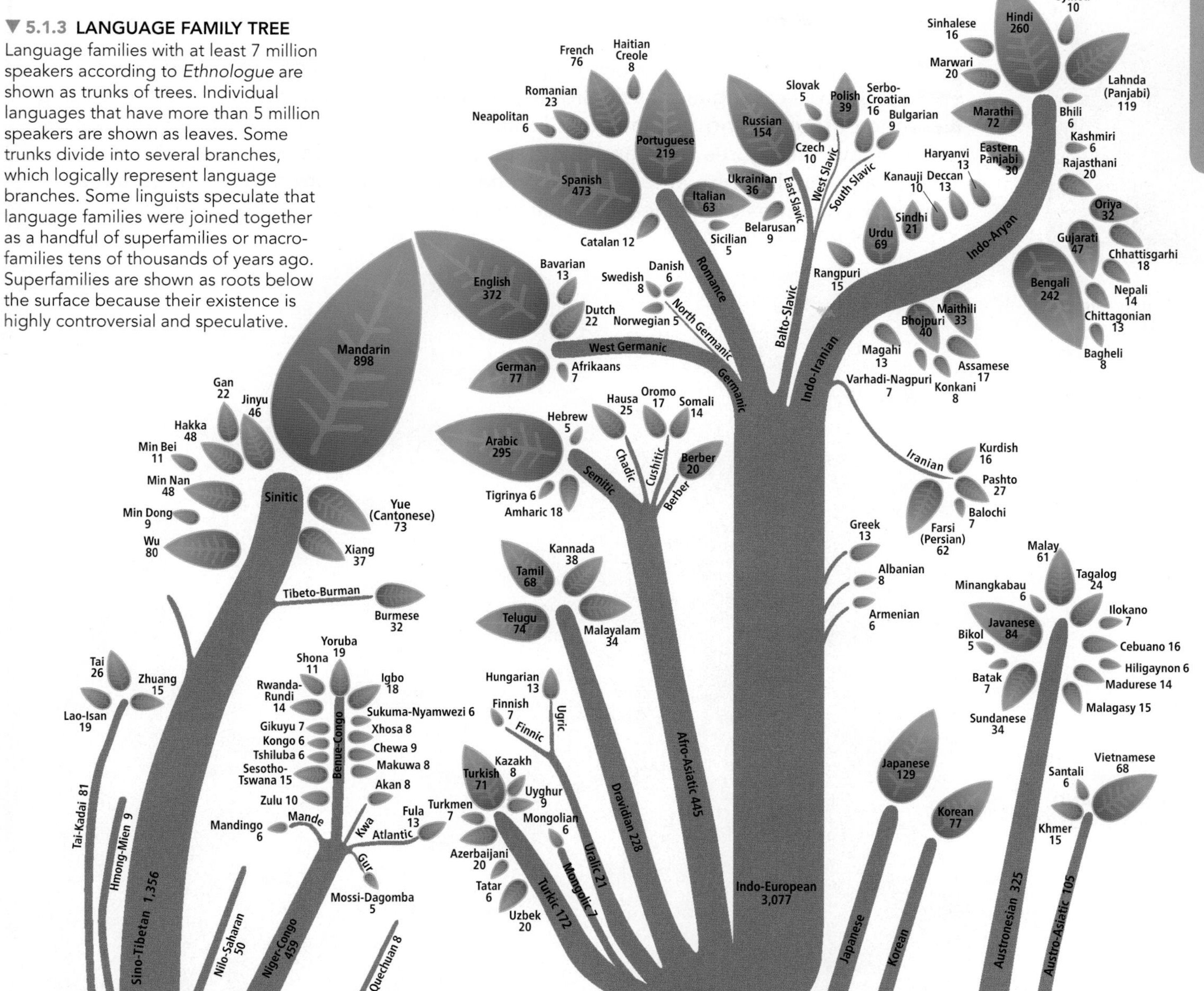

▼ **5.1.3 LANGUAGE FAMILY TREE**
Language families with at least 7 million speakers according to *Ethnologue* are shown as trunks of trees. Individual languages that have more than 5 million speakers are shown as leaves. Some trunks divide into several branches, which logically represent language branches. Some linguists speculate that language families were joined together as a handful of superfamilies or macro-families tens of thousands of years ago. Superfamilies are shown as roots below the surface because their existence is highly controversial and speculative.

Language Families

- **Summarize the distribution of language families and writing systems.**

Ethnologue identifies 3,856 writing systems, three of which are shown in Figure 5.2.1. Languages with literary traditions are most frequently written using one of four writing systems: Cyrillic and Latin (shown in Figures 5.2.2 and 5.2.3), Arabic (shown in Figures 5.2.1 and 5.2.2), plus Chinese (shown in Figure 5.1.1).

Language families with at least 7 million native speakers are shown in Figure 5.2.4. Individual languages with at least 50 million speakers are named on the map.

▲ 5.2.1 **THREE WRITING SYSTEMS** Sign in Hebrew (bottom), Arabic (upper left), and Latin (English).

▶ 5.2.2 **WRITING SYSTEMS OF EUROPE AND SOUTHWEST ASIA**

- Latin
- Cyrillic
- Arabic
- Greek
- Georgian
- Armenian
- Hebrew

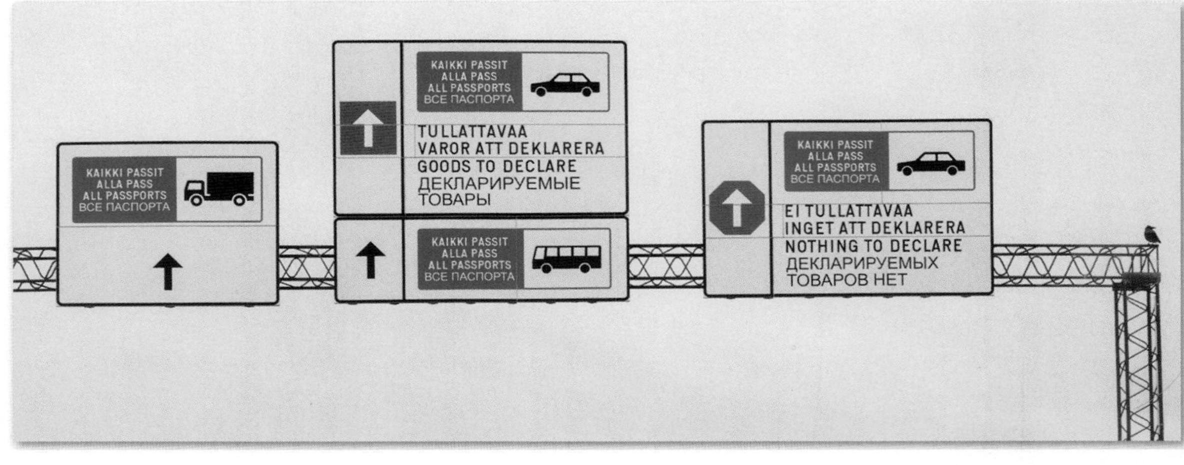

▶ 5.2.3 **SIGNS IN THREE LANGUAGES AND TWO WRITING SYSTEMS** The border between Russia and Finland. Signs are in Finnish and English (Latin writing system) and Russian (Cyrillic).

▼ 5.2.4 DISTRIBUTION OF LANGUAGE FAMILIES

Language families with at least 7 million native speakers

Afro-Asiatic	Nilo-Saharan
Austro-Asiatic	Quechuan
Austronesian	Sino-Tibetan
Dravidian	Tai-Kadai
Indo-European	Turkic
Japanese	Uralic
Korean	Other
Niger-Congo	Sparsely inhabited

SPANISH Languages with more than 100 million speakers

French Languages with 50–100 million speakers

URALIC
Traceable to a common language first used 7,000 years ago by people living in the Ural Mountains of present-day Russia. Migrants carried the Uralic languages to Europe, carving out homelands in the midst of Indo-European-speaking peoples.

TAI-KADAI
Once classified as a branch of Sino-Tibetan. The principal languages of this family are spoken in Thailand and neighboring portions of China.

TURKIC
Spoken in a wide band of Asia between China and Turkey. Turkish is by far the most widely used Turkic language. Turkic languages were once classified as "Altaic," but that name is no longer used.

INDO-EUROPEAN
The world's most widely spoken family, shown in more detail on the next page. English belongs to the Indo-European language family.

SINO-TIBETAN
Encompasses the languages of China and neighboring countries. There is no single spoken Chinese language. The most commonly used is Mandarin, which is by far the world's most-used language.

KOREAN
Each letter represents a sound, as in Western languages. More than half of the Korean vocabulary derives from Chinese words.

JAPANESE
Written in part with Chinese characters, Japanese also uses two systems of phonetic symbols.

ARCTIC OCEAN
ENGLISH
German
French
RUSSIAN
French
SPANISH
Italian
Turkish
PORTUGUESE
ENGLISH
Korean
MANDARIN
JAPANESE
Wu
Farsi
LAHNDA
Urdu HINDI
ARABIC
ARABIC
BENGALI
Yue
ATLANTIC OCEAN
SPANISH
Marathi
Telugu
Tamil
Vietnamese
TROPIC OF CANCER
PACIFIC OCEAN
PACIFIC OCEAN
Malay
EQUATOR
INDIAN OCEAN
Javanese
PORTUGUESE
SPANISH
ATLANTIC OCEAN
TROPIC OF CAPRICORN
ENGLISH

0 1,500 3,000 Miles
0 1,500 3,000 Kilometers

DRAVIDIAN
Languages spoken in southern India and northern Sri Lanka. The origin and historic distribution of the language family are unknown.

AUSTRO-ASIATIC
Spoken in Southeast Asia. Vietnamese, the most-spoken Austro-Asiatic language, uses the Latin writing system. The Vietnamese alphabet was devised in the seventeenth century by Roman Catholic missionaries.

AFRO-ASIATIC
The principal language family of Southwest Asia & North Africa. Arabic is the major language of the Afro-Asiatic family. In addition to its nearly 300 million native speakers, Arabic is also understood by many of the world's 1.8 billion Muslims, because the religion's holiest book, the Quran, was written in that language in the seventh century. The Afro-Asiatic family also includes Hebrew, the original language of Judaism's Bible and Christianity's Old Testament.

NILO-SAHARAN
Spoken by people in north-central Africa. Despite having relatively few speakers, the family is divided into six branches, plus numerous groups. The total number of speakers of each individual language is extremely small.

AUSTRONESIAN
Languages spoken mostly in Indonesia and nearby countries. Note it is also the language of Madagascar, off the east coast of Africa (refer ahead to Figure 5.4.1).

Indo-European Languages

- **Summarize the distribution of Indo-European branches.**

Indo-European is divided into eight branches. Four branches are spoken by large numbers: Romance (Figure 5.3.1), Germanic (Figure 5.3.2), Indo-Iranian (Figure 5.3.3), and Balto-Slavic (Figures 5.3.4 and 5.3.5). Figure 5.3.4 shows all eight branches, including the four used less extensively (Albanian, Armenian, Celtic, and Greek).

◀ **5.3.1 ROMANCE BRANCH**
The principal branch of southwestern Europe. Romance languages evolved from Latin spoken by the Romans 2,000 years ago. As they conquered much of Europe, Roman armies brought their language with them.

▲ **5.3.2 GERMANIC BRANCH**
The principal branch of northwestern Europe. English is part of the Germanic branch because of the language spoken by Germanic tribes that invaded England 1,500 years ago.

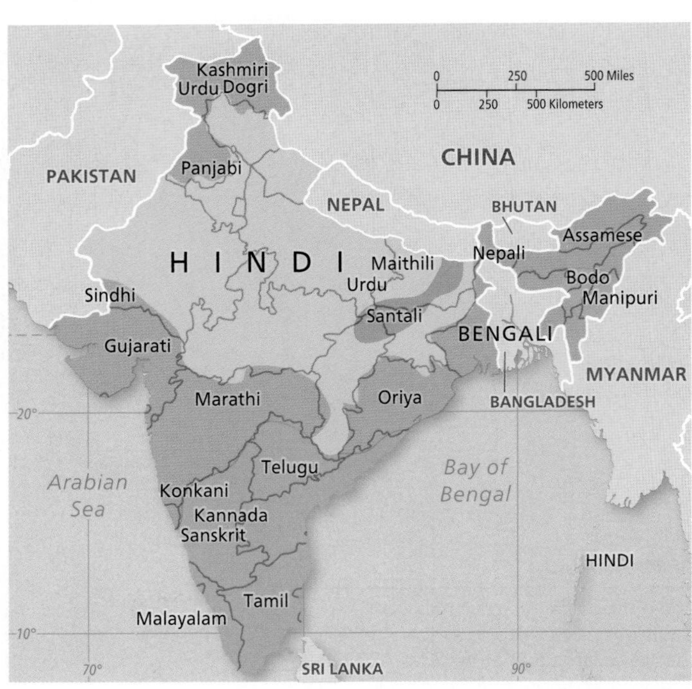

▲ **5.3.3 INDO-IRANIAN BRANCH**
Principally in western and South Asia. Hindi, an Indo-European language, is India's official language. India also recognizes 22 languages called scheduled languages that the government is required to protect and encourage.

Indo-European language family
- Hindi
- Other

Other language families
- Austro-Asiatic
- Dravidian
- Sino-Tibetan

— State boundary
BENGALI Bodo Scheduled language

▲ **5.3.4 INDO-EUROPEAN BRANCHES**

▼ **5.3.5 THE DAY OF SLAVIC WRITING AND CULTURE**

The festival is observed annually across Russia, including this procession in Novosibirsk.

Origin & Diffusion of Languages

- **Describe the origin and diffusion of language families.**

Like other cultural elements, the distribution of languages exists because of patterns of origin and diffusion. Individual languages and language branches have originated and diffused since recorded history began, so the processes leading to their current distribution can be documented.

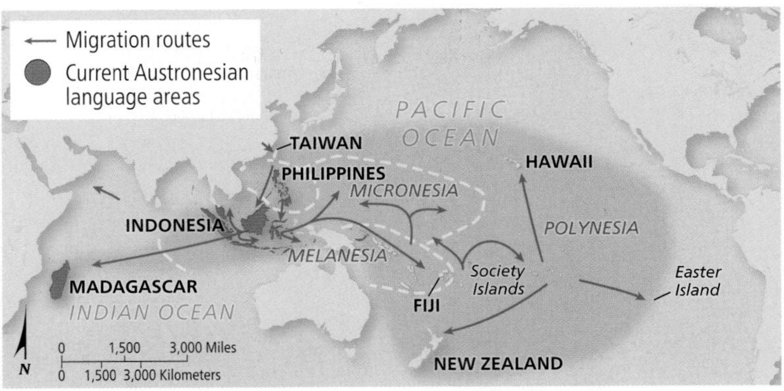

▲ 5.4.1 **ANCIENT MIGRATION OF A LANGUAGE FAMILY**
The current distribution of Austronesian languages is a function of migration of Austronesian people in the past.

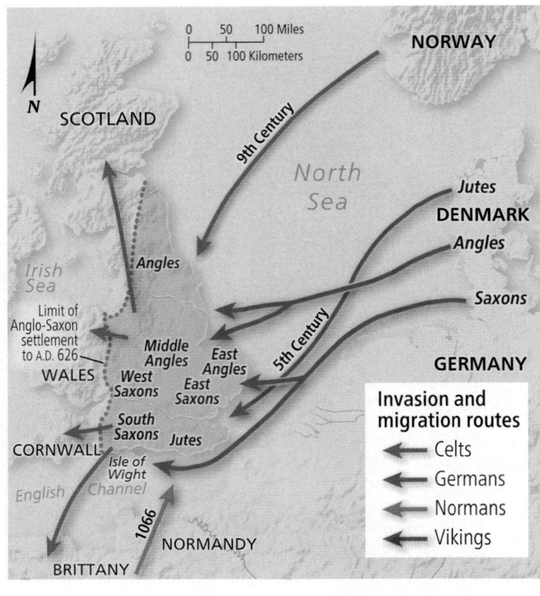

▶ 5.4.2 **INVASIONS OF ENGLAND**
The first speakers of the language that became known as English were invaders from present-day Germany and Denmark. Later invasions by Vikings and Normans brought new words to the language spoken in the British Isles.

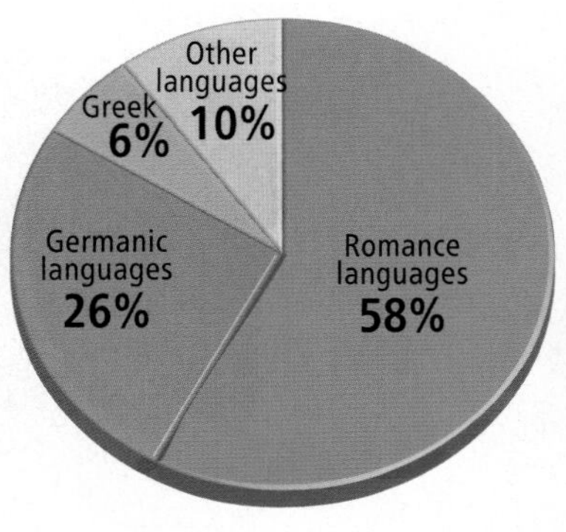

◀ 5.4.3 **ORIGIN OF ENGLISH WORDS**
Although classified in the Germanic branch, English actually has a higher percentage of Romance branch words.

Language and Migration

The people of Madagascar (the large island off the east coast of Africa) speak a language belonging to the same family as the languages of most of Indonesia and the Philippines (Figure 5.4.1). The shared language family between Indonesia and Madagascar is strong evidence of migration between these two places. Researchers have concluded that migrants sailed the 3,000 kilometers across the Indian Ocean from Indonesia to Madagascar approximately 2,000 years ago. Imagine sailing across 3,000 kilometers of ocean in tiny boats 1,500 years before Columbus sailed 6,000 kilometers across the Atlantic Ocean.

Origin and Diffusion of English

English is the language of England because of migration from various parts of Europe, including Angles, Saxons, and Jutes from northern Germany and southern Denmark around A.D. 450; Vikings from present-day Norway between A.D. 787 and 1171; and Normans from present-day Normandy in France in 1066 (Figure 5.4.2).

After the Norman invasion in 1066, French was the official language of England until 1362, when Parliament changed the official language to English. During the 300-year period that French was the official language of England, the Germanic languages used by the common people and the French used by the leaders mingled to form a new language. Modern English owes its simpler straightforward words, such as sky and horse, to its Germanic invaders, and more elegant words, such as celestial and equestrian, to its French invaders (Figure 5.4.3).

Emergence of Language Families

The emergence of distinct language families predates recorded history, so we can only speculate about their origin and initial diffusion. A biologist in New Zealand, Quentin Atkinson, argues that language originated in Africa (Figure 5.4.4). According to Atkinson, languages are most complex and diverse in Africa. Atkinson thinks humans outside Africa display less linguistic diversity because their languages have had a shorter time in which to evolve into new languages than have African languages.

Because the origin of language families predates recorded history, the evidence that Indo-European originated with a single language, which can be called Proto-Indo-European, comes primarily from words related to the physical environment. For example, individual Indo-European languages share common words for winter and snow but not for ocean. Therefore, linguists conclude that original Proto-Indo-European speakers probably lived in a cold climate, or one that had a winter season, but did not come in contact with oceans.

Linguists and anthropologists disagree on when and where Proto-Indo-European originated and the process and routes by which it diffused. Two theories are "nomadic warrior" (Figure 5.4.5) and "sedentary farmer" (Figure 5.4.6). The diffusion of Indo-European speaks to a fundamental question for humanity: do cultural elements such as language diffuse primarily through warfare and conquest, or primarily through peaceful sharing of food? Regardless of how Indo-European diffused, communication was poor among different peoples, whether warriors or farmers, but through the influence of Proto-Indo-European, languages developed over a wide area that shared some common words and structural characteristics. After generations of relative isolation, individual groups evolved increasingly distinct languages.

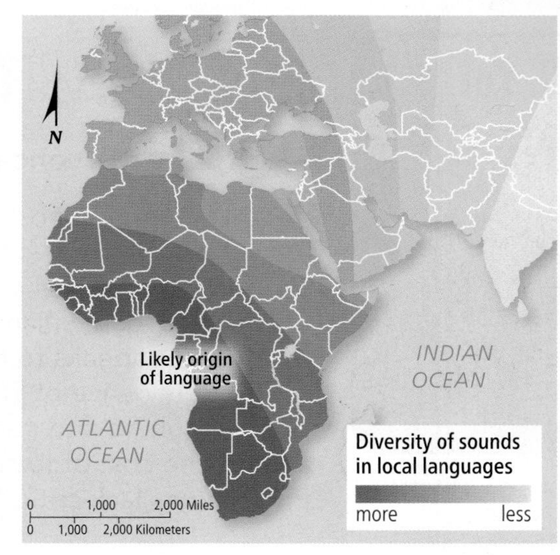

▲ 5.4.4 **ORIGIN OF LANGUAGES**
Biologist Quentin Atkinson argues that languages originated in Western Africa. Further from western Africa, languages are less diverse with fewer phonetic sounds.

Nomadic Warrior Theory

Archaeologist Marija Gimbutas argued that the first Proto-Indo-European speakers were the Kurgan people. The earliest archaeological evidence of the Kurgans dates to around 4300 B.C. near the border between present-day Russia and Kazakhstan. Among the first people to domesticate horses and cattle, the Kurgans migrated in search of grasslands for their animals. This took them westward through Europe, eastward to Siberia, and southeastward to Iran and South Asia. Between 3500 and 2500 B.C., Kurgan warriors, using their domesticated horses as weapons, conquered much of Europe and South Asia (Figure 5.4.5).

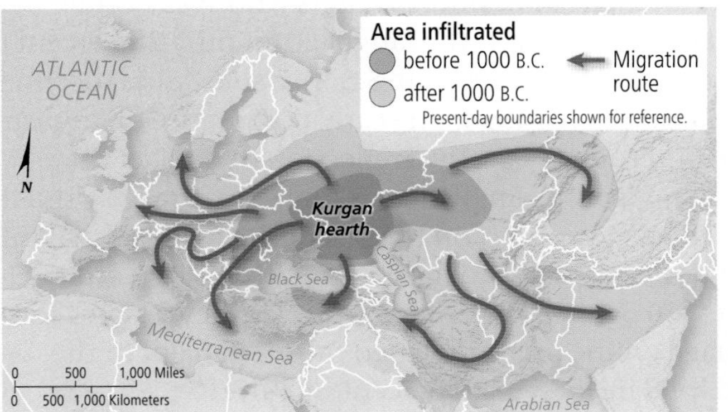

▲ 5.4.5 **ORIGIN AND DIFFUSION OF INDO-EUROPEAN: NOMADIC WARRIOR THEORY**

Sedentary Farmer Theory

Archaeologist Colin Renfrew argued that the first speakers of Proto-Indo-European lived 2,000 years before the Kurgans, in the eastern part of present-day Turkey (Figure 5.4.6). Supporting Renfrew, biologist Russell D. Gray dated the first speakers even earlier, at around 6700 B.C. This hypothesis argues that Indo-European diffused into Europe and South Asia along with agricultural practices rather than by military conquest. The language triumphed because its speakers became more numerous and prosperous by growing their own food instead of relying on hunting.

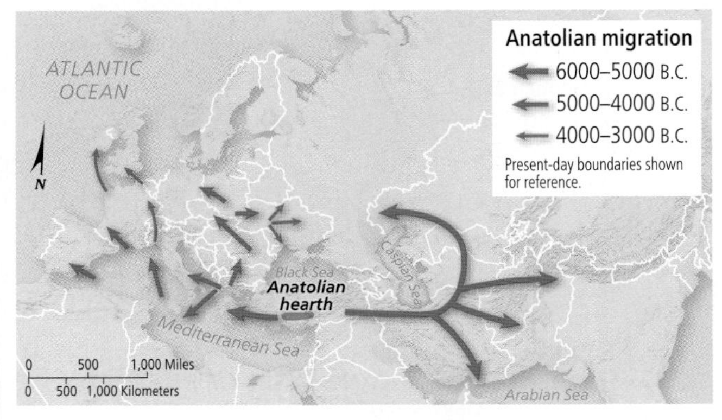

▲ 5.4.6 **ORIGIN AND DIFFUSION OF INDO-EUROPEAN: SEDENTARY FARMER THEORY**

▲ 5.5.1 **LINGUA FRANCA**
This sign on an electrical transformer in Tanzania displays four lingua franca languages: English, Arabic, Swahili, and Hindi.

English: The Leading Lingua Franca

- **Explain the concept of lingua franca.**

One of the most fundamental needs in a global society is a common language for communication. In the modern world, the most important language of international communication is English. English is included on signs at the border between Finland and Russia (refer to Figure 5.2.3). A Polish airline pilot who flies over France speaks to the traffic controller on the ground in English.

The dominance of English as an international language has facilitated the diffusion of popular culture and science. However, people must weigh the benefit of using English against the cost of forsaking their native language. And Americans who speak only English may lack critical knowledge of other countries' cultures and economies.

Lingua Franca

A **lingua franca** is a language mutually understood and commonly used to communicate by people who have different native languages. The leading lingua franca in the contemporary world is English. Others include Swahili in East Africa, Hindi in South Asia, Indonesian in Southeast Asia, and Chinese in Asia (Figure 5.5.1).

Some may speak a **pidgin language**, which is a form of speech that adopts a simplified grammar and limited vocabulary of a lingua franca. A pidgin language may be used for communication between speakers of two different languages who are not fluent in a lingua franca.

In the past, a lingua franca achieved widespread distribution through relocation diffusion, in other words, migration and conquest. The recent dominance of English is a result of expansion diffusion, the spread of a trait through the snowballing effect of an idea rather than through the relocation of people.

English 51.1
Other 11.4
Persian 1.7
Polish 1.7
Chinese 2.0
Italian 2.4
Portuguese 2.6
French 4.1
Spanish 5.1
German 5.6
Japanese 5.6
Russian 6.7

▲ 5.5.2 **LANGUAGES OF WEBSITES**
Figures are percent of all websites. More than one-half of all websites are in English.

English on the Internet

The emergence of the Internet as an important means of communication has strengthened the dominance of English. More than one-half of all Internet content is in English (Figure 5.5.2). Knowledge of English is essential for Internet users.

The dominance of English-language websites persists despite an increase in Internet users who speak other languages. English was the language for only 25 percent of Internet users in 2017 (Figure 5.5.3), a substantial decline from 71 percent in 1998. The early dominance of English on the Internet was partly a reflection of the fact that the most populous English-speaking country, the United States, had a head start on the rest of the world in making the Internet available to most of its citizens (refer to Figures 4.6.3 and 4.6.4). Meanwhile, Chinese (Mandarin) language online users increased from 2 percent of the world total in 1998 to 20 percent in 2017.

Other 23.1
English 25.3
Chinese 19.8
Spanish 8.0
Arabic 4.8
Portuguese 4.1
Japanese 3.0
Malay 4.1
Russian 2.8
French 2.8
German 2.2

▲ 5.5.3 **LANGUAGES OF INTERNET USERS, 2017**
Figures are percent of all speakers. English and Chinese speakers account for the largest shares of Internet users.

Global Distribution of English

English is an official language in 54 countries, more than any other language (Figure 5.5.4). Two billion people live in a country where English is an official language, even if they cannot speak it. In addition, English is the de facto (predominant but not official) language in several other of the most prominent English-speaking countries, including Australia, the United Kingdom, and the United States.

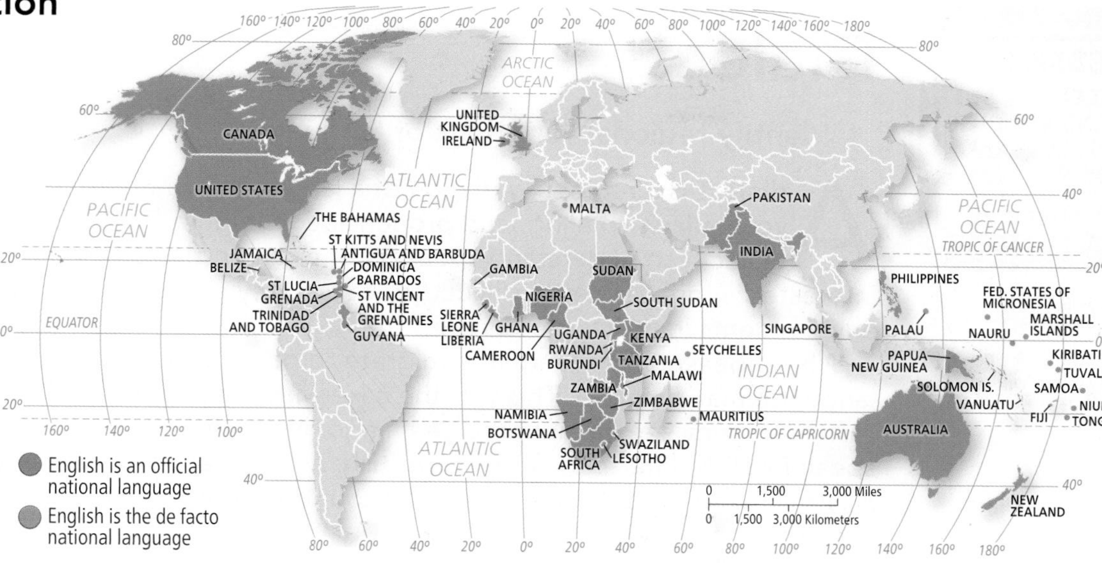

▲ **5.5.4 ENGLISH-SPEAKING COUNTRIES**
English is an official language in 54 countries and numerous territories and is predominant language in several other countries.

The contemporary distribution of English speakers around the world exists because the people of England migrated with their language when they established colonies during the past four centuries. More recently, the United States has been responsible for diffusing English to other places through the country's influence in many areas, including geopolitics, science and technology, entertainment, and social media.

Chinese: The Next Lingua Franca?

The future leadership of Chinese in social media comes in part from the large number of people worldwide who speak Chinese languages. The attraction of Chinese languages also comes from the way they are written. Rather than sounds (as in English), Chinese languages are written primarily with **logograms**, which are symbols that represent words, or meaningful parts of words. Ability to read a book requires understanding several thousand logograms. Most logograms are compounds; words related to bodies of water, for example, include a symbol that represents a river, plus additional strokes that alter the meaning in some way.

RESEARCH & ANALYZE
Languages of the United States

English is the de facto (predominant) language of the United States, but it is not official. However, 32 of the 50 states have laws that make English official (Figure 5.5.5). And at home, many Americans speak a language other than English.

1. Explore the American Community Survey, conducted by the U.S. Census Bureau. How many Americans speak English at home?
2. What is by a wide margin the second most commonly spoken language in American homes? Why is this the most popular language other than English?
3. In what region of the United States are speakers of this language clustered? What accounts for this distribution?
4. What other languages are spoken by at least 1 million people in American homes?

American Community Survey (ACS)
https://goo.gl/CyVrCU

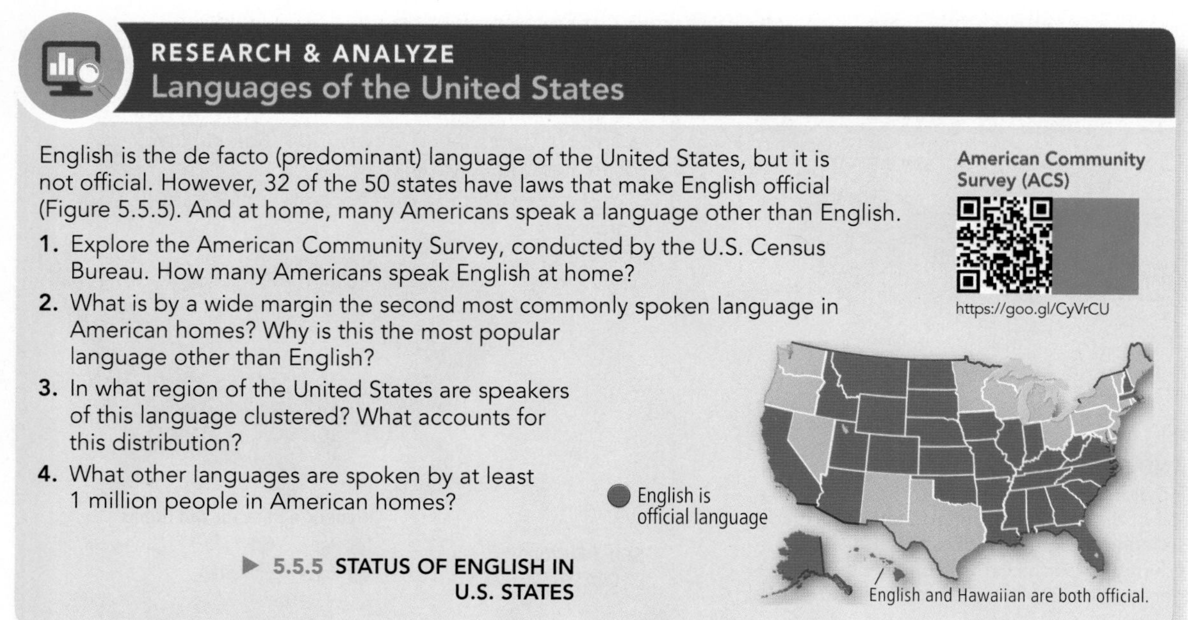

▶ **5.5.5 STATUS OF ENGLISH IN U.S. STATES**

5.6 KEY ISSUE 3 How do languages vary among places?

SEESTHA
BEATH KEEP DOG ONT
LEAD AN DEEANT PICK
FLUWERS LESS GAFFA
WILL ASK YE TI GAN
THANK YE

▲ 5.6.1 **UK DIALECT**
The sign is writen in Yorkshire dialect.

Dialects

- **Identify regional variations of languages.**

A **dialect** is a regional variation of a language distinguished by distinctive vocabulary, spelling, and pronunciation (Figure 5.6.1). Generally, speakers of one dialect can understand speakers of another dialect. Geographers are especially interested in differences in dialects because they reflect distinctive features of the environments in which groups live.

When speakers of a language migrate to other locations, various dialects of that language may develop. This was the case with the migration of English speakers to North America several hundred years ago. North Americans are well aware that they speak English differently from the British, not to mention people living in India, Pakistan, Australia, and other English-speaking countries. Further, English varies by regions within individual countries.

The distribution of dialects is documented through the study of particular words. Every word that is not used nationally has some geographic extent within the country and therefore has boundaries. Such a word-usage boundary, known as an **isogloss**, can be constructed for each word. Although every word has a unique isogloss, boundary lines of different words coalesce in some locations to form regions.

Dialects in the United States

Major differences in U.S. dialects originated because of differences in dialects among the original settlers along the Atlantic Coast colonies. The settlements can be grouped into three principal dialect regions: Northern (or New England), Midlands, and Southeastern. The national diffusion of distinctive dialects is a result of the westward movement of colonists from the three East Coast dialect regions. These have been joined by a fourth that developed in the West (Figure 5.6.2).

▲ 5.6.2 **U.S. DIALECTS AND SUBDIALECTS**
The United States has four major U.S. dialect regions. The most comprehensive classification of dialects in the United States was made by Hans Kurath in 1949. He found the greatest diversity of dialects in the eastern part of the country, especially in vocabulary used on farms. Kurath divided the three eastern U.S. dialect regions into several subdialects.

Many words that were once regionally distinctive are now national in distribution. Electronic and social media influence the adoption of the same words throughout the country. Nonetheless, regional dialect differences persist in the United States (see What's Your Language Geography? and Figure 5.6.3).

WHAT'S YOUR LANGUAGE GEOGRAPHY?

Do you have a strong regional dialect? Take a quiz constructed by the New York Times based on the Harvard Dialect Survey project by Professors Bert Vaux and Scott Golder.

1. What word do you use for a carbonated soft drink? Does your word match Figure 5.6.3? Why or why not?
2. Use your search engine, or the one at **www.nytimes.com**, to find *Harvard Dialect Survey Quiz. **Select** How Y'all, Youse and You Guys Talk.*
3. Take the quiz. Did the quiz accurately place you in your region of residence? Why or why not?

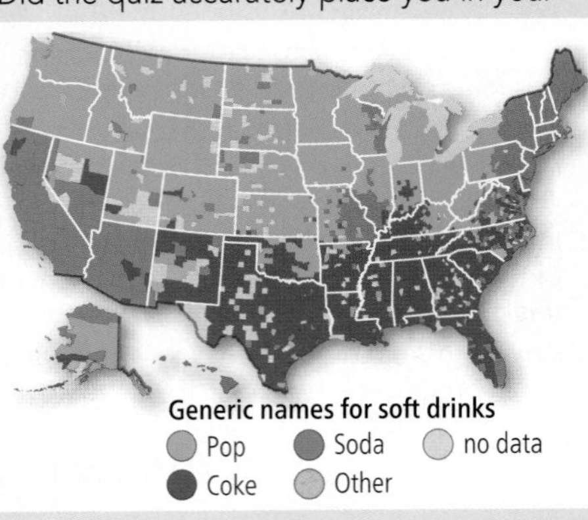

▶ 5.6.3 **SOFT-DRINK DIALECTS**

Dialects in the United Kingdom

Regional dialects of English are also found in the United Kingdom. The three principal ones are Northern, Midlands, and Southern (Figure 5.6.4b). The regional dialects are a legacy of the invasion of groups from Northern Europe who settled in different parts of Britain—the Angles in the north, the Jutes in the southeast, and the Saxons in the southwest. The language each spoke was the basis of distinct regional dialects of Old English—Kentish in the southeast, West Saxon in the southwest, Mercian in the center of the island, and Northumbrian in the north (Figure 5.6.4a).

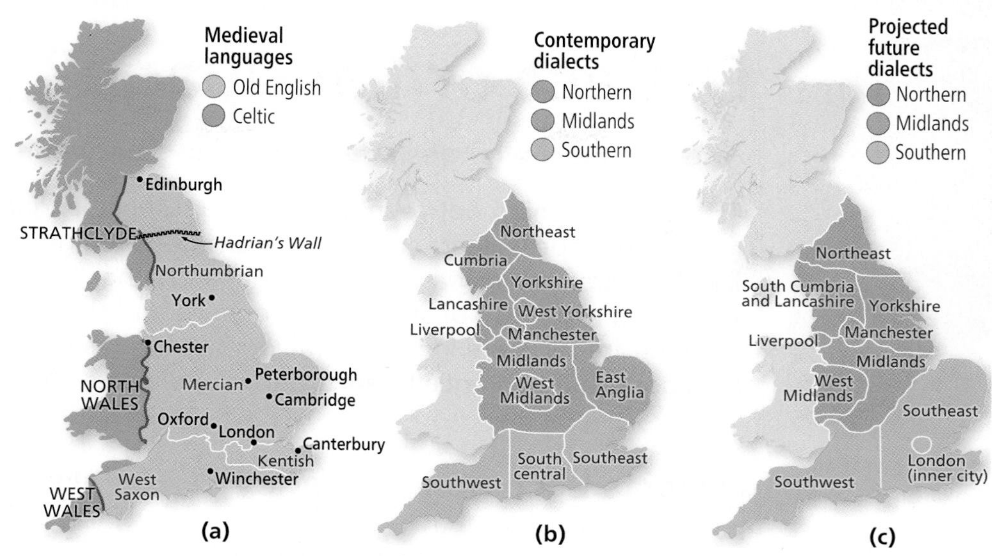

▲ 5.6.4 DIALECTS IN THE THE UNITED KINGDOM
The Southeast dialect based in London is forecast to expand because of migration of Londoners.

The isoglosses between English dialects have been moving and are projected to look different in 2030 (Figure 5.6.4c). The changes reflect patterns of migration. The emergence of a subdialect in London reflects migration of people from other countries into the capital city, and the northern expansion of the southeastern subdialect reflects the outmigration of Londoners.

Why are the dialects in the United States so different from those in the United Kingdom? As is so often the case with languages, the answer is migration and isolation. Separated by the Atlantic Ocean, English in the United States and in the United Kingdom evolved independently during the eighteenth and nineteenth centuries, with little influence on one another. Few residents of one country could visit the other, and the means to transmit the human voice over long distances would not become available until the twentieth century.

U.S. English differs from U.K. English in three significant ways:

- **Vocabulary.** The meaning of words differs because settlers in America encountered many new physical features, animals, and experiences unknown in the United Kingdom. As new inventions appeared in the nineteenth and early twentieth centuries, they acquired different names on either side of the Atlantic (Figure 5.6.5).
- **Spelling.** American spelling diverged from the British because of a strong national feeling in the United States for an independent identity. Noah Webster, the creator of the first comprehensive American dictionary, was determined to develop a uniquely American dialect of English. Webster argued that spelling and grammar reforms would help establish a national language, reduce cultural dependence on England, and inspire national pride.
- **Pronunciation.** From the time of their arrival in North America, colonists began to pronounce words differently from the British. Such divergence is normal, for interaction between the two groups was largely confined to exchange of letters and other printed matter rather than direct speech.

▲ 5.6.5 U.S. AND U.K CAR WORDS
Many words related to cars and motoring differ. (British words are in bold).

▲ 5.7.1 CATALÁN
Graffiti on Barcelona subway says "demand [to be written] in Catalán."

Dialect or Language?

- **Describe challenges in distinguishing between languages and dialects.**

Distinguishing between dialects and distinct languages is a good example of how language reflects cultural tensions between globalization and local diversity. Migration, increased interaction, and other globalization processes have resulted in wider use of standard languages and suppression of dialects. On the other hand, desire for more local cultural identity has resulted in the emergence of distinct languages that had once been considered dialects.

Dialects become Languages

It is sometimes difficult to distinguish whether a language is distinct or a dialect. The Romance language branch of Indo-European offers several examples.

Italy's languages. Several languages in Italy that have been traditionally considered dialects of Italian are now viewed by *Ethnologue* as sufficiently different to merit classification as languages distinct from Italian. Those with at least 1 million speakers include (number of speakers in parentheses) Lombard (3.6 million), Napoletano-Calebrese (5.7 million), Piemontese (1.6 million), Sicilian (4.7 million), and Venetian (3.8 million).

▲ 5.7.2 GALICIAN DIALECT
The mural, in Vigo, Spain, includes an image of Galician poet Maria do Carme Kruckenberg Sanjurjo and a poem he wrote in Galician.

Catalán. Once regarded as a dialect of Spanish, Catalán is now classified by linguists as a distinct Romance language. Catalán is the official language of Andorra, a tiny country of 70,000 inhabitants situated in the Pyrenees Mountains between Spain and France. Catalán is also spoken as the first language by 5 million people in Catalonia, centered on the city of Barcelona (Figure 5.7.1).

With the status of Catalán settled as a separate language, linguists are identifying its principal dialects. Linguists agree that Balear is a dialect of Catalán that is spoken in the Balearic Islands, which include Ibiza and Majorca.

Most linguists consider Valencian a dialect of Catalán. However, many in Valencia, including the Valencian Language Institute, consider Valencian a separate language, because it contains words derived from people who lived in the region before the Roman conquest. *Ethnologue* now calls the language Catalán-Valencian-Balear.

Galician. Whether Galician, which is spoken in northwestern Spain and northeastern Portugal, is a dialect of Portuguese or a distinct language is debated among speakers of Galician. The Academy of Galician Language considers it a separate language and a symbol of cultural independence. The Galician Association of the Language considers it a dialect, because it believes that as a dialect it can help influence one of the world's most widely used languages, whereas classified as a separate language it would be relegated to a minor and obscure status (Figure 5.7.2).

Official Languages

To promote national unity, governments have long promoted the designation of one dialect as the **official language** for the conduct of business and publication of documents. Here are two examples.

Spanish. As Spaniards conquered and colonized much of the Western Hemisphere, they brought their Spanish language with them. Consequently, Spanish is the official language of 18 Latin American states. But the dialects spoken in the Western Hemisphere differ from Spain's official version. The Spanish Royal Academy, housed in a mansion in Spain's capital Madrid, tries to promote a single standard language.

Portuguese. Portuguese-speaking countries, including Portugal, Brazil, and several in Africa, have tried to work together to create a single dialect. A 1994 agreement standardized the way Portuguese is written. Many people in Portugal were upset that the new standard language more closely resembled the Brazilian version, which eliminated some of the accent marks—such as tildes (as in São Paulo), cedillas (as in Alcobaça), circumflexes (as in Estância), and hyphens.

The standardization of Spanish and Portuguese is a reflection of the level of interaction that is possible in the modern world between groups of people who live tens of thousands of kilometers apart. Books, TV programs, and Internet posts originating in one country diffuse rapidly to other places where the same language is used.

Mixing Languages

Uncertainties can also exist in defining whether a way of speaking constitutes a separate dialect. Here are several examples of possible English dialects.

African American English. Some African Americans speak a form of English that is recognized as a distinct dialect known formally as African American Vernacular English (AAVE), or informally as **Ebonics**, a word that combines ebony and phonetics. Africans forced to migrate as slaves during the eighteenth century spoke in a distinctive dialect in part to communicate in a code not understood by their white masters. Black dialect words such as gumbo and jazz have long since diffused into the standard English language.

In the twentieth century, many African Americans migrated from the South to the large cities in the North (see Chapter 7). Living in racially segregated neighborhoods within northern cities and attending segregated schools, many African Americans preserved their distinctive dialect. The American Speech, Language and Hearing Association classifies AAVE as a distinct dialect, with recognized vocabulary, grammar, and word meaning. Among the distinctive elements of Ebonics is the use of double negatives, such as "ain't nothing".

Some African Americans argue that Ebonics should be recognized as an appropriate dialect that reflects the heritage of a cultural group. Others are reluctant to embrace Ebonics, fearing that its speakers are not treated with respect by other Americans. The determination of whether a language is standard or a dialect appropriate for usage takes place less through official organizations such as the Spanish Royal Academy and increasingly through informal communication, such as emulating an entertainer or a politician.

English and other languages. English has combined with other languages. Examples include **Franglais** (a mix of English and French, see Figure 5.7.3), **Spanglish** (a mix of English and Spanish), and **Denglish** (a mix of English and German). In Spanglish, for example, the verb "to text" is *textear* (English with a Spanish ending).

Creole languages. A language that results from the mixing of a colonizer's language with the indigenous language of the people being dominated is a **creole**, or **creolized language**. A creole language forms when the colonized group adopts the language of the dominant group but makes some changes, such as simplifying the grammar and adding words from the former language. Romance language examples include French Creole in Haiti, Papiamento (creolized Spanish) in Netherlands Antilles (West Indies), and Portuguese Creole in the Cape Verde Islands off the African coast.

▶ 5.7.3 FRANGLAIS
The name of the cafe in Nantes, France, is a mix of English ("death") and French ("porc").

Multilingual Places

- **Explain how different countries manage linguistic diversity.**

Difficulties can arise among cultural groups within a country if they speak different languages. However, countries have devised various strategies to promote peaceful coexistence among speakers of multiple languages.

Switzerland: Institutionalized Diversity

Figure 5.3.4 (Indo-European languages) shows a boundary between the Romance and Germanic branches running through the middle of two small European countries, Belgium and Switzerland. Belgium has had more difficulty than Switzerland in reconciling the interests of the different language speakers.

Switzerland has four official languages—German (used by 64 percent of the population), French (20 percent), Italian (7 percent), and Romansh (1 percent). These four languages predominate in different parts of the country (Figure 5.8.1). Swiss voters made Romansh an official language in a 1938 referendum, despite the small percentage of people who use the language.

Switzerland peacefully exists with multiple languages. Two-thirds of Swiss report that they use more than one language at least once a week. The Swiss, relatively tolerant of citizens who speak other languages, have institutionalized cultural diversity by creating a system of government that places considerable power in small communities. Decisions are frequently made by voter referenda.

▶ **5.8.1 LANGUAGE DIVERSITY IN SWITZERLAND**
Switzerland has four official languages that predominate in different regions of the country.

Predominant languages
- German
- Italian
- French
- Romansh

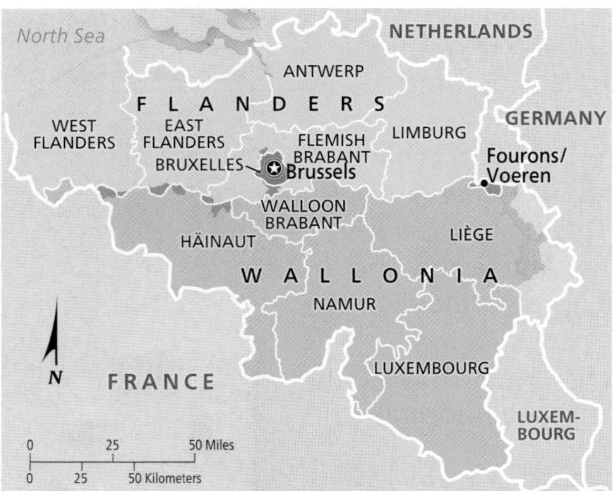

▶ **5.8.2 LANGUAGE DIVERSITY IN BELGIUM**
Flemings in the north speak Flemish, a Dutch dialect. Walloons in the south speak French.

- Flemings (speaking Flemish)
- Walloons (speaking French)
- Germans
- Flemings and Walloons (legally bilingual)

Protected minorities
- Walloons in Flanders
- Flemings in Wallonia
- Germans in Wallonia

Belgium: Barely Speaking

The language boundary sharply divides the country into two regions. Southern Belgians (known as Walloons) speak French, whereas northern Belgians (known as Flemings) speak Flemish, a dialect of the Germanic language Dutch (Figure 5.8.2). Brussels, the capital city, is officially bilingual, and signs are in both French and Flemish. In addition, a small area in eastern Belgium is German-speaking. Most Flemings can speak French but few Walloons can speak Dutch.

Economic and political differences have aggravated antagonism between the Flemings and Walloons. Historically, the Walloons dominated Belgium's economy and politics, and French was the official state language. But in recent years Flanders has been much more prosperous than Wallonia, and the Flemish-speaking northerners do not wish to see their taxes spent in the poorer south.

In response to pressure from Flemish speakers, Belgium has been divided into two autonomous regions, Flanders and Wallonia. Each elects an assembly that controls cultural affairs, public health, road construction, and urban development in its region. But for many in Flanders, regional autonomy is not enough. They want to see Belgium divided into two independent countries. Were that to occur, Flanders would be one of Europe's richest countries and Wallonia one of the poorest.

Canada: Bilingual Autonomy

English is the language most often spoken at home for 57 percent of Canadians, French for 21 percent, and another language for 22 percent. French speakers are clustered in Québec, where they account for 86 percent of the province's population (Figure 5.8.3). Colonized by the French in the seventeenth century, Québec was captured by the British in 1763, and in 1867 it became one of the provinces in the Confederation of Canada.

English and French are both official languages in Canada (Figure 5.8.4), but French is the sole official language of Québec. To minimize the diffusion of English, Québec avoids English words that are used in other French-speaking places, including France. For example, red octagonal road signs say STOP in France and ARRÊT in Québec, and unwanted email is spam in France and pourriel in Québec.

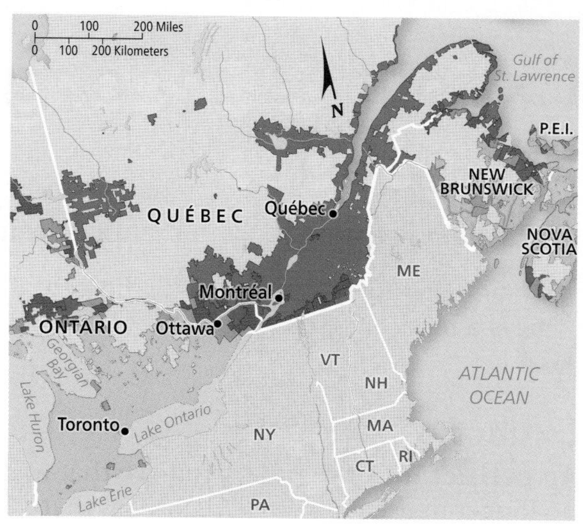

◀ **5.8.3 LANGUAGE DIVERSITY IN CANADA**
Canada has two official languages. French predominates in Québec and English elsewhere.

Percent French speakers
- 88–100
- 63.4–87.9
- 25.1–63.3
- 5.1–25
- 0–5
- Sparsely inhabited

▶ **5.8.4 BILINGUAL CANADA**
National Park sign in English and French, Canada's two official languages.

Nigeria: Spatial Compromise

Africa's most populous country, Nigeria, displays tensions that can arise from the presence of many speakers of many languages. Nigeria has 521 distinct languages, according to *Ethnologue*, but only three (Hausa, Igbo, and Yoruba) are used by more than 10 percent of the country's population (Figure 5.8.5).

Groups living in different regions of Nigeria have often battled. The southern Igbos attempted to secede from Nigeria during the 1960s, and northerners have repeatedly claimed that the Yorubas discriminate against them. To reduce these regional tensions, the government has moved the capital from Lagos in the Yoruba-dominated southwest to Abuja in the center of the country, where none of the three major languages predominates.

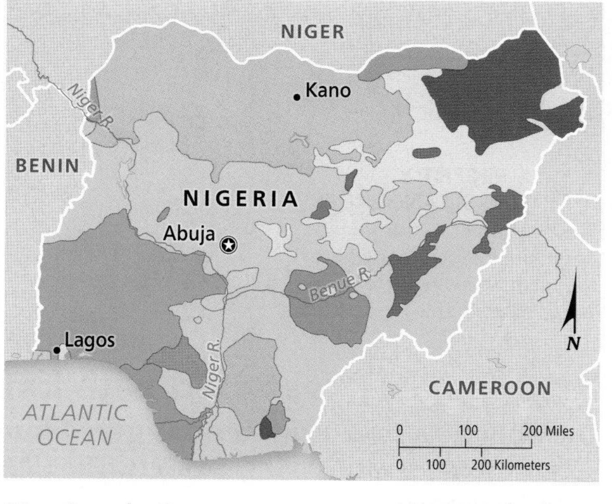

Niger-Congo family
- Adamawa-Fulfulde
- Anaang
- Berom
- Ebira
- Edo
- Ibibio
- Igbo
- Izon
- Nigerian Fulfulde
- Tiv
- Yoruba
- Other peoples

Afro-Asiatic family
- Hausa
- Other peoples

Nilo-Saharan family
- Kanuri
- Other peoples

All languages with over 1 million speakers

◀ **5.8.5 LANGUAGE DIVERSITY IN NIGERIA**
Hausa, Igbo, and Yoruba are the most widely used languages.

Extinct & Endangered Languages

- Explain reasons for the disappearance of languages.

Some languages disappear, whereas others flourish. The distribution of a language is a measure of the ability of a cultural group to retain a distinctive identity.

Extinct Languages

An **extinct language** is a language that was once used by people in daily activities but is no longer in use. *Ethnologue* estimates that 360 languages have become extinct since 1950. The United Nations identifies 228 recently extinct languages. For example, on Taiwan, a small island of 36,000 square kilometers (slightly larger than Maryland), nine languages belonging to the Austronesian family have recently become extinct (Figure 5.9.1).

In the United States, many of the nearly 300 languages once spoken by Native Americans have become extinct (Figure 5.9.2). For example, Edwin Benson was the last fluent speaker of Mandan, a language belonging to the Siouan family. Dr. Benson taught the language at Twin Buttes (North Dakota) Elementary School. When Dr. Benson died on December 9, 2016, the Mandan language became extinct.

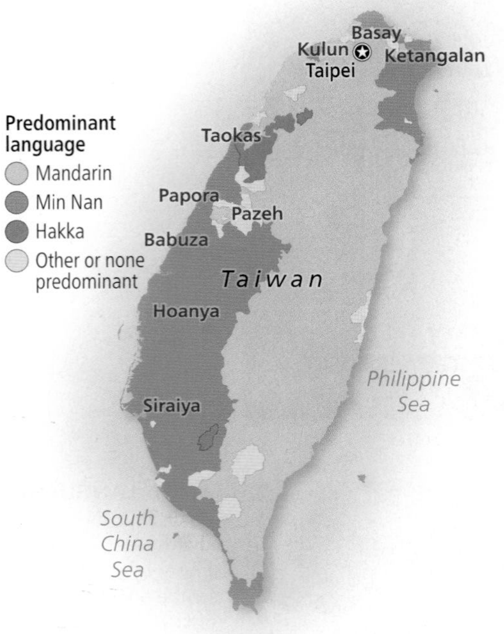

▲ 5.9.1 TAIWAN LANGUAGES The three most widely used languages (Mandarin, Min Nan, and Hakka) belong to the Sino-Tibetan family (refer to Figure 5.1.3). The languages named in red are extinct.

► 5.9.2 RECENTLY EXTINCT U.S. LANGUAGES The dots point to the approximate locations where the recently-extinct languages were last spoken.

Languages Threatened with Extinction

The United Nations defines **endangered language** as a language at risk of extinction because it has few surviving speakers. The UN considers 2,463 languages to face various levels of endangerment:

- 591 vulnerable languages are spoken by children, but only in some places.
- 639 endangered languages are no longer taught to children as their principal language at home.
- 537 severely endangered languages are spoken by older generations, but parents do not speak them with their children or among themselves.
- 576 critically endangered languages are spoken only by older people, and only infrequently.

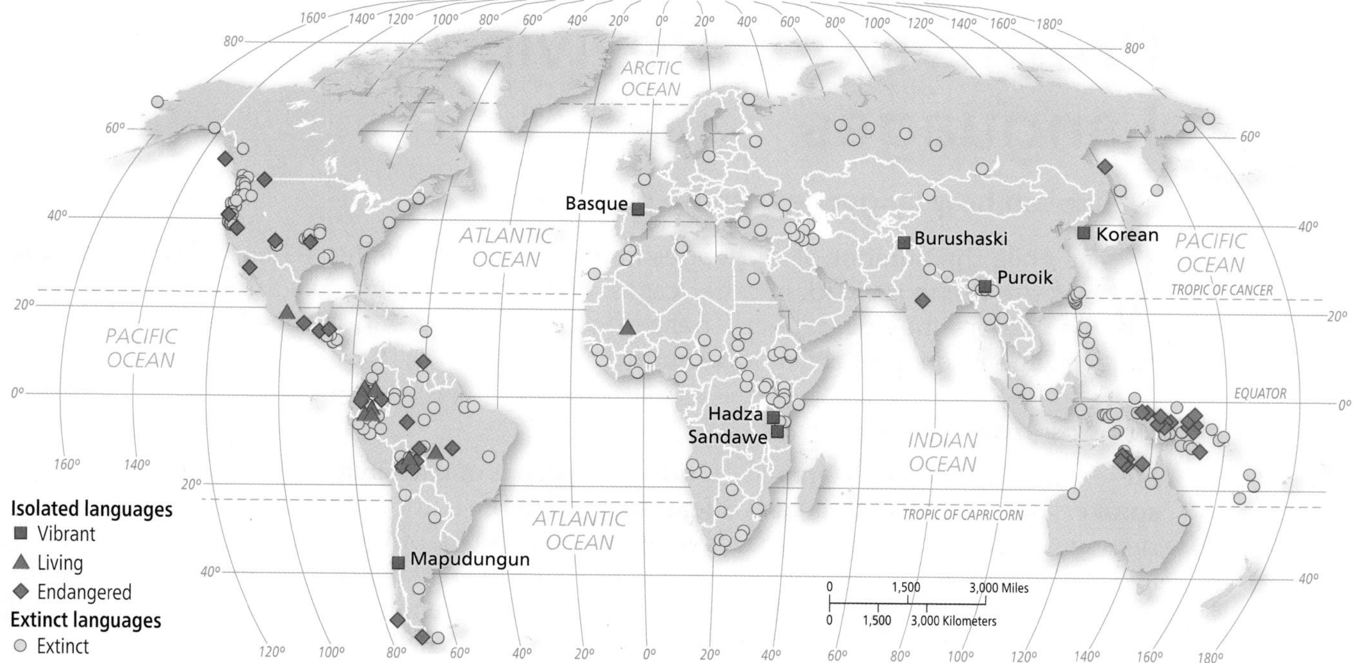

▲ 5.9.3 **EXTINCT AND ISOLATED LANGUAGES**

Isolated Languages

Some lesser-used languages have survived in the modern world, even in proximity to the leading world languages. An **isolated language** is a language unrelated to any other and therefore not attached to any language family. Similarities and differences between languages—our main form of communication—are a measure of the degree of interaction among groups of people. Isolated languages arise through lack of interaction with speakers of other languages.

The status of an isolated language is considered vibrant if it is in full use in the community, and it is being learned by children as their first language. Only seven isolated languages in the world are classified as vibrant: Hadza and Sandawe in Africa; Burushashki, Korean, and Puroik (also called Sulung) in Asia; Basque in Europe; and Mapudungun in South America (Figure 5.9.3). Other isolated languages are considered to be dying.

Basque, called Euskara by the Basque people, is the sole example of a vibrant isolated language in Europe. It is apparently the only language currently spoken in the region that survives from the period before the arrival of Indo-European speakers. No attempt to link Basque to the common origin of the other European languages has been successful.

Basque may have once been spoken over a wider area but was abandoned where its speakers came in contact with Indo-Europeans. It is now the first language of around 750,000 people in the Pyrenees Mountains of northern Spain and southwestern France (refer to Figure 5.3.1, the gray area in northern Spain). Basque's lack of connection to other languages reflects the isolation of the Basque people in their mountainous homeland. This isolation has helped them preserve their language in the face of the wide diffusion of Indo-European languages (Figure 5.9.4).

▶ 5.9.4 **BASQUE PROTEST**
Banner written in Basque says "Full amnesty for prisoners."

Preserving & Reviving Languages

- **Explain how languages can be preserved.**

While the number of languages in the world is declining, a handful of languages are being revived. In other cases, endangered languages are being preserved before they go extinct. These efforts reflect the importance that groups place on language as an element of local culture.

Preserving Languages

Preservation of the Celtic branch of Indo-European is of particular interest to English speakers because these languages offer insights into the cultural heritage of places that now speak English. Celtic languages were spoken in much of Western Europe 2,000 years ago. Today, Celtic languages survive in remote parts of Scotland, Wales, and Ireland, as well as on the Brittany peninsula of France (Figure 5.10.1). Recent efforts have prevented their extinction, but the numbers reported here are generally lower than a decade ago.

Welsh. Wales—the name derived from the Germanic invaders' word for foreign—was conquered by the English in 1283. Welsh was the dominant language of Wales until the nineteenth century, when many English speakers migrated there to work in coal mines and factories. A 2014 census found 580,000 Welsh speakers in Wales, 23 percent of the population, mostly in the western part of Wales, furthest from England. In 2011, the government of the United Kingdom made Welsh the official language in Wales. All local governments and utility companies are obliged to provide services in Welsh.

▼ 5.10.1 CELTIC LANGUAGES

Irish. Irish Gaelic is an official language of the Republic of Ireland, along with English. According to Ireland's 2016 Census, 74,000 people use Irish as a daily language and 1.8 million are able to speak it. Irish was once the principal language of Ireland, but when the country was a colony of the United Kingdom English was imposed. As in Wales, children are now required to learn Irish in school, signs are in Irish, and TV and radio broadcasts use the language.

Breton. In Brittany—like Cornwall, an isolated peninsula that juts out into the Atlantic Ocean—around 225,000 people speak Breton regularly, including around one-fourth of the people in the most isolated western-most portion of Brittany. Breton differs from the other Celtic languages in that it has more French words. Breton is not recognized as an official language in France.

Scottish. Around 59,000 people speak Scottish Gaelic. An extensive body of literature exists in the language, including the Robert Burns poem Auld Lang Syne ("old long since"), the basis for the popular New Year's Eve song. Gaelic was carried from Ireland to Scotland about 1,500 years ago.

Cornish. Cornish became extinct in 1777, with the death of the language's last known native speaker. The language was revived in the 1920s, but only a few hundred people are fluent, and no one uses it as their first language.

Growing Languages

Languages that have become extinct or nearly extinct can be revived and returned to daily use. Two examples are Hebrew and Myaamia.

Hebrew. Hebrew was once rarely used but is more commonly used now. Most of the Jewish Bible and Christian Old Testament were written in Hebrew. A language of daily activity in biblical times, Hebrew diminished in use in the fourth century B.C. and was thereafter retained primarily for Jewish religious services. At the time of Jesus, most people in present-day Israel spoke Aramaic, which in turn was replaced by Arabic.

When the State of Israel was established as an independent country in 1948, Hebrew became one of the new country's two official languages, along with Arabic. Hebrew was chosen because the Jewish population of Israel consisted of refugees and migrants from many countries who spoke many languages. Because Hebrew was still used in Jewish prayers, no other language could so symbolically unify the disparate cultural groups in the new country.

The task of making Hebrew a modern language was led by Eliezer Ben-Yehuda, who is credited with the invention of several thousand new Hebrew words—related when possible to ancient ones—and the creation of the first modern Hebrew dictionary.

Myaamia. The Miami Native American Tribe traditionally spoke the Myaamia language (listed in *Ethnologue* as Miami), bringing it with them until after their migration in the nineteenth century from their ancestral homelands in the Lower Great Lakes to northeastern Oklahoma. The last native speakers died in the 1960s.

▲ 5.10.2 **REVIVING THE MYAAMIA LANGUAGE**

Daryl Baldwin, a citizen of the Miami Tribe of Oklahoma and Director of the Myaamia Center at Miami University in Ohio, has acquired second language proficiency in Myaamia. Baldwin's children learned Myaamia as their first language in the home—the first in a half-century to be first-language speakers of the language (Figure 5.10.2). As part of the revival of the Myaamia language, an online dictionary has been created, accessible at myaamiadictionary.org.

Based on the language skills of the Baldwin family, as well as other Miami people, *Ethnologue* has reclassified Myaamia from an extinct language to a reawakening language. Before reclassifying Myaamia, *Ethnologue* first undertook an in-depth study of the Baldwin family's language skills by Dr. Wesley Leonard, a Native American language expert at the University of California, Riverside.

DEBATE IT!
Should U.S. students be required to learn a foreign language?

Immigrants to the United States speak many languages, but few people born in the United States speak a language other than English (Figures 5.10.3 and 5.10.4).

LEARN A FOREIGN LANGUAGE

- Many people in the world do not speak English.
- A foreign language is a competitive advantage in international business.
- Knowing a foreign language fosters understanding of and respect for other cultures.

▲ 5.10.3 **KOREATOWN, QUEENS, NEW YORK**

NO NEED FOR FOREIGN LANGUAGE

- Knowledge of English is sufficient for international communication.
- Time in school is better spent learning other subjects.
- Social media relies more on symbols and abbreviations than on official languages.

▲ 5.10.4 **AMERICANS LOST IN ROME**

CHAPTER 5

Review, Analyze, & Apply

KEY ISSUE 1 How Are Languages Distributed?

Languages are organized into families, branches, and groups. All but 1 percent of the world's people speak a language belonging to 1 of 14 language families. Nearly one-half of the world's people speak a language in the Indo-European family, and another one-fifth speak a language in the Sino-Tibetan family.

THINKING GEOGRAPHICALLY

1. This sign in England's Birmingham Airport says welcome in 12 languages. How many can you identify? How many writing systems appear to be represented in the sign?

◀ 5.CR.1 **"WELCOME" IN 12 LANGUAGES**

KEY ISSUE 2 How Do Languages Spread?

The origin and diffusion of individual languages can be documented. The origin of language families predates recorded history. In prehistoric times, languages may have diffused along with agriculture or through warfare.

THINKING GEOGRAPHICALLY

2. Which theory explaining the origin of Indo-European languages—nomadic warrior or sedentary farmer—seems more logical to you? Why?

◀ 5.CR.2 **KURGAN NOMADIC WARRIOR HOMELAND**
Horses, Altai Mountains, Russia.

GeoVideo

Log in to the Mastering Geography™ Study Area to view this video.

Israel: Reinventing Hebrew

The ancient language of Hebrew has been reinvented as a modern, living language.

1. What were the advantages to using Hebrew as the national language of Israel?
2. What are the disadvantages to using an ancient language in the modern world?
3. How does the video explain using a modernization of an ancient term (such as for "battery") and for using an English term (such as for "puncture")?

KEY ISSUE 3 How Do Languages Vary Among Places?

A dialect is a regional variation of a language. Dialects can vary in terms of vocabulary, spelling, and pronunciation. Some dialects become sufficiently different to justify classifying them as separate languages. This is important for some cultural groups as a symbol of cultural identity. Some countries peacefully embrace multiple languages, whereas in other places the multiplicity of languages is a source of tension.

THINKING GEOGRAPHICALLY

3. Natives of Appalachian communities, such as in rural West Virginia, have a distinctive dialect, pronouncing hollow as holler and creek as crick, for example. What positive elements and challenges might people of Appalachia experience as result of the distinctive dialect?

◀ 5.CR.3 **APPALACHIA**
Jug band performs in Asheville, NC.

KEY ISSUE 4 Why Do Languages Survive or Perish?

Many languages are endangered because not enough people continue to use them or teach them to children. Lack of interaction has helped a few isolated languages to survive, while interaction with other languages has caused the extinction of others. Some threatened languages, such as the Celtic branch of Indo-European, are being preserved with the help of governments.

THINKING GEOGRAPHICALLY

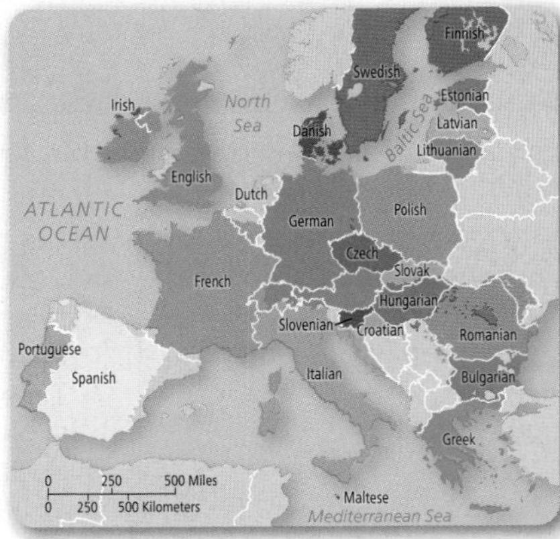

4. The European Union has 24 official and working languages (Figure 5.CR.4). What languages discussed in this chapter are not official EU languages? What languages would you expect these places to utilize? What might be the impact of the withdrawal of the United Kingdom from the EU on the distribution and usage of languages within the EU?

◀ 5.CR.4 **EUROPEAN UNION OFFICIAL LANGUAGES**

Mastering Geography

Looking for additional review and test prep materials? Visit the Study Area in Mastering Geography to enhance your geographic literacy, spatial reasoning skills, and understanding of this chapter's content. Access MapMaster™ interactive maps, video case studies, *In the News* current articles, flashcards, self-study quizzes, an eText of *Contemporary Human Geography*, and more. **pearson.com/mastering/geography**

Key Terms

Creole (or creolized) language (p. 127) A language that results from the mixing of a colonizer's language with the indigenous language of the people being dominated.

Denglish (p. 127) A combination of Deutsch (the German word for German) and English.

Developing language (p. 114) A language spoken in daily use with a literary tradition that is not widely distributed.

Dialect (p. 124) A regional variety of a language distinguished by vocabulary, spelling, and pronunciation.

Dying language (p. 114) A language used by older people, but is not being transmitted to children.

Ebonics (p. 127) A dialect spoken by some African Americans.

Endangered language (p. 130) A language at risk of extinction because it has few surviving speakers.

Extinct language (p. 130) A language that was once used by people in daily activities but is no longer used.

Franglais (p. 127) A combination of français and anglais (the French words for French and English, respectively).

Institutional language (p. 114) A language used in education, work, mass media, and government.

Isogloss (p. 124) A boundary that separates regions in which different language usages predominate.

Isolated language (p. 131) A language that is unrelated to any other languages and therefore not attached to any language family.

Language (p. 114) A system of communication through the use of speech, a collection of sounds understood by a group of people to have the same meaning.

Language branch (p. 114) A collection of languages related through a common ancestor that can be confirmed through archaeological evidence.

Language family (p. 114) A collection of languages related to each other through a common ancestor long before recorded history.

Language group (p. 114) A collection of languages within a branch that share a common origin in the relatively recent past and display relatively few differences in grammar and vocabulary.

Lingua franca (p. 122) A language mutually understood and commonly used in trade by people who have different native languages.

Literary tradition (p. 114) A language that is written as well as spoken.

Logogram (p. 123) A symbol that represents a word rather than a sound.

Official language (p. 127) The language adopted for use by a government for the conduct of business and publication of documents.

Pidgin language (p. 122) A form of speech that adopts a simplified grammar and limited vocabulary of a lingua franca; used for communications among speakers of two different languages.

Spanglish (p. 127) A combination of Spanish and English spoken by Hispanic Americans.

Threatened language (p. 114) A language used for face-to-face communication, but is losing users.

Vigorous language (p. 114) A language that is spoken in daily use but that lacks a literary tradition.

Geospatial Analysis

Log in to the Mastering Geography Study Area to access MapMaster 2.0

South America's indigenous languages

On a world map, most of South America appears in the Indo-European language family. Some diversity exists within the region, as shown in Figure 5.2.4.

1. ***Add*** the *Spanish as Official or De Facto Language* layer and ***zoom*** to Latin America.
1. What is the one large country in South America where Spanish is not the official language? If you do not know the answer, in the *Legend*, ***select*** the *Settings* icon, and ***select*** *Show Political Labels*.
2. ***Add*** the *Indigenous Languages (South America)* layer. ***Reset*** the map. ***Add*** the *Population Density* layer and select *Split Map Window*. Are indigenous languages more likely to be spoken in areas of high population density or low population density?
3. ***Add*** *World Elevations*, and ***replace*** the *Population Density* layer. ***Hover*** over the area of highest elevation on the *World Elevations* map. Describe the spatial association between high elevation and indigenous languages.

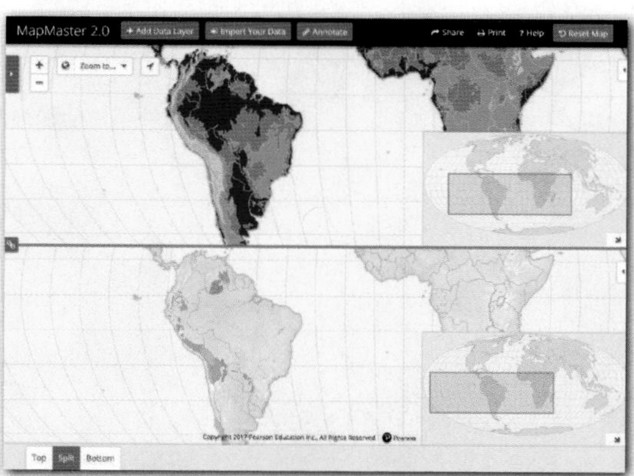

▲ 5.CR.6 **INDIGENOUS LANGUAGES AND WORLD ELEVATIONS**

Explore

Multilingual Belgium

Brussels, the capital of Belgium, is official bilingual, but many languages comingle there.

In Google Earth, ***search*** for *46 rue de Flandre, Brussels*.

1. What is housed in 46 rue de Flandre? ***Pan*** to the upper floors to read the sign. What language is displayed on the banner?
2. What language is displayed on the sign by the entrance to #46? What is next door at #44? Why might languages other than the two official ones be used at the entrance to these two buildings?
3. ***Scan up and down*** rue de Flandre. Which of Brussels' two official languages is more common? Why might that be the case? Can you find examples along the street where both official languages are displayed? Why might both official languages be used in these cases?

▶ 5.CR.7 **RUE DE FLANDRE, BRUSSELS**

CHAPTER

6 Religions

Religions interest geographers because understanding them is essential for recognizing spatial patterns underlying how humans occupy Earth. Many people care deeply about their religion and draw from religion their core values and beliefs, an essential element of the definition of culture. Geographers document the places where various religions are located in the world and offer explanations for why some religions have widespread distributions and others are highly clustered in particular places.

◀ Interfaith Vigil, London.

KEY ISSUES

1 Where Are Religions Distributed?

Some religions are highly clustered in one or two of Earth's regions, whereas others are distributed throughout the world. Individual religions also have distinctive distributions within regions.

2 Why Do Religions Have Distinctive Distributions?

Some religions have well-documented places of origin and have diffused extensively. Others have unknown origins and have experienced limited diffusion.

3 How Do Religions Organize Space?

Religious groups derive distinctive meaning from the physical landscape and construct places for worship and other religious practices.

4 Why Do Conflicts Arise Among Religions?

Adherents of various religions have disputes over Earth's territory. The attempt by adherents of one religion to organize a portion of Earth's surface can create conflicts with governments or with other religious groups.

LOCATIONS IN THIS CHAPTER

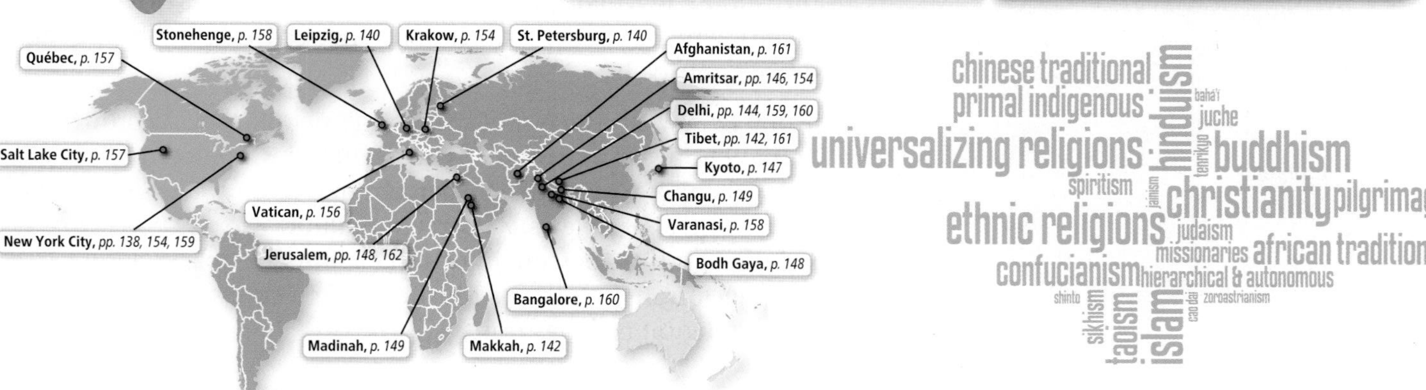

▲ 6.1.1 **JUDAISM** Central Synagogue, New York, designed to look like a synagogue in Budapest, Hungary.

Distribution of Religions

- **Summarize the distribution of the world's largest religions.**

A few religions claim the adherence of large numbers of people. This section identifies the major religions and their distributions.

Reliable statistics on the number of adherents are difficult to obtain. No official count of religious membership is taken in the United States or in many other countries. Some adherents may feel that their religion has been undercounted and therefore accorded less prominence than deserved in world and regional data.

Most international statistics in this chapter come from Adherents.com, the Association of Statisticians of American Religious Bodies, the Pew Research Center, and World Religion Database. None of these organizations is affiliated with a particular religion. The statistics are built on self-identification—that is, whatever people themselves view as the particular religious groups to which they belong. They do not measure how actively an individual practices a religion.

The world's religions can be grouped as follows:

- **Four largest religions.** Pew estimates that there are 2.3 billion Christians, 1.8 billion Muslims, 1.1 billion Hindus, and 488 million Buddhists. These four religions together claim the adherence of 77 percent of the world's people.
- **Folk religions.** A number of religions grouped by Pew under the title "folk religions" account for an estimated 6 percent of the world's population, although the number of adherents of these religions is especially difficult to measure. Adherents.com identifies the three largest groups of folk religions as Chinese traditional, primal-indigenous, and African traditional.
- **Other religions.** Another 1 percent of the world's people adhere to a number of other religions. The four most numerous of these other religions—Juche, Judaism (Figure 6.1.1), Sikhism, and Spiritism—have between 14 and 23 million adherents each. Six other religions have between 2 and 10 million adherents: Bahá'í, Cao Dai, Jainism, Shinto, Tenrikyo, and Zoroastrianism. Many other religions have fewer than 2 million adherents.
- **Unaffiliated.** The remaining 16 percent of the world's population are unaffiliated with a religion (Figure 6.1.2). According to Adherents.com, most people in this category affirm neither belief nor lack of belief in God or some other Higher Power. In the United States, many classified as unaffiliated believe in God and attend a religious service at least on occasion, but they do not have a formal association with a religious institution. In some countries, the unaffiliated are primarily people who express no religious interest or preference and do not participate in any organized religious activity. Some people in this group espouse **atheism**, which is belief that God does not exist, or **agnosticism**, which is belief that the existence of God can't be proven or disproven empirically.

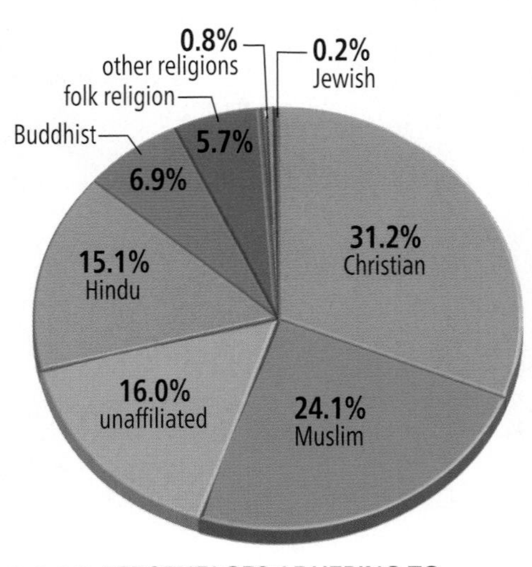

▲ 6.1.2 **PERCENTAGES ADHERING TO VARIOUS RELIGIONS**

According to Pew, 27 percent of the world's people live in countries where their religion is in the minority. This includes 3 percent of Hindus, 13 percent of Christians, 27 percent of Muslims, 29 percent of unaffiliated, 59 percent of Jews, 72 percent of Buddhists, 99 percent of folk religionists, and 100 percent of other religious groups. In addition, a large percentage of Christians and Muslims live in countries where their branch of the religion is the minority.

Universalizing and Ethnic Religions

Geographers distinguish between two types of religions:

- **Universalizing religions** attempt to appeal to all people, wherever they may live in the world, not just to those of one culture or location.
- **Ethnic religions** appeal primarily to one group of people living in one place.

Geographers consider the distinction between universalizing and ethnic religions to be significant because the two types of religions tend to display different spatial characteristics, including origin, diffusion, and distribution. In reality, the distinction between the two types of religions is not absolute because many religions can display both universalizing and ethnic elements.

Among the five largest religious groups, Christianity, Islam, and Buddhism are considered universalizing, whereas Hinduism and folk religions are considered ethnic. Most of the religions with fewer adherents are ethnic, but several are universalizing, and others display features of both and so are especially difficult to classify.

Figure 6.1.3 shows the most numerous religion in each country. The map must be viewed with caution because the distribution of religions is in reality more complex, especially at regional and local scales.

▼ 6.1.3 MOST NUMEROUS RELIGIONS BY COUNTRY AND WORLD REGION

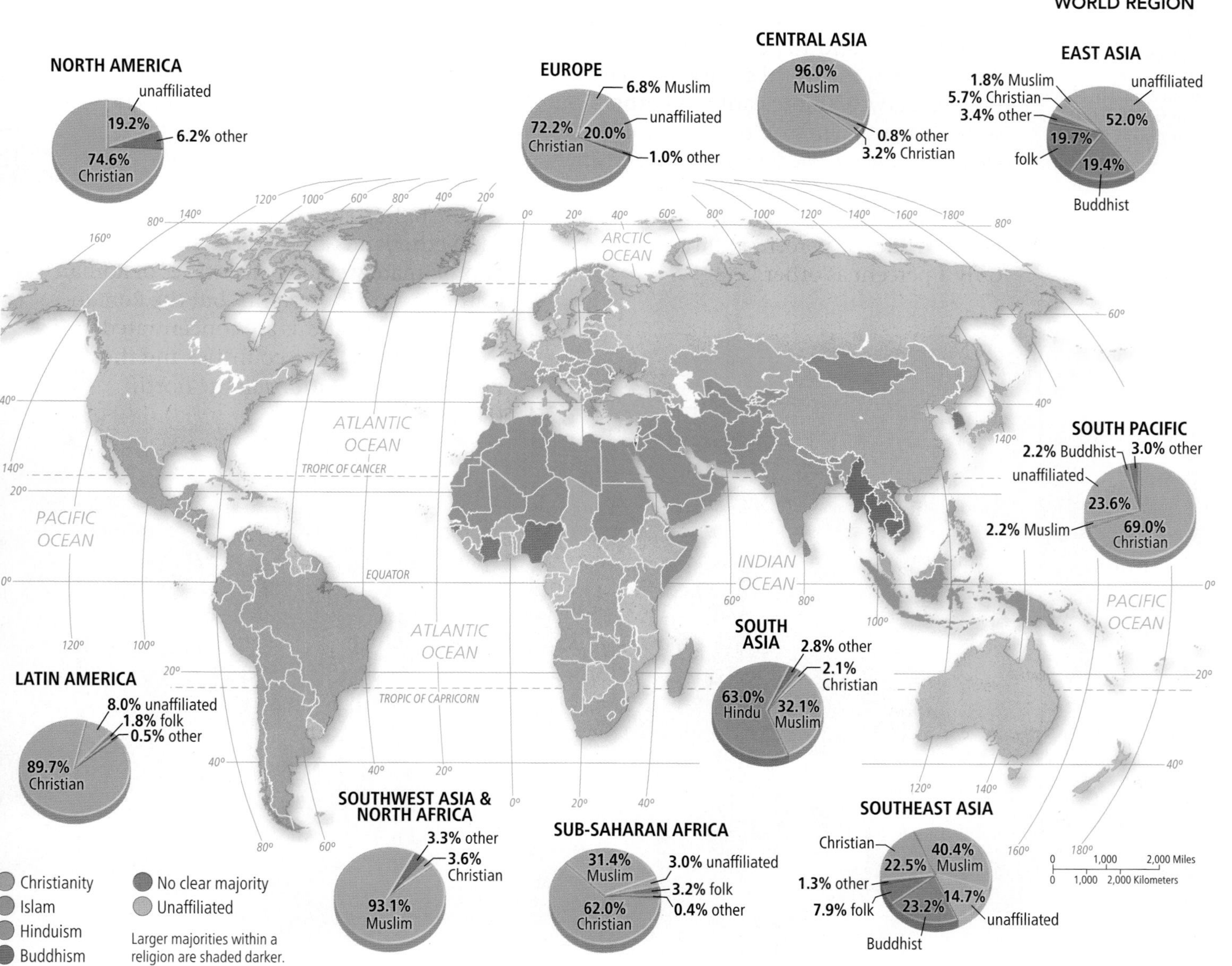

Distribution of Christians

- **Describe the distribution of Christianity's principal branches.**

Many religions, including the three most widely practiced universalizing religions, are divided into congregations, denominations, and branches. A **congregation** is a local assembly of persons brought together for common religious worship. A **denomination** unites a number of local congregations in a single legal and administrative body. A **branch** is a large and fundamental division within a religion.

▲ 6.2.1 **ORTHODOX CHRISTIANITY** Church of the Savior on Blood, St. Petersburg, Russia. The unusual name is because the church was built on the site of an attack in 1881 that fatally wounded Tsar Alexander II.

Branches of Christianity

Christianity has three major branches: Roman Catholic, Protestant, and Orthodox. In addition, many Christians belong to churches that do not consider themselves to be within any of these three branches. Roman Catholics comprise approximately 50 percent of the world's Christians and Orthodox around 12 percent. The other 38 percent of the world's Christians are divided between Protestants and others, but sources do not agree on the magnitude of each. The *Encyclopaedia Britannica* classifies 24 percent of the world's Christians as Protestant and 14 percent as other, whereas Pew classifies 37 percent as Protestant and only 1 percent as other.

Branches in Europe

Overall in Europe, 47 percent of Christians are Roman Catholics, 18 percent are Protestants, and 35 percent are Orthodox. Roman Catholicism is the most widely practiced branch of Christianity in the southwest and center of Europe, Protestantism in the northwest, and Orthodoxy in the east and southeast (Figure 6.2.1).

The regions of Roman Catholic and Protestant majorities frequently have sharp boundaries, even when they run through the middle of countries (Figure 6.2.2). For example, Germany, the Netherlands and Switzerland have approximately equal percentages of Roman Catholics and Protestants, but the Roman Catholic populations are concentrated in the south of these countries and the Protestant populations in the north (Figure 6.2.3).

Roman Catholic
Protestant
Orthodox
Other religions

▲ 6.2.2 **MOST NUMEROUS FAITHS IN EUROPE**

▲ 6.2.3 **PROTESTANT CHRISTIANITY: LUTHERAN** Old St. Peter's Church, Leipzig, Germany.

Branches in the Western Hemisphere

Christianity is by far the most widely practiced religion in the Western Hemisphere. Christians comprise 86 percent of the population of the Western Hemisphere. This includes 90 percent of Latin Americans and 75 percent of North Americans. People unaffiliated with any religion comprise 8 percent of Latin Americans and 19 percent of North Americans.

At the regional scale within the Western Hemisphere, a sharp boundary exists between North America and Latin America in the predominant branches of Christianity. Roman Catholics comprise 81 percent of Christians in Latin America and 32 percent in North America, whereas Protestants comprise 18 percent of Christians in Latin America and 63 percent in North America.

The diversity of faiths in the United States is displayed in Figure 6.2.4. Christian branches and denominations have distinctive distributions (Figure 6.2.5), as do non-Christian faiths (Figure 6.2.6 and What's Your Geography of Religion?).

▼ **6.2.4 RELIGIONS OF THE UNITED STATES**
Figures are percent of all Americans.

Religion			
Christian			70.6
Roman Catholic		20.8	
Evangelical Protestant		25.4	
Southern Baptist Convention	5.3		
Independent Baptist in the Evangelical Tradition	2.5		
Other Baptist in the Evangelical Tradition	1.4		
Lutheran in the Evangelical Tradition	1.5		
Assemblies of God	1.4		
Other Pentecostal in the Evangelical Tradition	2.2		
Restorationalist in the Evangelical Tradition (primarily Church of Christ)	1.6		
Nondenominational in the Evangelical Tradition	4.9		
Other Evangelical Protestant Traditions	6.0		
Mainline Protestant Churches		14.7	
Baptist in the Mainline Tradition	2.1		
Methodist in the Mainline Tradition	3.9		
Lutheran in the Mainline Tradition	2.1		
Presbyterian in the Mainline Tradition	1.4		
Anglican/Episcopal in the Mainline Tradition	1.2		
Other Mainline Protestant Traditions	4.0		
Historical Black Churches		6.5	
National Baptist Convention	1.4		
Other Baptist in the Historically Black Tradition	2.6		
Other Historically Black Churches	2.5		
Mormon		1.6	
Other Christian		1.7	
Jewish			1.9
Buddhist			0.7
Muslim			0.9
Hindu			0.7
Other religions or don't know			2.4
Unaffiliated			22.8

WHAT'S YOUR GEOGRAPHY OF RELIGION?

The U.S. Bureau of the Census does not collect information on people's religion, but the Association of Statisticians of American Religious Bodies conducts a U.S. Religion Census every 10 years (**http://www.usreligioncensus.org/**).

1. Does your immediate family have multiple faiths?
2. Do your immediate neighbors share the same faith as you?
3. What denomination or congregation are the five nearest places of worship to your house?
4. How many of the five nearest places of worship are part of the most widely practiced faith in your county?
5. Does the most widely practiced faith in your family and immediate neighbors match the county map, or does it differ?
6. Do you share the same faith, denomination, or congregation with your closest friends?

▲ **6.2.5 MOST NUMEROUS FAITHS BY U.S. COUNTY**

▲ **6.2.6 MOST NUMEROUS NON-CHRISTIAN FAITHS BY U.S. COUNTY**

Distribution of Buddhists & Muslims

- Describe the distribution of the principal branches of Islam and Buddhism.

Islam is the predominant religion of Central Asia and of Southwest Asia & North Africa (Figure 6.3.1). Buddhism is clustered primarily in East Asia and Southeast Asia. Like Christianity, Islam and Buddhism are divided into major branches with distinctive geographic distributions.

▲ 6.3.1 **MASJID AL-HARAM, MAKKAH, SAUDI ARABIA** Islam's largest mosque contains a cube called the Ka'ba, the holiest place in Islam.

Distribution of Buddhists

Buddhism split into more than one branch, as followers disagreed on interpreting statements by the founder, Siddhartha Gautama. The three main branches are Mahayana, Theravada, and Vajrayana (Figure 6.3.2). Mahayanists account for about 56 percent of Buddhists, primarily in China, Japan, and Korea. Theravadists comprise about 38 percent of Buddhists, especially in Cambodia, Laos, Myanmar, Sri Lanka, and Thailand. Vajrayanists, also known as Lamaists and Tantrayanists, comprise about 6 percent and are found primarily in Tibet and Mongolia (Figure 6.3.3).

An accurate count of Buddhists is especially difficult because only a few people participate in Buddhist institutions. Religious functions are performed primarily by monks rather than by the general public. The number of Buddhists is also difficult to count because Buddhism, although a universalizing religion, differs in significant respects from the Western concept of a formal religious system. Someone can be both a Buddhist and a believer in other Eastern religions, whereas Christianity and Islam both require exclusive adherence. Most Buddhists in China and Japan, in particular, believe at the same time in an ethnic religion.

▼ 6.3.2 **DISTRIBUTION OF BRANCHES OF BUDDHISM**

▼ 6.3.3 **BUDDHIST MONKS** Labrang Monastery, Tibet.

Distribution of Muslims

The word Islam in Arabic means "submission to the will of God," and it has a similar root to the Arabic word for "peace." An adherent of the religion of Islam is known as a Muslim, which in Arabic means "one who surrenders to God."

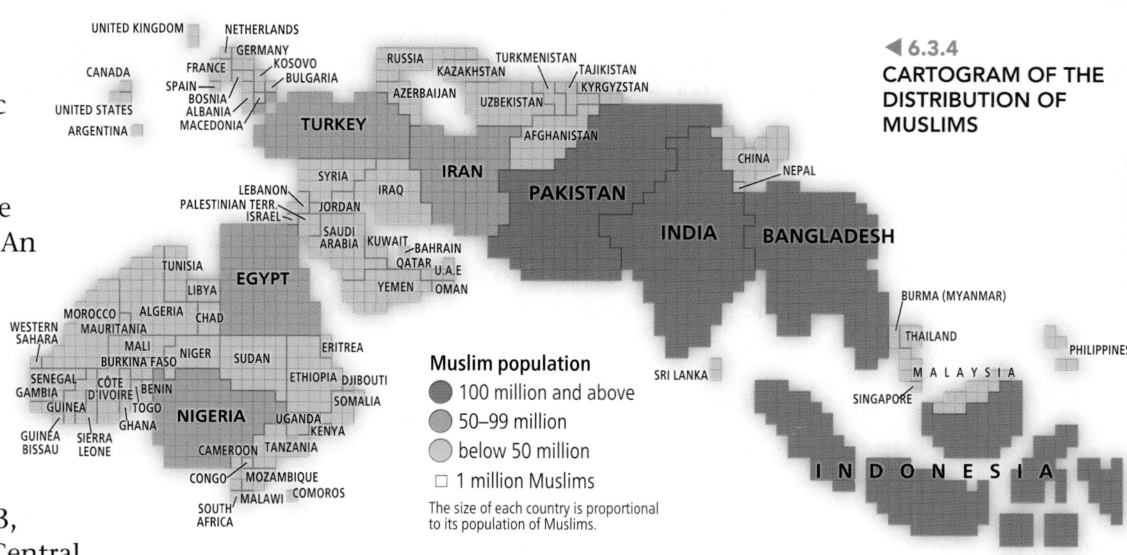

▲ 6.3.4 CARTOGRAM OF THE DISTRIBUTION OF MUSLIMS

On a standard world map, such as Figure 6.1.3, Islam predominates in Central Asia and in Southwest Asia & North Africa. However, on a cartogram, most of the world's Muslims live further east, in South and Southeast Asia (Figure 6.3.4). Indonesia, Pakistan, India, and Bangladesh together are home to more than 40 percent of the world's Muslims.

Islam is divided into two principal branches: Sunni and Shiite. The word Sunni comes from the Arabic for "people following the tradition of Muhammad." The word Shiite (sometimes spelled Shia) comes from the Arabic word for "party" or "support group." Sunnis comprise 88 percent of Muslims and are the most numerous branch in most Muslim countries in Southwest Asia & North Africa, as well as in Southeast Asia. Sunnis follow various schools of thought and religious law, which have distinctive regional distributions (Figure 6.3.5). The Hanafi, Hanbali, Maliki, and Shafi'i schools of thought and religious law are named for their founders.

Shiites are the most numerous branch in Azerbaijan, Bahrain, Iran, Iraq, Lebanon, and Yemen. Nearly 40 percent of all Shiites live in Iran, 15 percent in Pakistan, 12 percent in India, and 10 percent in Iraq. Shiite Islam is divided into three principal schools of thought, based in part on views of the succession of leadership after the Prophet Muhammad. The largest, known as Jafari, is the most widely followed tradition in Azerbaijan, Bahrain, Iran, Iraq, and Lebanon. Other traditions include the Ismaili and Zaidi. Ismailis are clustered in Pakistan and Zaidiyyahs in Yemen. A third branch of Islam, Ibadi, is the predominant form of Islam adhered to in Oman.

The Muslim populations of North America and Europe have increased rapidly in recent years. In Europe, Muslims account for 5 percent of the population. France has the largest Muslim population, about 4 million, a legacy of immigration from predominantly Muslim former colonies in North Africa.

Estimates of the number of Muslims in North America vary widely, from 1 million to 5 million, but in any event, the number has increased dramatically from only a few hundred thousand in 1990. Muslims in the United States come from a variety of backgrounds. According to the U.S. State Department, approximately one-third of U.S. Muslims trace their ancestry to Pakistan and other South Asian countries and one-fourth to Arab countries of Southwest Asia & North Africa. Many of these Muslims immigrated to the United States during the 1990s. Another one-fourth are African Americans.

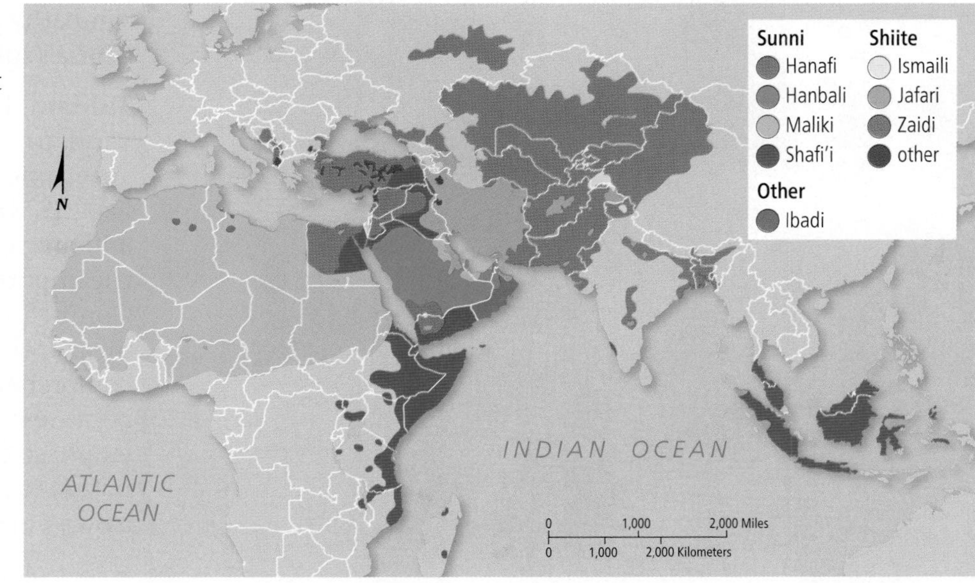

▲ 6.3.5 DISTRIBUTION OF BRANCHES OF ISLAM

Distribution of Ethnic Religions

- Summarize the distribution of ethnic religions.

Ethnic religions typically have much more clustered distributions than do universalizing religions. Unlike universalizing religions, which typically diffuse from one culture to another, most of the adherents of the world's leading ethnic religions have remained embedded in the culture where they originated.

Distribution of Hindus

The ethnic religion with by far the largest number of followers is Hinduism (Figure 6.4.1). In contrast to the large universalizing religions, 97 percent of Hindus are concentrated in just one country (India), 2 percent are in Nepal, 1 percent are in Bangladesh, and small numbers are elsewhere. Hindus comprise more than 80 percent of the population of India and Nepal, around 9 percent of the population of Bangladesh, and a small minority are found in every other country.

The average Hindu has allegiance to a particular god or concept within a broad range of possibilities. The manifestation of god with the largest number of adherents—an estimated 80 percent—is Vaishnavism, which worships the god Vishnu, a loving god incarnated as Krishna. The second-largest is Shaivism, dedicated to Shiva, a protective and destructive god.

Chinese Traditional Religions

Religions based in East Asia show the difficulty of classifying ethnic religions and counting adherents. Chinese traditional religions are **syncretic**, which means they combine several traditions. Adherents.com considers Chinese traditional religions to be a combination of Buddhism (a universalizing religion) and Confucianism, Taoism, and other traditional Chinese practices. Most Chinese who consider themselves religious blend together the religious cultures of these multiple traditions.

Confucianism. Confucius (551–479 B.C.) was a philosopher and teacher in the Chinese province of Lu. His sayings, which were recorded by his students, emphasized the importance of the ancient Chinese tradition of li, which can be translated roughly as "propriety" or "correct behavior." Confucianism prescribed a series of ethical principles for the orderly conduct of daily life in China, such as following traditions, fulfilling obligations, and treating others with sympathy and respect. These rules applied to China's rulers as well as to their subjects.

Taoism. Lao-Zi (604–531 B.C., also spelled Lao Tzu) organized Taoism. Although a government administrator by profession, Lao-Zi's writings emphasized the mystical and magical aspects of life rather than the importance of public service, which Confucius had emphasized. Tao, which means "the way" or "the path," cannot be comprehended by reason and knowledge because not everything is knowable. It emphasizes the importance of studying nature to find one's place in the world instead of striving to change the world.

◀ 6.4.1 HINDUS DURING THE CHHATH FESTIVAL, NEW DELHI, INDIA
The festival thanks the Sun for the bounties of life.

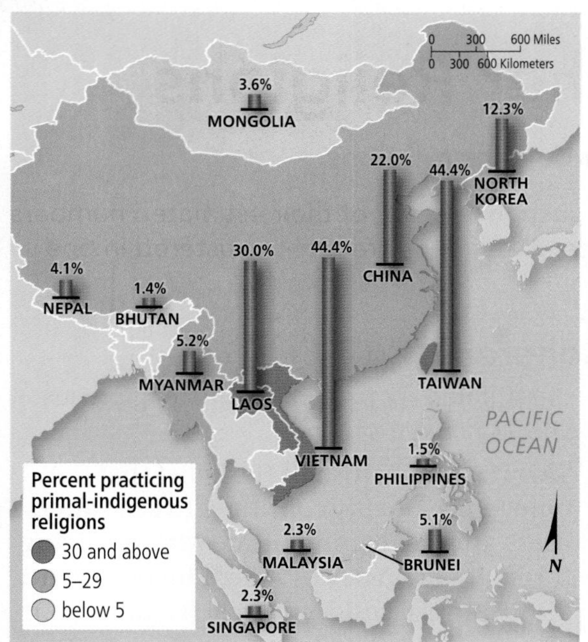

Primal-Indigenous Religions

Several hundred million people practice what Adherents.com has grouped into the category primal-indigenous religions. Most of these people reside in Southeast Asia (especially in Vietnam and Laos) or on South Pacific islands (Figure 6.4.2).

Followers of primal-indigenous religions believe that because God dwells within all things, everything in nature is spiritual. Narratives concerning nature are specific to the physical landscape where they are told. Included in this group are Shamanism and Paganism. According to Shamans, invisible forces or spirits affect the lives of the living. "Pagan" is used to refer to the practices of ancient peoples, such as the Greeks and Romans, who had multiple gods with human forms. The term is currently expanded to also include other beliefs that originated with religions that predate Christianity and Islam.

◀ 6.4.2 DISTRIBUTION OF PRIMAL-INDIGENOUS RELIGIONS IN EAST AND SOUTHEAST ASIA

African Traditional Religions

Approximately 27 million Africans, 2 percent of the continent's people, are estimated by Pew to follow traditional religions. African traditional religions are sometimes called **animism**, which is belief that inanimate objects such as plants and stones, or natural events such as thunderstorms and earthquakes, are "animated," or have discrete spirits and conscious life.

Today Africa is 50 percent Christian—split about evenly among Roman Catholic, Protestant, and other—and 44 percent Muslim. This distribution is in sharp contrast with the past. In 1900, more than 70 percent of Africans followed traditional folk religions (Figure 6.4.3a). As recently as 1980, one-half of Africans—around 200 million people—were still classified as folk religionists. The growth in the two universalizing religions at the expense of ethnic religions reflects fundamental geographic differences between the two types of religions. Remaining folk religionists in Africa are clustered primarily in a belt that separates predominantly Muslim North Africa from what has become predominantly Christian sub-Saharan Africa (Figure 6.4.3b).

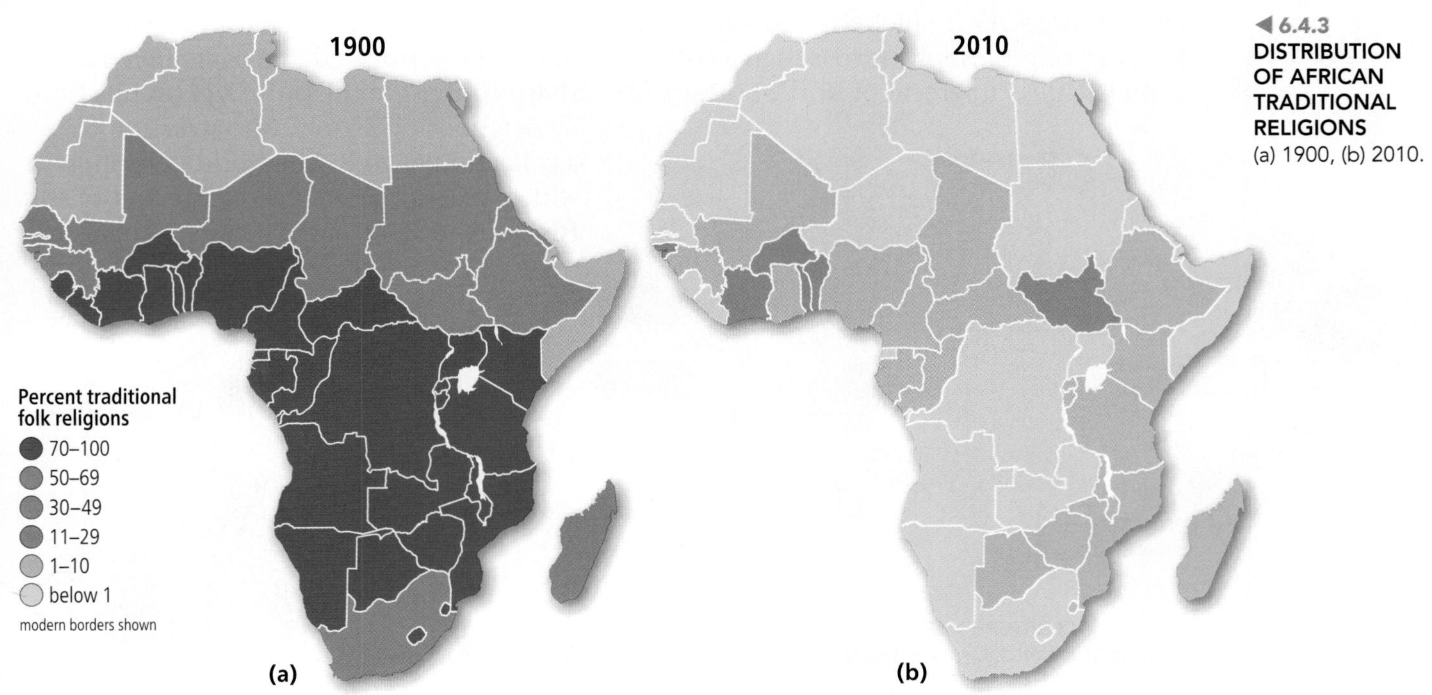

◀ 6.4.3 DISTRIBUTION OF AFRICAN TRADITIONAL RELIGIONS (a) 1900, (b) 2010.

▲ 6.5.1 **SIKHISM** The Golden Temple, Amritsar, India.

Distribution of Other Religions

- Describe the distributions of other important religions.

Ten religions are briefly described in this section in order of their estimated numbers of adherents. The adherents of 9 of these 10 religions are highly clustered in one or two countries. The exception is Bahá'í.

Religions with 14 to 23 Million Adherents

These four religions have an estimated 14 to 23 million adherents:

Sikhism. All but 3 million of the world's 23 million Sikhs are clustered in the Punjab region of India (Figure 6.5.1). The founder of Sikhism, Guru Nanak (1469–1538), lived in a village near the city of Lahore, in present-day Pakistan. God was revealed to Nanak as The One Supreme Being, or Creator, who rules the universe by divine will. Nanak traveled widely through South Asia around 500 years ago, preaching his new faith, and his many followers became known as Sikhs (Hindu for "disciples"). Nine other gurus succeeded Guru Nanak. In 1604, Arjan, the fifth guru, compiled and edited the Guru Granth Sa-hib (the Holy Granth of Enlightenment), which became the book of Sikh holy scriptures.

Juche. Most North Koreans are classified by Adherents.com as following Juche, which is Korean for "self-reliance." Juche was organized by Kim Il-sung, the leader of North Korea between 1948 and his death in 1994. Other sources regard Juche as a government ideology or philosophy rather than a religion. Pew classifies 71 percent of North Koreans as unaffiliated, 12 percent as folk religionists, and 13 percent as other.

Spiritism. Spiritism is the belief that the human personality continues to exist after death and can communicate with the living through the agency of a medium or psychic. Most Spiritists reside in Brazil (Figure 6.5.2).

Judaism. Roughly two-fifths of the world's 14 million Jews live in the United States and another two-fifths in Israel (Figure 6.5.3). The name Judaism derives from Judah, one of the Patriarch Jacob's 12 sons; Israel is another Biblical name for Jacob. The Tanakh recounts the ancient history of the Jewish people and the laws of the Jewish faith. Tanakh is an acronym for Torah (also known as the Five Books of Moses), Nevi'im ("Prophets") and Ketuvim ("Writings").

Judaism plays a more substantial role in Western civilization than its number of adherents would suggest. Judaism is the first recorded religion to espouse **monotheism**, belief that there is only one God. Fundamental to Judaism is belief in one all-powerful God. Judaism offered a sharp contrast to the **polytheism** practiced by neighboring people, who worshipped a collection of gods. The world's two most widely practiced religions—Christianity and Islam—find some of their roots in Judaism.

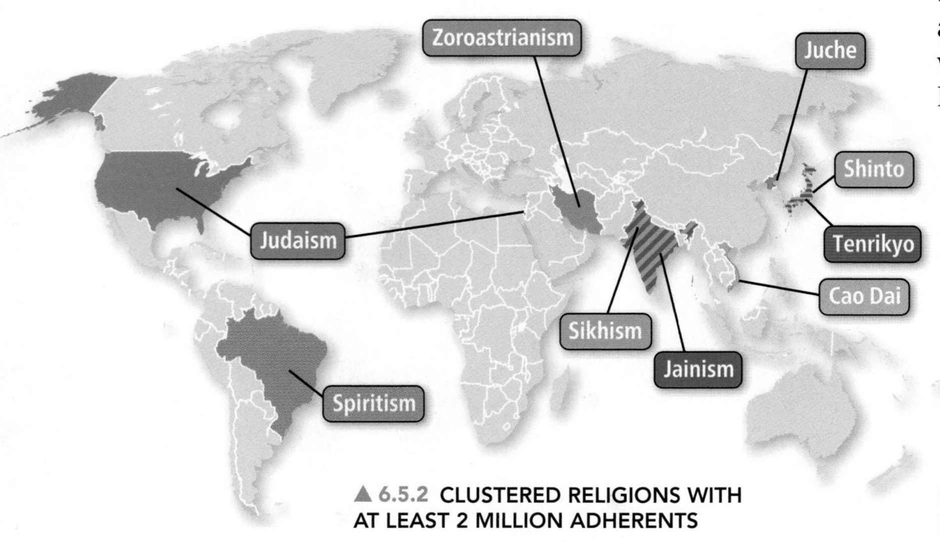

▲ 6.5.2 **CLUSTERED RELIGIONS WITH AT LEAST 2 MILLION ADHERENTS**

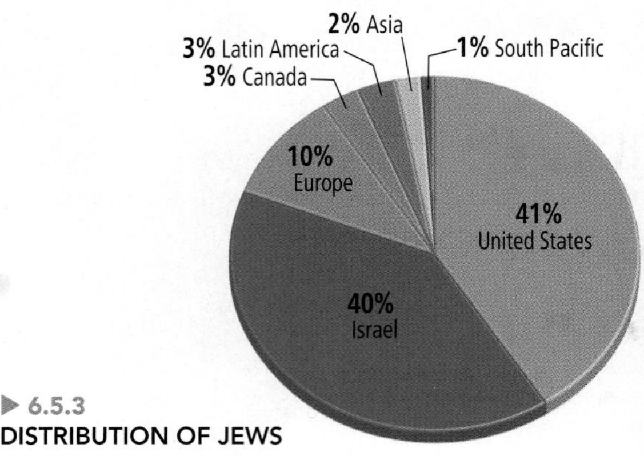

▶ 6.5.3 **DISTRIBUTION OF JEWS**

Religions with 2 to 10 Million Adherents

These six religions have an estimated 2 to 10 million adherents:

Bahá'í. Roughly equal numbers of Bahá'ís are found in India, other Asian countries, Africa, and the Western Hemisphere (Figure 6.5.4). The Bahá'í religion was established in Shíráz, Iran, in 1844. It grew out of the Bábi faith, under the leadership of Siyyid 'Ali Muhammad, known as the Báb (Persian for "gateway"). Bahá'í provoked strong opposition from Shiite Muslims, and the Báb was executed in 1850, as were 20,000 of his followers. Bahá'ís believe that one of the Báb's disciples, Husayn 'Ali Nuri, known as Bahá'u'lláh (Arabic for "Glory of God"), was the prophet and messenger of God.

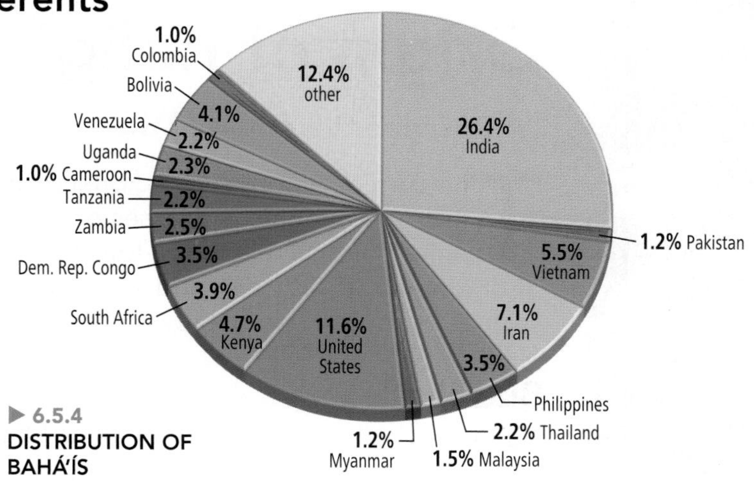

▶ 6.5.4 DISTRIBUTION OF BAHÁ'ÍS

Jainism. Jainism originated in South Asia around 2,500 years ago. Its importance declined with the rise in importance of Buddhism and Hinduism in the region, especially since the eighth century A.D. Jains believe that nonviolence and self-control are the means to achieve liberation. India is the home to 95 percent of the world's 4 million Jains, although Jain centers are located in 25 of the 50 U.S. states.

Shinto. As Japan's ethnic religion, Shinto is strongly rooted in the cultural history of the country (Figure 6.6.5). Japanese government statistics report around 100 million Shintos, or 78 percent of the country's population. However, in opinion polls only 4 million Japanese, or 3 percent of the population, identify themselves as Shinto. The large discrepancy stems in part from a seventeenth-century law in Japan that assigns Shinto organizations with the task of maintaining records on Japanese citizens. The discrepancy also stems from the perception by some Japanese people that Shinto is a cultural feature rather than a religion.

Cao Dai. The name refers to belief in God as the Supreme Being, Creator, and Ultimate Reality of the Universe. Cao Dai combines elements of Confucianism, Taoism, and Buddhism. Founded in Vietnam during the 1920s, Cao Dai found itself in opposition to a succession of rulers of Vietnam, including the French colonial administration and the Communists. Since Vietnam's Communist government granted Cao Dai legal status in 1997, the number of adherents has increased to an estimated 4 million, nearly all of whom live in Vietnam.

Zoroastrianism. The Prophet Zoroaster (or Zarathustra) founded the religion that bears his name around 3,500 years ago. The religion was more formally organized around 1,500 years ago in the Persian Empire (present-day Iran) and was the state religion for several ancient empires in Central Asia. The number of adherents declined after Muslims came to dominate Central Asia. Adherents.com estimates the number of Zoroastrians to be between 2 and 3 million.

Tenrikyo. Once regarded as a branch of Shinto, Tenrikyo was organized as a separate religion in 1854 by a woman named Nakayama Miki (1798–1887). Followers of Tenrikyo believe that God expressed the divine will through Nakayama's role as the Shrine of God. Adherents.com reports 2 million adherents around the world, 95 percent of whom are in Japan.

▼ 6.5.5 SHINTO PRIESTS Shimogamo Shrine, Kyoto, Japan.

▲ 6.6.1 **ORIGIN OF BUDDHISM**
Mahabodhi (Great Awakening) Temple was built in Bodh Gaya, the site in present-day India where Siddhartha Gautama Buddha attained enlightenment.

Origin of Religions

- **Describe the origin of the four largest religions.**

The current global and regional distributions of religions and their branches result from geographic processes of origin and diffusion. The most widely followed universalizing religions—Buddhism, Christianity, and Islam—have specific places of origin and widespread and well-documented patterns of diffusion. An ethnic religion such as Hinduism has unknown origins and limited diffusion.

Buddhism

Siddharta Gautama, was born about 563 B.C. in Lumbinī, in present-day Nepal, near the border with India. The son of a lord, he led a privileged existence, sheltered from life's hardships.

According to Buddhist tradition, Gautama's life changed after a series of four trips. He encountered a decrepit old man on the first trip, a disease-ridden man on the second trip, and a corpse on the third trip. After witnessing these scenes of pain and suffering, Gautama began to feel he could no longer enjoy his life of comfort and security.

At age 29 Gautama embarked on a fourth trip: he left his palace and lived in a forest for the next 6 years, thinking and experimenting with forms of meditation. Gautama emerged as the Buddha, the "awakened or enlightened one," and spent 45 years preaching his views across India. In the process, he trained monks, established monastic orders, and preached to the public (Figure 6.6.1).

Christianity

Christianity was founded upon the teachings of Jesus, who was born in Bethlehem between 8 and 4 B.C. and died on a cross in Jerusalem about A.D. 30. Raised as a Jew, Jesus gathered a small band of disciples and preached the coming of the Kingdom of God. He was referred to as Christ, from the Greek word for the Hebrew word *messiah*, which means "anointed."

According to the Gospels, in the third year of his mission, Jesus was betrayed to the authorities by one of his companions, Judas Iscariot. After sharing the Last Supper (which may have been the Jewish Passover Seder) with his disciples in Jerusalem, Jesus was arrested and put to death as an agitator. On the third day after his death, his tomb was found empty (Figure 6.6.2). Christians believe that Jesus was the messiah, that he died to atone for human sins, that he was raised from the dead by God, and that his Resurrection from death provides people with hope for salvation.

▶ 6.6.2 **ORIGIN OF CHRISTIANITY**
The tomb in the center of the Church of the Holy Sepulchre in Jerusalem was erected at the place Christians accept to be where Jesus was buried and resurrected.

Islam

Islam traces its origin to the same narrative as Judaism and Christianity. All three religions consider Adam to have been the first man and Abraham to have been one of his descendants. According to the Jewish Torah and Christian Old Testament narrative, Abraham married Sarah, who did not bear children. As polygamy was a custom of the culture, Abraham then married Hagar, who bore a son, Ishmael. Sarah's fortunes changed, and she bore a son, Isaac.

Jews and Christians trace their story through Abraham's original wife Sarah and her son Isaac. Muslims trace their story through his second wife, Hagar, and her son Ishmael. The Islamic tradition tells that Abraham brought Hagar and Ishmael to Makkah (spelled Mecca on many English-language maps), in present-day Saudi Arabia.

Centuries later, according to the Muslim narrative, one of Ishmael's descendants, Muhammad, was born in Makkah about 570. At age 40, while engaged in a meditative retreat, Muhammad is believed by Muslims to have received his first revelation from God through the Angel Gabriel. The Quran, the holiest book in Islam, is accepted by Muslims to be a record of God's words, as revealed to the Prophet Muhammad through Gabriel. Arabic is the lingua franca, or language of communication, within the Muslim world, because it is the language in which the Quran is written.

Islam teaches that as he began to preach the truth that God had revealed to him, Muhammad and his followers suffered persecution, and in 622 he was commanded by God to emigrate. His migration from Makkah to the city of Yathrib—an event known as the Hijra (from the Arabic word for "migration," sometimes spelled hegira)—marks the beginning of the Muslim calendar. Yathrib was subsequently renamed Madinah, Arabic for "the City." After several years, Muhammad and his followers returned to Makkah and established Islam as the city's religion. By Muhammad's death, in 632 at about age 63, Islam had spread through most of present-day Saudi Arabia (Figure 6.6.3).

▲ 6.6.3 **ORIGIN OF ISLAM**
Muhammad is buried under the green dome in Al-Masjid an-Nabawī (Prophet's Mosque) in Madinah, Saudi Arabia.

Hinduism

As an ethnic religion based in India, Hinduism has unknown origins. The word Hinduism originated in the sixth century B.C. to refer to people living in what is now India, but religious practices existed prior to recorded history.

Elements of Hinduism may have originated in the Indus Valley civilization, which flourished between approximately 2500 B.C. and 1500 B.C. in the valley along the Indus River in present-day eastern Pakistan. Archaeological evidence of possible rituals from that era includes bathing rituals, animal sacrifices, and sculptures that may depict Hindu gods.

Aryan tribes from Central Asia invaded South Asia about 1400 B.C. and brought with them Indo-European languages, as discussed in Chapter 5. In addition to their language, the Aryans brought their religion. The Aryans first settled in the area now called the Punjab in northwestern India and later migrated east to the Ganges River valley, as far as Bengal. Centuries of intermingling with the Dravidians already living in the area modified their religious beliefs.

The earliest surviving Hindu texts, known as Vedas, were written around 1100 B.C. Some rituals from this era survive in contemporary Hinduism, including worship of various gods representing Earth, atmosphere, and sky.

By around 2,000 years ago, key texts were composed, and rituals were developed that remain central to contemporary Hinduism. The earliest surviving Hindu temples were constructed between 1,500 and 2,000 years ago (Figure 6.6.4).

▶ 6.6.4 **UNKNOWN ORIGIN OF HINDUISM**
Changu Narayan is the oldest surviving Hindu temple in Nepal. It was built in A.D. 325 and dedicated to Lord Vishnu.

Historical Diffusion of Religions

- **Summarize the process of diffusion of universalizing religions.**

The three main universalizing religions diffused from specific hearths to other regions of the world. Followers transmitted the messages preached in the hearths to people elsewhere, diffusing them across Earth's surface along distinctive paths (Figure 6.7.1).

Diffusion of Christianity

Christianity's diffusion has been rather clearly recorded since Jesus first set forth its tenets in the Roman province known at the time as Judea. Consequently, geographers can examine its diffusion by reconstructing patterns of communications, interaction, and migration.

In Chapter 1 two processes of diffusion were identified: relocation (diffusion through migration) and expansion (diffusion through an additive effect). Within expansion diffusion, we distinguished between hierarchical diffusion (diffusion through key leaders) and contagious diffusion (widespread diffusion). Christianity diffused through a combination of these forms of diffusion.

Relocation Diffusion of Christianity. Christianity first spread from its hearth in Judea through relocation diffusion. **Missionaries**—individuals who help to transmit a universalizing religion through relocation diffusion—carried the teachings of Jesus along the Roman Empire's protected sea routes and excellent road network to people in other locations (Figure 6.7.2). People in commercial towns and military settlements that were directly linked by the communications network received the message first from Paul and other missionaries.

Expansion Diffusion of Christianity. The dominance of Christianity throughout the Roman Empire was assured during the fourth century through the two types of expansion diffusion:

- **Hierarchical diffusion.** The spread of Christianity was encouraged when the Roman Empire's key elite figure, Emperor Constantine (274?–337), embraced the religion in 313, and Emperor Theodosius proclaimed it the empire's official religion in 380. In subsequent centuries, Christianity further diffused into Europe through conversion of kings or other elite figures.
- **Contagious diffusion.** Christianity also spread widely within the Roman Empire through daily contact between believers in the towns and nonbelievers in the surrounding countryside. Since the year 1500, contagious diffusion, especially through migration and missionary activity by Europeans, has extended Christianity around the world.

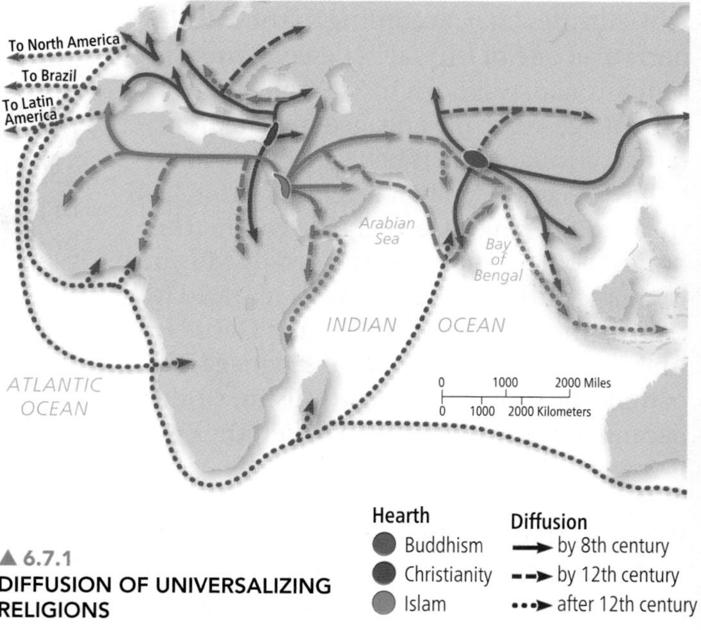

▲ 6.7.1
DIFFUSION OF UNIVERSALIZING RELIGIONS

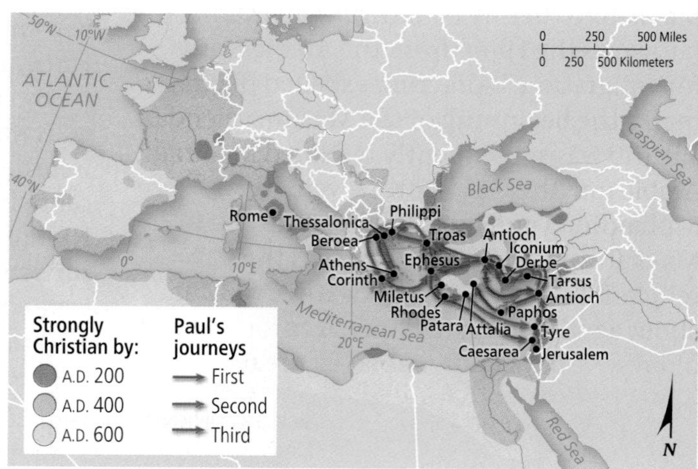

▶ 6.7.2 EARLY DIFFUSION OF CHRISTIANITY
Christianity began to diffuse throughout Europe during the time of the Roman Empire and continued after the empire's collapse. Paul of Tarsus, a disciple of Jesus, traveled extensively through the Roman Empire as a missionary.

Diffusion of Islam

Muhammad's successors organized followers who extended the region of Muslim control over an extensive area of Africa, Asia, and Europe (Figure 6.7.3). Within a century of Muhammad's death, Muslims controlled Palestine, the Persian Empire, and much of India, resulting in the conversion of many non-Arabs to Islam, often through intermarriage.

To the west, Muslims diffused across North Africa, and crossed the Strait of Gibraltar into present-day Spain, which they retained until 1492. During the same century in which the Christians regained all of Western Europe, Muslims took control of much of southeastern Europe and Turkey.

▲ 6.7.3 **EARLY DIFFUSION OF ISLAM**

As was the case with Christianity, Islam, as a universalizing religion, diffused well beyond its hearth in Southwest Asia through relocation diffusion of missionaries and traders to portions of sub-Saharan Africa and Southeast Asia. Although it is spatially isolated in Southeast Asia from the Islamic core region, Indonesia is predominantly Muslim. The world's fourth-most-populous country is home to more Muslims than any other country because Arab traders took the religion there in the thirteenth century.

Diffusion of Buddhism

Buddhism did not diffuse rapidly from its point of origin in northeastern India (Figure 6.7.4) Three centuries after its origin, it began a process of hierarchical diffusion, primarily through the efforts of Asoka, emperor of the Magadhan Empire from about 273 to 232 B.C. The Magadhan Empire formed the nucleus of several powerful kingdoms in South Asia between the sixth century B.C. and the eighth century A.D.

About 257 B.C., at the height of the Magadhan Empire's power, Asoka became a Buddhist and thereafter attempted to put into practice Buddha's social principles. A council organized by Asoka at Pataliputra decided to send missionaries to territories neighboring the Magadhan Empire. Emperor Asoka's son, Mahinda, led a mission to the island of Ceylon (now Sri Lanka), where the king and his subjects were converted to Buddhism. As a result, Sri Lanka is the country that claims the longest continuous tradition of practicing Buddhism. Missionaries were also sent in the third century B.C. to Kashmir, the Himalayas, Burma (Myanmar), and elsewhere in India.

▼ 6.7.4 **EARLY DIFFUSION OF BUDDHISM**

In the first century A.D., merchants along the trading routes from northeastern India introduced Buddhism to China. Many Chinese were receptive to the ideas brought by Buddhist missionaries, and Buddhist texts were translated into Chinese languages. Chinese rulers allowed their people to become Buddhist monks during the fourth century A.D., and in the following centuries Buddhism turned into a genuinely Chinese religion. Buddhism further diffused from China to Korea in the fourth century and from Korea to Japan two centuries later. During the same era, Buddhism lost its original base of support in India.

Recent Diffusion of Religions

- **Describe contemporary migration patterns of several religious groups.**

Migration continues in modern times to alter the distribution of religions. Although most people do not migrate primarily for religious reasons, when they do migrate, they take their religion with them.

The religious composition of international migrants does not match the overall share of adherents of various religions. Christians comprise only one-third of the world's population but account for one-half of the world's international migrants. Muslims and Jews also comprise higher percentages of the world's migrants than their shares of the world's population. Buddhists, Hindus, folk religionists, and unaffiliated people are less likely to migrate (Figure 6.8.1).

Buddhism 7,310,000 3%
2% Judaism 3,650,000
other religions 9,110,000 4%
Hinduism 10,700,000 5%
9% unaffiliated 19,330,000
Christianity 105,670,000 49%
Islam 58,580,000 27%

▲ 6.8.1 **RELIGION OF INTERNATIONAL MIGRANTS**

Jews are much more likely to migrate internationally than their share of the world's population would suggest. Around 25 percent of all Jews have migrated from one country to another at some point in their lives. In comparison, only 3 percent of all people alive today have migrated internationally. Among the more numerous religious groups, around 5 percent of all Christians and 4 percent of all Muslims have migrated, compared to only 1 or 2 percent of other religious groups (Figure 6.8.2).

▲ 6.8.2 **PERCENTAGE OF PEOPLE ALIVE TODAY WHO HAVE MIGRATED**

Migration Patterns of Christians

Christians who migrate internationally favor some predominantly Christian regions over others. North America and Europe attract relatively large numbers of Christians, whereas Latin America and sub-Saharan Africa attract relatively few Christian migrants compared to the share of the world's Christians living in those two regions. The largest migration flows of Christians are into the United States and into and out of Russia (Figure 6.8.3).

Most immigrants to the United States are Christians. In 2012, approximately 61 percent of immigrants were Christian, according to Pew. Muslims comprised 10 percent of immigrants, Hindus 7 percent, Buddhists 6 percent, other religions 3 percent, and unaffiliated 14 percent. Unauthorized immigrants were 83 percent Christian, 7 percent other religions, and 9 percent unaffiliated. The percentage of immigrants to the United States who are Christians declined from 68 percent in 1992 to 61 percent in 2012. The decline has been offset by increases in the percentage who are Muslim or Hindu.

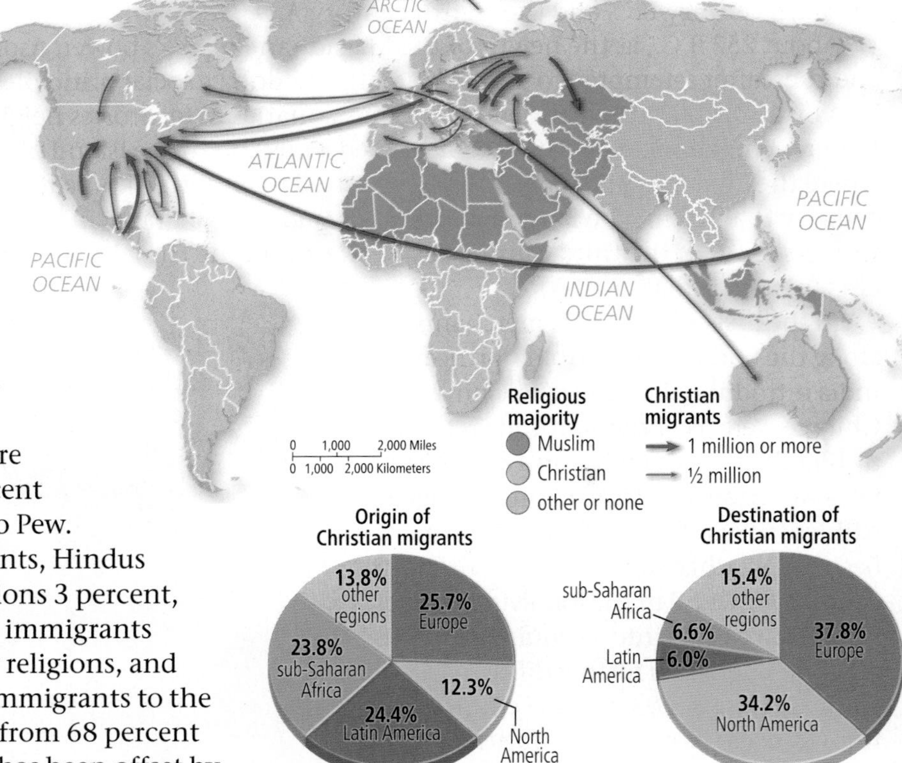

▲ 6.8.3 **INTERNATIONAL MIGRATION OF CHRISTIANS**
(a) Largest flows of Christian migrants (b) Origin and destination of Christian migrants.

Migration Patterns of Muslims

The migration patterns of Muslims vary from their distribution. Europe and Southwest Asia & North Africa attract much higher shares of migrants than their shares of the world's Muslims. Saudi Arabia is the country that attracts the largest number of Muslim migrants; Egypt sends the largest number of migrants there (Figure 6.8.4). Among European countries, Russia, Germany, and France are all leading destinations for Muslims. The largest numbers of Muslims who have migrated to Europe have come from Turkey to Germany and from Algeria to France. Morocco has been the origin of a large number of Muslim migrants to France and Spain.

On the other hand, the four countries with the largest Muslim populations—Indonesia, Pakistan, Bangladesh, and India—attract much fewer Muslim migrants compared with their share of the world's Muslim population. North America receives only around 1 percent of Muslim migrants.

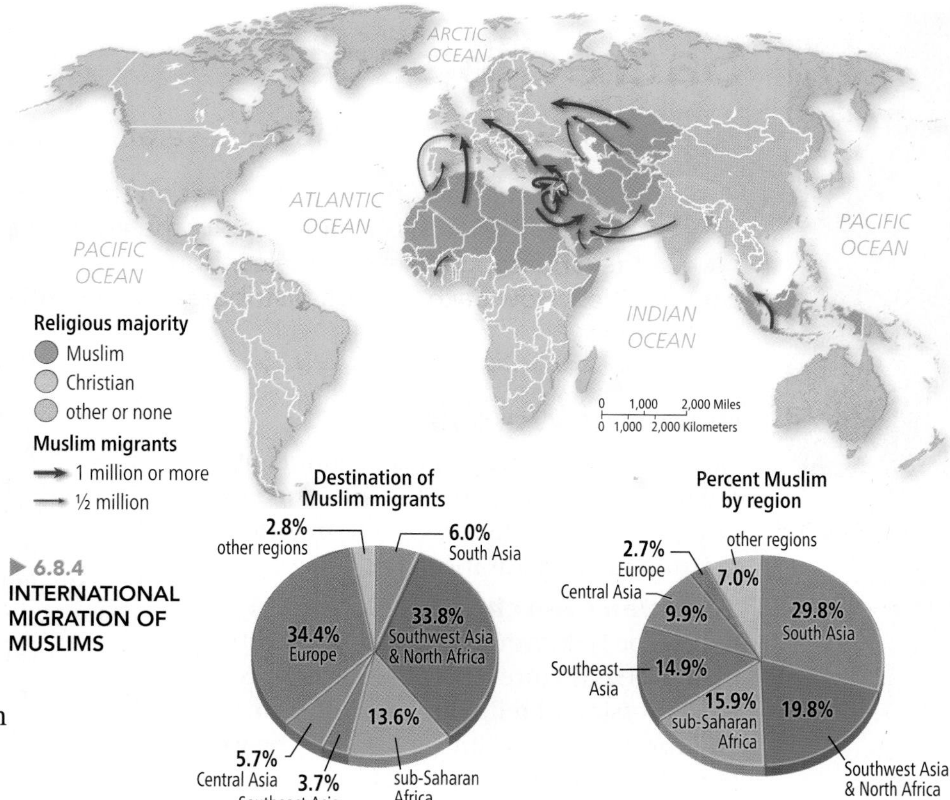

▶ 6.8.4 **INTERNATIONAL MIGRATION OF MUSLIMS**

Migration Patterns of Jews

Israel is the destination for nearly three-fourths of Jews who migrate internationally. As the world's only state with a Jewish majority, Israel offers an especially strong pull factor for Jewish migrants (see Key Issue 4). North America is the destination for most of the remainder.

Only since the creation of the State of Israel in 1948 has a significant percentage of the world's Jews lived in that territory. Most Jews have not lived there since A.D. 70, when the Romans forced them to disperse throughout the world, an action known as the diaspora, from the Greek word for "dispersion."

Most Jews migrated from the eastern Mediterranean to Europe. Having been exiled from the home of their religion, Jews lived among other nationalities, retaining separate religious practices but adopting other cultural characteristics of the host country, such as language.

Other nationalities often persecuted the Jews living in their midst. Historically, the Jews of many European countries were forced to live permanently in **ghettos**, defined as city neighborhoods set up by law to be inhabited only by Jews. The term ghetto originated during the sixteenth century in Venice, Italy, as a reference to the city's former copper foundry or metal-casting district, where Jews were forced to live. Ghettos were frequently surrounded by walls, and the gates were locked at night to prevent escape.

Beginning in the 1930s, but especially during World War II (1939–1945), the Nazis systematically rounded up a large percentage of European Jews, transported them to concentration camps, and exterminated them in the Holocaust. About 4 million Jews died in the camps and 2 million in other ways. Many of the survivors migrated to territory that became the State of Israel. Today, less than 15 percent of the world's 14 million Jews live in Europe, compared to 90 percent a century ago (Figure 6.8.5).

▼ 6.8.5 **DISTRIBUTION OF JEWS, 1910 AND 2012**

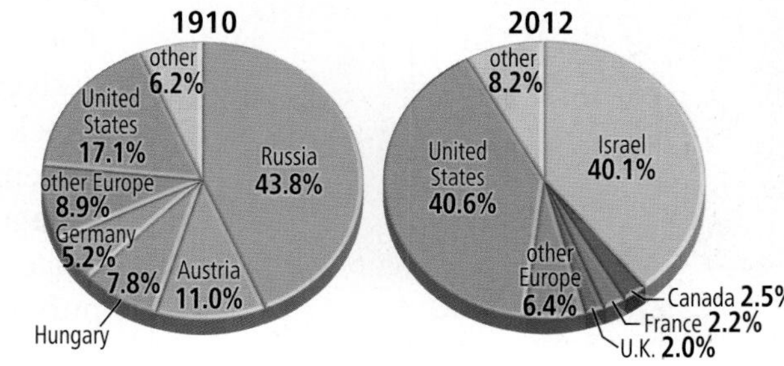

▲ 6.9.1
CHRISTIAN CHURCH
Church of Our Lady Assumed into Heaven, Krakow, Poland.

Sacred Space

- **Describe places of worship for several religions.**

Geographers study the major impact on the landscape made by religions. The impact of religion is clearly seen in the arrangement of human activities on the landscape at several scales, from relatively small parcels of land to entire communities. How each religion distributes its elements on the landscape is influenced by its beliefs.

Places of Worship

Sacred structures are physical anchors of religions. Some structures are designed for a group to gather, whereas others are intended for individual meditation.

Christian Churches. The Christian landscape is dominated by a high density of churches (Figure 6.9.1). The church is an expression of religious principles, an environment in the image of God. The word church derives from a Greek term meaning "lord," "master," and "power." Church also refers to a gathering of believers, as well as to the building at which the gathering occurs.

Since Christianity split into many denominations, no single style of church construction has dominated. Churches reflect both the cultural values of the denomination and the region's architectural heritage. Orthodox churches follow an architectural style that developed in the Byzantine Empire during the fifth century. Byzantine-style Orthodox churches tend to be highly ornate, topped by prominent domes. Many Protestant churches in North America, on the other hand, are simple, with little ornamentation. This austerity is a reflection of the Protestant conception of a church as an assembly hall for preaching to the congregation.

▲ 6.9.2 **JEWISH SYNAGOGUE**
Eldridge Street Synagogue, New York.

Jewish Synagogues. The word synagogue derives from the Greek word for "assembly." A synagogue is a place for study and public assembly, as well as for prayer (Figure 6.9.2). The origin of the synagogue is unknown; it possibly came to be during the sixth century B.C., when Jews were living in exile in Babylonia, after the destruction of the First Temple in 586 B.C. Synagogues took on more importance as the place for communal prayer after the destruction of the Second Temple in A.D. 70.

Hindu Temples. Important Hindu religious functions are more likely to take place at home within the family. A Hindu temple is a structure designed to bring individuals closer to their gods. It serves as a shrine to one or more gods and as a place for individual reflection and meditation, in accordance with one's personal practices within the faith.

As with many other elements of Hinduism, the time and place of origin of temples are unknown. Detailed evidence of the existence of temples dates from the first century B.C. Size and number of temples are determined by local preferences and commitment of resources rather than standards imposed by religious doctrine (Figure 6.9.3).

▼ 6.9.3 **HINDU TEMPLE**
Mata Lal Devi Mandir, Amritsar, India.

Places of Pilgrimage

Buddhism and Islam place strong emphasis on identifying shrines. Places are holy because they are the locations of important events in the life of Buddha or Muhammad. Making a **pilgrimage** to these holy places—a journey for religious purposes to a place considered sacred—is incorporated into the rituals of these religions.

Buddhist Shrines. Eight places are holy to Buddhists because they were the locations of important events in Buddha's life (see Research & Analyze and Figure 6.9.4). The four most important of the eight places are concentrated in a small area of northeastern India and southern Nepal:

- Lumbinī in southern Nepal is where Buddha was born around 563 B.C.
- Bodh Gaya is the site where Buddha reached Enlightenment (freedom from lust, hatred, and delusion).
- Deer Park in Sarnath is where Buddha gave his first sermon.
- Kushinagar is where Buddha died at age 80 and passed into Nirvana, a state of peaceful extinction.

Four other sites in northeastern India are particularly sacred because they were the locations of Buddha's principal miracles:

- Śrāvastī is where Buddha performed his greatest miracle. Before an assembled audience of competing religious leaders, Buddha created multiple images of himself and visited heaven.
- Sankashya is where Buddha is said to have ascended to heaven, preached to his mother, and returned to Earth.
- Rājagrha is holy because Buddha tamed a wild elephant there, and shortly after Buddha's death, it became the site of the first Buddhist Council.
- Vaiśālī is the site of Buddha's announcement of his impending death and the second Buddhist Council.

Pagodas contain relics that Buddhists believe to be a portion of Buddha's body or clothing. After Buddha's death, his followers scrambled to obtain these relics. As part of the process of diffusing the religion, Buddhists carried these relics to other countries and built pagodas for them. Pagodas typically include tall, many-sided towers arranged in a series of tiers, balconies, and slanting roofs. Pagodas are not designed for congregational worship. Individual prayer or meditation is more likely to be undertaken at an adjacent temple, at a remote monastery, or in a home.

Islam Holy Cities. The holiest locations in Islam are in cities associated with the life of Muhammad.

- **Makkah.** The holiest city for Muslims is Makkah (Mecca), the birthplace of Muhammad. Every healthy Muslim who has adequate financial resources is expected to undertake a pilgrimage, called a hajj, to Makkah. Makkah contains the holiest object in the Islamic landscape, a cube-shaped structure encased in silk known as al-Ka'ba (refer to Figure 6.3.1). The Ka'ba, thought by Muslims to have been built by Abraham and Ishmael, contains a black stone that Muslims believe was given to Abraham by Gabriel as a sign of a covenant with Ishmael and the Muslim people.

  The Ka'ba stands at the center of the Great Mosque, Masjid al-Haram, Islam's largest mosque. The Masjid al-Haram mosque also contains the well of Zamzam, considered to have the same source as the water given to Hagar by the Angel Gabriel to quench the thirst of her infant, Ishmael.
- **Madinah.** The second-most-holy geographic location in Islam is Madinah (Medina), site of Muhammad's tomb. Muhammad received his first support from the people of Madinah and became the city's chief administrator (refer to Figure 6.6.3).

RESEARCH & ANALYZE
Buddhist shrines

Buddhists regard the eight places named in Figure 6.9.4 as especially important because of events in Buddha's life.

Buddhanet
https://goo.gl/4nXqr2

1. Use your search engine to look up *Buddha Bodh Gaya*. Describe the structure that currently occupies the site.

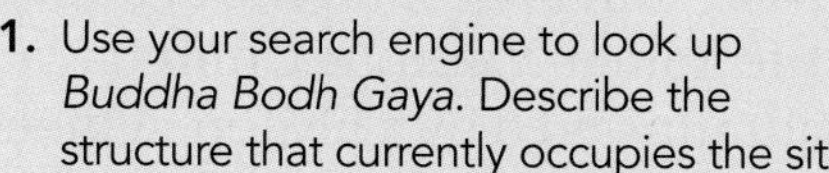

2. Look up each of the other seven important sites and describe what you see there.

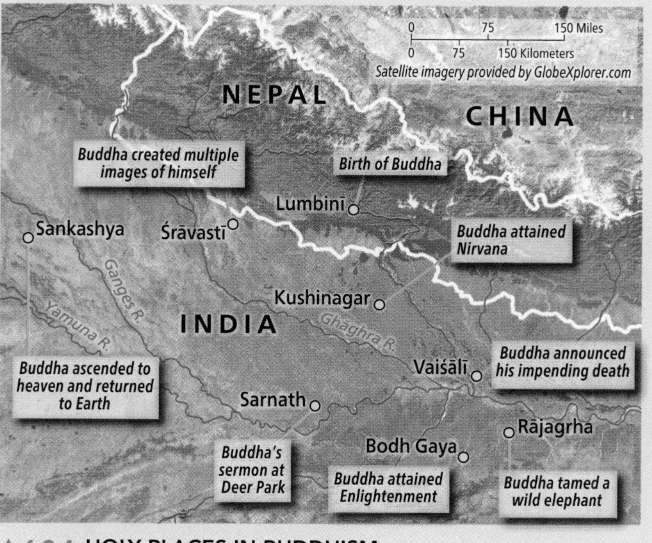

▲ 6.9.4 HOLY PLACES IN BUDDHISM

▲ 6.10.1 ST. PETER'S BASILICA AND SQUARE, VATICAN CITY, DURING AUDIENCE WITH THE POPE

Administration of Space

- Describe how different religions are organized across space.

Followers of a universalizing religion must be connected in order to ensure communication and consistency of doctrine. The method of interaction varies among universalizing religions, branches, and denominations. Ethnic religions tend not to have organized, central authorities.

Examples of Hierarchical Religions

A **hierarchical religion** has a well-defined geographic structure and organizes territory into local administrative units. The Church of Jesus Christ of Latter-Day Saints and Roman Catholicism are examples of hierarchical religions.

Latter-Day Saints. Latter-day Saints (Mormons) exercise strong organization of the landscape. The territory occupied by Mormons, primarily Utah and portions of surrounding states, is organized into wards, with populations of approximately 750 each. Several wards are combined into a stake of approximately 5,000 people. The highest authority in the Church—the board and president—frequently redraws ward and stake boundaries in rapidly growing areas to reflect the ideal population standards.

Roman Catholic Hierarchy. The basic unit of geographic organization in the Roman Catholic Church is a diocese, administered by a bishop. A diocese is spatially divided into parishes, each headed by a priest. A province, which combines several dioceses, is headed by an archbishop, who reports to the pope (Figure 6.10.1).

The area and population of parishes and dioceses vary according to the distribution of Roman Catholics across Earth's surface, though heavily influenced by historical factors. In parts of Europe, where the density is high, a typical parish may encompass only a few square kilometers and fewer than 1,000 people. On the other hand, portions of Latin America where the population is dispersed, may have parishes that encompass several hundred square kilometers and 5,000 people.

Changing distribution of the Roman Catholic population provides a challenge to the church. In the United States, for example, the Roman Catholic population is increasing in the Southwest and some suburbs, whereas it is declining in inner cities and rural areas (Figure 6.10.2). It can be difficult to add new parishes in the growing areas and to close churches in declining areas.

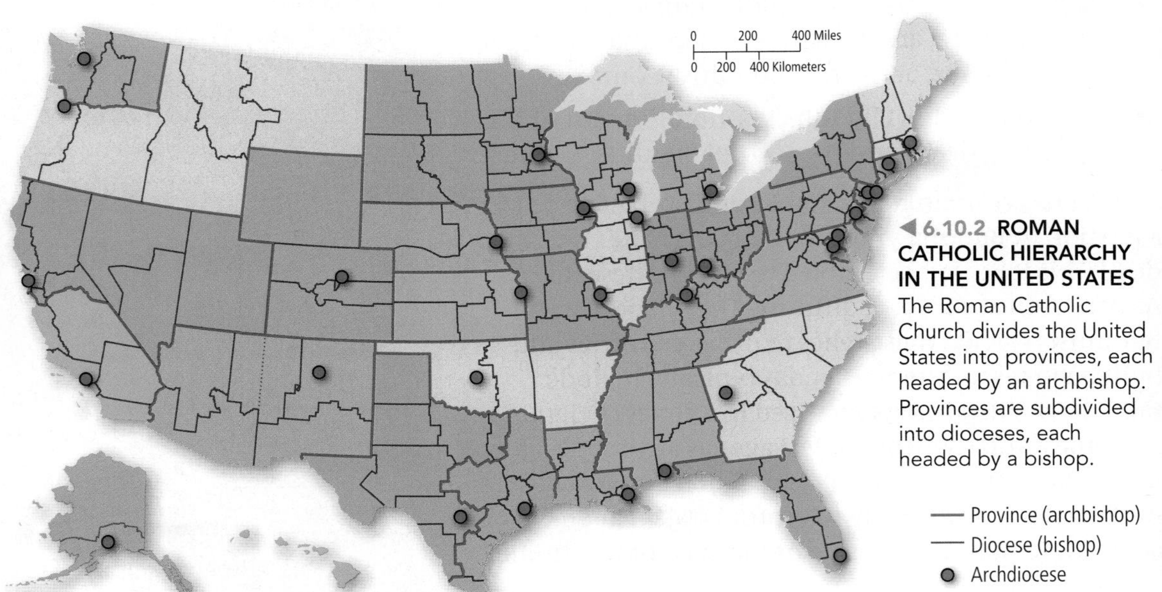

◀ 6.10.2 ROMAN CATHOLIC HIERARCHY IN THE UNITED STATES
The Roman Catholic Church divides the United States into provinces, each headed by an archbishop. Provinces are subdivided into dioceses, each headed by a bishop.

Locally Autonomous Religions

Some universalizing religions are highly **autonomous religions**, or self-sufficient, and interaction among communities is confined to little more than loose cooperation and shared ideas. Islam and some Protestant denominations are good examples.

Islam. Among the three large universalizing religions, Islam provides the most local autonomy. Like other locally autonomous religions, Islam has neither a religious hierarchy nor a formal territorial organization. A mosque is a place for public ceremony, and a leader known as a muezzin calls the faithful to prayer, but everyone is expected to participate equally in the rituals and is encouraged to pray privately.

Some Protestant Denominations. Extremely autonomous denominations including Baptists and United Church of Christ are organized into self-governing congregations. Each congregation establishes the precise form of worship and selects the leadership.

Presbyterian churches represent an intermediate degree of autonomy. Individual churches are united in a presbytery, several of which in turn are governed by a synod, with a general assembly as ultimate authority over all churches. Each Presbyterian church is governed by an elected board of directors with lay members.

Ethnic Religions. Hinduism is highly autonomous because worship is usually done alone or with others in the household. Hinduism has no centralized structure of religious control. Hindus share ideas primarily through undertaking pilgrimages and reading traditional writing.

Utopian Settlements

Most human settlements serve an economic purpose (see Chapter 12), but some are established primarily for religious reasons. A **utopian settlement** is an ideal community built around a religious way of life. Buildings are sited and economic activities organized to integrate religious principles into all aspects of daily life. More than 100 utopian communities were begun in the United States during the nineteenth century, in conformance with a group's distinctive religious beliefs. Examples include Oneida, New York; Ephrata, Pennsylvania; Nauvoo, Illinois; and New Harmony, Indiana.

The culmination of the utopian movement in the United States was the construction of Salt Lake City by the Mormons, beginning in 1848. The layout of Salt Lake City is based on a plan of the city of Zion given to the church elders in 1833 by the Mormon prophet Joseph Smith. The city has a regular grid pattern, unusually broad boulevards, and church-related buildings situated at strategic points (Figure 6.10.3).

▲ 6.10.3 **SALT LAKE TEMPLE, DOWNTOWN SALT LAKE CITY**
The Salt Lake Temple is located at the headquarters for the Church of Jesus Christ of Latter-day Saints.

Most utopian communities declined in importance or disappeared altogether. Some disappeared because the inhabitants were celibate and could not attract new adherents; in other cases, residents moved away in search of better economic conditions.

Religious Place Names

Roman Catholic immigrants have frequently given religious place names, or toponyms, to their settlements in the New World, particularly in Québec and the U.S. Southwest. Québec's boundaries with Ontario and the United States clearly illustrate the difference between toponyms selected by Roman Catholic and Protestant settlers. Religious place names are common in Québec but rare in the two neighbors (Figure 6.10.4).

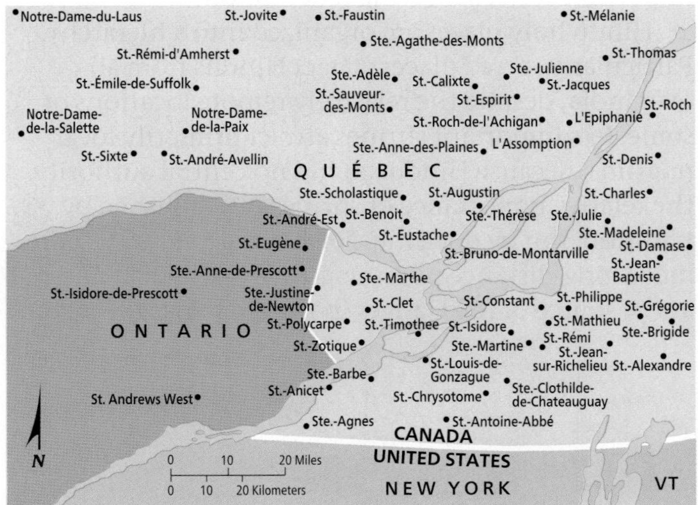

▲ 6.10.4 **RELIGIOUS TOPONYMS IN QUÉBEC**
Place names near Quebéc's boundaries with Ontario and the United States show the imprint of religion on the landscape. In Québec, a province with a predominantly Roman Catholic population, a large number of settlements are named for saints, whereas relatively few religious toponyms are found in predominantly Protestant Ontario, New York, and Vermont.

▲ 6.11.1 **HINDUS BATHE AND PRAY IN THE GANGES RIVER**
Varanasi, India.

Religions & the Physical Environment

- **Examine relationships of religions to the calendars and the physical landscape.**

Cosmogony is a set of beliefs concerning the origin of the universe. The universalizing religions Christianity and Islam consider that God (or Allah, for Islam) created the universe, including Earth's physical environment and human beings. To followers of ethnic religions such as primal-indigenous animists, the powers of the universe are mystical, and only a few people on Earth can harness these powers for medical or other purposes. Rather than attempt to transform the environment, animists accept environmental hazards as normal and unavoidable. Spirits or gods can be placated, however, through prayer and sacrifice.

Hinduism's South Asian Landscape

One of the principal reasons that ethnic religions are highly clustered is that they are closely tied to the physical geography of a particular place. Pilgrimages are undertaken to these physical features as an act of devotion.

As an ethnic religion of India, Hinduism is closely tied to the physical geography of India. According to a survey conducted by the geographer Surinder Bhardwaj, the natural features most likely to rank among the holiest shrines in India are riverbanks and coastlines. Hindus consider a pilgrimage, known as a tirtha, to be an act of purification. Although not a substitute for meditation, the pilgrimage is an important act in achieving redemption.

Hindu holy places are organized into a hierarchy. Particularly sacred places attract Hindus from all over India, despite the relatively remote locations of some; less important shrines attract primarily local pilgrims. Because Hinduism has no central authority, the relative importance of shrines is established by tradition, not by doctrine. For example, many Hindus make long-distance pilgrimages to Mt. Kailash, located at the source of the Ganges in the Himalayas, which is holy because Shiva lives there. Other mountains may attract only local pilgrims: Local residents may consider a nearby mountain to be holy if Shiva is thought to have visited it at one time.

Hindus believe that they achieve purification by bathing in holy rivers. The Ganges is the holiest river in India because it is supposed to spring forth from the hair of Shiva, one of the main deities (Figure 6.11.1). Indians come from all over the country to Hardwar, the most popular location for bathing in the Ganges.

Hindus generally practice cremation rather than burial. The body is washed with water from the Ganges River and then burned with a slow fire on a funeral pyre. Motivation for cremation may have originated from unwillingness thousands of years ago to leave a dead body exposed to attack by wild beasts or evil spirits.

The Solstice

The **solstice** has special significance in some ethnic religions. A major holiday in some pagan religions is the winter solstice, December 21 or 22 in the Northern Hemisphere. The winter solstice is the shortest day and longest night of the year, when the Sun appears lowest in the sky, and the apparent movement of the Sun's path north or south comes to a stop before reversing direction (solstice comes from the Latin to "stand still"). Stonehenge, a collection of stones erected in southwestern England some 4,500 years ago, is a prominent remnant of a pagan structure apparently aligned so the Sun rises between two stones on the summer and winter solstices (Figure 6.11.2).

◀ 6.11.2 **SUMMER SOLSTICE, STONEHENGE, UNITED KINGDOM**

The Calendar in Universalizing Religions

The principal purpose of the holidays in universalizing religions is to commemorate events in the founder's life. Here are some examples:

▲ 6.11.3 **END OF RAMADAN**
Muslims at Jama Masjid mosque, Delhi, India, observe Eid-al-Fitr Festival, which marks the end of Ramadan.

Christianity. Some Christians associate the major holidays of Easter (the resurrection of Jesus) and Christmas (the birth of Jesus) with distinctive seasons, but climate and the agricultural cycle are not central to the liturgy and rituals of these holidays. For example, Christians living in the U.S. North, Canada, and Northern Europe associate Christmas with winter. But for Christians in the Southern Hemisphere, December 25 is the height of summer.

Islam. As a universalizing religion with 1.8 billion adherents, Islam is practiced in various climates and latitudes (Figure 6.11.3). Islam uses a lunar calendar, which has 354 or 355 days. As a result, Muslim holidays arrive in different seasons from generation to generation. For example, Ramadan (commemorating the first revelation of the Quran to Muhammad) starts in 2020 on April 23, in the North Hemisphere spring. But Ramadan started in 2010 on August 11 and will start in 2030 on January 6.

The Calendar in Judaism

Judaism's major holidays are based on events in the agricultural calendar of the religion's homeland in present-day Israel. These agricultural holidays later gained importance because they also commemorated events in the Exodus of the Jews from Egypt, as recounted in the Bible. The reinterpretation of agricultural holidays in light of historical events has been especially important for Jews in North America, Europe, and other regions who are unfamiliar with the agricultural calendar of Southwest Asia.

Examples include:

- Pesach (Passover) derives from traditional agricultural practices in which farmers offered God the first fruits of the new spring harvest. It also recalls the liberation of the Jews from slavery in Egypt and the miracle of their successful flight under the leadership of Moses.
- Sukkot celebrates the final gathering of fruits for the year, and prayers, especially for rain, are offered to bring success in the upcoming agricultural year (Figure 6.11.4). It derives from the Hebrew word for the "booths," or "temporary shelters," occupied by Jews during their wandering in the wilderness for 40 years after fleeing Egypt.
- Shavuot (Feast of Weeks) comes at the end of the grain harvest. It is also considered the date during the wandering when Moses received the Ten Commandments from God.

Like Islam, Judaism uses a lunar calendar rather than a solar calendar. The Jewish calendar inserts an extra month every few years to match the agricultural and solar calendars, whereas Islam retains a strict lunar calendar.

◄ 6.11.4 **AGRICULTURAL HOLIDAYS IN JUDAISM**
Jews bless the *etrog* (citron) and *lulav* (date palm branches) during the holiday Sukkot at a synagogue in Brooklyn, New York.

6.12 KEY ISSUE 4 Why do conflicts arise among religions?

▲ 6.12.1 **DALIT** A Dalit cleans the street in Delhi, India.

Challenges for Religions

- **Interpret some challenges faced by religions in society.**

Religion is an element of cultural diversity that has led to conflict in many localities. Attempts by intense adherents of one religion to organize Earth's surface can conflict with the spatial expression of other religious or nonreligious ideas.

Contributing to more intense religious conflict has been a resurgence of religious **fundamentalism**, which is a literal interpretation and a strict and intense adherence to what the fundamentalists define as the basic principles of a religion (or a religious branch, denomination, or sect). In a world increasingly dominated by a global culture and economy, religious fundamentalism is one way for a group to maintain distinctive cultural identity. A group convinced that its religious view is the correct one may spatially intrude upon the territory controlled by other religious groups.

Hinduism and Social Equality

Hinduism has been strongly challenged since the 1800s, when British colonial administrators introduced their social and moral concepts to India. The most vulnerable aspect of the Hindu religion was its rigid **caste** system, which was the class or distinct hereditary order into which a Hindu was assigned, according to religious law. Castes included Brahmans (priests and top administrators), Kshatriyas (warriors), Vaisyas (merchants), and Shudras (agricultural workers and artisans).

Below the four castes were the Dalits (outcasts or untouchables), who did work considered too dirty for other castes (Figure 6.12.1). In theory, the Dalits were descended from the indigenous people who dwelled in India prior to the Aryan conquest. Until recently, social relations among the castes were limited, and the rights of non-Brahmans, especially Dalits, were restricted (Figure 6.12.2). Since India's independence in 1947, the rigid caste system has been considerably relaxed, but some people still take it into consideration in activities such as marriage.

▶ 6.12.2 **HINDU CASTE SYSTEM** Women demonstrate for Dalit rights, Bangalore, India.

Religion and Communism

Organized religion was challenged in the twentieth century by the rise of communism in Eastern Europe and Asia. Communist regimes generally discouraged religious belief and practice. Communist leaders shared the view of Karl Marx, who had called religion "the opium of the people. " The end of Communist rule in the late twentieth century brought a religious revival in Eastern Europe, especially where Roman Catholicism is the most prevalent branch of Christianity. Countries in Central Asia, where Islam is the predominant religion, are struggling to find a balance between secular laws and values of the former Soviet Union and Islamic traditions.

Conflict between communism and religion remains especially acute in China. The dispute centers around the role of Buddhism and its spiritual leader the Dalai Lama in the territory known as Tibet in most of the world but called Xizang by the government of China. China, which had ruled Tibet from 1720 until its independence in 1911, invaded the rugged, isolated country in 1950 and installed a Communist government in 1953. Before the Communist takeover, daily life in Tibet was traditionally dominated by Buddhist rites. The Chinese Communists sought to reduce the domination of Buddhist monks. After crushing a rebellion in 1959, China executed or imprisoned tens of thousands and forced another 100,000, including the Dalai Lama, to emigrate (Figure 6.12.3).

▲ 6.12.3 **RELIGION AND COMMUNISM** Tibet Uprising Day in London (March 10) commemorates a failed rebellion against the takeover of Tibet by the People's Republic of China.

Islamic Fundamentalism and Democratic Values

Islamic fundamentalists control of portions of Central and Southwestern Asia. The Taliban (which means "religious students") gained power in Afghanistan in 1996 and imposed very strict laws inspired by Islamic values as they interpreted them. "Western, non-Islamic" leisure activities were banned, such as playing music, flying kites, watching television, and surfing the Internet. Soccer stadiums were converted to settings for executions and floggings.

A U.S.-led coalition overthrew the Taliban in 2001 and replaced it with a democratically elected government. However, the Taliban was able to regroup and has regained control of parts of Afghanistan and Pakistan (Figure 6.12.4) (see Chapter 8).

The Islamic State (also known as ISIS and ISIL) is an example of terrorist group that professes to adhere to fundamentalist Islam. The Islamic State has gained control of portions of Iraq and Syria and has imposed harsh laws backed by violence that the organization considers consistent with its views of Islam. The vast majority of the world's Muslims do not consider organizations such as the Taliban and Islamic State to reflect the true teachings of Islam.

▶ 6.12.4 **ISLAMIC FUNDAMENTALISM** Taliban fighters at a surrender ceremony in Afghanistan.

▲ 6.13.1 **JERUSALEM** The Western Wall, which remains from the ancient Jewish Temple, is situated immediately below the mount containing Islam's Dome of the Rock and al-Aqsa Mosque. A ramp allows visitors to reach Islam's holy structures without passing through Jews praying at the Western Wall.

Geographic Perspectives on Religious Conflicts in the Middle East

- Understand geographic elements of conflict in Israel.

Religious conflict in the Middle East is among the world's longest-standing and most intractable.

Religious Importance

Jews, Christians, and Muslims have fought for more than 1,000 years to control the same small strip of land, most of which is now part of the State of Israel.

Judaism. Jews make a special claim to the territory they call the Promised Land. The major events in the development of Judaism took place there, and the religion's customs and rituals acquired meaning from the agricultural life of the ancient Israelite tribes. Jerusalem is especially holy to Jews as the location of the Temple, their center of worship in ancient times.

Christianity. Christians consider Palestine the Holy Land and Jerusalem the Holy City because the major events in Jesus's life, death, and resurrection were concentrated there.

Islam. Muslims regard Jerusalem as their third-holiest city, after Makkah and Madinah, because it is the place from which Muhammad is thought by Muslims to have ascended to heaven. Islam became the region's most widely practiced religion beginning in the seventh century A.D.

Jerusalem: Challenging Geography

The geography of Jerusalem makes it especially difficult to settle long-standing religious conflicts. The challenge is that the most sacred space in Jerusalem for Muslims was literally built on top of the most sacred space for Jews (Figures 6.13.1 and 6.13.2).

Jerusalem is especially holy to Jews as the location of the Temple, their center of worship in ancient times. The First Temple, built by King Solomon in approximately 960 B.C., was destroyed by the Babylonians in 586 B.C. After the Persian Empire, led by Cyrus the Great, gained control of Jerusalem, Jews were allowed to build a Second Temple in 516 B.C. The Romans destroyed the Jewish Second Temple in A.D. 70. The Western Wall of the Temple survives.

The most important Muslim structure in Jerusalem is the Dome of the Rock, built in A.D. 691. Muslims believe that the large rock beneath the building's dome is the place from which Muhammad ascended to heaven, as well as the altar on which Abraham prepared to sacrifice his son Isaac (according to Jews and Christians) or his son Ishmael (according to Muslims). Immediately south of the Dome of the Rock is the al-Aqsa Mosque.

The challenge facing Jews and Muslims is that al-Aqsa Mosque was built on the site of the ruins of the Jewish Second Temple. Thus, the surviving Western Wall of the Jewish Temple is situated immediately beneath holy Muslim structures. Because the holy Muslim structures sit literally on top of Judaism's holiest structure, the two sets of holy structures cannot be logically divided by a line on a map.

▼ 6.13.2 **OLD CITY OF JERUSALEM**

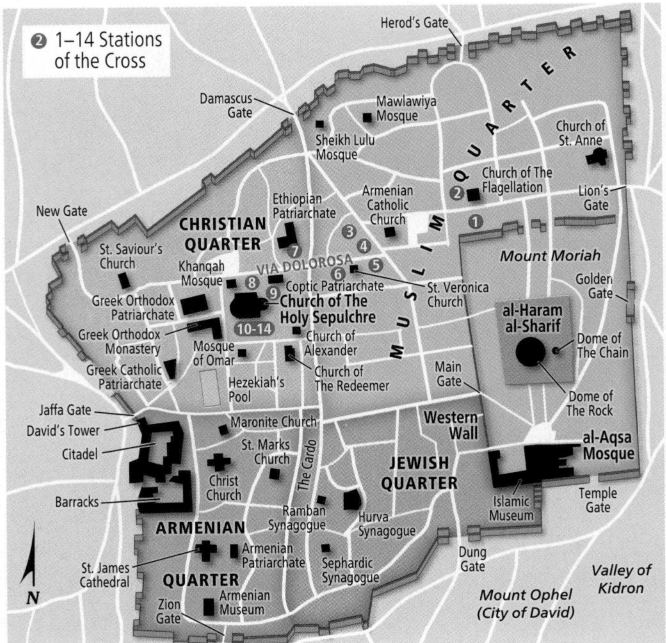

Competing Israeli and Palestinian Perspectives

The Holy Land was incorporated into a succession of empires, culminating with the British after World War I. The United Nations voted in 1947 to partition the British Mandate for Palestine into two independent states, one Jewish and one Arab. Jerusalem was to be an international city, open to all religions, and run by the U.N. (Figure 6.13.3a).

When the British withdrew in 1948, Jews declared an independent State of Israel within the boundaries prescribed by the U.N. resolution (Figure 6.13.3b). Over the next quarter-century, Israel was forced to fight for its survival in four wars with its neighbors in 1948-49, 1956, 1967, and 1973. During the 1967 Six-Day War, Israel captured territory from its neighbors. Israel has returned some of the captured territory and retains control of some of it (Figure 6.13.3c).

After the 1973 War, the Palestinians emerged as Israel's principal opponent. Five groups of people consider themselves Palestinians: people living in the territories captured by Israel in 1967; some citizens of Israel who are Arabs; people who fled from Israel to other countries after the 1948–1949 war; people who fled from the West Bank or Gaza to other countries after the 1967 Six-Day War; and some citizens of other countries, especially Jordan, Lebanon, Syria, Kuwait, and Saudi Arabia.

Israel has permitted the organization of a limited form of government in much of the West Bank and Gaza, called the Palestinian Authority, but Palestinians are not satisfied with either the territory or the power they have received thus far. Some Palestinians are willing to recognize the State of Israel with its Jewish majority in exchange for return of all territory taken by Israel in the 1967 Six-Day War. Other Palestinians do not recognize the right of Israel to exist and want to continue fighting for control of the entire territory between the Jordan River and the Mediterranean Sea. The United States, European countries, and Israel consider the Palestinian organization Hamas to be a terrorist organization.

Israeli Jews have been divided between those who wished to retain some of the West Bank and those who wished to make compromises with the Palestinians in return for formal recognition and a stable peace. In recent years, a large majority of Israelis have supported construction of a barrier to deter Palestinian attacks (see Debate It! feature and Figures 6.13.4 and 6.13.5).

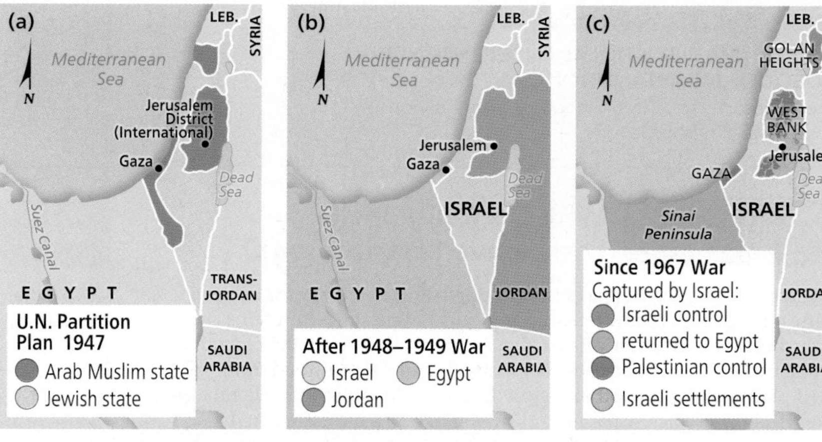

▲ 6.13.3 TERRITORIAL CHANGES IN ISRAEL AND ITS NEIGHBORS

DEBATE IT!
The Separation Barrier

Israel has built a security fence along 70 percent of the boundary with the West Bank.

KEEP THE SECURITY FENCE

- Israel is a small country with a Jewish majority surrounded by a a region of mostly hostile neighbors.
- To protect its citizens after repeated attacks by its neighbors, Israel constructed a fence near its borders to help keep out attackers (Figure 6.13.4).
- Israel has made numerous adjustments to the location of the fence in response to humanitarian concerns.

► 6.13.4 SEPARATION BARRIER

REMOVE THE SEGREGATION WALL

- The wall has helped Jewish settlers to increase the territory under their control.
- Palestinians living in the West Bank consider Israel's construction of settlements and the wall to be hostile acts.
- The wall that Israel built prevents some Palestinians from reaching their fields and workplaces (Figure 6.13.5).

▲ 6.13.5 SEPARATION BARRIER IN JERUSALEM
PALESTINIAN TOWN OF AL-RAM IS IN THE BACKGROUND.

CHAPTER 6

Review, Analyze, & Apply

KEY ISSUE 1 Where Are Religions Distributed?

Religions are classified as universalizing or ethnic. The three universalizing religions with the largest number of adherents are Christianity, Islam, and Buddhism. Each is divided into branches and denominations. Hinduism is the largest ethnic religion. Other ethnic religions with the largest numbers of followers are clustered primarily elsewhere in Asia.

THINKING GEOGRAPHICALLY

▲ 6.CR.1 **MASJID ISTIQLAL (INDEPENDENCE MOSQUE), JAKARTA, INDONESIA**
The largest mosque in the country with the world's largest Muslim population.

1. The percentage of the world's people adhering to Islam is forecast by the Pew Research Forum to increase from 23 percent in 2010 to 30 percent in 2050. What demographic factors presented in Chapter 2 (Population & Health) would underlie this increase? Conversely, why might the percentage who are Christians not be increasing?

KEY ISSUE 2 Why Do Religions Have Distinctive Distributions?

A universalizing religion has a known origin and clear patterns of diffusion, whereas ethnic religions typically have unknown origins and little diffusion. The three most widely practiced universalizing religions originated with single historical individuals and have diffused from their places of origin to other regions of the world. An ethnic religion like Hinduism typically has unknown origins and a more clustered distribution that is often tied to the physical landscape.

THINKING GEOGRAPHICALLY

▲ 6.CR.2 **EDICULE, CHURCH OF THE HOLY SEPULCHRE, JERUSALEM**
Undergoing investigation and restoration work.

2. Most Christians accept that Jesus was buried and resurrected from a tomb called the Edicule that is now housed inside the Church of the Holy Sepulchre in Jerusalem. In 2016, researchers unsealed the burial site. What did they find? Use your Internet browser or go to **news.nationalgeographic.com/2016/10/jesus-christ-tomb-burial-church-holy-sepulchre/**.

KEY ISSUE 3 How Do Religions Organize Space?

The holiest places in universalizing religions typically relate to events in the life of the founder. In an ethnic religion, holy places typically derive from the physical geography where the religion's adherents are clustered. Holidays typically derive from the physical geography where an ethnic religion is clustered, whereas they derive from the founder's life in a universalizing religion.

THINKING GEOGRAPHICALLY

3. Based on your understanding of reasons for migration discussed in Chapter 3, as well as the distribution of Muslims by country, what factors might account for the distinctive origin of pilgrims?

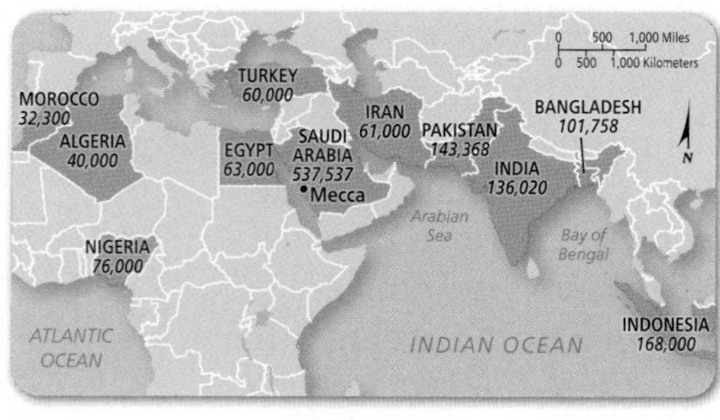

◀ 6.CR.3 **ORIGINS OF PILGRIMS TO MAKKAH, 2015**

KEY ISSUE 4 Why Do Conflicts Arise Among Religions?

Some religions have competed for control of territory with nonreligious ideas, notably communism and economic modernization. Conflict in the Middle East goes back many centuries. Jews, Muslims, and Christians have fought for control of land in the Middle East that is now part of the State of Israel. The most sacred space in Jerusalem for Muslims was built on top of the most sacred space for Jews.

THINKING GEOGRAPHICALLY

▲ 6.CR.4 **POTALA PALACE, LHASA, TIBET**

4. Three-fourths of the Chinese people adhere to a Chinese traditional religion or are unaffiliated with any religion. Given the relatively small percentage of Chinese who adhere to the principal universalizing religions, why might the government of China be engaged in conflicts with Tibetan Buddhists and Muslims living in the western portion of the country?

Mastering Geography

Looking for additional review and test prep materials? Visit the Study Area in Mastering Geography to enhance your geographic literacy, spatial reasoning skills, and understanding of this chapter's content. Access MapMaster™ interactive maps, video case studies, *In the News* current articles, flashcards, self-study quizzes, an eText of *Contemporary Human Geography*, and more. **pearson.com/mastering/geography**

Key Terms

Agnosticism (p. 138) The belief that the existence of God can't be proven or disproven empirically.

Animism (p. 145) The belief that objects, such as plants and stones, or natural events, like thunderstorms and earthquakes, have a discrete spirit and conscious life.

Atheism (p. 138) The belief that God does not exist.

Autonomous religion (p. 157) A religion that does not have a central authority but shares ideas and cooperates informally.

Branch (p. 140) A large and fundamental division within a religion.

Caste (p. 160) The class or distinct hereditary order into which a Hindu is assigned, according to religious law.

Congregation (p. 140) A local assembly of persons brought together for common religious worship.

Cosmogony (p. 158) A set of beliefs concerning the origin of the universe.

Denomination (p. 140) A division of a branch that unites a number of local congregations into a single legal and administrative body.

Ethnic religion (p. 139) A religion with a relatively concentrated spatial distribution whose principles are likely to be based on the physical characteristics of the particular location in which its adherents are concentrated.

Fundamentalism (p. 160) Literal interpretation and strict adherence to basic principles of a religion (or a religious branch, denomination, or congregation).

Ghetto (p. 153) During the Middle Ages, a neighborhood in a city set up by law to be inhabited only by Jews; now used to denote a section of a city in which members of any minority group live because of social, legal, or economic pressure.

Hierarchical religion (p. 156) A religion in which a central authority exercises a high degree of control.

Missionary (p. 150) An individual who helps to diffuse a universalizing religion.

Monotheism (p. 146) The doctrine of or belief in the existence of only one God.

Pilgrimage (p. 155) A journey to a place considered sacred for religious purposes.

Polytheism (p. 146) Belief in or worship of more than one god.

Solstice (p. 158) An astronomical event that happens twice each year, when the tilt of Earth's axis is most inclined toward or away from the Sun, causing the Sun's apparent position in the sky to reach its northernmost or southernmost extreme, and resulting in the shortest and longest days of the year.

Syncretic (p. 144) Combining several religious traditions.

Universalizing religion (p. 139) A religion that attempts to appeal to all people, not just those living in a particular location.

Utopian settlement (p. 157) A community built around an ideal way of life, often based on a religion.

GeoVideo

Log in to the Mastering Geography™ Study Area to view this video.

Christians of the Holy Land

Christians living in Israel and the West Bank represent a community that dates backs to Christianity's early centuries, but today is experiencing stress.

1. How has the number of Christians in Jerusalem's Old City and Bethlehem changed in recent decades? How does the video explain this change?
2. What does the video imply about the size of the Christian population of Nazareth, and what possible explanations are discussed?

Explore

Masjid's surroundings

Use Google Earth to explore the surrounding of Masjid al-Haram, Islam's most important mosque, in Makkah, Saudi Arabia.

Search *for Masjid al-Haram, Makkah.*

1. What is the name of the tall building complex immediately the south of the Masjid? Click on the name. What is in the building complex?
2. Why might this building complex be located immediately next to Islam's holiest place (refer to page 155)?

▶ 6.CR.5 ABRAJ AL BAIT

Geospatial Analysis

Log in to the Mastering Geography Study Area to access MapMaster 2.0.

South Asia's religions

South Asia has several religious boundaries that appear to be sharp on a world map.

Add *Religions* and ***zoom*** to South Asia. In the *Legend,* ***select*** the *Settings* icon, and ***select*** *Show Political Labels.* ***Add*** *The British Empire, Early 1920s* layer, ***select*** *Add Group Data Layers to Map,* ***select*** *Split Map Window.*

1. What present-day countries in *South Asia* were part of the British Empire in the early 1920s?
2. What religions were contained within the British Empire? Why might this have been a challenge for the Empire rulers? Why might this have been a challenge when the Empire was broken into independent countries?

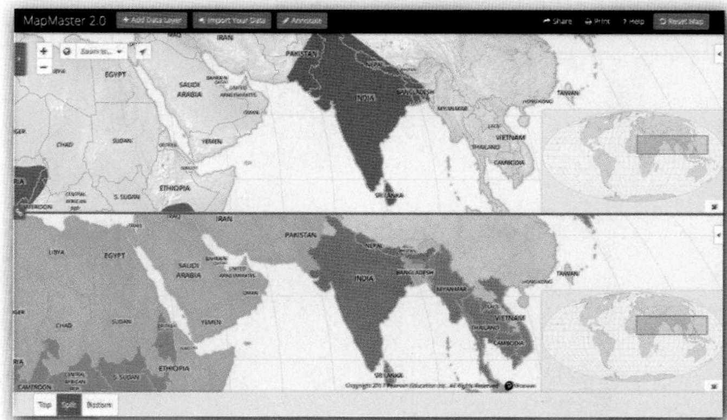

▲ 6.CR.6 SOUTH ASIA RELIGIONS

CHAPTER

7 Ethnicities

Our ethnicity is an important element of our cultural identity. It is a link to the experiences of our ancestors and to our cultural traditions. Geographers are especially interested in ethnicity, because the concept is place-based. Ethnic identity is rooted in the geography of a particular place on Earth, but can remain important even when people live far from the place where their ethnicity originated.

◀ 1 mile race, Nitro Athletics event, Melbourne, Australia.

KEY ISSUES

1 Where Are Ethnicities Distributed?

An ethnic group draws identity and meaning from the physical and cultural features of a particular place that it currently lives or where it once inhabited.

2 Why Do Ethnicities Have Distinctive Distributions?

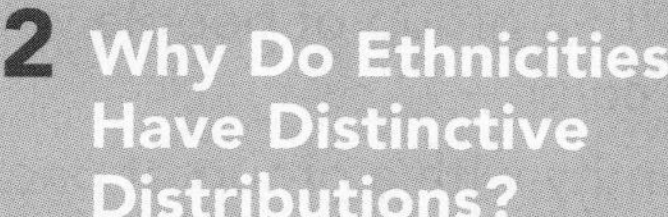

African Americans have a distinctive ethnic history shaped by forced migration from Africa and enforced segregation within the United States.

3 Why Might Ethnicities Face Conflicts?

Conflicts may arise among ethnic groups trying to live in the same area.

4 Why Do Ethnic Cleansing and Genocide Occur?

Conflicts among ethnic groups have sometimes led to mass killings and forced relocation.

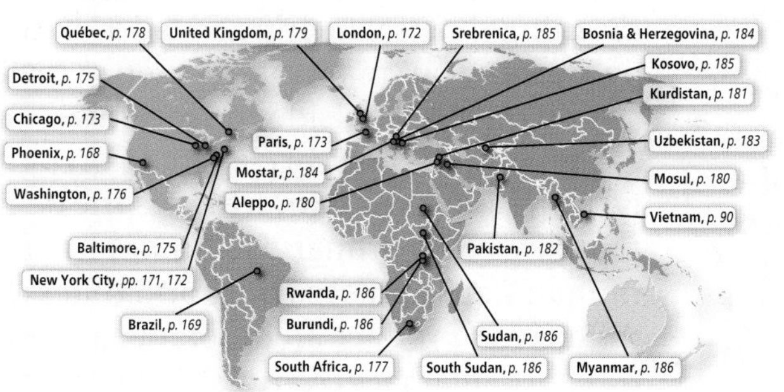

social construction
separate but equal
ethnicity
sharecropper
white flight
hispanic
black lives matter
racism
nationalism centripetal force
genocide
nationality
latino/latina
ethnophobia
sharecropper
ethnic cleansing
race
ethnoburb
apartheid
triangular slave trade
asian american
blockbusting
homelands
ethnic enclave
african american

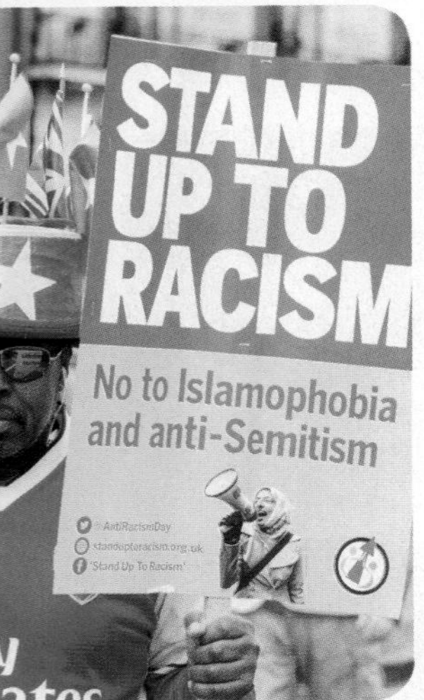

▲ 7.1.1 RALLY IN SUPPORT OF UNITED NATIONS INTERNATIONAL DAY FOR THE ELIMINATION OF RACIAL DISCRIMINATION

Ethnicity & Race

- Distinguish between ethnicity and race.

The meaning of ethnicity, the subject of this chapter, is frequently confused with definitions of race and nationality:

- **Ethnicity** is identity with a group of people who share the cultural traditions of a particular homeland or hearth. An ethnicity could refer to a group occupying a very small area, such as the Tutsis of Central Africa, or it could refer to a large heterogeneous group, such as Asian Americans.
- **Race** is identity with a group of people who are perceived to share a physiological trait, such as skin color.
- **Nationality** is identity with a group of people who share legal attachment to a particular country.

The title of this chapter is "Ethnicities," because it is the cultural feature that is place-based. "Nationality," which is also place-based, is introduced in this chapter and is discussed in more detail in Chapter 8. Though not place-based, "race" is an important concept because it is often misused as a synonym for "ethnicity."

Ethnicity and Race

In principle, ethnicity, nationality, and race are distinct concepts. Nationality refers to a person's country of citizenship, race to a person's biological composition, and ethnicity to a person's place of cultural heritage. In actuality, differences among the three concepts are not always clear-cut. Some individuals are not in a position to identify one or more of their personal traits. For example, an individual's two parents may identify with different ethnicities, races, and nationalities. Furthermore, many societies muddle the three concepts, either through unclear language or deliberate decisions.

Features of race, such as skin color, hair type and color, blood traits, and shape of body, head, and facial features, were once thought to be scientifically classifiable. Contemporary geographers reject the discredited biological basis of classifying humans into a handful of races because these features are not rooted in specific places (Figure 7.1.1).

One feature of race is especially important for geographers: the color of skin. The distribution of persons by skin color is studied by geographers because it is the fundamental basis by which people in many societies sort out where they reside, attend school, spend their leisure time, and perform many other activities of daily life (Figure 7.1.2).

▼ 7.1.2 CESAR CHAVEZ HIGH SCHOOL PERCUSSION ENSEMBLE, PHOENIX, ARIZONA

At best, biological features are so highly variable among members of a race that any prejudged classification is meaningless. Perhaps many tens or hundreds of thousands of years ago, early "humans" (however they emerged as a distinct species) lived in such isolation from other early "humans" that they were truly distinct genetically. But the degree of isolation needed to keep biological features distinct genetically vanished when the first human crossed a river or climbed a hill. The attempt to classify people according to race is regarded by geographers as a **social construction**, which is an idea or a meaning that is widely accepted as natural by a society but may not represent a reality shared by those outside the society.

At worst, biological classification by race is the basis for **racism**, which is the belief that race is the primary determinant of human traits and capacities and that racial differences produce an inherent superiority of a particular race. A **racist** is a person who displays discrimination or feels prejudice against people of particular races.

Ethnicities and Races in Brazil

Brazil struggles with defining its population by race or ethnicity. Like the United State, Brazil is composed of people whose ancestors emigrated from many places. Portugal and West Africa have been the leading places of origin, but large numbers have come from other European countries, Japan, Southwest Asia, and elsewhere. In addition, a large number of indigenous people lived in Brazil prior to large-scale emigration from other continents.

Brazil's census classifies people according to skin color. The Brazilian Institute of Geography and Statistics, a government agency that conducts the official census, asks Brazilians to identify themselves as belonging to one of five so-called races: branco (white), pardo (brown), preto (black), amarelo (yellow), and indigenous (Figure 7.1.3a). Brancos and pardos each comprise more than 40 percent of Brazil's population and together account for more than 90 percent.

Further complicating Brazil's racial classifications, Brazilian Institute of Geography and Statistics researcher José Luiz Petrucelli found that Brazilians don't care for the census choices. When asked an open-ended question about their race, Brazilians responded with 143 different answers. Most significant were the large numbers who identified themselves as moreno (brunette or olive) or moreno claro (light brown), races not even included in the census. A number of Brazilians also identified with two races that both translate into English as black: preto and negro. On the other hand, few Brazilians considered themselves pardo, which the official census uses for brown (Figure 7.1.3b).

Brazil also displays sharp regional differences in the distribution of races (Figure 7.1.4). Brancos are clustered in the south and pardos in the north.

Genetic studies show that roughly 70 percent of Brazilians have predominantly European ancestry, 20 percent predominantly African, and 10 percent predominantly Native American. However, through many generations of marriages and births, most Brazilians have a mix of backgrounds (Figure 7.1.5).

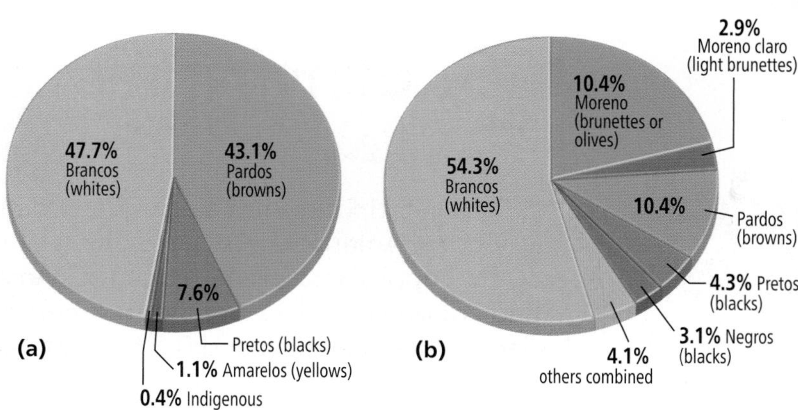

▲ 7.1.3 RACES IN BRAZIL
(a) Official results from the 2010 census. (b) Results of a self-identification survey by Brazilian Institute of Geography and Statistics.

◀ 7.1.4 DISTRIBUTION OF RACES IN BRAZIL
Whites are clustered in the south and browns in the north.

▶ 7.1.5 BRAZILIAN UNIVERSITY STUDENTS

U.S. Ethnicities

- Compare the distribution of U.S. ethnicities.

The United States has always been defined, in part, by its ethnic and racial diversity. Today, Americans are more diverse than ever before. The Census Bureau estimates that approximately 61 percent of Americans are white, 18 percent Hispanic or Latino, 13 percent black or African American, 6 percent Asian, 1 percent American Indian or Alaska Native, and 0.2 percent Native Hawaiian or Other Pacific Islander.

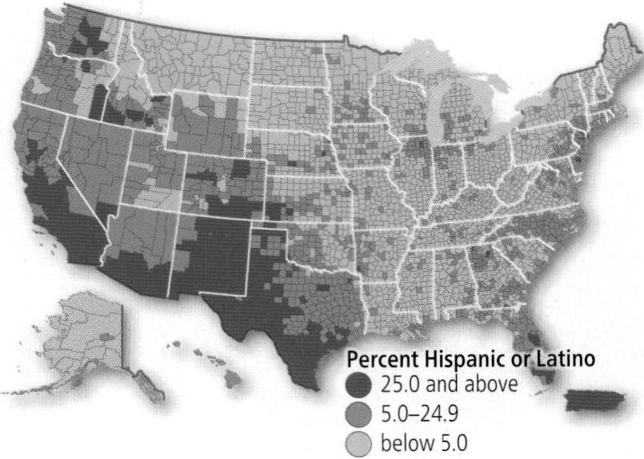

▲ 7.2.1 **DISTRIBUTION OF HISPANICS IN THE UNITED STATES**
Hispanics are clustered in the Southwest, near the Mexican border.

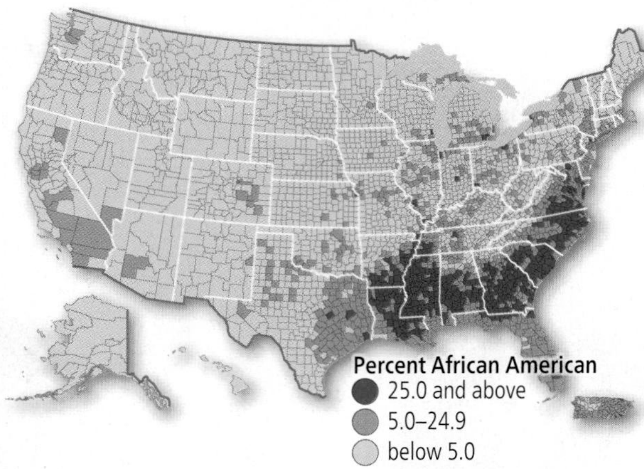

▲ 7.2.2 **DISTRIBUTION OF AFRICAN AMERICANS IN THE UNITED STATES**
African Americans are clustered in the Southeast.

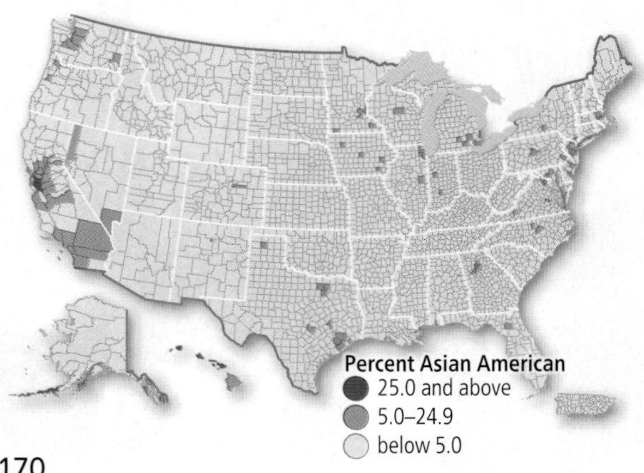

◀ 7.2.3 **DISTRIBUTION OF ASIAN AMERICANS IN THE UNITED STATES**
Asian Americans are clustered in the West.

Distribution of U.S. Ethnicities

The distribution of the ethnicities varies within the United States.

Hispanics. Clustered in the Southwest, Hispanics exceed one-third of the population of Arizona, New Mexico, and Texas and one-quarter of California (Figure 7.2.1). California is home to one-third of the nation's Hispanics, Texas one-fifth, and Florida and New York one-sixth each.

Hispanic is a term that the U.S. government chose in 1973 to describe the group because it is an inoffensive label that can be applied to all people from Spanish-speaking countries. Some Americans of Latin American descent have instead adopted the terms Latino (males) and Latina (females). A 1995 U.S. Census Bureau survey found that 58 percent of Americans of Latin American descent preferred the term Hispanic and 12 percent Latino/Latina. Preferences vary by region: Easterners prefer Hispanic, whereas Westerners prefer Latino/Latina.

African Americans. Most black Americans are descended from Africans and therefore also belong to an African American ethnicity. Some American blacks, however, trace their cultural heritage to regions other than Africa, including Latin America, Asia, and Pacific islands.

The term African American identifies a group with an extensive cultural tradition, whereas the term black in principle denotes nothing more than dark skin. Because many Americans categorize people by observing skin color, black is substituted for African American in daily language.

African Americans are clustered in the Southeast, comprising at least one-fourth of the population in several states (Figure 7.2.2). At the other extreme, nine states in upper New England and the West have less than 1 percent African Americans.

Asian Americans. Clustered in the West and in cities, Asian Americans also include more than 40 percent of the population of Hawaii (Figure 7.2.3). One-half of all Asian Americans live in California, where they comprise 12 percent of the population.

WHAT'S YOUR ETHNIC GEOGRAPHY?

Race and Ethnicity in the U.S. Census

Every 10 years, the U.S. Bureau of the Census asks people to classify themselves according to the ethnicity or ethnicities with which they most closely identify (Figure 7.2.4). The Census form in use through 2010 mixed ethnicity with race and was increasingly difficult for many Americans to answer (Figure 7.2.5).

Beginning in 2020, the Census form is expected to offer only ethnicity-based choices. Note the use of the term "categories" rather than race or ethnicity in 2020.

1. Are you able to answer questions 8 and 9 on the 2010 census? Are you able to answer the questions for your mother? For your father?
2. Does the proposed 2020 census form change the ease of answering for you? Why or why not? Does the proposed form change the answers for your mother and your father?
3. What changes would need to be made to the 2010 census to clarify the difference between ethnicity and race, as defined by geographers? Does the proposed 2020 census help to clarify or muddle the difference between ethnicity and race? Why?
4. Figure 7.2.6 depicts the most prevalent ethnicity or race in each location in the United States. You can zoom in on the dot map at **demographics.virginia.edu/DotMap/index.html**. Does the color on the map for where you live correspond with your race/ethnicity?
5. As you zoom in on where you live, how does the map change? When you zoom in as much as possible, does the map reflect your race/ethnicity?

▲ 7.2.4 PUERTO RICAN DAY PARADE, BROOKLYN, NEW YORK, ENCOURAGING PEOPLE TO COMPLETE THE CENSUS FORM

8. Is the person of Hispanic, Latino, or Spanish origin?
- ☐ No, not of Hispanic, Latino, or Spanish origin
- ☐ Yes, Mexican, Mexican American, Chicano
- ☐ Yes, Puerto Rican
- ☐ Yes, Cuban
- ☐ Yes, another Hispanic, Latino, or Spanish origin

9. What is the person's race?
- ☐ White
- ☐ Black, African American, or Negro
- ☐ American Indian or Alaska Native
- ☐ Asian Indian
- ☐ Chinese
- ☐ Filipino
- ☐ Other Asian
- ☐ Japanese
- ☐ Korean
- ☐ Vietnamese
- ☐ Native Hawaiian
- ☐ Guamanian or Chamorro
- ☐ Samoan
- ☐ Other Pacific Islander
- ☐ Other race

Respondents who select American Indian, Other Asian, Other Pacific Islander, Other race, or Another Hispanic are asked to write in the specific names on the census form.

▲ ▶ 7.2.5 U.S. CENSUS FORM (ABOVE) 2010, (RIGHT) PROPOSED 2020

Which categories describe Person1?
*Mark all boxes that apply **AND** print details in the spaces below. Note, you may report more than one group.*

☐ **WHITE** – *Provide details below.*
☐ German ☐ Irish ☐ English
☐ Italian ☐ Polish ☐ French
Print, for example, Scottish, Norwegian, Dutch, etc.

☐ **HISPANIC, LATINO, OR SPANISH** – *Provide details below.*
☐ Mexican or Mexican American ☐ Puerto Rican ☐ Cuban
☐ Salvadoran ☐ Dominican ☐ Colombian
Print, for example, Guatemalan, Spaniard, Ecuadorian, etc.

☐ **BLACK OR AFRICAN AM.** – *Provide details below.*
☐ African American ☐ Jamaican ☐ Haitian
☐ Nigerian ☐ Ethiopian ☐ Somali
Print, for example, Ghanaian, South Afrian, Barbadian, etc.

☐ **ASIAN** – *Provide details below.*
☐ Chinese ☐ Filipino ☐ Asian Indian
☐ Vietnamese ☐ Korean ☐ Japanese
Print, for example, Pakistani, Cambodian, Hmong, etc.

☐ **AMERICAN INDIAN OR ALASKA NATIVE** – *Provide details below.*
☐ American Indian ☐ Alaska Native ☐ Central or South American Indian
Print, for example, Navajo Nation, Blackfeet Tribe, Mayan, Aztec, Native Village of Barrow Inupiat, Nome Eskimo Community, etc.

☐ **MIDDLE EASTERN OR NORTH AFRICAN** – *Provide details below.*
☐ Lebanese ☐ Iranian ☐ Egyptian
☐ Syrian ☐ Moroccan ☐ Algerian
Print, for example, Israeli, Iraqi, Tunisian, etc.

☐ **NATIVE HAWAIIAN OR OTHER PACIFIC ISLANDER** – *Provide details below.*
☐ Native Hawaiian ☐ Samoan ☐ Chamorro
☐ Tongan ☐ Fijian ☐ Marshallese
Print, for example, Palauan, Tahitian, Chuckese, etc.

☐ **SOME OTHER RACE, ETHNICITY,OR ORIGIN** – *Print below.*

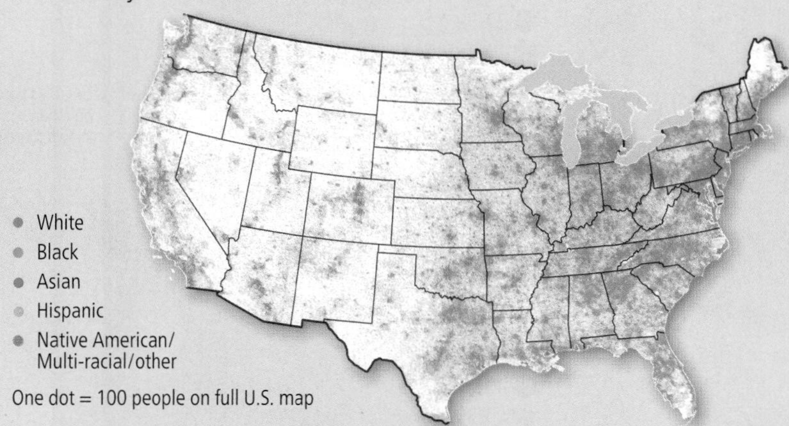

▲ 7.2.6 PREVALENT ETHNICITY OR RACE, 2010 CENSUS

Ethnic Enclaves

- Describe the distribution of ethnic enclaves within urban areas.

Ethnicities are defined in part by their possession of distinct cultural features, including languages, religions, and social customs such as food and art. These cultural features can influence the creation of a place with physical appearance and social structure reflective of a particular ethnicity.

▲ 7.3.1 **ETHNIC ENCLAVE, LONDON** Bangladeshis celebrate Bengali new year in East London's South Asia ethnic enclave (the eastern cluster in Figure 7.3.3b).

Ethnic Enclaves

An **ethnic enclave** is a place with a high concentration of an ethnic group that is distinct from those in the surrounding area. Most ethnic enclaves are neighborhoods within large cities. Ethnic enclaves with distinctive physical appearances and social structures typically form through migration. As immigrants arrive in a new country, many follow the process of chain migration, discussed in Chapter 3. That is, new immigrants often locate in places where people of the same ethnicity have already clustered.

In the ethnic enclave, newcomers can find people who speak the same language, practice the same religion, and prepare the same foods. They can also get help from people who know how to fill out forms, obtain assistance from public and private agencies, and adapt to the culture of the receiving country. Most importantly, ethnic enclaves offer newcomers economic support, such as employment opportunities, affordable housing, and loans.

Large cities like New York and London display a mosaic of ethnic enclaves. Most of New York's ethnic enclaves are located in Brooklyn and Queens (Figure 7.3.2). Manhattan has fewer ethnic enclaves, because much of that island is devoted to offices and residences occupied by wealthy people whose ancestors immigrated in the more distant past. Similarly, Central London has fewer ethnic enclaves than the outer boroughs (Figure 7.3.3).

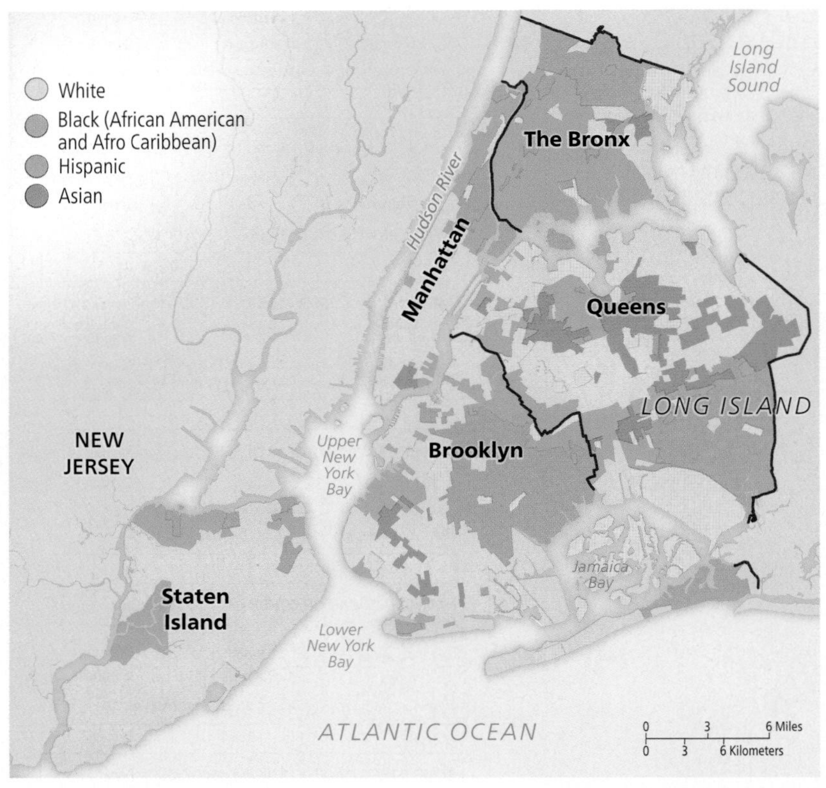

▲ 7.3.2 **ETHNIC ENCLAVES, NEW YORK**

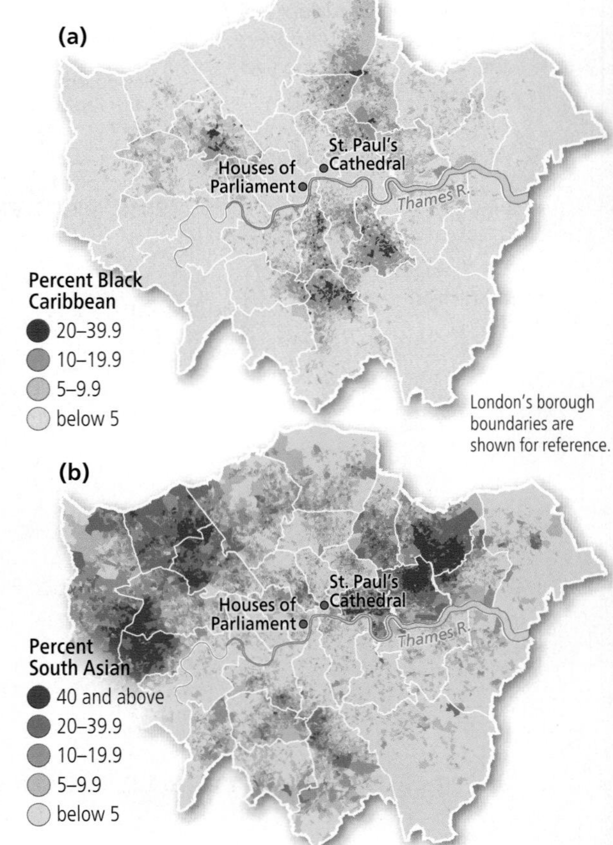

▶ 7.3.3 **ETHNIC ENCLAVES, LONDON** (a) Black Caribbean (b) South Asian.

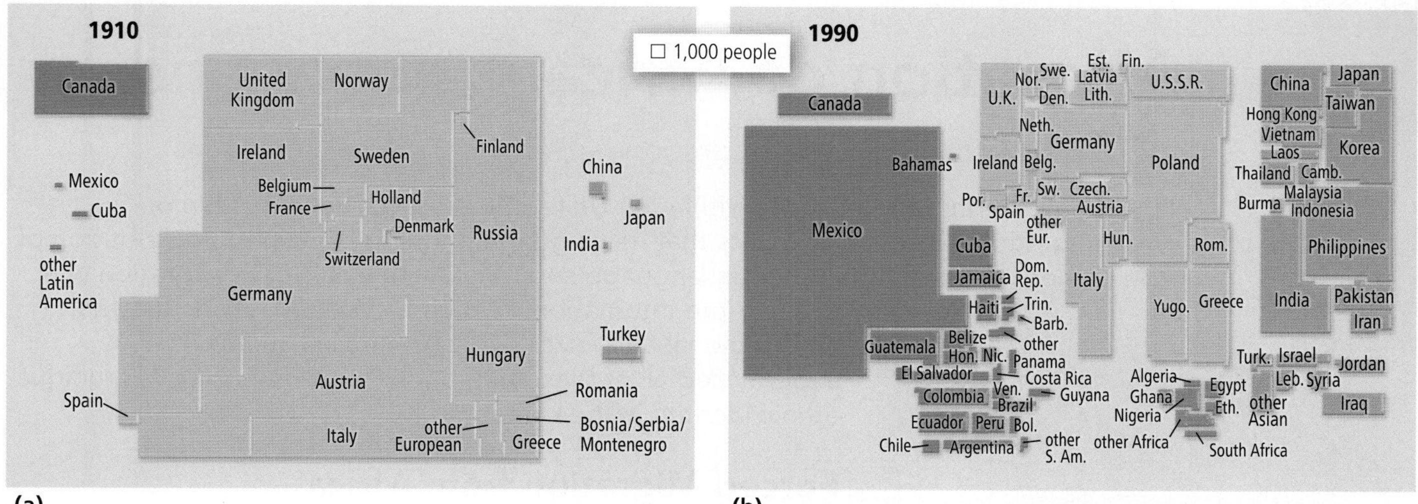

▲ 7.3.4 **CARTOGRAMS OF ETHNIC ENCLAVES, CHICAGO**
(a) In 1910, most immigrants were from Europe. (b) In 1990, origins were more diverse.

Changing Ethnic Enclaves

The areas occupied by ethnicities have changed over time. In the early twentieth century, Chicago, Cleveland, Detroit, and other Midwest cities attracted ethnic groups primarily from Southern and Eastern Europe, many of whom found work in the rapidly growing steel, automotive, and related industries. In 1910, when Detroit's auto production was expanding, three-fourths of the city's residents were immigrants and children of immigrants. Southern and Eastern European ethnic groups clustered in neighborhoods named for their predominant ethnicities, such as Detroit's Greektown and Poletown.

As recently as the middle of the twentieth century, large U.S. cities still had ethnic enclaves established by European immigrants. By the late twentieth century, most of the children and grandchildren of European immigrants had moved out of the inner-city enclaves to suburbs, in some cases forming **ethnoburbs**. An ethnoburb is a suburban area with a cluster of a particular ethnic population.

For descendants of European immigrants, ethnic identity is more likely to be retained through religion, food, and other cultural traditions than through location of residence. A visible remnant of early-twentieth-century European ethnic neighborhoods is the clustering of restaurants in such areas as Little Italy and Greektown.

Cartograms depict the change in Chicago. In 1910, most residents of the city were descendants of immigrants from Europe, but by 1990, descendants of immigrants from Latin America and Asia were comparable in number (Figure 7.3.4).

Similarly, ethnic enclaves have arisen in recent years in European cities, such as the Goutte d'Or neighborhood of Paris. One-third of the residents of the neighborhood belong to ethnicities who have emigrated from former African colonies of France. Paris is an attractive destination for several African ethnicities because as emigrants from one-time French colonies, they already speak the French language. However, they arrive in Paris with other distinctive customs, such as religion (primarily Islam), and food and clothing preferences (Figure 7.3.5).

▼ 7.3.5 **ETHNIC ENCLAVE, PARIS**
Muslim immigrants from Africa pray in a street in the Goutte d'Or neighborhood, because the local mosque isn't large enough to accommodate everyone who wants to pray.

Migration of African Americans

- **Describe the distinctive migration patterns of African Americans.**

The clustering of ethnicities within the United States is partly a function of migration—the same process that helps geographers to explain the distribution of other cultural factors, such as language and religion. In Chapter 3, migration was divided into international (voluntary or forced) and internal (interregional and intraregional). African Americans have experienced all of these migration patterns, and have a unique ethnic identity in the United States as a result.

▲ 7.4.1 **TRIANGULAR SLAVE TRADE**
Ships left Europe for Africa with cloth and other goods used to buy the slaves. The same ships transported the slaves across the Atlantic. Completing the triangle, the ships returned to Europe with sugar and molasses. Some ships carried molasses from the Caribbean to the North American colonies and rum from the colonies to Europe, forming a rectangular trading pattern.

Forced Migration from Africa

Most African Americans are descended from Africans forced to migrate to the Western Hemisphere as slaves during the eighteenth century. A number of European countries adopted a trading pattern called the **triangular slave trade** (Figure 7.4.1). At the height of the triangular slave trade between 1710 and 1810, at least 10 million Africans were uprooted from their homes and sent on European ships to the Western Hemisphere for sale in the slave markets. Different European countries operated in various regions of Africa, each sending slaves to different destinations in the Americas (Figure 7.4.2).

The large-scale forced migration of Africans caused them unimaginable hardship, separating families, destroying villages, and erasing cultural memories. The Africans were packed onto ships at extremely high density, kept in chains, and provided with minimal food and sanitary facilities. Approximately one-fourth died crossing the Atlantic (Figure 7.4.3).

▼ 7.4.3 **SLAVE SHIP**
This drawing made around 1845 for a French magazine shows the high density and poor conditions of Africans transported to the Western Hemisphere to become slaves.

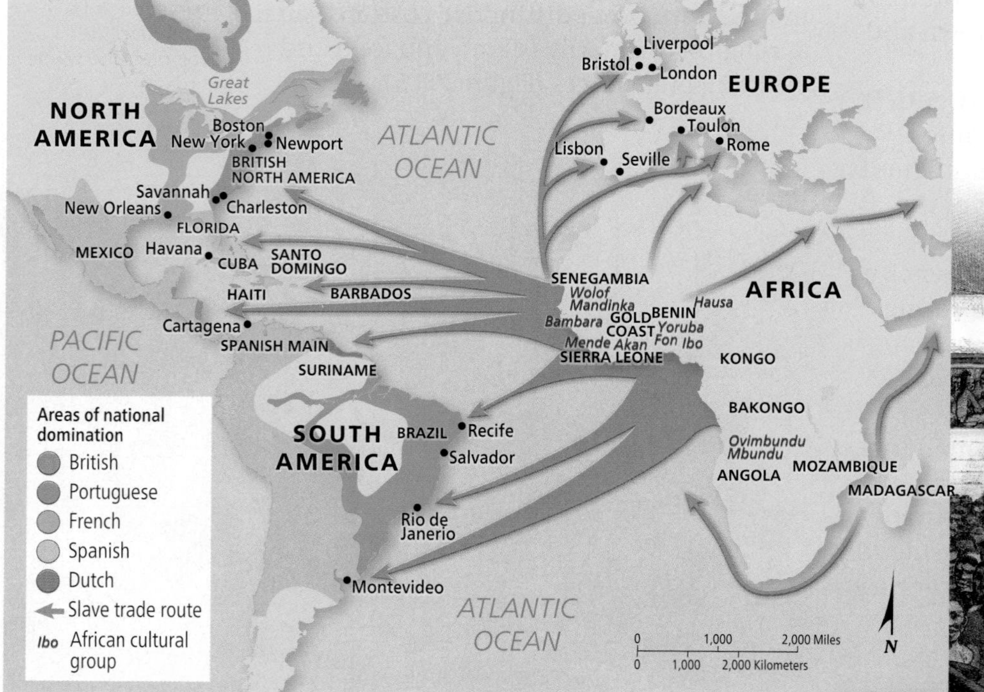

▲ 7.4.2 **ORIGINS AND DESTINATION OF SLAVES**
Ships sailed from Africa to the Western Hemisphere, from the Americas to Europe, and from Europe to Africa. From Africa slaves and gold were transported to the Western Hemisphere, primarily to the Caribbean islands.

Interregional Migration of African Americans

At the time of Emancipation and the end of the Civil War, most African Americans were concentrated in the rural South. Today, as a result of interregional migration, many African Americans live in cities throughout the Northeast, Midwest, and West as well.

Freed as slaves, most African Americans remained in the rural South during the late nineteenth century, working as sharecroppers. A **sharecropper** works fields rented from a landowner and pays the rent by turning over to the landowner a share of the crops. Sharecropping became less common into the twentieth century, as farm machinery reduced labor demand, and industrial jobs pulled migrants to the North.

Southern African Americans migrated north and west in two main waves, the first in the 1910s and 1920s before and after World War I and the second in the 1940s and 1950s before and after World War II. The world wars stimulated expansion of factories to produce war material, while the demands of the armed forces created shortages of factory workers. After the wars, factories produced steel, motor vehicles, and other goods demanded in civilian society. African Americans migrated out of the South along several clearly defined channels (Figure 7.4.4).

▲ 7.4.4 **INTERREGIONAL MIGRATION OF AFRICAN AMERICANS**
Migration followed four distinct channels along the East Coast and east-central, west-central, and southwestern regions of the country.

Intraregional Migration of African Americans

Intraregional migration—migration within cities and metropolitan areas—also changed the distribution of African Americans and people of other ethnicities. When they reached the big cities, African American immigrants clustered in the one or two neighborhoods where the small numbers who had arrived in the nineteenth century were already living. These areas became known as ghettos, after the term for neighborhoods in which Jews were forced to live in the Middle Ages (see Chapter 6).

American ghettos expanded during the 1950s and 1960s (Figure 7.4.5). The expansion of the black ghettos in American cities was made possible by "white flight," the emigration of whites from an area in anticipation of blacks immigrating into the area. Rather than integrate, whites fled (Figure 7.4.6).

White flight was encouraged by unscrupulous real estate practices, especially blockbusting and redlining. Under **blockbusting**, real estate agents convinced white homeowners living near a black area to sell their houses at low prices, preying on their fears that black families would soon move into the neighborhood and cause property values to decline. The agents then sold the houses at much higher prices to black families desperate to escape the overcrowded ghettos.

Redlining is a process by which financial institutions draw red-colored lines on a map and refuse to lend money for people to purchase or improve property within the lines. Through redlining, African Americans were prevented from getting mortgages to buy houses in the neighborhoods to which whites fled.

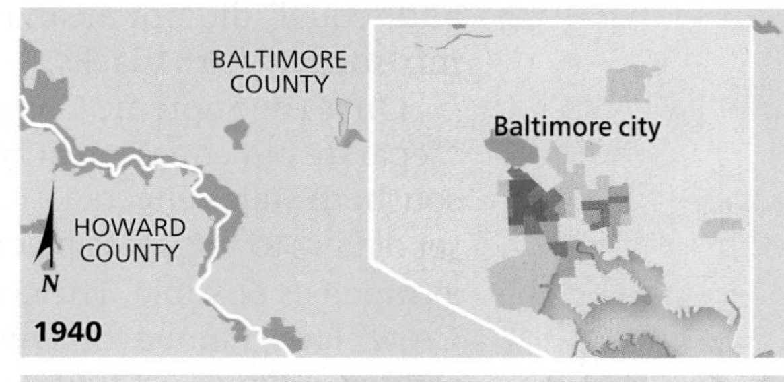

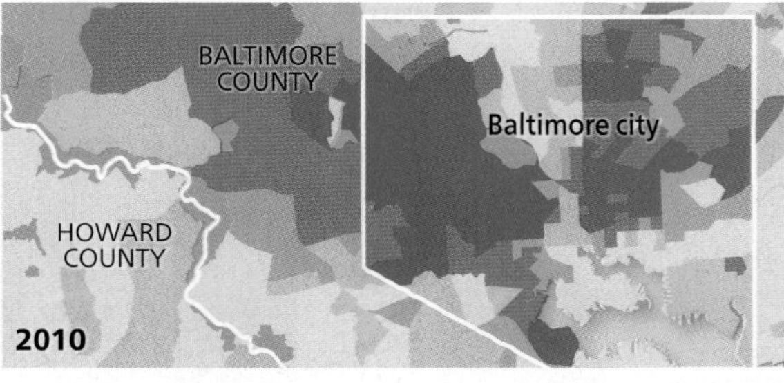

▲ 7.4.5 **EXPANSION OF THE GHETTO IN BALTIMORE**
Percent African American
90 and above
60–89
30–59
10–29
below 10
few or none
Parks

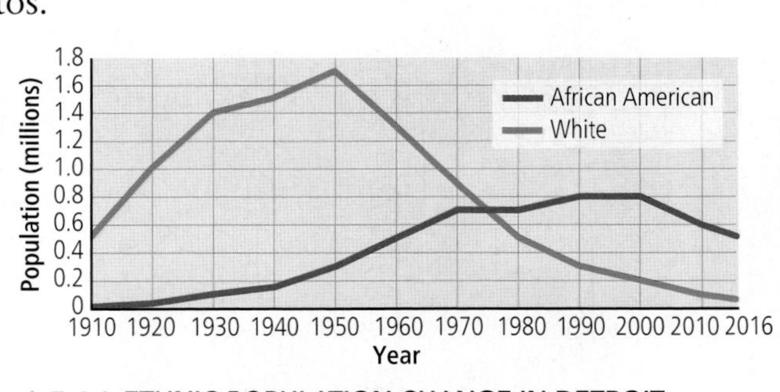

▲ 7.4.6 **ETHNIC POPULATION CHANGE IN DETROIT**

Segregation by Race

- Describe laws that once segregated races.

In explaining spatial regularities, geographers look for patterns of spatial interaction. A distinctive feature of ethnic relations in the United States and South Africa has been the strong discouragement of spatial interaction between whites and blacks—in the past through legal means and today through cultural preferences or discrimination.

▲ 7.5.1 **SEGREGATION IN THE UNITED STATES** Until the 1960s in the U.S. South, whites and blacks had to use separate drinking fountains, as well as separate restrooms, bus seats, hotel rooms, and other public facilities.

"Separate but Equal" in the United States

The concept of "separate but equal" was upheld by the U.S. Supreme Court in 1896. Louisiana had enacted a law that required black and white passengers to ride in separate train cars. In *Plessy v. Ferguson*, the Supreme Court stated that Louisiana's law was constitutional because it provided separate, but equal, treatment of blacks and whites, and "equal" did not mean that whites had to mix socially with blacks.

Once the Supreme Court permitted "separate but equal" treatment of the races, southern states enacted a comprehensive set of laws to segregate blacks from whites as much as possible. These were called "Jim Crow" laws, named for a nineteenth-century song-and-dance act that depicted blacks offensively. Blacks had to sit in the backs of buses, and shops, restaurants, and hotels could choose to serve only whites (Figure 7.5.1). Separate schools were established for blacks and whites. Throughout the country, not just in the South, house deeds contained restrictive covenants that prevented the owners from selling to blacks, as well as to Roman Catholics or Jews in some places.

The landmark Supreme Court decision *Brown v. Board of Education of Topeka*, Kansas, in 1954, found that having separate schools for blacks and whites was unconstitutional because no matter how equivalent the facilities, racial separation branded minority children as inferior and therefore was inherently unequal. A year later, the Supreme Court further ruled that schools had to be desegregated "with all deliberate speed."

A nationwide movement in favor of civil rights forced elimination of U.S. segregation laws during the 1950s and 1960s (Figure 7.5.2). Civil Rights Acts during the 1960s outlawed racial discrimination. The civil rights movement continues through Black Lives Matter, founded in 2013 after several unarmed African American men were killed by people of other ethnicities. The objectives of **Black Lives Matter** include campaigning against violence and perceived racism toward black people and educating others about the challenges that African Americans continue to face in the United States.

Consequences of racial discrimination are still felt in the United States. A recent example of environmental racism is the contamination of the drinking water in Flint, Michigan. Flint's residents, who are predominantly African American, have been exposed to a high concentration of lead in the drinking water because of insufficient treatment of the water source. Public officials have faced legal charges of negligence for endangering the health of the citizens of Flint in order to save money. Flint's water supply was judged acceptable to drink in 2017, but residents have been instructed to use bottled or filtered water until at least the year 2020.

▼ 7.5.2 **CIVIL RIGHTS MARCH** Washington D.C., 1969.

Apartheid in South Africa

Discrimination by race in the twentieth century reached its peak in South Africa. The cornerstone of the South Africa's institutional racism was the creation of **apartheid**, which was the legal separation of races into different geographic areas. Under apartheid, a newborn baby was classified as being one of four government-designated races: black, white, colored (mixed white and black), or Asian.

The apartheid system was created by descendants of whites who arrived in South Africa from the Netherlands in 1652 and settled in Cape Town, at the southern tip of the territory. They were known either as Boers, from the Dutch word for "farmer," or Afrikaners, from the word "Afrikaans," the name of their language, which is a dialect of Dutch.

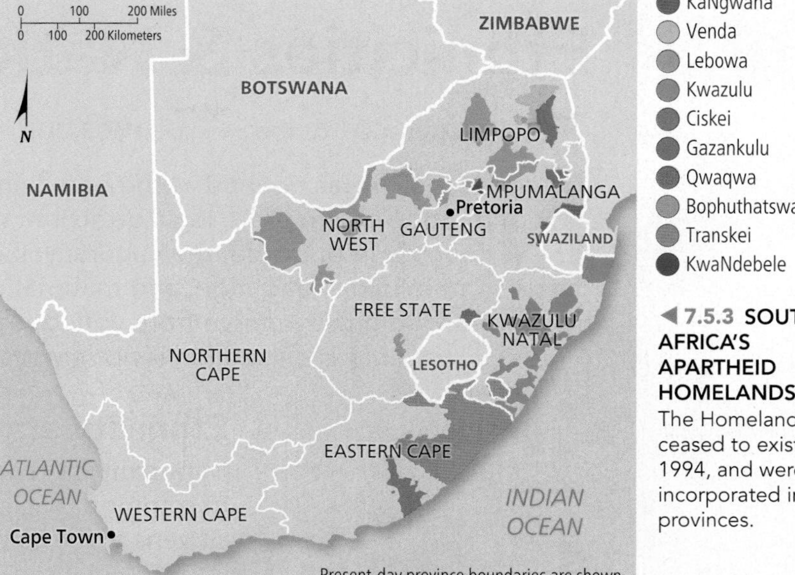

◀ **7.5.3 SOUTH AFRICA'S APARTHEID HOMELANDS** The Homelands ceased to exist in 1994, and were incorporated into provinces.

The British seized the Dutch colony in 1795 and controlled South Africa's government until 1948, when the Afrikaner-dominated white minority Nationalist Party won elections. The Afrikaners gained power at a time when colonial rule was being replaced in the rest of Africa by a collection of independent states run by the local black population. The Afrikaners vowed to resist pressures to turn over South Africa's government to blacks, and the Nationalist Party created the apartheid laws in the next few years to perpetuate white dominance of the country.

To ensure geographic isolation of these groups, the South African government designated 10 so-called homelands for blacks (Figure 7.5.3). The white minority government expected every black to become a citizen of one of the homelands and to move there. More than 99 percent of the population in the 10 homelands was black. The apartheid laws determined where different races could live, attend school, work, shop, travel, and own land (Figure 7.5.4). Blacks were restricted to certain occupations and were paid far lower wages than were whites for similar work. They could not vote or run for political office in national elections.

▼ **7.5.4 APARTHEID IN SOUTH AFRICA** Separate buses for blacks and whites, 1975.

The white-minority government of South Africa repealed the apartheid laws in 1991. The principal antiapartheid organization, the African National Congress, was legalized, and its leader, Nelson Mandela, was released from jail after more than 27 years of imprisonment. When all South Africans were permitted to vote in national elections for the first time, in 1994, Mandela was overwhelmingly elected the country's first black president.

Though South Africa's apartheid laws have been dismantled and the country is governed by its black majority, the legacy of apartheid will linger for many years. South Africa's blacks have achieved political equality, but they are much poorer than white South Africans. As one example, South Africa is a major producer of wine, but only a small number of vineyards and wineries are owned by blacks.

Ethnicities & Nationalities

- Distinguish between ethnicities and nationalities

Nationality was defined at the beginning of this chapter as identity with a group of people who share legal attachment and personal allegiance to a particular country. In principle, the cultural values shared with others of the same ethnicity derive from religion, language, and material culture, whereas those shared with others of the same nationality derive from voting, obtaining a passport, and performing civic duties. However, this distinction is not always clear.

▲ 7.6.1 RALLY IN SUPPORT OF QUÉBEC INDEPENDENCE, 1995

Ethnicity and Nationality in North America

Nationality is generally kept reasonably distinct from ethnicity in common usage in the United States. Nationality identifies citizens of the United States of America, including those born in the country and those who immigrated and became citizens. Ethnicity identifies groups with distinct ancestry and cultural traditions, such as African Americans, Mexican Americans, or Chinese Americans.

In Canada, the distinction between ethnicity and nationality is less clear. Québécois are clearly distinct from other Canadians in cultural traditions, especially language. But do the Québécois form a distinct ethnicity within the Canadian nationality or a second French-speaking nationality separate altogether from English-speaking Canadian? The distinction is critical because if Québécois is recognized as a separate nationality from English-speaking Canadian, the Québec government would have a much stronger justification for breaking away from Canada to form an independent country (Figure 7.6.1).

Clarifying Ethnicity and Nationality

Sorting out ethnicity and nationality can be challenging for many individuals. Consider professional soccer player Sydney Rae Leroux Dwyer. Leroux's mother is white and her nationality is Canadian. Leroux's father is African American and his nationality is United States of America. Because of her parents, Leroux holds dual nationality, and has been eligible to play soccer for either the United States or Canada. At various times, she has played for teams representing Canada and teams representing the United States.

Leroux is married to professional soccer player Dom Dwyer, who was born a citizen of the United Kingdom to parents who had emigrated from Jamaica (Figure 7.6.2). In 2017, Dwyer became a U.S. citizen and also holds dual citizenship. Their son Cassius, born in 2016, also has multiple nationalities.

▲ 7.6.2 SYDNEY RAE LEROUX AND DOM DWYER

Ethnicity and Nationality in the British Isles

Sorting out the inhabitants of the British Isles into nationalities is increasingly controversial. The British Isles are divided between two countries—the United Kingdom of Great Britain and Northern Ireland and the Republic of Ireland. The Republic of Ireland comprises the southern 84 percent of the island of Ireland (called Eire in Irish). The United Kingdom includes Great Britain (divided into England, Scotland, Wales) and the northern portion of Eire (Figure 7.6.3).

The nationality of the citizens of the Republic of Ireland is clearly Irish. However, the nationality of the citizens of the United Kingdom is disputed. Does the United Kingdom contain one nationality (called British)? Or does it contain four nationalities—English, Scottish, Welsh, and the Irish of Northern Ireland? International sports organizations permit each of the four parts of the United Kingdom to field its own separate national teams in soccer and rugby.

Tensions among the U.K. units have increased in recent years. Scots voted in 2014 to remain part of the U.K., but political differences between Scotland and England have increased since then. Most Irish, Scots, and Welsh voted in 2016 to remain in the European Union, whereas most English voted to leave (see Chapter 8).

▲ 7.6.3 **BRITISH ISLES**
The British Isles comprises two countries: The Republic of Ireland and the United Kingdom. See Figure 5.10.1 for a language map of the British Isles.

Nationalism

A nationality, once established, must hold the loyalty of its citizens to survive. Politicians and governments try to instill loyalty through **nationalism**, which is loyalty and devotion to a nationality. Nationalism promotes a national consciousness that exalts one nation above all others and emphasizes its culture and interests as opposed to those of other nations.

Nationalism is an important example of a **centripetal force**, which is an attitude that tends to unify people and enhance support for a state. (The word centripetal means "directed toward the center"; it is the opposite of centrifugal, which means "to spread out from the center.") States foster nationalism by promoting symbols of the country, such as flags and songs. In recent years, nationalism has been a rallying cry for people opposed to forces promoting political, economic, and cultural globalization.

DEBATE IT!
Should ethnicities be encouraged to pursue national independence?

A country may contain many ethnicities that are able to live together peacefully. However, in other places an ethnic group may seek independence because it is unable to live peacefully as a minority in countries dominated by other ethnicities.

ENCOURAGE INDEPENDENCE

- In an independent country, a vulnerable ethnic group can protect itself from being dominated by others (Figure 7.6.4).
- The government is more likely to represent the group's interests.
- People's desire to associate and organize with others of the same ethnicity should be respected.

► 7.6.4 **SUPPORTING INDEPENDENCE FOR KURDS**
Shopkeeper displays fabric with the flag of Kurdistan. Kurds hope Kurdistan will be an independent country some day.

DO NOT ENCOURAGE INDEPENDENCE

- Ethnic groups intermingle in space, so cannot be realistically separated into distinct territories (Figure 7.6.5).
- Peace requires ethnic groups to interact and cooperate.
- An ethnic group espousing hatred and discrimination could use the power of a state to inflict harm on other ethnic groups.

◄ 7.6.5 **ETHNIC GROUPS JOIN TOGETHER**
Children prepare for peace march, New York.

▲ 7.7.1 **WAR IN IRAQ**
Victims of fighting in the city of Mosul.

Ethnic Diversity in Western Asia

- Identify the principal ethnic conflicts in Western Asia.

Few ethnicities inhabit an area that matches the territory of a nationality. The lack of correspondence between the territories occupied by ethnicities and by nationalities is especially severe in Western Asia (discussed in this section) and West-central Asia (discussed in the next section).

Western Asia has been the center of long-standing conflicts among ethnicities. Ethnic diversity is intermixed with religious diversity, as discussed in the previous chapter. The region has also experienced military intervention by states outside of the region. The terrorist organization Islamic State is also an important source of conflict in the region, as discussed in the next chapter.

Ethnicities in Turkey

Ethnic Turks comprise approximately three-fourths of the population of Turkey. The Republic of Turkey was created in the 1920s to encompass the territory inhabited by ethnic Turks, but other numerous ethnicities live there. The most populous minority in Turkey is the Kurds, who make up 18 percent of the population and are clustered in the eastern portion of Turkey (see next page).

Ethnicities in Iraq

Iraqi Arabs comprise 90 percent of Iraq's population, but they are divided by branches of Islam. Iraqi Shiites claim a history of discrimination at the hands of Iraqi Sunnis since the 1930's. As President (1979-2003), Saddam Hussein, a Sunni, violently suppressed Shiite and Kurdish movements for representation within Iraq. The United States led an attack against Iraq in 2003 that resulted in the removal and death Saddam Hussein. Having invaded Iraq and removed Hussein from power, the United States became embroiled in a complex and violent struggle among ethnicities (Figure 7.7.1).

Ethnicities in Syria

Syria's government has been controlled since 1963 by the minority Alawites, including Hafez-al-Assad (President 1971-2000) and his son Bashar al-Assad (President beginning in 2000). The Alawites have exercised control through suppression of the rights of the majority Sunni Muslim population, as well as the other minority groups. As a result, a civil war has raged in the country since 2011, pitting the Alawite-controlled government against other groups. Complicating Syria's civil war has been the presence of the Islamic State terrorists, who have seized control over a portion of the country (Figure 7.7.2).

Ethnicities in Lebanon

Lebanon is divided among around 55 percent Muslims, 40 percent Christians, and 5 percent Druze. The Druze are sometimes classified as Muslims, but they do not follow Islam's five pillars of faith described in Chapter 6 and therefore do not self-identify as Muslims. Lebanon's religious groups have tended to live in different regions of the country. During a civil war between 1975 and 1990, several religious groups formed private militias to guard their territory. The territory controlled by each militia changed according to battles with other religious groups.

Lebanon's Christians and Muslims consider themselves ethnically distinct from each other. The Christians regard themselves as descendants of the ancient Phoenicians who once occupied present-day Lebanon, whereas the country's Muslims are regarded as ethnically Arab. Lebanon's Constitution officially recognizes 18 religions and requires that each be represented in the Chamber of Deputies according to its percentage in the 1932 census.

▼ 7.7.2 **WAR IN SYRIA**
Damage in the city of Aleppo.

Kurds

The Kurds are the most numerous ethnicity in Western Asia without a country that they control. An independent Kurdistan was created after World War I, but Turkey took control of most of it in 1923. Repeated attempts to gain an independent state have failed. The Kurdish struggle for independence is marked with violence, committed both by and against the group (Figure 7.7.3).

Mapping Western Asia's Ethnicities

Figure 7.7.4 depicts the diversity of ethnicities in Western Asia. The most numerous ethnicities in the region are Turks, Iraqi Arabs, Azerbaijanis, Kurds, and Syrian Arabs. But numerous others appear on the map.

▲ 7.7.3 **KURDISTAN**
Kurds in Turkey celebrate Newroz (Kurdish New Year).

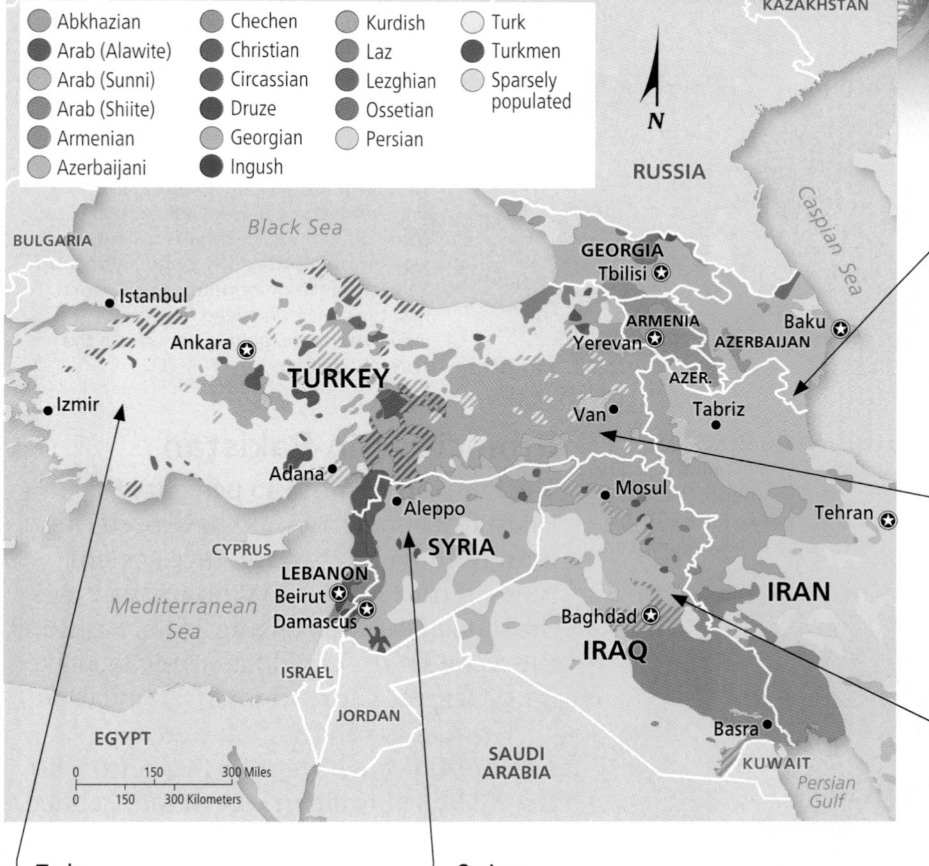

◀ 7.7.4 **ETHNICITIES IN WESTERN ASIA**

Azerbaijanis

Azerbaijanis trace their roots to Turkish invaders who migrated from Central Asia in the eighth and ninth centuries and merged with the existing Persian population. Azerbaijanis are predominantly Shiite Muslims and speak Azerbaijani, a Turkic language.

Kurds

The Kurds are predominantly Sunni Muslims who speak Kurdish, a language in the Indo-Iranian branch of Indo-European. The Kurds have inhabited Western Asia since ancient times.

Iraqi Arabs

Iraqi Arabs are descended from Arabs who immigrated in ancient times from Arabia and mingled with peoples already living in the area known then as Mesopotamia. Iraqi Arabs are predominantly Muslim, divided between Shiite and Sunni.

Turks

Ethnic Turks are descended from migrants to present-day Turkey around 1,000 years ago, most likely from Siberia. Turks are predominantly Sunni Muslims and speak Turkish, a Turkic language.

Syrians

Arabs comprise 90 percent of Syria's population. The ethnic Arabs are divided by religion: 75 percent are Sunni Muslim, 10 percent Alawite Muslim, 10 percent Christian, 3 percent Druze, and 2 percent other branches of Islam. The most numerous Christian denominations are Greek Orthodox and Greek Catholic.

Ethnic Diversity in West-Central Asia

- **Identify the principal ethnic conflicts in West-Central Asia.**

Dozens of ethnicities inhabit the region, allocated among eight nationalities (Figure 7.8.1). The five most numerous ethnicities are Punjabis, Persians, Pashtuns, Uzbeks, and Azerbaijanis. Azerbaijanis were described in Figure 7.7.4.

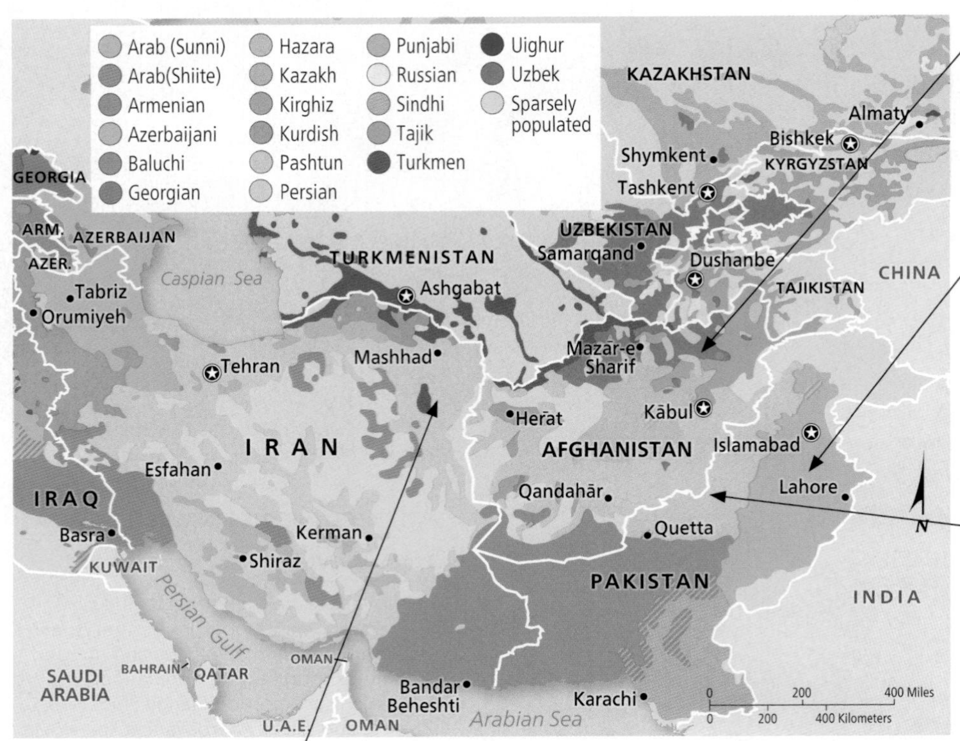

▲ 7.8.1 ETHNICITIES IN WEST-CENTRAL ASIA

Uzbeks

Turkic people migrated here from China around 1,500 years ago. They were among the first people of Central Asia to convert to Islam around 900 years ago. They speak a Turkic language.

Punjabis

Punjabi is a term applied 200 years ago to people of varying cultural heritages inhabiting the Punjab region of South Asia. Cultural unity was forged initially through sharing the Punjabi language, which is classified in the Indo-Iranian branch of Indo-European. The partition of South Asia in 1947 divided the Punjab between the newly independent countries of India and Pakistan.

Pashtuns

The Pashtuns have inhabited this region since prehistoric times. Cultural unity has come primarily from speaking various dialects of Pashto, a language in the Indo-Iranian branch of Indo-European. Most Pashtuns have practiced Islam since the arrival of that religion in the area in the seventh century.

Persians

Persians are believed to be descendants of Indo-European peoples who migrated from Central Asia into what is now Iran several thousand years ago. Persians are predominantly Shiite Muslims and speak Persian, a language in the Indo-Iranian branch of Indo-European.

▼ 7.8.2 PUNJABI FAMILY, PAKISTAN

Ethnicities in Pakistan

The Punjabi comprise 45 percent of Pakistan's population and have been the most numerous ethnicity since ancient times in the territory that now constitutes the state of Pakistan (Figure 7.8.2). Pashtuns, the second most populous ethnicity, make up 15 percent of the country's population.

The border between Pakistan and Afghanistan was imposed by the British in the 1890s before either was an independent country. The border, called the Durand line, is named for the British diplomat principally responsible for setting the line. The Durand line, which is not recognized by the government of Afghanistan, is a source of tension, because it divides the Pashtun and Baluchi ethnic groups between the two countries.

▲ 7.8.3 PERSIAN MOTHER AND CHILD, IRAN

Ethnicities in Iran

Most people in Iran are ethnic Persians, who comprise 61 percent of Iran's population (Figure 7.8.3). Iran's other principal ethnicities include 16 percent Azerbaijanis in the northwest, 10 percent Kurds in the west, 6 percent Lurs in the west, 2 percent Turkmen in the north, 2 percent Shiite Arabs in the southwest, and 2 percent Baluchi in the southeast.

Relations between Iran and the United States have been poor since 1979, when a revolution brought to power fundamentalist Shiites, and some of their supporters seized the U.S. Embassy, holding 52 Americans hostage for more than a year. More recently, other countries have struggled to keep Iran from creating nuclear weapons (discussed in more detail in Chapter 8).

Ethnicities in Afghanistan

The most numerous ethnicities in Afghanistan include 42 percent Pashtun, 27 percent Tajik, and 9 percent each Hazara and Uzbek. Afghanistan's ethnic diversity can be attributed to its position as a key trading route between Central, Southern, and Western Asia.

The current unrest among Afghanistan's ethnicities dates from 1979, with the start of a rebellion by several ethnic groups against the government. After many years of infighting among ethnicities, a Pashtun faction called the Taliban gained control over most of the country in 1995. The Taliban imposed strict laws on Afghanistan, according to Islamic values as the Taliban interpreted them (see chapter 6). The United States invaded Afghanistan in 2001 and overthrew the Taliban-led government because it was harboring terrorists (see chapter 8). Removal of the Taliban unleashed a new struggle for control of Afghanistan among the country's many ethnicities.

Ethnicities in the Caucasus

The Caucasus region, an area about the size of Colorado, was once part of the Soviet Union. The breakup of the Soviet Union resulted in the creation of the three small states of Armenia, Azerbaijan, and Georgia.

Armenians have inhabited this territory since prehistoric times. All but 2 percent of the population of Armenia are ethnic Armenians. Most speak Armenian, which is a branch of Indo-European (see Chapter 5), and adhere to Orthodox Christianity.

Azerbaijanis comprise more than 90 percent of the population of Azerbaijan. They trace their roots to Turkish invaders who migrated from Central Asia in the eighth and ninth centuries and merged with the existing Persian population. Azerbaijanis are predominantly Shiite Muslims and speak Azerbaijani, a Turkic language (refer to Figure 7.7.4).

Armenians and Azerbaijanis have fought a war over possession of Nagorno-Karabakh, a 5,000-square-kilometer (2,000-square-mile) enclave within Azerbaijan that is inhabited primarily by Armenians but placed under Azerbaijan's control by the Soviet Union during the 1920s.

Georgia is more ethnically diverse. Ethnic Georgians comprise 82 percent of Georgia's population. The country also includes about 6 percent Aerbaijani, 5 percent Armenian, 3 percent Abkhazian, 2 percent Ossetian, and 1 percent Russian. Georgia's cultural diversity has been a source of unrest, especially among the Ossetians and Abkhazians. Russia has recognized Abkhazia and South Ossetia as independent countries and sent troops there. Only a handful of other countries recognize the independence of Abkhazia and South Ossetia, although the two operate as if they were independent of Georgia.

Ethnicities in Central Asia States

The five states in Central Asia carved out of the former Soviet Union display varying degrees of ethnic diversity. Tajiks and Turkmens comprise more than 80 percent of the population of Tajikistan and Turkmenistan, respectively; Kyrgyz and Uzbeks more than 70 percent of Kyrgyzstan and Uzbekistan, respectively (Figure 7.8.4); and Kazakhs more than 60 percent of Kazakhstan. Conflicts among these ethnicities have occurred primarily between Uzbeks and Kyrgyz.

▼ 7.8.4 UZBEK WOMEN, UZBEKISTAN

Ethnic Cleansing in Europe

- Summarize how conflict among ethnic groups led to ethnic cleansing in the former Yugoslavia.

Conflicts sometimes result in the forced migration of ethnic groups. **Ethnophobia** is a fear of people of a particular ethnicity. It can overlap with **xenophobia**, which is a fear of people who are from other countries.

Ethnic cleansing is a process in which a more powerful ethnic group forcibly removes a less powerful one in order to create an ethnically homogeneous region. Ethnic cleansing is undertaken to rid an area of an entire ethnicity so that the surviving ethnic group can be the sole inhabitants. **Genocide** is the mass killing of a group of people in an attempt to eliminate the entire group from existence. In recent years, instances of ethnic cleansing and genocide have occurred in Europe, Asia, and Africa.

▶ **7.9.1 BREAKUP OF YUGOSLAVIA** Yugoslavia was organized into republics that in some (but not all) cases matched the homelands of ethnicities.

Yugoslavia: Many Ethnicities

Ethnic cleansing in the former Yugoslavia is part of a complex pattern of ethnic diversity in the region of southeastern Europe known as the Balkans, named for the Balkan Mountains. The Balkan Peninsula, a complex assemblage of ethnicities, has long been a hotbed of unrest.

Yugoslavia was created after World War I to unite several Balkan ethnicities that spoke similar South Slavic languages. Longtime leader Josip Broz Tito (prime minister 1943–63 and president 1953–80) was instrumental in forging a Yugoslav nationality. Central to Tito's vision of a Yugoslav nationality was acceptance of ethnic cultural diversity.

Rivalries among ethnicities resurfaced in Yugoslavia during the 1980s after Tito's death, leading to its breakup initially into six small countries: Bosnia & Herzegovina, Croatia, Macedonia, Montenegro, Serbia, and Slovenia (Figure 7.9.1). The creation of a viable nationality has proved especially difficult for Bosnia & Herzegovina (Figure 7.9.2).

(a)

(b)

(c)

▶ **7.9.2 ETHNIC CLEANSING IN BOSNIA & HERZEGOVINA** (a) The Stari Most (old bridge), in the city of Mostar, Bosnia & Herzegovina, was built by the Turks in 1566 across the Neretva River. (b) The bridge was blown up by Croats in 1993 as part of their ethnic cleansing against the Bosniaks. The goal was to demoralize the Bosniaks. (c). With the end of the war in Bosnia & Herzegovina, the bridge was rebuilt in 2004 nearly identical to the old one, to boost morale after the devastating war.

Ethnic Cleansing in Bosnia

At the time of the breakup of Yugoslavia, the population of Bosnia & Herzegovina was 48 percent Bosniaks, 37 percent Serbs, and 14 percent Croats. Bosniaks are frequently called Bosnian Muslims, in recognition of their predominant religion. Rather than live in an independent multiethnic state with a Muslim plurality, Bosnia & Herzegovina's Serbs and Croats fought to unite the portions of the republic that they inhabited with Serbia and Croatia, respectively. To strengthen their cases for breaking away from Bosnia & Herzegovina, Serbs and Croats engaged in ethnic cleansing of Bosniaks (see Research & Analysis feature and Figure 7.9.3).

Accords reached in Dayton, Ohio, in 1995 by leaders of the various ethnicities divided Bosnia & Herzegovina into three entities: one dominated by Serbs (Republika Srpska), one a mix of Bosniaks and Croats (Federation of Bosnia & Herzegovina), and one mixed (Brčko District). The accords rewarded ethnic cleansing: Bosnian Serbs received nearly half of the country, although they comprised one-third of the population, and Bosnian Croats got one-fourth of the land, although they comprised one-sixth of the population. Bosniaks, one-half of the population before the ethnic cleansing, got only one-fourth of the land (Figure 7.9.4).

RESEARCH & ANALYZE
Srebrenica Massacre

The Srebrenica massacre is considered the largest single ethnic cleansing and genocide event in Bosnia & Herzegovina.

1. Do a web search for *Srebrenica Massacre*. Summarize what happened at the massacre. How many people were killed during the massacre?
2. What were the nationality, ethnicity, and religion of the victims?
3. What were the nationality, ethnicity, and religion of the people who committed the massacre?
4. How did international peacekeepers fail to prevent the massacre from taking place?

▲ 7.9.3 **SREBRENICA RESIDENTS ROUNDED UP BEFORE BEING MASSACRED**

Ethnic Cleansing in Kosovo

After the breakup of Yugoslavia, Serbia remained an ethnically diverse country. Particularly troubling was the province of Kosovo, where ethnic Albanians comprised 90 percent of the population. Serbia had a historical claim to Kosovo, having controlled it between the twelfth and fourteenth centuries.

With the breakup of Yugoslavia, Serbia took direct control of Kosovo and launched a campaign of ethnic cleansing of the Albanian majority. The process of ethnic cleansing involved four steps:

1. Move a large amount of military equipment and personnel into a village that has no strategic value.
2. Round up all the people in the village.
3. Force the people to leave the village in a convoy, some in the vehicles and others on foot, heading for the Albanian border.
4. Destroy the vacated village by setting it on fire.

Outraged by the evidence of ethnic cleansing, the United States and Western European countries, operating through the North Atlantic Treaty Organization (NATO), launched an air attack against Serbia. The bombing campaign ended when Serbia agreed to withdraw all of its soldiers and police from Kosovo. Kosovo declared its independence from Serbia in 2008.

(a)

(b)

▲ 7.9.4 **BOSNIA & HERZEGOVINA BEFORE AND AFTER ETHNIC CLEANSING**
(a) Distribution of ethnicities in Bosnia & Herzegovina before the war during the 1990s. (b) Distribution of ethnicities after Serbs and Croats undertook ethnic cleansing to seize territory from Bosniaks.

Ethnic Cleansing & Genocide in Asia & Africa

- Identify examples of genocide in Asia and Africa

Competition among ethnicities can lead in a handful of the most extreme cases to genocide. Several areas of Asia and Africa have been plagued by conflicts among ethnicities that have resulted in genocide in recent years. Other countries have been either unable or unwilling to stop the genocide.

Ethnic Cleansing and Genocide in Myanmar

Asia's most extreme example of ethnic cleansing and genocide in recent years has been in Myanmar, a country of 53 million inhabitants. The attacks have been directed against the Rohingya, an ethnic group living in Myanmar's far western Rakhine State (Figure 7.10.1). Rakhine is the poorest State in Myanmar, which in turn is one of the world's poorest countries.

The Rohingya are predominantly Sunni Muslims who speak an Indo-European language. In contrast, the largest number of people in Myanmar are Theravada Buddhists who speak Sino-Tibetan languages.

Most Rohingya migrated in the nineteenth century from present-day Bangladesh to present-day Myanmar, when both were British colonies. The Myanmar government claims that because the Rohingya immigrated during the British colonial era, they are living in Myanmar illegally. In 1982, the Myanmar government enacted laws that took away the Rohingya's citizenship, land, and rights to attend school and hold jobs.

In 2016, Rohingyas attacked some police and military posts. In retaliation, the Myanmar military launched a massive ethnic cleansing operation against the Rohingya. The pretext was to eliminate the group that had attacked the police and military, but in reality more than 1 million Rohingya have been ethnically cleansed. Their villages have been destroyed, and they have been forced to move from Rakhine to other countries, primarily Bangladesh (Figure 7.10.2).

◄ 7.10.1 FORCED MIGRATION OF ROHINGYA

▲ 7.10.2 DESTINATIONS OF ETHNICALLY CLEANSED ROHINGYA

▲ 7.10.3 HONORING THE MEMORY OF TUTSI VICTIMS OF 1994 GENOCIDE

Ethnic Cleansing and Genocide in Africa

Several wars in Africa have resulted in genocide and ethnic cleansing. Two are summarized here.

Sudan and South Sudan. A war from 1983 until 2005 between Sudan's northern and southern ethnicities resulted in two million deaths and four million forcibly relocated. The war was sparked when southern ethnicities resisted northerners' attempts to impose a legal system based on Muslim religious practice.

The north-south war ended with the establishment of South Sudan as an independent state in 2011. However, since independence South Sudan has suffered from its own ethnic conflict, primarily between the predominantly Christian Dinka and the predominantly folk religionist Nuer. The United Nations has accused the Dinka of ethnic cleansing against the Nuer.

Elsewhere in Sudan, black African ethnic groups in the country's Darfur region launched a rebellion in 2003, accusing the Arab-dominated national government of discrimination and neglect. In response, the national government army engaged in ethnic cleansing.

Rwanda and Burundi. Long-standing conflicts between the Hutus and Tutsis, the two ethnic groups in these tiny countries, have resulted in severe ethnic cleansing and genocide (Figure 7.10.3). Hutus constituted a majority of the population historically, but Tutsis controlled kingdoms there for several hundred years and turned the Hutus into their serfs.

When Rwanda became an independent country in 1962, Hutus gained power and undertook ethnic cleansing and genocide against the Tutsis. Meanwhile in Burundi, where the Tutsis were still in power, a civil war resulted in genocide committed by and against both Hutus and Tutsis.

After the assassination of the presidents of Burundi and Rwanda in 1994, Hutus launched a genocide campaign, killing an estimated 800,000 Tutsis. The genocide ended after Tutsis gained control of Rwanda (Figure 7.10.3).

Africa's Complex Map

Traditionally, the most important element of cultural identity in Africa was ethnicity rather than nationality. Africa contains several thousand ethnicities with distinct languages, religions, and social customs. The precise number of ethnicities is impossible to determine because boundaries separating them can be hard to define. Further, it is hard to determine whether a particular group forms a distinct ethnicity or is part of a larger collection of similar groups.

During the late nineteenth and early twentieth centuries, European countries carved up the continent into a collection of colonies, with little regard for the distribution of these ethnicities. When the European colonies in Africa became independent states, especially during the 1950s and 1960s, the areas of the new states typically matched the colonial administrative units imposed by the Europeans rather than the historical distribution of ethnicities (Figure 7.10.4). As a result, most states contained a large collection of often dissimilar ethnicities, and some ethnic groups were divided among more than one state.

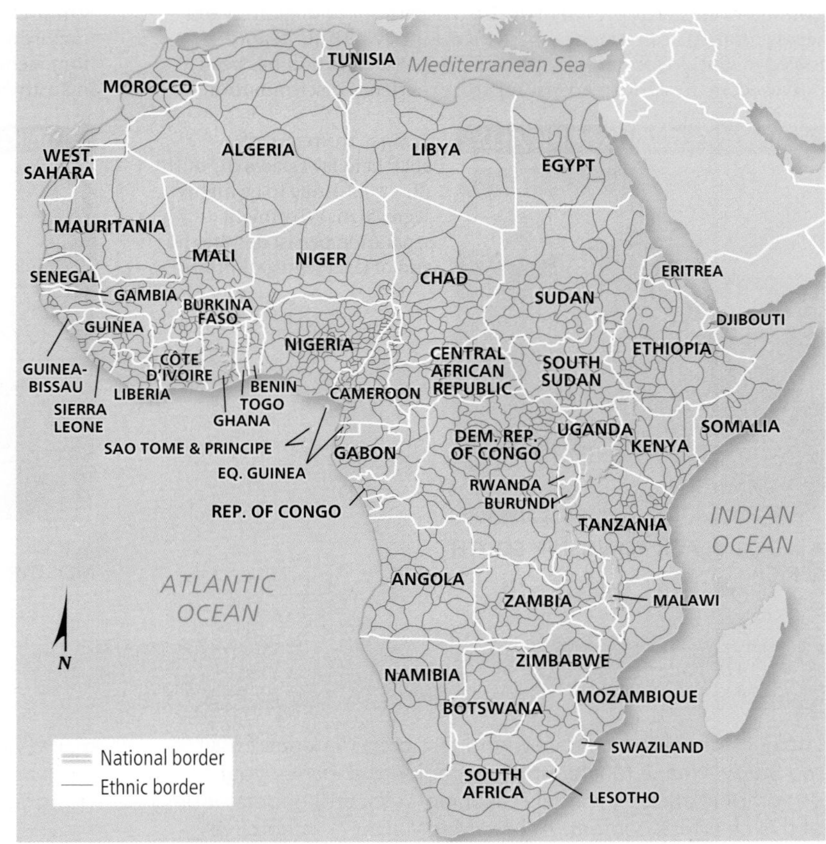

▲ 7.10.4 ETHNICITIES AND NATIONALITIES IN AFRICA

CHAPTER 7

Review, Analyze, & Apply

KEY ISSUE 1 Where Are Ethnicities Distributed?

Ethnicity is identity with a group of people who share the cultural traditions of a particular homeland or hearth. Ethnicity refers to a person's place of cultural heritage, whereas race refers to biological traits such as skin color. The three most numerous ethnic groups in the United States are Hispanics, African Americans, and Asian Americans.

THINKING GEOGRAPHICALLY

▲ 7.CR.1 POLISH ETHNIC ENCLAVE, CHICAGO

1. A century ago, European immigrants to the United States created ethnic enclaves within U.S. cities. Why have most of these European ethnic enclaves become much less prominent in U.S. cities, or disappeared altogether?

KEY ISSUE 2 Why Do Ethnicities Have Distinctive Distributions?

Ethnicities cluster as a result of distinctive patterns of migration and segregation. African Americans have a distinctive ethnic history of forced migration for slavery. Although formal segregation has been outlawed, many African Americans still experience discrimination.

THINKING GEOGRAPHICALLY

▲ 7.CR.2 BLACK TOWNSHIP, SOUTH AFRICA

2. Since the repeal of apartheid laws, races in South Africa continue to be highly segregated. Why might separation persist despite the end of legal segregation?

KEY ISSUE 3 Why Might Ethnicities Face Conflicts?

Conflicts can arise when a country contains several ethnicities competing with each other for control or dominance. Conflicts also arise when an ethnicity is divided among more than one country.

THINKING GEOGRAPHICALLY

▲ 7.CR.3 KURDS CELEBRATE NEWROZ FESTIVAL

3. The Kurds claim to be the world's largest ethnic group not in control of a country. Based on Figures 7.7.4 and 7.8.1, what other ethnic groups might have a strong claim to reorganize territorial boundaries so that they could become the majority? What are some of the obstacles that might be faced in sharing power with other ethnicities?

KEY ISSUE 4 Why Do Ethnic Cleansing and Genocide Occur?

Ethnic cleansing is a process in which a more powerful ethnic group forcibly removes a less powerful one in order to create an ethnically homogeneous region. Genocide is the mass killing of a group of people in an attempt to eliminate the entire group from existence.

THINKING GEOGRAPHICALLY

▲ 7.CR.4 STARI MOST BRIDGE DIVE, MOSTAR

4. The Stari Most bridge in Mostar, Bosnia & Herzegovina, was rebuilt to look almost precisely like the original bridge (refer to Figure 7.9.2). Why do you think it was important to Bosniaks to replicate the original bridge? Professional divers jump off the bridge as part of competitions. Why might the bridge be an important place to hold professional diving competitions?

Mastering Geography

Looking for additional review and test prep materials? Visit the Study Area in Mastering Geography to enhance your geographic literacy, spatial reasoning skills, and understanding of this chapter's content. Access MapMaster™ interactive maps, video case studies, *In the News* current articles, flashcards, self-study quizzes, an eText of *Contemporary Human Geography*, and more. **pearson.com/mastering/geography**

Key Terms

Apartheid (p. 177) Laws (no longer in effect) in South Africa that physically separated different races into different geographic areas.

Black Lives Matter (p. 176) Movement that campaigns against violence and perceived racism toward black people and educates others about the challenges that African Americans continue to face in the United States.

Blockbusting (p. 175) A process by which real estate agents convince white property owners to sell their houses at low prices because of fear that persons of color will soon move into the neighborhood.

Centripetal force (p. 179) An attitude that tends to unify people and enhance support for a state.

Ethnic cleansing (p. 184) A purposeful policy designed by one ethnic or religious group to remove by violent and terror-inspiring means the civilian population of another ethnic or religious group from certain geographic areas.

Ethnic enclave (p. 172) A place with a high concentration of an ethnic group that is distinct from those in the surrounding area.

Ethnicity (p. 168) Identity with a group of people who share the cultural traditions of a particular homeland or hearth.

Ethnoburb (p. 173) A suburban area with a cluster of a particular ethnic population.

Ethnophobia (p. 184) Fear of people of a particular ethnicity.

Genocide (p. 184) The mass killing of a group of people in an attempt to eliminate the entire group from existence.

Nationalism (p. 179) Loyalty and devotion to a particular nationality.

Nationality (p. 168) Identity with a group of people who share legal attachment to a particular country.

Race (p. 168) Identity with a group of people who are perceived to share a physiological trait, such as skin color.

Racism (p. 168) The belief that race is the primary determinant of human traits and capacities and that racial differences produce an inherent superiority of a particular race.

Racist (p. 168) A person who subscribes to the beliefs of racism.

Redlining (p. 175) A process by which financial institutions draw red-colored lines on a map and refuse to lend money for people to purchase or improve property within the lines.

Sharecropper (p. 175) A person who works fields rented from a landowner and pays the rent and repays loans by turning over to the landowner a share of the crops.

Social construction (p. 168) An idea or a meaning that is widely accepted as natural by a society but may not represent a reality shared by those outside the society.

Triangular slave trade (p. 174) A practice, primarily during the eighteenth century, in which European ships transported slaves from Africa to Caribbean islands, molasses from the Caribbean to Europe, and trade goods from Europe to Africa.

Xenophobia (p. 184) Fear of people who are from other countries.

GeoVideo

Log in to the Mastering Geography™ Study Area to view this video.

People in the Altai

The sparsely populated Altai Republic in southern Siberia, Russia, is a mountainous, forested region that is home to an ethnic group known as the Altai.

1. What are some of the distinctive cultural elements of the Altai ethnicity?
2. Describe the role of horses in the everyday life of the Altai's inhabitants.
3. How do the Altai people describe their culture's relationship to the natural environment? Is this similar to or different from your own culture's relationship to nature? Explain.

Explore

Lingering apartheid in South Africa

Use Google Earth to explore a township where only blacks lived during South Africa's apartheid period.

Search for *500 Barracuda Road, Lawley, Gauteng, South Africa.*

1. Continue east along Barracuda Road until you reach the end. What nonresidential activities did you see along the road?
2. Describe the condition of the houses. Large or small? Modern or old? In good shape or poor?
3. Describe the landscaping around the houses, especially when you get to the end of the road.
4. Why is it important for people to erect fences or walls around their houses?

▲ 7.CR.6 **LAWLEY TOWNSHIP, SOUTH AFRICA**

Geospatial Analysis

Log in to the Mastering Geography Study Area to access MapMaster 2.0.

Ethnic diversity in sub-Saharan Africa

Sub-Saharan Africa has the world's most ethnically diverse countries.

Add the *Ethnic Diversity* layer. ***Select*** the *Settings* icon from the *Legend*, and ***select*** *Show Political Labels.* ***Zoom*** to Sub-Saharan Africa.

1. ***Select*** one country that is most ethnically diverse and one country that is least or less ethnically diverse. Place the cursor over these two countries. How do the data show that one country is more ethnically diverse than the other?
2. ***Add*** the *Refugees, by Country of Origin* layer, ***select*** *Split map window.* Does the spatial association between the two maps appear to be strong or weak? Why might that be the case?

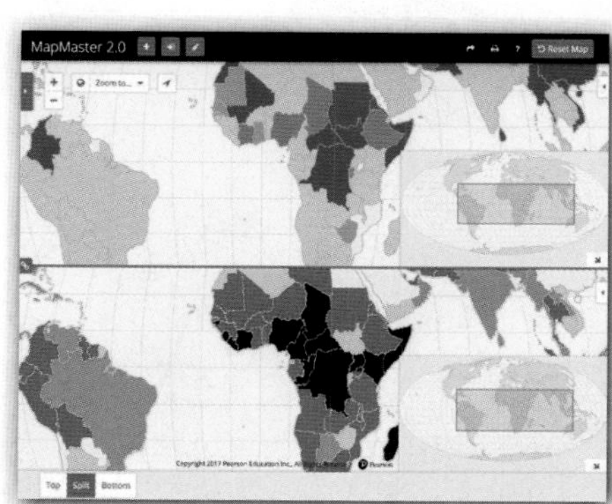

▶ 7.CR.7 **ETHNIC DIVERSITY AND REFUGEES IN AFRICA**

CHAPTER 8

Political Geography

How many states of the world can you name? Old-style geography sometimes required memorization of countries and their capitals. Human geographers now emphasize a thematic approach that studies the locations of activities in the world, the reasons for particular spatial distributions, and the significance of the arrangements. Despite this change in emphasis, you still need to know the locations of states. Without such knowledge, you lack a basic frame of reference—knowing where things are.

◀ A woman votes in general election, Nairobi, Kenya.

KEY ISSUES

1 Where Are States Distributed?

Earth's land area is divided into states, although what constitutes a state is not always clear-cut.

2 How Are States Created?

The organization of Earth's surface into a collection of sovereign states is recent. In principle, states are designed to match the territory occupied by cultural groups. But in practice, the creation of nation-states is sometimes difficult.

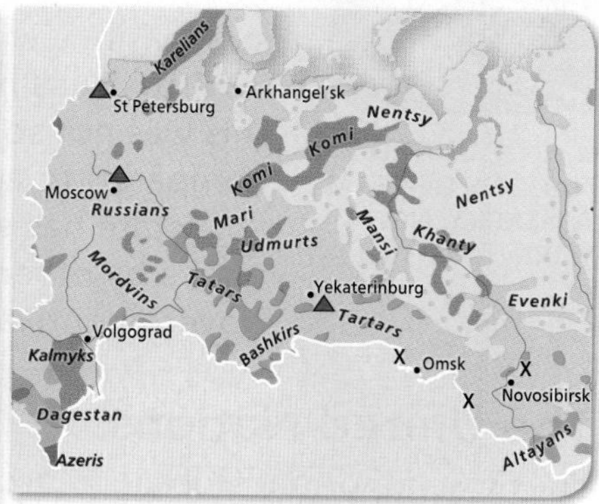

3 How Are States Organized?

Boundaries divide Earth's surface into a collection of states that assume various shapes. Individual states assume varying forms of governance.

4 What Threats Do States Face?

States have come together in international organizations, but many people do not feel connected to some of these organizations. Some recent conflicts have been initiated by terrorist organizations.

LOCATIONS IN THIS CHAPTER

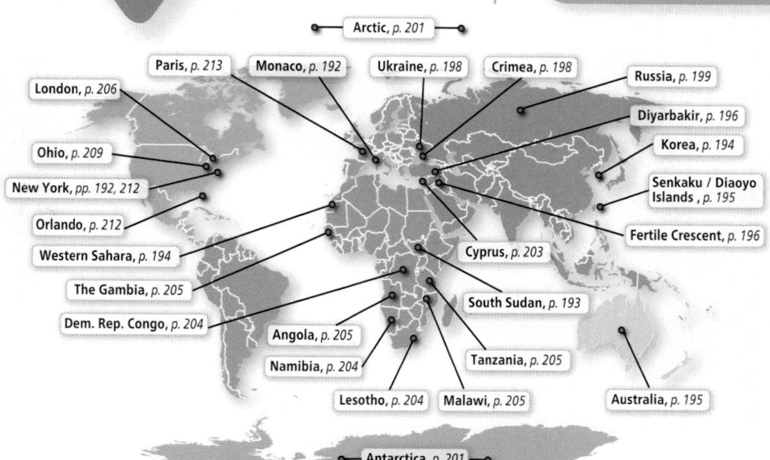

nation · fragmented state · terrorism · unitary state · landlocked state · democracy · autocracy · colony · boundary · perforated state · microstate · frontier · multinational state · compact state · federal state · nation state · sovereignty · anocracy · balance of power · gerrymandering · prorupted state · self determination · elongated state · state

A World of States

- **Define "state" as used in political geography.**

▲ 8.1.1 UNITED NATIONS GENERAL ASSEMBLY, NEW YORK

A **state** is an area organized into a political unit and ruled by an established government that has control over its internal and foreign affairs. It occupies a defined territory on Earth's surface and contains a permanent population. The term country is a synonym for state.

The term state, as used in political geography, does not refer to the 50 local governments inside the United States. The 50 states of the United States are subdivisions within a single state—the United States of America.

Virtually all habitable land belongs to some country or other. But for most of history, this was not so. As recently as the 1940s, the world contained only about 50 countries, compared to approximately 200 today.

A state has **sovereignty**, which means independence from control of its internal affairs by other states. Because the entire area of a state is managed by its national government, laws, army, and leaders, it is a good example of a formal or uniform region.

The United Nations

The most important global organization is the United Nations, created at the end of World War II by the victorious Allies (Figure 8.1.1). During this era of rapid changes in states and their relationships, the UN has provided a forum for the discussion of international problems. On occasion, the UN has intervened in conflicts between or within member states, authorizing military and peacekeeping actions. In addition, the UN seeks to promote international cooperation to address global economic problems, promote human rights, and provide humanitarian relief.

The land area occupied by the states of the world varies considerably. The largest state is Russia, which encompasses 17.1 million square kilometers (6.6 million square miles). At the other extreme are about two dozen **microstates**, which are states with very small land areas (Figure 8.1.2).

▼ 8.1.2 MICROSTATE
Monaco occupies only 2 square kilometers (0.8 square mile).

UN Growth

When it was organized in 1945, the UN had only 51 members, including 49 sovereign states plus Byelorussia (now Belarus) and Ukraine, then part of the Soviet Union (Figure 8.1.3). Much of the world consisted of colonies and other territories controlled by European states (see Section 8.5 later in this chapter). As these areas gained independence, UN membership grew. With the admission of South Sudan in 2011 (Figure 8.1.4), the number of UN members reached 193 (Figure 8.1.5).

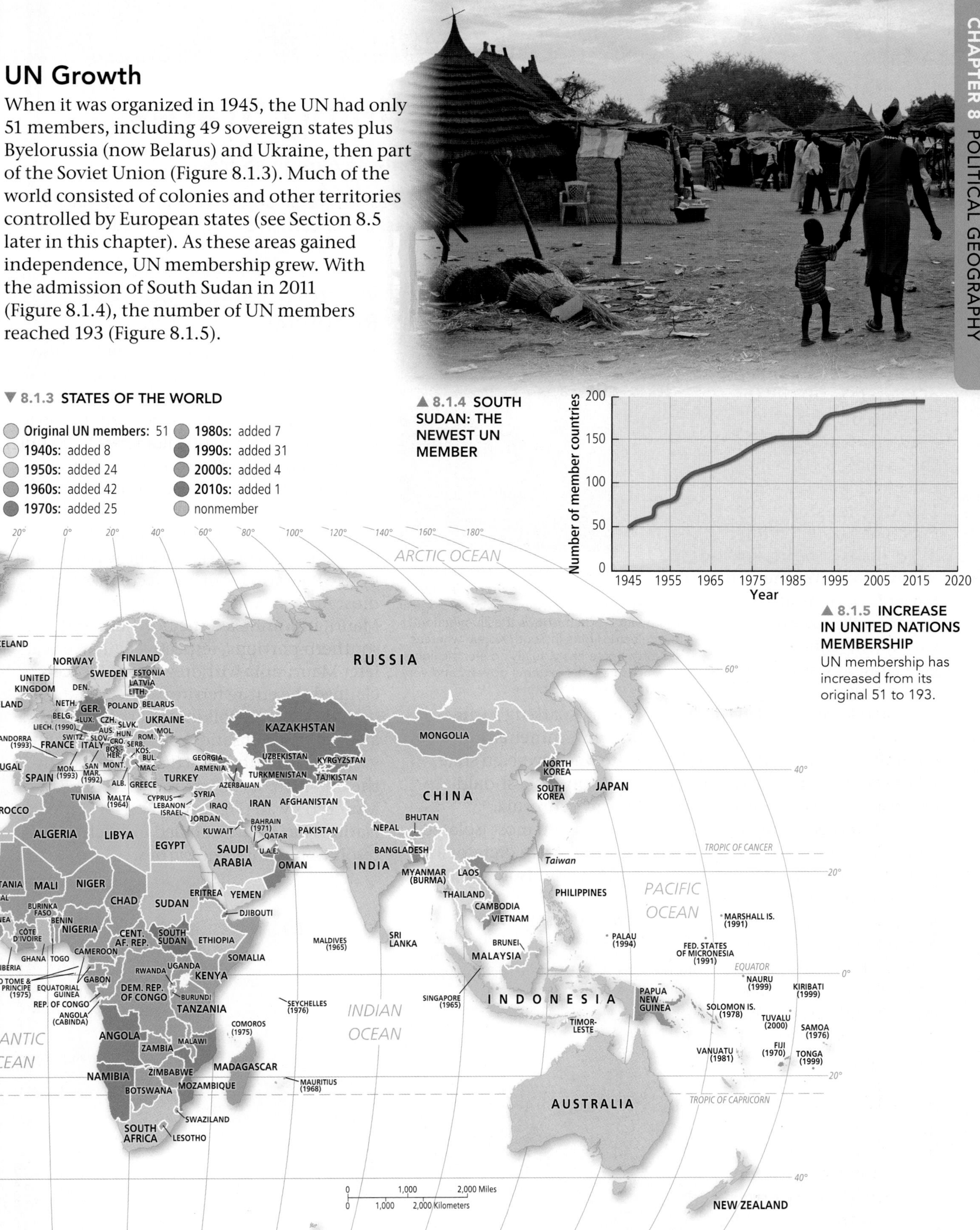

▼ 8.1.3 STATES OF THE WORLD

▲ 8.1.4 SOUTH SUDAN: THE NEWEST UN MEMBER

▲ 8.1.5 INCREASE IN UNITED NATIONS MEMBERSHIP
UN membership has increased from its original 51 to 193.

Challenges in Defining States

- Explain difficulties in identifying some sovereign states.

Most of the world has been allocated to sovereign states. A handful of places, however, have complicated histories and uncertain or disputed status, straining the definition of sovereignty.

Korea

The Korean peninsula is divided between the Democratic People's Republic of Korea (North) and the Republic of Korea (South). After the United States and the former Soviet Union defeated Japan in World War II, the victors divided Korea, which had been a colony of Japan for 35 years, into two occupation zones. The Soviet Union installed a pro-Communist government in the North, while a pro-U.S. government was established in the South.

▲ 8.2.1 NORTH AND SOUTH KOREA
A nighttime satellite image recorded by the U.S. Air Force Defense Meteorological Satelite Program shows the illumination of electric lights in South Korea, whereas North Korea has virtually no electric lights, a measure of its extreme poverty and very low level of development.

North Korea invaded the South in 1950, sparking a three-year war that ended in a cease-fire. Both governments are committed to reuniting the country into one sovereign state. However, both maintain that they are the one that should exercise sovereignty over the entire Korean peninsula.

North Korea is one of the world's poorest and most isolated countries, and since 1948 it has been governed as a dictatorship by Kim Il-sung, his son Kim Jong-il, and his grandson Kim Jong-un. Further aggravating reconciliation, North Korea has built and tested nuclear weapons and long-range missiles, even though the country lacks the ability to provide its citizens with food, electricity, and other basic needs (Figure 8.2.1). As generations of Koreans in the South without direct family connections to Koreans in the North come of voting age, public support in South Korea for reunification is declining.

Western Sahara (Sahrawi Republic)

The Sahrawi Arab Democratic Republic, also known as Western Sahara, is considered by most African countries as a sovereign state. Morocco, however, claims the territory and to prove it has built a 2,700-kilometer (1,700-mile) wall around the territory to keep out rebels.

Spain controlled the territory on the continent's west coast between Morocco and Mauritania until withdrawing in 1976. An independent Sahrawi Republic was declared by the Polisario Front and recognized by most African countries, but Morocco and Mauritania annexed the northern and southern portions, respectively. Three years later Mauritania withdrew, and Morocco claimed the entire territory.

Morocco controls most of the populated area, but the Polisario Front operates in the vast, sparsely inhabited deserts, especially the one-fifth of the territory that lies east of Morocco's wall (Figure 8.2.2). The United Nations has tried but failed to reach a resolution among the parties.

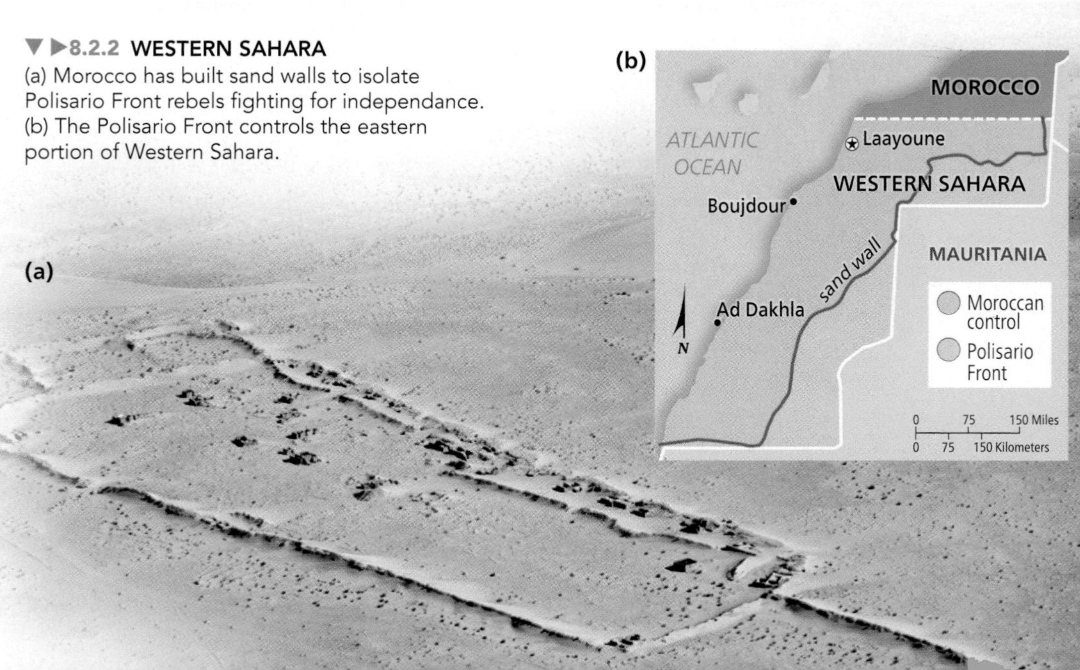

▼ ▶8.2.2 WESTERN SAHARA
(a) Morocco has built sand walls to isolate Polisario Front rebels fighting for independance. (b) The Polisario Front controls the eastern portion of Western Sahara.

China and Taiwan

Most other countries consider China (officially the People's Republic of China) and Taiwan (officially the Republic of China) as separate and sovereign states. According to China's government, Taiwan is not sovereign but a part of China. The government of Taiwan agrees.

The current status arises from a civil war in China during the late 1940s between the Nationalists and the Communists. After losing in 1949, Nationalist leaders fled to Taiwan, 200 kilometers (125 miles) off the China coast, and proclaimed that they were still the legitimate rulers of the entire country of China. Until some future occasion when they could defeat the Communists and recapture all of China, the Nationalists argued, at least they could continue to govern one island of the country.

The United States had supported the Nationalists during the civil war, so many Americans opposed acknowledging that China was firmly under the control of the Communists. Consequently, the United States continued to regard the Nationalists as the official government of China until 1971, when U.S. policy finally changed and the United Nations voted to transfer China's seat from the Nationalists to the Communists.

Senkaku / Diaoyu Islands

The People's Republic of China, Taiwan, and Japan all claim sovereignty over several small uninhabited islands in the East China Sea. These islands are known as Diaoyu in China, Diaoyutai in Taiwan, and Senkaku in Japan (Figure 8.2.3). The largest of five islands is only 4.3 square kilometers (1.7 square miles).

▲ 8.2.3 DISPUTED ISLANDS
The Senkaku/Diaoyo Islands are all claimed by China, Taiwan, and Japan.

Japan has controlled the islands since 1895, except between 1945 and 1972 when the United States administered them after defeating Japan in World War II. China and Taiwan claim that the islands historically belonged to China until the Japanese government illegally seized them in 1895. Japan's position is that China did not state that it had sovereignty over the uninhabited islands in 1895 when Japan claimed them. To bolster their claims, China and Japan have both established air defense zones in the East China Sea with conflicting boundaries.

The Law of the Sea

States that border an ocean can claim vast areas of it for defense and for control of valuable fishing areas. The dispute over the East China Sea islands shows the importance of territorial waters to many countries. Sovereign rights to the islands are important to China and Japan, because the country that controls them has a stronger claim to the territorial waters around them, including control over fishing rights.

The Law of the Sea, signed by 167 countries, has standardized the territorial limits for most countries at 12 nautical miles (about 22 kilometers, or 14 land miles). Under the Law of the Sea, states also have exclusive rights to the fish and other marine life within 200 nautical miles (320 kilometers). Disputes such as the location of boundaries between Australia and Timor-Leste can be taken to a tribunal for the Law of the Sea or to the International Court of Justice (Figure 8.2.4).

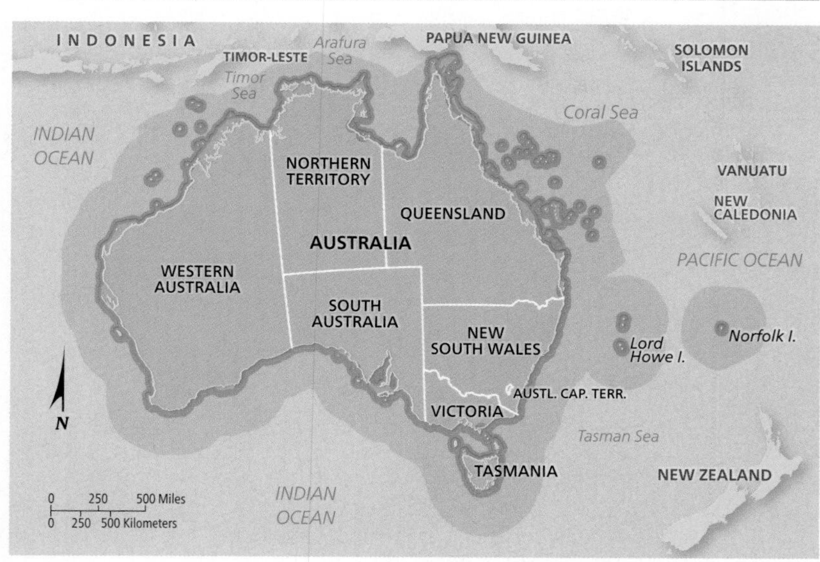

▲ 8.2.4 LAW OF THE SEA APPLIED TO AUSTRALIA

Evolution of States

- **Summarize how states developed historically.**

The concept of dividing the world into a collection of independent states is recent. Prior to the 1800s, Earth's surface was organized in other ways, such as into city-states, empires, kingdoms, and small land areas controlled by a hereditary class of nobles. Much of it consisted of unorganized territory.

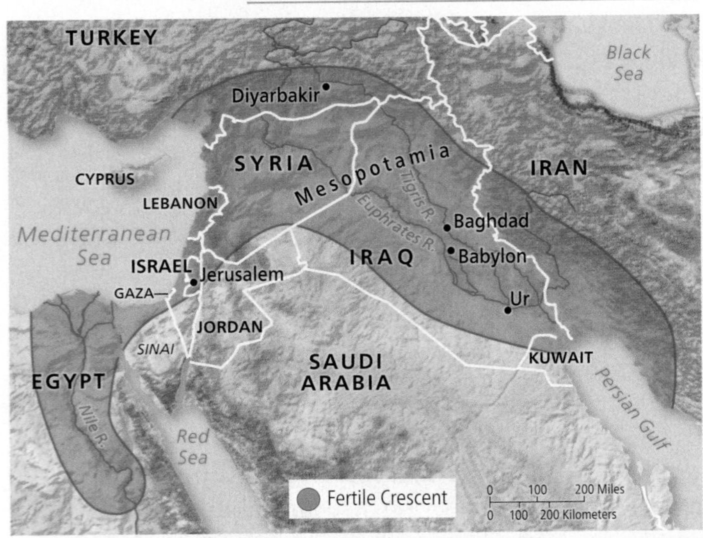

▲ 8.3.1 **THE FERTILE CRESCENT**
The crescent-shaped area of relatively fertile land was organized into a succession of empires starting several thousand years ago.

▼ 8.3.2 **THE FERTILE CRESCENT AT DIYARBAKIR, TURKEY**
The earliest reference to the city is 3,300 years ago.

Ancient States

The development of states can be traced to the ancient Middle East, in an area known as the Fertile Crescent. The ancient Fertile Crescent formed an arc between the Persian Gulf and the Mediterranean Sea (Figure 8.3.1). Situated at the crossroads of Europe, Asia, and Africa, the Fertile Crescent was a center for land and sea communications in ancient times (Figure 8.3.2).

The first states to evolve in Mesopotamia were known as city-states. A **city-state** is a sovereign territory that comprises a town and the surrounding countryside. Walls clearly delineated the boundaries of the city, and outside the walls the city controlled agricultural land to produce food for urban residents. The countryside also provided the city with an outer line of defense against attack by other city-states.

Periodically, one city or tribe in Mesopotamia would gain military dominance over the others and form an empire. Mesopotamia was organized into a succession of empires by the Sumerians, Assyrians, Babylonians, and Persians.

From the Roman Empire to Medieval States

Political unity in the ancient world reached its height with the establishment of the Roman Empire, which controlled most of Europe, North Africa, and Southwest Asia, from modern-day Spain to Iran and from Egypt to England. At its maximum extent, the empire comprised 38 provinces, each using the same set of laws that had been created in Rome. Massive walls helped the Roman army defend many of the empire's frontiers.

The Roman Empire collapsed in the fifth century, after a series of attacks by people living on its frontiers and because of internal disputes. The European portion of the Roman Empire was fragmented into a large number of estates owned by competing kings, dukes, barons, and other nobles. A handful of powerful kings emerged as rulers over large numbers of these European estates beginning around the year 1100 (Figure 8.3.3). The consolidation of neighboring estates under the unified control of a king formed the basis for the development of such modern European states as England, France, and Spain (Figure 8.3.4).

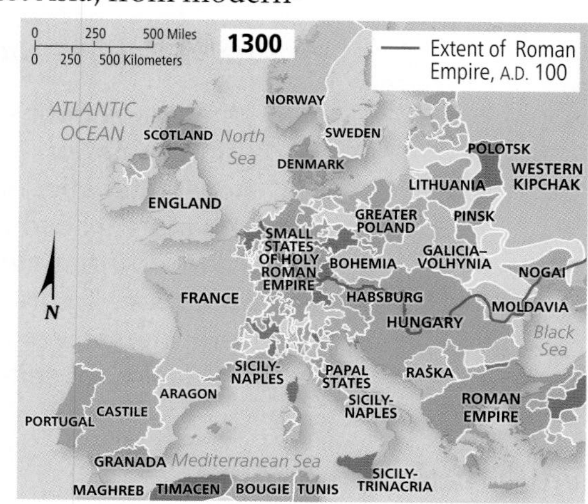

▲ 8.3.3 **EUROPE, 1300**
Much of Europe was fragmented into small estates controlled by nobles. Until the fifth century, the Roman Empire controlled the land south of the red line.

States in Twentieth Century Europe

Into the twentieth century, most of Europe's territory was ruled by a handful of emperors, kings, and queens. After World War I ended in 1918, leaders of the victorious countries met at the Versailles Peace Conference to redraw the map of Europe (Figure 8.3.5). One of the chief advisers to President Woodrow Wilson, the geographer Isaiah Bowman, played a major role in the decisions.

The redrawn map of Europe was not a recipe for peace. During the 1930s, German National Socialists (Nazis) claimed that all German-speaking parts of Europe constituted one nationality and should be unified into one state. After it was defeated in World War II, Germany was divided into two countries, and two Germanys existed from 1949 until 1990 (Figure 8.3.6). Germany was reunified in 1990 into a single state, but its area bears little resemblance to the territory occupied by German-speaking people prior to the upheavals of the twentieth century.

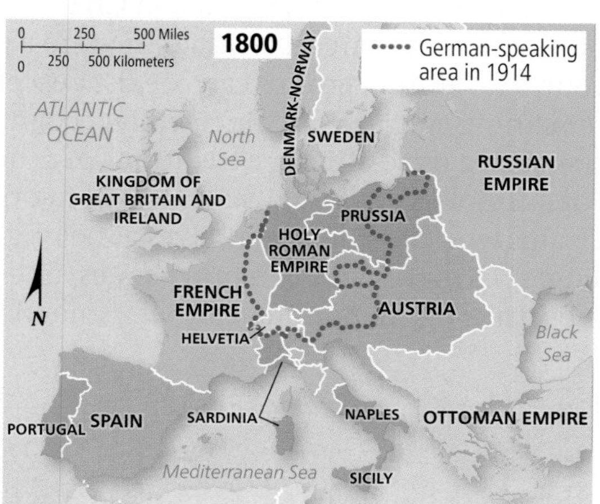

▲ 8.3.4 **EUROPE, 1800**
Much of Europe was organized into empires.

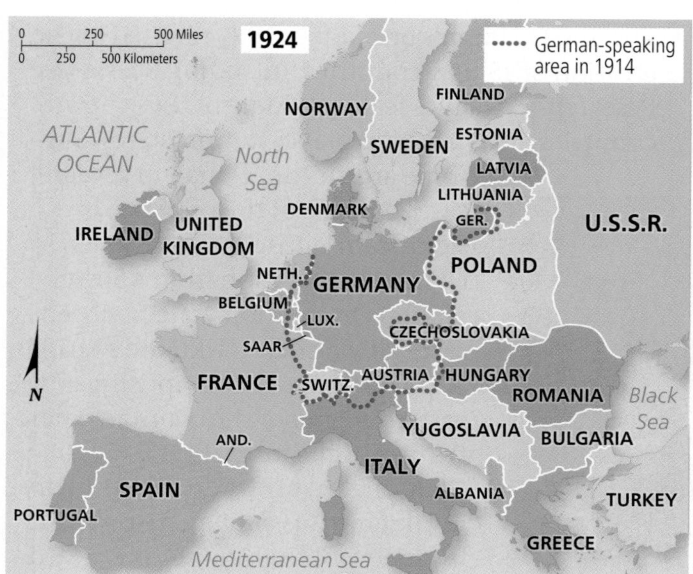

▲ 8.3.5 **EUROPE, 1924**
Much of Europe was organized into nation-states.

▲ 8.3.6 **EUROPE, 1980**
Germany was divided into two states after its defeat in World War II.

Nation-States

- Analyze challenges in creating nation-states.

A state was defined earlier in the chapter as an area organized into a political unit. A **nation** is a large group of people who are united by common cultural characteristics, such as language and ethnicity, or by shared history. A **nation-state** is a state whose territory corresponds to that occupied by a particular nation.

The concept that nations have the right to govern themselves is known as **self-determination**. To preserve and enhance distinctive cultural characteristics, nations seek to govern themselves without interference. Nations have pushed to create nation-states because desire for self-rule is a very important shared attitude for many of them.

Multinational States

A **multinational state** is a state that contains more than one nation. In some states, nations all contribute cultural features to the formation of a single nationality, which was defined in Chapter 7 as a group of people who share legal attachment to a particular country. Cultural groups can coexist peacefully, remaining culturally distinct while recognizing and respecting the distinctive traditions of other groups. For example, the United States has numerous cultural groups who consider themselves as belonging to a single U.S. nationality. In other states, one cultural group may try to dominate others, sometimes by force.

▲ 8.4.1 **ETHNICITIES IN A MULTINATIONAL STATE: UKRAINE** Many ethnic Ukrainians, as well as ethnic Russians, speak Russian as their primary language in the eastern portion of Ukraine. When Ukraine was part of the Soviet Union, the government required the use of the Russian language.

▲ 8.4.2 **RUSSIAN SOLDIERS TAKE CONTROL OF CRIMEA**

Dismantling Multinational States

Some multinational states face complex challenges in maintaining unity and preventing discontented cultural groups from trying to break away and form their own nation-states. In Europe, the breakup of the Soviet Union, Czechoslovakia, and Yugoslavia in the late twentieth century demonstrated both success and failure in creating new nation-states.

- Czechoslovakia was peacefully transformed in 1993 from a multinational state to two nation-states—Czechia (Czech Republic) and Slovakia. Slovaks comprise only 1 percent of Czechia's population, and Czechs less than 1 percent of Slovakia's population.
- Yugoslavia's breakup included a peaceful conversion of Slovenia in 1991 from a republic in multinational Yugoslavia to a nation-state. However, other portions of former Yugoslavia became nation-states only after ethnic cleansing and other atrocities, as discussed on pages 184–85.
- The Soviet Union's breakup in 1991 resulted in the creation of 15 new countries, including Russia (see Research & Analyze feature). Some of these new countries are good examples of nation-states and some are multinational, in several cases because of the presence of a significant minority of Russians. Ukraine's transition from a Soviet republic to a nation-state has been especially difficult. Ukraine's Russian population started an uprising in the eastern region of the country, where they were clustered (Figure 8.4.1). Claiming that the Russian ethnicity in Ukraine was endangered, Russia invaded eastern Ukraine and seized Crimea in 2014 (Figure 8.4.2).

Russia: The Largest Multinational State

Russia's 2010 census recorded 43 ethnic groups with at least 100,000 people and 31 with between 10,000 and 100,000. Ethnicities other than Russian are clustered in two principal locations: on the borders with neighboring states and in the center of Russia especially between the Volga River basin and the Ural Mountains (Figure 8.4.3).

Slavic peoples
- Russians
- Ukrainians

Turkic peoples
- Tatars, Bashkirs
- Azerbaijanis
- other Turkic peoples

Other Indo-European peoples
- Lithuanians, Armenians, Ossetians
- X Germans
- ▲ Jews

Paleo-Siberian peoples
- Chukchi, Koryaks, Nivkhi
- Eskimos

Caucasian peoples
- Georgians, Chechens, Ingush, peoples of Dagestan

Other Uralic and Altaic peoples
- Karelians, Mari, Komi, Mordvins, Udmurts, Mansi, Khanty, Nentsy, Buryats, Kalmyks, Evenki, Eveny, Nganasany
- uninhabited or sparsely settled

▲ 8.4.3 **SOME OF RUSSIA'S MANY ETHNICITIES**

Russians are clustered in Western Russia, and the percentage declines to the east. The largest numbers of non-Russians are found between the Volga River and the Ural Mountains and near the southern borders.

RESEARCH & ANALYZE

Nation-states in the former Soviet Union

The Soviet Union (U.S.S.R.) was an especially prominent example of a multinational state until its collapse in the early 1990s. Are the states carved out of the Soviet Union good examples of nation-states (Figure 8.4.4)?

CIA World Factbook

https://goo.gl/mYPVk5

At CIA World Factbook (**cia.gov/library/publications/theworld-factbook**), ***open*** *Please select a country to view*, then ***select*** in turn each of the six former Soviet Republics along Russia's western (European) border. ***Scroll down*** the page and ***select*** *People and society*.

1. For each of the six countries, what percentage of the population belongs to the principal ethnic group?
2. What percentage is Russian?
3. Which two of these six countries contain a second ethnicity that is more numerous than Russian?
4. Which two of these six countries appear from the data to be the best examples of nation-states?
5. ***Select*** one of the six countries that appears to be a good example of a nation-state and one that appears to be multinational. ***Read*** the *Background, Military & Security, and Transnational Issues* sections of the CIA briefing. Which appears to be more stable, peaceful, and democratic? What role might the ethnic uniformity or diversity be playing in this condition?

▲ 8.4.4 **SOVIET UNION**

The U.S.S.R. consisted of 15 republics that have become independent states.

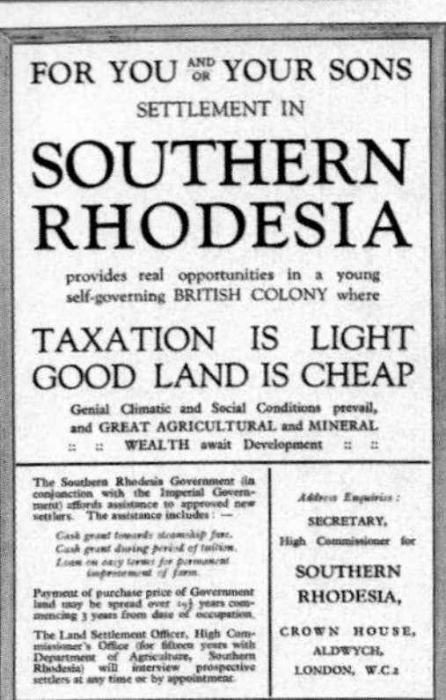
FOR YOU AND/OR YOUR SONS
SETTLEMENT IN
SOUTHERN RHODESIA
provides real opportunities in a young self-governing BRITISH COLONY where
TAXATION IS LIGHT
GOOD LAND IS CHEAP
Genial Climatic and Social Conditions prevail, and GREAT AGRICULTURAL and MINERAL :: :: WEALTH await Development :: ::

The Southern Rhodesia Government (in conjunction with the Imperial Government) affords assistance to approved new settlers. The assistance includes: —

Cash grant towards steamship fare.
Cash grant during period of tuition.
Loan on easy terms for permanent improvement of farm.

Payment of purchase price of Government land may be spread over 19½ years commencing 3 years from date of occupation.

The Land Settlement Officer, High Commissioner's Office (for fifteen years with Department of Agriculture, Southern Rhodesia) will interview prospective settlers at any time or by appointment.

Address Enquiries:
SECRETARY,
High Commissioner for
SOUTHERN RHODESIA,
CROWN HOUSE,
ALDWYCH,
LONDON, W.C.2

▲ **8.5.1 BRITISH COLONY**
British newspaper ad from the 1920s encouraging people to move to the British colony of Southern Rhodesia (now Zimbabwe).

Colonies

- **Explain the concept of colonies and describe their current distribution.**

Although most of Earth's land area has been allocated to sovereign states, some territories have not achieved self-determination and statehood. A **colony** is a territory that is legally tied to a sovereign state rather than being an independent sovereign state in its own right. The military and foreign policy of a colony are run by a sovereign state, and sometimes its internal affairs as well.

Colonialism

European states came to control much of the world through **colonialism**, which is an effort by one country to establish settlements in a territory and to impose its political, economic, and cultural principles on that territory. European states established colonies elsewhere in the world for three basic reasons: to promote Christianity; to extract useful resources and create captive markets for their own products; and to gain prestige through the number of their colonies. These three motives were summarized as God, gold, and glory.

The colonial era began in the 1400s, when European explorers sailed around Africa to reach India, then sailed westward for Asia but encountered and settled in the Western Hemisphere instead. Eventually, the European states lost most of their Western Hemisphere colonies: Independence was declared by the United States in 1776 and by most Latin American states between 1800 and 1824.

European states later again turned their attention to Africa and Asia (Figure 8.5.1). The United Kingdom planted colonies through much of eastern and southern Africa, South Asia, the Middle East, Australia, and Canada. With by far the largest colonial empire, the British proclaimed that the "Sun never set" on their empire. France had the second-largest overseas territory, primarily in West Africa and Southeast Asia (Figure 8.5.2). France attempted to assimilate its colonies into French culture and educate an elite group to provide local administrative leadership. After independence, most of these leaders retained close ties with France.

Most African and Asian colonies became independent after World War II. Only 15 African and Asian states were members of the United Nations in 1945, compared to 106 in 2017. The boundaries of the new states frequently coincide with former colonial provinces, although not always.

▶ **8.5.2 COLONIES IN 1914**
At the outbreak of World War I in 1914, European states held colonies in much of the world.

Present-day boundaries are shown.

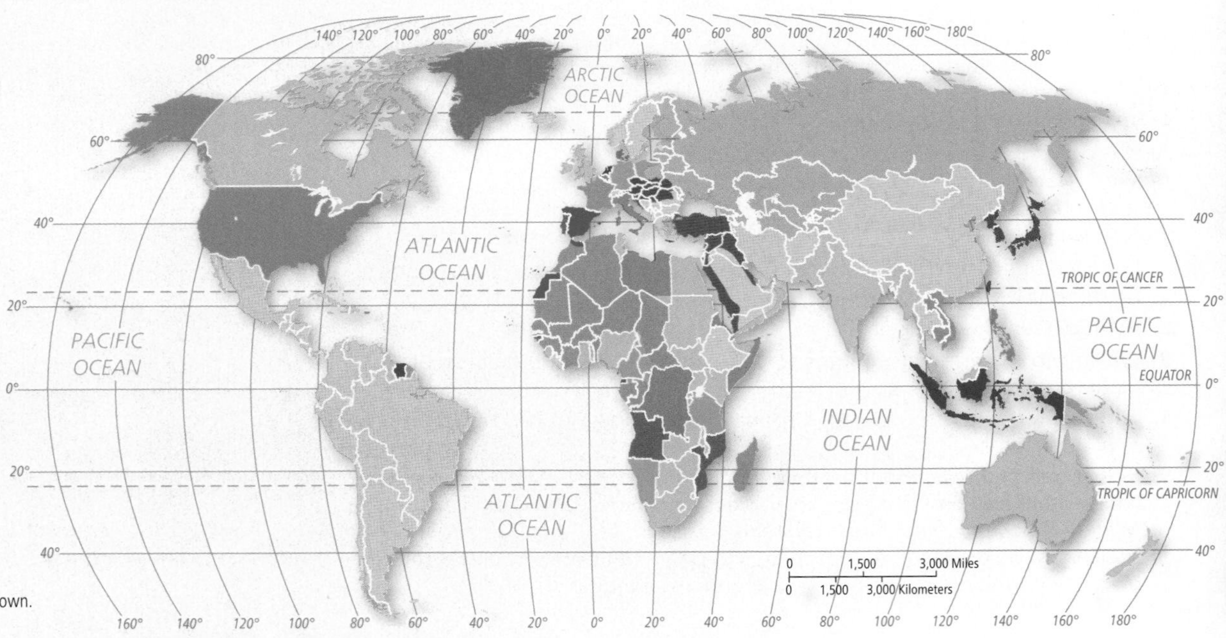

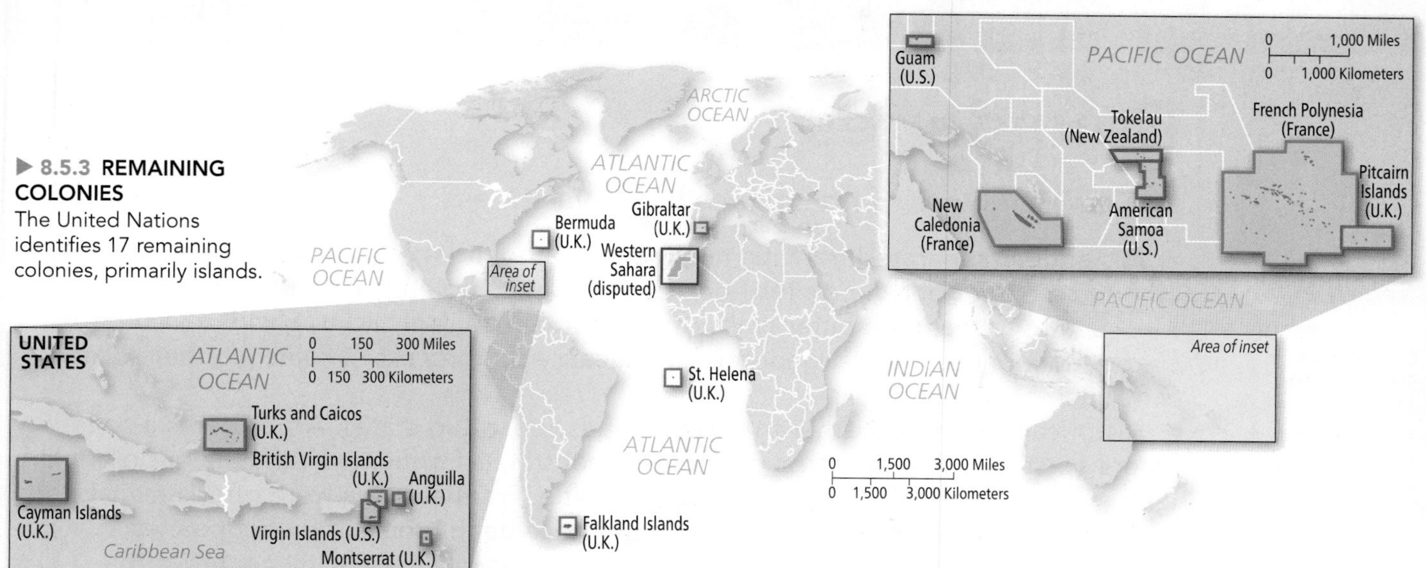

▶ **8.5.3 REMAINING COLONIES**
The United Nations identifies 17 remaining colonies, primarily islands.

The Remaining Colonies

The United Nations lists 17 places in the world that it calls "non-self-governing territories" (Figure 8.5.3). Of the seventeen, Western Sahara is by far the most extensive (266,000 square kilometers) and most populous (531,000). The two next most populous are French Polynesia and New Caledonia, both controlled by France, with less than 300,000 inhabitants each. All but Western Sahara are islands.

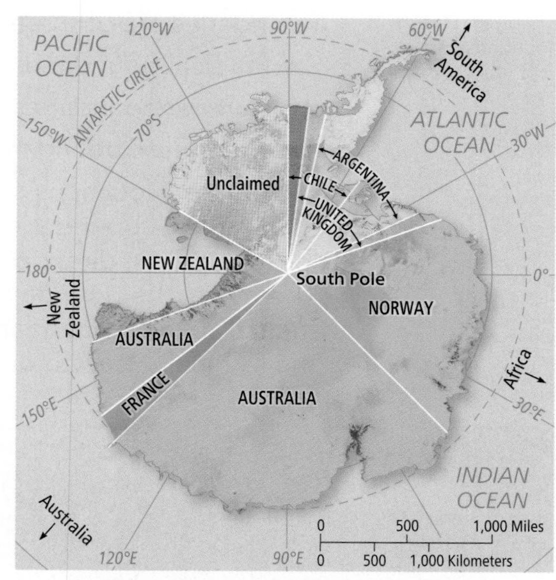

▲ **8.5.4 NATIONAL CLAIMS TO ANTARTICA**

Polar Regions: Many Claims

The South Pole region contains the only large landmass on Earth's surface that is not part of a state. Several states claim portions of the region, and some claims are overlapping and conflicting.

Several states, including Argentina, Australia, Chile, France, New Zealand, Norway, and the United Kingdom, claim portions of Antarctica (Figure 8.5.4). Argentina, Chile, and the United Kingdom have made conflicting, overlapping claims. The United States, Russia, and a number of other states do not recognize the claims of any country to Antarctica. The Antarctic Treaty, signed in 1959 and entered into force two years later, provides a legal framework for managing Antarctica. States may establish research stations there for scientific investigations, but no military activities are permitted. The treaty is currently signed by 53 states.

As for the Arctic Ocean, the 1982 United Nations Convention on the Law of the Sea permitted countries to submit claims inside the Arctic Circle by 2009 (Figure 8.5.5). The Arctic Ocean's seafloor is thought to be rich in energy resources.

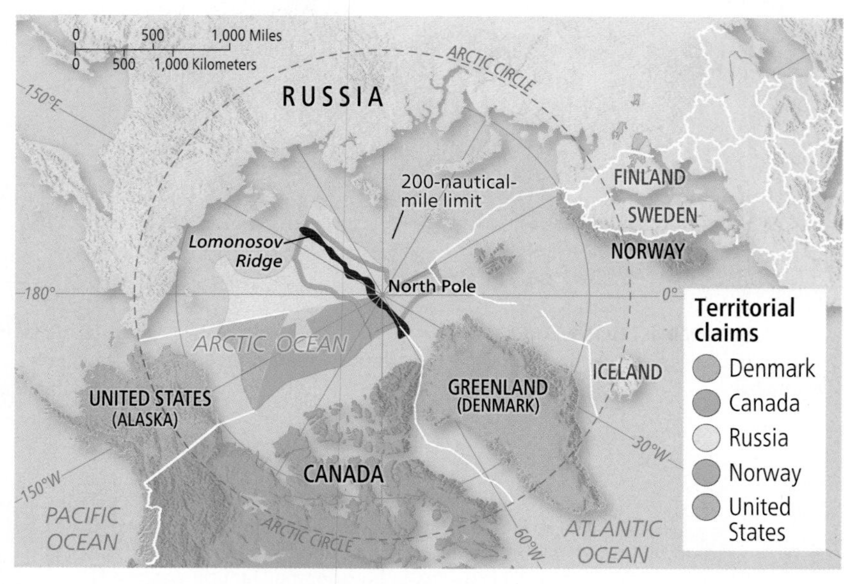

▲ **8.5.5 NATIONAL CLAIMS TO THE ARCTIC OCEAN**

▲ 8.6.1 **DESERT BOUNDARY: SUDAN AND ERITREA**
A boundary drawn in a desert, such as between Sudan and Eritrea, can effectively divide two states because deserts are hard to cross and sparsely inhabited. Desert boundaries are common in Africa and Asia.

Boundaries

- Describe types of boundaries between states.

A state is separated from its neighbors by a **boundary**, an invisible line that marks the extent of a state's territory. Boundaries completely surround an individual state to mark the outer limits of its territorial control and to give it a distinctive shape. Boundaries interest geographers because the process of selecting their location is frequently difficult.

Historically, frontiers rather than boundaries separated states. A **frontier** is a zone where no state exercises complete political control. A frontier is a tangible geographic area, whereas a boundary is an infinitely thin line. Frontier areas were often uninhabited or sparsely settled. Frontiers between states have been replaced by boundaries, because modern communications and electronic surveillance permit countries to monitor and guard boundaries effectively, even in previously inaccessible locations. Boundaries are of three types:

- Physical boundaries coincide with significant features of the natural landscape.
- Cultural boundaries follow the distribution of cultural characteristics.
- Geometric boundaries are based on human constructs, such as straight lines.

Boundary locations can generate conflict, both within a country and with its neighbors. A boundary line, which must be shared by more than one state, is the only location where direct physical contact must take place between two neighboring states. Therefore, the boundary has the potential to become the focal point of conflict between them. The best boundaries are those to which all impacted states agree, regardless of the rationale used to draw the line, and may combine more than one type.

▲ 8.6.2 **MOUNTAIN BOUNDARY**
The border between Argentina and Chile runs through the Andes Mountains.

Physical Boundaries

A physical boundary coincides with significant features of the natural landscape. Important physical features on Earth's surface can make good boundaries because they are easily seen, both on a map and on the ground. Three types of physical elements serve as boundaries between states: deserts (Figure 8.6.1), mountains (Figure 8.6.2), and water (Figure 8.6.3).

▶ 8.6.3 **WATER BOUNDARIES**
Rivers, lakes, and oceans are the physical features most commonly used as boundaries. Water boundaries are readily visible on maps and aerial imagery. In Europe, the Danube and Rhine rivers serve as boundaries between several countries.

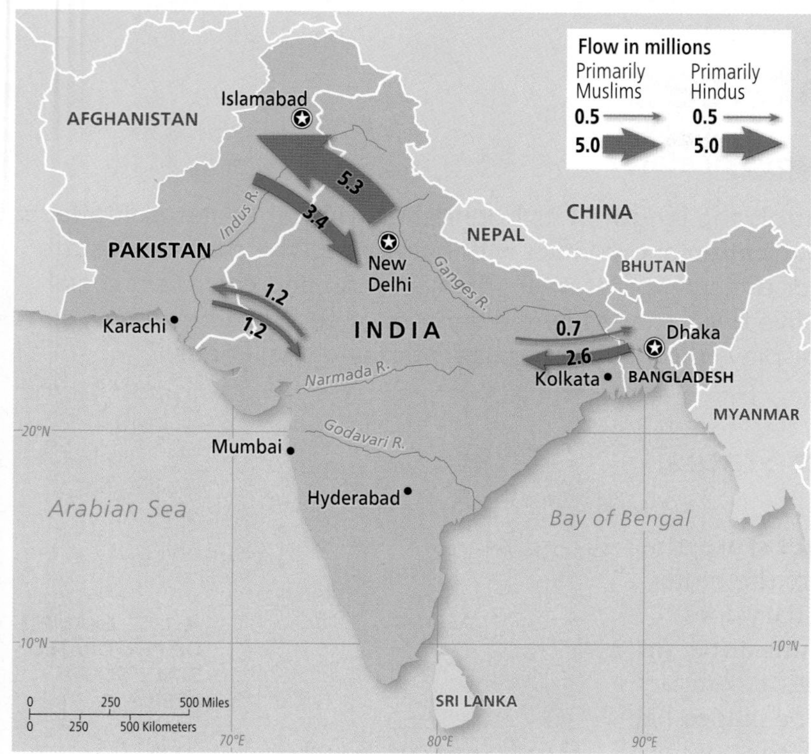

▲ 8.6.4 **RELIGIOUS BOUNDARY: SOUTH ASIA**
When the British ended their colonial rule in South Asia in 1947, they divided the colony into two irregularly shaped countries: India and Pakistan. Present-day Pakistan was initially known as West Pakistan. Present-day Bangladesh was initially part of Pakistan, known as East Pakistan, until it became a separate country in 1971. The basis for separating East and West Pakistan from India was religion. The people living in East and West Pakistan were predominantly Muslim, whereas those in India were predominantly Hindu. The partition resulted in massive migration of Muslims from India into East and West Pakistan and Hindus from East and West Pakistan into India.

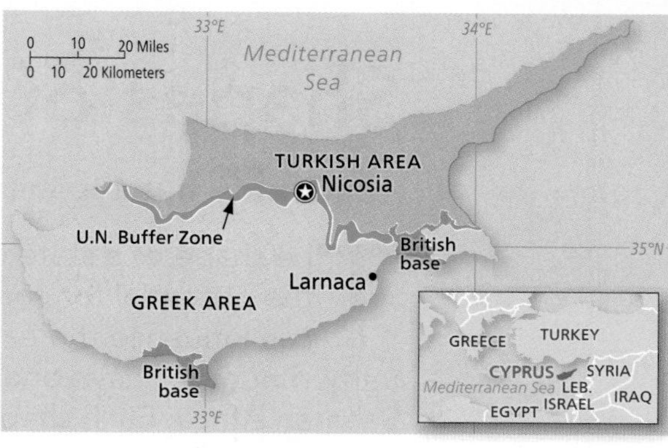

▲ 8.6.5 **ETHNIC BOUNDARY: CYPRUS**
Cyprus is divided between 58 percent Greeks clustered in the south, and 25 percent Turks clustered in the north. When Cyprus gained independence from the United Kingdom in 1960, the Turkish minority was guaranteed considerable autonomy, but after Greek Cypriot military officers, hoping to unify Cyprus with Greece, seized control of the government in 1974, Turkey invaded Cyprus. An elected government was restored a few months later, but the north declared itself the independent Turkish Republic of Northern Cyprus in 1983. A wall and a frontier patrolled by the United Nations were delineated across the country.

Cultural Boundaries

Some boundaries between countries have been placed to separate speakers of different languages, followers of different religions (Figure 8.6.4), or members of different ethnicities (Figure 8.6.5).

Geometric Boundaries

Part of the northern U.S. boundary with Canada is a 2,100-kilometer (1,300-mile) line along the parallel of 49° north latitude, running from Lake of the Woods between Minnesota and Manitoba to the Strait of Georgia between Washington State and British Columbia (Figure 8.6.6). This boundary was established in 1846 by a treaty between the United States and the United Kingdom, which still controlled Canada. The two countries share an additional 1,100-kilometer (700-mile) geometric boundary between Alaska and the Yukon Territory along the north–south meridian of 141° west longitude.

▼ 8.6.6 **GEOMETRIC BOUNDARY: U.S. AND CANADA**
Peace Arch between Blaine, Washington, and Surrey, British Columbia.

Shapes of States

- Identify five typical shapes of states.

The shape of a state controls the length of its boundaries with other states. It affects the potential for communication and conflict with neighbors. The shape of a state can influence the ease or difficulty of internal administration and can affect social unity. Countries have one of five basic shapes, and examples of each can be seen in sub-Saharan Africa. Each shape displays distinctive characteristics and challenges.

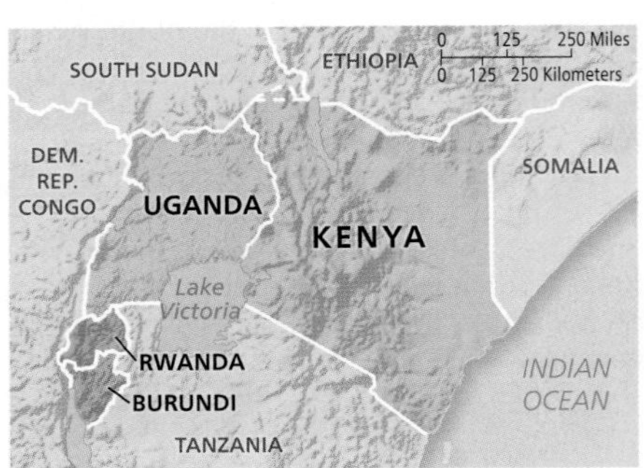

▲ 8.7.1 EXAMPLES OF COMPACT STATES: BURUNDI, KENYA, RWANDA, AND UGANDA

Compact States: Efficient

In a **compact state**, the distance from the center to any boundary does not vary significantly. An ideal theoretical compact state would be shaped like a circle, with the capital at the center and with the shortest possible boundaries to defend. Examples of compact states in sub-Saharan African include Burundi, Kenya, Rwanda, and Uganda (Figure 8.7.1).

Compactness can be a beneficial characteristic for smaller states because good communications can be more easily established with all regions, especially if the capital is located near the center. However, compactness does not necessarily mean peacefulness, as compact states are just as likely as others to experience civil wars and ethnic rivalries.

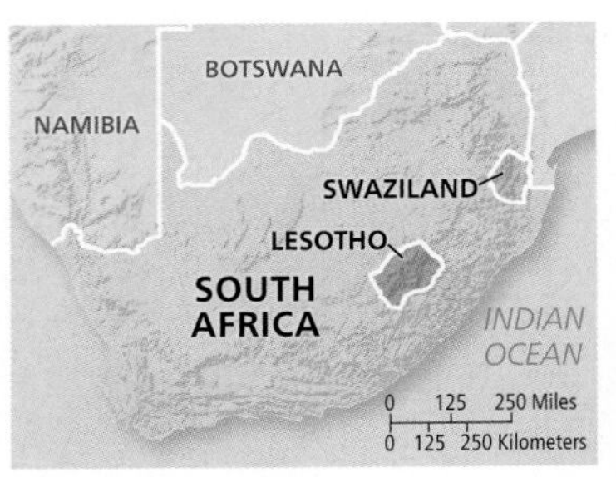

◄ 8.7.2 EXAMPLE OF PERFORATED STATE: SOUTH AFRICA

Perforated State: South Africa

A state that completely surrounds another one is a **perforated state**. The surrounded state may face problems of dependence on, or interference from, the surrounding state. A clear example in sub-Saharan Africa is South Africa, which completely surrounds Lesotho, which is a compact state (Figure 8.7.2). Lesotho must depend almost entirely on South Africa for the import and export of goods. Dependency on South Africa was especially difficult for Lesotho when South Africa had a government controlled by whites who discriminated against the black majority population.

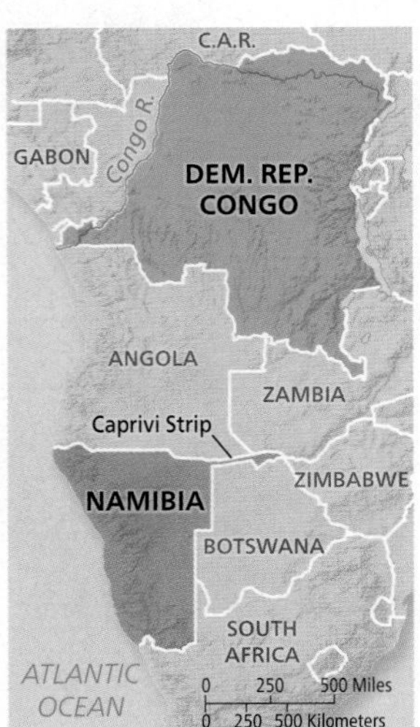

▲ 8.7.3 EXAMPLES OF PRORUPTED STATES: DEMOCRATIC REPUBLIC OF THE CONGO AND NAMIBIA

Prorupted States: Access or Disruption

An otherwise compact state with a large projecting extension is a **prorupted state**. Proruptions are created for two principal reasons, and examples of both are found in sub-Saharan Africa (Figure 8.7.3):

- To provide a state with access to a resource. The Democratic Republic of Congo has a 500-kilometer (300-mile) proruption to the west along the Zaire (Congo) River. The Belgians created the proruption to give their colony access to the Atlantic.
- To separate two states that otherwise would share a boundary. Namibia has a 500-kilometer (300-mile) proruption to the east called the Caprivi Strip. When Namibia was a colony of Germany, the proruption disrupted communications among the British colonies of southern Africa. It also provided the Germans with access to the Zambezi, one of Africa's most important rivers. Elsewhere, Afghanistan similarly has a proruption approximately 300 kilometers (200 miles) long and as narrow as 20 kilometers (12 miles) wide, created by the British to prevent Russia from sharing a border with Pakistan.

Elongated States: Potential Isolation

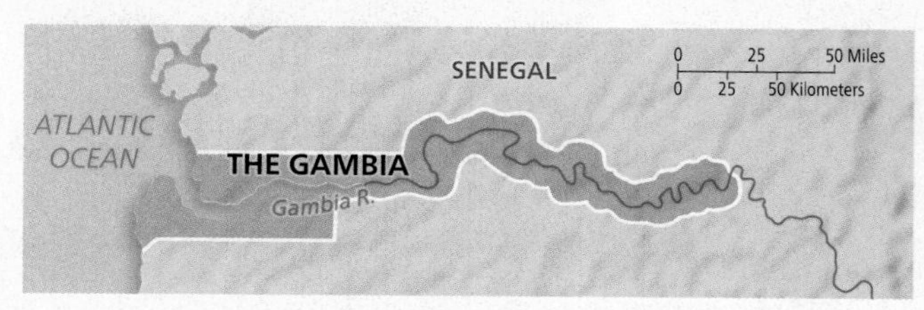

▲ 8.7.4 EXAMPLE OF ELONGATED STATE: THE GAMBIA

A handful of **elongated states** have a long and narrow shape. Examples in sub-Saharan Africa include:

- The Gambia, which extends along the banks of the Gambia River about 500 kilometers (300 miles) east–west but is only about 25 kilometers (15 miles) north–south (Figure 8.7.4); the shape was determined in the late nineteenth century, when the British controlled the mouth of the river and the French most of the surrounding area.
- Malawi, which measures about 850 kilometers (530 miles) north–south but only 100 kilometers (60 miles) east–west; in 1891, the British declared the territory a Protectorate in order to deter Portuguese on the west side of Lake Malawi from staking their own claim.

Elongated states may suffer from poor internal communications. A region located at an extreme end of the elongation might be isolated from the capital, which is usually placed near the center.

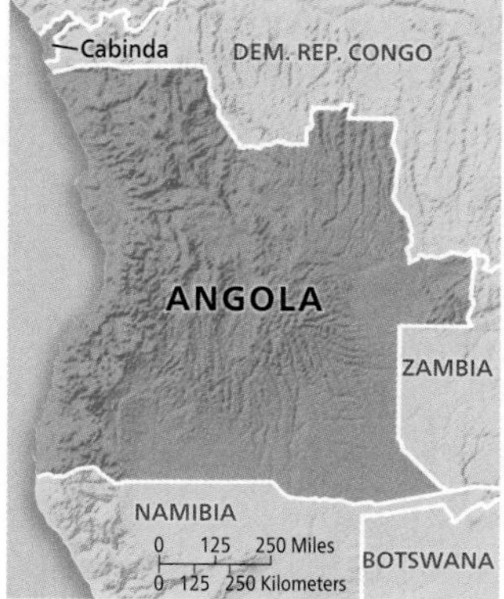

▲ 8.7.5 EXAMPLE OF FRAGMENTED STATE: ANGOLA

Fragmented States: Problematic

A **fragmented state** includes several discontinuous pieces of territory. Technically, all states that have offshore islands as part of their territory are fragmented. However, fragmentation is particularly significant for some states that face problems and costs associated with communications and maintaining national unity.

There are two kinds of fragmented states, and both can be seen in sub-Saharan Africa:

- Fragmented by water. Tanzania was created in 1964 as a union of the island of Zanzibar with the mainland territory of Tanganyika. Although home to different ethnic groups, the two entities agreed to join together because they shared common development goals and political priorities.
- Fragmented by other states. Angola is divided into two fragments by the Democratic Republic of Congo. An independence movement is trying to detach Cabinda as a separate state from Angola, with the justification that its population belongs to distinct ethnic groups (Figure 8.7.5).

Landlocked States

A **landlocked state** lacks a direct outlet to a sea because it is completely surrounded by other countries. Direct access to an ocean is critical to states because it facilitates international trade. Bulky goods, such as petroleum, grain, ore, and vehicles, are normally transported long distances by ship. This means that a country needs a seaport where goods can be transferred between land and sea. To send and receive goods by sea, a landlocked state must arrange to use another country's seaport.

Landlocked states are common in Africa, where 15 of the continent's 55 states have no direct ocean access (Figure 8.7.6). The prevalence of landlocked states in Africa is a remnant of the colonial era, when Britain and France controlled extensive regions that were eventually divided into independent states without regard for whether they were landlocked. The European powers built railroads in their colonial empires to connect the interior of Africa with the sea (refer to Figure 8.5.2). Railroads moved minerals from interior mines to seaports, and in the opposite direction, rail lines carried mining equipment and supplies from seaports to the interior.

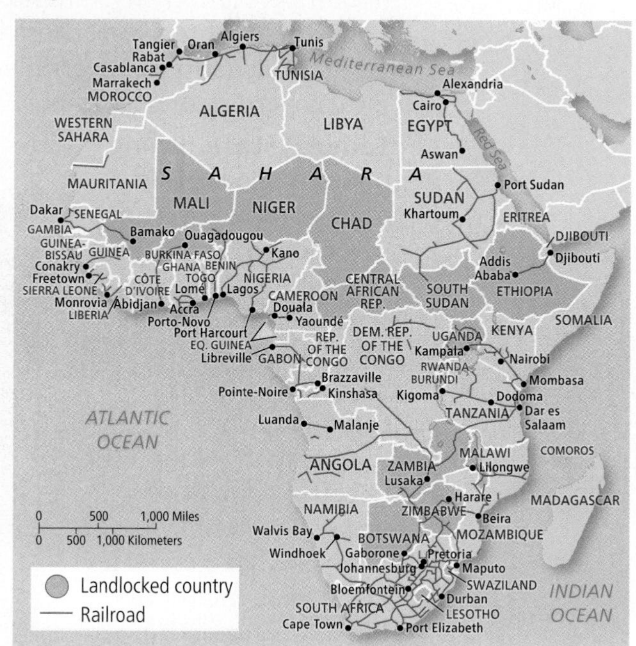

▲ 8.7.6 LANDLOCKED STATES IN AFRICA
Landlocked states must import and export goods by land-based transportation, primarily rail lines, to reach ocean ports in cooperating neighbor states. South Africa is the only state in Africa with a dense rail network.

▲ 8.8.1 **UNITARY STATE**
Presidential election voting, France.

Governing States

- **Explain differences among three regime types.**

A state has two levels of government: a national government and local governments. At the national scale, a government can be more or less democratic. At the local scale, the national government can determine how much power to allocate to local governments.

Local Scale: Unitary and Federal

The internal governments of states are organized according to one of two approaches: unitary and federal. The size of the state is not always an accurate predictor of the form of government: Tiny Belgium is a federal state (to accommodate the two main cultural groups, the Flemish and the Walloons, as discussed in Chapter 5), whereas China is a unitary state (to promote Communist values).

Unitary state. In a **unitary state**, most power is placed in the hands of central government officials (Figure 8.8.1). In principle, a unitary government works best in a relatively compact nation-state characterized by few internal cultural differences and a strong sense of national unity. Unitary states are especially common in Europe. France, for example, has a long tradition of unitary government in which a very strong national government dominates local government decisions.

Federal state. Strong power is allocated to units of local government in a **federal state**. In principle, the federal system is more suitable for very large states because the national capital may be too remote to provide effective control over isolated regions. Most of the world's largest states are federal, including Russia, Canada, the United States, Brazil, and India (Figure 8.8.2). For example, the federal state principle is embedded in the Tenth Amendment to the United States Constitution, which states: "The powers not delegated to the United States by the Constitution, nor prohibited by it to the States, are reserved to the States respectively, or to the people."

In recent years there has been a strong global trend toward federal government. Unitary systems have been sharply curtailed in a number of countries and scrapped altogether in others. In the face of increasing demands by ethnicities for more self-determination, states have restructured their governments to transfer some authority from the national government to local government units. An ethnicity that is not sufficiently numerous to gain control of the national government may be content with control of its territory through a regional or local unit of government.

▶ 8.8.2 **FEDERAL STATE**
Town Hall meeting to ask questions of elected officials, City of London, Ontario, Canada.

National Scale: Regime Types

Some national governments are better able than others to provide the leadership needed to promote peace and prosperity. In contrast, a corrupt repressive government embroiled in wars is less able to respond effectively to economic challenges.

National governments can be classified as democratic, autocratic, or anocratic (Figure 8.8.3).

- A **democracy** is a country in which citizens elect leaders and can run for office.
- An **autocracy** is a country that is run according to the interests of the ruler rather than the people.
- An **anocracy** is a country that is not fully democratic or fully autocratic, but rather displays a mix of the two types.

According to the Center for Systemic Peace, democracies and autocracies differ in three essential elements: selection of leaders, citizen participation, and checks and balances (Figure 8.8.4).

The world has become more democratic (Figure 8.8.5). The Center for Systemic Peace cites these reasons: The replacement of increasingly irrelevant and out-of-touch monarchies with elected governments that broaden individual rights and liberties, the widening of participation in policymaking to all citizens through rights to vote and to serve in government, and the diffusion of democratic government structures created in Europe and North America to other regions.

The Fragile States Index, calculated by the Fund for Peace, measures the relative stability of every country. The index combines several factors, including fairness of the legal system, extent of youth unemployment, level of violence, and freedom to express diverse political views (Figure 8.8.6). The most fragile states are clustered in sub-Saharan Africa. This is not surprising, as we have already seen the region to have the world's highest population growth and poorest health (Chapter 2), the greatest extent of ethnic cleansing and genocide (Chapter 7), and the most problematic shapes of states (the previous page). The region also has the largest number of recent civil wars.

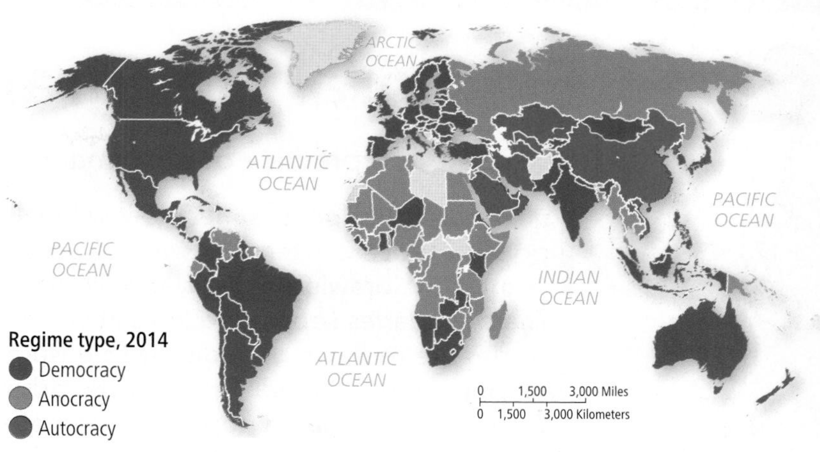

▲ 8.8.3 REGIME TYPES

Element	Democracy	Autocracy
Selection of leaders	Institutions and procedures through which citizens can express effective preferences about alternative policies and leaders	Leaders are selected according to clearly defined (often hereditary) rules of succession from within the established political elite
Citizen participation	Institutionalized constraints on the exercise of power by the exectutive	Citizens' participation is sharply restricted or suppressed
Checks and balances	Guarantee of civil liberties to all citizens in their daily lives and in acts of political participation	Leaders exercise power with no meaningful checks from legislative, judicial, or civil society institutions

▲ 8.8.4 COMPARING DEMOCRACY AND AUTOCRACY

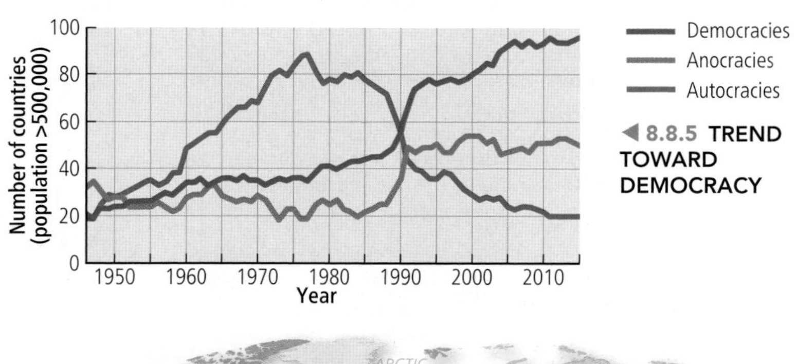

◀ 8.8.5 TREND TOWARD DEMOCRACY

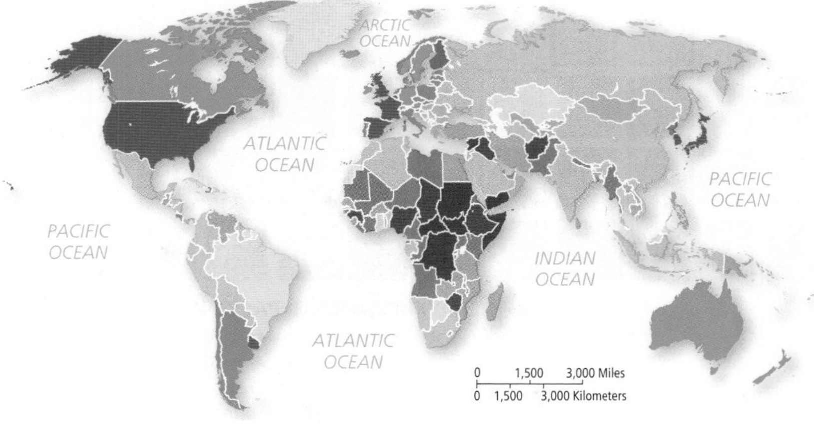

▲ 8.8.6 STATE FRAGILITY INDEX, 2017

Electoral Geography

- **Explain the practice of gerrymandering and ways in which it is done.**

▲ 8.9.1 THE ORIGINAL GERRYMANDERING CARTOON

In democracies, politics must follow legally prescribed rules. But all parties to the political process often find ways of bending those rules to their advantage. A case in point is the drawing of legislative district boundaries.

The boundaries separating legislative districts within the United States and other countries are redrawn periodically to ensure that each district has approximately the same population. Boundaries must be redrawn because migration inevitably results in some districts gaining population and others losing population. The 435 districts of the U.S. House of Representatives are redrawn every 10 years, following the Census Bureau's release of official population figures.

Gerrymandering

Redrawing legislative boundaries to benefit the party in power is called **gerrymandering**. The term gerrymandering was named for Elbridge Gerry (1744–1814), governor of Massachusetts (1810–1812) and vice president of the United States (1813–1814).

As governor, Gerry signed a bill that redistricted the state to benefit his party. An opponent observed that an oddly shaped new district looked like a "salamander," whereupon another opponent responded that it was a "gerrymander." A newspaper subsequently printed a cartoon of a monster named "gerrymander" with a body shaped like the district (Figure 8.9.1).

Gerrymandering takes two forms:

- **Cracking.** Like-minded voters are spread across several districts to prevent them from reaching a majority in any of them, thus wasting their votes (Figure 8.9.2).
- **Packing.** Like-minded voters are stacked in one district to prevent them from affecting elections in other districts (Figure 8.9.3).

▲ 8.9.2 **GERRYMANDERING: CRACKING** Like-minded voters are spread across many districts as a minority. Assume there are 50 voters, 20 supporters of the Red Party and 30 supporters of the Blue Party. If the Blue Party controls the redistricting process, it could create five districts all with slender majorities of Blue Party voters. As a result, the votes of all Red Party supporters are wasted.

▲ 8.9.3 **GERRYMANDERING: PACKING** Like-minded voters are stacked into a few districts. Assume there are 50 voters, 20 supporters of the Red Party and 30 supporters of the Blue Party. If the Blue Party controls the redistricting process, it could pack most of the Red Party voters into one district with an overwhelming majority, leaving four districts with solid Blue Party majorities.

Packing has been especially attractive for creating districts inclined to elect ethnic minorities. Because the two largest ethnic groups in the United States (African Americans and most Hispanics other than Cubans) tend to vote Democratic—in some elections more than 90 percent of African Americans vote Democratic—creating a majority African American district virtually guarantees election of a Democrat. Republicans support a "packed" Democratic district because they are better able to draw boundaries that are favorable to their candidates in the rest of the state. A score was given by the Washington Post to each Congressional district according to the extent of gerrymandering (see What's Your Political Geography?).

Redrawing Boundaries

The job of redrawing boundaries in most European countries is entrusted to independent commissions. Commissions typically try to create compact homogeneous districts without regard for voting preferences or incumbents. In the United States, Iowa is an exception to the gerrymandering practice. Nonpartisan employees of the state legislature create the maps without reference to past election data. The result is compact districts that follow county lines.

In most U.S. states the job of redrawing boundaries is entrusted to the state legislature. The political party in control of the state legislature naturally attempts to redraw boundaries to improve the chances of its supporters to win (Figure 8.9.4). GIS has been an especially useful tool for creating gerrymandered districts. Only about one-tenth of congressional seats across the United States are competitive, making a shift of more than a few seats unlikely from one election to another in the United States, except in unusual circumstances.

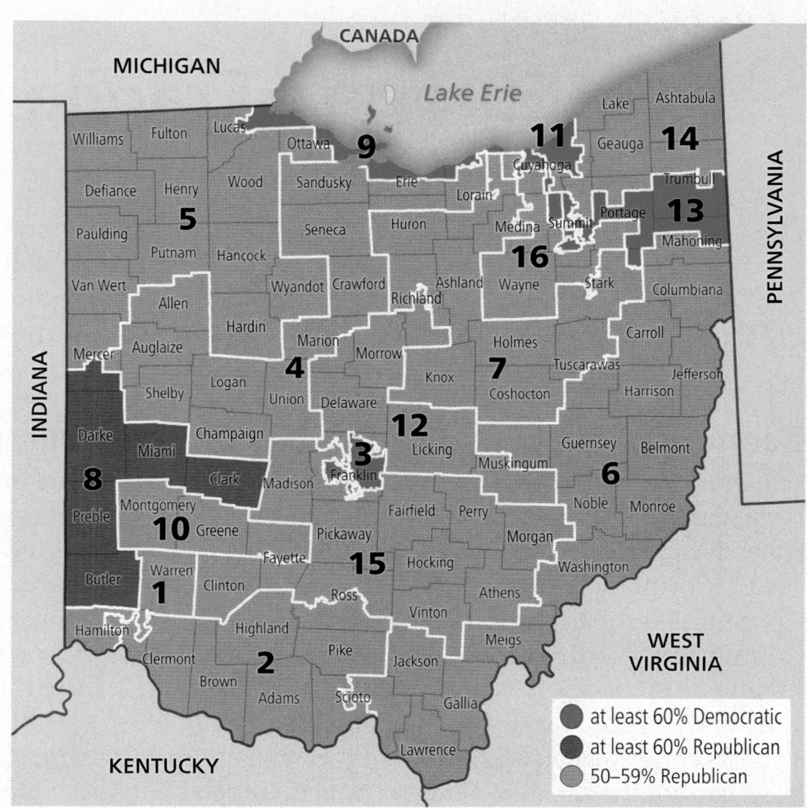

▲ 8.9.4 **OHIO GERRYMANDERING**
Ohio's Congressional map was drawn to pack Democrats into a handful of districts.

WHAT'S YOUR POLITICAL GEOGRAPHY?

Check out the shape of your state's legislative districts.

1. In your search engine, ***enter*** *[your state] congressional district map*. If you live in a state with only one state-wide at large Representative (Alaska, Delaware, Montana, North Dakota, South Dakota, Vermont, and Wyoming), enter another state.
2. Are the districts compact and geometrically shaped, or are they irregularly shaped? If irregularly shaped, can you see a geographical reason for the shape, perhaps a natural feature such as a body of water, or a cultural boundary such as between ethnicities?
3. A gerrymander score has been calculated for each Congressional district (Figure 8.9.5). Use your Internet browser to ***search*** for *gerrymander score*. Or ***search*** *How gerrymandered is your Congressional district?* at **www.washingtonpost.com**. The higher the score, the more severe the gerrymandering. What is the gerrymander score for your Congressional district? Did you expect your district to have a higher score or a lower score? Why?

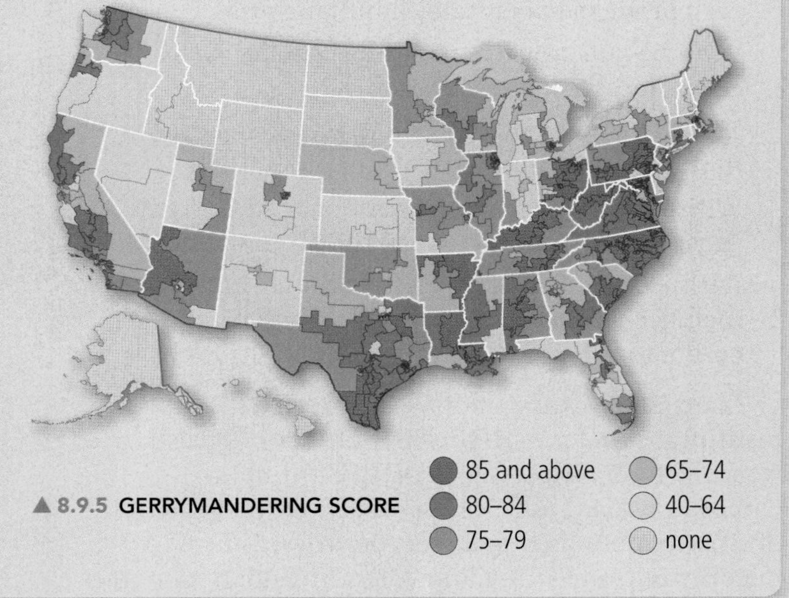

▲ 8.9.5 **GERRYMANDERING SCORE**

Europe's Fragile Cooperation

- Describe the principal alliances in Europe.

States cooperate with each other for economic and military reasons. An economic alliance enlarges markets for one state's goods, services, and labor. A military alliance offers protection to one state through the threat of retaliation by the combined force of its allies. European states have been especially active in creating economic and military alliances.

Economic Cooperation in Europe

The most important economic alliance in Europe is the European Union (EU), which had 28 member states as of 2018 (Figure 8.10.1). The predecessor of the EU (formerly known as the European Economic Community, the Common Market, and the European Community) formed in 1958 with six members. The EU and its predecesors helped to heal Western Europe's scars from World War II (which had ended only 13 years earlier) when Nazi Germany, in alliance with Italy, conquered the other four original members.

Meanwhile in Eastern Europe, six Communist countries formed an economic alliance in 1949, during the Cold War era, called the Council for Mutual Economic Assistance (COMECON). Five other Communist countries later joined. With the end of the Cold War, COMECON disbanded, and economic cooperation across Europe has become increasingly important through the EU.

The main task of the European Union is to promote economic and political cooperation. For example:

- A European Parliament is elected by the people in each of the member states simultaneously.
- Subsidies are provided to farmers and to economically depressed regions.
- Most goods move across borders of member states in trucks and trains without stopping.
- With a few exceptions, a citizen of one EU state is permitted to work and live in the other states.
- A bank or retailer can open branches in any member country with supervision only by the corporation's home country.

Many Europeans do not feel connected to the institutions that govern the EU, or to the officials working in EU offices (see Debate It! feature). Opposition to EU policies, especially free movement of citizens among EU member countries, induced a majority of United Kingdom voters in 2016 to support the country's withdrawal from the EU in 2019, a move known as "Brexit."

The Eurozone

The most dramatic step taken toward integrating Europe's nation-states into a regional organization was the creation of a common currency, the euro. France's franc, Germany's mark, and Italy's lira—powerful symbols of sovereign nation-states—disappeared, replaced by the single currency. Twenty-five countries use the euro, including 19 EU members, plus 6 others (Andorra, Kosovo, Monaco, Montenegro, San Marino, and Vatican City).

European leaders expected that every country in the region would be stronger economically if it replaced its national currency with the euro. In recent years, the future of the euro has been called into question. The economically weaker countries within the eurozone, such as Greece, Ireland, Italy, and Spain, have had to implement harsh and unpopular policies, such as drastically cutting services and raising taxes, whereas the economically strong countries, especially Germany, have had to subsidize the weaker states.

▲ 8.10.1 EUROPEAN UNION

Military Cooperation in Europe

During the Cold War era (the late 1940s until the early 1990s), when the United States and the Soviet Union were the world's two superpowers, most European states joined one of two military alliances. The North Atlantic Treaty Organization (NATO) comprised the United States, Canada, and Western European allies. The Warsaw Pact comprised the Soviet Union and its Eastern European allies.

A condition of roughly equal strength between opposing alliances is known as a **balance of power**. NATO and the Warsaw Pact were designed to maintain a bipolar balance of power in Europe. For NATO allies, the principal objective was to prevent the Soviet Union from overrunning West Germany and other smaller countries. The Warsaw Pact provided the Soviet Union with a buffer of allied states between it and Germany to discourage a third German invasion of the Soviet Union in the twentieth century.

After the breakup of the Soviet Union in 1991, in a Europe no longer dominated by military confrontation between two blocs, the Warsaw Pact was disbanded, and the number of troops under NATO command was sharply reduced. NATO expanded its membership to include most of the former Warsaw Pact countries (Figure 8.10.2). Membership in NATO offered Eastern European countries an important sense of security against any future Russian threat, especially after Russia annexed Crimea from Ukraine and threatened other parts of Ukraine.

Expansion of NATO
- Original members, 1949
- Joined 1952–1982
- Joined 1999–2017
- Potential new members

▲ 8.10.2 **NATO MEMBERS IN EUROPE**
Canada and the United States are also members.

DEBATE IT!

Does the European Union benefit Europeans?

Europe has become the world's wealthiest market, but many Europeans question whether the EU has improved their lives.

BENEFITS OF THE EU

- EU citizens can live, work, and travel freely among all EU countries (Figure 8.10.3).
- Businesses can hire workers from a larger pool of talented people.
- By sticking together, EU countries have stronger bargaining power in reaching international agreements.

▲ 8.10.3 **EU SUPPORTERS**

SHORTCOMINGS OF THE EU

- Decisions are made by EU bureaucrats rather than locally elected officials directly answerable to voters (Figure 8.10.4).
- The free movement of people makes it harder to control terrorism.
- Countries have not shared equally in the benefits of EU membership.

▲ 8.10.4 **EU OPPONENTS**

Terrorism by Individuals & Organizations

▲ 8.11.1 TERRORIST ATTACK ON THE WORLD TRADE CENTER, 2001

- **Explain the concept of terrorism and identify major terrorist organizations.**

Terrorism is the systematic use of violence by a group calculated to create an atmosphere of fear and alarm among a population. Terrorists also act to try to coerce a government into actions it would not otherwise undertake or refrain from actions it wants to take. Distinctive characteristics of terrorists include:

- Performing organized acts that spread fear and anxiety among the population, such as bombing, kidnapping, hijacking, taking of hostages, and assassination.
- Viewing violence as a means of bringing widespread publicity to goals and grievances that are not being addressed through peaceful means.
- Believing in a cause so strongly that they do not hesitate to attack despite knowing they will probably die in the act.

▶ 8.11.2 TERRORIST ATTACK, ORLANDO, JUNE 12, 2016
Memorials left at Pulse nightclub after a terrorist attack killed 49 and injured 53.

Terrorism against Americans

The most dramatic terrorist attack against the United States came on September 11, 2001 (Figure 8.11.1). The tallest buildings in the United States, the 110-story twin towers of the World Trade Center in New York City were destroyed, and the Pentagon in Washington, D.C., was damaged. The attacks resulted in nearly 3,000 fatalities. The United States has suffered several terrorist attacks since 1990 (Figures 8.11.2 and 8.11.3).

▼ 8.11.3 TERRORIST ATTACKS IN THE UNITED STATES, 1993–2017

MARCH 25, 2006
Six people were killed and 2 injured at a party in Seattle's Capitol Hill neighborhood.

AUGUST 5, 2012
Six people were killed and 4 injured in an attack at a Sikh Temple in Oak Creek, Wisconsin.

FEBRUARY 26, 1993
A car bomb parked in the underground garage damaged New York's World Trade Center, killing 6 and injuring 1,042.

OCTOBER 31, 2017
A man drove a truck onto a crowded bike path, killing 8 and wounding 11.

APRIL 15, 2013
Two bombs were detonated near the finish line of the Boston Marathon, killing 5 and injuring more than 280.

DECEMBER 2, 2015
A mass shooting at the Inland Regional Center in San Bernardino, California, killed 14 and injured 21.

SEPTEMBER 11, 2001
Attacks that destroyed the World Trade Center towers and damaged the Pentagon resulted in the deaths of 2,977 civilians, plus 19 terrorists.

OCTOBER 1, 2017
A gunman opened fire on concertgoers in Las Vegas, killing 58 and injuring 546.

JUNE 17, 2015
Nine people were killed and 1 wounded in an attack in Emanuel AME Church in Charleston, South Carolina.

APRIL 19, 1995
A car bomb killed 168 people and injured at least 680 in the Alfred P. Murrah Federal Building in Oklahoma City.

NOVEMBER 5, 2009
Thirteen people were killed and 32 injured in an attack on the military base at Fort Hood, Texas.

NOVEMBER 5, 2017
A gunman killed 26 and injured 20 in a church in Sutherland Springs, Texas.

JULY 16, 2015
Five U.S. military personnel were killed in an attack on two installations in Chattanooga, Tennessee.

JUNE 12, 2016
An attack at a gay nightclub in Orlando, Florida, killed 49 and injured 53.

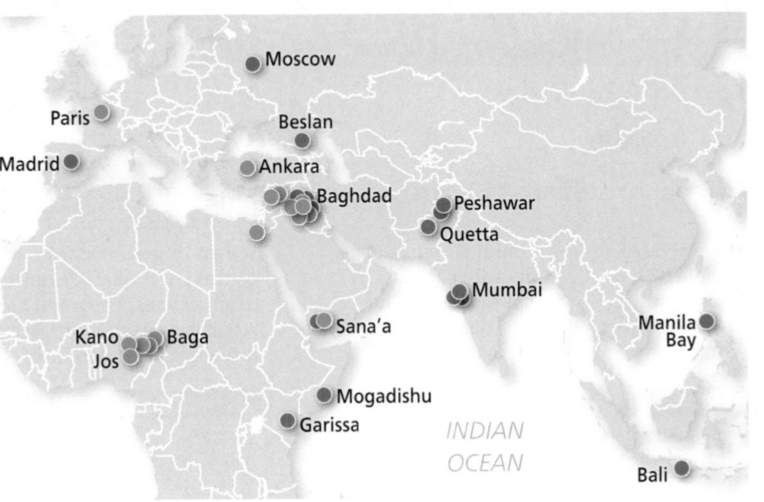

◀ 8.11.4 **TERRORIST ATTACKS WITH AT LEAST 100 FATALITIES, 2000–2016**

- Al-Qaeda and affiliates
- Islamic State and affiliates
- Other

Al-Qaeda

Two terrorist organizations are responsible or implicated in most of the attacks in Figures 8.11.3 and 8.11.4: al-Qaeda or the Islamic State. Al-Qaeda's founder Osama bin Laden (1957–2011) issued a declaration of war against the United States. In a 1998 decree, bin Laden argued that Muslims had a duty to wage a holy war against U.S. citizens because the United States was responsible for maintaining the Saud royal family as rulers of Saudi Arabia and a State of Israel dominated by Jews. Destroying the Saudi monarchy and the Jewish state of Israel would liberate from their control Islam's three holiest sites of Makkah (Mecca), Madinah, and Jerusalem. Al-Qaeda was responsible for the 9/11 attacks in the United States.

Al-Qaeda is not a single unified organization. It has loosely affiliated "franchises" in many countries, as well as imitators and emulators ideologically aligned with, but not financially tied to, al-Qaeda. In recent years, al-Qaeda's most active affiliate has been in Yemen, where it controls a large portion of Yemen's territory.

The Islamic State

The Islamic State is a terrorist organization that originated in 1999 and became an affiliate of al-Qaeda in 2004. The two organizations split in 2014 because of lack of agreement on how to cooperate and consult with each other. The Islamic State is also known as the Islamic State of Iraq and Syria (ISIS) and the Islamic State of Iraq and the Levant (ISIL).

Members of the Islamic State have carried out violent attacks in several countries, overrun territory in Syria and Iraq, and tried to impose their own, extremist version of Muslim religious laws (Figure 8.11.5).

They have maintained control of territory through human rights violations, such as beheadings, massacres, and torture. The organization claims that it has authority to rule Muslims around the world. The Islamic State has had success recruiting members through Internet and social media communications that show beheadings and destruction of sites of historical importance, such as Shiite Muslim shrines.

Islamic extremist groups and individuals around the world have pledged allegiance to the Islamic State, identifying with its vision and objectives. One example is Boko Haram, which was founded in 2002 in northeastern Nigeria to try to transform Nigeria into an Islamic state. Boko Haram has been responsible for killing 20,000 people and causing the forced migration of 2.3 million.

The use of religion by groups such as al-Qaeda, the Islamic State, and their allies to justify attacks has posed challenges to Muslims and non-Muslims alike. For many Muslims, the challenge has been to express disagreement with the policies of governments in the United States and Europe yet disavow the use of terrorism. For many Americans and Europeans, the challenge has been to distinguish between the peaceful but unfamiliar principles and practices of the world's 1.8 billion Muslims and the misuse and abuse of Islam by a handful of terrorists.

◀ 8.11.5 **PARIS TERRORIST ATTACK**
On November 13, 2015, as the Eagles of Death Metal were playing a sold-out concert at the Bataclan theatre in Paris, terrorists entered the theatre and killed 89 and wounded 368 of the 1,500 in the audience. A few months later, the group performed again in Paris. Survivors of the Bataclan attack were admitted free.

CHAPTER 8

Review, Analyze, & Apply

KEY ISSUE 1 Where Are States Distributed?

Nearly all of Earth's land area is divided among around 200 sovereign states. Nearly all states are members of the United Nations. "State" is a synonym for country, an area organized into a political unit. The fifty U.S. states are a form of local government. Some disputes exist concerning whether an area belongs to one state or to two.

THINKING GEOGRAPHICALLY

▲ 8.CR.1 CRIMEA RESIDENTS WAIT IN LONG LINES TO GET RUSSIAN PASSPORTS AFTER RUSSIA'S INVASION OF CRIMEA

1. In 2014, Russia invaded Crimea and annexed it, claiming that the majority of the Crimean people, who are ethnic Russians, supported the action. Nearly every other country in the world continues to recognize Ukraine's sovereignty over Crimea. Should Crimea appear on maps as part of Ukraine, or as part of Russia? Why?

KEY ISSUE 2 How Are States Created?

A nation-state is a state whose territory corresponds to that occupied by a particular cultural group. Ancient and medieval states were organized as city-states, kingdoms, and other forms of government. The creation of nation-states began in Europe in modern times. A colony is territory legally tied to a state. The world once contained a large number of colonies, but only a few remain.

THINKING GEOGRAPHICALLY

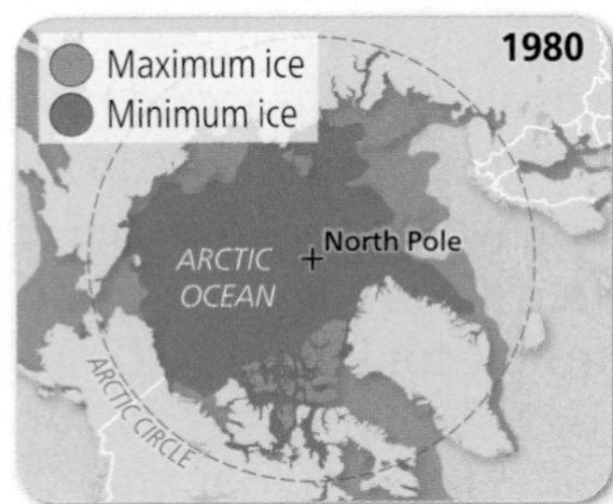

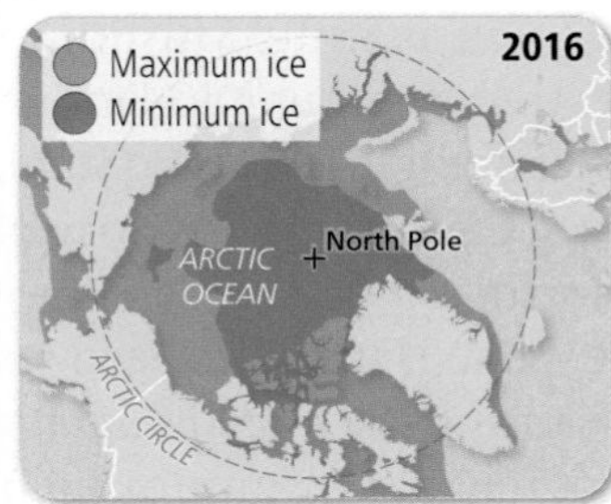

▲ 8.CR.2 RECEDING ARCTIC SEA ICE

2. The Arctic Ocean sea ice has receded in recent decades as a result of climate change. How might the reduction in sea ice affect claims by states to the Arctic region? How might states benefit or be harmed by the loss of the ice?

KEY ISSUE 3 How Are States Organized?

States are separated from each other by boundaries. Boundaries can be cultural or physical. Countries are considered democracies, autocracies, or anocracies. The trend has been toward more democracies. Legislative districts are sometimes gerrymandered to benefit the party in power and influence the outcome of elections.

THINKING GEOGRAPHICALLY

▲ 8.CR.3 NINTH CONGRESSIONAL DISTRICT, OHIO

3. Legal challenges to gerrymandering have focused on the fact that many districts do not have a compact shape. What are some of the challenges faced by states of the world that are not compact? How might some of those challenges apply to the shapes of legislative and Congressional districts within U.S. states?

KEY ISSUE 4 What Threats Do States Face?

Most European states are united in the European Union, but opposition to continuing membership in the EU is strong in several states. Terrorism is the systemic use of violence against the entire population. The world's two most active terrorist organizations are currently al-Qaeda and the Islamic State, as well as terrorist organizations affiliated with the two.

THINKING GEOGRAPHICALLY

▲ 8.CR.4 CYBERSECURITY

4. In what ways might cybersecurity measures such as cell phone encryption or privacy of social media accounts aid terrorists on the one hand and counterterrorism on the other hand?

GeoVideo

Log in to the Mastering Geography™ Study Area to view this video.

Iraq & Saudi Arabia: Defining the Border

The state of Iraq was created after WWI following the fall of the Ottoman Empire.

1. Before WWI, there were no linear boundaries in the middle east. Explain why.
2. After WWI, what were the two proposals for creating borders for the new state of Iraq? Describe each.
3. The video implies that some of the problems facing Iraq today can be traced back to the decisions about its borders made in 1922. Do you agree? Why or why not?

Key Terms

Anocracy (p. 207) A country that is not fully democratic or fully autocratic but rather displays a mix of the two types.

Autocracy (p. 207) A country that is run according to the interests of the ruler rather than the people.

Balance of power (p. 211) A condition of roughly equal strength between opposing countries or alliances of countries.

Boundary (p. 202) An invisible line that marks the extent of a state's territory.

City-state (p. 196) A sovereign state comprising a city and its immediately surrounding countryside.

Colonialism (p. 200) An attempt by one country to establish settlements and to impose its political, economic, and cultural principles in another territory.

Colony (p. 200) A territory that is legally tied to a sovereign state rather than completely independent.

Compact state (p. 204) A state in which the distance from the center to any boundary does not vary significantly.

Democracy (p. 207) A country in which citizens elect leaders and can run for office.

Elongated state (p. 205) A state with a long, narrow shape.

Federal state (p. 206) An internal organization of a state that allocates most powers to units of local government.

Fragmented state (p. 205) A state that includes several discontinuous pieces of territory.

Frontier (p. 202) A zone separating two states in which neither state exercises political control.

Gerrymandering (p. 208) The process of redrawing legislative boundaries for the purpose of benefiting the party in power.

Landlocked state (p. 205) A state that does not have a direct outlet to the sea.

Microstate (p. 192) A state that encompasses a very small land area.

Multinational state (p. 198) A state that contains two or more cultural groups with traditions of self-determination that agree to coexist peacefully by recognizing each other as distinct nationalities.

Nation (p. 198) A large group of people who are united by common cultural characteristics, such as language and ethnicity, or by shared history

Nation-state (p. 198) A state whose territory corresponds to that occupied by a particular nation.

Perforated state (p. 204) A state that completely surrounds another one.

Prorupted state (p. 204) An otherwise compact state with a large projecting extension.

Self-determination (p. 198) The concept that ethnicities have the right to govern themselves.

Sovereignty (p. 192) Ability of a state to govern its territory free from control of its internal affairs by other states.

State (p. 192) An area organized into a political unit and ruled by an established government that has control over its internal and foreign affairs.

Terrorism (p. 212) The systematic use of violence by a group calculated to create an atmosphere of fear and alarm among a population or to coerce a government into actions it would not otherwise undertake or refrain from actions it wants to take.

Unitary state (p. 206) An internal organization of a state that places most power in the hands of central government officials.

Geospatial Analysis

Log in to the Mastering Geography Study Area to access MapMaster 2.0.

Unity and diversity in Europe

Most countries in Europe have joined economic and military alliances. But differences persist among the member countries.

Add the *NATO* layer. ***Select*** the *Settings* icon from the *Legend*, and ***select*** *Show Political Labels*. ***Add*** the *Gross National Income Per Capita* layer and ***select*** *Split map window*. ***Zoom*** to Europe.

1. What differences in GNI per capita do you see between countries in the eastern countries of NATO and the western countries?
2. What historical factor accounts for the income difference between east and west? Refer to Figure 8.4.4 or view Former Warsaw Pact Members in MapMaster 2.0.

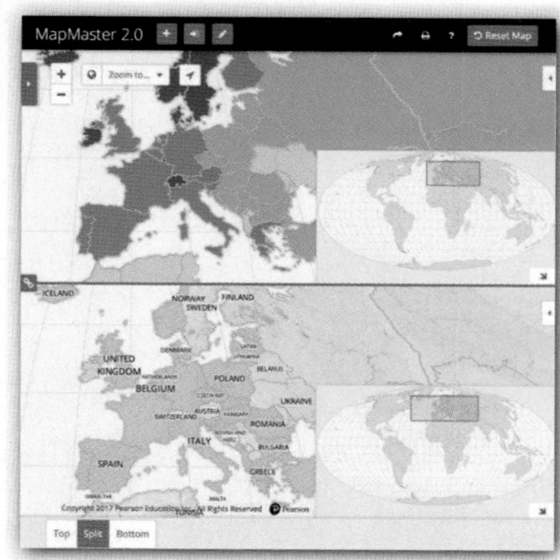

▲ 8.CR.6 **NATO MEMBERS AND GROSS NATIONAL INCOME PER CAPITA IN EUROPE**

Explore

Europe's international boundaries

Use Google Earth to view the international boundary formed by the Rhine River.

Search for *Le Jardin-des-Deux-Rives* (Two Rivers Garden).

1. In what country is the garden? What country is on the other side of the Rhine River?
2. Drop to *Street View* at the red pin marking the garden. Move the photo across the bridge. How do the border controls across the Rhine compare with those illustrated in Chapter 3 between the United States and Mexico?
3. Why do you think the border crossing at the Rhine differs from border crossings between the United States and Mexico?

▶ 8.CR.7 **LE JARDIN-DES-DEUX-RIVES**

Mastering Geography

Looking for additional review and test prep materials? Visit the Study Area in Mastering Geography to enhance your geographic literacy, spatial reasoning skills, and understanding of this chapter's content. Access MapMaster™ interactive maps, video case studies, *In the News* current articles, flashcards, self-study quizzes, an eText of *Contemporary Human Geography*, and more.
pearson.com/mastering/geography

CHAPTER 9

Food & Agriculture

All humans need food to survive. We have two choices in obtaining our food: Buy it from others or produce it ourselves. For most of human history, people had to search out their food. Around 10,000 years ago, humans figured out how to deliberately grow their own food. In the modern world, most people buy their food.

With greater separation between growing food and consuming it, humans are less aware of the connections between their food choices and impacts on the physical environment. People may also be less aware of the connections between their food choices and the businesses that grow and distribute the food.

◀ A coffee-bean harvester in Zambia removes unripe and overripe coffee beans prior to weighing.

KEY ISSUES

1 How Did Agriculture Originate?

Agriculture was invented around 10,000 years ago in multiple places. Prior to the agricultural revolution, people survived by hunting and gathering their food.

2 What Do People Eat?

People consume a wide variety of food, depending on their income, growing conditions in the physical environment, and cultural preferences. Most people are consuming enough food, but the UN estimates that 815 million people are undernourished.

3 Where Is Agriculture Distributed?

The world can be divided into 11 principal agricultural regions, including 5 that are important in developing countries and 6 in developed countries.

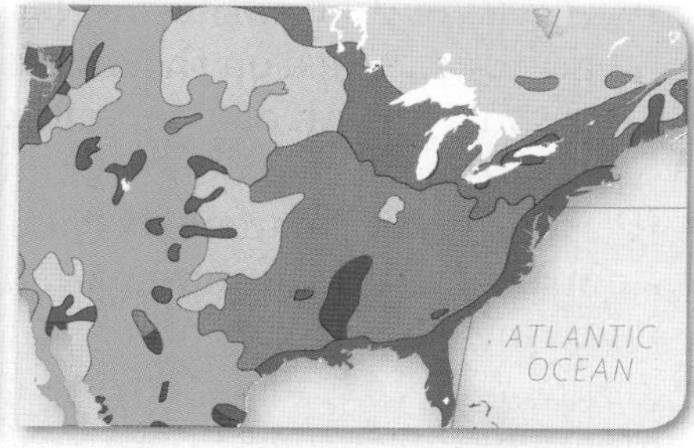

4 What Challenges Do Farmers Face?

Globally, food production and trade have increased to meet the needs of a growing population. The environmental impacts of increasing food production are debated.

LOCATIONS IN THIS CHAPTER

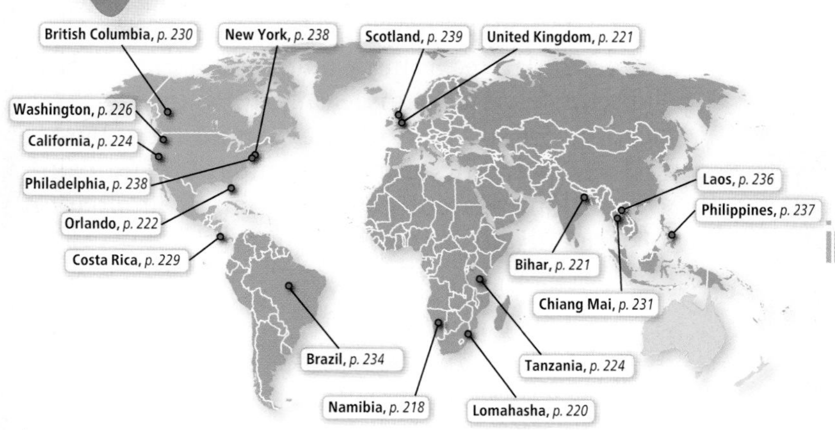

undernourishment
agribusiness
the dirty dozen
commercial agriculture
nutrients
conservation tillage
ranching
dairying
mixed crop & livestock
hunting & gathering
subsistence agriculture
shifting cultivation
pastoral nomadism
commercial gardening
intensive subsistence
plantation
agricultural revolution
organic farming
diet
mediterranean
agricultural hearth
genetically modified organism
food security
dietary energy consumption

Origin of Agriculture

- Explain how agriculture may have originated.

Agriculture is deliberate modification of Earth's surface through cultivation of plants and raising of animals for sustenance or economic gain. Agriculture originated when humans domesticated plants and animals for their use. The word cultivate means "to care for," and a **crop** is any plant cultivated by people.

Hunters and Gatherers

Before the invention of agriculture, all humans probably obtained the food they needed for survival through hunting for animals, fishing, or gathering plants (such as berries, nuts, fruits, and roots). Hunters and gatherers lived in small groups of usually fewer than 50 persons because a larger number would quickly exhaust the available resources within walking distance.

These groups traveled frequently, establishing new home bases or camps. The direction and frequency of migration depended on the movement of game and the seasonal growth of plants at various locations. We can assume that groups communicated with each other concerning matters such as hunting rights and intermarriage. For the most part, they kept the peace by steering clear of each other's territory.

The group collected food often, perhaps daily. The amount of time needed for each day's food search varied, depending on local conditions. The men hunted game or fished, and the women collected berries, nuts, and roots. This division of labor sounds like a stereotype but is based on evidence from archaeology and anthropology.

Today, perhaps a quarter-million people, or less than 0.005 percent of the world's population, still survive by hunting and gathering rather than by agriculture. Contemporary hunting and gathering societies are isolated groups that live on the periphery of world settlement, but they provide insight into human customs that prevailed in prehistoric times, before the invention of agriculture (Figure 9.1.1).

Agricultural Revolution

The time when human beings first domesticated plants and animals and no longer relied entirely on hunting and gathering was the **agricultural revolution**. Geographers and other scientists believe that the agricultural revolution occurred around the year 8000 B.C., because the world's population began to grow at a more rapid rate than it had in the past. By growing plants and raising animals, human beings created larger and more stable sources of food, so more people could survive.

Scientists do not agree on whether the agricultural revolution originated primarily because of environmental factors or cultural factors. Probably a combination of both factors contributed:

- **Environmental factors.** The first domestication of crops and animals coincided with climate change that marked the end of the last ice age. At that time, permanent ice cover receded from Earth's mid-latitudes to the polar regions, resulting in a massive redistribution of humans, other animals, and plants.
- **Cultural factors.** A preference for living in a fixed place rather than as nomads may have led hunters and gatherers to build permanent settlements and to store surplus vegetation there. In gathering wild vegetation, people inevitably cut plants and dropped berries, fruits, and seeds. These hunters probably observed that, over time, damaged or discarded food produced new plants. They may have deliberately cut plants or dropped berries on the ground to see if they would produce new plants. Subsequent generations learned to pour water over the site and to introduce manure and other soil improvements. Over thousands of years, plant cultivation apparently evolved from a combination of accident and deliberate experiment.

◀ 9.1.1 HUNTING AND GATHERING
San people of Namibia.

Agriculture Hearths

Scientists agree that agriculture originated in multiple hearths around the world: Southwest Asia, East Asia, sub-Saharan Africa, and Latin America (Figure 9.1.2). Even within these hearths, scientists have determined that agriculture was invented independently by multiple groups.

- **Southwest Asia.** The earliest crops domesticated in Southwest Asia around 10,000 years ago are thought to have been barley, wheat, lentil, and olive. Southwest Asia is also thought to have been the hearth for the domestication of the largest number of animals that would prove to be most important for agriculture, including cattle, goats, pigs, and sheep, between 8,000 and 9,000 years ago. Domestication of the dog is thought to date even earlier, around 12,000 years ago. From this hearth, cultivation diffused west to Europe and east to Central Asia.
- **East Asia.** Rice is now thought to have been domesticated in East Asia more than 10,000 years ago, along the Yangtze River in eastern China. Millet was cultivated at an early date along the Yellow River.
- **Central and South Asia.** Chickens are thought to have diffused from South Asia around 4,000 years ago. The horse is considered to have been domesticated in Central Asia. Diffusion of the domesticated horse is thought to be associated with the diffusion of the Indo-European language, as discussed in Chapter 5.
- **Sub-Saharan Africa.** Sorghum was domesticated in central Africa around 8,000 years ago. Yams may have been domesticated even earlier. Millet and rice may have been domesticated in sub-Saharan Africa independently of the hearth in East Asia. From central Africa, domestication of crops probably diffused further south in Africa.
- **Latin America.** Two important hearths of crop domestication are thought to have emerged in Mexico and Peru around 4,000 to 5,000 years ago. Mexico is considered a hearth for beans and cotton, and Peru for potato. The most important contribution of the Americas to crop domestication, maize (corn), may have emerged in the two hearths independently around the same time. From these two hearths, cultivation of maize and other crops diffused northward into North America and southward into tropical South America. Some researchers place the origin of squash in the southeastern present-day United States.

That agriculture had multiple origins means that, from earliest times, people have produced food in distinctive ways in different regions. This diversity derives from a unique legacy of wild plants, climatic conditions, and cultural preferences in each region. Improved communications in recent centuries have encouraged the diffusion of some plants to varied locations around the world. Many plants and animals thrive across a wide portion of Earth's surface, not just in their place of original domestication. Only after 1500, for example, were wheat, oats, and barley introduced to the Western Hemisphere and maize to the Eastern Hemisphere.

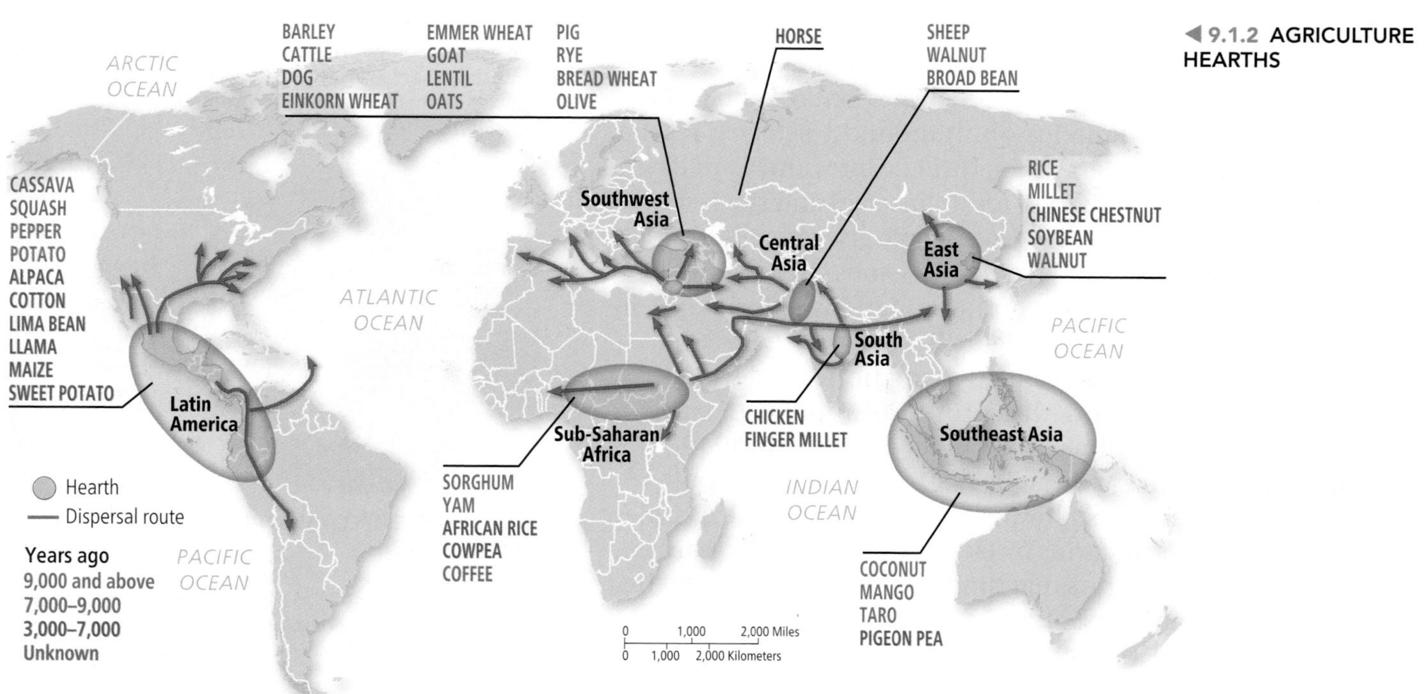

◀ 9.1.2 AGRICULTURE HEARTHS

Subsistence & Commercial Agriculture

▲ 9.2.1 **SUBSISTANCE AGRICULTURE** Lomahasha, Swaziland.

- **Compare and contrast subsistence and commercial agriculture.**

The most fundamental differences in agricultural practices are between those in developing countries and those in developed countries. Farmers in developing countries generally practice subsistence agriculture, whereas farmers in developed countries practice commercial agriculture.

Subsistence agriculture, found in developing countries, is the production of food primarily for consumption by the farmer's family (Figure 9.2.1). **Commercial agriculture**, found in developed countries, is the production of food primarily for sale off the farm. The main features that distinguish commercial agriculture from subsistence agriculture include the percentage of farmers in the labor force, the use of machinery, and farm size.

Farmers: Fewer Grow More

All people must secure food in order to survive. In developing countries a large percentage of people are subsistence farmers who work in agriculture to produce the food they and their families require. In developed countries relatively few people are engaged in farming, and most people buy food with money earned by working in factories or offices or by performing other services.

▲ 9.2.2 **AGRICULTURAL WORKERS**
The percentage of the workforce engaged in agriculture is much higher in developing countries with subsistence agriculture than in developed countries with commercial agriculture.

In developed countries, around 3 percent of workers are engaged directly in farming, compared to around 42 percent in developing countries (Figure 9.2.2). The percentage of farmers is even lower in North America—only around 1 percent. Yet the small percentage of farmers in the United States and Canada produces not only enough food for themselves and the rest of the region but also a surplus to feed people elsewhere. Although farmers account for only 1 percent of U.S. jobs, 10 percent of U.S. jobs are in other elements of the food industry, primarily in restaurants and supermarkets (Figure 9.2.3).

The number of farmers declined dramatically in developed countries during the twentieth century. The number of farms in the United States declined from about 6 million in 1940 to 4 million in 1960 and 2 million in 1980. Both push and pull migration factors have been responsible for the decline: People were pushed away from farms by lack of opportunity to earn a decent income, and at the same time they were pulled to higher-paying jobs in urban areas. The number of U.S. farmers has stabilized since 1980, though, at around 2 million.

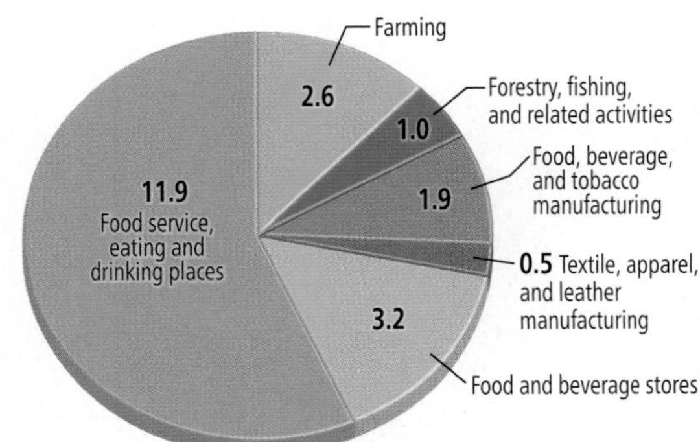

▲ 9.2.3 **U.S. EMPLOYMENT IN FOOD AND AGRICULTURE**
Figures are in millions of jobs. Employment in food and agriculture total 21 million jobs and represent 11 percent of all U.S. employment. Most of the jobs are in restaurants and stores, rather than on farms.

Technology: Agriculture's Game Changer

In developed countries, a small number of commercial farmers can feed many people because they rely on machinery to perform work rather than on people or animals (Figure 9.2.4). In developing countries, subsistence farmers do much of the work with hand tools and animal power (Figure 9.2.5).

Traditionally, the farmer or local craftspeople made equipment from wood, but beginning in the late eighteenth century, factories produced farm machinery. The first all-iron plow was made in the 1770s and was followed in the nineteenth and twentieth centuries by inventions that made farming less dependent on human or animal power. Today, farmers use tractors, combines, corn pickers, planters, and other factory-made farm machines to increase productivity.

Experiments conducted in university laboratories, industry, and research organizations generate new fertilizers, herbicides, hybrid plants, animal breeds, and farming practices, which lead to higher crop yields and healthier animals. Access to other scientific information has enabled farmers to make more intelligent decisions concerning proper agricultural practices. Some farmers conduct their own on-farm research.

Electronics also help commercial farmers. Farmers use Global Positioning System (GPS) devices to determine the precise coordinates for planting seeds and for spreading different types and amounts of fertilizers. On large ranches, they also use GPS devices to monitor the locations of cattle and tractors. They use satellite imagery to measure crop progress and yield monitors attached to combines to determine the precise number of bushels being harvested.

▲ 9.2.4 TECHNOLOGY: COMMERCIAL AGRICULTURE
A British farmer uses electronics mounted in his tractor to control and monitor planting operations.

Farm Size: Is Bigger Better?

In commercial agriculture, the average farm is relatively large. Farms average 178 hectares (441 acres) in the United States, compared to about 1 hectare (2.5 acres) in South Asia. Farm size partly depends on mechanization. Combines, pickers, and other machinery perform most efficiently at very large scales, and their considerable expense cannot be justified on a small farm. As a result of the large size and the high level of mechanization, commercial agriculture is an expensive business. Farmers spend hundreds of thousands of dollars to buy or rent land and machinery before beginning operations. This money is frequently borrowed from a bank and repaid after output is sold.

Commercial agriculture is increasingly dominated by a handful of large farms. In the United States, the largest 3 percent of farms produce 42 percent of the country's total agriculture. Despite their size, most commercial farms in developed countries—99 percent in the United States—are family owned and operated. Commercial farmers frequently expand their holdings by renting nearby fields.

Although the United States had fewer farms and farmers in 2000 than in 1900, the amount of land devoted to agriculture increased by 13 percent, primarily due to irrigation and reclamation. However, in the twenty-first century, the United States has been losing 400,000 hectares (1 million acres) per year of its 365 million hectares (910 million acres) of farmland, primarily because of the expansion of urban areas.

▲ 9.2.5 TECHNOLOGY: SUBSISTENCE AGRICULTURE
Demonstrating the use of a row-scoring rake, Bihar, India.

▲ 9.3.1
SUPERMARKET
Orlando, Florida.

Diet

- **Explain variations in what and how much people eat.**

When you buy food in a supermarket, are you reminded of a farm? Not likely. The meat is carved into pieces that no longer resemble an animal and is wrapped in paper or plastic film. Often the vegetables are canned or frozen. The milk and eggs are in cartons (Figure 9.3.1).

Consumption of food varies around the world, both in total amount and source of nutrients. The variation results from a combination of:

- **Level of development.** People in developed countries tend to consume more food and from different sources than do people in developing countries.
- **Physical conditions.** Climate is important in influencing what can be most easily grown and therefore consumed in developing countries. In developed countries, though, food is shipped long distances to locations with different climates.
- **Cultural preferences.** Some food preferences and avoidances are expressed without regard for physical and economic factors, as discussed in Chapter 4.

Total Consumption of Food

Dietary energy consumption is the amount of food that an individual consumes. The unit of measurement of dietary energy is the kilocalorie (kcal), or Calorie in the United States. One gram (or ounce) of each food source delivers a kilocalorie level that nutritionists can measure.

Most humans derive most of their kilocalories through consumption of **cereal grain** (or simply cereal), which is a grass that yields grain for food. **Grain** is the seed from a cereal grass. The three leading cereal grains—wheat, rice, and maize (corn in North America)—together account for nearly 90 percent of all grain production and more than 40 percent of all dietary energy consumed worldwide (Figure 9.3.2).

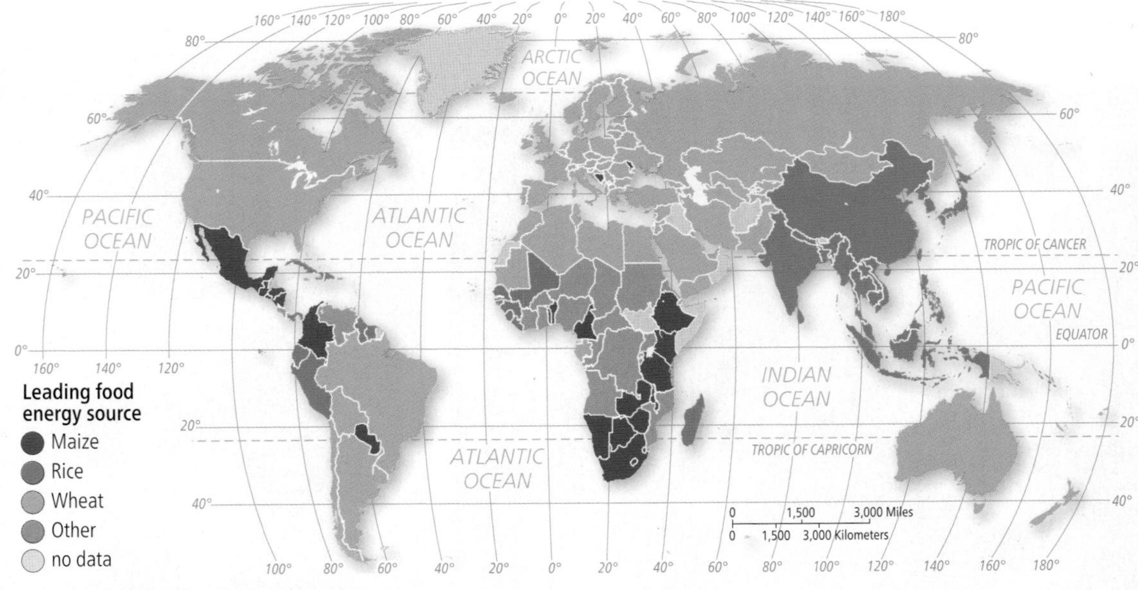

▲ 9.3.2 **DIETARY ENERGY BY SOURCE**
Wheat is the principal cereal grain consumed in the developed regions of Europe and North America through bread, pasta, cake, and many other forms. Rice is the principal cereal grain consumed in the developing regions of East, South, and Southeast Asia. Maize (called corn in North America) is grown primarily as animal feed.

Dietary Energy Needs

To maintain a moderate level of physical activity, according to the UN Food and Agricultural Organization, an average individual needs to consume on a daily basis at least 1,844 kcal. Average consumption worldwide is 2,902 kcal per day, well above the recommended minimum. Thus, most people get enough food to survive (Figure 9.3.3).

In developing regions, average daily consumption is 2,800 kcal, still above the recommended minimum. However, the average in sub-Saharan Africa is only 2,400, an indication that a large percentage of Africans are not getting enough to eat. Diets are more likely to be deficient in countries where people have to spend a high percentage of their income to obtain food (Figure 9.3.4).

On the other hand, people in developed countries are consuming on average nearly twice the recommended minimum, 3,400 kcal per day. The United States has the world's highest consumption, 3,800 kcal per day per person. The consumption of so much food is one reason that obesity rather than hunger is more prevalent in the United States, as well as other developed countries (refer to stage 4 of the epidemiologic transition and Figure 2.8.5 on page 51). Americans are also ingesting large quantities of pesticides in their produce, according to the U.S. Department of Agriculture (see Research & Analyze feature).

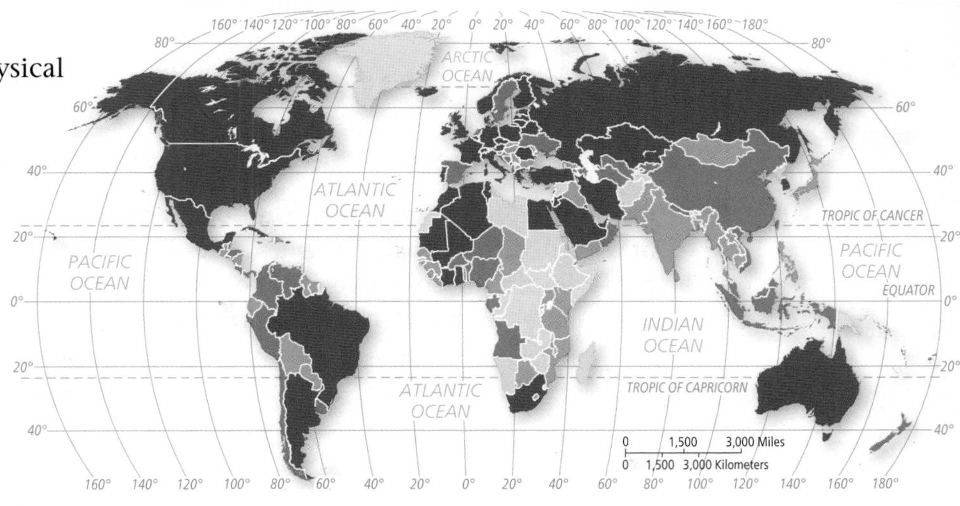

▲ 9.3.3 ADEQUACY OF AVERAGE DIETARY ENERGY SUPPLY (%)

Percent consumed of daily dietary minimum
- 130 and above
- 120–129
- 100–119
- below 100
- no data

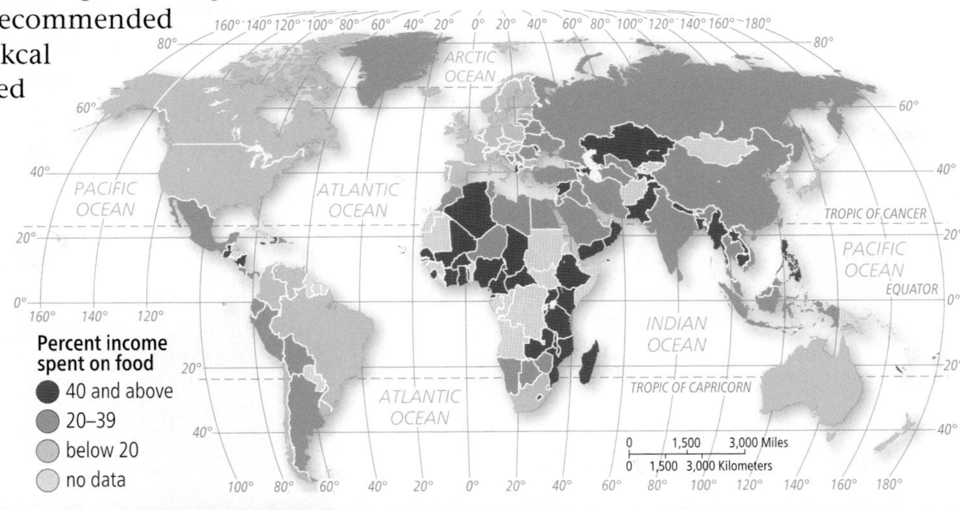

◀ 9.3.4 INCOME SPENT ON FOOD

RESEARCH & ANALYZE
The dirty dozen

The Environmental Working Group ranks 48 types of produce according to level of pesticides, based on tests conducted by the U.S. Department of Agriculture (Figure 9.3.5). The 12 most pesticide-contaminated fruits and vegetables are called "the dirty dozen," and the 15 least contaminated are called "the clean fifteen." To see the complete list, go to the website **ewg.org/foodnews/list** or use your web browser to ***search*** for *Environmental Working Group dirty dozen.*

1. What are the six most pesticide-contaminated fruits and vegetables?
2. ***Scroll*** to the bottom of the list. Which are the six cleanest?
3. What characteristics differentiate the produce with the most contamination from those with the least?
4. According to the Environmental Working Group's FAQ, why should someone be concerned about pesticides?

▲ 9.3.5 STRAWBERRIES: ONE OF THE DIRTY DOZEN

Environmental Working Group
https://goo.gl/Ph6Qjb

Food Security

- Explain variations in source of nutrients and nourishment.

The United Nations defines **food security** as physical, social, and economic access at all times to safe and nutritious food sufficient to meet dietary needs and food preferences for an active and healthy life. By this definition, around 10 percent of the world's inhabitants do not have food security.

Source of Nutrients

Protein is a nutrient needed for growth and maintenance of the human body. Many food sources provide protein of varying quantity and quality. One of the most fundamental differences between developed and developing regions is the primary source of protein (Figure 9.4.1).

The leading source of protein in developed countries is meat products, including beef, pork, and poultry (Figure 9.4.2). In most developing countries, cereal grains provide the largest share of protein (Figure 9.4.3). Otherwise stated, meat accounts for only one-tenth of all protein intake in developing countries, compared with around one-third in developed countries (Figure 9.4.4).

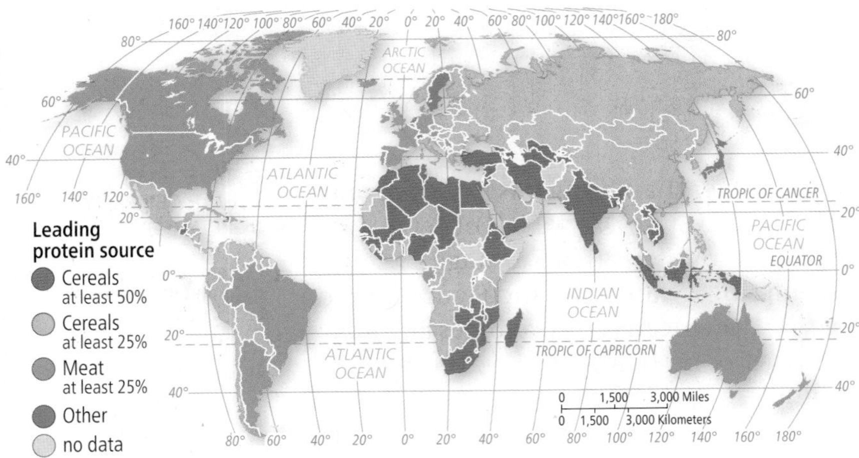

▲ 9.4.1 PROTEIN BY SOURCE
People get most of their protein from meat in developed countries and from cereals in developing countries.

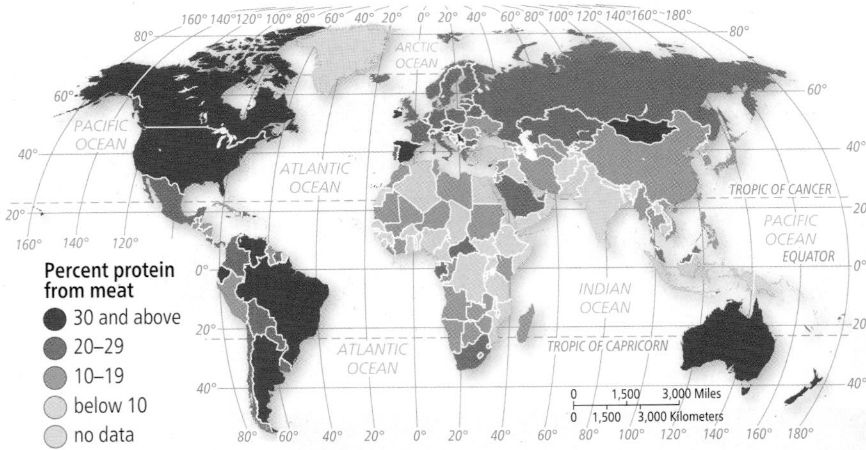

▲ 9.4.2 PROTEIN FROM MEAT
The percentage of protein from meat is much higher for people in developed countries than for those in developing countries.

▲ 9.4.3 PROTEIN FROM CEREAL: TANZANIA

◀ 9.4.4 PROTEIN FROM MEAT: CATTLE RANCH, CALIFORNIA

Undernourishment

The level of dietary energy consumption that is continuously below the minimum requirement for maintaining a healthy life and carrying out light physical activity is called **undernourishment**. The U.N. estimates that 815 million people in the world are undernourished, one-half of them in India and China (Figure 9.4.5). Overall, 98 percent of the world's undernourished people are in developing countries. As a percentage of a region's population, undernourishment is most prevalent in sub-Saharan Africa and South Asia. One-fourth of the population in sub-Saharan Africa and one-fifth in South Asia are undernourished (Figure 9.4.6).

The world as a whole has made progress in reducing hunger during the twenty-first century. Between 2000 and 2016, the number of undernourished people declined from 924 million to 815 million, and the percentage of people who are undernourished declined from 15 percent in 2000 to 11 percent (Figure 9.4.7). East Asia, led by China, has had by far the largest decrease in the number and percentage undernourished, followed by Southeast Asia. On the other hand, calorie consumption in developed countries can be extremely high (see What's Your Geography?).

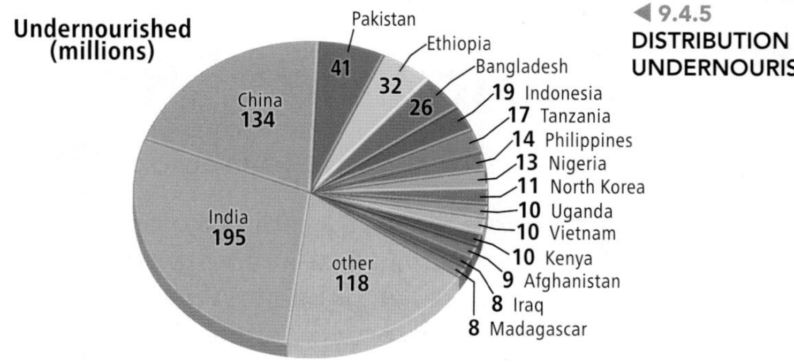

▲ 9.4.5 DISTRIBUTION OF UNDERNOURISHMENT

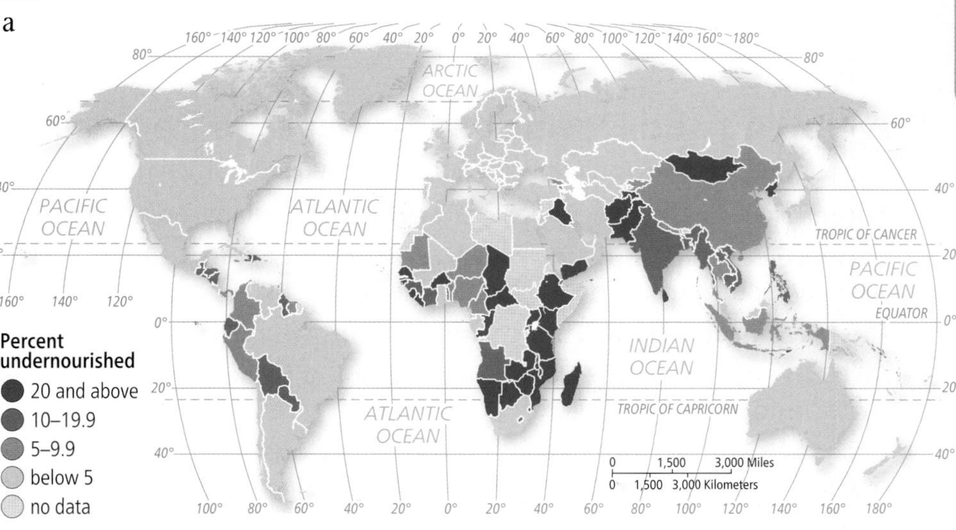

▲ 9.4.6 PERCENTAGE OF POPULATION UNDERNOURISHED

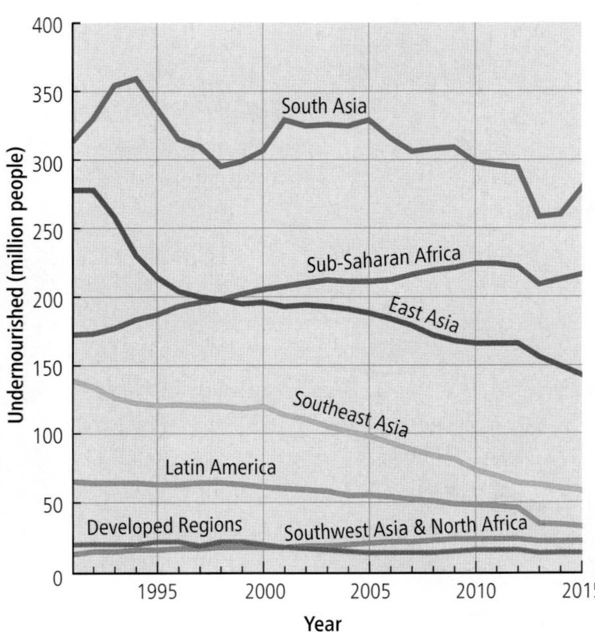

▲ 9.4.7 CHANGE IN UNDERNOURISHMENT

WHAT'S YOUR FOOD & AGRICULTURE GEOGRAPHY?

Your Calorie Counter

Select a calorie calculator from several available online, such as **calculator .net/calorie-counter**. Record all of the food you have consumed on a recent day, from the time you awoke to the time you went to sleep. Don't forget to record the snacks.

1. For each item on your list, estimate the number of calories you consumed.
2. How many calories did you consume through the day?
3. How does your calorie count compare with the average in the United States?

▶ 9.4.8 DOUBLE CHEESEBURGER: AROUND 430 CALORIES

Agricultural Regions

- Describe agricultural regions and their relationships to climate regions.

People have been able to practice agriculture in a wide variety of places. The most widely used map of world agricultural regions is based on work done by geographer Derwent Whittlesey in 1936. Whittlesey identified 11 main agricultural regions, plus an area where agriculture was nonexistent. Whittlesey's 11 regions are divided between 5 that are important in developing countries and 6 that are important in developed countries (Figure 9.5.1).

Developing and Developed Agriculture Regions

The five agricultural regions that predominate in developing countries are:

- **Intensive subsistence, wet rice dominant:** The large population concentrations of East Asia and South Asia.
- **Intensive subsistence, crops other than rice dominant:** The large population concentrations of East Asia and South Asia, where growing rice is difficult.
- **Pastoral nomadism:** The drylands of Southwest Asia & North Africa, Central Asia, and East Asia.
- **Shifting cultivation:** The tropical regions of Latin America, sub-Saharan Africa, and Southeast Asia.
- **Plantation:** The tropical and subtropical regions of Latin America, sub-Saharan Africa, South Asia, and Southeast Asia.

The six agricultural regions that predominate in developed countries are:

- **Mixed crop and livestock:** The U.S. Midwest and central Europe.
- **Dairying:** Near population clusters in the northeastern United States, southeastern Canada, and northwestern Europe.
- **Grain:** The north-central United States, south-central Canada, and Eastern Europe (Figure 9.5.2).
- **Ranching:** The drylands of western North America, southeastern Latin America, Central Asia, sub-Saharan Africa, and the South Pacific.
- **Mediterranean:** Lands surrounding the Mediterranean Sea, the western United States, the southern tip of Africa, and Chile.
- **Commercial gardening:** The southeastern United States and southeastern Australia.

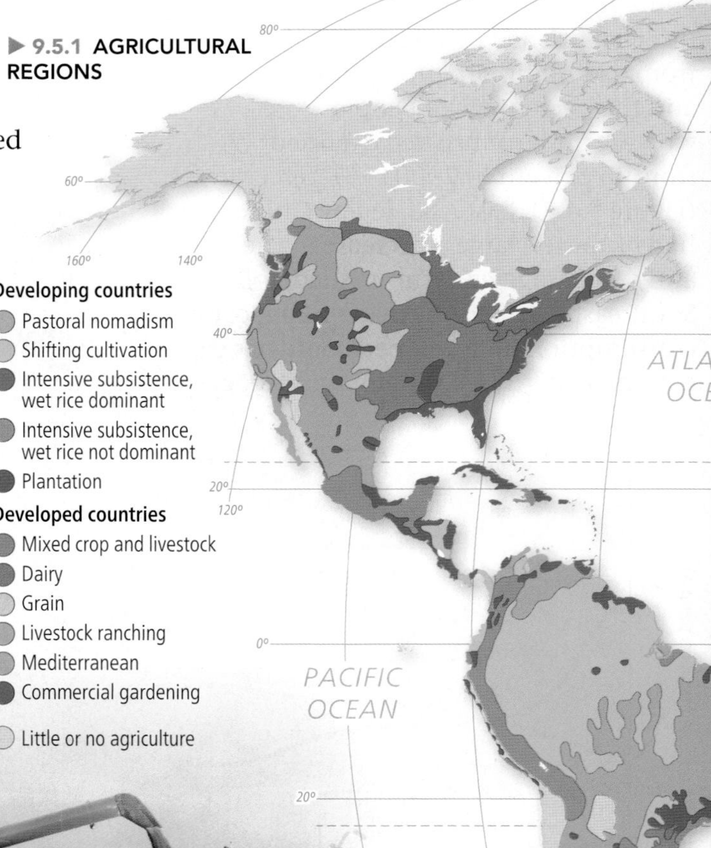

▶ 9.5.1 AGRICULTURAL REGIONS

◀ 9.5.2 GRAIN FARMING, WASHINGTON STATE

Agricultural Regions and Climate

Similarities between the agriculture and climate maps are striking (Figure 9.5.3). For example, pastoral nomadism is the predominant type of agriculture in Southwest Asia & North Africa, which has a dry climate, whereas shifting cultivation is the predominant type of agriculture in sub-Saharan Africa, which has a tropical climate. Note the division between southeastern China (warm mid-latitude climate, intensive subsistence agriculture with wet-rice dominant) and northeastern China (cold mid-latitude climate, intensive subsistence agriculture with wet rice not dominant).

In the United States, much of the West is distinguished from the rest of the country according to climate (dry) and agriculture (livestock ranching). Thus, agriculture varies between the drylands and the tropics within developing countries—as well as between the drylands of developing countries and developed countries.

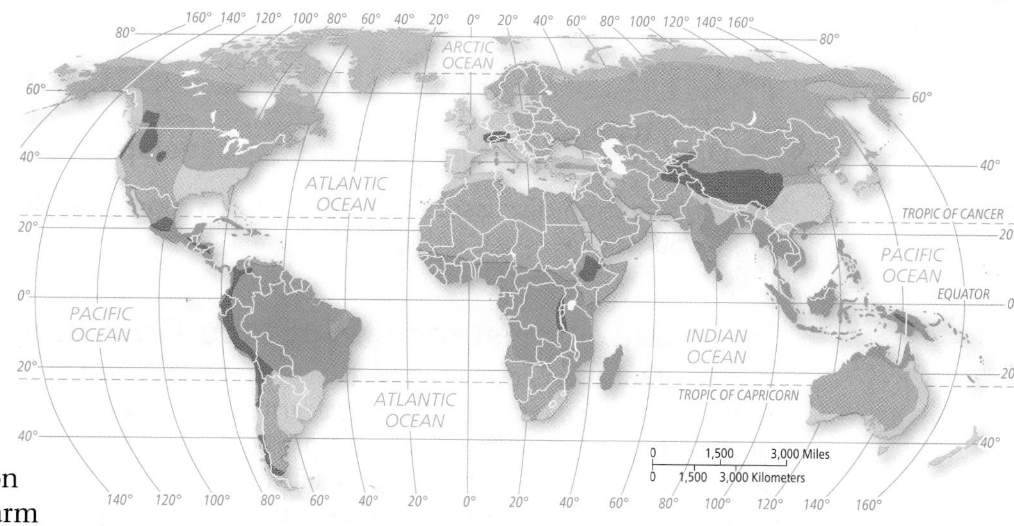

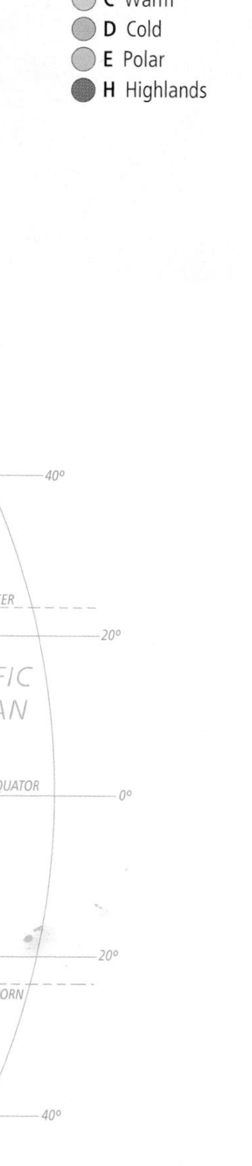

▲ 9.5.3 **CLIMATE REGIONS**

- A Tropical
- B Dry
- C Warm
- D Cold
- E Polar
- H Highlands

Agriculture in Developing Regions

- Describe agricultural practices in developing countries.

This section discusses the five most common agricultural regions in developing countries.

Intensive Subsistence, Wet Rice Dominant

A form of subsistence agriculture in which farmers expend a relatively large amount of effort to produce the maximum feasible yield from the land is known as **intensive subsistence**. It is the typical form of agriculture in the densely populated regions of East, South, and Southeast Asia, where more than half of the world's people live (Figures 9.6.1 and 9.6.2).

▲ 9.6.1 FLOODED RICE FIELDS, INDIA

Four main steps are involved in growing **wet rice**, the region's most important crop. As the name implies, all four steps are intensive.

1. The field is prepared, typically with a plow drawn by water buffalo or oxen. Flat land is needed to grow rice, so hillsides are terraced.
2. The field is flooded with water. The flooded field is called a **sawah** in Indonesia, and is sometimes incorrectly called a **paddy**, which is actually the Malay word for wet rice.
3. Rice seedlings grown for the first month in a nursery are transplanted into the flooded field.
4. Rice plants are harvested with knives. The chaff (husks) are separated from the seeds by threshing (beating) them on the ground. The threshed rice is placed in a tray and the lighter chaff is winnowed (allowed to be blown away by the wind).

Intensive Subsistence, Wet Rice Not Dominant

Agriculture in much of the interior of India and northeastern China is devoted to crops other than wet rice, because the climate is too harsh to grow wet rice. Wheat and barley are the most important crops.

Rice production (million metric tons)
- 100 and above
- 10–99
- 1–9.9
- below 1
- no data

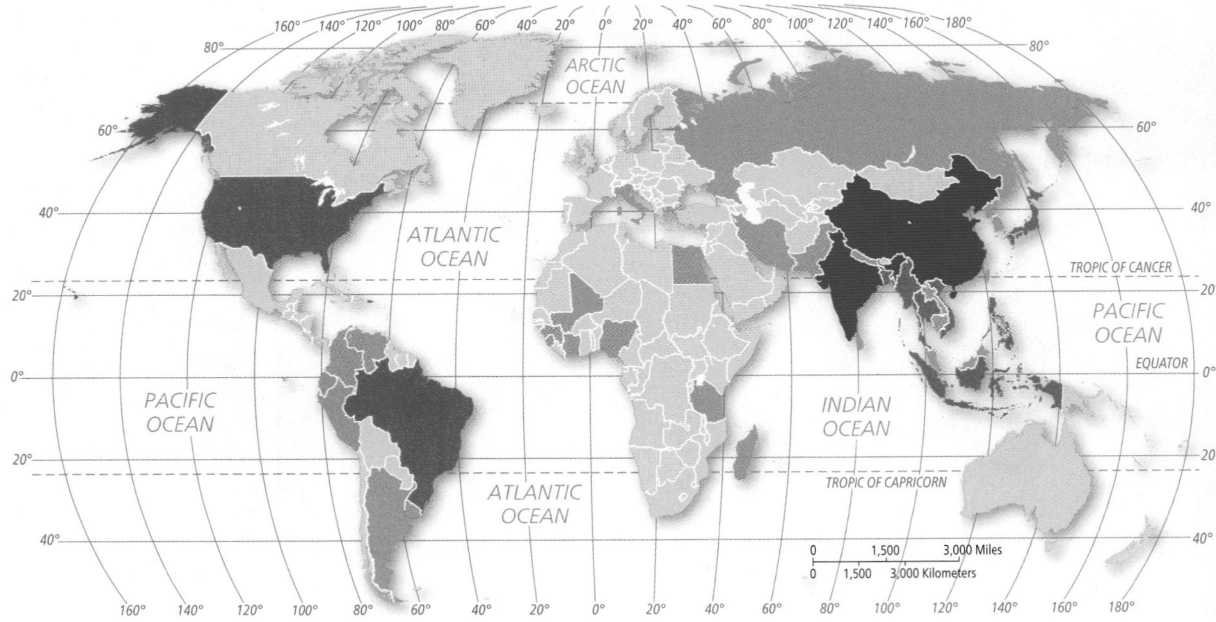

▶ 9.6.2 RICE PRODUCTION

Pastoral Nomadism

A form of subsistence agriculture based on the herding of domesticated animals is known as **pastoral nomadism**. It is adapted to dry climates, where planting crops is impossible. Pastoral nomads live primarily in the large belt of arid and semiarid land that includes most of North Africa and Southwest Asia, and parts of Central Asia. The Bedouins of Saudi Arabia and North Africa and the Maasai of East Africa are examples of nomadic groups.

Like other subsistence farmers, pastoral nomads consume mostly grain rather than meat. Their animals are usually not slaughtered, although dead ones may be consumed. Instead, the animals provide milk, and their skins and hair are used for clothing and tents. To nomads, the size of their herd is both an important measure of power and prestige and their main security during adverse environmental conditions.

Nomads used to be the most powerful inhabitants of the dry lands. Before recent transportation and communications inventions, they were the carriers of goods and information across the sparsely inhabited dry lands. Today, national governments control the nomadic population, using force, if necessary. Governments force groups to give up pastoral nomadism because they want the land for other uses.

Shifting Cultivation

In the form of subsistence agriculture known as **shifting cultivation**, people frequently shift farming from one field to another. It is practiced in much of the world's tropical rainforests, where temperatures are high and rainfall abundant, especially in Latin America, sub-Saharan Africa, and Southeast Asia (refer ahead to Figure 9.10.1).

Two distinctive features of shifting cultivation are:

- **Slash and burn.** Farmers clear land for planting by slashing vegetation and burning the debris; rain washes the ashes into the soil to provide needed nutrients.
- **Frequent relocation.** Farmers grow crops on a cleared field for only a few years, until soil nutrients are depleted, and then leave it fallow (with nothing planted) for many years so the soil can recover.

Land devoted to shifting cultivation is declining. Development agencies like the World Bank once supported projects to clear tropical rainforests for other more lucrative types of agriculture, such as raising cattle to sell meat to fast-food restaurants. As evidence mounts that the loss of the rainforests contributes to global warming and destruction of tropical ecosystems, shifting cultivation is increasingly regarded as a more environmentally sound approach to tropical agriculture.

Plantation Farming

A **plantation** is a large commercial farm in a developing country that specializes in one or two crops. Most plantations are located in the tropics and subtropics, especially in Latin America, sub-Saharan Africa, and Asia. Although generally situated in developing countries, plantations are often owned or operated by Europeans or North Americans, and they grow crops for sale primarily to developed countries. Among the most important crops grown on plantations are cotton, sugarcane, coffee, rubber, and tobacco. Also produced in large quantities are cocoa, jute, bananas, tea, coconuts, and palm oil (Figure 9.6.3).

Until the Civil War, plantations were important in the U.S. South, where the principal crop was cotton, followed by tobacco and sugarcane. Slaves brought from Africa performed most of the labor until the abolition of slavery and the defeat of the South in the Civil War. Thereafter, plantations declined in the United States; they were subdivided and either sold to individual farmers or worked by tenant farmers.

▼ 9.6.3 BANANA PLANTATION, COSTA RICA

▲ 9.7.1 WILD SALMON FISHING, BRITISH COLUMBIA

Fishing

- Explain the contribution of fishing to our food supply.

Food acquired from Earth's waters includes fish, crustaceans (such as shrimp and crabs), mollusks (such as clams and oysters), and aquatic plants (such as watercress). Developing countries are responsible for most production and consumption of fish. Historically the sea has provided only a small percentage of the world food supply, but Earth's vast oceans have become an increasing source of food for developing countries.

Fish Production

Water-based food is acquired in two ways. **Fishing** is the capture of wild fish and other seafood living in the waters (Figure 9.7.1). **Aquaculture** is the cultivation of fish and seafood under controlled conditions.

The world's oceans are divided into 16 major fishing regions, including six each in the Atlantic and Pacific oceans, two in the Indian Ocean, and the Mediterranean (Figure 9.7.2). The fishing regions with the largest yields are Pacific Northwest and Pacific Western Central. Fishing is also conducted in inland waterways, such as lakes and rivers. China is responsible for one-third of the world's yield of fish (Figure 9.7.3).

▼ 9.7.2 MAJOR FISHING REGIONS

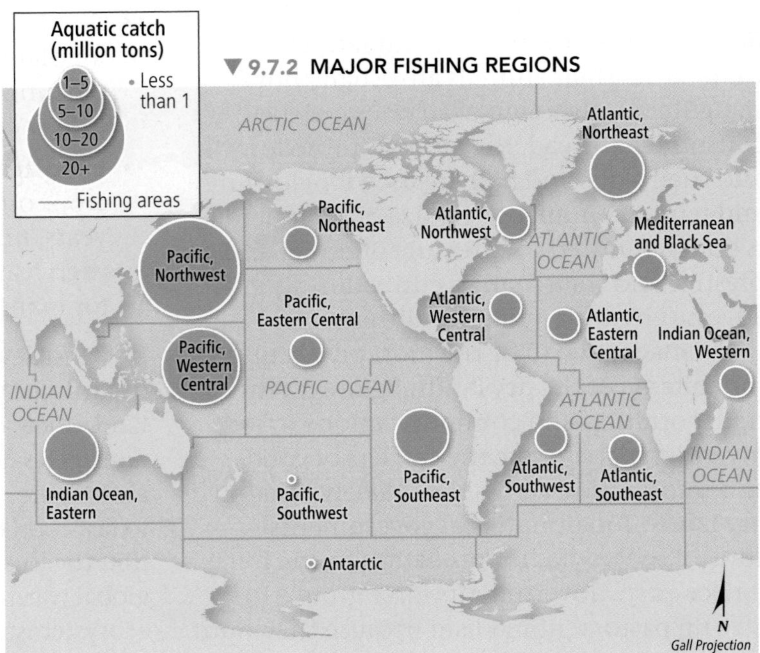

▶ 9.7.3 FISH CAPTURE

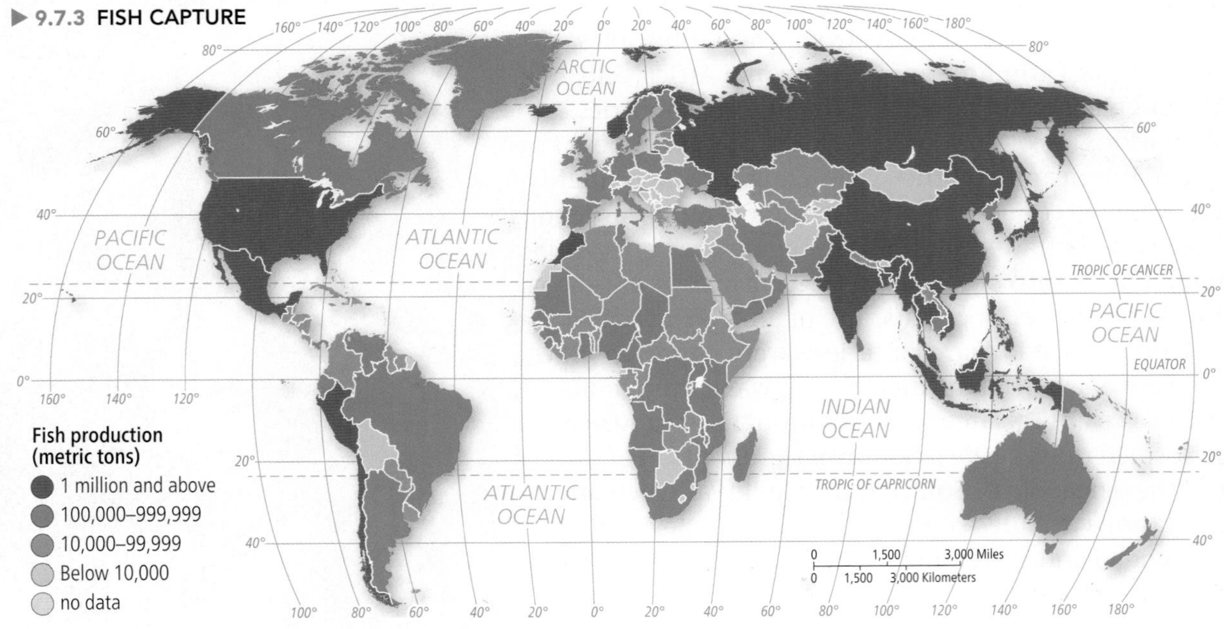

Fish Consumption

Human consumption of fish and seafood has increased from 27 million metric tons in 1960 to 132 million metric tons in 2012 (Figure 9.7.4). Developing countries are responsible for five-sixths of the increase.

Fish consumption has increased more rapidly than population growth. During the past half-century, per capita consumption of fish has nearly doubled in both developed and developing countries. Still, fish and seafood account for only 1 percent of all calories consumed by humans.

Fish production has increased even more rapidly than fish consumption (Figure 9.7.5). The growth results entirely from expansion of aquaculture (Figure 9.7.6). A comparison of Figures 9.7.4 and 9.7.5 shows that production of fish is around one-fourth higher than human consumption of it. Around three-fourths of the fish are consumed directly by humans. The remainder is converted to fish meal and fed to poultry and hogs.

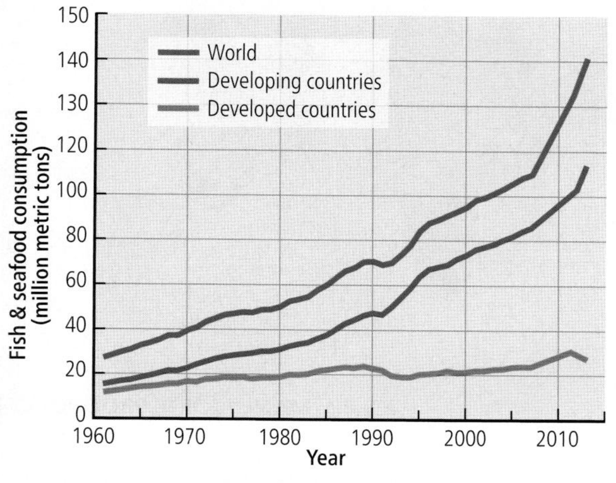

▲ 9.7.4 GROWTH IN HUMAN CONSUMPTION OF FISH

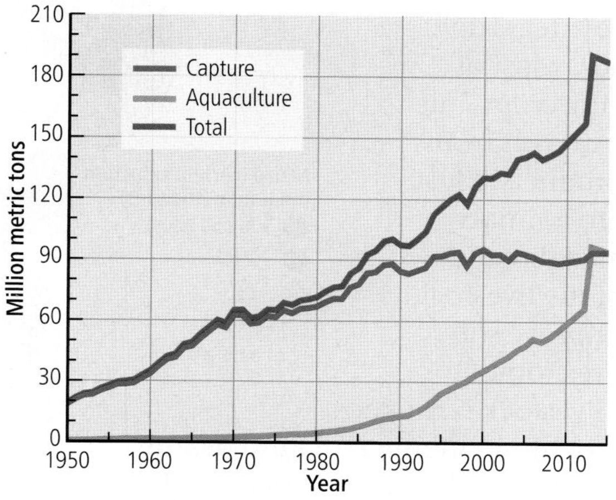

▲ 9.7.5 GROWTH IN FISH PRODUCTION

Overfishing

The population of some fish species in the oceans and lakes has declined because of **overfishing**, which is capturing fish faster than they can reproduce. Overfishing has been particularly acute in the North Atlantic and Pacific oceans. Overfishing has reduced the population of tuna and swordfish by 90 percent in the past half-century, for example. The UN estimates that one-quarter of fish stocks have been overfished and one-half fully exploited, leaving only one-fourth underfished.

▼ 9.7.6 AQUACULTURE
Mae Ping River, Chiang Mai, Thailand.

Agriculture in Developed Regions

- **Describe agricultural practices in developed countries.**

The system of commercial farming found in developed countries is called **agribusiness** because farming is integrated into a large food-production industry. Commercial agriculture in developed countries can be divided into six main types. Each type is predominant in distinctive regions, depending somewhat on climate.

Mixed Crop and Livestock

The form of commercial farming called **mixed crop and livestock** is characterized by the integration of crops and livestock. Most of the land is for growing crops, but most of the income derives from the sale of animal products. Most of the crops are fed to animals rather than consumed directly by humans. In turn, the livestock supply manure to improve soil fertility to grow more crops.

Mixed crop and livestock is the most common form of agriculture in much of Europe and in the United States between the Appalachians and 98° west longitude (a boundary between wetter and drier climates, as shown in Figure 9.5.3). Maize (corn) is the crop most frequently planted, followed by soybeans (Figure 9.8.1). Crops are typically rotated or varied to help maintain fertility, because various crops deplete the soil of some nutrients but restore others.

▲ 9.8.1 MAIZE (CORN) PRODUCTION

Dairy Farming

The most important agriculture practiced near large urban areas in developed countries is **dairy farming**, a form of commercial agriculture that specializes in the production of milk and other dairy products (Figure 9.8.2). Dairy farms must be closer to their markets than other products because milk is highly perishable. The ring surrounding a city from which milk can be supplied without spoiling is known as the **milkshed**.

Traditionally most milk was produced and consumed in developed countries (Figure 9.8.3). However, the share of the world's dairy farming conducted in developing countries has risen dramatically in recent years, surpassing the total in developed countries. Rising incomes permit urban residents in developing countries to buy more milk products.

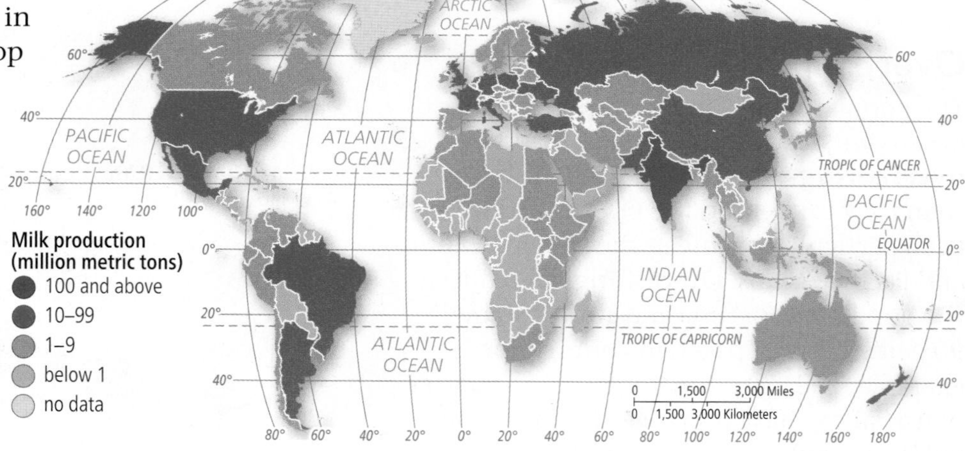

▲ 9.8.2 MILK PRODUCTION

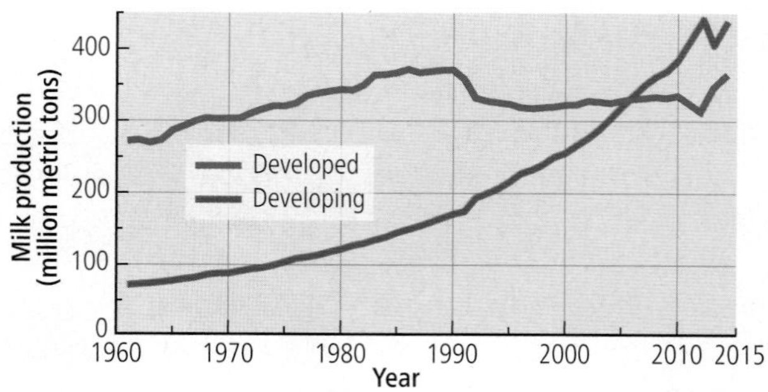

▲ 9.8.3 CHANGING MILK PRODUCTION

Grain Farming

Commercial grain farms tend to locate in regions that are too dry for mixed crop and livestock, such as North America's Great Plains (refer to Figure 9.5.3). Crops on a grain farm are grown primarily for consumption by humans rather than by livestock. The most important crop grown is wheat, used to make flour (Figure 9.8.4).

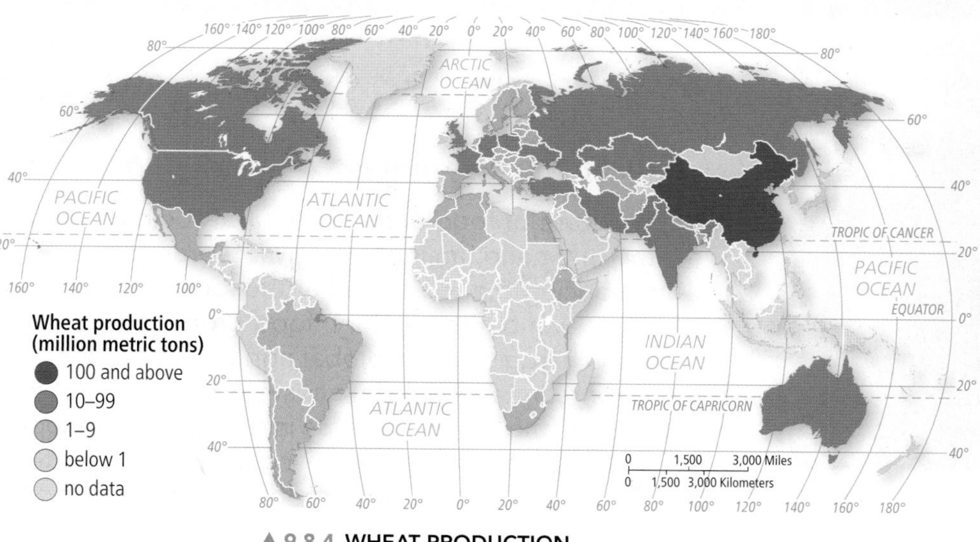

▲ 9.8.4 WHEAT PRODUCTION

Livestock Ranching

The commercial grazing of livestock over an extensive area is called **ranching**. This form of agriculture is adapted to semiarid or arid land and is practiced in developed countries where the vegetation is too sparse and the soil too poor to support crops. The United States is the leading producer of chicken and beef, but like other forms of commercial agriculture the growth in ranching has been in developing countries, and China is the leading producer of pig meat (Figure 9.8.5).

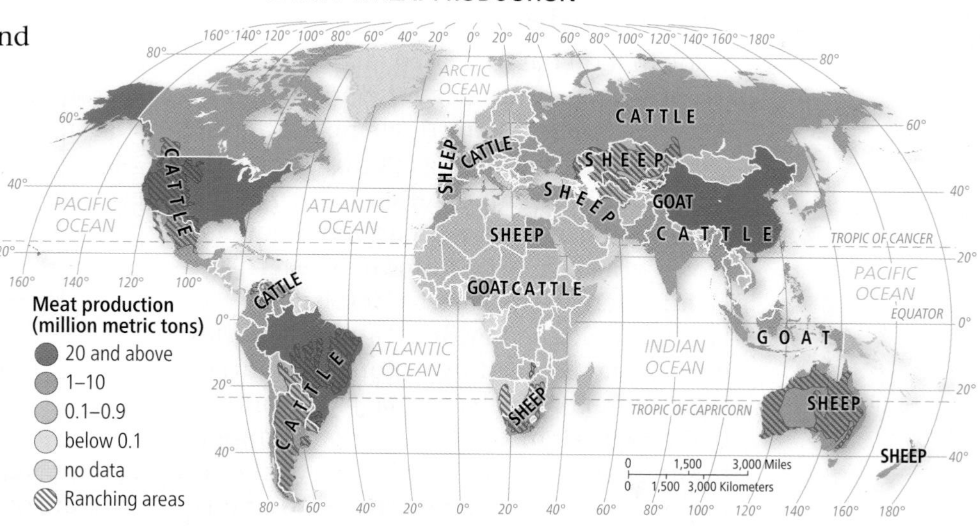

▲ 9.8.5 MEAT PRODUCTION

Commercial Gardening and Fruit Farming

Commercial gardening and fruit farming are the predominant types of agriculture in the U.S. Southeast. The region has a long growing season and humid climate and is accessible to the large markets in the big cities along the East Coast. It is frequently called **truck farming**, because "truck" was a Middle English word meaning bartering or the exchange of commodities.

Truck farms grow many of the fruits and vegetables that consumers demand in developed countries, such as lettuce, peaches, and tomatoes. A form of truck farming called specialty farming has spread to New England.

Mediterranean Agriculture

Mediterranean agriculture exists primarily on lands that border the Mediterranean Sea and other places with a similar physical geography, such as California and central Chile, where winters are moist and mild, summers hot and dry. The land is very hilly, and mountains frequently plunge directly to the sea, leaving very little flat land. The two most important crops are olives (primarily for cooking oil) and grapes (primarily for wine).

Von Thünen Model

Because the purpose of commercial farming is to sell produce off the farm, the distance from the farm to the market influences the choice of crop to plant. Geographers use the von Thünen model to help explain the importance of proximity to market in the choice of crops on commercial farms (Figure 9.8.6). Johann Heinrich von Thünen developed the model for a small region with a single market center, but the model is also applicable on a national or global scale.

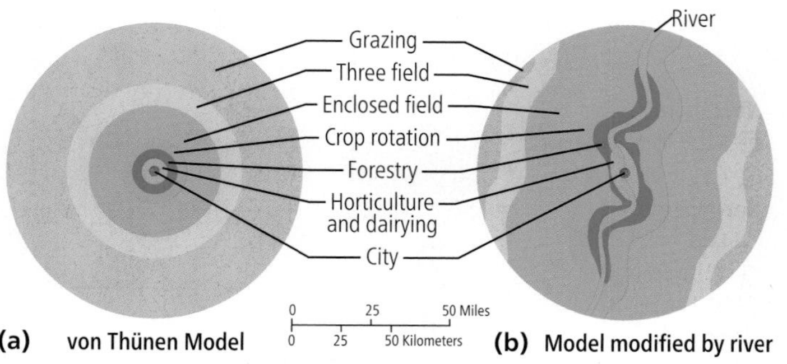

▲ 9.8.6 VON THÜNEN MODEL

Trade in Food & Agriculture

- **Explain the contribution of agriculture to the global economy.**

▲ 9.9.1 **SOYBEAN PRODUCTION, BRAZIL**
Brazil is the world's leading exporter of soybeans.

The future of food and agriculture is being pulled in global and local directions. On the one hand, an increasingly integrated global agricultural system is devoted to producing the most food at the lowest cost for the world's nearly 8 billion humans. And in the twenty-first century, food production is higher and undernourishment is lower. But critics charge that the global agriculture system is causing major long-run damage to the environment and to local ecosystems for the sake of short-term production.

Meanwhile, the biggest increase in demand in developed countries is for locally grown food produced through sustainable farming methods. But critics charge that the local and organic movements are not capable of providing affordable food for the world's nearly 8 billion humans.

Food Trade

Trade in food has increased rapidly in the twenty-first century (Figures 9.9.1 and 9.9.2). Exporting countries benefit from the revenues, and importing countries meet the food needs of their people.

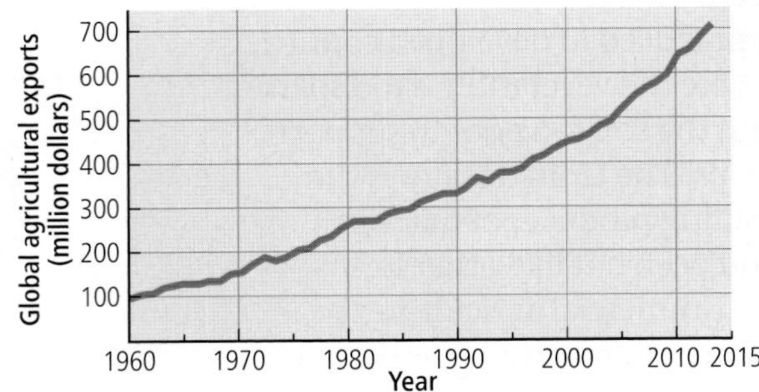

▲ 9.9.2 **GLOBAL AGRICULTURAL EXPORTS**

On a global scale, agricultural products are moving primarily from the Western Hemisphere to the Eastern Hemisphere. Latin America, led by Brazil and Argentina, is the by far the leading region for export of agricultural products; China, Japan, and the United Kingdom are the leading net importers (Figure 9.9.3). The United States is the world's leading exporter, but it is also the world's leading importer. U.S. supermarkets increasingly import fruits and vegetables when domestic sources are out of season.

To expand agricultural production in developing countries, subsistence farmers need higher-yield seeds, fertilizer, pesticides, and machinery. These supplies are typically imported from other countries. To generate money to buy agricultural supplies, governments in developing countries encourage farmers to grow crops for sale in developed countries. Consumers in developed countries may be willing to pay high prices for fruits and vegetables that would otherwise be out of season or for crops such as coffee and tea that cannot be grown in developed countries because of the climate.

The sale of export crops brings a developing country foreign currency, a portion of which can be used to buy agricultural supplies. But if more land is devoted to growing export crops, less is available to grow crops for domestic consumption. Rather than help to increase productivity, the funds generated through the sale of export crops may be needed to feed the people who switched from subsistence farming to growing export crops.

▶ 9.9.3 **TRADE IN AGRICULTURE**

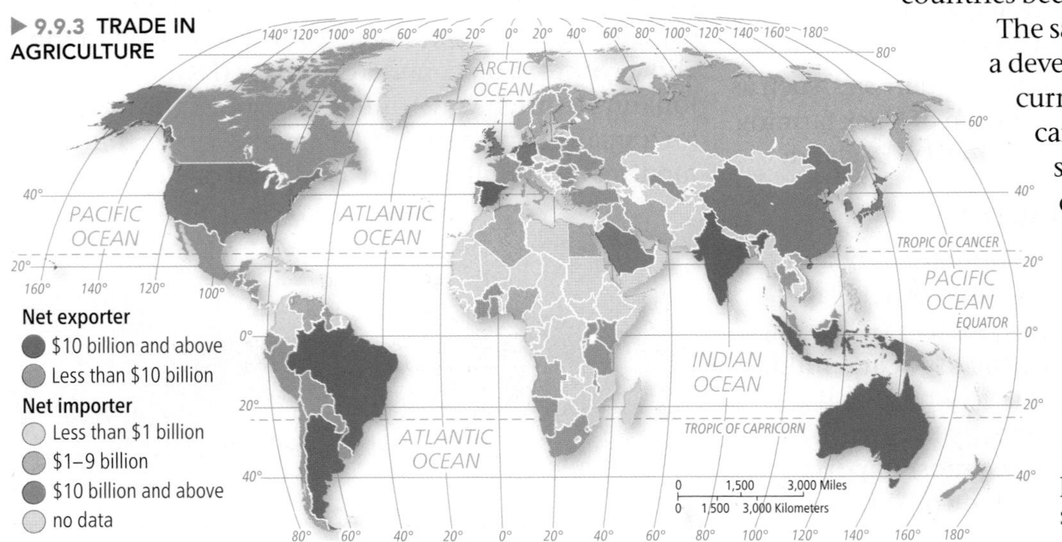

Drug Trade

The export crops grown in some developing countries are those that can be converted to drugs, especially cocaine, heroin, and marijuana. Cocaine is derived from coca leaf, more than 98 percent of which is grown in Colombia or the neighboring countries Peru and Bolivia. Heroin is derived from raw opium gum, which is produced by the opium poppy plant. Afghanistan is the source of more than 90 percent of the world's opium; most of the remainder is grown in Myanmar (Burma) and Laos. Marijuana, produced from the Cannabis sativa plant, is cultivated widely around the world. The overwhelming majority of the marijuana that reaches the United States is grown in Mexico (Figure 9.9.4).

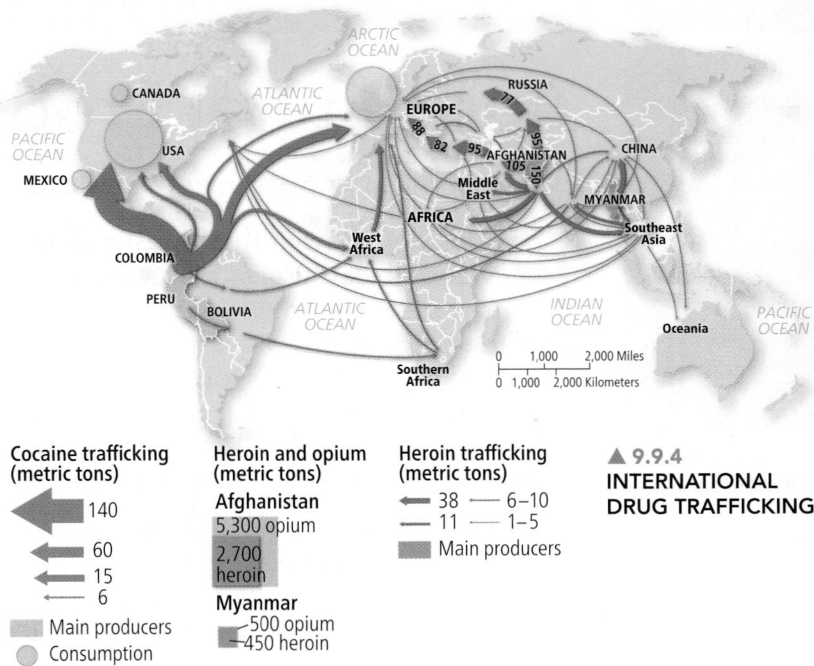

▲ 9.9.4 INTERNATIONAL DRUG TRAFFICKING

Government Policies

The U.S. government has three agriculture policies designed to improve the financial position of farmers:

- Farmers are encouraged to avoid producing crops that are in excess supply. Because soil erosion is a constant threat, the government encourages planting fallow crops, such as clover, to restore nutrients to the soil and to help hold the soil in place. These crops can be used for hay or forage for pigs, or to produce seeds for sale.
- The government pays farmers when certain commodity prices are low. The government sets a target price for a commodity and pays farmers the difference between the price they receive in the market and the target price set by the government as a fair level for the commodity. The target prices are calculated to give farmers the same price for the commodity today as in the past, when compared to other consumer goods and services.
- The government buys surplus production and sells or donates it to foreign governments. In addition, low-income Americans receive food stamps in part to stimulate their purchase of additional food.

The United States has averaged about $25 billion a year on farm subsidies in recent years. Annual spending varies considerably from one year to the next. Subsidy payments are lower in years when market prices rise and production is down, typically as a result of poor weather conditions in the United States or political problems in other countries.

Farming in Europe is subsidized even more than in the United States. More farmers receive subsidies in Europe, and they receive more than American farmers. The high subsidies are a legacy of a long-standing commitment by the European Union to maintain agriculture in its member states, especially in France. Supporters point to the preservation of rural village life in parts of Europe, while critics charge that Europeans pay needlessly high prices for food as a result of the subsidies.

Food Prices

The greatest challenge to world food supply in the twenty-first century has been food prices rather than food supply. Food prices more than doubled between 2006 and 2008, remained at record high levels through 2014, declined sharply in 2015, and increased in 2017 (Figure 9.9.5).

The U.N. attributes the record high food prices to four factors: Poor weather, especially in major crop-growing regions of North America and Australia; higher demand, especially in China and India; smaller growth in productivity, especially without major new "miracle" breakthroughs; and use of crops as biofuels instead of food, especially in Latin America.

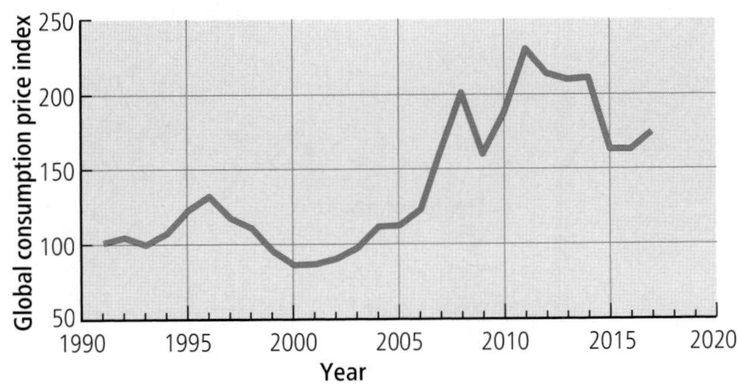

▲ 9.9.5 GLOBAL FOOD PRICE INDEX

▲ 9.10.1 SHIFTING CULTIVATION, LAOS

Agricultural Productivity

- Explain the importance of the green revolution.

Population grew at the fastest rate in human history during the second half of the twentieth century, as discussed in Chapter 2. With the amount of land devoted to agriculture not increasing, many experts forecasted massive global famine. But these dire predictions did not come true. Instead, increased productivity has resulted in an expansion of food supply. New agricultural practices have permitted farmers worldwide to achieve much greater yields from the same amount of land.

Supply of Agricultural Land

Historically, world food production increased primarily by expanding the amount of land devoted to agriculture (Figure 9.10.1). People believed that good agricultural land would always be available for willing pioneers. Today few scientists believe that further expansion of agricultural land can feed the growing world population. In recent decades, population has increased much more rapidly than agricultural land (Figure 9.10.2).

In some regions, farmland is abandoned for lack of water. Especially in semiarid regions, human actions are causing land to deteriorate to a desert-like condition, a process called **desertification** (or, more precisely, semiarid land degradation). Semiarid lands that can support only a handful of pastoral nomads are overused because of rapid population growth. Excessive crop planting, animal grazing, and tree cutting exhaust the soil's nutrients and preclude agriculture.

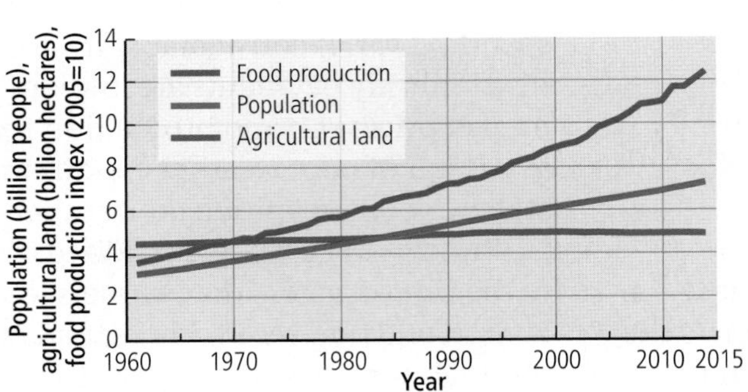

▶ 9.10.2 WORLD POPULATION GROWTH, AGRICULTURAL LAND, AND FOOD PRODUCTION

The Earth Policy Institute estimates that 2 billion hectares (5 billion acres) of land have been degraded around the world (Figure 9.10.3). Overgrazing is thought to be responsible for 34 percent of the total, deforestation for 30 percent, and agricultural use for 28 percent. The U.N. estimates that desertification removes 27 million hectares (70 million acres) of land from agricultural production each year.

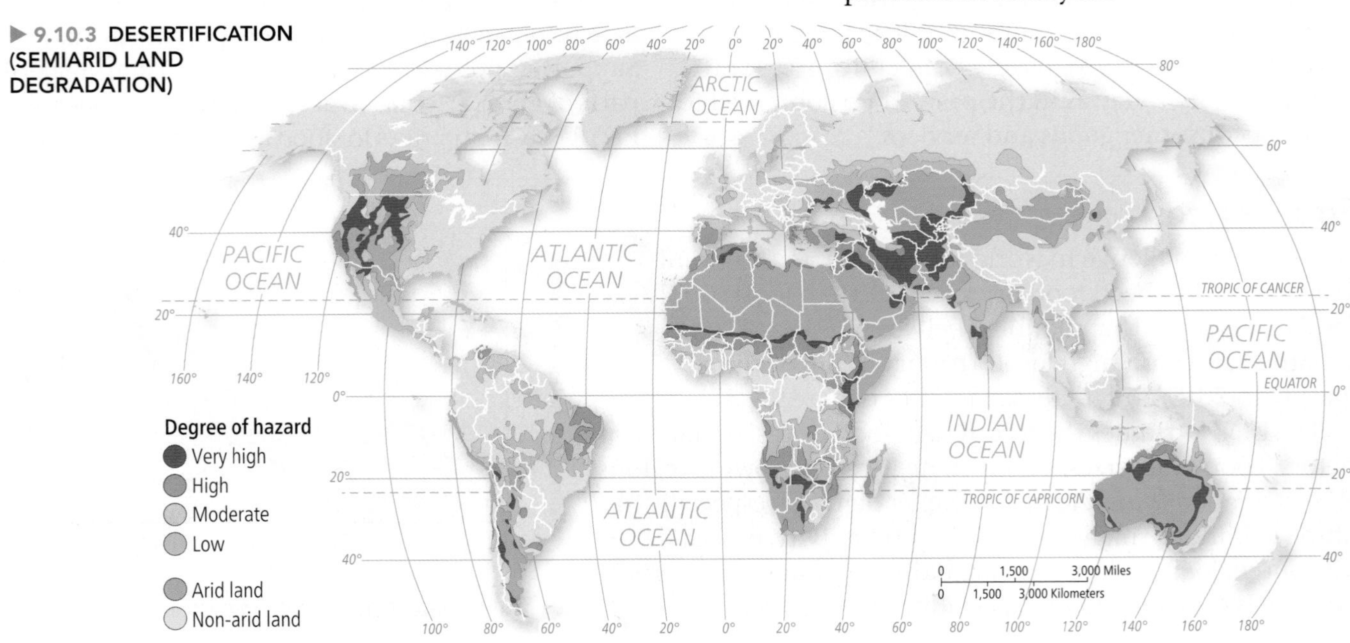

▶ 9.10.3 DESERTIFICATION (SEMIARID LAND DEGRADATION)

Intensification

For hundreds if not thousands of years, subsistence farming in developing countries yielded enough food for people living in rural villages to survive, assuming that no drought, flood, or other natural disaster occurred. Suddenly in the late twentieth century, subsistence farming practices needed to provide enough food for a rapidly increasing population as well as for the growing number of urban residents who cannot grow their own food.

According to economist Ester Boserup, subsistence farmers increase the supply of food through intensification of production, achieved in two ways. First, land is left fallow for shorter periods. Second, new farming methods are adopted. Plows replace axes and sticks. More weeding is done, more manure is applied, more terraces are carved out of hillsides, and more irrigation ditches are dug. Farmers adopt **crop rotation**, which varies the crop planted in a field each year to avoid exhausting the soil, as well as **double cropping**, which is the ability to harvest twice a year from the same field.

▲ 9.10.4 INTERNATIONAL RICE RESEARCH INSTITUTE, THE PHILIPPINES

The Green Revolution

The invention and rapid diffusion of more productive agricultural techniques during the 1970s and 1980s is called the green revolution. The **green revolution** involves two main practices: the introduction of new higher-yield seeds and the expanded use of fertilizers. Because of the green revolution, agricultural productivity at a global scale has increased faster than population growth.

Scientists began an intensive series of experiments during the 1950s to develop a higher-yield form of wheat. A decade later, the "miracle wheat seed" was ready. Shorter and stiffer than traditional breeds, the new wheat was less sensitive to variation in day length, responded better to fertilizers, and matured faster. The Rockefeller and Ford foundations sponsored many of the studies, and the program's director, Dr. Norman Borlaug, won the Nobel Peace Prize in 1970.

The International Rice Research Institute, established in the Philippines by the Rockefeller and Ford foundations, worked to create a miracle rice seed (Figure 9.10.4). During the 1960s, their scientists introduced a hybrid of Indonesian rice and Taiwan dwarf rice that was hardier and that increased yields. More recently, scientists have developed new high-yield maize (corn).

Farmers need fertilizers, tractors, irrigation pumps, and other machinery to make the most effective use of the new miracle seeds. In developing countries, farmers cannot afford such equipment and cannot, in view of high energy costs, buy fuel to operate the equipment. To maintain the green revolution, governments in developing countries must allocate scarce funds to subsidize the cost of seeds, fertilizers, and machinery.

Commercial Agriculture Productivity

Productivity has also increased among commercial farmers in recent years. New seeds, fertilizers, pesticides, mechanical equipment, and management practices have enabled commercial farmers to obtain greatly increased yields per area of land.

The experience of dairy farming in the United States demonstrates the growth in productivity. The number of dairy cows in the United States decreased from 10.8 million to 9.3 million between 1980 and 2016. But milk production increased from 58 to 96 million metric tons. Thus, yield per cow nearly doubled during this 36-year period, from 5.4 to 10.4 metric tons per cow (Figure 9.10.5).

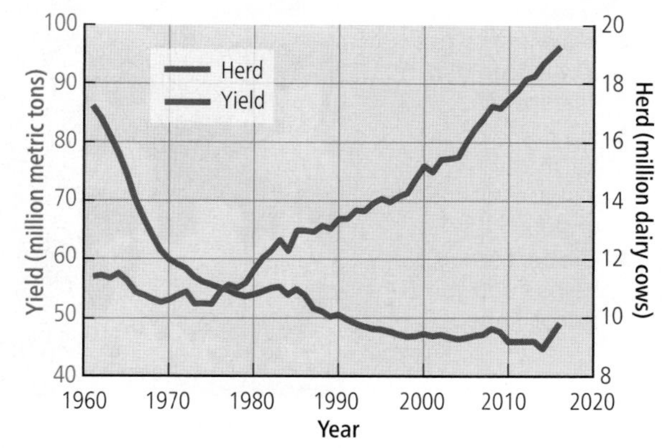

▲ 9.10.5 U.S. DAIRY PRODUCTIVITY

Biotechnology & Sustainability

- Explain principles of organic farming.

One of the most challenging issues in contemporary agriculture is the extent to which seeds should be genetically modified. Alternatively, demand has increased for organic crops that have not been genetically modified.

Farmers have been manipulating crops and livestock for thousands of years. The fundamental purpose of agriculture is to deliberately manipulate nature. Humans control selective reproduction of plants and animals in order to produce a larger number of stronger, hardier survivors.

Genetically Modified Organisms

A **genetically modified organism (GMO)** is a living organism that possesses a novel combination of genetic material obtained through the use of modern biotechnology. GMO seeds are genetically modified to survive when herbicides and insecticides are sprayed on fields to kill weeds and insects. A GMO mixes genetic material of two or more species that would not otherwise mix in nature.

GMO marks a sharp break with the agricultural practices of the past several thousand years. Today, scientists do not merely alter organisms incrementally through selective breeding, but directly engineer specific genetic changes.

North America is responsible for one-half of the world's genetically modified foods, and developing countries—especially in Latin America—are responsible for the other one-half. Genetic modification is especially widespread in the United States, including 94 percent of soybeans, 90 percent of cotton, and 88 percent of maize (Figure 9.11.1).

▼ 9.11.1 GENETICALLY MODIFIED CROPS IN THE UNITED STATES

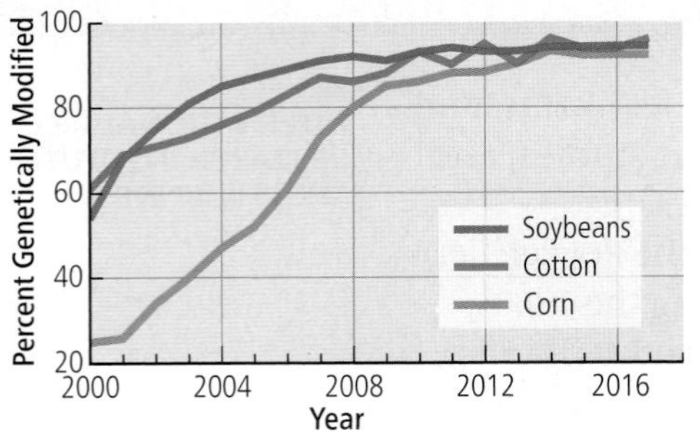

Most medical studies conclude that consuming large quantities of GMOS is not injurious to human health. However, GMOs may reduce the effectiveness of antibiotics and may destroy longstanding ecological balances in local agriculture. As a result of these concerns, many countries require GMO labeling (including China, India, and nearly all in Europe), and they make it difficult to sell GMO food. The United States is an exception: three-fourths of the processed food that Americans consume have GMO ingredients. Americans are also debating the importance of consuming local food (see Debate It! feature).

DEBATE IT!

Should you consume local or global food?

CONSUME GLOBAL

- It is easier to eat a balanced diet year-round.
- No place on Earth can grow all types of food (Figure 9.11.2).
- Global sourcing helps keep food prices lower.

▲ 9.11.2 GLOBAL: BANANAS FROM LATIN AMERICA IN DETROIT GROCERY STORE

CONSUME LOCAL

- Many foods transported long distance lose their nutritional value.
- Buying local supports the local farm economy and helps to preserve local farmland (Figure 9.11.3).
- Local food is fresher and tastes better.

▲ 9.11.3 LOCAL: FARMERS MARKET, PHILADELPHIA

Organic Farming

The most rapid growth in demand has been for organic food, including non-GMO food. Some consumers in developed countries are questioning the health risks in consuming biotech food produced through heavy application of chemicals, as well as the long-term adverse environmental impacts for agriculture.

Worldwide, the Research Institute of Organic Agriculture classified 51 million hectares (127 million acres), or 1 percent of farmland, as organic in 2015. Australia was the leader, with 23 million hectares (Figure 9.11.4). In the United States, organic food sales spiked from $3.4 billion in 1997 to an estimated $40 billion in 2015. Organic food accounted for 5 percent of food purchases in the United States in 2014, compared with less than 1 percent in 1997.

Organic farming is sensitive to the complexities of biological and economic interdependencies between crops and livestock. Growing crops and raising livestock is integrated as much as possible at the level of the individual farm. This integration reflects a return to the historical practice of mixed crop and livestock farming, in which growing crops and raising animals were regarded as complementary activities on the farm. This was the common practice for centuries, until the mid-1900s, when technology, government policy, and economics encouraged farmers to become more specialized.

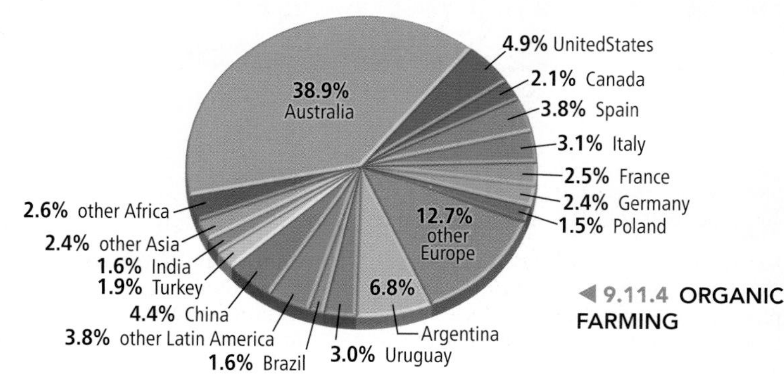

◀ 9.11.4 ORGANIC FARMING

In organic farming, crops are grown without application of herbicides and pesticides to control weeds. GMO seeds are not used. In organic farming, animals consume crops grown on the farm and are not confined to small pens. The moral and ethical debate over animal welfare is particularly intense regarding confined livestock production systems. Confining livestock leads to surface water and groundwater pollution, particularly where the density of animals is high. If animals are not confined, manure can contribute to soil fertility.

In organic farming, antibiotics are administered to animals only for therapeutic purposes. Many conventional livestock farms have fed animals antibiotics to foster weight gain. The European Union has banned the use of antibiotics in livestock for reasons other than medical. The United States has permitted the practice, but the U.S. Food & Drug Administration has ordered the practice to be phased out.

Sustainable Land Management

After harvesting, conventional farming clears away crop residue, such as corn stalks. The soil is churned up or tilled before the next year's seeds are planted. This practice loosens the soil particles, making them susceptible to being washed away by rain or blown away by wind.

Conservation tillage is a method of soil cultivation that reduces soil erosion and runoff. Under conservation tillage, some or all of the previous harvest is left on the fields through the winter. **No tillage**, as the name implies, leaves all of the soil undisturbed, and the entire residue of the previous year's harvest is left untouched on the fields. **Ridge tillage** is a system of planting crops on ridge tops. Crops are planted on 10- to 20-centimeter (4- to 8-inch) ridges that are formed during cultivation or after harvest (Figure 9.11.5). A crop is planted on the same ridges, in the same rows, year after year.

▼ 9.11.5 RIDGE TILLAGE, SCOTLAND

CHAPTER

9 Review, Analyze, & Apply

KEY ISSUE 1 How Did Agriculture Originate?

Before the invention of agriculture, humans were hunters and gatherers. Agriculture originated in multiple hearths and diffused to numerous places independently. Subsistence agriculture is the production of food primarily for consumption by the farmer's family. Commercial agriculture is the production of food primarily for sale off the farm. Commercial agriculture involves larger farms, fewer farmers, and more mechanization than does subsistence agriculture.

THINKING GEOGRAPHICALLY

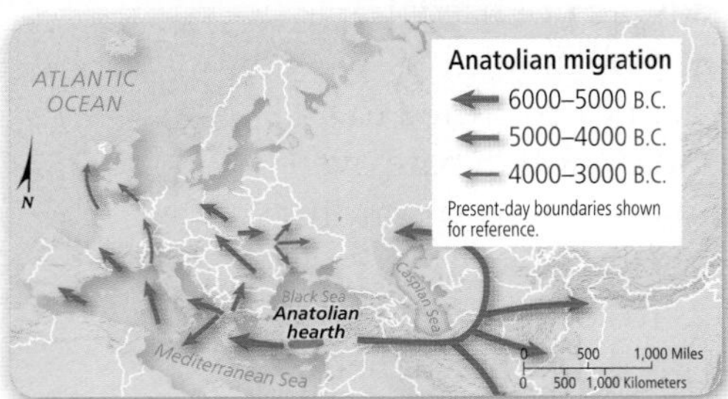

▲ 9.CR.1 ANATOLIAN MIGRATION

1. How does the diffusion of agriculture compare with the diffusion of the Indo-European language family (refer to Figures 5.4.5, 5.4.6, and 9.1.2)? What might account for similarities and differences in the two distributions?

KEY ISSUE 2 What Do People Eat?

What people eat is influenced by a combination of level of development, cultural preferences, and environmental constraints. Most humans derive most of their dietary energy from grains, but the amount consumed varies widely. People in developed countries consume more protein through animal products like meat and dairy. One in 10 humans is undernourished, though the percentage has been declining.

THINKING GEOGRAPHICALLY

2. People in developed countries consume a lot more meat than do people in developing countries. What might be some of the environmental and health challenges of relying on meat for a large share of protein?

◀ 9.CR.2 COWS
A major source of protein in developed countries.

KEY ISSUE 3 Where Is Agriculture Distributed?

The distribution of major agricultural regions is closely related to the distribution of climate regions. The principal forms of subsistence agriculture in developing countries are intensive subsistence, pastoral nomadism, and shifting cultivation. Commercial agriculture in developed countries includes three principal crop-based forms (grain, Mediterranean, and commercial gardening and fruit farming) and three principal animal-based forms (mixed crop and livestock, dairy, and ranching).

THINKING GEOGRAPHICALLY

▲ 9.CR.3 SLASH AND BURN, MYANMAR

3. Land devoted to shifting cultivation is declining rapidly. Why might critics of shifting cultivation argue that it does not meet the food needs of a rapidly growing population? Why might defenders argue that it is the most environmentally sound approach for agriculture in the tropics? How might the people's cultural values and folk customs be impacted by a shift away from shifting cultivation?

KEY ISSUE 4 What Challenges Do Farmers Face?

Subsistence and commercial farmers are challenged to produce food in sustainable ways. The global food production system is expanding and feeding more people. The green revolution has increased production in subsistence agriculture through higher-yield seeds and expanded use of fertilizers. At the same time, demand is increasing for local and organic foods.

THINKING GEOGRAPHICALLY

4. What might be some of the obstacles to introducing or expanding organic food service at your school or university?

◀ 9.CR.4 STUDENT CAFETERIA, UNIVERSITY OF CALIFORNIA, BERKELEY

GeoVideo

Log in to the Mastering Geography™ Study Area to view this video.

Zambia Farm Land

As demand for food increases worldwide, the fertile soils of African countries such as Zambia are being developed for commercial farming for exports, affecting the lives of subsistence farmers.

1. Describe the form of agriculture that Zambian farmers have traditionally practiced. What are its advantages and disadvantages?
2. What are the characteristics of commercial farming in Zambia and how does it affect local subsistence farmers?
3. Should the government of Zambia continue leasing land to foreign agribusiness companies? Explain why or why not.

Mastering Geography

Looking for additional review and test prep materials? Visit the Study Area in Mastering Geography to enhance your geographic literacy, spatial reasoning skills, and understanding of this chapter's content. Access MapMaster™ interactive maps, video case studies, *In the News* current articles, flashcards, self-study quizzes, an eText of *Contemporary Human Geography*, and more. **pearson.com/mastering/geography**

Key Terms

Agribusiness (p. 232) Commercial agriculture characterized by the integration of different steps in the food-processing industry, usually through ownership by large corporations.

Agricultural revolution (p. 218) The time when human beings first domesticated plants and animals and no longer relied entirely on hunting and gathering.

Agriculture (p. 218) The deliberate effort to modify a portion of Earth's surface through the cultivation of crops and the raising of livestock for sustenance or economic gain.

Aquaculture (p. 230) The cultivation of seafood under controlled conditions.

Cereal grain (p. 222) A grass that yields grain for food.

Commercial agriculture (p. 220) Agriculture undertaken primarily to generate products for sale off the farm.

Conservation tillage (p. 239) A method of soil cultivation that reduces soil erosion and runoff.

Crop (p. 218) Any plant gathered from a field as a harvest during a particular season.

Crop rotation (p. 237) The practice of rotating use of different fields from crop to crop each year to avoid exhausting the soil.

Dairy farm (p. 232) A form of commercial agriculture that specializes in the production of milk and other dairy products.

Desertification (p. 236) Degradation of land, especially in semiarid areas, primarily because of human actions such as excessive crop planting, animal grazing, and tree cutting. Also known as semiarid land degradation.

Dietary energy consumption (p. 222) The amount of food that an individual consumes, measured in kilocalories (Calories in the United States).

Double cropping (p. 237) Harvesting twice a year from the same field.

Fishing (p. 230) The capture of wild fish and other seafood living in the waters.

Food security (p. 224) Physical, social, and economic access at all times to safe and nutritious food sufficient to meet dietary needs and food preferences for an active and healthy life.

Genetically modified organism (GMO) (p. 238) A living organism that possesses a novel combination of genetic material obtained through the use of modern biotechnology.

Grain (p. 222) Seed of a cereal grass.

Green revolution (p. 237) Rapid diffusion of new agricultural technology, especially new high-yield seeds and fertilizers.

Intensive subsistence agriculture (p. 228) A form of subsistence agriculture characteristic of Asia's major population concentrations in which farmers must expend a relatively large amount of effort to produce the maximum feasible yield from a parcel of land.

Milkshed (p. 232) The area surrounding a city from which milk is supplied.

Mixed crop and livestock farming (p. 232) Commercial farming characterized by integration of crops and livestock; most of the crops are fed to animals rather than consumed directly by humans.

No tillage (p. 239) A farming practice that leaves all of the soil undisturbed and the entire residue of the previous year's harvest left untouched on the fields.

Overfishing (p. 231) Capturing fish faster than they can reproduce.

Paddy (p. 228) The Malay word for wet rice, increasingly used to describe a flooded field.

Pastoral nomadism (p. 229) A form of subsistence agriculture based on herding domesticated animals.

Plantation (p. 229) A large farm in tropical and subtropical climates that specializes in the production of one or two crops for sale, usually to a more developed country.

Ranching (p. 233) A form of commercial agriculture in which livestock graze over an extensive area.

Ridge tillage (p. 239) A system of planting crops on ridge tops in order to reduce farm production costs and promote greater soil conservation.

Sawah (p. 228) A flooded field for growing rice.

Shifting cultivation (p. 229) A form of subsistence agriculture in which people shift activity from one field to another; each field is used for crops for a relatively few years and left fallow for a relatively long period.

Subsistence agriculture (p. 220) Agriculture designed primarily to provide food for direct consumption by the farmer and the farmer's family.

Truck farming (p. 233) Commercial gardening and fruit farming, so named for the Middle English word truck, meaning "barter" or "exchange of commodities."

Undernourishment (p. 225) Dietary energy consumption that is continuously below the minimum requirement for maintaining a healthy life and carrying out light physical activity.

Wet rice (p. 228) Rice planted on dry land in a nursery and then moved to a deliberately flooded field to promote growth.

Explore

Rice fields in Asia

Use Google Earth to examine how rice is grown in Asia.

Search for *Pura Desa Banjar Calo, Indonesia*. ***Zoom*** in to around 800 meters. Move the image so that *Pura Desa Banjar Calo* is on the far left of the screen.

1. Immediately to the east of Pura Desa Banjar Calo is patch of dense forest. Describe the landscape to the east of the forest patch. What do the many parallel features represent?
2. ***Search*** for *Jl. Melati, Indonesia*, which is the north-south road to the east of the parallel features in question 1. ***Drag*** *Street View* to *Jl. Melati*. ***Zoom*** in on the west side of the road. Why is the west side of the road wet?

▶ **9.CR.6 RICE FIELD, INDONESIA**

Geospatial Analysis

Log in to the Mastering Geography Study Area to access MapMaster 2.0.

Agriculture and climate in China

Eastern China is divided into three principal agricultural regions. How closely do they follow climate regions?

Add the *Agricultural Regions* layer. ***Select*** the *Settings* icon from the *Legend*, and select *Show Political Labels*. ***Add*** the *Climate Zones* data layer and ***select*** *Split map window*. ***Zoom*** to East Asia.

1. What is the principal form of agriculture in southeastern China? Hover over this area. What is the predominant climate?
2. What are the principal forms of agriculture in northeastern China? What is the most common climate?
3. What are the principal forms of agriculture in inland China? What is the predominant climate?
4. Why does the predominant agriculture vary among the climate regions (refer to pages 228-299)?

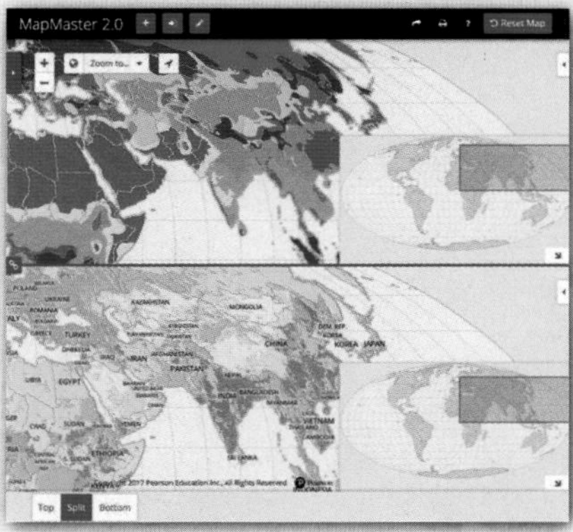

◀ **9.CR.7 AGRICULTURE REGIONS, AND CLIMATE ZONES OF EAST ASIA**

CHAPTER

10 Development

The average person in the world is better off today than in the twentieth century. The average person possesses more wealth, has had more education, and will live longer than someone in the previous century. But not everyone is better off. Development is considered a process of improving people's prospects of leading long and healthy lives, acquiring knowledge, and obtaining adequate resources.

◀ Selling fruit alongside road construction, Cameroon.

KEY ISSUES

1 How Does Development Vary Among Countries?

The United Nations divides countries according to their level of development. The UN's Human Development Index is the basis for the allocation.

2 What Inequalities Are Found In Development?

According to UN development measures, the status of women is lower than that of men in every country. Within countries, the level of development also varies by place of residence.

3 How Do Countries Become More Developed?

Self-sufficiency and international trade are two paths to development. International trade has become more important, although countries have had increasing concerns with the path.

4 What Progress Towards Development Are Countries Achieving?

By most measures, the level of development has improved. The UN has adopted goals that emphasize sustainable development.

LOCATIONS IN THIS CHAPTER

London, *p. 253*
Canterbury, *p. 263*
France, *p. 248*
Turkey, *p. 251*
Delhi, *pp. 256, 257*
South Korea, *p. 259*
South Sudan, *p. 247*
Hong Kong, *p. 258*
Laos, *p. 262*
Singapore, *p. 257*
Brazil, *p. 251*
Bolivia, *p. 244*
Uganda, *p. 248*
São Paulo, *p. 251*
Kenya, *p. 262*
Islamabad, *p. 252*
Kerala, *p. 260*
Tiruppar, *p. 263*

maternal mortality rate
gross national income
literacy rate
primary sector
tertiary sector
foreign direct investment
gender inequality index
sustainable development goals
gender related development index
education
secondary sector
fair trade
reproductive health
developed country
structural adjustment program
empowerment
human development index
world trade organization
developing country
international monetary fund
international trade
self sufficiency
inequality adjusted HDI
microfinance

▲ 10.1.1 A DEVELOPING COUNTRY: BOLIVIA

Development Regions

- Measure a country's level of development.

Earth's nearly 200 countries can be classified according to their level of **development**, which is the process of improving the material conditions of people through diffusion of knowledge and technology. Every place lies at some point along a continuum of development.

The development process is continuous, involving never-ending actions to constantly improve the health and prosperity of the people. Because many countries cluster at the high or low end of the continuum of development, they can be divided into two groups:

- A **developed country**, also known as a more developed country (MDC) and by the UN as a very high developed country, has progressed further along the development continuum.
- A **developing country**, also frequently called a less developed country (LDC), has made some progress toward development, though less than the developed countries (Figure 10.1.1).

Recognizing that progress has varied widely among developing countries, the UN divides them into high, medium, and low developing.

Human Development Index

To measure the level of development of every country, the UN has created the **Human Development Index (HDI)**. The UN has computed HDIs for countries every year since 1980, although it has occasionally modified the method of computation. The highest HDI possible is 1.0, or 100 percent. The HDI considers development to be a function of three factors:

- A decent standard of living.
- A long and healthy life.
- Access to knowledge.

Each country gets an overall HDI score based on these three factors (Figure 10.1.2).

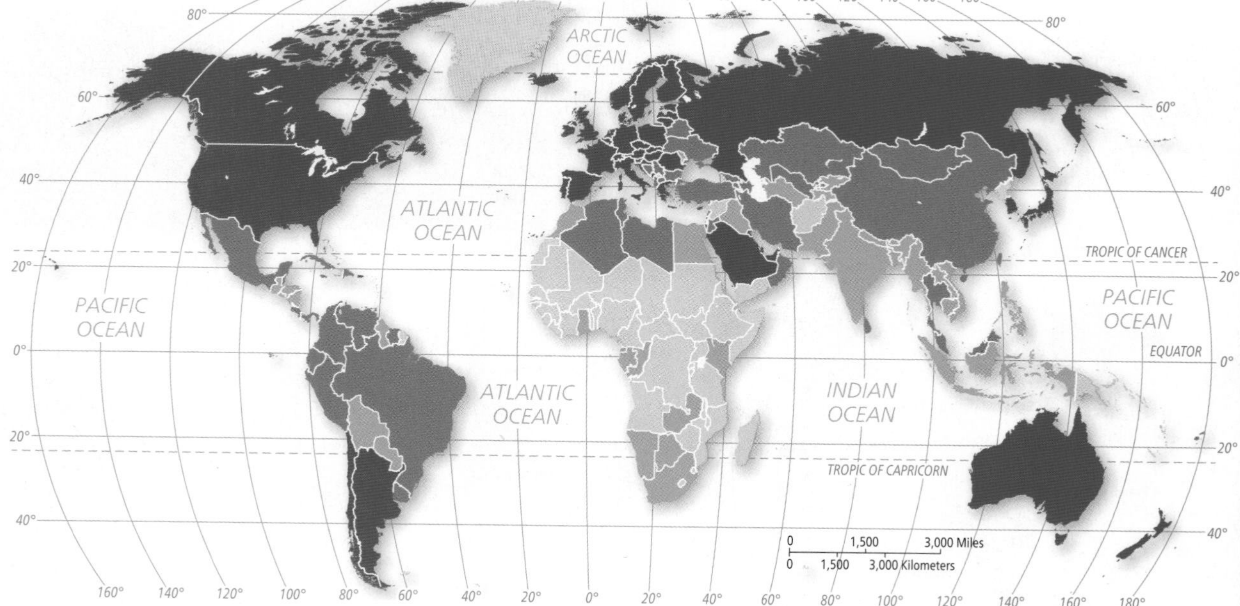

▶ 10.1.2 HUMAN DEVELOPMENT INDEX (HDI)

- Very high developed (above 0.80)
- High developing (0.70–0.80)
- Medium developing (0.55–0.69)
- Low developing (below 0.55)
- no data

Regional Differences in Development

Geographers divide the world into two developed and seven developing regions (Figure 10.1.3). Each region has an overall HDI score, although as we will see in this chapter regions sometimes have unexpectedly high or low scores in particular factors.

In addition to the nine regions, three other distinctive areas can be identified. Japan and South Korea are classified separately rather than included with the rest of East Asia, because their level of development is much higher than that of their neighbors. The South Pacific is a much less populous area than the nine development regions; Australia (its most populous country), and New Zealand are developed, but the area's other countries are developing. The UN classifies Russia as a developed country.

▼ 10.1.3 **DEVELOPMENT REGIONS**
The nine world regions are shown with their regional HDI score.

NORTH AMERICA
HDI = .92
Both the United States and Canada are very high developed.

▲ **DISNEY WORLD, ORLANDO, FLORIDA**

EUROPE
HDI = .86
All but a handful are very high developed.

▲ **MERCEDES-BENZ FACTORY, BREMEN, GERMANY**

SOUTHWEST ASIA & NORTH AFRICA
HDI = .73
Medium developing on average, but wide variation between high developing (Saudi Arabia) and low developing (Yemen).

▲ **OIL DRILL, BAHRAIN**

CENTRAL ASIA
HDI = .86
Medium developing on average, but wide variation between high developing (Iran) and low developing (Afghanistan).

▲ **ASTANA, KAZAKHSTAN**

EAST ASIA
HDI = .74
China is high developing.

▲ **SHANGHAI, CHINA**

SOUTHEAST ASIA
HDI = .70
Most are medium developing.

▲ **PORT OF SINGAPORE**

LATIN AMERICA
HDI = .73
Most are high developing.

▲ **SÃO PAULO, BRAZIL**

SUB-SAHARAN AFRICA
HDI = .51
Most are low developing.

▲ **RAILWAY UNDER CONSTRUCTION BETWEEN NAIROBI AND MOMBASA, KENYA**

SOUTH ASIA
HDI = .63
Most are medium developing.

▲ **MUMBAI, INDIA**

A Decent Standard of Living

- **Explain standard of living as a factor in the HDI.**

Having enough wealth for a decent standard of living is key to development. The average individual in a developed country earns a much higher income than the average individual in a developing one. Geographers observe that people generate and spend their wealth in different ways in developed countries than in developing countries.

Income

The UN measures the standard of living in countries through a complex index called *gross national income per capita at purchasing power parity* (Figure 10.2.1):

- **Gross national income (GNI)** is the value of the output of goods and services produced in a country in a year, including money that leaves and enters the country.
- **Purchasing power parity (PPP)** is an adjustment made to the GNI to account for differences among countries in the cost of goods. For example, if a resident of country A has the same income as a resident of country B but must pay more for a Big Mac or a Starbucks latte, the resident of country B is better off.

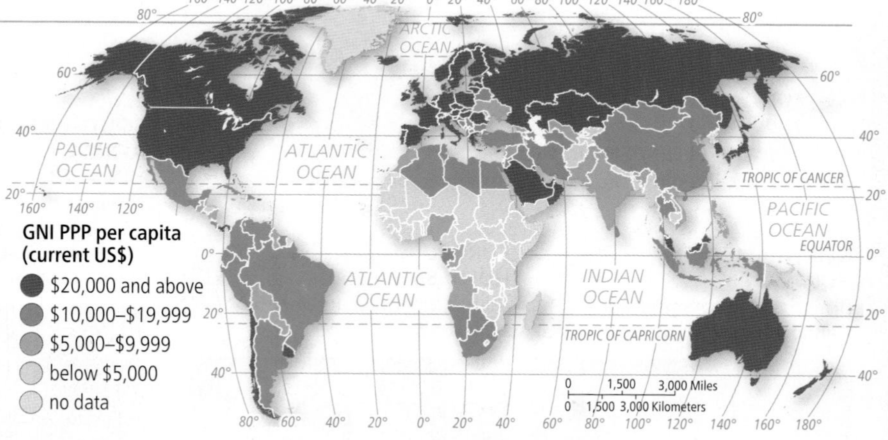

▲ 10.2.1 **INCOME**
GNI per capita PPP is highest in developed countries. The lowest figures are in sub-Saharan Africa and South Asia.

Dividing GNI by total population estimates the contribution made by the average individual toward generating a country's wealth in a year. Some studies refer to **gross domestic product**, which also measures the value of the output of goods and services produced in a country in a year, but it does not account for money that leaves and enters the country.

The higher the per capita GNI, the greater is the potential for ensuring that all citizens can enjoy a comfortable life. Per capita GNI measures average (mean) wealth, not the distribution of wealth. So if only a few people receive much of the GNI, then the standard of living for the majority may be lower than the average figure implies.

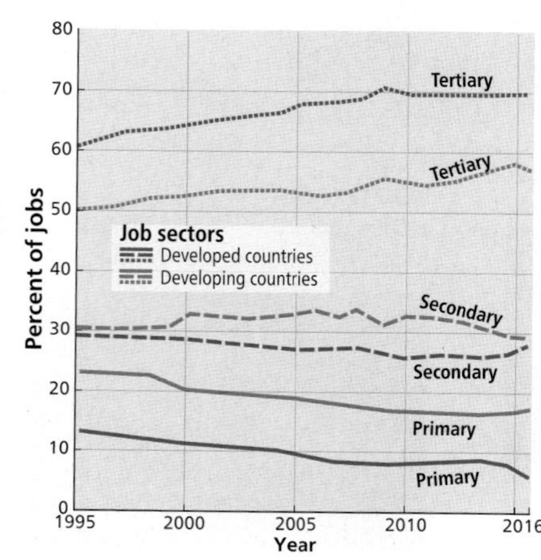

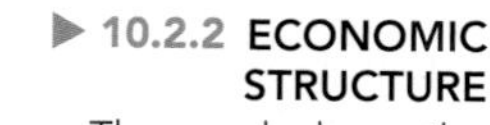

▶ 10.2.2 **ECONOMIC STRUCTURE**
The graph shows the changing contribution to GNI by the three sectors of jobs.

Economic Structure

Average per capita income is higher in developed countries because people typically earn their living by different means than in developing countries. Jobs fall into three categories:

- **Primary sector:** Directly extracting materials from Earth through agriculture or through mining, fishing, and forestry. The share of GNI accounted for by the primary sector is relatively high in developing countries, though the share is decreasing (Figure 10.2.2). The low share in developed countries indicates that a handful of farmers produce enough food for the rest of society.
- **Secondary sector:** Manufacturing raw materials into products. The share of GNI accounted for by the secondary sector has decreased in developed countries.
- **Tertiary sector:** Providing goods and services to people in exchange for payment, such as retailing, banking, law, education, and government. The share of GNI accounted for by the tertiary sector is relatively large and increasing in both developing and developed countries.

Productivity

Workers in developed countries are more productive than those in developing countries. **Productivity** is the value of a particular product compared to the amount of labor needed to make it. Productivity can be measured by the **value added** per capita. The value added in manufacturing is the gross value of a product minus the costs of raw materials and energy. Workers in developed countries produce more with less effort because they have access to more machines, tools, and equipment to perform much of the work.

Consumer Goods

Part of the wealth generated in developed countries is used to purchase goods and services. Products such as motor vehicles (Figure 10.2.3) and electronic devices (Figure 10.2.4) that promote better transportation and communications, are accessible to nearly all residents in developed countries and are vital to the economy's functioning and growth. Most people in developing countries are familiar with these goods, but may not have enough income to purchase them.

Technological change is helping to reduce the gap between developed and developing countries in access to communications. Cell phone ownership is expanding rapidly in developing countries because these phones obtain service from a tower or satellite and therefore do not require the costly investment of connecting wires to each individual building (Figures 10.2.5 and 10.2.6).

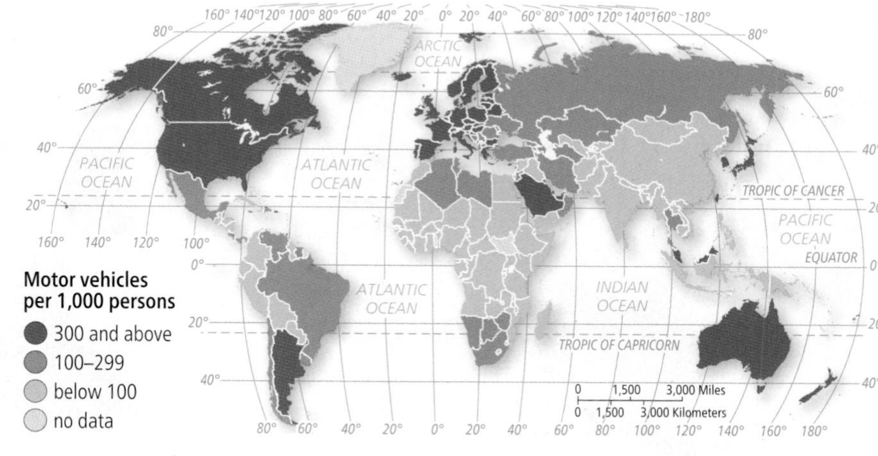

▲ **10.2.3 MOTOR VEHICLES**
The highest level of motor vehicle ownership is in North America, and the lowest is in South Asia.

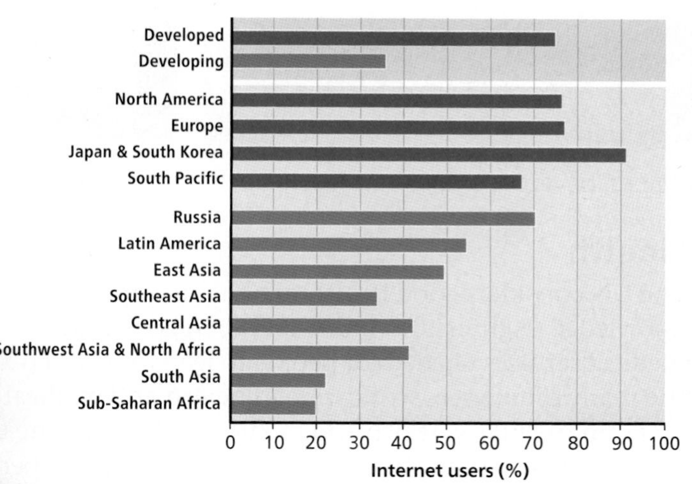

◀ **10.2.4 INTERNET USERS**
The highest level of internet users is in North America, and the lowest is in sub-Saharan Africa.

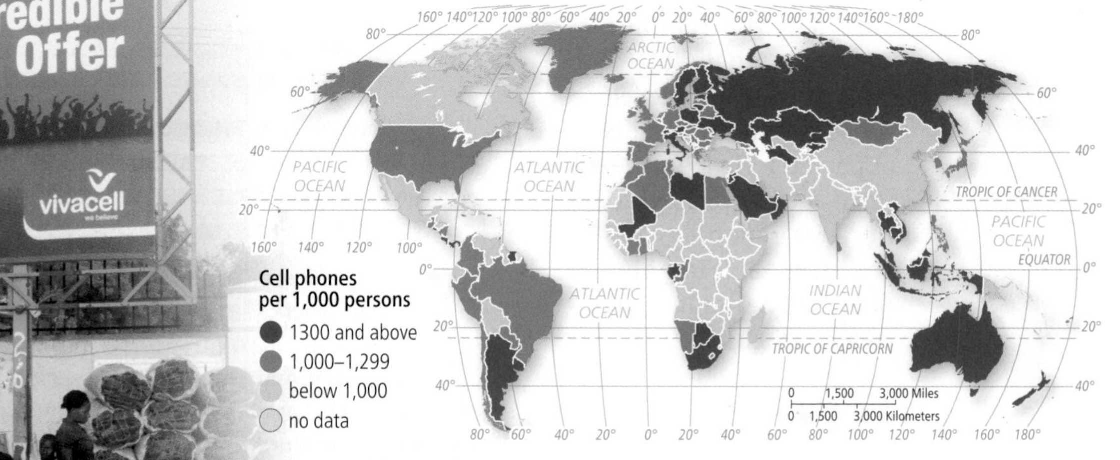

▲ **10.2.5 CELL PHONES**

◀ **10.2.6 CELL PHONES: SOUTH SUDAN**
Cell phone service is increasing even in South Sudan, which is classified as a low developing country, with one of the world's lowest HDI scores.

Access to Knowledge & Health

- **Explain education and health as factors in the HDI.**

Development is about more than wealth. The UN believes that development is about people becoming healthier and wiser, not just wealthier.

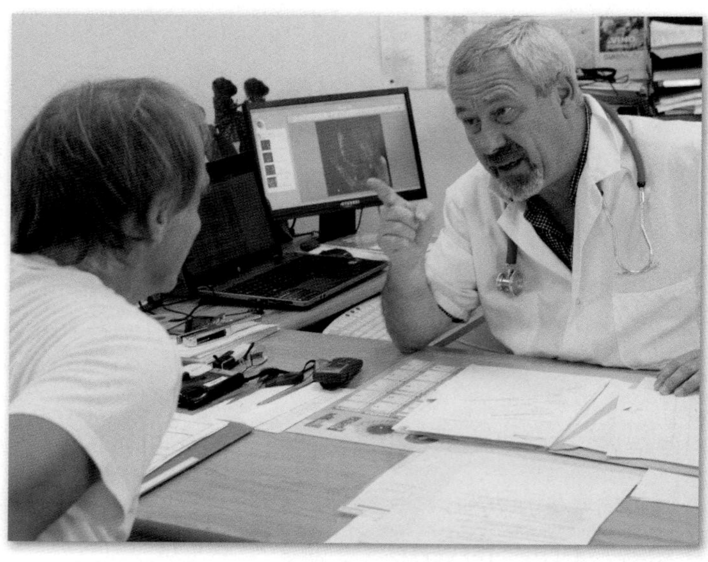

▲ 10.3.1 MEDICAL SERVICES, DEVELOPED COUNTRY: FRANCE

▲ 10.3.2 MEDICAL SERVICES, DEVELOPING COUNTRY: UGANDA

Health

The UN considers good health to be as an important a measure of development as wealth and knowledge (Figures 10.3.1 and 10.3.2). A goal of development is to provide the nutrition and medical services needed for people to lead long and healthy lives. Chapter 2 discussed in detail the many differences worldwide in health and medical services.

From the many health and medical indicators, the UN has selected life expectancy at birth as the contributor to the HDI (Figure 10.3.3). Life expectancy at birth was defined in Chapter 2 as the average number of years a newborn infant can expect to live at current mortality levels. A baby born this year is expected to live on average until age 71 worldwide, until 80 in developed countries, and to only 60 in sub-Saharan Africa (refer to Figure 2.6.4).

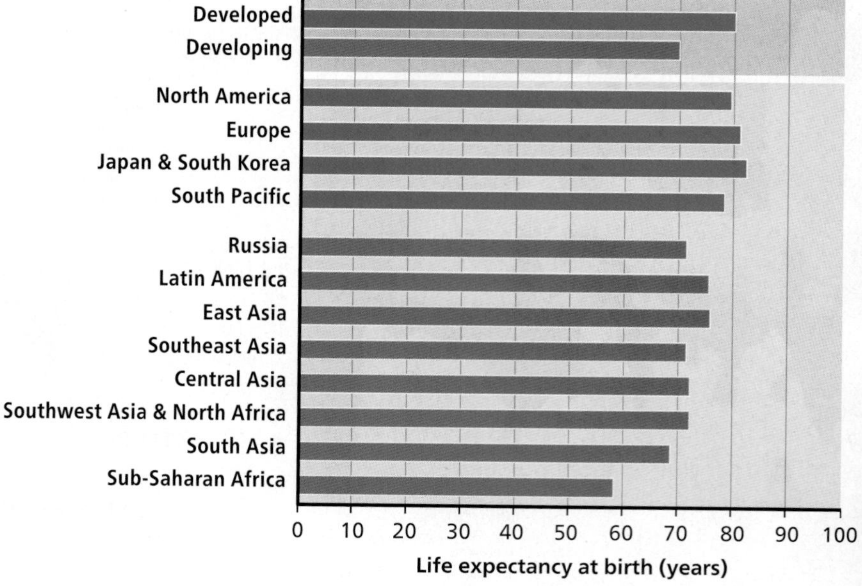

▶ 10.3.3 LIFE EXPECTANCY AT BIRTH BY DEVELOPMENT REGION
The highest life expectancy among the nine development regions is in North America, and the lowest is in sub-Saharan Africa.

Education

The UN considers years of schooling to be the most critical measure of the ability of an individual to gain access to knowledge needed for development. The assumption is that no matter how poor the school, the longer the pupils attend, the more likely they are to learn something. To form the access to knowledge component of HDI, the UN combines two measures of quantity of schooling:

- **Years of schooling for today's adults.** The number of years that the average person aged 25 or older in a country has spent in school (Figure 10.3.4). Adults have spent an average of 11.5 years in school in developed countries, compared to only 4.7 years in South Asia and sub-Saharan Africa.
- **Expected years of schooling for today's youth.** The number of years that the UN forecasts an average 5-year-old will spend in school. The UN expects that 5-year-olds will spend an average of 16.3 years in school; in other words, roughly half of today's 5-year-olds will graduate from college in developed countries. On the other hand, the expected average is 9.3 years in sub-Saharan Africa and 10.2 years in South Asia—an improvement over current figures but a smaller increase than in developed countries.

Though not calculated in the HDI, other indicators can measure regional variations in access to knowledge:

- **Pupil/teacher ratio.** The fewer pupils a teacher has, the more likely that each student will receive effective instruction (Figure 10.3.5).
- **Literacy rate.** The **literacy rate** is the percentage of a country's people who can read and write (Figure 10.3.6).

Improved education is a major goal of many developing countries, but funds are scarce. Education may receive a higher percentage of GNI in developing countries, but those countries' GNI is far lower to begin with, so they spend far less per pupil than do developed countries.

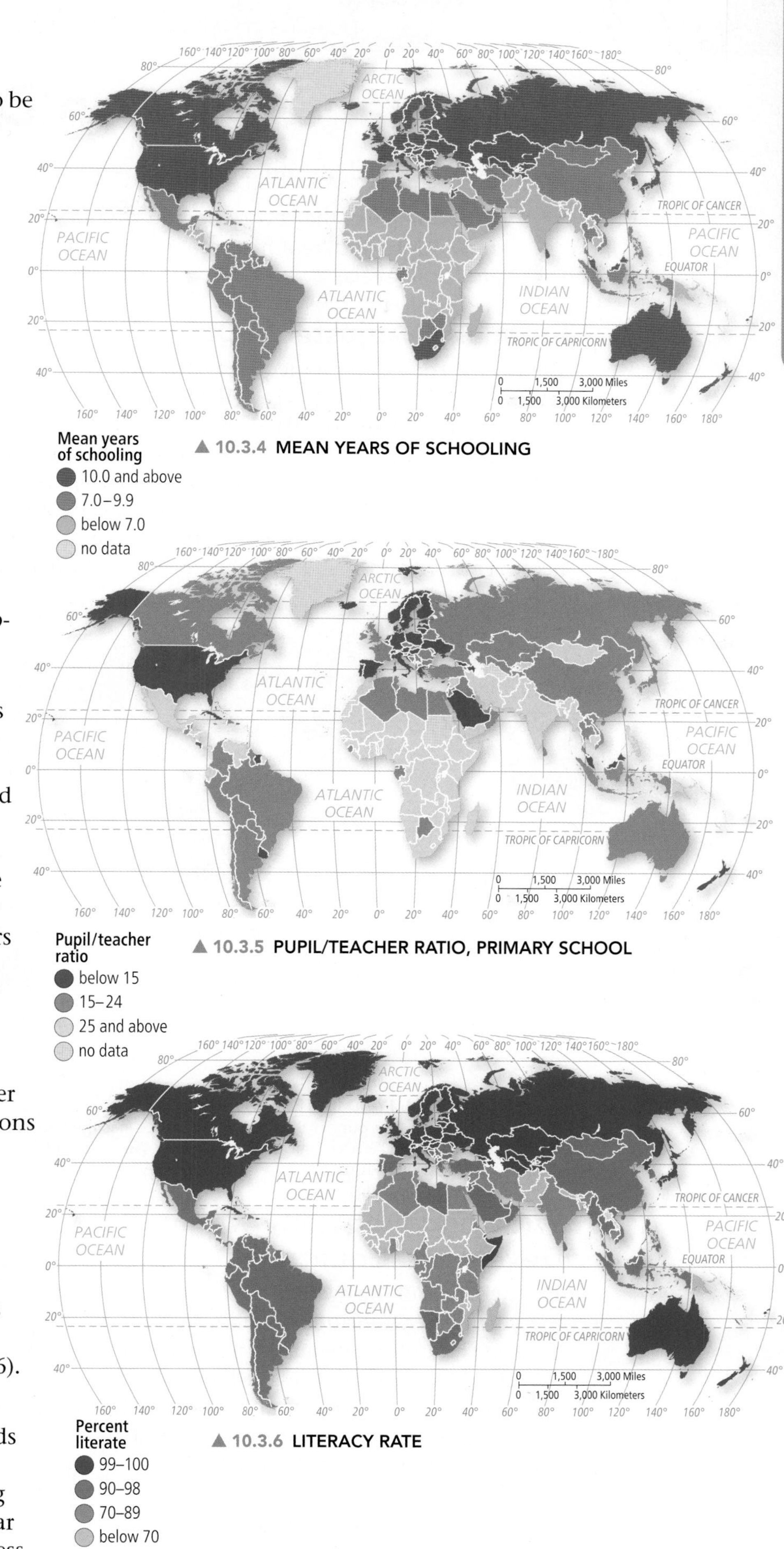

▲ 10.3.4 MEAN YEARS OF SCHOOLING

▲ 10.3.5 PUPIL/TEACHER RATIO, PRIMARY SCHOOL

▲ 10.3.6 LITERACY RATE

Unequal & Uneven Development

- Describe the UN's measures of inequality.

The UN believes that every person should have access to decent standards of living, knowledge, and health. In reality, inequality occurs at the international, regional, and local levels.

Inequality-Adjusted HDI

To measure the extent of inequality, the UN has created the **inequality-adjusted HDI (IHDI)**. The IHDI modifies the HDI to account for inequality within a country. Under perfect equality, the HDI and the IHDI are the same.

If the IHDI is lower than the HDI, the country has some inequality; the greater the difference in the two measures, the greater the inequality. For example, a country where only a few people have high incomes, college degrees, and good health care would have a lower IHDI than a country where differences in income, level of education, and access to health care are minimal. Developed countries have the lowest gap between HDI and IHDI, indicating a relatively modest level of inequality by worldwide standards (Figure 10.4.1). The lowest scores (highest inequality) are in sub-Saharan Africa and South Asia. The score may be low in Southwest Asia & North Africa, but the UN is unable to assign a score because it lacks data from many of the region's countries.

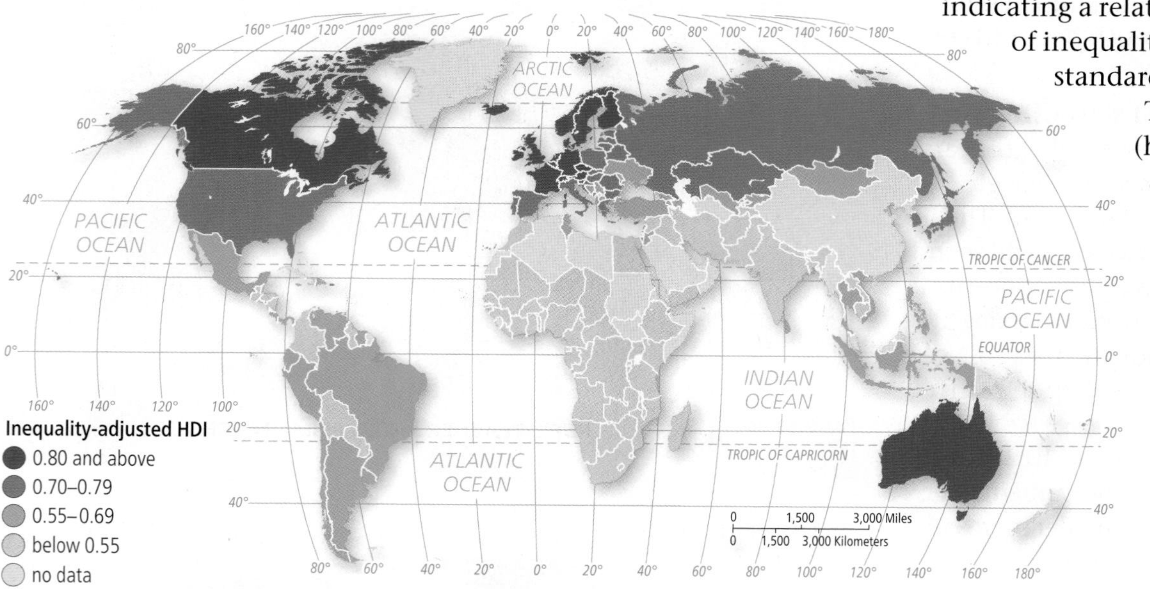

▲ 10.4.1 INEQUALITY-ADJUSTED HDI
The lower the score, the greater the inequality. Europe has the highest score, hence the least inequality. South Asia and sub-Saharan Africa have the lowest scores and therefore the greatest degree of inequality.

Widening Inequality within Developed Countries

Through most of the twentieth century, the gap between rich and poor narrowed in developed countries. Inequality was reduced because developed countries used some of their wealth to extend health care and education to more people, and to provide some financial assistance to poorer people. Since 1980, however, inequality has increased in most developed countries, including the United States and the United Kingdom (Figure 10.4.2).

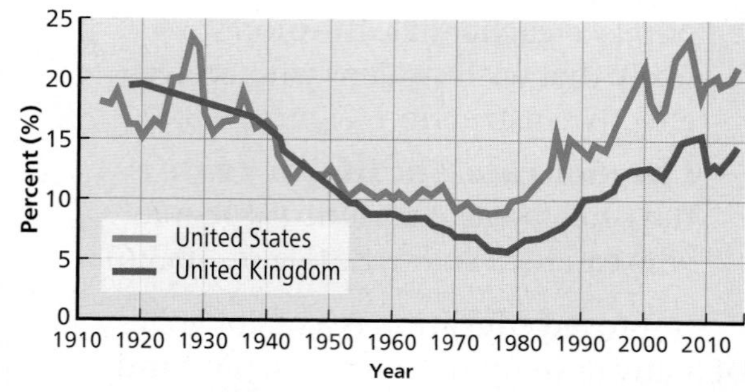

▲ 10.4.2 WIDENING INEQUALITY IN THE U.S. AND U.K.
The share of total national income received by the richest 1 percent declined in the United States and the United Kingdom for most of the twentieth century but has increased in recent decades.

Inequality within Developing Countries

Brazil and Turkey are among the world's largest and most populous countries. At the national scale, the two countries fall somewhere in the middle of the pack in HDI. Among the 188 countries with HDI scores, Brazil ranks 79 and Turkey 71.

The extent of inequality within these countries can be seen in two ways. First is the difference between the HDI and IHDI. The two countries have similar HDI scores, but the gap between HDI and IHDI is much higher in Brazil than in Turkey, indicating that Brazil has a higher degree of inequality than does Turkey.

▲ 10.4.3 INEQUALITY WITHIN TURKEY

Inequality can also be seen through differences in GDP per capita among states or provinces within the countries. In both Turkey (Figure 10.4.3) and Brazil (Figure 10.4.4), the GDP per capita is around $20,000 in the wealthiest areas and only $4,000 in the poorest areas. This is a much larger difference among regions than is found within developed countries. Brazil's wealthiest regions are clustered in the southeast coast, including the country's two largest cities São Paulo and Rio de Janeiro.

Inequality can also be seen in contrasts among neighborhoods within the largest cities of developing countries (see Chapter 13). Wealthy people may live in modern high-rise apartments or single-family homes, while poor people live in primitive structures (Figure 10.4.5).

Developed countries also have regional internal variations in GDP per capita, but they are less extreme than in developing countries. In the United States, for example, the GDP per capita is 22 percent above the national average in the wealthiest region (New England) and 10 percent below the national average in the poorest region (Southeast).

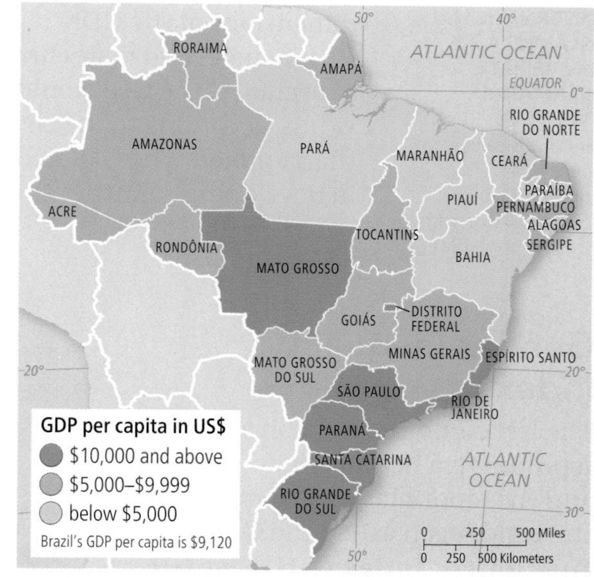

▲ 10.4.4 INEQUALITY WITHIN BRAZIL

▼ 10.4.5 INEQUALITY WITHIN BRAZIL: SÃO PAULO, BRAZIL

Gender Inequality

- Describe the UN's measures of gender inequality.

▲ **10.5.1 FEMALE CAMPUS, INTERNATIONAL ISLAMIC UNIVERSITY, ISLAMABAD, PAKISTAN**
Separate campuses were established for men and women, in accordance with Muslim principles.

A country's overall level of development can mask inequalities in the status of men and women (Figure 10.5.1). The UN uses two indexes to measure gender inequality: the Gender-related Development Index (GDI) and the Gender Inequality Index (GII).

Gender-Related Development Index

The UN combines Human Development Index data on income, education, and life expectancy in a measure of the gender gap called the **Gender-related Development Index (GDI)**. The GDI uses the same methodology as the HDI, described in the previous section. Countries are ranked based on their deviation from gender parity in the three dimensions of the HDI.

If females and males had precisely the same levels of income, education, and life expectancy, the GDI would be 1.000. In fact, the overall GDI in the world is 0.920. In other words, according to the UN index, the level of achievement is 8 percent lower for women than for men. The GDI in developed regions is nearly the same for women and men, whereas in developing countries the index is 10 percent lower for women than for men (Figure 10.5.2).

Gender Inequality Index

The UN combines data on reproductive health, empowerment, and the labor market in a measure of the gender gap called the **Gender Inequaltiy Index (GII)**. The GII uses similar methodology to the IHDI discussed on the previous page. The higher the GII, the greater is the inequality between men and women. A score of 0 would mean that men and women fare equally, and a score of 1.0 would mean the maximum degree of inequality between women and men.

The GII is higher in developing countries than in developed ones (Figure 10.5.3). Reproductive health is the largest contributor to gender inequality in some developing regions. At the other extreme, 10 countries in Europe have GIIs less than 0.1, meaning that men and women are nearly equal. In general, countries with high HDIs have low GIIs and vice versa.

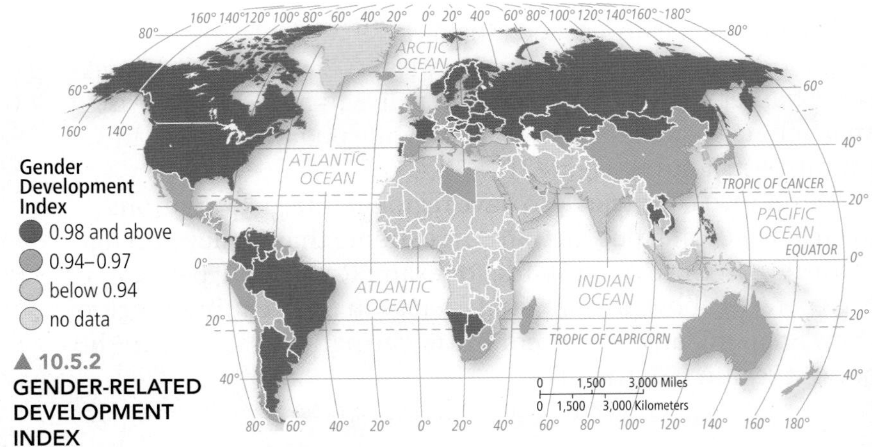

▲ **10.5.2 GENDER-RELATED DEVELOPMENT INDEX**

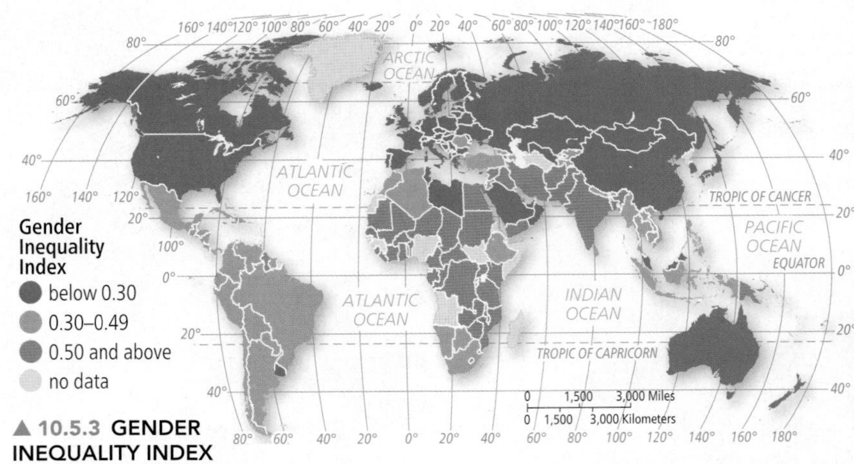

▲ **10.5.3 GENDER INEQUALITY INDEX**

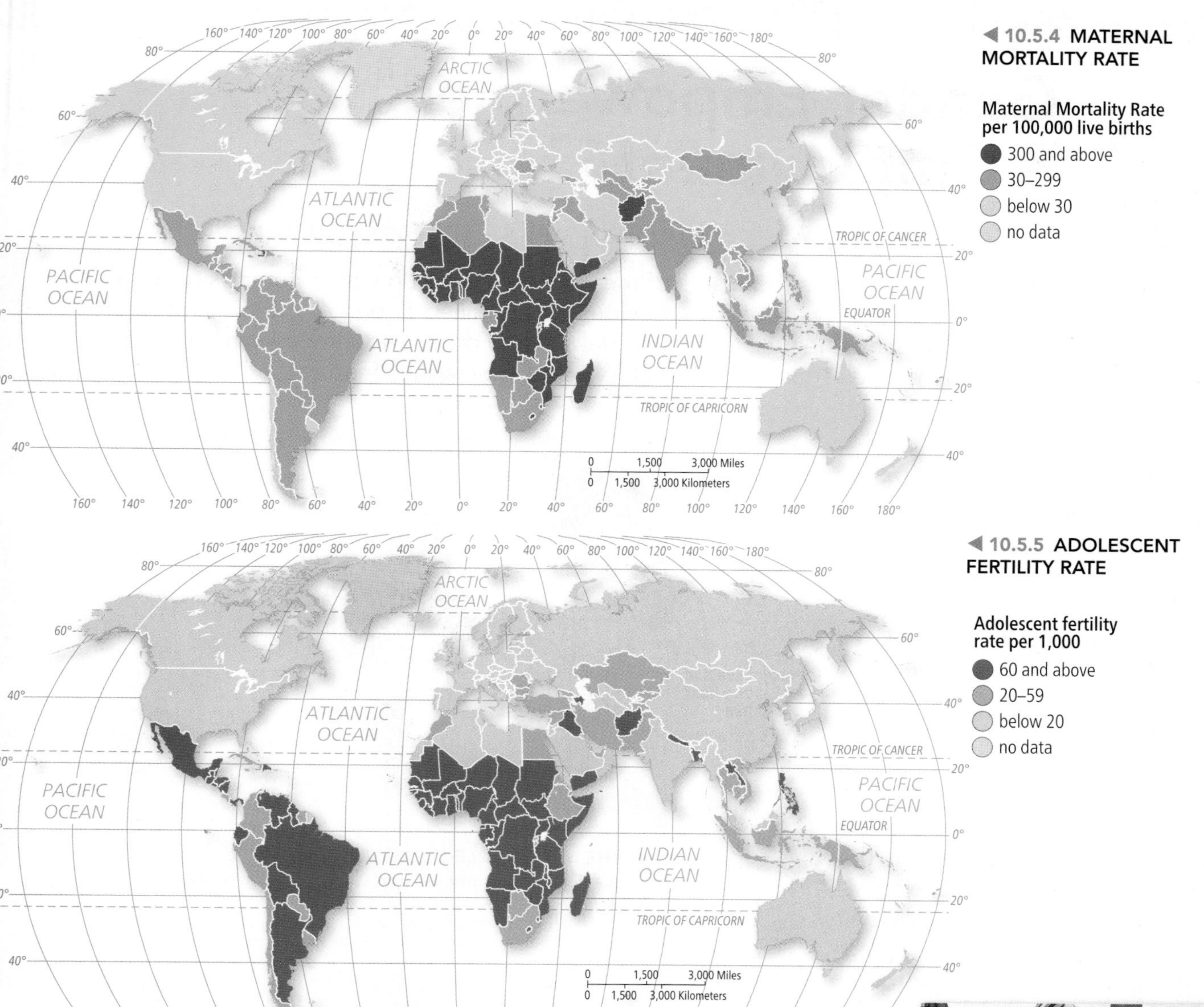

◀ 10.5.4 MATERNAL MORTALITY RATE

Maternal Mortality Rate per 100,000 live births
- 300 and above
- 30–299
- below 30
- no data

◀ 10.5.5 ADOLESCENT FERTILITY RATE

Adolescent fertility rate per 1,000
- 60 and above
- 20–59
- below 20
- no data

Reproductive Health

The effects of reproduction are significantly greater for females by nature. The reproductive health dimension of the GII is based on two indicators: The maternal mortality rate was defined in Chapter 2 as the number of women who die giving birth per 100,000 births. The ratio is 16 deaths of mothers per 100,000 live births in developed countries and 171 in developing countries. The highest rates (most deaths per births) are in sub-Saharan Africa (Figure 10.5.4). The UN estimates that 150,000 women and 1.6 million children die each year between the onset of labor and 48 hours after birth.

The **adolescent fertility rate** is the number of births per 1,000 women ages 15 to 19. The rate is 19 births per 1,000 women ages 15 to 19 in developed countries and 53 in developing countries. The teenage pregnancy rate is below 10 per 1,000 in most European countries, where most couples use some form of contraception. In sub-Saharan Africa, where gender inequality is high, contraceptive use is below 10 percent, and the teenage pregnancy rate is 110 per 1,000 (Figure 10.5.5).

The UN includes reproductive health as a contributor to GII because in countries where effective control of reproduction is universal, women have fewer children, and maternal and child health are improved (Figure 10.5.6). Women in developing regions are more likely than women in developed regions to die in childbirth and to give birth as teenagers. Every country that offers women a full range of reproductive health options has a very low total fertility rate.

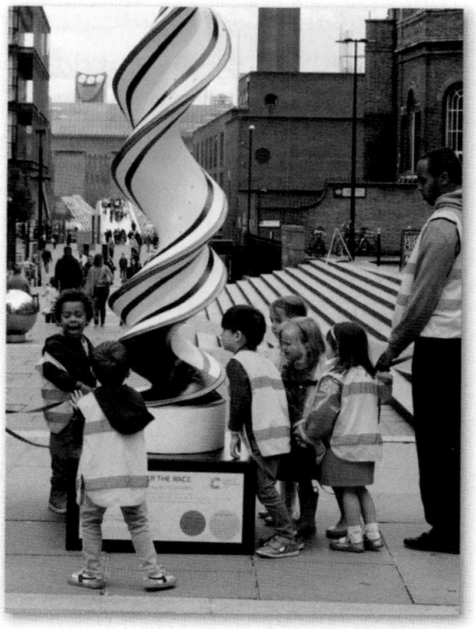

▲ 10.5.6 CHILD CARE: DEVELOPED COUNTRY
Nursery school children wear high visibility jackets as they are escorted on a walk, London, United Kingdom.

Gender Empowerment & Employment

- Describe empowerment-related components of gender inequality.

The GII combines three sets of measures to come up with a composite score for gender inequality. The previous page looked at one of the three measures, reproductive health. This page looks at the other two: empowerment and employment (see What's Your Development Geography? feature).

Empowerment

In the context of gender inequality, empowerment refers to the ability of women to achieve improvements in their own status—that is, to achieve economic and political power. The empowerment dimension of GII is measured by two indicators: The percentage of seats held by women in the national legislature and the percentage of women who have completed some secondary school.

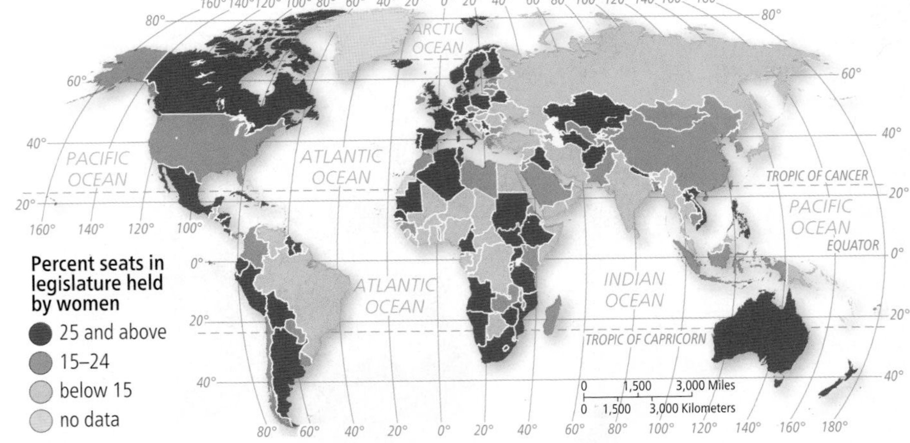

▲ 10.6.1 WOMEN IN THE NATIONAL LEGISLATURE
The highest percentages are in Europe, and the lowest are in Southwest Asia and North Africa.

National Legislature. No particular gender-specific skills are required to be elected as a representative and to serve effectively. But in every country of the world, both developed and developing, fewer women than men hold positions of political power (Figure 10.6.1).

Although more women than men vote in most places, only one country has a national parliament or congress with a majority of women: Rwanda. With a few exceptions, the highest percentages are in Europe, where women comprise approximately one-fourth of the members of national parliaments. The lowest rates are in Southwest Asia & North Africa.

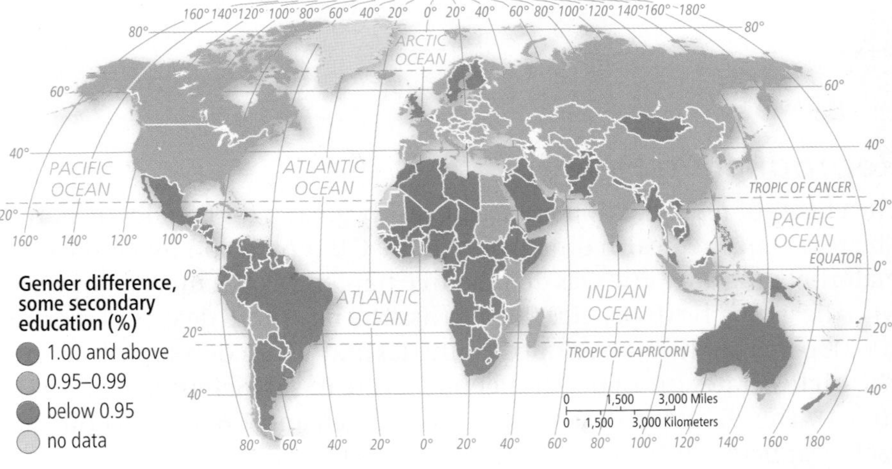

▲ 10.6.2 GENDER DIFFERENCES IN SECONDARY SCHOOL
A figure above 1.00 means that more girls than boys have some secondary school.

In the United States, 19 percent of the House of Representatives (84 of 435 members) were women in 2017. The percentage is much lower than the average of "houses" in other developed countries and slightly below average for all countries in the world. For example, in 2017 Canada's House of Commons included 27 percent women, and the United Kingdom's House of Commons included 32 percent women.

Secondary School. Worldwide, 54 percent of women have completed some secondary (high) school, compared to 64 percent of men. In North America, girls are more likely than boys to complete some high school, and boys are slightly ahead in Europe. In developing countries, boys are much more likely than girls to be high school graduates. For every 10 boys who attend high school in developing countries, only 6 girls attend (Figure 10.6.2). The gap in education between girls and boys is especially high in South Asia.

Employment

The **female labor force participation rate** is the percentage of women holding full-time jobs outside the home. Worldwide, 51 percent of women work outside the home, compared to 77 percent of men. In general, women in developed countries are more likely than women in developing countries to hold full-time jobs outside the home.

Figures vary widely among developing regions. South Asia and Southwest Asia & North Africa have substantial gaps between male and female labor participation, whereas East Asia and sub-Saharan Africa have smaller gaps (Figure 10.6.3). Women hold jobs in agriculture or services in sub-Saharan Africa, even while they have the world's highest fertility rates.

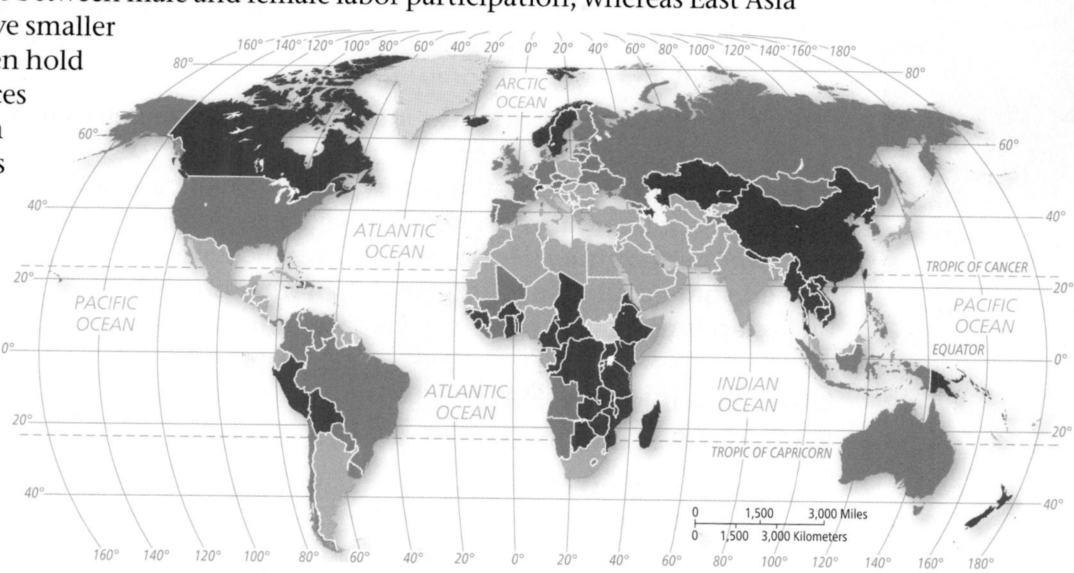

10.6.3 LABOR FORCE PARTICIPATION
A lower number means that relatively few women participate in the labor force compared with men.

Percent of women in the labor force
- 60 and above
- 50–59
- below 50
- no data

WHAT'S YOUR DEVELOPMENT GEOGRAPHY?

Your Community's Gender Inequality Index (GII)

The UN has found that gender inequality has declined since the 1990s in all but 3 of 157 countries for which time-series data are available (Figure 10.6.4). The improvement has been relatively modest in the United States. Furthermore, the United States has a GII rank of only 43, although it ranks tenth in the world on HDI. The UN points to two factors accounting for the relatively low U.S. GII ranking:

1. Compared with other very high HDI countries, the United States has a much higher birth rate among teenage women and a higher mortality rate among women during childbirth. The rate of teen births in the United States was 22 per 1,000 in 2015. The rate varies widely among U.S. states. Go to **www.cdc.gov** and ***search*** teen births. **Select** *Fast Stats-Teen Births*, then ***select*** *Births: Final Data*
   a. Is your state higher or lower than the national average?
   b. What might account for the variation?
2. The percentage of women in the national legislature is lower in the United States than in other high HDI countries. Women account for around 20 percent of the U.S. Congress.
   a. What percentage of your state's legislature are women?
   b. What percentage of your local community's elected body are women?
   c. Are these percentages higher or lower than the national average?

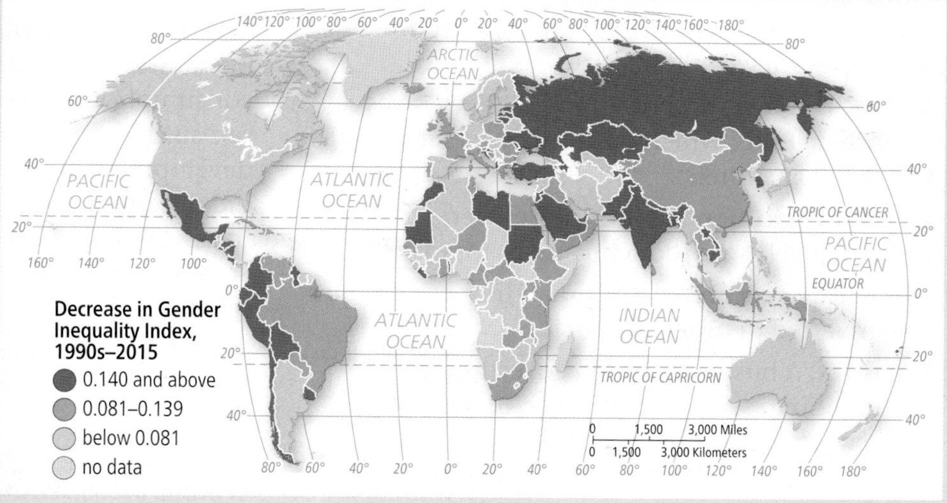

Decrease in Gender Inequality Index, 1990s–2015
- 0.140 and above
- 0.081–0.139
- below 0.081
- no data

10.6.4 TREND IN GENDER INEQUALITY
The map shows the change in GII from the late 1990s to 2015. Most countries have seen an improvement in the GII.

▲ 10.7.1 **SELF-SUFFICIENCY IN INDIA: BUREAUCRACY** Bureaucrats lacking office space work on the sidewalk in Delhi.

Two Paths to Development

- **Compare and contrast the principal development strategies.**

To promote development, most developing countries choose one of two models:

- **Self-sufficiency.** Countries encourage domestic production of goods, discourage foreign ownership of businesses and resources, and protect their businesses from international competition.
- **International trade.** Countries open themselves to foreign investment and international markets.

For most of the twentieth century, self-sufficiency was the more popular of the development alternatives. International trade became more popular beginning in the late twentieth century. However, the global economic slowdown that began in 2008 caused some countries to rethink the international trade approach. Each path has advantages and challenges (see Debate It! feature).

Self-Sufficiency Path

Key elements of the self-sufficiency path to development include the following:

- **Balanced growth.** Investment is spread as equally as possible across all sectors of a country's economy and in all regions.
- **Import barriers.** The import of goods is limited through barriers, including setting high taxes (tariffs) on imported goods to make them more expensive than domestic goods, fixing quotas to limit the quantity of imported goods, and requiring licenses in order to restrict the number of legal importers.

Self-Sufficiency Example: India

For several decades after it gained independence from the United Kingdom in 1947, India was a leading example of the self-sufficiency path. Among India's strategies were the following:

- **Import licenses.** To import goods into India, a company needed a license, which was hard to get because several dozen government agencies had to approve the request (Figure 10.7.1).
- **Quotas.** Companies with import licenses were severely restricted by the government in the quantities they could import.
- **Taxes.** The government imposed heavy taxes on imported goods, which doubled or even tripled the prices to consumers.
- **Export limits.** Indian businesses were discouraged from producing goods for export.
- **Currency restrictions.** Indian money could not be converted to other currencies.
- **Permits.** A business needed government permission to sell a new product, modernize a factory, expand production, set prices, hire or fire workers, and change the job classification of existing workers.
- **Subsidies.** Unprofitable private companies were kept in business with government subsidies, such as cheap electricity or forgiveness of debts.
- **Government ownership.** The government owned not just communications, transportation, and power companies, which is common around the world, but it also owned businesses such as insurance companies and carmakers, which are left to the private sector in most countries.

Effectively cut off from the world economy, businesses were supposed to produce goods for consumption inside India. But by following the self-sufficiency path, India achieved only modest development and did not produce internationally competitive goods (Figure 10.7.2).

▶ 10.7.2 **SELF-SUFFICIENCY IN INDIA: INEFFICIENCY** Textile manufacturing, Delhi.

International Trade Path

The international trade model of development calls for a country to identify its distinctive or unique economic assets. What animal, vegetable, or mineral resources does the country have in abundance that other countries are willing to buy? What product can the country manufacture and distribute at a higher quality and a lower cost than other countries?

The international trade path derives from a five-step model proposed by W.W. Rostow in 1960. Each country is thought to be in one of these five stages:

1. **The traditional society.** A very high percentage of people engaged in agriculture and a high percentage of national wealth allocated to what Rostow called "nonproductive" activities, such as the military and religion.
2. **The preconditions for takeoff.** An elite group of well-educated leaders initiates investment in technology and infrastructure, such as water supplies and transportation systems, designed to increase productivity.
3. **The takeoff.** Rapid growth is generated in a limited number of economic activities, such as textiles or food products.
4. **The drive to maturity.** Modern technology, previously confined to a few takeoff industries, diffuses to a wide variety of industries.
5. **The age of mass consumption.** The economy shifts from production of heavy industry, such as steel and energy, to consumer goods, such as motor vehicles and refrigerators.

Among the first places to adopt the international trade path were South Korea, Singapore, Taiwan, and Hong Kong—known as the "four dragons" (Figure 10.7.3). Lacking many natural resources, the four dragons promoted development by concentrating on producing a handful of manufactured goods, especially clothing and electronics, as well as financial services. Low labor costs enabled these countries to sell products inexpensively in developed countries.

▲ 10.7.3 **TRADE: SINGAPORE**
The port of Singapore is the world's second busiest. Singapore's modern skyline reflects the wealth generated by its pursuit of international trade.

DEBATE IT!

Strengths of the two development paths?

Which development path (Figures 10.7.4 and 10.7.5) is more beneficial for people? Both self-sufficiency and international trade development paths are sharply criticized for not meeting the needs of ordinary people.

SELF-SUFFICIENCY CRITICS

- An inefficient and unresponsive bureaucracy controls the availability of goods.
- Consumers are unable to get some desired products.
- What is available can be old-fashioned and out-of-date.

▲ 10.7.4 **SELF-SUFFICIENCY IN INDIA**
Old-fashioned Maruti cars made in India.

INTERNATIONAL TRADE CRITICS

- Decisions are made by large corporations with no ties to local communities.
- Foreign governments make decisions without regard for local sentiment.
- More immigrants may be permitted to enter the country and take jobs away from locals.

▲ 10.7.5 **INTERNATIONAL TRADE IN INDIA**
Transferring containers between train and trucks, Delhi, India.

World Trade

- **Analyze reasons for success of international trade.**

Most countries have adopted the international trade approach as the preferred alternative for stimulating development. Many long-time advocates of self-sufficiency converted to international trade, especially during the 1990s.

Shortcomings of Self-Sufficiency

During the late twentieth and early twenty-first centuries trade increased more rapidly than wealth (as measured by GDP), an indication of the growing importance of the international trade approach (Figures 10.8.1 and 10.8.2). International trade was embraced both because of its perceived benefits and the shortcomings of self-sufficiency.

Self-sufficiency was rejected for a number of reasons:

- **Inefficient industries.** Businesses could sell all they made, at high government-controlled prices, to customers culled from long waiting lists, so they had little incentive to improve quality, lower production costs, reduce prices, or increase production.
- **Lack of competitiveness.** Companies protected from international competition were not pressured to keep abreast of rapid technological changes or give high priority to sustainable development and environmental protection.
- **Corruption.** A large, complex bureaucracy administered rules and processed documents for permits. The system gave unmonitored power to bureaucrats, thus encouraging abuse and corruption.
- **Black market.** Ambitious businessmen found that struggling to produce goods was less rewarding than illegally importing goods and selling them at inflated prices on the black market.

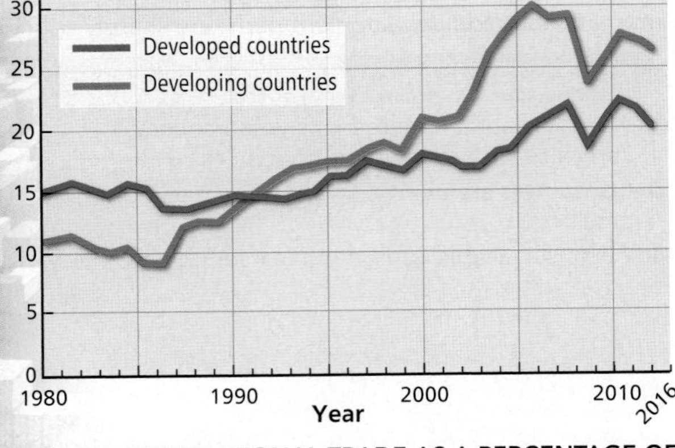

▲ 10.8.1 INTERNATIONAL TRADE AS A PERCENTAGE OF INCOME

◀ 10.8.2 INTERNATIONAL TRADE: HONG KONG
The world's fifth busiest port.

Transition to International Trade

International trade attracted many developing countries during the late twentieth century. International trade exposes a country's people and businesses to the demands, needs, and preferences of people and businesses in other countries. India, for example, dismantled many of its formidable collection of barriers to international trade through the following changes:

- **Permits.** Foreign companies were allowed to set up factories and sell in India.
- **Taxes and quotas.** Tariffs and restrictions on the import and export of goods were reduced or eliminated.
- **Competition.** Monopolies in communications, insurance, and other industries were eliminated.

Countries like India converted from self-sufficiency to international trade during the 1990s because of overwhelming evidence at the time that international trade better promoted development. After converting to international trade, India's GDP per capita increased much more rapidly than it had under self-sufficiency (Figure 10.8.3). With exposure to international trade, Indian companies have improved the quality and competitiveness of their products.

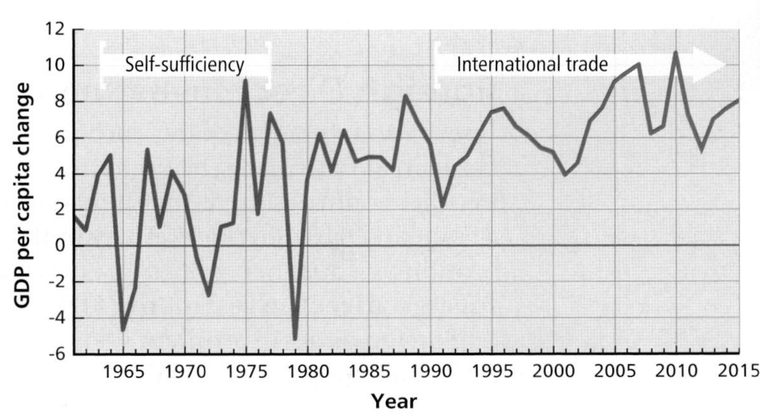

▲ 10.8.3 **GDP PER CAPITA CHANGE IN INDIA**
The graph shows the percentage change in GDP from the previous year.

World Trade Organization

To promote the international trade development model, countries representing 97 percent of world trade established the World Trade Organization (WTO) in 1995. The WTO enforces agreements designed to reduce barriers to international trade. Through the WTO, countries agree to reduce or eliminate restrictions on the trade of manufactured goods, such as unfair subsidies, quotas, and tariffs. Also reduced or eliminated are restrictions on the international movement of money by banks, corporations, and wealthy individuals.

International Trade Critics

Critics have sharply attacked international trade. Progressive critics charge that international trade promotes the interests of large corporations rather than poor people. Conservatives charge that international trade compromises the power and sovereignty of individual countries by transferring authority to organizations like the WTO. Protesters routinely gather in the streets outside high-level meetings of the WTO (Figure 10.8.4).

▼ 10.8.4 **SOUTH KOREAN FARMERS PROTEST AGAINST THE WTO**

Financing Development

- Identify the main sources for financing development.

Developing countries lack money to fund development, so they obtain financial support from developed countries. Finance comes from two primary sources: direct investment by transnational corporations and loans from banks and international organizations.

Foreign Direct Investment

International trade requires corporations based in a particular country to invest in other countries. Investment made by a company based in one country in the economy of another country is known as **foreign direct investment (FDI)**.

Foreign direct investment grew from $172 billion in 2002 to $646 billion in 2016 (Figure 10.9.1). FDI does not flow equally around the world (Figure 10.9.2). Most FDI both originates and is invested in developed countries. China (including Hong Kong) receives one-third of all FDI destined for developing countries. The United States is by far the leading source of FDI investment, and at the same time is virtually tied with China as the leading destination for FDI.

The major sources of FDI are transnational corporations that invest and operate in countries other than the one in which the company headquarters are located. Of the 100 largest transnational corporations in 2016, 87 had headquarters in developed countries, including 55 in the United States and 22 in Europe. China (including Hong Kong) was the location of 11 of the 13 with headquarters in developing countries.

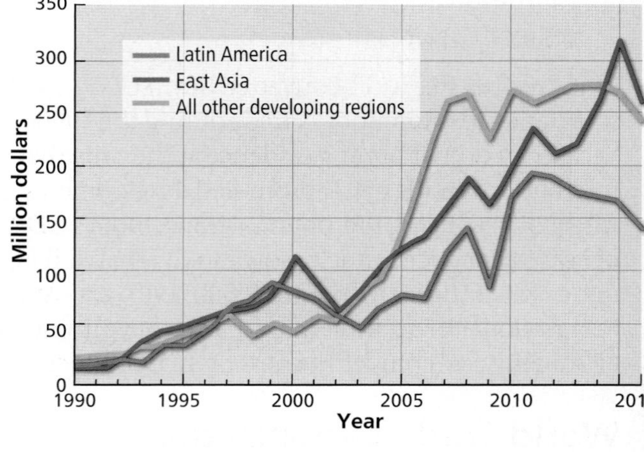

▲ 10.9.1 GROWTH IN FDI
East Asia and Latin America have received the most FDI.

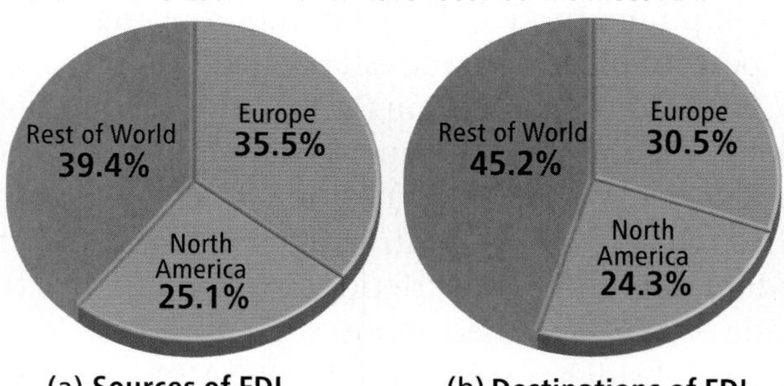

▲ 10.9.2 SOURCES AND DESTINATIONS OF FDI

Large transnational corporations have access to financing, but would-be business owners in developing countries are too poor to qualify for regular bank loans. An alternative source of loans is **microfinance**, which is provision of small loans and other financial services to individuals and small businesses in developing countries that are unable to obtain loans from commercial banks (Figure 10.9.3).

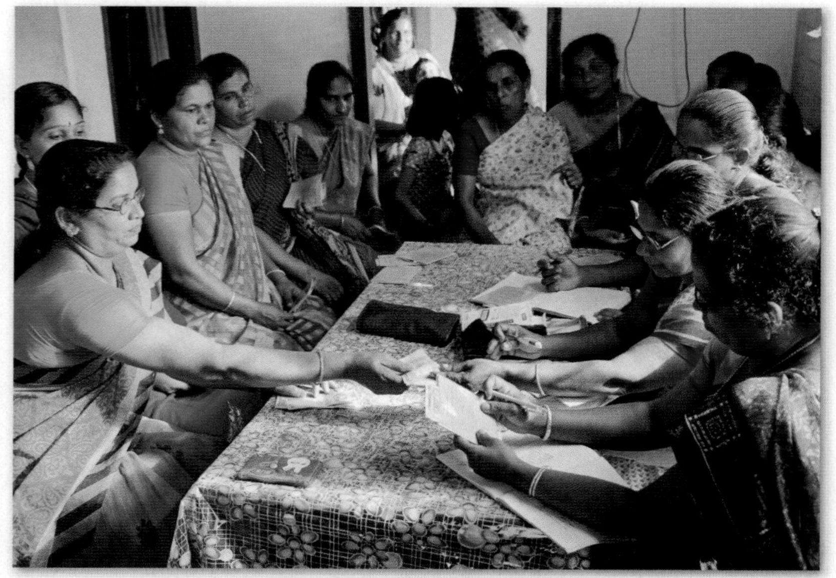

◀ 10.9.3 MICROFINANCE
The Peermade Development Society, Kerala, India, makes microloans to women trying to start small businesses.

Loans

The two major lenders to developing countries are the World Bank and the International Monetary Fund (IMF). The World Bank and IMF were conceived at a 1944 United Nations Monetary and Financial Conference in Bretton Woods, New Hampshire, to promote economic development and stability after the devastation of World War II and to avoid a repetition of the disastrous economic policies contributing to the Great Depression of the 1930s. The IMF and World Bank became specialized agencies of the UN when it was established in 1945.

Developing countries borrow money to build new infrastructure, such as hydroelectric dams, electric transmission lines, flood-protection systems, water supplies, roads, and hotels. The theory is that new infrastructure will make conditions more favorable for domestic and foreign businesses to open or expand. After all, no business wants to be located in a place that lacks paved roads, running water, and electricity. Half of the loans have gone to seventeen countries, including nine in Africa, seven in Asia, and one in Latin America (Figure 10.9.4).

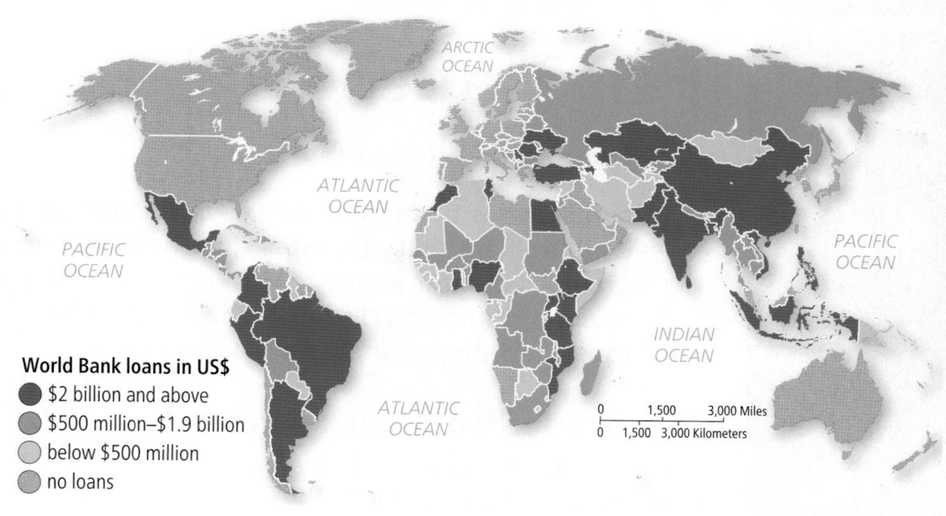

▲ 10.9.4 WORLD BANK LOANS

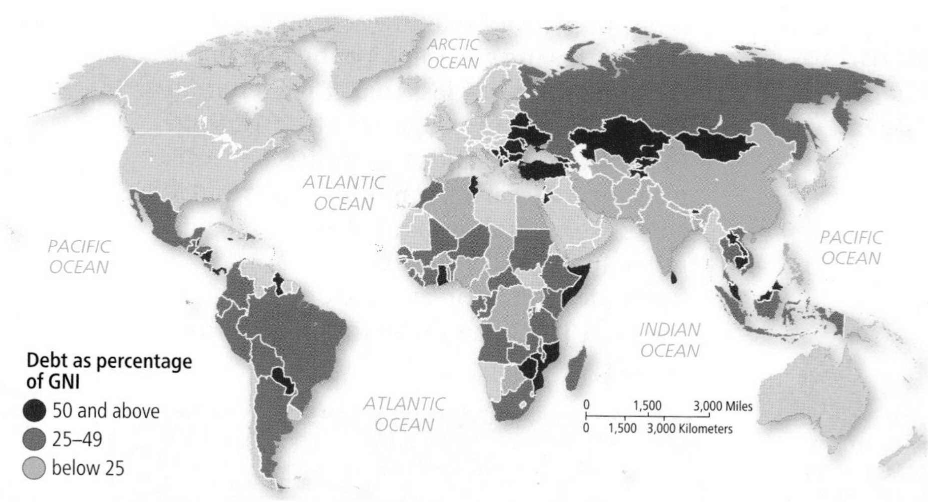

▲ 10.9.5 DEBT AS PERCENTAGE OF GNI

Structural Adjustment Programs

Some countries have had difficulty repaying their loans, especially those countries with very high debt compared to their GNI (Figure 10.9.5). The IMF, World Bank, and developed countries fear that granting, canceling, or refinancing debts without strings attached will perpetuate bad habits in developing countries. Therefore, to apply for debt relief, a developing country is required to prepare a Policy Framework Paper (PFP). The PFP outlines a **structural adjustment program**, a detailed plan of economic reforms (or "adjustments") that includes economic goals, strategies for achieving them, and external financing requirements.

Critics charge that poverty worsens under structural adjustment programs. By placing priority on reducing government spending, structural adjustment programs cause higher unemployment and cuts in health, education, and social services that benefit the poor.

International organizations respond that the poor suffer more when a country does not undertake reforms. Economic growth is what benefits the poor the most in the long run. Nevertheless, in response to criticisms, the IMF and the World Bank now encourage innovative programs to reduce poverty and corruption and consult more with average citizens. A safety net must be included to ease short-term pain experienced by poor people.

▲ 10.10.1 FAIR TRADE COFFEE BEANS, LAOS

Fair Trade

- Explain principles of fair trade.

Fair trade has been proposed as a variation of the international trade model of development that promotes sustainability. **Fair trade** is international trade that provides greater equity to workers and small businesses in developing countries.

Two sets of standards distinguish fair trade: One set applies to workers on farms and in factories and the other applies to producers.

Fair Trade Producer Standards

Critics of international trade charge that only a tiny percentage of the price a consumer pays for a good reaches the individual in the developing country who is responsible for making or growing it. A Haitian sewing clothing for the U.S. market, for example, earns less than 1 percent of the retail price of the garment, according to the National Labor Committee. The rest goes to wholesalers, importers, distributors, advertisers, retailers, and others who did not actually make the item. In contrast, fair trade returns on average one-third of the price to the producer in the developing country.

▶ 10.10.2 FAIR TRADE MACADAMIA NUTS, KENYA

Fair Trade is a set of business practices designed to advance a number of economic, social and environmental goals. These include:

- Raising the incomes of small-scale farmers and artisans by eliminating some of the middlemen (Figure 10.10.1).
- Distributing the profits and risks associated with production and sale of goods more fairly among producers, distributors, retailers, and financiers.
- Increasing the entrepreneurial and management skills of the producers (Figure 10.10.2).
- Promoting safe and sustainable farming methods and working conditions, such as by prohibiting the use of dangerous pesticides and herbicides and promoting the production of certified crops.

International fair trade organizations set standards for implementing these principles, and they monitor, audit, and certify that practices comply with the standards.

Many small-scale farmers and artisans join democratically managed cooperatives. Cooperatives offer several advantages:

- The cooperative can qualify for credit so that funds can be borrowed to buy equipment and invest in improving farms.
- Materials can be purchased at a lower cost.
- The people who grow or make the products democratically manage allocation of resources and assure safe and healthy working conditions.
- Profits are reinvested in the community instead of going to absentee corporate owners.

Fair Trade Worker Standards

Fair trade requires that workers be:

- Paid fair wages, at least enough to cover food, shelter, education, health care, and other basic needs (Figure 10.10.3).
- Permitted to organize a union and to have the right to collective bargaining.
- Protected by high environmental and safety standards.

Protection of workers' rights is not a high priority in the international trade development approach, according to its critics. Critics charge that:

- Oversight of workers' conditions by governments and international lending agencies is minimal.
- Workers allegedly work long hours in poor conditions for low pay.
- Children or forced labor may be in the workforce.
- Health problems may result from poor sanitation and injuries from inadequate safety precautions.
- Injured, ill, or laid-off workers are not compensated.

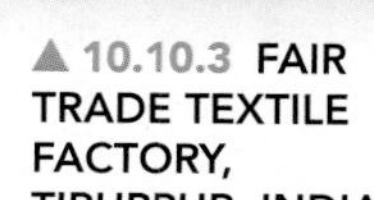

▲ 10.10.3 FAIR TRADE TEXTILE FACTORY, TIRUPPUR, INDIA

Fair Trade and Consumers

Most fair trade sales are in food, including coffee, tea, banana, chocolate, cocoa, juice, sugar, and honey products (Figure 10.10.4). In North America, fair trade products have been primarily craft products such as decorative home accessories, jewelry, textiles, and ceramics. Ten Thousand Villages is the largest fair trade organization in North America, specializing in handicrafts.

Buying fair trade products helps consumers connect more directly with the producers of the food, clothing, and household items that they buy. Fair trade products do not necessarily cost the consumer more than conventionally grown or produced alternatives. Because fair trade organizations bypass exploitative intermediaries and work directly with producers, they are able to cut costs and return a greater percentage of the retail price to the producers. The cost remains the same as for traditionally traded goods, but the distribution of the cost of the product is different because the large percentage taken by intermediaries is removed from the equation.

◀ 10.10.4 SHOP SELLING FAIR TRADE PRODUCTS, CANTERBURY, UNITED KINGDOM

Progress in Development

- Describe measures of progress in development.

Since the UN began measuring HDI in 1980, both developed and developing regions have made progress.

The overall HDI score has increased by about the same level in developed countries and in developing countries (Figure 10.11.1). All regions have increased their HDI scores ((see Research & Analyze feature and Figure 10.11.2).

GNI per capita has increased much more rapidly in developed countries than in developing countries (refer to Figure 1.10.5). With life expectancy, developing countries have narrowed the gap, but progress has slowed in recent years. Since 1980, people are expected to live 9 years longer in developing countries and 8 years longer in developed countries. With education, the average number of years that a five-year-old is expected to attend school has increased since 1980 by 3.1 years in developed and by 3.6 years in developing countries. Again, the gap has been narrowed only slightly.

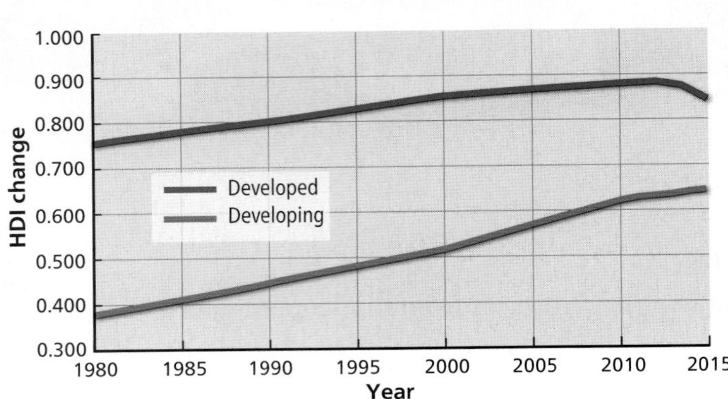

▶ 10.11.1 CHANGE IN HDI

RESEARCH & ANALYZE
Build Your Own HDI

The UN lets you change the numbers used to calculate the HDI and IHDI to see the impact on a country's level of development. Go to **http://hdr.undp.org/** and ***select*** *Data*, then *Calculating the Indices*, or ***select*** HDI in your search engine and ***select*** *Calculating the Indices* twice.

Select *Download the Tool*, then *Open*. ***Select*** the HDI worksheet.

Country A is an example of a high developing country. The UN's cut-off to be a developed country is 0.80. Change one or more of the four data columns until you get an HDI above 0.80. Which of the four columns needs to change the most in order for Country A to be reclassified from high developing to developed?

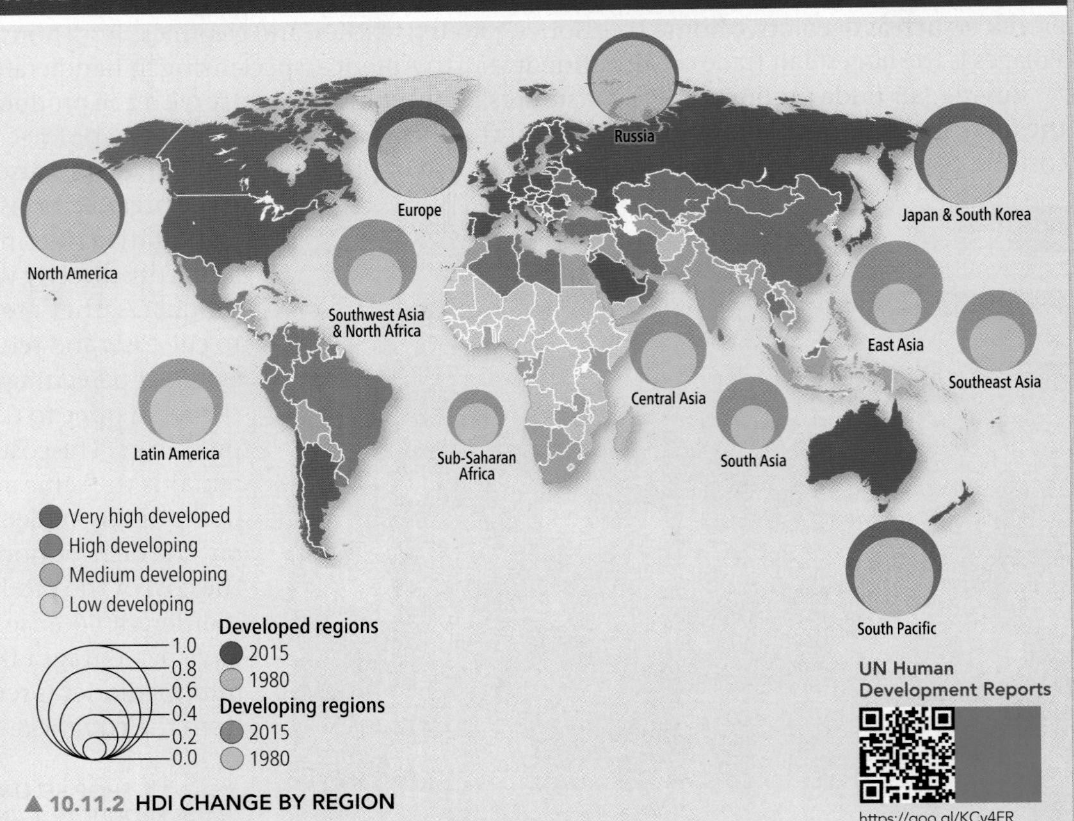

▲ 10.11.2 HDI CHANGE BY REGION

UN Human Development Reports

https://goo.gl/KCy4FR

Sustainable Development Goals

To reduce disparities between developed and developing countries, the 193 members of the United Nations in 2015 adopted 17 Sustainable Development Goals (Figure 10.11.3). All UN members agreed to achieve these goals by 2030. The **Sustainable Development Goals** replaced eight **Millennium Development Goals** adopted in 2002.

UN Sustainable Development Goals	
Goal	**Comment**
1. End poverty in all its forms everywhere.	Poverty was cut in half between 1990 and 2010, but 767 million people still live in extreme poverty, which the UN defines as earning less than $1.75 per day.
2. End hunger, achieve food security and improved nutrition, and promote sustainable agriculture.	The UN estimates 795 million people are undernourished. It wants to double agricultural productivity by 2030.
3. Ensure healthy lives and promote well-being for all at all ages.	Progress has been made in reducing infant mortality and maternal mortality, but the UN hopes to reduce these rates further by 2030.
4. Ensure inclusive and quality education for all and promote lifelong learning.	The UN wants to ensure that all children attend school; 57 million children currently do not attend school, more than half of whom are in sub-Saharan Africa.
5. Achieve gender equality and empower all women and girls.	Gender inequalities have been reduced but linger in all regions, as discussed in Key Issue 2.
6. Ensure access to water and sanitation for all.	663 million people lack access to drinking water, and 2.4 billion lack access to toilets or latrines.
7. Ensure access to affordable, reliable, sustainable, and modern energy for all.	One in five people lack access to electricity, and fossil fuels are the principal contributor to climate change.
8. Promote inclusive and sustainable economic growth, employment, and decent work for all.	The UN wants an increase in GDP per capita in developing countries of at least 7 percent per year.
9. Build resilient infrastructure, promote sustainable industrialization, and foster innovation.	In addition to electricity and sanitation issues cited in earlier goals, the UN also estimates that 1-to-1.5 billion people lack access to reliable phones.
10. Reduce inequality within and among countries.	Income inequality has increased since 1990 within and between countries.
11. Make cities inclusive, safe, resilient, and sustainable.	Rapid urbanization has put pressure on water, sewage, and health; 828 million people live in what the UN defines as slums.
12. Ensure sustainable consumption and production patterns.	The UN estimates that one-third of food rots or spoils because of poor transportation or harvesting methods.
13. Take urgent action to combat climate change and its impacts.	It is not too late to reverse the recent sharp increase in carbon dioxide emissions that is producing climate change.
14. Conserve and sustainably use the oceans, seas, and marine resources.	Progress has been made in water quality, but overfishing is a problem.
15. Sustainably manage forests, combat desertification, halt and reverse land degradation, halt biodiversity loss.	Drought, desertification, and deforestation are negatively impacting agriculture and biodiversity.
16. Promote just, peaceful, and inclusive societies.	The UN estimates that corruption, bribery, theft, and tax evasion cost developing countries $1.26 trillion annually.
17. Revitalize the global partnership for sustainable development.	Overall aid has increased from developed countries to developing countries.

◀ **10.11.4 UN SUSTAINABLE DEVELOPMENT GOALS**

UN Sustainable Development Goals
https://goo.gl/hDFtjE

CHAPTER

10 Review, Analyze, & Apply

KEY ISSUE 1 How Does Development Vary Among Countries?

The UN's Human Development Index (HDI) measures the level of development of every country. The HDI is based on three factors: a decent standard of living, a long and healthy life, and access to knowledge.

THINKING GEOGRAPHICALLY

1. What economic, demographic, and literacy measures presented in this chapter or in earlier chapters do you feel would be better measures of a country's level of development? Why?

◀ **10.CR.1 UGANDAN CHILDREN**

KEY ISSUE 2 What Inequalities Are Found In Development?

At least some degree of gender and economic inequality is found in every country. The inequality-adjusted HDI (IHDI) modifies the HDI to account for inequality within a country. The GDI measures the gender gap in the level of achievement for the three dimensions of the HDI. The GII measures the gender gap in the level of achievement in terms of reproductive health, empowerment, and the labor market.

THINKING GEOGRAPHICALLY

2. According to the maps in Key Issue 2, sub-Saharan Africa and South Asia appear to have the highest levels of gender inequality. What factors discussed in earlier chapters might be contributing to the high level of gender inequality in these two regions? Why?

◀ **10.CR.2 CLEANERS, JAIPUR, INDIA**

KEY ISSUE 3 How Do Countries Become More Developed?

To promote development, developing countries choose between self-sufficiency and international trade paths. In recent years, both developed and developing countries have expressed increasing concern with some of the consequences of the international trade path.

THINKING GEOGRAPHICALLY

3. Although the international trade development path has proved more successful at promoting development in the developing world, why might developed countries like the United States and the United Kingdom take steps to reduce their commitment to the path?

◀ **10.CR.3 BREXIT SUPPORTERS**

KEY ISSUE 4 What Progress Towards Development Are Countries Achieving?

Most countries have a higher HDI now than in the twentieth century. The gap between developing and developed countries in life expectancy has narrowed, but the gap in income has increased. The UN has adopted 17 Sustainable Development Goals that it hopes all countries will achieve by 2030.

THINKING GEOGRAPHICALLY

4. Which of the 17 Sustainable Development Goals appear to be realistic, and which appear unlikely to be achieved? Why?

◀ **10.CR.4 CONSTRUCTION, KINSHASA, DEMOCRATIC REPUBLIC OF THE CONGO**

Explore

The World's lowest HDI

Central African Republic has the world's lowest HDI score. Let's examine its development possibilities.

In Google Earth, ***search*** for *Bayanga, Central African Republic*

1. Describe the image that Google Earth supplies for Bayanga.
2. Does Google Earth offer Street View for Bayanga? Why do you think this is the situation?
3. ***Zoom*** in to around 5 km. What transportation features are visible? How might these features help Bayanga become more economically developed?

▲ **10.CR.5 CENTRAL AFRICAN REPUBLIC**

Mastering Geography

Looking for additional review and test prep materials? Visit the Study Area in Mastering Geography to enhance your geographic literacy, spatial reasoning skills, and understanding of this chapter's content. Access MapMaster™ interactive maps, video case studies, *In the News* current articles, flashcards, self-study quizzes, an eText of *Contemporary Human Geography*, and more.
pearson.com/mastering/geography

Key Terms

Adolescent fertility rate (p. 253) The number of births per 1,000 women ages 15 to 19.

Developed country (p. 244) A country that has progressed relatively far along a continuum of development.

Developing country (p. 244) A country that is at a relatively early stage in the process of development.

Development (p. 244) A process of improvement in the conditions of people through diffusion of knowledge and technology.

Fair trade (p. 262) A variation of international trade that provides greater equity to workers, small businesses, and consumers, focusing primarily on products exported from developing countries to developed countries.

Female labor force participation rate (p. 255) The percentage of women holding full-time jobs outside the home.

Foreign direct investment (FDI) (p. 260) Investment made by a foreign company in the economy of another country.

Gender-related Development Index (GDI) (p. 252) An indicator constructed by the U.N. to measure the gender gap in the level of achievement in terms of income, education, and life expectancy.

Gender Inequality Index (GII) (p. 252) An indicator constructed by the U.N. to measure the extent of each country's gender inequality in terms of reproductive health, empowerment, and the labor market.

Gross domestic product (GDP) (p. 246) The value of the total output of goods and services produced in a country in a year, not accounting for money that leaves and enters the country.

Gross national income (GNI) (p. 246) The value of the output of goods and services produced in a country in a year, including money that leaves and enters the country.

Human Development Index (HDI) (p. 244) An indicator constructed by the U.N. to measure the level of development for a country through a combination of income, education, and life expectancy.

Inequality-adjusted Human Development Index (IHDI) (p. 250) A modification of the HDI to account for inequality.

Literacy rate (p. 249) The percentage of a country's people who can read and write.

Microfinance (p. 260) Provision of small loans and financial services to individuals and small businesses in developing countries.

Millennium Development Goals (p. 265) Eight goals adopted by the U.N. in 2002 to reduce disparities between developed and developing countries by 2015.

Primary sector (p. 246) The portion of the economy concerned with the direct extraction of materials from Earth, generally through agriculture.

Productivity (p. 247) The value of a particular product compared to the amount of labor needed to make it.

Purchasing power parity (PPP) (p. 246) The amount of money needed in one country to purchase the same goods and services in another country.

Secondary sector (p. 246) The portion of the economy concerned with manufacturing useful products through processing, transforming, and assembling raw materials.

Structural adjustment program (p. 261) Economic policies imposed on less developed countries by international agencies to create conditions that encourage international trade.

Sustainable Development Goals (p. 265) Seventeen goals adopted by the U.N. in 2015 to reduce disparities between developed and developing countries by 2030.

Tertiary sector (p. 246) The portion of the economy concerned with transportation, communications, and utilities, sometimes extended to the provision of all goods and services to people in exchange for payment.

Value added (p. 247) The gross value of a product minus the costs of raw materials and energy.

Geospatial Analysis

Log in to the Mastering Geography Study Area to access MapMaster 2.0

HDI in Southwest Asia

The HDI for Southwest Asia & North Africa overall ranks in the middle among developing regions. The region's mid-range HDI masks wide variations among the region's individual countries and factors contributing to the HDI.

Add the *Human Development Index (HDI)* layer. ***Select*** the *Settings* icon from the *Legend*, and ***Select*** *Show Political Labels*. ***Add*** the *Per Capita Gross Domestic Product* layer and ***Select*** *Split map window*. ***Zoom*** to Southwest Asia and North Africa.

1. Do most of the countries with relatively high HDI have GDP that is relatively, low, or in the middle?
2. ***Remove*** *Per Capita Gross Domestic Product* layer. ***Add*** *Life Expectancy* and ***select*** *Split map window*. Do the countries with the highest HDI have the highest life expectancy? What might account for this situation?
3. ***Remove*** the *Life Expectancy* layer. ***Add*** the *Literacy Rate* layer, ***select*** *Split map window*. Do the countries with the highest HDI have the highest literacy rate? What might account for this situation?

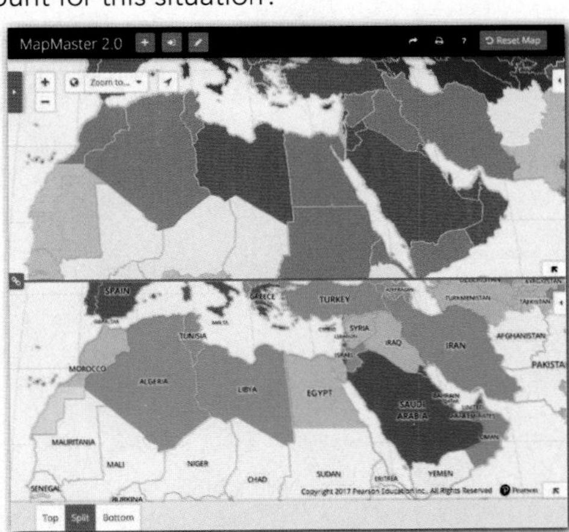

▲ **10.CR.6 HDI AND LITERACY RATES, SOUTHWEST ASIA & NORTH AFRICA**

GeoVideo

Log in to the Mastering Geography™ Study Area to view this video.

China: Economic Growth and Communism

In just a few decades, China has become an industrial powerhouse by following a model of growth very different from that of the United States and most other industrial countries.

1. What has been the relationship between market forces and government policy throughout China's recent rapid economic growth?
2. Describe the role of the city of Wenzhou in China's "new Industrial Revolution."
3. According to the video, what two problems must China solve to ensure continued economic growth and social stability?

CHAPTER

11 Industry

Industry was once highly clustered in a handful of communities within a handful of developed countries. But industry has diffused to many communities in many developing countries. Communities around the world view manufacturing jobs as a special asset. They mourn when factories close and rejoice when new ones open.

◀ Jeep assembly plant, Detroit.

KEY ISSUES

1 Where Is Industry Distributed?

Industry is clustered in three regions: Europe, East Asia, and North America. Europe was the first region to industrialize, and East Asia is the fastest growing.

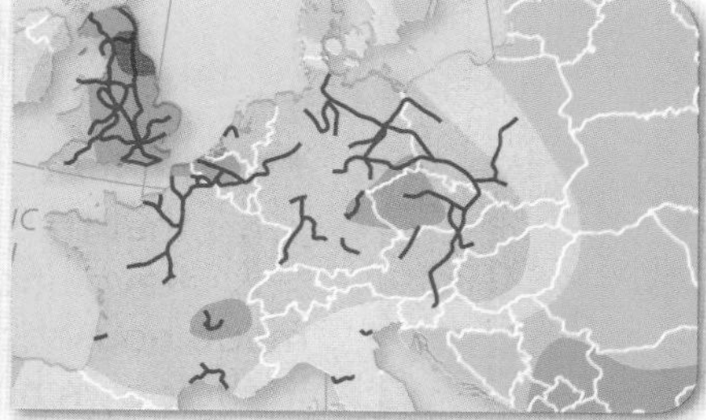

2 Why Are Site Factors Important For Industry?

Site factors are related to the costs of factors of production inside a factory. The three production factors that may vary among locations are labor, land, and capital.

3 Why Are Situation Factors Important For Industry?

Situation factors involve transporting materials to and from a factory. Some industries locate near inputs, whereas other choose locations near their markets.

4 Why Are Industries Changing Locations?

Manufacturing is increasing in some developing countries, attracted by low-wage labor. Industries requiring skilled labor are more likely to remain in industrial regions in developed countries.

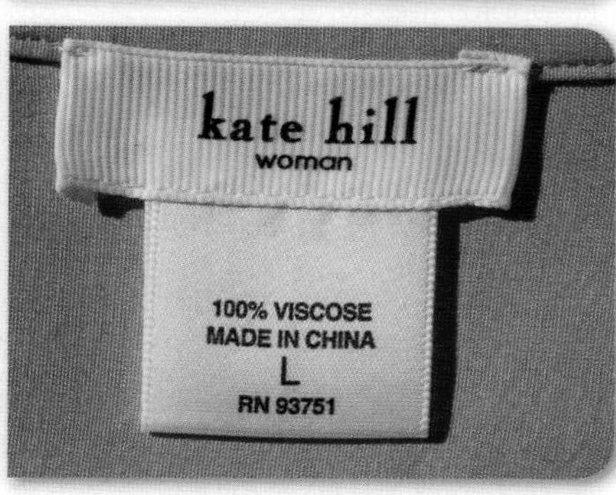

LOCATIONS IN THIS CHAPTER

Memphis, p. 283
Wolverhampton, p. 270
Aston Clinton, p. 273
Japan, p. 278
Arizona, p. 276
Cambodia, p. 274
Indonesia, p. 272
Chattanooga, p. 287
India, pp. 274, 275
Singapore, p. 282

right to work law
new international division of labor
industry
outsourcing
auto production
transport mode
planes
just in time delivery
maquiladora
minimills
steel mills
bulk gaining industry
NAFTA
bulk reducing industry
trucks, trains, ships, planes
situation factors
fordist and post-fordist production
vertical integration
labor intensive industry
capital
BRIC countries
industrial clusters
land
break of bulk point
site factors
industrial revolution

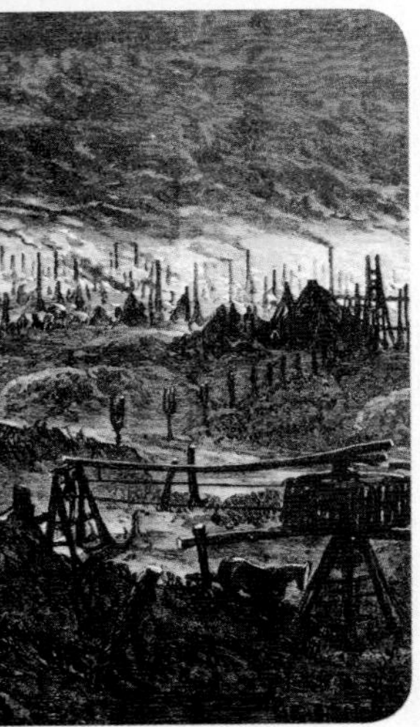

▲ 11.1.1 **THE INDUSTRIAL REVOLUTION** Factories belching smoke, Wolverhampton, England, 1866.

Industry Past & Present

• Describe past and current distributions of industry.

The **Industrial Revolution** was a series of improvements in industrial technology that transformed the process of manufacturing goods. Prior to the Industrial Revolution, industry was geographically dispersed across the landscape. People made household tools and agricultural equipment in their own homes or obtained them in the local village. Home-based manufacturing was known as the **cottage industry** system.

Europe: Birthplace of the Industrial Revolution

Europe was the first region to industrialize, during the nineteenth century. The catalyst of the Industrial Revolution was technology, with several inventions transforming the way in which goods were manufactured (Figure 11.1.1). The opening of railroads reflects the diffusion of the Industrial Revolution from the United Kingdom to the European continent (Figure 11.1.2). Numerous industrial centers emerged in Europe as countries competed with each other for supremacy (Figure 11.1.3).

First railway opened by
1826
1836
1846
1856
1876
After 1876
Rail lines constructed by 1848
0 200 400 Miles
0 200 400 Kilometers
50°N
ATLANTIC OCEAN
10°W
40°N
Mediterranean Sea
0°
20°E

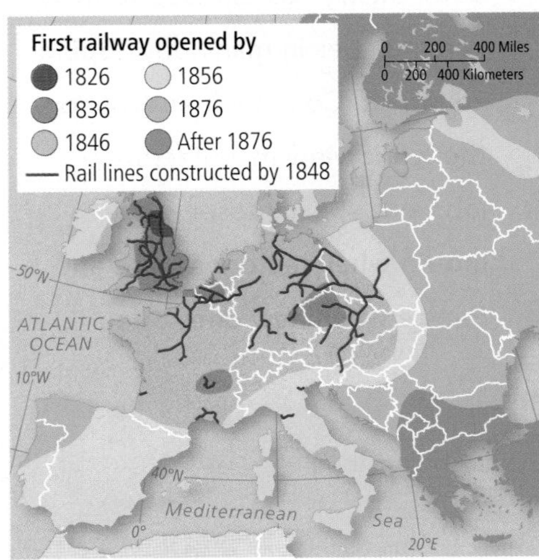

▲ 11.1.2 **DIFFUSION OF THE INDUSTRIAL REVOLUTION**

▶ 11.1.3 **EUROPE'S INDUSTRIAL AREAS**

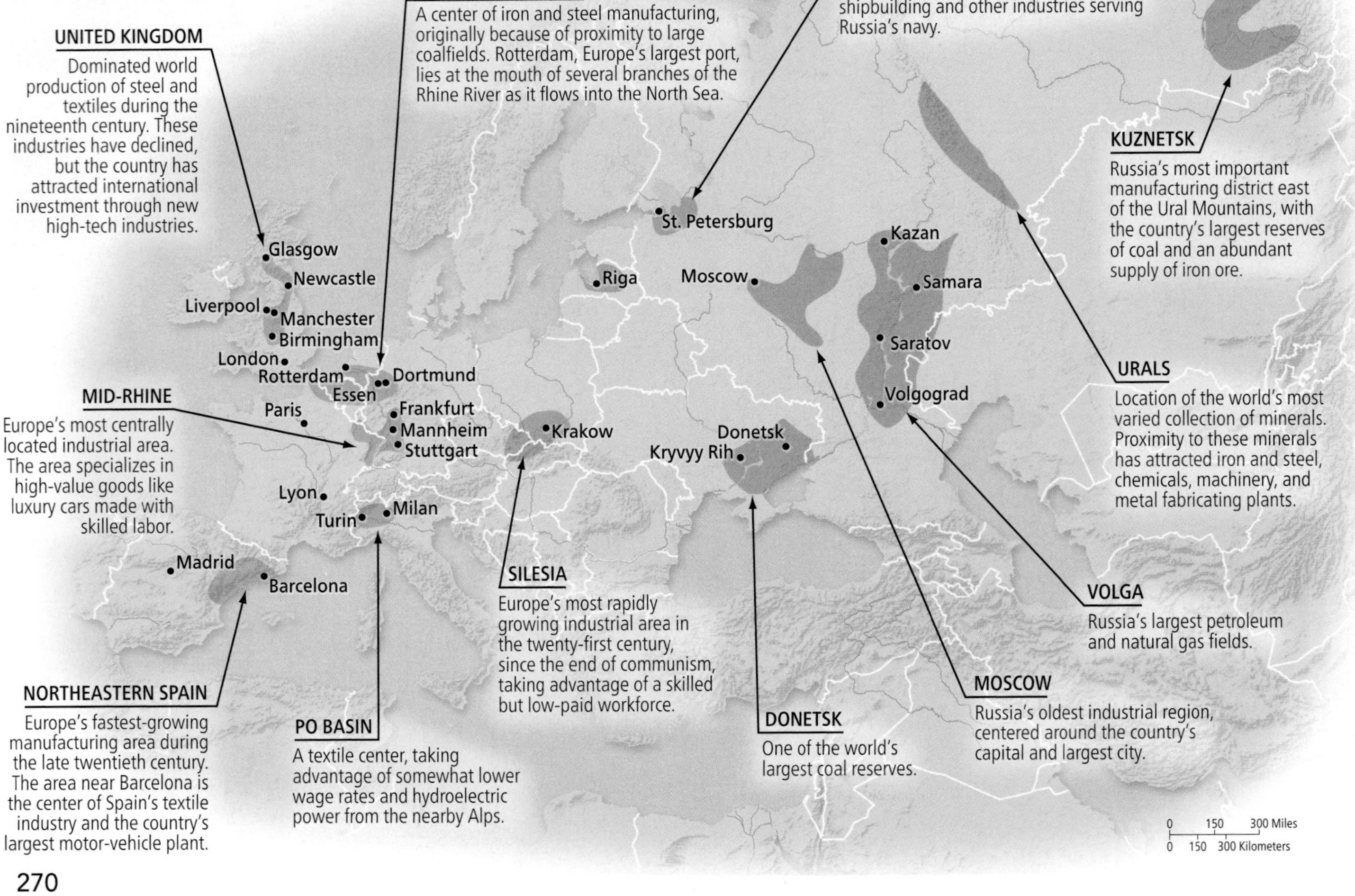

UNITED KINGDOM
Dominated world production of steel and textiles during the nineteenth century. These industries have declined, but the country has attracted international investment through new high-tech industries.
RHINE-RUHR VALLEY
A center of iron and steel manufacturing, originally because of proximity to large coalfields. Rotterdam, Europe's largest port, lies at the mouth of several branches of the Rhine River as it flows into the North Sea.
ST. PETERSBURG
Russia's second-largest city, specializing in shipbuilding and other industries serving Russia's navy.
KUZNETSK
Russia's most important manufacturing district east of the Ural Mountains, with the country's largest reserves of coal and an abundant supply of iron ore.
URALS
Location of the world's most varied collection of minerals. Proximity to these minerals has attracted iron and steel, chemicals, machinery, and metal fabricating plants.
MID-RHINE
Europe's most centrally located industrial area. The area specializes in high-value goods like luxury cars made with skilled labor.
VOLGA
Russia's largest petroleum and natural gas fields.
MOSCOW
Russia's oldest industrial region, centered around the country's capital and largest city.
SILESIA
Europe's most rapidly growing industrial area in the twenty-first century, since the end of communism, taking advantage of a skilled but low-paid workforce.
DONETSK
One of the world's largest coal reserves.
NORTHEASTERN SPAIN
Europe's fastest-growing manufacturing area during the late twentieth century. The area near Barcelona is the center of Spain's textile industry and the country's largest motor-vehicle plant.
PO BASIN
A textile center, taking advantage of somewhat lower wage rates and hydroelectric power from the nearby Alps.
Glasgow
Newcastle
Liverpool
Manchester
Birmingham
London
Rotterdam
Essen
Dortmund
Paris
Frankfurt
Mannheim
Stuttgart
Lyon
Turin
Milan
Madrid
Barcelona
Krakow
Riga
St. Petersburg
Moscow
Kazan
Samara
Saratov
Volgograd
Donetsk
Kryvyy Rih
0 150 300 Miles
0 150 300 Kilometers

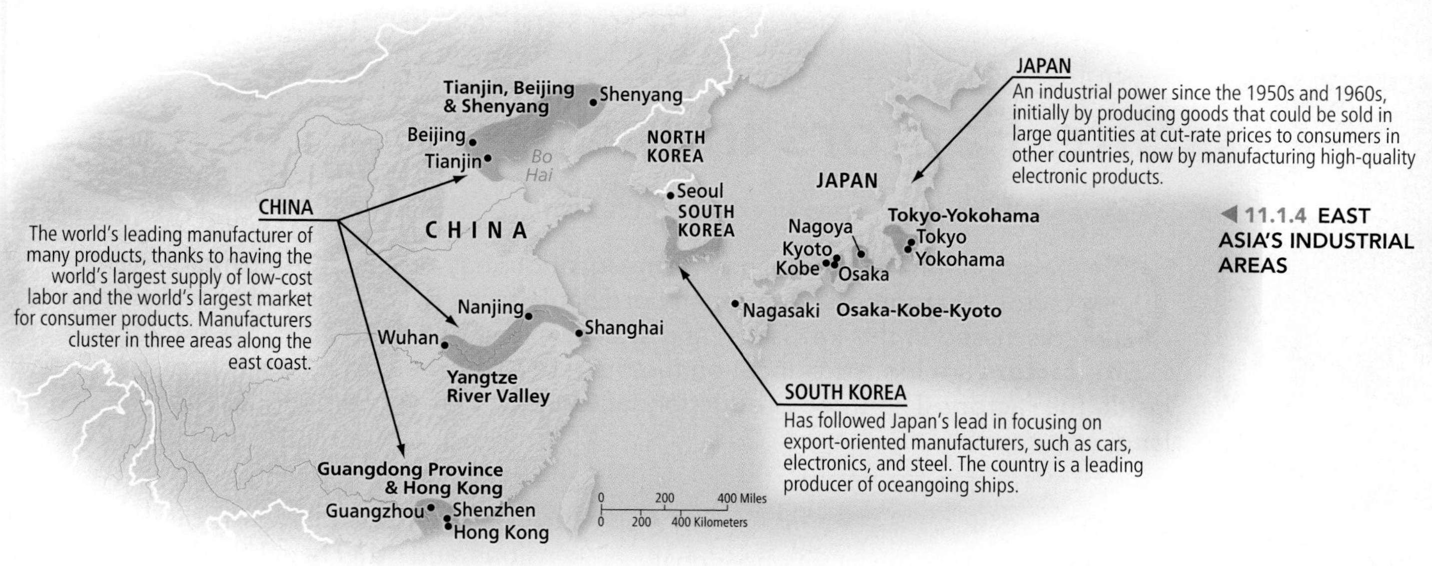

JAPAN
An industrial power since the 1950s and 1960s, initially by producing goods that could be sold in large quantities at cut-rate prices to consumers in other countries, now by manufacturing high-quality electronic products.
CHINA
The world's leading manufacturer of many products, thanks to having the world's largest supply of low-cost labor and the world's largest market for consumer products. Manufacturers cluster in three areas along the east coast.
SOUTH KOREA
Has followed Japan's lead in focusing on export-oriented manufacturers, such as cars, electronics, and steel. The country is a leading producer of oceangoing ships.
Tianjin, Beijing & Shenyang
Shenyang
Beijing
Tianjin
Bo Hai
NORTH KOREA
Seoul
SOUTH KOREA
CHINA
JAPAN
Nagoya
Kyoto
Kobe
Osaka
Tokyo-Yokohama
Tokyo
Yokohama
Nagasaki
Osaka-Kobe-Kyoto
Nanjing
Shanghai
Wuhan
Yangtze River Valley
Guangdong Province & Hong Kong
Guangzhou
Shenzhen
Hong Kong
0 200 400 Miles
0 200 400 Kilometers

◀ 11.1.4 EAST ASIA'S INDUSTRIAL AREAS

SOUTHEASTERN ONTARIO
Canada's most important industrial area, central to the Canadian and U.S. markets and near the Great Lakes and Niagara Falls.
MOHAWK VALLEY
Takes advantage of inexpensive electricity generated at nearby Niagara Falls.
NEW ENGLAND
A cotton textile center in the early nineteenth century. Cotton was imported from southern states, and finished cotton products were shipped to Europe.
NORTHERN CALIFORNIA
A leading center for social media, biotech, software, and electronic devices.
WESTERN GREAT LAKES
Centered on Chicago, the hub of the nation's transportation network and now the center of steel production.
MIDDLE ATLANTIC
The largest U.S. market, so attracts industries that need proximity to a large number of consumers and depend on foreign trade through one of this region's large ports.
SOUTHERN CALIFORNIA
Now the country's largest area of clothing and textile production, the second-largest furniture producer, and a major food-processing center.
PITTSBURGH-LAKE ERIE
The leading steel-producing area in the nineteenth century because of its proximity to Appalachian coal and iron ore.
CANADA
NORTH AMERICA
MEXICO
Toronto
Buffalo
Boston
Detroit
Milwaukee
Chicago
Cleveland
New York City
Philadelphia
Pittsburgh
Baltimore
San Francisco
Los Angeles
0 200 400 Miles
0 200 400 Kilometers

◀ 11.1.5 NORTH AMERICA'S INDUSTRIAL AREAS

East Asia: Twenty-First Century's Industrial Leader

East Asia has become the world's most important industrial region, beginning with Japan in the late twentieth century (Figure 11.1.4). By most measures, China is now the world's leading manufacturing country.

North America: Industrial Powerhouse

The United States became the world's leading industrial power in the late nineteenth century and retained that position through the twentieth century. North America's manufacturing was traditionally highly concentrated in northeastern United States and southeastern Canada (Figure 11.1.5).

ARCTIC OCEAN
PACIFIC OCEAN
ATLANTIC OCEAN
TROPIC OF CANCER
PACIFIC OCEAN
EQUATOR
INDIAN OCEAN
TROPIC OF CAPRICORN
ATLANTIC OCEAN
Industrial output
$1 trillion and above
$1 billion–$999 billion
below $1 billion
0 1,500 3,000 Miles
0 1,500 3,000 Kilometers

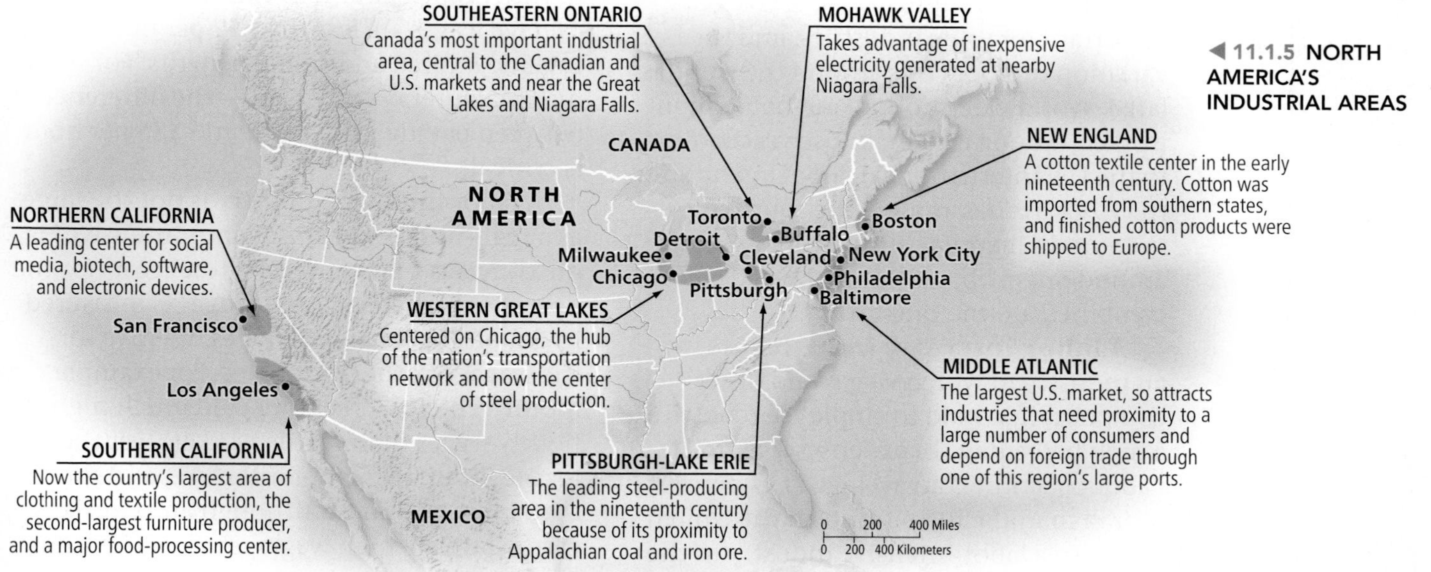

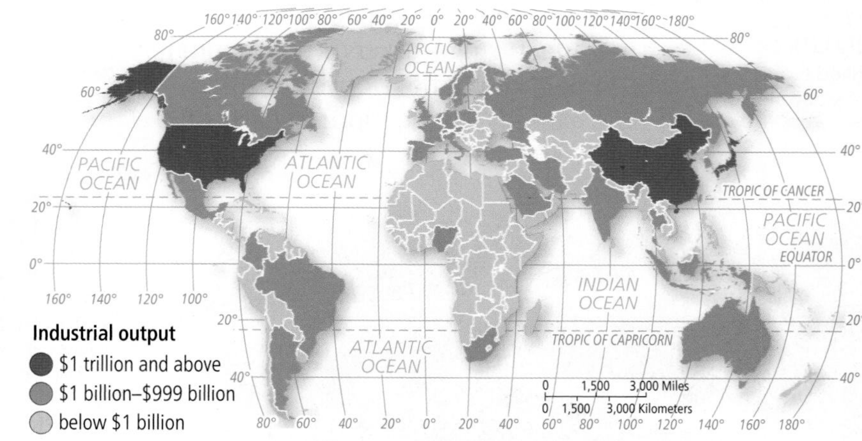

▲ 11.1.6 INDUSTRIAL OUTPUT

Industrial Clusters

Industry is clustered in three of the nine world regions identified in Chapter 10: Europe, East Asia, and North America. Each of the three regions accounts for roughly one-fourth of the world's total industrial output (Figure 11.1.6).

▲ 11.2.1 LABOR-INTENSIVE INDUSTRY
Kitchen utensil factory, Indonesia.

Site Factors in Industry

- Analyze the three types of site factors.

Geographers try to explain why one location may prove more profitable for a factory than others. A company ordinarily faces two geographic costs: site (discussed in this key issue) and situation (see Key Issue 3).

Site factors are industrial location factors related to the costs of factors of production inside the factory. The three production factors that may vary among locations are labor, land, and capital.

Labor

The most important site factor on a global scale is labor. Minimizing labor costs is important for some industries, and the variation of labor costs around the world is large. Worldwide, around one-half billion workers are engaged in industry, according to the UN International Labor Organization (ILO). China has around one-fourth of the world's manufacturing workers, India around one-fifth, and all developed countries combined around one-fifth.

A **labor-intensive industry** is an industry in which wages and other compensation paid to employees constitute a high percentage of expenses (Figure 11.2.1). Labor constitutes an average of 11 percent of overall manufacturing costs in the United States, so a labor-intensive industry in the United States would have a much higher percentage than that. The reverse case, an industry with a much lower-than-average percentage of expenditures on labor, is considered capital intensive (Figure 11.2.2).

The average wage paid to manufacturing workers is approximately $35 per hour in developed countries and exceeds $40 per hour in parts of Europe (Figure 11.2.3). Health-care, retirement pensions, and other benefits add substantially to the compensation. In China and India, average wages are less than $2 per hour and include limited additional benefits. For some manufacturers—but not all—the difference between paying workers $2 and $35 per hour is critical.

A labor-intensive industry is not the same as a high-wage industry. "Labor-intensive" is measured as a percentage of total costs for the operation, whereas "high-wage" is measured in dollars (or other currencies) relative to the wages of other industries. For example, motor-vehicle workers are paid much higher hourly wages than textile workers, yet the textile industry is labor intensive, and the auto industry is not. Although auto workers earn relatively high wages, most of the value of a car is accounted for by the parts and the machinery needed to put together the parts. On the other hand, labor accounts for a large percentage of the cost of producing a towel or shirt compared with materials and machinery.

▼ 11.2.2 CAPITAL INTENSIVE INDUSTRY
Skilled high-wage aerospace factory workers.

▲ 11.2.3 HOURLY WAGES
The chart shows average hourly wages for workers in manufacturing in 14 of the 15 countries with the largest industrial production in 2016.

Capital

Manufacturers typically borrow capital—the funds to establish new factories or expand existing ones. The most important factor in the clustering of high-tech industries in California's Silicon Valley—even more important than proximity to skilled labor—was the availability of capital.

Banks in Silicon Valley have long been willing to provide money for new software and communications firms, even though lenders elsewhere have hesitated. High-tech industries have been risky propositions—roughly two-thirds of them fail. However, because potential returns on investment are high, Silicon Valley financial institutions continue to lend money to engineers who have good ideas. Engineers use the loans to buy the software, communications, and networks they need to get started. One-fourth of all capital in the United States is currently spent on new industries in Silicon Valley.

The ability to borrow money has become a critical factor in the distribution of industry in developing countries. Financial institutions in many developing countries are short of funds, so new industries must seek loans from banks in developed countries. But enterprises may not get loans if they are located in a country that is perceived to have an unstable political system, a high debt level, or ill-advised economic policies.

Land

Land suitable for constructing a factory can be found in many places. Geographers consider "land" a critical site factor that includes a site's natural resources as well as the land itself.

Early factories located inside cities due to a combination of situation and site factors. A city offered an attractive situation—proximity to a large local market and convenience in shipping to a national market by rail. A city also offered an attractive site—proximity to a large supply of labor as well as to sources of capital.

The site factor that cities have always lacked is abundant land. To get the necessary space in cities, early factories were typically multistory buildings. Raw materials were hoisted to the upper floors to make smaller parts, which were then sent downstairs on chutes and pulleys for final assembly and shipment. Water was stored in tanks on the roof.

Contemporary factories operate most efficiently when laid out in one-story buildings (Figure 11.2.4). Raw materials are typically delivered at one end and moved through the factory on conveyors or forklift trucks. Products are assembled in logical order and shipped out at the other end. The land needed to build one-story factories is now more likely to be available in suburban and rural locations. Also, land is much cheaper in suburban and rural locations than near the center of a city.

In addition to providing enough space for one-story buildings, locations outside cities are also attractive because they facilitate delivery of inputs and shipment of products. In the past, when most material moved in and out of a factory by rail, a central location was attractive because rail lines converged there. With trucks now responsible for transporting most inputs and products, proximity to major highways is more important for a factory.

Especially attractive is the proximity to the junction of a long-distance route and the beltway that encircles most cities. Thus, factories cluster in industrial parks located near suburban highway junctions.

▼ **11.2.4 MODERN ONE-STORY FACTORY**
Arla Dairy Products, Aston Clinton, United Kingdom.

▲ 11.3.1 FEMALE TEXTILE WORKERS, CAMBODIA

Changing Site Factors: Clothing

- Explain the distribution of clothing production.

Production of **textiles** (woven fabrics) and **apparel** (clothing) is a prominent example of a labor-intensive industry that generally requires less-skilled, low-cost workers. The textile and apparel industry accounts for 6 percent of the dollar value of world manufacturing but a much higher 14 percent of world manufacturing employment, an indicator that it is a labor-intensive industry. The percentage of the world's women employed in this type of manufacturing is even higher (Figure 11.3.1).

Textile and apparel production involves three principal steps:

- Spinning of fibers to make yarn.
- Weaving or knitting of yarn into fabric.
- Assembly of fabric into products.

Spinning, weaving, and sewing are all labor intensive compared to other industries, but the importance of labor varies somewhat among them. As a result, their global distributions are not identical because the three steps are not equally labor intensive.

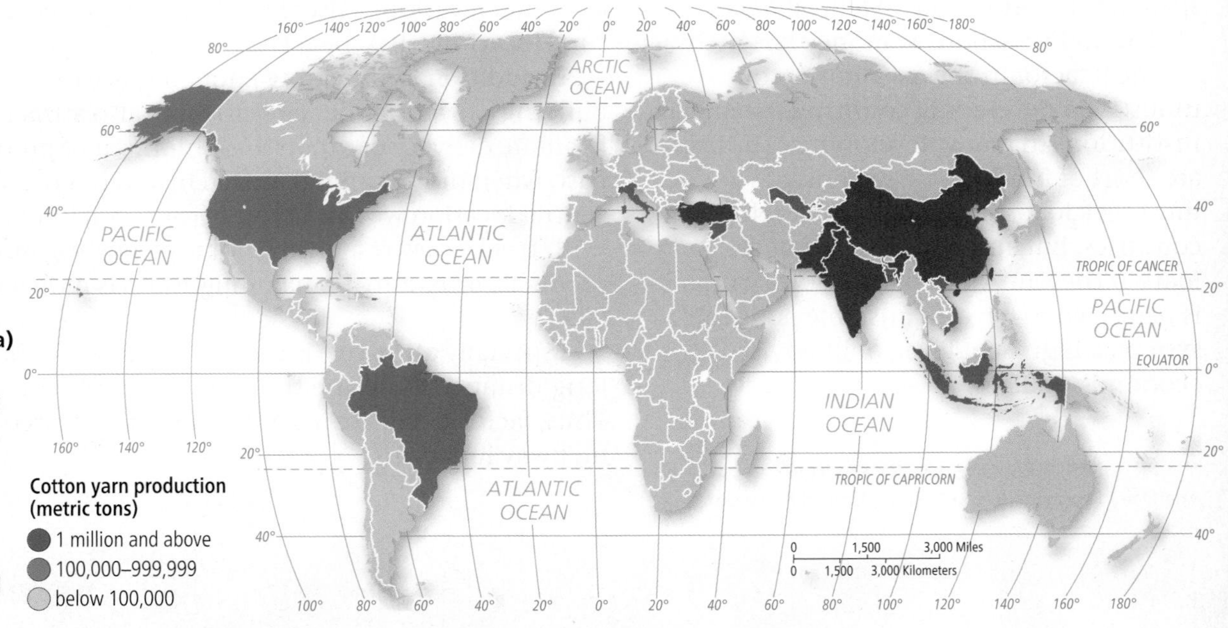

(a)

▶ ▼11.3.2 COTTON SPINNING
(a) Nearly one-half of world cotton yarn is spun in China and India. (b) Factory in Indore, India, spins yarn from organic and fair trade cotton.

(b)

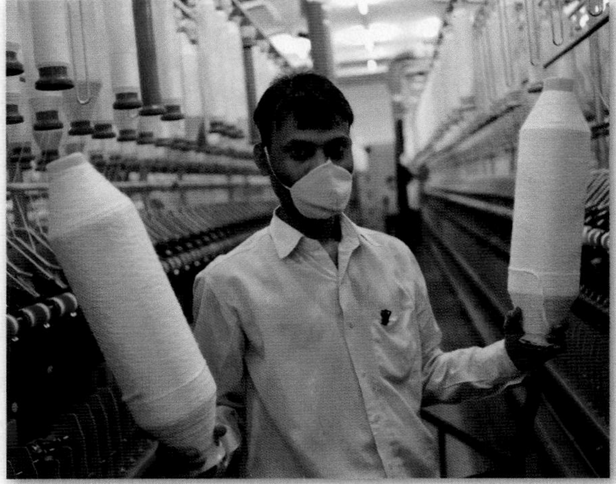

Spinning

Fibers can be spun from natural or synthetic elements. The principal natural fiber is cotton, though synthetics now account for three-fourths of world thread production. Because it is a labor-intensive industry, spinning is done primarily in low-wage countries (Figure 11.3.2). China produces two-thirds of the world's cotton thread.

Weaving

For thousands of years, fabric has been woven or laced together by hand on a loom, which is a frame on which two sets of threads are placed at right angles to each other. One set of threads, called the warp, is strung lengthwise. A second set of threads, called the weft, is carried in a shuttle that is inserted over and under the warp.

For mechanized weaving, labor constitutes a high percentage of the total production cost. Consequently, weaving is highly clustered in low-wage countries (Figure 11.3.3). China accounts for nearly 60 percent of the world's woven cotton fabric production and India another 30 percent. Despite their remoteness from European and North American markets, China and India have become the dominant fabric producers because their lower labor costs offset the expense of shipping inputs and products long distances.

Cotton woven fabric (million square meters)
1,000 and above
1–999
below 1

(a)

(b)

▲◄ 11.3.3
COTTON WEAVING
(a) China and India account for 90 percent of world cotton weaving. (b) Factory in India weaves textiles.

Assembly

Sewing by hand is a very old human activity. Needles made from animal horns or bones date back tens of thousands of years, and iron needles date from the fourteenth century. The first functional sewing machine was invented by French tailor Barthelemy Thimonnier in 1830. Isaac Singer manufactured the first commercially successful sewing machine in the United States during the 1850s.

Textiles are cut and sewn to be assembled into four main types of products: garments, carpets, home products such as bed linens and curtains, and industrial items such as headliners for inside motor vehicles (Figure 11.3.4). Developed countries play a larger role in assembly than in spinning and weaving because most of the consumers of assembled products are located in developed countries. Nonetheless, overall production costs are generally lower in developing countries because substantially lower labor costs compared to developed countries offset higher shipping and taxation costs (Figure 11.3.5).

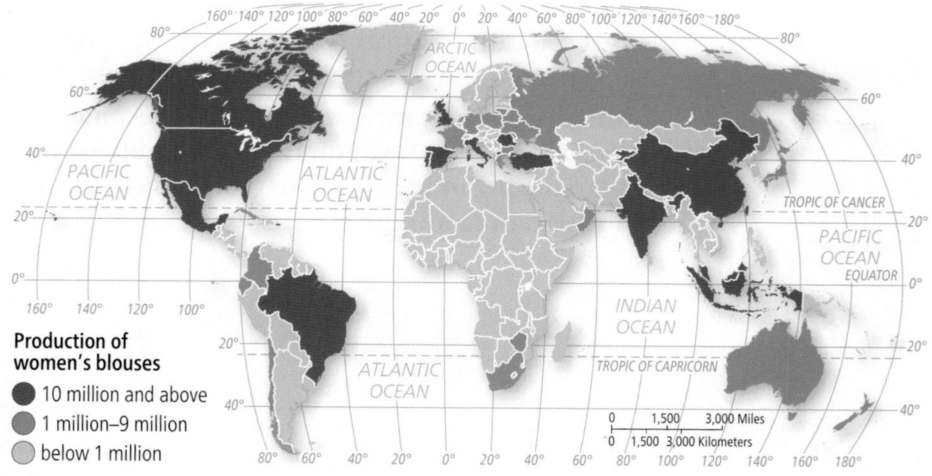

▲ **11.3.4 WOMEN'S BLOUSE PRODUCTION**
The United States is the leading producer of women's blouses.

$17.40
$3.20
$17.00
$0.50
U.S. TOTAL COST
$38.10
(a)

$18.40
$2.30
$5.50
$3.50
$1.70
ASIA TOTAL COST
$31.40
(b)

◄ **11.3.5 HOODIE PRODUCTION COST**
The cost of production is higher in (a) the United States than in (b) Asia, because of higher wages paid to clothing workers.

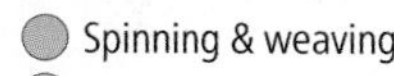
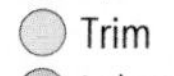
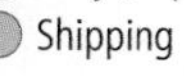

Spinning & weaving
Trim
Labor
Duty (Import tax)
Shipping

▲ 11.4.1 COPPER MINE, ARIZONA

Proximity to Inputs

- Explain why some industries locate near inputs.

For many companies, the most critical factors influencing their choice of factory locations are situation factors. **Situation factors** involve transporting materials to and from a factory. A firm seeks a location that minimizes the cost of transporting inputs to the factory and finished goods to consumers.

Proximity to inputs is the most critical situation factor for some manufacturers, whereas proximity to market is more important for others. The optimal plant location is as close as possible to inputs if the cost of transporting raw materials to the factory is greater than the cost of transporting the product to consumers. Conversely, the optimal plant location is as close as possible to the customer if the cost of transporting raw materials to the factory is less than the cost of transporting the product to consumers.

Bulk-Reducing Industry: Copper

An industry in which the inputs weigh more than the final products is a **bulk-reducing industry**. To minimize transport costs, a bulk-reducing industry locates near its sources of inputs. An example of a bulk-reducing industry is most of the steps of copper production.

Copper production involves several steps:

1. **Mining.** Mining in general is bulk reducing because the heavy, bulky ore extracted from mines contains less than 0.7 percent copper, so is mostly waste (Figure 11.4.1).
2. **Concentration.** The ore is crushed and ground into fine particles, mixed with water and chemicals, filtered, and dried. Concentration mills are near copper mines because concentration transforms the heavy, bulky copper ore into a product of much higher value per weight. The concentrated ore is now around 25 percent copper.
3. **Smelting.** The concentrated copper becomes the input for smelters, which remove more impurities. The result is ore that is up to 60 percent copper. Because smelting is a bulk-reducing industry, smelters are built near their main inputs—the concentration mills—again to minimize transportation costs.
4. **Refining.** The purified copper produced by smelters is treated at refineries to produce copper cathodes, which are least 99.5 percent pure copper.
5. **Manufacturing.** Copper is used primarily in factories that manufacture either wire or brass (an alloy of copper and zinc).

Figure 11.4.2 shows the distribution of the U.S. copper industry. Mining, concentration, smelting, and refining are bulk-reducing industries; because two-thirds of U.S. copper is mined in Arizona, the state also has most of the concentration mills and smelters. The two largest refineries are in west Texas. The first four steps are good examples of bulk-reducing activities that need to be located near their sources of inputs. The fifth step—manufacturing—is not bulk reducing, so factories are sited elsewhere in the country rather than near inputs.

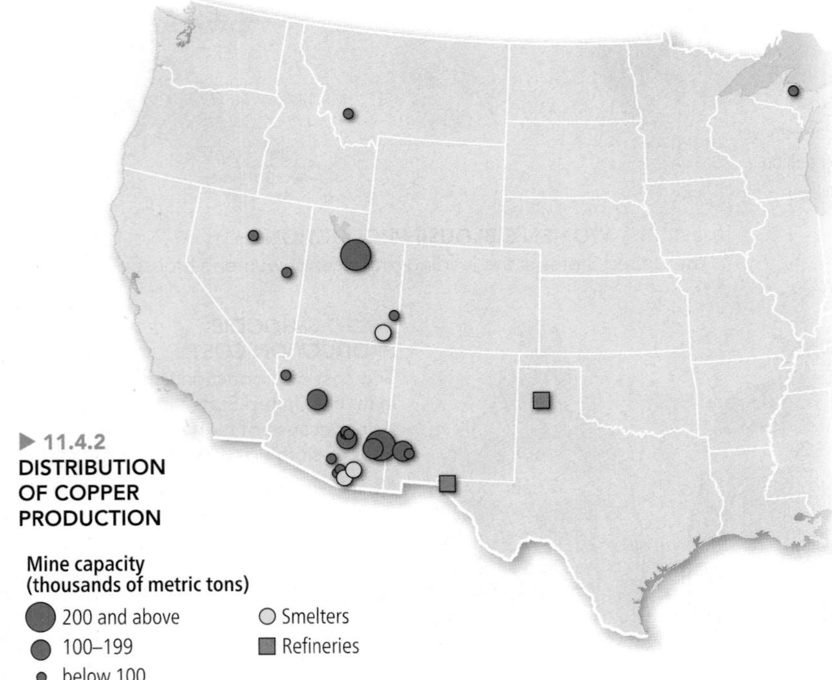

▶ 11.4.2 DISTRIBUTION OF COPPER PRODUCTION

Mineral Resources

Minerals are especially important inputs for many industries, especially bulk reducing ones such as copper production. Earth has 92 natural elements, but about 99 percent of the crust is composed of 8 of them (Figure 11.4.3). The 8 most common elements combine with several dozen less common elements to form approximately 3,000 different minerals, all with their own properties of hardness, color, and density, as well as spatial distribution. Many of these minerals have important industrial uses.

Minerals are either nonmetallic or metallic:

- **Nonmetallic minerals.** By weight, more than 90 percent of the minerals that humans use are nonmetallic. Important nonmetallic minerals include building stones, gemstones such as diamonds, and minerals used in the manufacture of fertilizers such as nitrogen, phosphorus, potassium, calcium, and sulfur.
- **Metallic minerals.** Metallic minerals have properties that are especially valuable for fashioning machinery, vehicles, and other elements essential to contemporary society. They are to varying degrees malleable (able to be hammered into thin plates) and ductile (able to be drawn into fine wire) and are good conductors of heat and electricity.

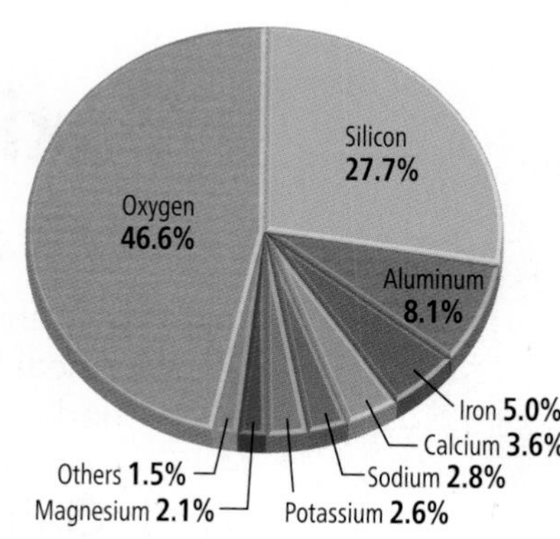

▲ 11.4.3 ELEMENTS IN EARTH'S CRUST

Many metals are capable of combining with other metals to form alloys with distinctive properties that are important for industry. Alloys are known as ferrous or nonferrous:

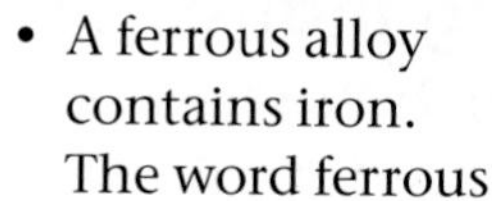

- A ferrous alloy contains iron. The word ferrous comes from the Latin for "iron." Iron is extracted from iron ore, by far the world's most widely used ore. Humans began fashioning tools and weapons from iron 4,000 years ago. Important metals used to make ferrous alloys include chromium, manganese, molybdenum, nickel, tin, titanium, and tungsten.
- A nonferrous alloy does not contain iron. Important nonferrous alloys include aluminum, copper, lead, lithium, magnesium, zinc, precious metals (silver, gold, and the platinum group), and rare earth metals used in cell phones and rechargeable batteries.

Mineral resources are not distributed uniformly across Earth (Figure 11.4.4). Few important minerals are found in Europe, Central Asia, and Southwest Asia & North Africa.

▼ 11.4.4 DISTRIBUTION OF MINERALS

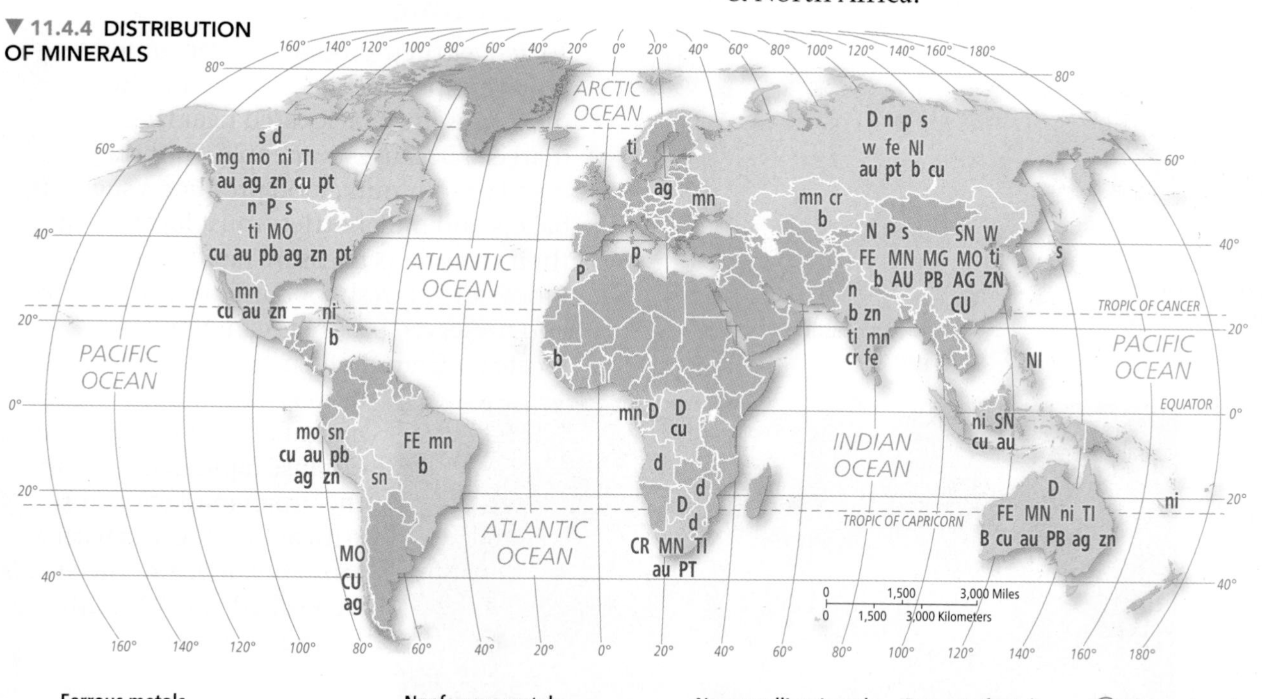

Proximity to Markets

- Explain why some industries locate near markets.

For many firms, the optimal location is close to customers. Proximity to markets is a critical locational factor for three types of industries: bulk-gaining industries, single-market manufacturers, and perishable-products companies.

Bulk-Gaining Industries

A **bulk-gaining industry** makes something that gains volume or weight during production. To minimize transport costs, a bulk-gaining industry needs to locate near where the product is sold.

A good example of a bulk-gaining industry is beverage bottling. Because water is the principal ingredient in beer or cola, a filled container is much heavier than an empty one. Shipping filled containers is more expensive than shipping empty ones, so to minimize shipping costs, bottlers locate near their customers rather than the manufacturers of the containers (Figure 11.5.1).

Persons per square kilometer
1,000 and above
500–999
250–449
100–249
25–99
6–24
below 6

Anheuser-Busch InBev
MillerCoors

▲ 11.5.1 BULK-GAINING INDUSTRY: BEER PRODUCTION
Containers are filled mostly with water. Most beer is bottled near major metropolitan areas, where most of the consumers are clustered. The darker areas on the map have relatively high population density.

Single-Market Manufacturers

A single-market manufacturer is a specialized manufacturer with only one or two customers. The optimal location for these factories is often in close proximity to the customers.

An example of a single-market manufacturer is a producer of buttons, zippers, clips, pins, or other specialized components attached to clothing. The clothing manufacturer may need additional supplies of these pieces on very short notice. The world's largest manufacturer of zippers, YKK, for example, has factories in 68 countries in order to be near its customers, the manufacturers of clothing (Figure 11.5.2).

Perishable-Products Companies

To deliver their products to consumers as rapidly as possible, perishable-products industries must be located near their markets. Because few people want stale bread or sour milk, food producers such as bakers and milk bottlers must locate near their customers to assure rapid delivery. Processors of fresh food into frozen, canned, and preserved products can, however, locate far from their customers. Cheese and butter, for example, are manufactured in Wisconsin because rapid delivery to the urban markets is not critical for products with a long shelf life, and the area is well suited agriculturally for raising dairy cows.

◀ 11.5.2 SINGLE-MARKET MANUFACTURER
YKK Zipper factory, Japan.

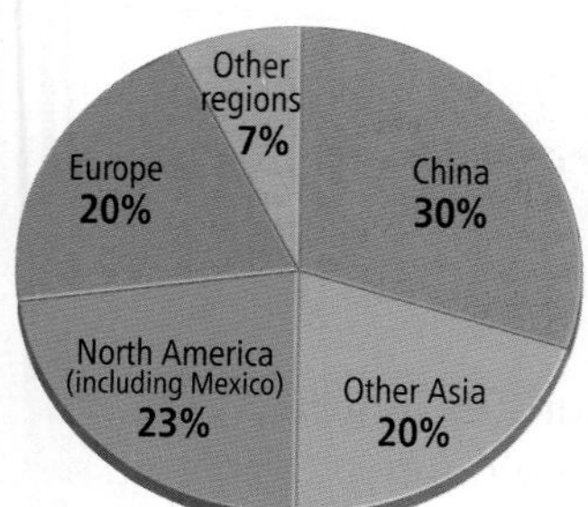

◀ **11.5.3 MOTOR VEHICLE SALES**
China, the rest of Asia, North America, and Europe account for more than 90 percent of world vehicles sales.

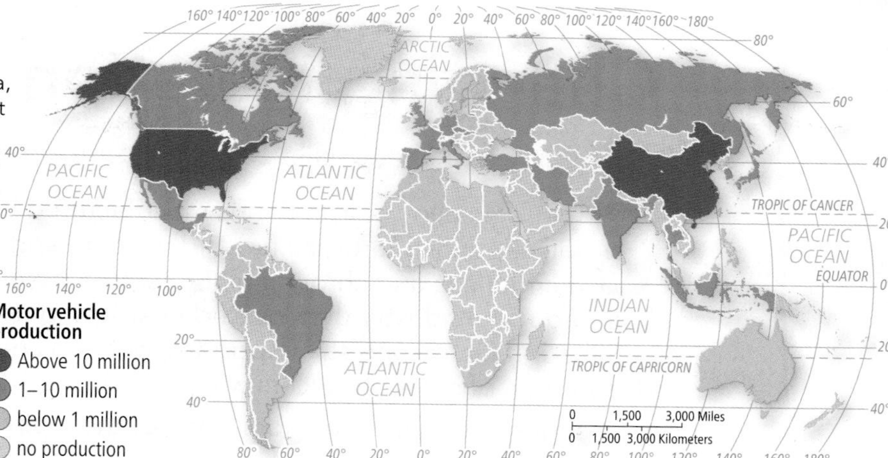

▲ **11.5.4 MOTOR VEHICLE PRODUCTION**
The regional distribution of vehicle production closely matches the regional distribution of sales.

Motor Vehicle Production

The motor vehicle is a prominent example of a bulk-gaining industry that is likely to be built near its market. Around 90 million new vehicles are sold annually worldwide. China accounts for 30 percent of those sales, other Asian countries 20 percent, North America (including Mexico) 23 percent, and Europe 20 percent (Figure 11.5.3).

Not surprisingly, in view of the importance of producing vehicles near their markets, the regional distribution of production is extremely close to that for sales (Figure 11.5.4) (see Research & Analyze feature). Asia has around one-half of world production and Europe and the Americas around one-quarter each. For example, around 85 percent of vehicles sold in the Americas are produced in the Americas. Around 10 percent come from Asia and 5 percent from Europe (Figure 11.5.5). Similarly, most vehicles sold in Europe are assembled in Europe, most vehicles sold in Japan are assembled in Japan, and most vehicles sold in China are assembled in China.

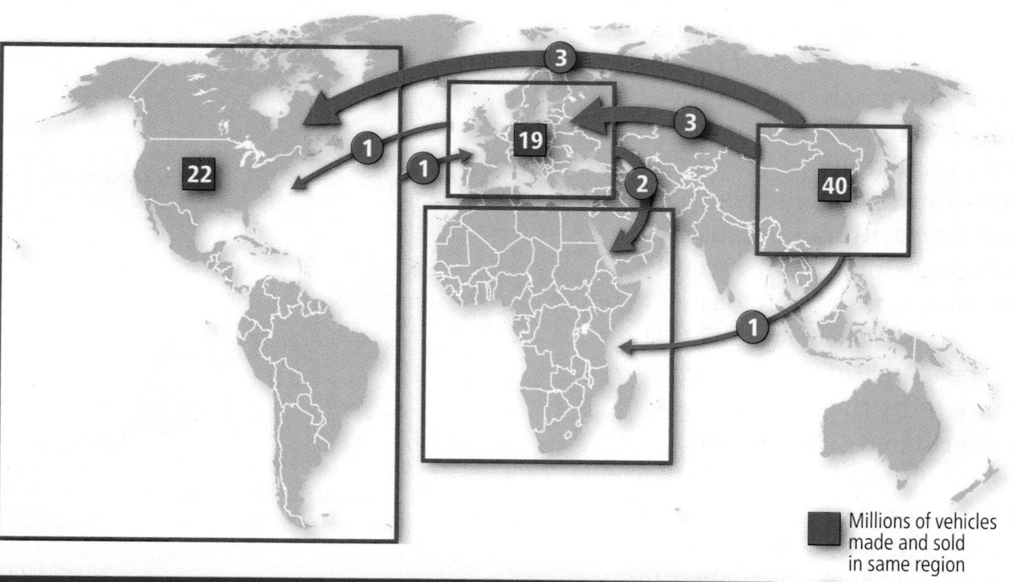

▶ **11.5.5 REGIONAL DISTRIBUTION OF VEHICLE SALES AND ASSEMBLY**

RESEARCH & ANALYZE
Where was your vehicle assembled?

Every car has a 17-digit vehicle identification number (VIN) that tells a lot about the vehicle (Figure 11.5.6). Among other information, the VIN pinpoints the country and city where the car was assembled. Obtain the VIN number for your car or for someone else's. You will find it on a metal plate near the front windshield on the driver's side.

1. In your search engine, enter the brand of the vehicle and VIN. In what country was your vehicle assembled?
2. Does this match your expectation as to whether the vehicle is "American" or "foreign"?
3. In what city was the vehicle assembled?
4. If in the United States, is that city in Auto Alley? (Refer to page 286 and Figure 11.9.2).
5. Was the location where the vehicle was assembled important to the purchaser of the car? Why or why not?

▲ **11.5.6 VIN NUMBER**

History of the VIN (NISR)
https://goo.gl/7bJcQD

Changing Situation Factors: Steel

- Summarize changes in the distribution of steel production.

Steel is an alloy of iron that is manufactured by removing impurities in iron, such as silicon, phosphorus, sulfur, and oxygen, and adding desirable elements, such as manganese and chromium. In the past, steel production was a good example of a bulk-reducing industry that located near its inputs.

Situation factors are still important, but two changes in these factors have altered the distribution of steel producers within the United States and worldwide:

- Changes in the relative importance of the main inputs.
- Increasing importance of proximity to markets.

Changing Distribution of U.S. Steel Production

The two principal inputs in steel production are iron ore and coal. Because of the need for large quantities of bulky, heavy iron ore and coal, steelmaking traditionally clustered near sources of the two key raw materials. Within the United States, the distribution of steel production changed several times during the nineteenth and twentieth centuries because of changing inputs. More recently, steel production has relocated to be closer to markets (Figure 11.6.1).

The increasing importance of proximity to markets is also demonstrated by the recent growth of steel minimills, which have captured one-fourth of the U.S. steel market. Rather than iron ore and coal, the main input into minimill production is scrap metal. In the past, most steel was produced at large integrated mill complexes. They processed iron ore, converted coal into coke, converted the iron into steel, and formed the steel into sheets, beams, rods, or other shapes. Minimills, generally limited to one step in the process—steel production—are less expensive than integrated mills to build and operate, and they can locate near their markets because their main input—scrap metal—is widely available (Figure 11.6.2).

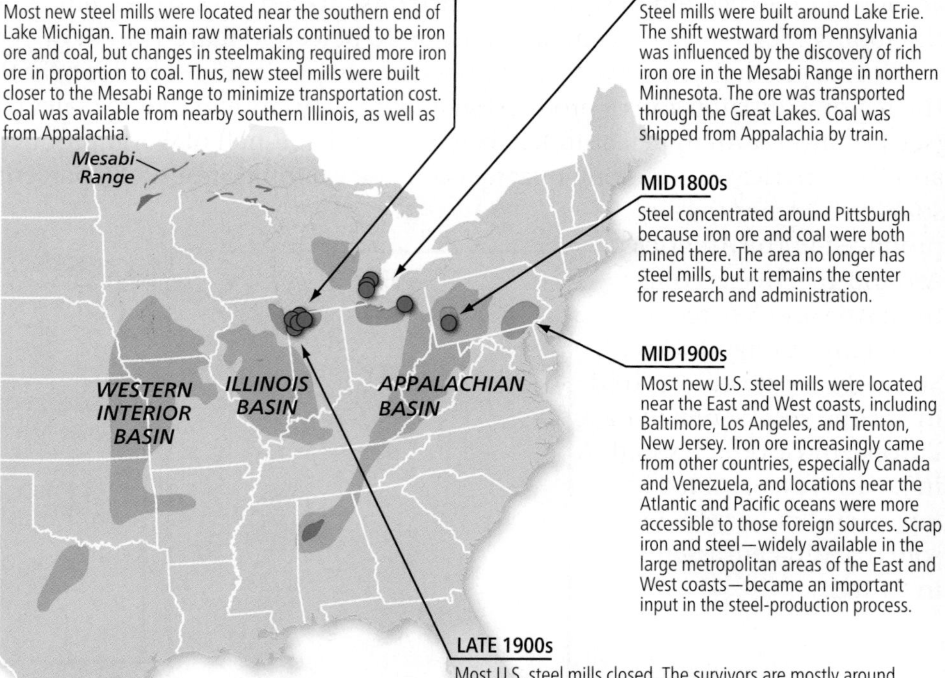

▲ 11.6.1 INTEGRATED STEEL MILLS IN THE UNITED STATES
Integrated steel mills are highly clustered near the southern Great Lakes, especially Lake Erie and Lake Michigan. Historically, the most critical factor in situating a steel mill was to minimize transportation cost for raw materials, especially heavy, bulky iron ore and coal. In recent years, many integrated steel mills have closed. Most surviving mills are in the southern Great Lakes to maximize access to consumers.

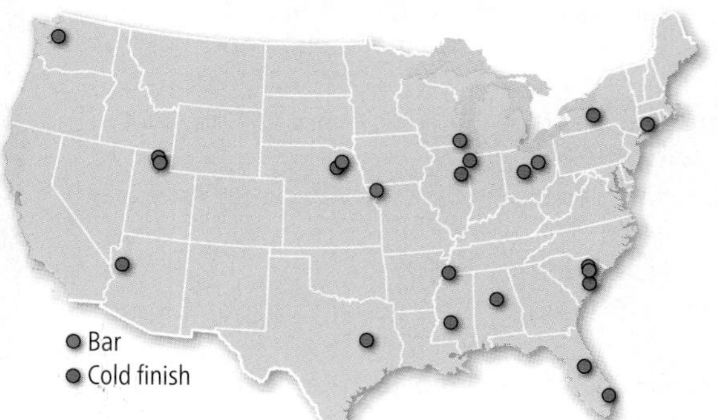

◀ 11.6.2 MINIMILLS
Minimills, which produce steel from scrap metal, are more numerous than integrated steel mills, and they are distributed around the country near local markets. Shown are the plants of Nucor Corporation, the largest minimill operator in the United States.

Changing Distribution of World Steel Production

The shift of world manufacturing to new industrial regions can be seen clearly in steel production. In 1980, 81 percent of world steel was produced in developed countries and 19 percent in developing countries (Figure 11.6.3). Between 1980 and 2016, the share of world steel production declined to 35 percent in developed countries and increased to 65 percent in developing countries (Figure 11.6.4).

World steel production more than doubled between 1980 and 2016, from 0.7 billion to 1.6 billion metric tons. China was responsible for 0.8 billion of the 0.9 billion metric ton increase, and other developing countries (primarily India and South Korea) for another 0.2 billion. Production in developed countries declined by 0.1 billion metric tons. China's steel industry has grown in part because of access to the primary inputs iron ore and coal. However, the principal factor in recent years has been increased demand by growing industries in China that use a lot of steel, such as motor vehicles.

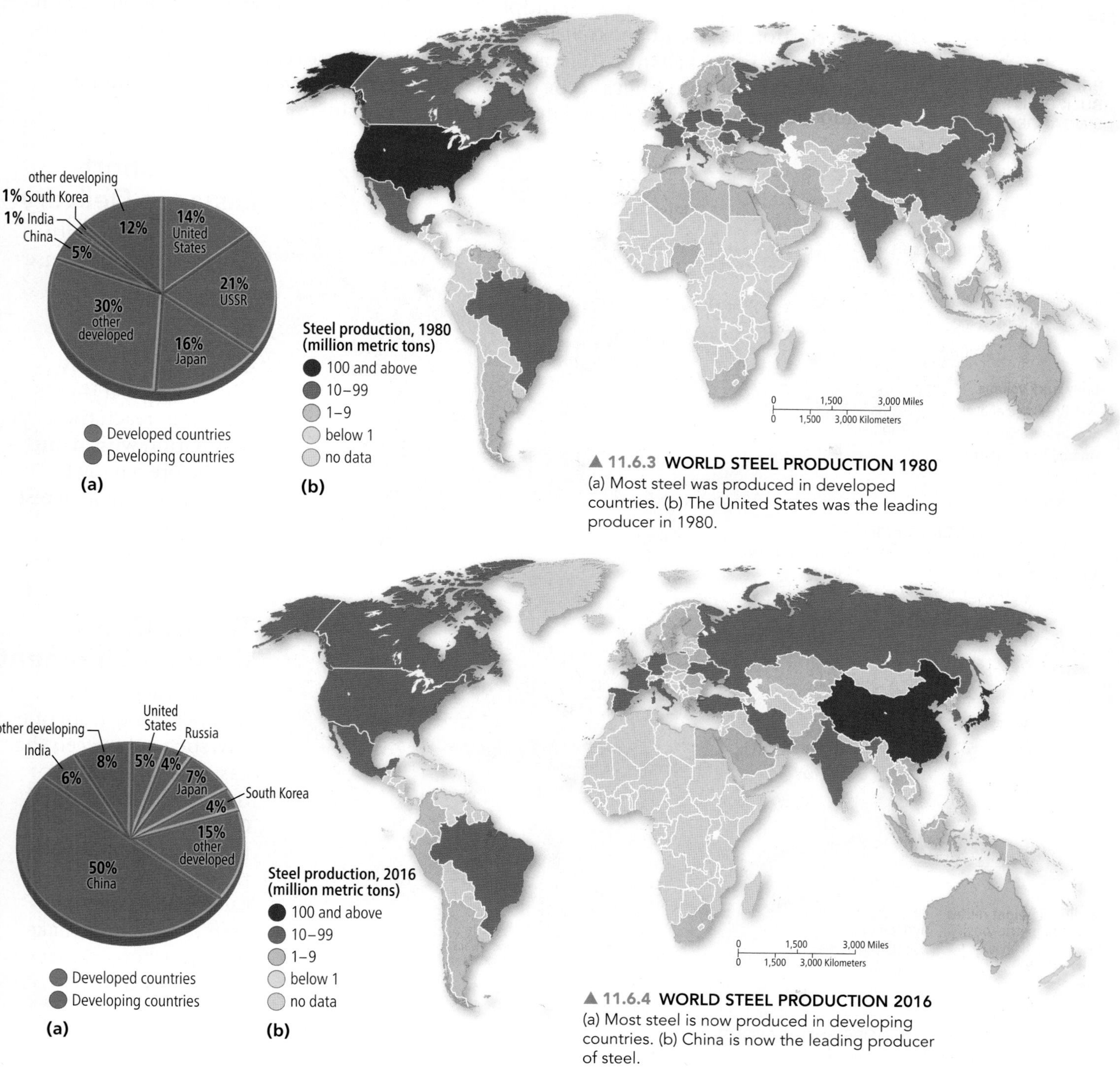

▲ **11.6.3 WORLD STEEL PRODUCTION 1980**
(a) Most steel was produced in developed countries. (b) The United States was the leading producer in 1980.

▲ **11.6.4 WORLD STEEL PRODUCTION 2016**
(a) Most steel is now produced in developing countries. (b) China is now the leading producer of steel.

▲ 11.7.1 BREAK-OF-BULK POINT: SINGAPORE

Ship by Boat, Rail, Truck, or Air?

- Compare industries' use of different modes of transportation.

Inputs and products are transported in one of four modes: ship, rail, truck, or air. Firms seek the lowest-cost mode of transport, but which of the four alternatives is cheapest changes with the distance that goods are being sent.

Break-of-Bulk Points

Cost rises each time inputs or products are transferred from one of the four modes to another. A **break-of-bulk point** is a place where transfer among transportation modes is possible. Many companies that use multiple transport modes locate at a break-of-bulk point. Containerization has facilitated transfer of packages between modes at break-of-bulk points. Containers may be packed into a rail car, transferred quickly to a container ship to cross the ocean, and unloaded into trucks at the other end. Large ships have been specially built to accommodate large numbers of rectangular, box-like containers (Figure 11.7.1).

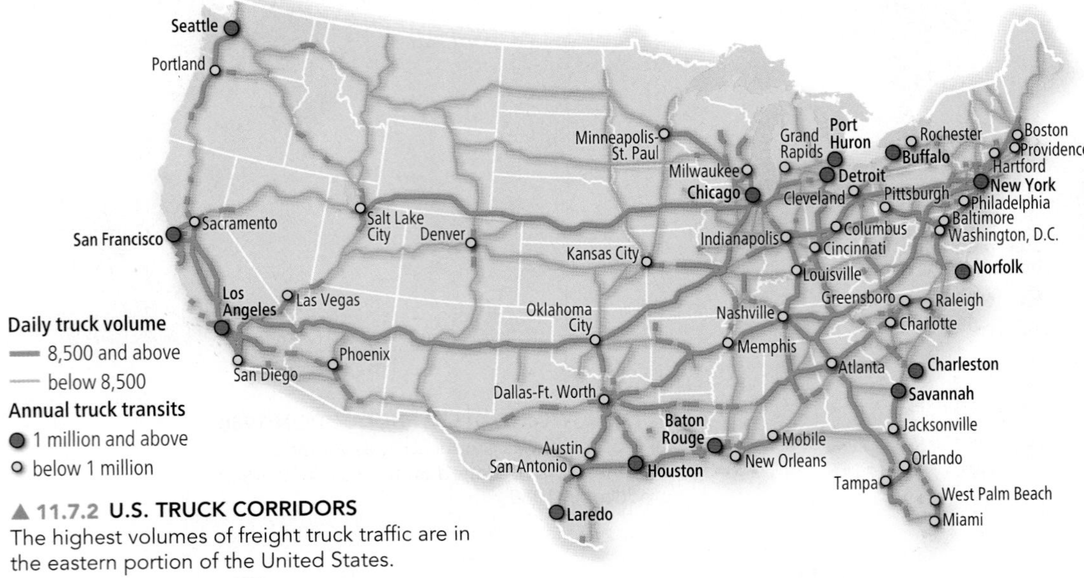

▲ 11.7.2 U.S. TRUCK CORRIDORS
The highest volumes of freight truck traffic are in the eastern portion of the United States.

Trucks: Short-Distance Delivery

Trucks are optimal for short distances, because they can be loaded and unloaded quickly and cheaply. Truck delivery is especially advantageous if the driver can reach the destination within one day, before having to stop for an extended rest (Figure 11.7.2).

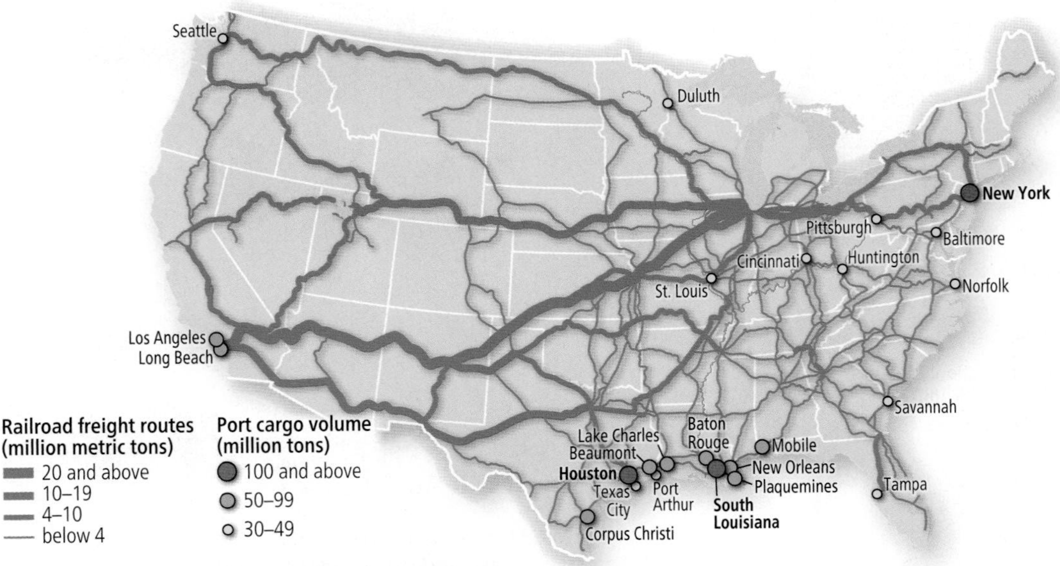

▲ 11.7.3 U.S. RAIL CORRIDORS AND SEAPORTS
Most rail traffic moves long distances east-west within the United States.

Trains: Cross-Country Shipment

Journeys across land that take more than one day, such as between the East and West coasts of the United States and Canada, are suitable for trains. Trains take longer than trucks to load, but once under way, they aren't required to make daily rest stops like trucks (Figure 11.7.3).

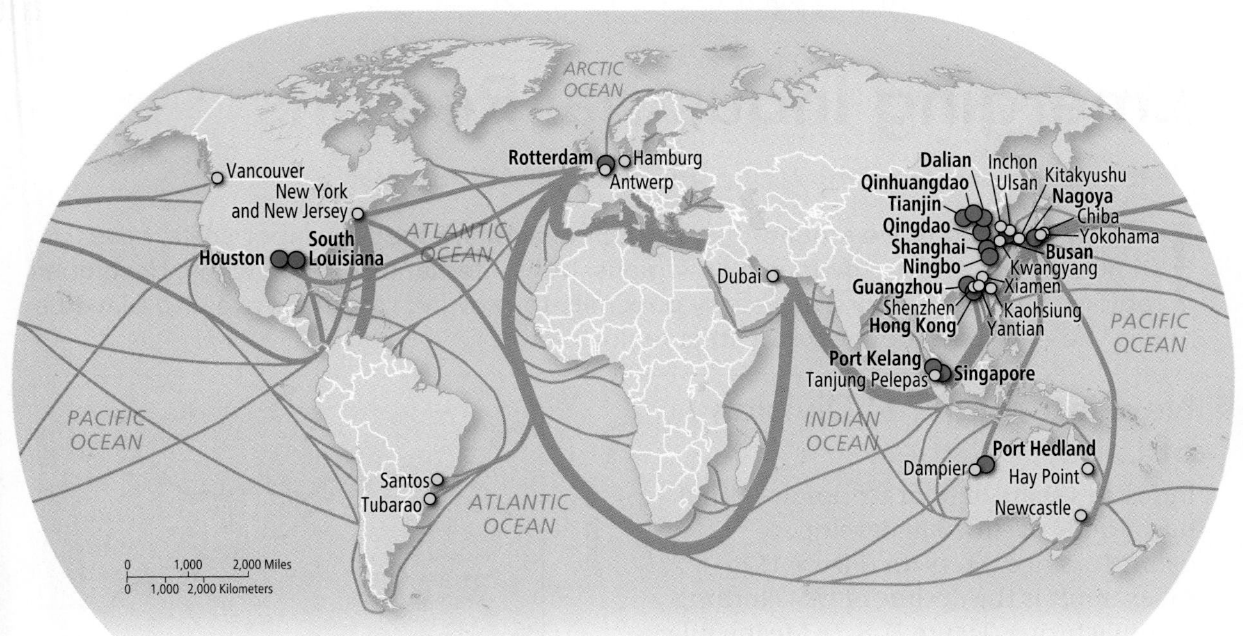

◀ **11.7.4 WORLD SHIPPING ROUTES AND PORTS** Most freight is moved between continents by ship.

Ships: For Crossing Oceans

Ships are slower than land-based transportation, but unlike trains or trucks, they can cross oceans, such as to North America from Europe or Asia (Figure 11.7.4). The cost per kilometer (or mile) is very low.

Airplanes: For Small Valuable Packages

Air transport is the most expensive option for all distances, so it usually reserved for speedy delivery of small-bulk, high-value packages (Figure 11.7.5).

Just-in-Time Delivery

Proximity to market has become more important in recent years because of the rise of **just-in-time delivery**. As the name implies, just-in-time is shipment of parts and materials to arrive at a factory moments before they are needed. Just-in-time delivery is especially important for delivery of inputs, such as parts and raw materials, to manufacturers of fabricated products, such as cars and computers.

Under just-in-time, parts and materials arrive at a factory frequently, in many cases daily or even hourly. Suppliers of the parts and materials are told a few days in advance how much will be needed over the next week or two, and first thing each morning, they are told exactly what will be needed at precisely what time that day. To meet a tight timetable, a supplier of parts and materials must locate factories near its customers. If given only an hour or two of notice, a supplier has no choice but to locate a factory within 50 miles or so of the customer.

Just-in-time delivery reduces the money that a manufacturer must tie up in wasteful inventory. Manufacturers also save money through just-in-time delivery by reducing the size of the factory because space does not have to be wasted on piling up a mountain of inventory. Leading computer manufacturers have eliminated inventory altogether. They build computers only in response to customer orders placed primarily over the Internet or by telephone.

Just-in-time delivery means that producers have lower inventory to cushion against disruptions in the arrival of needed parts. Three kinds of disruptions can result from reliance on just-in-time delivery:

- Natural hazards. Poor weather conditions can affect deliveries anywhere in the world. Blizzards can close highways, rail lines, and airports.
- Traffic. Deliveries may be delayed when traffic is slowed by accident, construction, or unusually heavy volume.
- Labor unrest. A strike at one supplier plant can shut down the entire production within a couple of days.

▼ **11.7.5 FEDEX, MEMPHIS, TENNESSEE**

Emerging Industrial Regions

- Identify changes in the global distribution of industry.

Industry is on the move around the world. Site factors, especially labor costs, have stimulated industrial growth in new regions, both internationally and within developed regions. Situation factors, especially proximity to growing markets, have also played a role in the emergence of new industrial regions.

New International Division of Labor

Industry's share of total economic output has steadily declined in developed countries since the 1970s (Figure 11.8.1). An example is the decline of U.S. clothing manufacturing (Figure 11.8.2). Meanwhile, the share of world industry in other regions has increased—from one-sixth in 1970 to one-half in 2010.

Transnational corporations have been especially aggressive in using low-cost labor in developing countries. Despite the greater transportation cost, transnational corporations can profitably transfer some work to developing countries, given their substantially lower wages compared to those in developed countries. At the same time, operations that require highly skilled workers remain in factories in developed countries. The selective transfer of some jobs to developing countries is known as the **new international division of labor**.

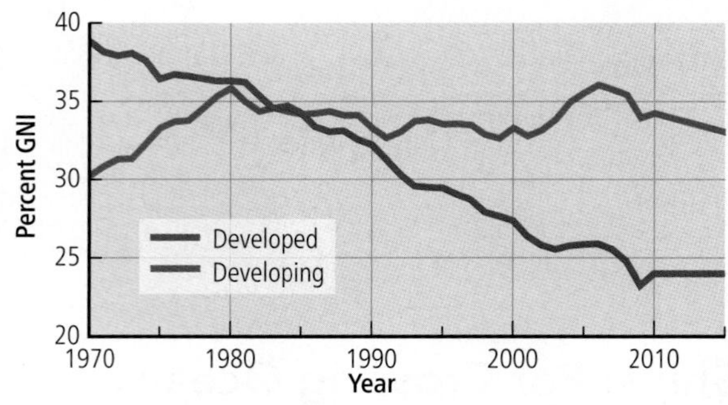

▲ 11.8.1 **MANUFACTURING VALUE ADDED AS PERCENTAGE OF GNI**
Manufacturing has accounted for a higher share of GNI in developing countries than in developed countries since the 1980s.

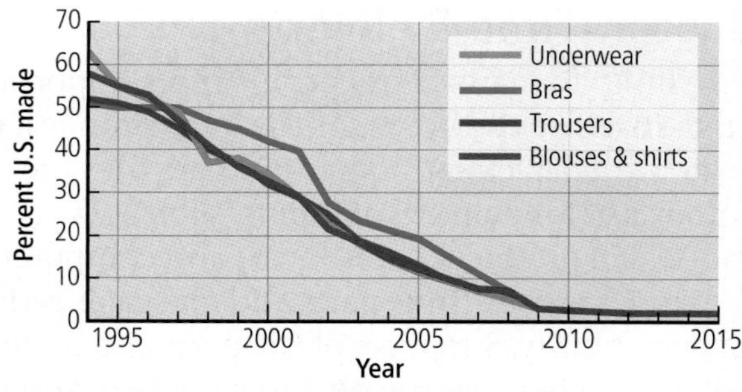

▲ 11.8.2 **U.S. CLOTHING MANUFACTURING**
The percentage of clothing sold in the United States that was made in the United States has declined from around 50 percent in the 1990s to 3 percent today.

Outsourcing

Transnational corporations allocate production to low-wage countries through **outsourcing**, which is turning over much of the responsibility for production to independent suppliers. Outsourcing has had a major impact on the distribution of manufacturing because each step in the production process is now scrutinized closely in order to determine the optimal location.

Outsourcing contrasts with the approach typical of traditional mass production, called **vertical integration**, in which a company controls all phases of a highly complex production process. Vertical integration was traditionally regarded as a source of strength for manufacturers because it gave them the ability to do and control everything.

Outsourcing is especially important in the electronics industry. The world's largest electronics contractor is Foxconn, a major supplier of chips and other electronics components for such companies as Apple and Intel. Foxconn's largest factory complex in China employs around 300,000 workers. A large percentage of Foxconn's employees live in dormitories near the factories, working long hours, for low wages and limited benefits.

Mexico and NAFTA

Manufacturing has increased rapidly in Mexico. The North American Free Trade Agreement (NAFTA), effective in 1994, eliminated most barriers to moving goods among Mexico, the United States, and Canada. Because it is the nearest low-wage country to the United States, Mexico attracts labor-intensive industries that also need proximity to the U.S. market. Nearly all of the growth of motor vehicle production in North America, for example, has been located in Mexico rather than the United States or Canada (Figure 11.8.3).

Plants in Mexico near the U.S. border are known as **maquiladoras**. Under U.S. and Mexican laws, companies receive tax breaks if they ship materials from the United States, assemble components at a maquiladora plant in Mexico, and export the finished product back to the United States (Figure 11.8.4). More than 1 million Mexicans are employed at over 3,000 maquiladoras.

Integration of North American industry has generated fear in the United States and Canada that companies are relocating production to Mexico to take advantage of lower wage rates. Environmentalists charge that environmental protection laws are not strictly enforced in Mexico.

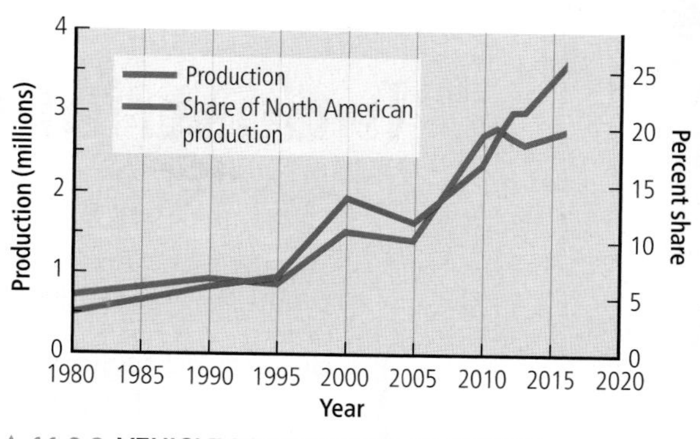

▲ 11.8.3 VEHICLE PRODUCTION IN MEXICO

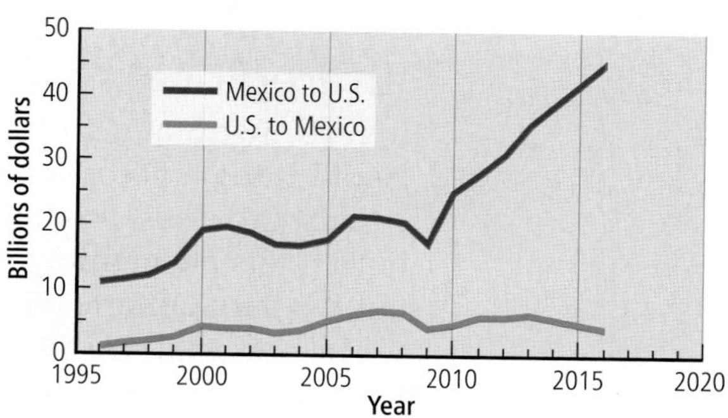

▲ 11.8.4 U.S.-MEXICO TRADE IN VEHICLES

BRICS Countries

Much of the world's future growth in manufacturing is expected to cluster in a handful of countries known as BRICS, which is an acronym coined by the investment banking firm Goldman Sachs for Brazil, Russia, India, China, and South Africa.

The five BRICS countries together contain 42 percent of the world's inhabitants but account for only 23 percent of world GDP. However, their share of world GDP is expected to increase rapidly in the future, especially those of China and India (Figure 11.8.5). China and India have the two largest labor forces, whereas Russia and Brazil are rich in inputs critical for industry.

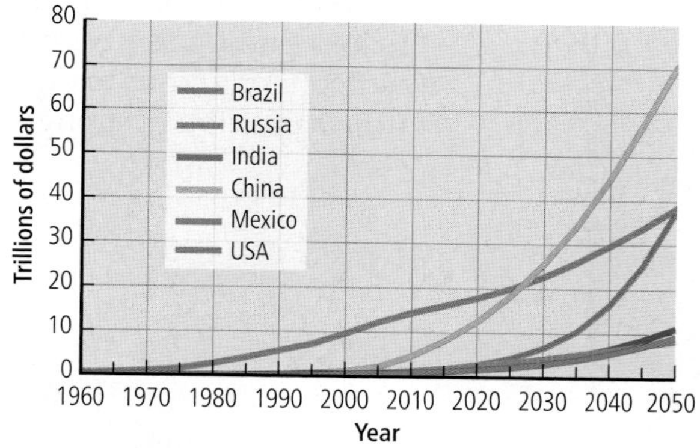

▲ 11.8.5 GDP FOR BRICS COUNTRIES, MEXICO, AND THE UNITED STATES

China is expected to have the world's largest GDP during the 2020s, and India is expected to be second in the 2050s.

WHAT'S YOUR INDUSTRIAL GEOGRAPHY?

NATIONAL ORIGIN OF YOUR CLOTHING

Clothing sold in the United States has a label showing national origin (Figure 11.8.6).

1. Take a look at the labels in 10 of your t-shirts. For each t-shirt, record the world region in which it was made (Africa, Asia, Europe, Latin America, or North America). Record the total number of t-shirts made in each of the five regions.
2. Sum the total t-shirts made in each of the five regions. Which region has the highest number? Which has the lowest?
3. Compare the results with others in your class. How do your results compare with those of the overall class?
4. Which of the three developing regions (Africa, Asia, or Latin America) has the highest total? Which has the lowest total? What might account for the sharp difference between these developing regions?

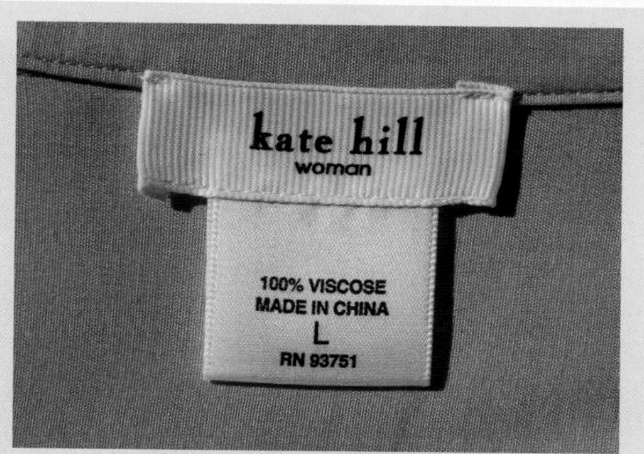

▲ 11.8.6 NATIONAL ORIGIN, CHINA

Industrial Change in Developed Regions

- Explain industrial location changes within developed regions.

In developed regions, industry is shifting away from the traditional industrial areas of northwestern Europe and the northeastern United States.

Intraregional Shifts in North America

In the United States, industry has shifted from the Northeast toward the South and West (Figure 11.9.1). Motor vehicle production is an example of an industry that has been attracted to the South. Most production is located in a corridor known as Auto Alley formed by north–south interstate highways 65 and 75 between Michigan and Alabama, with an extension into southwestern Ontario (Figure 11.9.2). Newer plants are in the southern portion of auto alley.

The principal lure for many manufacturers has been right-to-work laws. A **right-to-work law** requires a factory to maintain an "open shop" and prohibits a "closed shop." In a closed shop, a company and a union agree that everyone must join the union to work in the factory. In an open shop, a union and a company may not negotiate a contract that requires workers to join a union as a condition of employment. Right-to-work laws that make it much more difficult for unions to organize factory workers, collect dues, and bargain with employers from a position of strength.

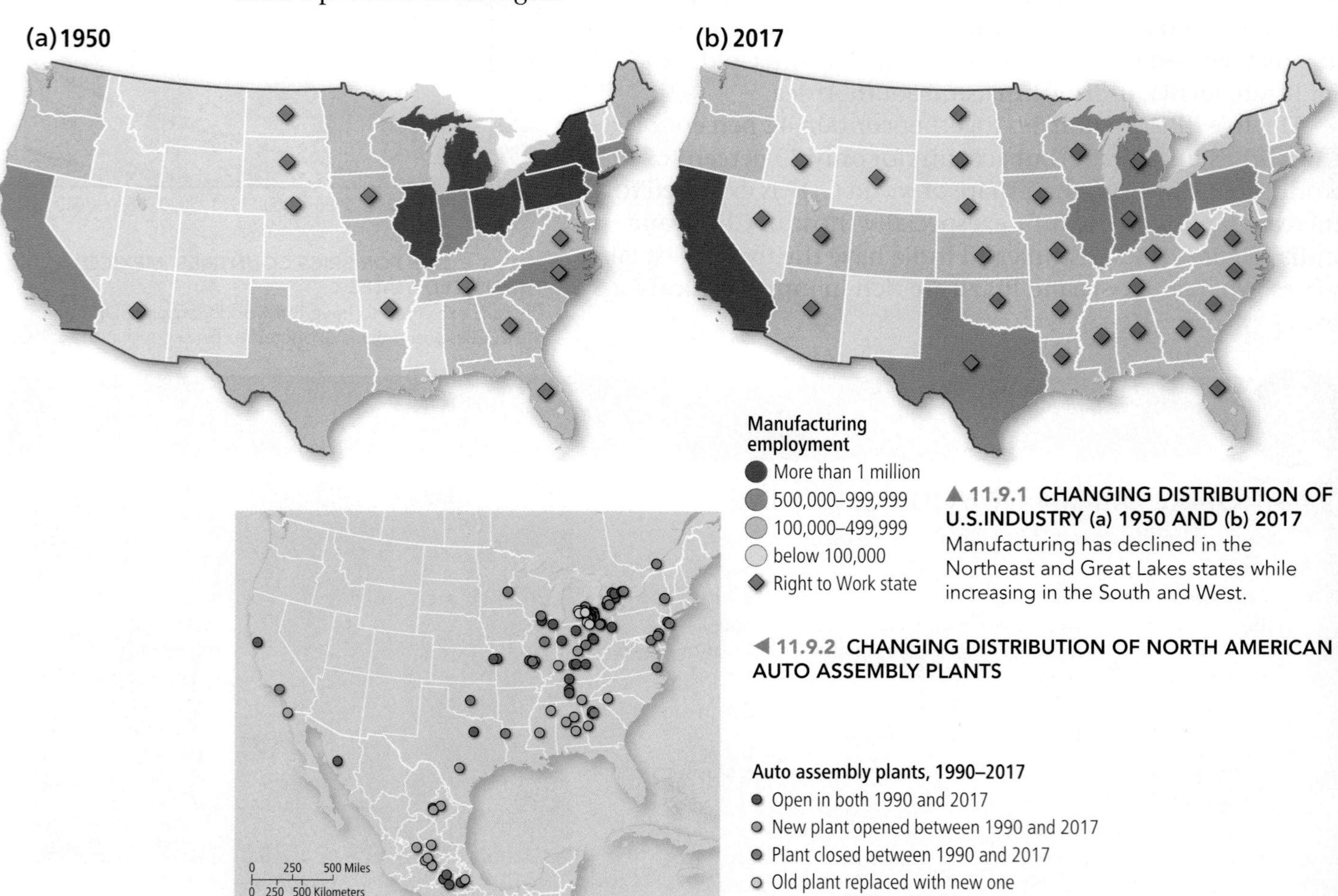

▲ 11.9.1 CHANGING DISTRIBUTION OF U.S.INDUSTRY (a) 1950 AND (b) 2017
Manufacturing has declined in the Northeast and Great Lakes states while increasing in the South and West.

◀ 11.9.2 CHANGING DISTRIBUTION OF NORTH AMERICAN AUTO ASSEMBLY PLANTS

Intraregional Shifts in Europe

Manufacturing has diffused from traditional industrial centers in northwestern Europe toward Southern and Eastern Europe. Government policies have encouraged relocation toward economically distressed peripheral areas.

The Western European country with the most rapid manufacturing growth during the late twentieth century was Spain, especially after its admission to the European Union in 1986. Since the fall of communism in the early 1990s, investment in industry has increased rapidly in Central Europe, especially Czechia, Hungary, Poland and Slovakia (Figure 11.9.3). Central Europe offers manufacturers two important site and situation factors: low-wage but relatively skilled labor and proximity to Western Europe markets.

Skilled Labor

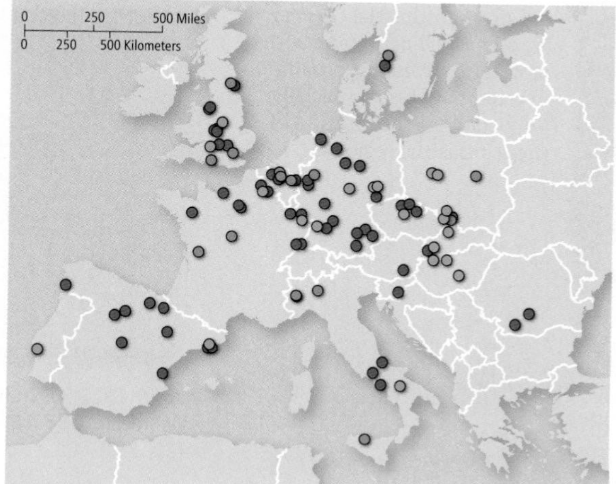

Auto assembly plants, 1990–2017

- Open in both 1990 and 2017
- Opened between 1990 and 2017
- Closed beween 1990 and 2017

◀ 11.9.3 CHANGING DISTRIBUTION OF EUROPEAN AUTO ASSEMBLY PLANTS

Former manufacturing centers of Northeastern United States and northwestern Europe still attract industries that depend on skilled labor and rapid delivery to market. Skilled labor has important geographic implications because it is an asset found principally in the older industrial regions.

Traditionally, factories assigned each worker one task to perform repeatedly. Some geographers call this approach **Fordist production**, or mass production, because the Ford Motor Co. was one of the first companies to organize its production this way early in the twentieth century.

Many industries now follow a lean, or flexible, production approach. The term **post-Fordist** production is sometimes used to describe flexible production, in contrast with Fordist production. Post-Fordist flexible production organizes workers into teams that perform a variety of tasks and solve problems through consensus. Increasingly, factory workers need skills such as computer literacy, and many now have college degrees.

DEBATE IT!

Should corporations receive government subsidies to build a new industry?

Corporations such as Foxcomm, Amazon, and Toyota have received substantial subsidies from state and local governments to build new industrial facilities.

GOVERNMENT SHOULD PROVIDE SUBSIDIES

- The new industry brings many jobs to the community (Figure 11.9.4).
- The new employees will spend more at the community's existing businesses.
- Everyone in the community benefits from new roads, expanded broadband, and other infrastructure provided for the new industry.

▶ 11.9.4 VW PLANT, CHATTANOOGA, TENNESSEE

GOVERNMENT SHOULD NOT PROVIDE SUBSIDIES

- The community often spends more on subsidies than it gets back in tax revenues.
- Arrival of many newcomers causes prices to rise for housing and other services.
- The new industry and its workers may change the character of a small close-knit community (Figure 11.9.5).

◀ 11.9.5 WATCHING JULY 4 PARADE

CHAPTER 11

Review, Analyze, & Apply

KEY ISSUE 1 Where Is Industry Distributed?

Industry is not distributed uniformly around the world. Most of the world's industry is clustered in the three regions: Europe, North America, and East Asia. The concept of manufacturing goods in a factory originated with the Industrial Revolution in the United Kingdom.

THINKING GEOGRAPHICALLY

▲ 11.CR.1 GRAIN ELEVATORS AT SHIP TERMINALS, LAKE SUPERIOR

1. The world's three most important industrial clusters are all located near some body of water. Why might proximity to water have been especially important for the location of these industrial regions?

KEY ISSUE 2 Why Are Site Factors Important For Industry?

A company ordinarily considers a combination of situation and site factors in deciding where to locate a factory or to find suppliers. Site factors are related to the costs of factors of production inside a factory. The three site factors are labor, capital, and land.

THINKING GEOGRAPHICALLY

▲ 11.CR.2 "MADE IN" LABEL: READ THE FINE PRINT

2. Check your clothing labels. Do you have any clothing made in the United States or a developed country in Europe? What might account for that clothing being made in a developed country rather than in Asia or Latin America?

KEY ISSUE 3 Why Are Situation Factors Important For Industry?

Situation factors involve transporting inputs into a factory and transporting manufactured goods to the markets. Inputs and products are transported by ship, rail, truck, or air. The optimal choice depends on the distance something is being transported.

THINKING GEOGRAPHICALLY

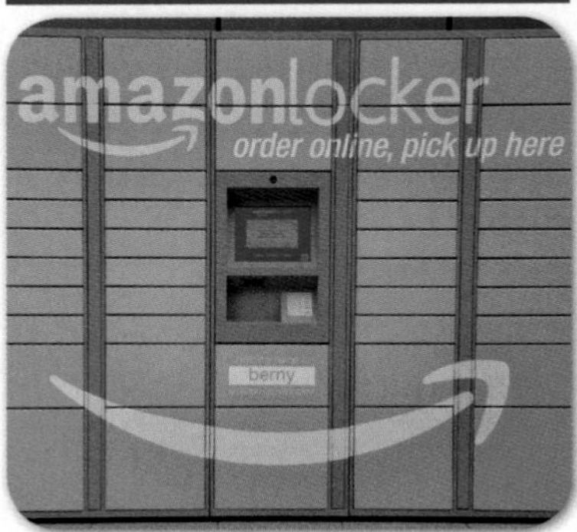

▲ 11.CR.3 ON-LINE RETAIL: FROM WAREHOUSE TO YOU

3. How has the increase in delivery of goods ordered on-line affect the various modes of transport?

KEY ISSUE 4 Why Are Industries Changing Locations

The location of manufacturing has changed. Industry is increasing in some developing countries and in some areas within developed regions. Site factors, especially labor costs, have stimulated industrial growth in new regions, especially the BRICS countries. Within North America and Europe, manufacturing is growing in areas where it had not traditionally clustered.

THINKING GEOGRAPHICALLY

▲ 11.CR.4 TRANSPORTING COPPER ORE IN ZAMBIA

4. Refer to material in Chapter 8 about landlocked states and regime types. How might the distribution of landlocked states and regime types impact the ability of African countries to emerge as new industrial regions?

Mastering Geography

Looking for additional review and test prep materials? Visit the Study Area in Mastering Geography to enhance your geographic literacy, spatial reasoning skills, and understanding of this chapter's content. Access MapMaster™ interactive maps, video case studies, *In the News* current articles, flashcards, self-study quizzes, an eText of *Contemporary Human Geography*, and more. **pearson.com/mastering/geography**

Key Terms

Apparel (p. 274) An article of clothing.

Break-of-bulk point (p. 282) A location where transfer is possible from one mode of transportation to another.

Bulk-gaining industry (p. 278) An industry in which the final product weighs more or comprises a greater volume than the inputs.

Bulk-reducing industry (p. 276) An industry in which the final product weighs less or comprises a lower volume than the inputs.

Cottage industry (p. 270) Manufacturing based in homes rather than in factories, commonly found prior to the Industrial Revolution.

Fordist production (p. 287) A form of mass production in which each worker is assigned one specific task to perform repeatedly.

Industrial Revolution (p. 270) A series of improvements in industrial technology that transformed the process of manufacturing goods.

Just-in-time delivery (p. 283) Shipment of parts and materials to arrive at a factory moments before they are needed.

Labor-intensive industry (p. 272) An industry for which labor costs comprise a high percentage of total expenses.

Maquiladora (p. 285) A factory built by a U.S. company in Mexico near the U.S. border, to take advantage of the much lower labor costs in Mexico.

New international division of labor (p. 284) Transfer of some types of jobs, especially those requiring low-paid, less-skilled workers, from developed to developing countries.

Outsourcing (p. 284) A decision by a corporation to turn over much of the responsibility for production to independent suppliers.

Post-Fordist production (p. 287) Adoption by companies of flexible work rules, such as the allocation of workers to teams that perform a variety of tasks.

Right-to-work law (p. 286) A law in some U.S. states that prevents a union and a company from negotiating a contract that requires workers to join the union as a condition of employment.

Site factors (p. 272) Location factors related to the costs of factors of production inside a plant, such as land, labor, and capital.

Situation factors (p. 276) Location factors related to the transportation of materials into and from a factory.

Textile (p. 274) A fabric made by weaving, used in making clothing.

Vertical integration (p. 284) An approach typical of traditional mass production in which a company controls all phases of a highly complex production process.

GeoVideo

Log in to the Mastering Geography™ Study Area to view this video.

China: New Industrial Power

Economists project that by 2025, China's economy will be the world's largest, raising questions about how China's dominance will affect the United States economy.

1. Summarize the reasons presented in the video for the recent perceived decline in the United States' position as the world's leading economy.
2. What is one strategy the United States has used recently to cope with China's rise as an industrial power? How does China plan to counter that strategy?
3. Explain what is meant by the phrase "globalization in reverse." Would this process necessarily be bad for the United States?

Explore

Auto assembly plants

Auto assembly plants take up a lot of land. Let's compare one of the oldest and newest in the United States.

1. In Google Earth, ***search*** for *7777 Kia Parkway, West Point, Georgia*. This is a Kia assembly plant opened in 2009. Describe the use of land surrounding the factory.
2. ***Search*** for *12600 S. Torrence Ave., Chicago*. This is a Ford assembly plant opened in 1924. ***Zoom*** out to around 2 km. Describe the uses of land that surround the factory. How do the surroundings differ from those around the Kia plant?

▲ 11.CR.6 **KIA MOTORS, WEST POINT, GEORGIA**

Geospatial Analysis

Log in to the Mastering Geography Study Area to access MapMaster 2.0.

Railroads and industries

U.S. manufacturers make heavy use of railroads.

Add the *Major Manufacturing Regions (North America)* layer. ***Select*** the *Settings* icon from the *Legend*, ***select*** *Change Map Projection* and ***select*** *Albers*, and ***select*** *Show City Labels*. ***Zoom*** to North America..

1. What major cities in the United States appear to be within major manufacturing regions?
2. ***Add*** the *World Railroads* layer. In which city do the largest number of railroads appear to converge? What industry discussed in this chapter is highly clustered near this city? What might account for this clustering?

▲ 11.CR.7 **MAJOR MANUFACTURING REGIONS AND RAILROADS OF NORTH AMERICA**

CHAPTER

12 Services

Most employed people in the world work in services, such as shops, offices, restaurants, universities, and hospitals. Services are closely linked with settlements because most services are located in settlements. Geography plays an especially important role in the provision of services. For example, service providers apply geographic principles to determine the best place to locate.

◀ Street market, Seoul, South Korea.

KEY ISSUES

1 Where Are Services Distributed?

Three types of services are consumer, business, and public. Services account for a relatively high share of GDP in developed countries.

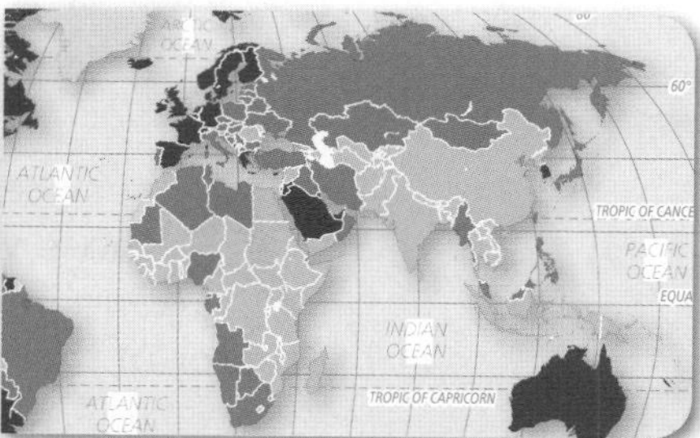

2 Where Are Consumer Services Distributed?

Consumer services are distributed in a regular pattern, especially in developed countries. Central place theory helps to explain the distribution of consumer services.

3 Where Are Business Services Distributed?

Business services tend to cluster in a relatively small number of large settlements, known as global cities. Developing countries specialize in some forms of business services.

4 Why Do Services Cluster In Settlements?

Services cluster in settlements, which could be rural or urban. An increasing number and an increasing percentage of humans live in urban settlements.

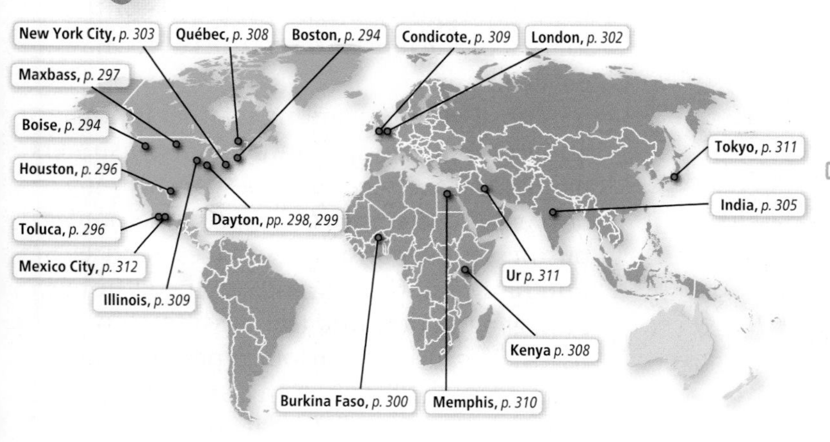

basic business
primate city
hinterland
offshore financial services
dispersed rural settlement
public services
clustered rural settlement
central place theory
threshold
business process outsourcing
gravity model
food desert
urbanization
business services
global cities
rank size rule
range
periodic markets
hexagons
consumer services
economic base
sharing services
nonbasic business
market area analysis

Types of Services

- Identify the three types of services.

A **service** is any activity that fulfills a human want or need and returns money to those who provide it. As fewer people in developed countries work in agriculture and industry, more are employed in services, otherwise known as the tertiary sector of the economy.

▼ 12.1.1 **U.S. EMPLOYMENT BY SECTOR**
Approximately one-half of jobs in the United States are in consumer services and one-fourth in business services. The remainder are in public services, manufacturing, and agriculture.

Percent of all U.S. jobs	Sector
	SERVICES
	CONSUMER SERVICES
14.6%	**Retail and Wholesale** Department stores, grocers, and motor vehicle sales and service account for nearly one-half of this sector. Another one-fourth are wholesalers that provide merchandise to retailers.
13.1%	**Health and Social Services** One-third are in hospitals, one-half in other health-care services, such as doctors' offices and nursing homes, and one-sixth in social assistance.
9.4%	**Education Services** This figure includes educators at both public and private schools.
10.7%	**Leisure and Hospitality Services** Three-fourths of these jobs are in restaurants, bars, and lodging; the other one-fourth are in the arts and entertainment.
3.9%	**Other Consumer Services**
	BUSINESS SERVICES
13.9%	**Professional Services** Technical services, including law, management, accounting, architecture, engineering, design, and consulting, comprise 60 percent of professional service jobs. Support services, such as clerical, secretarial, and custodial work, account for the other 40 percent.
5.6%	**Transportation and Information Services** Transportation, primarily trucking and warehousing, account for 60 percent of these jobs. The other 40 percent are in information services such as publishing and broadcasting, as well as utilities such as water and electricity.
5.7%	**Financial Services** This sector is often called "FIRE," an acronym for finance, insurance, and real estate. One-half of the financial services jobs are in banks and other financial institutions, one-third in insurance companies, and the remainder in real estate.
8.0%	PUBLIC SERVICES
13.0%	**MANUFACTURING AND CONSTRUCTION**
2.0%	**AGRICULTURE AND MINING**

Three Types of Services

The service sector of the economy is subdivided into three types—consumer services, business services, and public services. Each of these sectors is subdivided into several major subsectors (Figure 12.1.1).

Consumer Services. The principal purpose of **consumer services** is to provide services to individual consumers who desire them and can afford to pay for them. Around one-half of all jobs in the United States are in consumer services. Four main types of consumer services are retail, education, health, and leisure.

Business Services. The principal purpose of **business services** is to facilitate the activities of other businesses. One-fourth of all jobs in the United States are in business services. Professional services, financial services, and transportation services are the three main types of business services.

Public Services. The purpose of **public services** is to provide security and protection for citizens and businesses. About 8 percent of all U.S. jobs are in the public sector. Excluding educators, one-sixth of public-sector employees work for the federal government, one-fourth for one of the 50 state governments, and three-fifths for one of the tens of thousands of local governments.

The distinction among services is not absolute. For example, individual consumers use business services, such as consulting lawyers and keeping money in banks, and businesses use consumer services, such as purchasing stationery and staying in hotels. Still, geographers find the classification useful, because the various types of services have different distributions, and different factors influence locational decisions.

Services and Settlements

Services generate more than two-thirds of GDP in most developed countries, compared to less than one-half in most developing countries (Figure 12.1.2). Logically, the distribution of service workers is opposite that of the percentage of primary workers (refer to Figure 9.2.2).

However, if services were located merely where people lived, then China and India would have the most, rather than the United States and other developed countries. Services cluster in developed countries because more people who are able to buy services live there. Within developed countries, larger cities offer a larger scale of services than do small towns because more customers reside there.

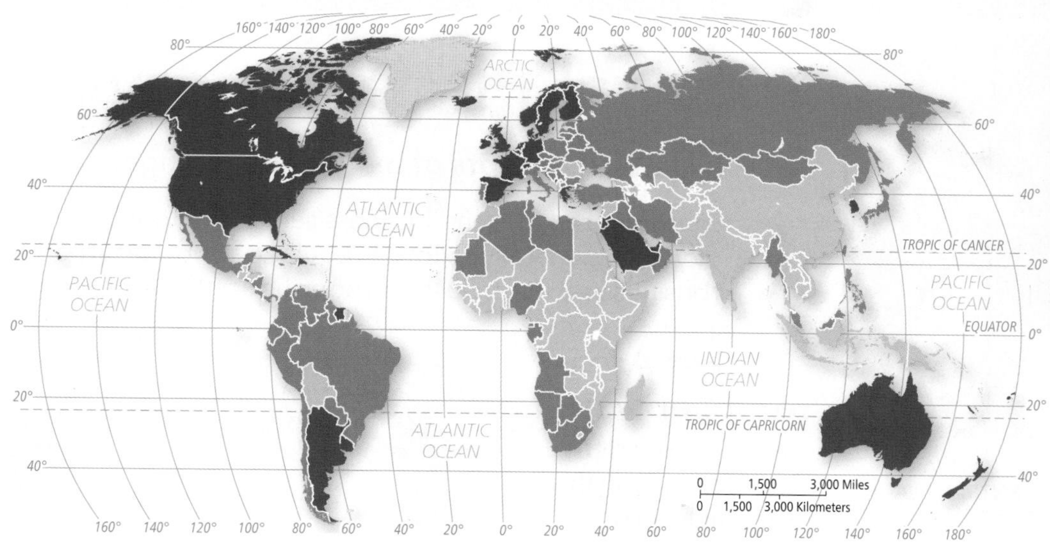

▲ **12.1.2 PERCENTAGE OF GDP FROM SERVICES**

Geographers see a close link between services and settlements because services are located in settlements. A **settlement** is a permanent collection of buildings where people reside, work, and obtain services. They occupy a very small percentage of Earth's surface, well under 1 percent, but settlements are home to nearly all humans because few people live in isolation.

Explaining why services are clustered in settlements is at one level straightforward for geographers. In geographic terms, only one locational factor is critical for a service: proximity to the market. The optimal location of industry, described in Chapter 11, requires balancing a number of site and situation factors, but the optimal location for a service is simply near its customers.

On the other hand, locating a service calls for far more precise geographic skills than locating a factory. The optimal location for a factory may be an area of several hundred square kilometers, whereas the optimal location for a service may be a very specific place, such as a street corner.

Changes in Job Sectors

Figure 12.1.3 shows changes in U.S. employment. All the growth in employment in the United States has been in services, whereas employment in primary- and secondary-sector activities has declined. Within business services, jobs expanded most rapidly in professional services and more slowly in finance and transportation services because of improved efficiency; fewer workers are needed to run trains and answer phones, for example. On the consumer services side, the most rapid increase has been in the provision of health care, education, entertainment, and recreation.

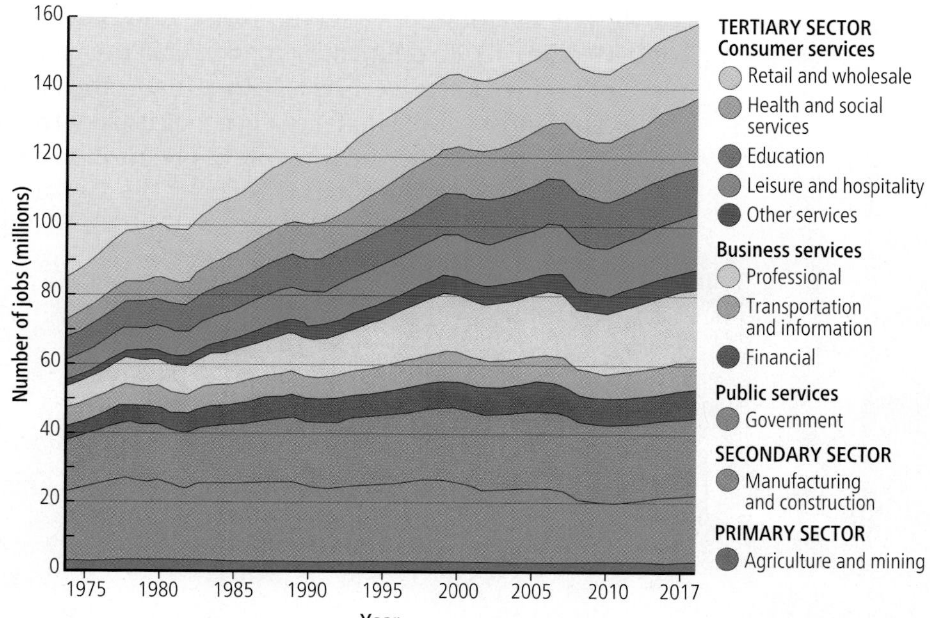

▲ **12.1.3 CHANGE IN U.S. EMPLOYMENT**
Jobs have increased in the tertiary sector, especially consumer services.

▲ 12.2.1 A CENTRAL PLACE: BOSTON

Central Place Theory

- Define the concepts of market area, range, and threshold.

Consumer services and business services do not have the same distributions. Consumer services generally follow a regular pattern based on size of settlements, whereas business services cluster in specific settlements creating a specialized pattern.

Market Area of a Service

Selecting the right location is probably the single most important factor in the profitability of a consumer service. **Central place theory** helps to explain how the most profitable location can be identified.

Central place theory was first proposed in the 1930s by German geographer Walter Christaller, based on his studies of southern Germany. August Lösch in Germany and Brian Berry and others in the United States further developed the concept during the 1950s.

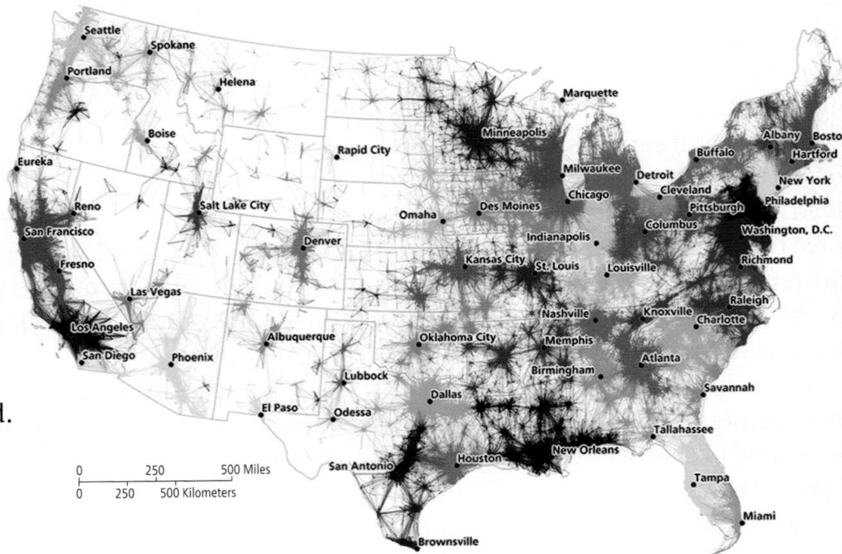

▲ 12.2.2 U.S. MEGAREGIONS
The map shows areas around cities from which commuters are attracted.

A **central place** is a market center where people cluster to buy and sell goods and services. The place is named “central” because it is centrally located to maximize accessibility from a surrounding area (Figure 12.2.1).

The area surrounding a service from which customers are attracted is the **market area** (or **hinterland**). To delineate a market area on a map, a circle can be drawn around a central place or node of a service. The territory inside the circle is its market area.

Because most people prefer to get services from the nearest location, the closer to the center of the circle, the greater the percentage of consumers who will choose to obtain services from that node. People on the circumference of the market-area circle are equally likely to use the service or go elsewhere. A market area is thus a good example of a functional region—a region with a node where the characteristic is most intense (refer to Figure 1.7.4).

The United States can be divided into market areas based on the hinterlands surrounding the largest urban settlements (Figure 12.2.2). Studies conducted by geographers Alasdair Rae and Garrett Nelson use U.S. Census data for travel from home to work to depict what they call megaregions, such as the market area centered on Boise, Idaho (Figure 12.2.3).

▼ 12.2.3 BOISE, IDAHO: CENTRAL PLACE OF A MEGAREGION

Range of a Service

The market area of every service varies. To determine the extent of a market area, geographers need two pieces of information about a service: its range and its threshold.

How far are you willing to travel for a pizza? To see a doctor for a serious problem? To watch a ball game? The **range** is the maximum distance people are willing to travel to use a service. The range is the radius of the circle drawn to delineate a service's market area.

People are willing to go only a short distance for everyday consumer services, such as groceries and pharmacies. But they will travel longer distances for other services, such as a concert or professional ball game. Thus a convenience store has a small range, whereas a stadium has a large range.

As a rule, people tend to go to the nearest available service: Someone in the mood for a McDonald's hamburger is likely to go to the nearest McDonald's. Therefore, the range of a service must be determined from the radius of a circle that is irregularly shaped rather than perfectly round, taking in the territory for which the proposed site is closer than competitors' sites.

The range must be modified further because most people think of distance in terms of time: "One hour" may translate into 100 kilometers (60 miles) of driving on an expressway but only 50 kilometers (30 miles) on city streets.

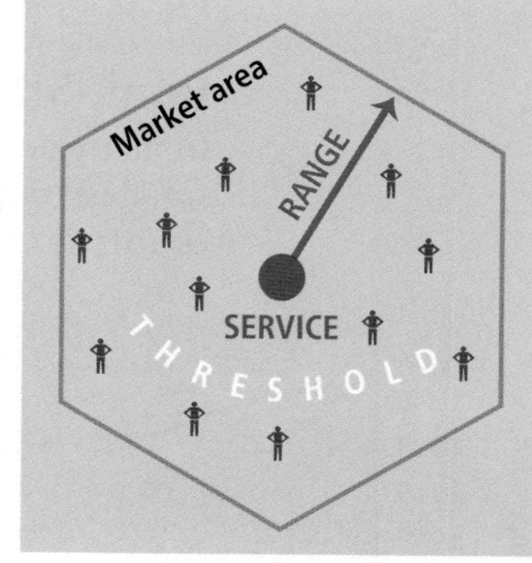

▲ 12.2.4 **MARKET AREA, RANGE, AND THRESHOLD**
The market area is the area of the hexagon, the range is the radius, and the threshold is a sufficient number of people inside the area to support the service.

Threshold of a Service

The second piece of geographic information needed to compute a market area is the **threshold**, which is the minimum number of people needed to support the service. Every enterprise has a minimum number of customers required to generate enough sales to make a profit. So once the range has been determined, a service provider must determine whether a location is suitable by counting the potential customers inside the irregularly shaped circle—often estimated using census data.

How expected consumers inside the range are counted depends on the product. Convenience stores and fast-food restaurants appeal to nearly everyone, whereas other goods and services appeal primarily to certain consumer groups. For example:

- Movie theaters attract younger people; chiropractors attract older folks.
- Poorer people are drawn to thrift stores; wealthier ones might frequent upscale department stores.
- Amusement parks attract families with children; nightclubs appeal to singles.

Developers of shopping malls, department stores, and large supermarkets may count only higher-income people, perhaps those whose annual incomes exceed $50,000. Even though the stores may attract individuals of all incomes, higher-income people are likely to spend more and purchase items that carry higher profit margins for the retailer.

The Geometry of Market Areas

To represent market areas in central place theory, geographers draw hexagons around settlements (Figure 12.2.4). Hexagons represent a compromise between circles and squares (Figure 12.2.5).

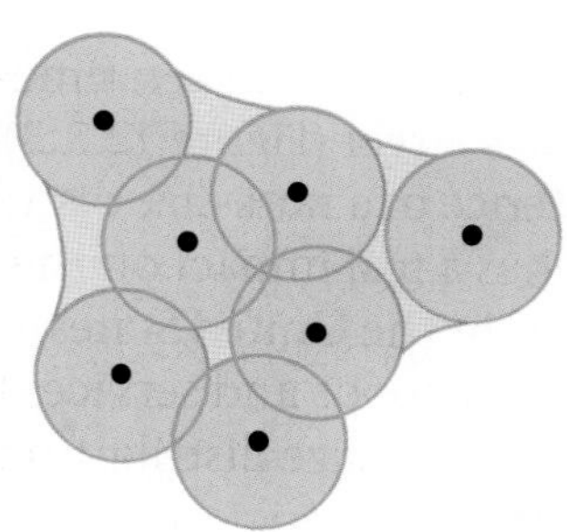

(a) THE PROBLEM WITH CIRCLES
Circles are equidistant from center to edge, but they overlap or leave gaps. An arrangement of circles that leaves gaps indicates that people living in the gaps are outside the market area of any service, which is obviously not true. Overlapping circles are also unsatisfactory, for one service or another will be closer, and people will tend to patronize it.

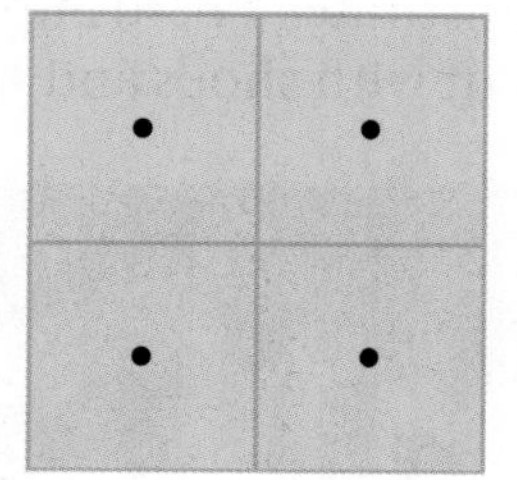

(b) THE PROBLEM WITH SQUARES
Squares nest together without gaps, but their sides are not equidistant from the center. If the market area is a circle, the radius—the distance from the center to the edge—can be measured because every point around a circle is the same distance from the center. But in a square, the distance from the center varies among points along a square.

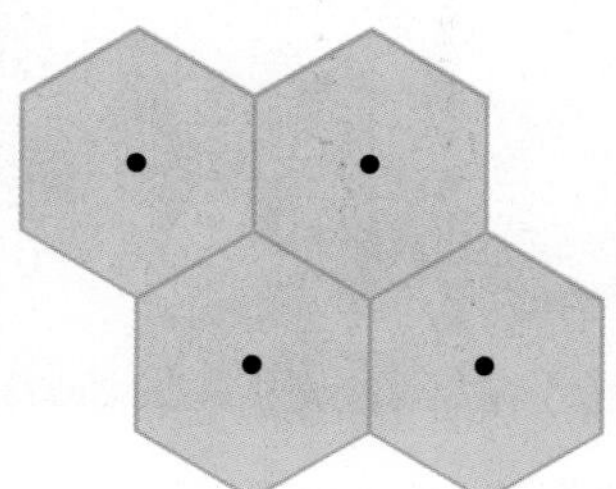

(c) THE HEXAGON COMPROMISE
Geographers use hexagons to depict the market area of a good or service because hexagons offer a compromise between the geometric properties of circles and squares. Like squares, hexagons nest without gaps. Although all points along the hexagon are not the same distance from the center, the variation is less than with a square.

▲ 12.2.5 **WHY GEOGRAPHERS USE HEXAGONS TO DELINEATE MARKET AREAS**

Hierarchy of Consumer Services

- **Describe the distribution of different-sized settlements.**

We spend as little time and effort as possible in obtaining consumer services and thus go to the nearest place that fulfills our needs. There is no point in traveling to a distant store if the same merchandise is available at a nearby one. We travel greater distances only if the price is much lower or if the item is unavailable locally.

Rank-Size Distribution of Settlements

In many developed countries, geographers observe that ranking settlements from largest to smallest (population) produces a regular pattern. This is the **rank-size rule**, in which the country's nth-largest settlement is 1/n the population of the largest settlement.

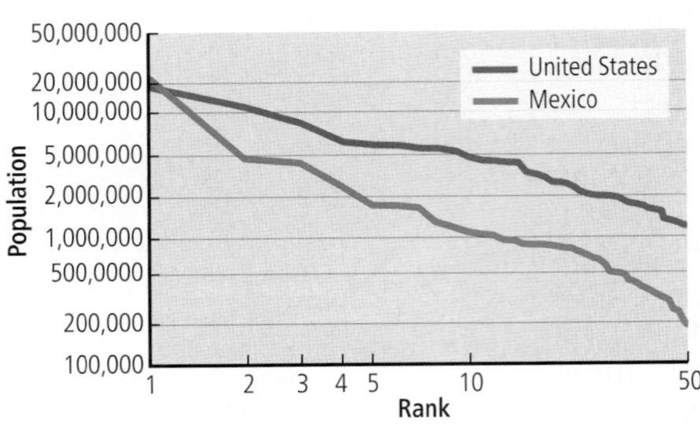

▲ 12.3.1 **RANK-SIZE DISRIBUTION OF SETTLEMENTS IN THE UNITED STATES AND MEXICO**
The size of settlements follows the rank-size rule in the United States and the primate city rule in Mexico.

According to the rank-size rule, the second-largest city is one-half the size of the largest, the fourth-largest city is one-fourth the size of the largest, and so on. When plotted on logarithmic paper, the rank-size distribution forms a fairly straight line (Figure 12.3.1). In the United States and a handful of other countries, the distribution of settlements closely follows the rank-size rule (Figure 12.3.2).

If the settlement hierarchy does not graph as a straight line, then the country does not follow the rank-size rule. Instead, it may follow the **primate city rule**, in which the largest settlement has more than twice as many people as the second-ranking settlement. In this distribution, the country's largest city is called the **primate city**. Mexico is an example of a country that follows the primate city distribution. Its largest settlement, Mexico City, is ten times larger than its fifth-largest settlement, Toluca, rather than five times larger (Figure 12.3.3).

The existence of a rank-size distribution of settlements is not merely a mathematical curiosity. It has a real impact on the quality of life for a country's inhabitants. A regular hierarchy—as in the United States—indicates that the society is sufficiently wealthy to justify the provision of goods and services to consumers throughout the country. Conversely, the absence of the rank-size distribution in a developing country indicates that there is not enough wealth in the society to pay for a full variety of services. The absence of a rank-size distribution constitutes a hardship for people who must travel long distances to reach an urban settlement with shops and such services as hospitals.

▲ 12.3.2 **RANK-SIZE DISTRIBUTION: UNITED STATES**
Houston is the 5th largest settlement in the United States and has an even larger population than the rank-size rule predicts.

▲ 12.3.3 **PRIMATE CITY DISRIBUTION: MEXICO**
Toluca is Mexico's 5th largest settlement but has a smaller population than the rank-size rule would suggest.

Nesting of Services and Settlements

According to central place theory, market areas across a developed country would be a series of hexagons of various sizes, unless interrupted by physical features such as mountains and bodies of water. Developed countries have numerous small settlements with small thresholds and ranges and far fewer large settlements with large thresholds and ranges. In his original study, Walter Christaller showed that the distances between settlements in southern Germany followed a regular pattern (Figure 12.3.4).

The nesting pattern can be illustrated with overlapping hexagons of different sizes. Four different levels of market area—hamlet, village, town, and city—are shown in Figure 12.3.4. Hamlets with very small market areas are represented by the smallest contiguous hexagons. Larger hexagons represent the market areas of larger settlements and are overlaid on the smaller hexagons because consumers from smaller settlements shop for some goods and services in larger settlements.

Businesses in central places compete against each other to serve as markets for goods and services for the surrounding region. According to central place theory, this competition creates a regular pattern of settlements.

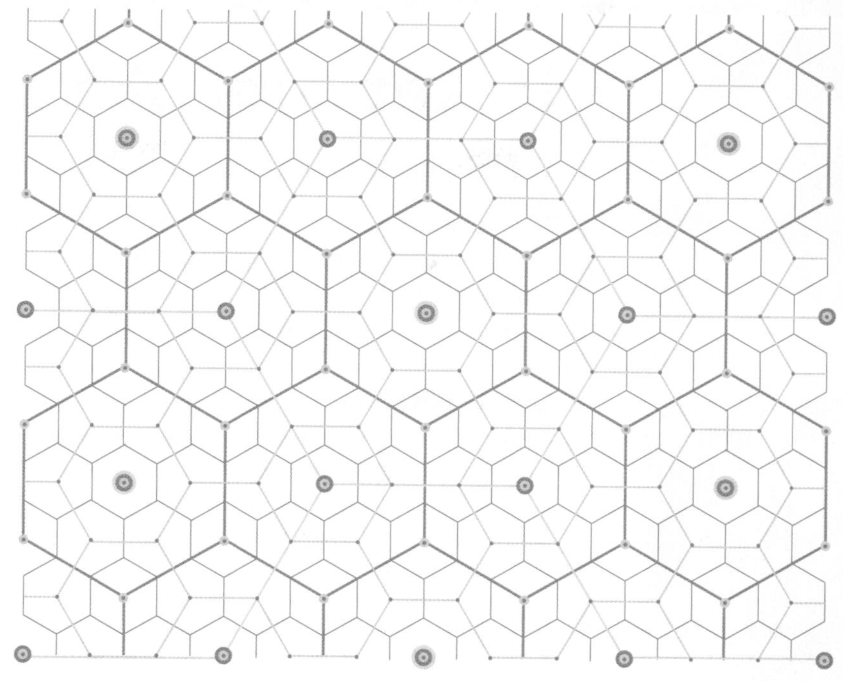

▲ 12.3.4 **CENTRAL PLACE THEORY**

▲ 12.3.5 **CENTRAL PLACE THEORY IN NORTH DAKOTA** Central place theory helps explain the distribution of settlements of varying sizes in North Dakota.

Across much of the interior of the United States, a regular pattern of settlements can be observed, even if not precisely the same as the generalized model shown in Figure 12.3.4. North-central North Dakota is an example (Figure 12.3.5). Minot—the largest city in the area, with 49,000 inhabitants—is surrounded by:

- 11 small towns of between 1,000 and 3,000 inhabitants, with average ranges of 30 kilometers (20 miles) and market areas of around 2,800 square kilometers (1,200 square miles).
- 20 villages of between 100 and 999 inhabitants, with ranges of 20 kilometers (12 miles) and market areas of around 1,200 square kilometers (500 square miles).
- 22 hamlets of fewer than 100 inhabitants, with ranges of 15 kilometers (10 miles) and market areas of around 800 square kilometers (300 square miles), including Maxbass, illustrated in Figure 12.3.6.

Larger settlements provide consumer services that have larger thresholds, ranges, and market areas. Only consumer services that have small thresholds, short ranges, and small market areas are found in small settlements because too few people live in small settlements to support many services. A large store cannot survive in a small settlement because the threshold (the minimum number of people needed) exceeds the population within range of the settlement. For example, Minot is the only settlement in Figure 12.3.5 that has a Walmart.

▼ 12.3.6 **HAMLET: MAXBASS, NORTH DAKOTA** North of Minot, near the junction of routes 83 and 5, in Figure 12.3.5.

▲ 12.4.1 CENTRAL PLACE OF A MARKET AREA: DAYTON, OHIO

Market Area Analysis

- Explain how to find the optimal location for a consumer service.

Geographers apply central place theory to create market area studies that assist service providers with opening and expanding their facilities (see What's Your Services Geography? feature). And in a severe economic downturn, market area analysis helps determine where to close facilities.

Gravity Model

Geographers have adapted the **gravity model** from physics. The gravity model predicts that the optimal location of a service is directly related to the number of people in the area and inversely related to the distance people must travel to access it. The best location will be the one that minimizes the distances that all potential customers must travel to reach the service.

According to the gravity model, consumer behavior reflects two patterns:

1. The greater the number of people living in a particular place, the greater the number of potential customers for a service. A neighborhood that contains 100 families will generate more customers than an individual house containing only 1 family.
2. The farther people are from a particular service, the less likely they are to use it. People who live 1 kilometer from a store are more likely to patronize it than people who live 10 kilometers away.

WHAT'S YOUR SERVICES GEOGRAPHY?

Food Deserts

Retailers are less likely to place shops in low-income neighborhoods. This can lead to the existence of food deserts. The U.S. government defines a **food desert** as an area that has a substantial amount of low-income residents and has poor access to a grocery store. Poor access is defined by the government in most cases as further than 1 mile. A distance of 1 mile is not far for people to travel in a car, but it is far for low-income people who do not own cars. Not surprisingly, food deserts in Dayton, Ohio, are located in low-income areas (Figures 12.4.1 and 12.4.2).

1. What is the distance from your home to the grocery store most frequently used by your family?
2. By what means of transportation does your family usually shop at the grocery store?
3. Does your family shop at the nearest grocery store? If not, why not?
4. Map the food deserts in your community. ***Search*** the Internet using key words *Food Access Research Atlas* or go to the U.S. Department of Agriculture's Food Access web page. ***Zoom*** in on your community.
5. Is your home in a food desert? Is your neighborhood accurately classified as being within or outside a food desert? Why or why not?

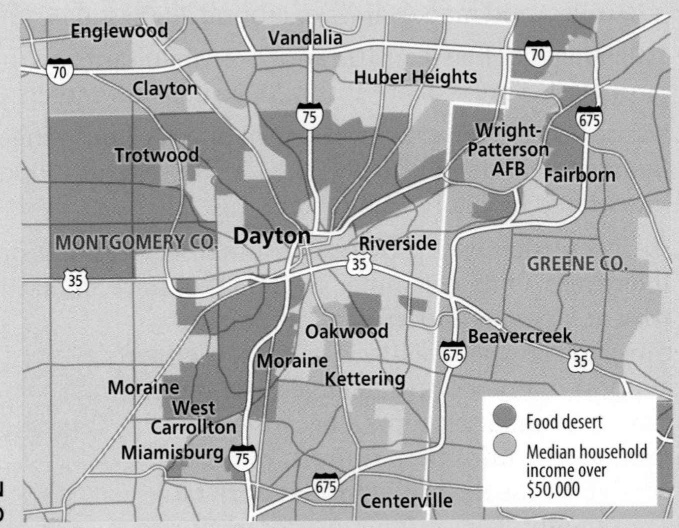

▶ 12.4.2 FOOD DESERTS IN DAYTON, OHIO

Profitability of a Location

The best location for a factory is typically described as a large region, such as auto alley. For service providers, the optimal location is much more precise: One corner of an intersection can be profitable and another corner of the same intersection unprofitable.

Major U.S. consumer services, such as supermarkets and department stores, employ geographers to determine the best location to build new stores. Geographers use the two components of central place theory—range and threshold—to determine whether a location would be profitable. Here's how:

- **Define the market area.** The first step in forecasting sales for a proposed new consumer service is to define the market or trade area where the store would derive most of its sales. The market area of a department store is often defined as the zip codes where two-thirds to three-fourths of the customers live.
- **Estimate the range.** Based on the zip codes of credit-card customers, geographers can estimate the range for the service (Figure 12.4.3). The range is around 15 minutes for a store like Family Dollar (Figure 12.4.4) and 30 minutes for a store like Target (Figure 12.4.5).
- **Estimate the threshold.** The threshold varies for each service. The threshold is around 25,000 for a store like Family Dollar and 100,000 for a store like Target. People are counted only if they have sufficient income to shop regularly at the store.
- **Predict the market share.** The proposed new consumer service will have to share customers with competitors. Geographers typically predict market share through the so-called analog method. The geographer identifies one or more existing stores in locations judged to be comparable to the location of the proposed store. The geographer then applies the market share of the comparable stores to the proposed new store.

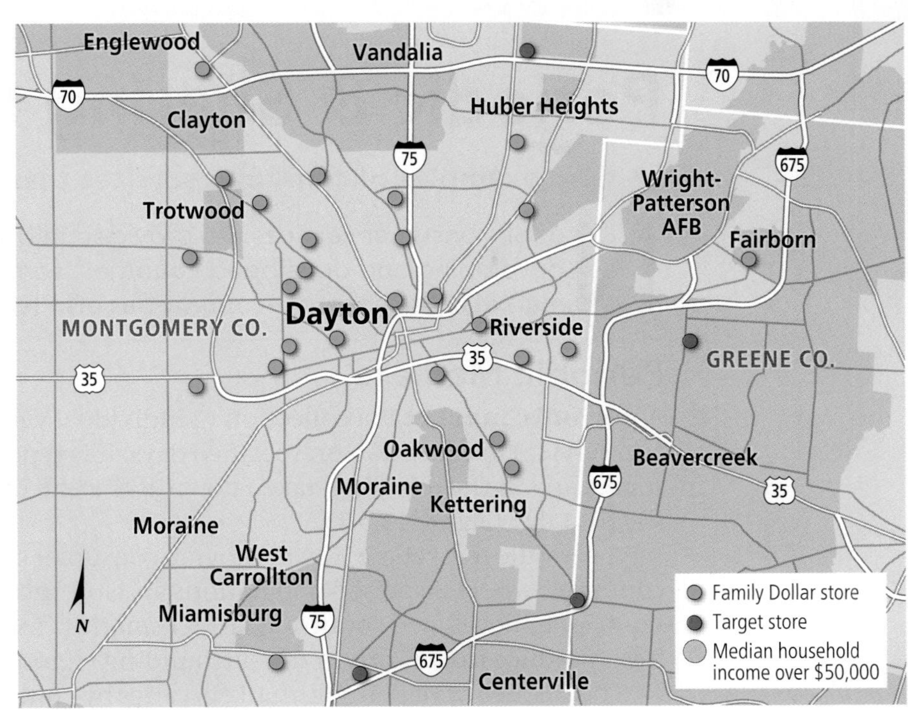

▲ 12.4.3 RETAILERS IN DAYTON, OHIO
Compared with Target, Family Dollar has a lower threshold and lower range. Family Dollar stores are more likely to be located in lower income areas than are Target stores.

◀ 12.4.4 FAMILY DOLLAR HAS A RELATIVELY LOW THRESHOLD AND RANGE

◀ 12.4.5 TARGET HAS A RELATIVELY HIGH THRESHOLD AND RANGE

Periodic & Sharing Services

- Give examples of consumer services that do not have a fixed location.

Not all consumer services are provided in buildings in fixed locations. In both developing and developed countries, some groceries are sold in periodic markets. The sharing economy has also led to more flexible consumer services.

Periodic Markets

A **periodic market** is a collection of individual vendors who come together to offer goods and services in a location on specified days. It is typically set up in a street or other public space early in the morning, taken down at the end of the day, and set up in another location the next day (Figure 12.5.1).

A periodic market is a way to provide consumer services to residents of developing countries, where dispersed populations and low incomes may not be able to support full-time services. In developed countries, farmers markets may be set up one or two days a week to sell fresh produce from farms in the surrounding region to consumers living in urban areas.

The frequency of periodic markets varies by culture:

- **Muslim countries.** Markets are once a week in each of six cities, with no market on Friday, the Muslim day of rest.
- **Rural China.** Markets operate in one location on days 1, 4, and 7; in a second location on days 2, 5, and 8; in a third location on days 3, 6, and 9; and no market on the tenth day. Three cycles fit in a lunar month.
- **Korea.** Two 15-day market cycles fit in a lunar month.
- **Sub-Saharan Africa.** Markets occur every 3 to 7 days. Variations in the cycle stem from ethnic differences.

▼ 12.5.1 WEEKLY PERIODIC MARKET, BURKINA FASO

Sharing Services

Services that involve sharing have expanded rapidly, especially in transportation and lodging. These sharing services are challenging the traditional classification of services between consumer and business (see Debate It! feature).

Ride sharing services, such as Uber and Lyft, match people looking for a ride with people who are willing to transport them in their cars (Figure 12.5.2). They compete with taxis which are typically summoned through a phone call or a hit-or-miss process of flagging one down on the street. In contrast, ride sharing services are summoned by using a smart phone app. The driver's smart phone shows the passenger's current location and desired destination, as well as the optimal route. It also confirms that the passenger has already paid for the ride.

▲ 12.5.2 RIDE SHARING SERVICE: UBER

Uber claims that its several million drivers are independent contractors, essentially one-person businesses providing transportation business service. Some government regulators have ruled that ridesharing drivers should instead be classified as employees. The classification matters because it is the ridesharing company's responsibility to screen, train, and insure them if they are consumer service employees, but not if they are independent business service contractors.

DEBATE IT!
Is Airbnb a business service or a consumer service?

Airbnb matches people looking for lodging with people who have spaces for rent (Figures 12.5.3 and 12.5.4). Should Airbnb be considered a consumer service or a business service? The distinction matters, because it affects issues of insurance and liability. Who is at fault if something goes wrong?

AIRBNB IS A BUSINESS SERVICE

- Airbnb employees are primarily computer operators, a type of employment classified under transportation and information business services.
- People access Airbnb through their electronic devices.
- The owners of the rented rooms and homes are not Airbnb employees, nor are the people who might clean and repair the rooms and homes.

▲ 12.5.3 AIRBNB HEADQUARTERS

AIRBNB IS A CONSUMER SERVICE

- Airbnb competes with hotels, which are clearly classified as a leisure and hospitality consumer service.
- Airbnb offers nightly rentals, and does not have leases, unlike regular residential rental units.
- Airbnb units cause a reduction in availability of long-term rentals, especially for lower-income people.

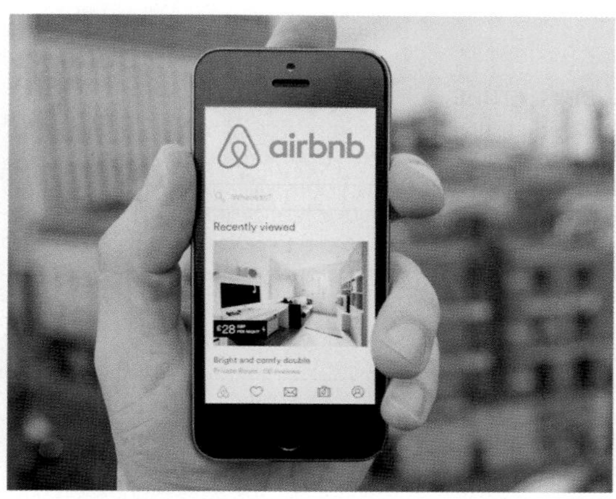

▲ 12.5.4 AIRBNB APP

▲ 12.6.1 THEATER DISTRICT, LONDON

Hierarchy of Business Services

- Explain the clustering of business services in global cities.

Every urban settlement provides consumer services to people in a surrounding area, but not every settlement of a given size has the same number and types of business services. Business services disproportionately cluster in a handful of urban settlements, and individual settlements specialize in particular business services.

Levels of Global Cities

A combination of economic, political, cultural, and infrastructure factors define a **global city** (also known as a world city), which is a major center for the provision of services in the global economy:

- **Economic factors.** Number of headquarters for multinational corporations, financial institutions, and law firms that influence the global economy.
- **Political factors.** Hosting headquarters for international organizations and capitals of countries that play a leading role in international events.
- **Cultural factors.** Presence of renowned cultural institutions, influential media outlets, sports facilities, and educational institutions (Figure 12.6.1).
- **Infrastructural factors.** A major international airport, health-care facilities, and advanced communications systems.

Technology was expected to reduce the need for clustering of services in large cities:

- **Communications.** The telegraph and telephone in the nineteenth century and the computer in the twentieth century made it possible to communicate immediately with coworkers, clients, and customers around the world.
- **Transportation.** The railroad in the nineteenth century and the motor vehicle and airplane in the twentieth century made it possible to deliver people, inputs, and products quickly.

Modern transportation and communications enable industry to decentralize, as discussed in Chapter 11, but they reinforce rather than diminish the primacy of global cities in the world economy.

Global cities are divided into three levels: alpha, beta, and gamma. These three levels in turn are further subdivided (Figure 12.6.2). The same hierarchy of business services can be used within countries and continents (Figure 12.6.3).

Global city hierarchy
- Alpha++
- Alpha+
- Alpha
- Alpha–
- Beta
- Gamma

▲ 12.6.2 GLOBAL CITIES
Geographers distinguish various ranks of global cities. London and New York, the two dominant global cities are ranked as alpha++. Other alpha, beta, and gamma cities play somewhat less central roles in the provision of services than the two dominant global cities. Cities ranked alpha++ and alpha+ are labeled on the map.

▶ 12.6.3 GLOBAL CITIES IN NORTH AMERICA
Atop the hierarchy of business services is New York, followed by Chicago, Los Angeles, and Toronto.

Consumer and Public Services in Global Cities

Because of their large size, global cities have consumer services with extensive market areas, but they may have even more consumer services than large size alone would predict. A disproportionately large number of wealthy people live in global cities, so luxury and highly specialized products are especially likely to be sold there.

Leisure services of national significance are especially likely to cluster in global cities, in part because they require large thresholds and large ranges and in part because of the presence of wealthy patrons. Global cities typically offer the most plays, concerts, operas, night clubs, restaurants, bars, and professional sporting events. They contain the largest libraries, museums, and theaters.

Global cities may be centers of national or international political power. Most are national capitals, and they contain mansions or palaces for the head of state, imposing structures for the national legislature and courts, and offices for the government agencies. Also clustered in global cities are offices for groups having business with the government, such as representatives of foreign countries, trade associations, labor unions, and professional organizations.

Unlike other global cities, New York is not a national capital. But as the home of the world's major international organization, the United Nations, it attracts thousands of diplomats and bureaucrats, as well as employees of organizations with business at the United Nations. Brussels, Belgium, is a global city because it is the most important center for European Union activities.

Business Services in Global Cities

Global cities play an especially important role in global business services (Figure 12.6.4). Global cities are most closely integrated into the global economic system because they are at the center of the flow of information and capital. Business services that concentrate in disproportionately large numbers in global cities include:

- **Financial institutions.** As centers for finance, global cities attract the headquarters of the major banks, insurance companies, and specialized financial institutions where corporations obtain and store funds for expansion of production.
- **Headquarters of large corporations.** Shares of these corporations are bought and sold on stock exchanges located in global cities. Obtaining information in a timely manner is essential in order to buy and sell shares at attractive prices. Executives of manufacturing firms meeting far from the factories make key decisions concerning what to make, how much to produce, and what prices to charge. Support staff also far from the factory accounts for the flow of money and materials to and from the factories. This work is done in offices in global cities.
- **Lawyers, accountants, and other professional services.** Professional services cluster in global cities to provide advice to major corporations and financial institutions. Advertising agencies, marketing firms, and other services concerned with style and fashion locate in global cities to help corporations anticipate changes in taste and to help shape those changes.

▼ 12.6.4 FINANCIAL DISTRICT, NEW YORK

Business Services in Developing Countries

- Describe the types of business services in developing countries.

In the global economy, developing countries specialize in two distinctive types of business services: offshore financial services and back-office functions. These businesses tend to locate in developing countries for a number of reasons, including the presence of supportive laws, weak regulations, and low-wage workers.

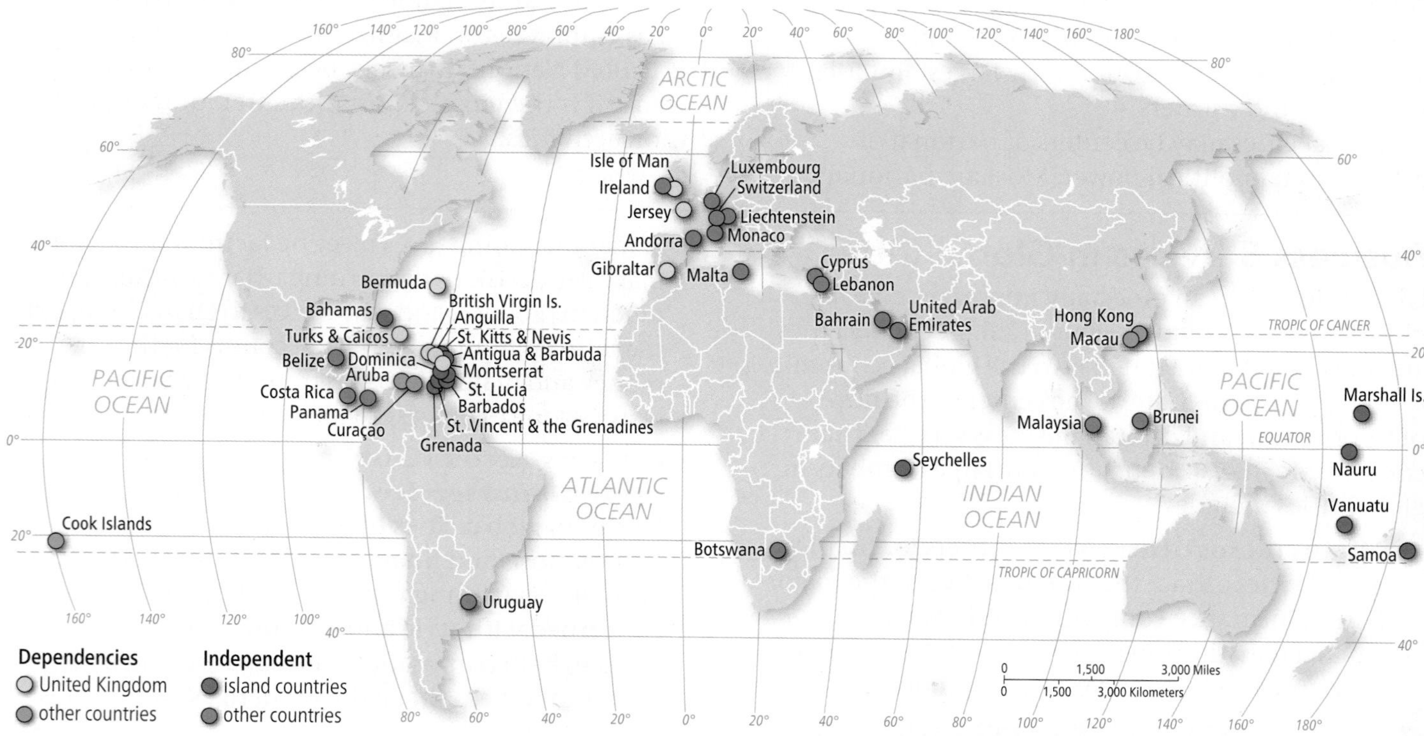

▲ 12.7.1 **OFFSHORE FINANCIAL SERVICE CENTERS**
The International Monetary Fund, the Tax Justice Network's Financial Secrecy Index, and the Organization for Economic Co-operation and Development all maintain lists of offshore financial service centers. The map shows locations that appear on all three organizations' lists. These include independent countries and dependencies of other countries. Many of the independent countries are small islands. The largest number of dependencies are tied to the United Kingdom.

Offshore Financial Services

Small countries, usually islands and microstates, exploit niches in the circulation of global capital by offering offshore financial services (Figure 12.7.1). Offshore centers provide two important functions in the global circulation of capital:

- **Taxes.** Taxes on income, profits, and capital gains are typically low or nonexistent. Companies incorporated in an offshore center also have tax-free status, regardless of the nationality of the owners. The United States loses an estimated $150 billion in tax revenue each year because companies operating in the country conceal their assets in offshore tax havens.
- **Privacy.** Bank secrecy laws can help individuals and businesses evade disclosure in their home countries. People and corporations in litigious professions, such as a doctor or lawyer accused of malpractice, or the developer of a collapsed building, can protect some of their assets from lawsuits by storing them in offshore centers. So can a wealthy individual who wants to protect assets in a divorce. Creditors cannot reach such assets in bankruptcy hearings. Short statutes of limitation protect offshore accounts from long-term investigation.

The privacy laws and low tax rates in offshore centers can also provide havens to tax dodges and other illegal schemes. By definition, the extent of illegal activities is unknown and unknowable.

Business-Process Outsourcing

A second distinctive type of business service found in peripheral regions is business-process outsourcing (BPO), also known as back-office functions (Figure 12.7.2). Typical back-office functions include insurance claims processing, payroll management, transcription work, and other routine clerical activities. Back-office work also includes centers for responding to billing inquiries related to credit cards, shipments, and claims, or technical inquiries related to installation, operation, and repair.

Traditionally, companies housed their back-office staff the same office building downtown as their management staff, or at least in nearby buildings. A large percentage of the employees in a downtown bank building, for example, would be responsible for sorting paper checks and deposit slips. Proximity was considered important to assure close supervision of routine office workers and rapid turnaround of information.

▲ 12.7.2 CALL CENTER, INDIA

Rising rents downtown have induced many business services to move routine work to lower-rent buildings elsewhere. In most cases, sufficiently low rents can be obtained in buildings in the suburbs or nearby small towns. However, for many business services, improved telecommunications have eliminated the need for spatial proximity.

Selected developing countries have attracted back offices for two reasons related to labor:

- **Low wages.** Most back-office workers earn a few thousand dollars per year—higher than wages paid in most other sectors of the economy, but only one-tenth the wages paid for workers performing similar jobs in developed countries. As a result, what is regarded as menial and dead-end work in developed countries may be considered relatively high-status work in developing countries and therefore able to attract better-educated, more-motivated employees in developing countries than would be possible in developed countries.
- **Ability to speak English.** Many developing countries offer lower wages than developed countries, but only a handful of developing countries possess a large labor force fluent in English. In Asia, countries such as India, Malaysia, and the Philippines have substantial numbers of workers with English-language skills, a legacy of British and American colonial rule. Major multinational companies such as American Express and General Electric have extensive back-office facilities in those countries.

The ability to communicate in English over the telephone is a strategic advantage in competing for back offices with neighboring countries, such as Indonesia and Thailand, where English is less commonly used. Familiarity with English is an advantage not only for literally answering the telephone but also for gaining a better understanding of the preferences of American consumers through exposure to English-language music, movies, and television.

Workers in back offices are often forced to work late at night, when it's daytime in the United States, peak demand for inquiries. Many employees must arrive at work early and stay late because they lack their own transportation, so they depend on public transportation, which typically does not operate late at night. Sleeping and entertainment rooms are provided at work to fill the extra hours.

Economic Specialization of Settlements

- Define the concept of economic base.

Settlements can be classified by the distinctive types of economic activities that take place there. All sectors of the economy—be they the various types of agriculture, manufacturers, or services—have distinctive geographic distributions.

Economic Base

The economic activities in a settlement can be divided into two types:

- **Basic businesses** export primarily to customers outside the settlement.
- **Nonbasic businesses** serve primarily customers living in the same settlement.

The **economic base** of a settlement is its unique cluster of basic businesses.

A settlement's economic base is important because exporting by the basic businesses brings more money into the local economy, thus stimulating the provision of more nonbasic services for the settlement. It works like this:

- New basic businesses attract new workers to a settlement.
- The new basic business workers bring their families with them.
- New nonbasic services are opened to meet the needs of the new workers and their families.

For example, when a new car assembly plant opens, new supermarkets, restaurants, and other consumer services soon follow. But the opposite doesn't occur: a new supermarket does not induce construction of a new car plant.

Settlements in the United States can be classified by their distinctive collection of basic businesses. The concept of basic businesses originally referred to manufacturing, but with the growth of the service sector of the economy, the basic businesses of many communities are in consumer, business, and public services (Figure 12.8.1).

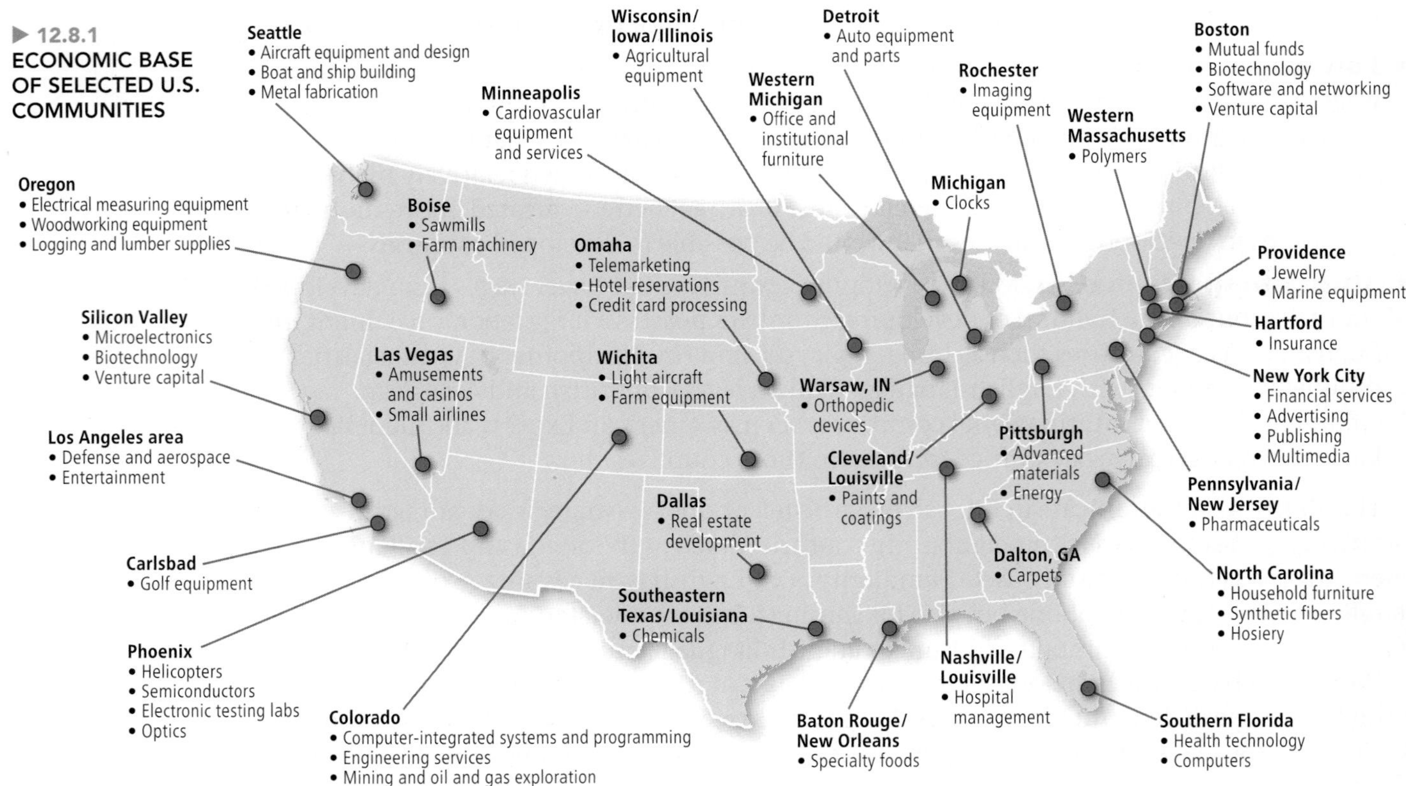

▶ 12.8.1 ECONOMIC BASE OF SELECTED U.S. COMMUNITIES

Distribution of Talent

Individuals possessing special talents are not distributed uniformly among cities. Some cities have a higher percentage of talented individuals such as scientists and professionals (Figures 12.8.2 and 12.8.3). Attracting talented individuals is important for a city because these individuals are responsible for promoting economic innovation. They are likely to start new businesses and infuse the local economy with fresh ideas.

To some extent, talented individuals are attracted to the cities with the most job opportunities and financial incentives. But the principal enticement for talented individuals to cluster in some cities more than others is cultural rather than economic, according to research conducted by Richard Florida. Florida found that individuals with special talents gravitate toward cities that offer more cultural diversity. He used a "coolness" index developed by POV Magazine that combined the percentage of population in their 20s, the number of bars and other nightlife places per capita, and the number of art galleries per capita (Figure 12.8.4).

Job opportunities are more likely to be found in settlements where basic businesses are growing. For example, Boston's basic sector in biotechnology consists of a cluster of business sectors that complement each other (Figure 12.8.5).

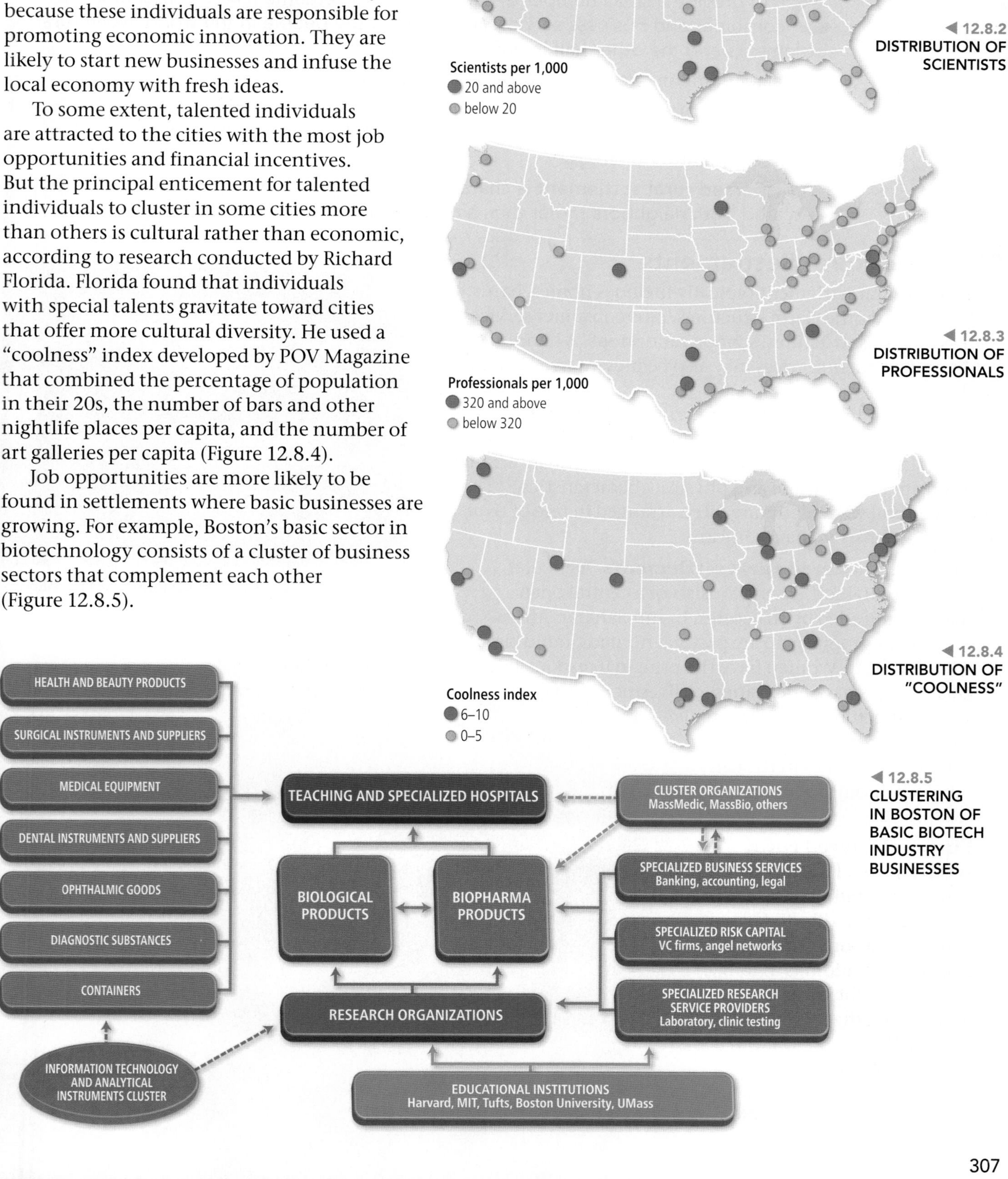

◀ 12.8.2 DISTRIBUTION OF SCIENTISTS

◀ 12.8.3 DISTRIBUTION OF PROFESSIONALS

◀ 12.8.4 DISTRIBUTION OF "COOLNESS"

◀ 12.8.5 CLUSTERING IN BOSTON OF BASIC BIOTECH INDUSTRY BUSINESSES

Services in Rural Settlements

- **Compare clustered and dispersed rural settlements.**

Services are clustered in settlements. Rural settlements are centers for agriculture and provide a small number of services. Urban settlements are centers for consumer and business services. One-half of the people in the world live in rural settlements and the other half in urban settlements

Rural settlements are either clustered or dispersed:

- **A clustered rural settlement** is an agricultural-based community in which a number of families live in close proximity to each other, with fields surrounding the collection of houses and farm buildings.
- **A dispersed rural settlement** is characterized by farmers living on individual farms isolated from neighbors rather than alongside other farmers in settlements.

Clustered Rural Settlements

A clustered rural settlement typically includes homes, barns, tool sheds, and other farm structures, plus consumer services, such as religious structures, schools, and shops. A handful of public and business services may also be present in a clustered rural settlement.

Each person living in a clustered rural settlement is allocated strips of land in the surrounding fields. Homes, public buildings, and fields in a clustered rural settlement are arranged according to local cultural and physical characteristics. Clustered rural settlements are often arranged in one of two types of patterns: circular or linear.

▲ 12.9.1 CIRCULAR CLUSTERED RURAL SETTLEMENT: KRAAL VILLAGE, KENYA

- **Circular clustered rural settlements.** A circular clustered rural settlement consists of a central open space surrounded by structures. In sub-Saharan Africa, the Maasai people, who are pastoral nomads, build circular settlements known as kraal (Figure 12.9.1). Women have the principal responsibility for constructing them. The kraal villages have enclosures for livestock in the center, surrounded by a ring of houses. Von Thünen observed this circular pattern in Germany in his landmark agricultural studies in the early nineteenth century (refer to Figure 9.8.6).
- **Linear clustered rural settlements.** Linear rural settlements comprise buildings clustered along a road, river, or dike to facilitate communications. The fields extend behind the buildings in long, narrow strips. Long-lot farms can be seen today along the St. Lawrence River in Québec (Figure 12.9.2). Québec got the system from the French.

▶ 12.9.2 LINEAR CLUSTERED RURAL SETTLEMENT: QUÉBEC

▲ 12.9.3 U.K. RURAL VILLAGE: CANDICOTE

Dispersed Rural Settlements

Isolated farms are typical of most of the rural United States. In Europe, some clustered settlements were converted to dispersed settlements in order to make agriculture more efficient. Clustered rural settlements worked when the population was low, but they had no spare land to meet the needs of a growing population. With the introduction of machinery, farms operated more efficiently at a larger scale.

- **U.K. dispersed rural settlements.** A number of European countries converted much of their rural landscapes from a clustered to a dispersed pattern (Figure 12.9.3). In the United Kingdom between 1750 and 1850, the **enclosure movement** consolidated individually owned strips of land surrounding a village into a large farm owned by a single individual. The population of clustered rural settlements declined drastically as displaced farmers moved to urban settlements. Because the enclosure movement coincided with the Industrial Revolution, villagers displaced from farming became workers in urban factories.
- **U.S. dispersed rural settlements.** A dispersed pattern developed from the time of initial settlement of the Middle Atlantic colonies, because most immigrants to these colonies arrived individually rather than as members of a cohesive group, as in New England. As people moved westward from the Middle Atlantic region, they took with them their preference for isolated individual farms. Land was plentiful and cheap, so people bought as much as they could manage (Figure 12.9.4).

▼ 12.9.4 U.S. DISPERSED RURAL SETTLEMENT: ILLINOIS

Services in Early Urban Settlements

- Summarize important urban settlements through history.

No one knows the precise sequence of events through which settlements were established to provide services. The first urban settlements existed prior to the beginning of recorded history around 5,000 years ago.

▲ 12.10.1
MEMPHIS, EGYPT
World's largest city 5,000 years ago.

Prehistoric Urban Settlements

Based on archaeological research, urban settlements probably originated to provide consumer and public services. Business services probably came later.

- **Consumer services.** The first permanent settlements may have been places for nomads to bury and honor their dead. The group might then leave some of their group at the site to perform rituals in honor of the deceased. They were also places to house women and children while males hunted for food. Women made tools, clothing, and containers.
- **Business services.** Early urban settlements were places where groups could store surplus food and trade with other groups. People brought plants, animals, and minerals, as well as tools, clothing, and containers, to the urban settlements, and exchanged them for items brought by others. To facilitate this trade, officials in the settlement set fair prices, kept records, and created currency.
- **Public services.** Early settlements housed cultural and political leaders, as well as military forces to guard the residents of the urban settlement and defend the surrounding hinterland from seizure by other groups.

Urban settlements may have originated in Mesopotamia, part of the Fertile Crescent of Southwest Asia (Figure 12.10.1), and diffused at an early date west to Egypt and east to China and South Asia's Indus Valley. Or they may have originated independently in each of the four hearths. In any case, from these four hearths the concept of urban settlements diffused to the rest of the world (Figure 12.10.2).

▼ 12.10.2 LARGEST URBAN SETTLEMENTS THROUGH HISTORY

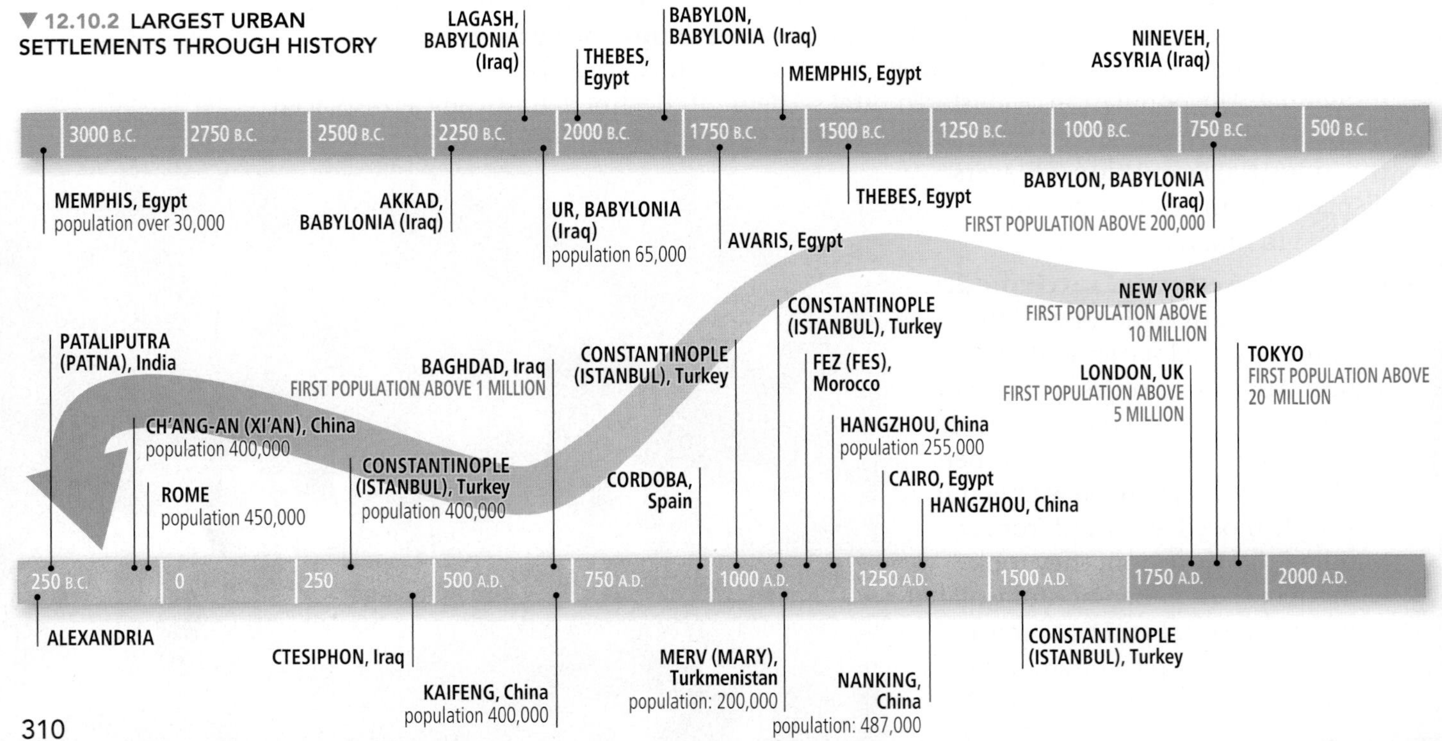

Urban Settlements Since Ancient Times

Until around 350 B.C, the world's largest urban settlements were in the Fertile Crescent and Egypt (Figure 12.10.3). Ur was one of the largest prehistoric urban settlements (Figure 12.10.4). Beginning around 2,400 years ago, the largest settlements were likely to be in China or Europe (Figure 12.10.5). During the past three centuries, the title of world's largest urban settlement has been shared by London, New York, and Tokyo (Figures 12.10.6 and 12.10.7).

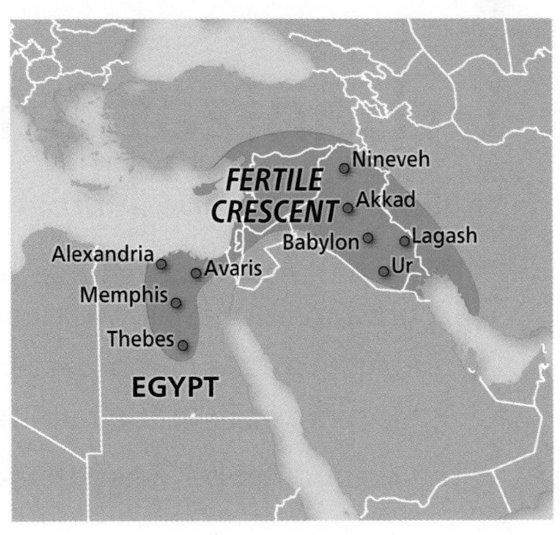

◀ 12.10.3 LARGEST URBAN SETTLEMENTS BEFORE 350 B.C.

▼ 12.10.4 UR ZIGGURAT

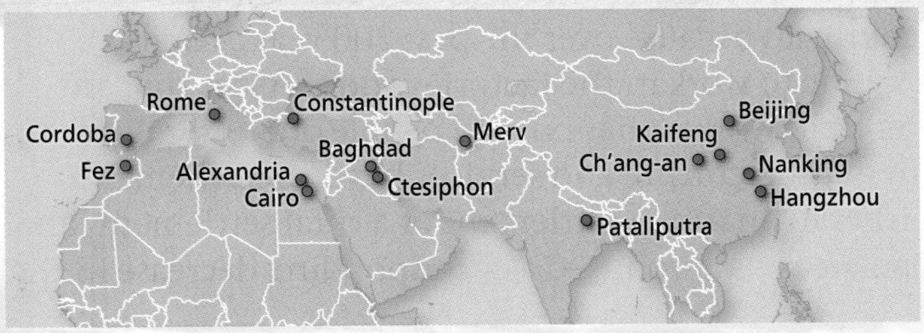

▲ 12.10.5 LARGEST URBAN SETTLEMENTS 350 B.C. – A.D. 1750

▲ 12.10.6 LARGEST URBAN SETTLEMENTS 1750 – 2018

▼ 12.10.7 TOKYO: LARGEST URBAN SETTLEMENT IN 2018

▲ 12.11.1 **MEXICO CITY**
More than 1 out of 6 Mexicans lives in Mexico City and its surrounding Federal District, which has a population of more than 20 million.

Urbanization

- **Compare trends in urbanization in developed and developing countries.**

The process by which the population of urban settlements grows, known as **urbanization**, has two dimensions:

- An increase in the percentage of people living in urban settlements.
- An increase in the number of people living in urban settlements.

The distinction between these two factors is important because they occur for different reasons and have different global distributions.

Percentage in Urban Settlements

The percentage of people living in urban settlements reflects a country's level of development. In developed countries, 78 percent of the people live in urban areas, compared to 49 percent in developing countries. The major exception to the global pattern is Latin America, where the urban share is 80 percent, which is higher than the level in developed countries (Figure 12.11.1).

The population of urban settlements exceeded that of rural settlements for the first time in human history in 2008 (Figure 12.11.2). The percentage of people living in urban settlements had increased from 3 percent in 1800 to 6 percent in 1850, 14 percent in 1900, 30 percent in 1950, 47 percent in 2000, and 54 percent in 2017.

The higher percentage of urban residents in developed countries is a consequence of changes in economic structure during the past two centuries—first the Industrial Revolution in the nineteenth century and then the growth of services in the twentieth. The percentage of urban dwellers is high in developed countries because over the past 200 years, rural residents have migrated from the countryside to work in the factories and services that are concentrated in cities. The need for fewer farm workers has pushed people out of rural areas, and rising employment opportunities in manufacturing and services have lured them into urban areas. Because everyone resides either in an urban settlement or a rural settlement, an increase in the percentage living in urban areas has produced a corresponding decrease in the percentage living in rural areas.

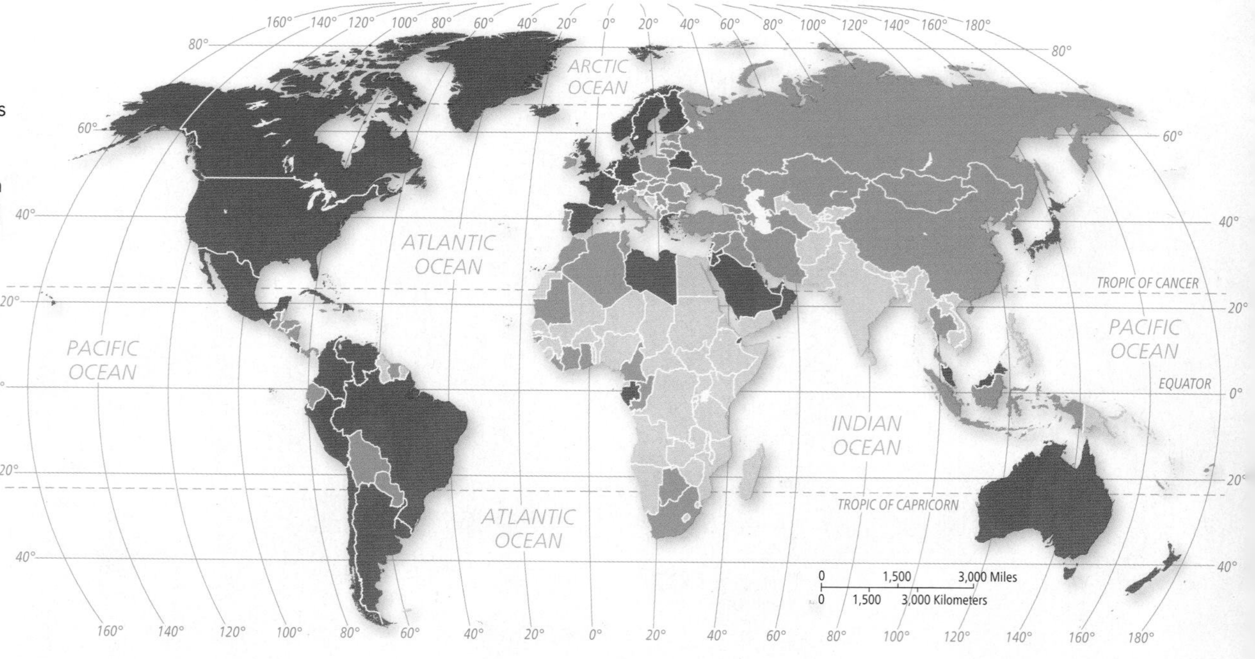

▶ 12.11.2 **PERCENTAGE LIVING IN URBAN SETTLEMENTS**
Developed countries have higher precentages of urban residents than do most developing countries, though Latin America has a percentage comparable to that of developed countries.

Percent urban
- 75 and above
- 50–74
- below 50
- no data

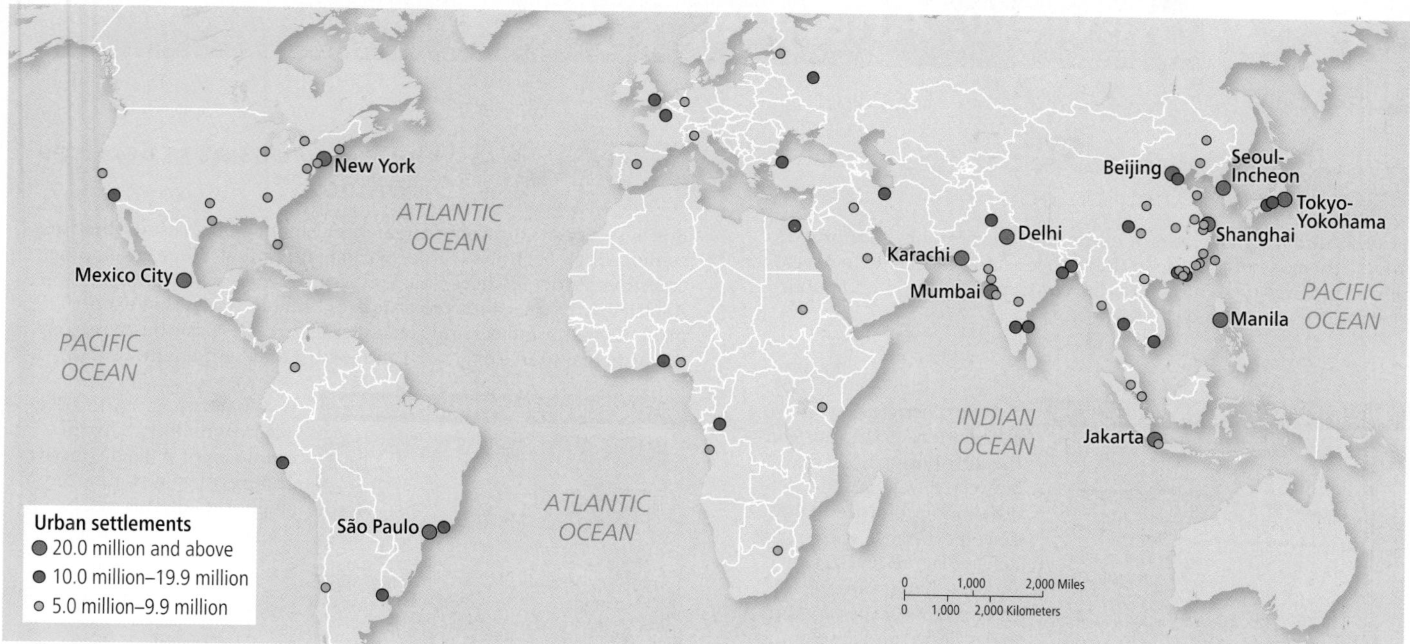

▲ 12.11.3 **URBAN SETTLEMENTS WITH AT LEAST 5 MILLION INHABITANTS**

Number in Urban Settlements

Developed countries have a higher percentage of urban residents, but developing countries have more of the very large urban settlements (Figure 12.11.3). Eight of the 10 most populous cities are currently in developing countries: Cairo, Delhi, Jakarta, Manila, Mexico City, São Paulo, Seoul, and Shanghai. New York and Tokyo are the two large cities in developed countries. In addition, 44 of the 50 largest urban settlements are in developing countries, as are 98 of the 100 fastest growing urban settlements (see Research & Analyze feature).

That developing countries dominate the list of largest urban settlements is remarkable because urbanization was once associated with economic development. In 1800, 7 of the world's 10 largest cities were in Asia. In 1900, after diffusion of the Industrial Revolution from the United Kingdom to today's developed countries, all 10 of the world's largest cities were in Europe and North America.

In developing countries, migration from the countryside is fueling half of the increase in population in urban settlements, even though job opportunities may not be available. The other half results from high natural increase rates; in Africa, the natural increase rate accounts for three-fourths of urban growth.

RESEARCH & ANALYZE
The world's fastest growing urban settlements

The world's largest and fastest growing urban settlements are ranked at **http://www.citymayors.com**. Go to the site and ***search*** *urban growth.*

Scroll down *to Fastest growing cities and urban areas (1 to 100).*

1. What is the world's fastest growing city? In what country is it? Use your search engine to find this city's current population.
2. Of the 100 fastest growing cities, only two are in developed countries (both in the United States). What are they? What economic geography factors might help to explain why these are the two fastest-growing cities in the United States?

▲ 12.11.4 **WORLD'S FASTEST GROWING CITY**

City Mayors Statistics
https://goo.gl/nMoe9t

CHAPTER

12 Review, Analyze, & Apply

KEY ISSUE 1 Where Are Services Distributed?

Services fulfill human wants or needs and return money to those who provide them. Most jobs are in the service sector, especially in developed countries. Three types of services are consumer, business, and public. Most services are located in settlements.

THINKING GEOGRAPHICALLY

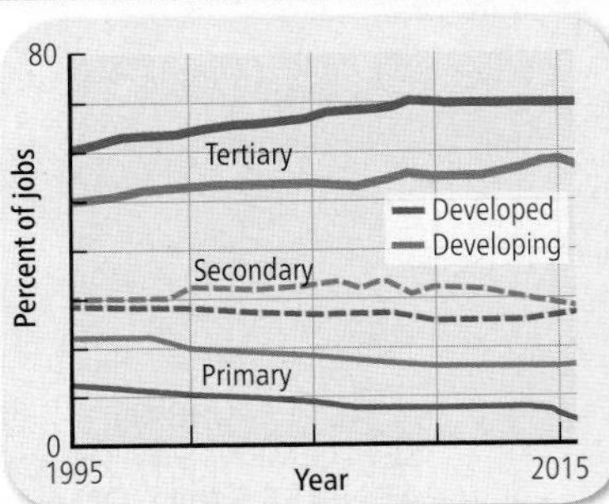

▲ 12.CR.1 CHANGES IN JOB SECTORS IN DEVELOPED AND DEVELOPING COUNTRIES

1. What changes do you expect to see in the future in the distribution of services between developed and developing countries? Why do you expect these changes? Refer to Figure 10.2.2, which showed changes among the three sectors of the economy in developed and developing countries. Figure 12.CR.1 is a simplified version of Figure 10.2.2.

KEY ISSUE 2 Where Are Consumer Services Distributed?

Consumer services generally follow a regular pattern, based on size of settlements. The range is the maximum distance people are willing to travel to use a service. The threshold is the minimum number of people needed to support a service. The market area is the area surrounding a service from which customers are attracted. Larger settlements provide consumer services that have larger thresholds, ranges, and market areas.

THINKING GEOGRAPHICALLY

▲ 12.CR.2 CONSUMER SERVICE: FRANCHISE RESTAURANT

2. What consumer services are lacking in your community that you would like to see added? How might the concepts of range and threshold help to explain its absence or possible addition to your community?

KEY ISSUE 3 Where Are Business Services Distributed?

Business services disproportionately cluster in global cities, which are centers for global flows of information and capital. Some developing countries attract offshore financial services and back-office operations. A settlement's basic industries are economic activities that export primarily to businesses and consumers elsewhere. Basic businesses are the principal source of growth and wealth for a settlement.

THINKING GEOGRAPHICALLY

▲ 12.CR.3 MAYO CLINIC
Basic industry of Rochester, Minnesota.

3. What basic industries does your community have in abundance? What distinctive features of your community might explain this base?

KEY ISSUE 4 Why Do Services Cluster In Settlements?

Services cluster in rural and urban settlements. Rural settlements may be either clustered or dispersed. Few people lived in urban settlements until modern times. Urbanization involves an increase in the percentage of people living in urban settlements. Developed countries have higher percentages of urban residents than do developing countries. Urbanization also involves an increase in size of settlements. Most very large settlements are in developing countries.

THINKING GEOGRAPHICALLY

▲ 12.CR.4 SERVICES IN URBAN SETTLEMENTS: PROFESSIONAL SPORTS

4. Professional sports teams are leisure services with large ranges, thresholds, and areas. They tend to cluster in large urban settlements. Go online to find a list of the largest U.S. Metropolitan Statistical Areas. Compare the list with the locations of the 32 National Football League teams. How many of the 32 largest metropolitan areas do not have an NFL team? How many teams are outside the 32 largest metropolitan areas? What factors might account for the discrepancy between the two lists?

GeoVideo

Log in to the Mastering Geography™ Study Area to view this video.

Ukraine: Serhiy's Leap

In a Ukrainian village, people raise much of their own food, and jobs other than farming are scarce. Like most of the village's young people, Serhiy plans to leave when he finishes school.

1. How does Serhiy's family earn its living? What is Serhiy's contribution?
2. How does Serhiy rate the advantages and disadvantages of village life versus city life?
3. Describe Serhiy's plan for his life. Does it seem reasonable? What is the alternative?

Key Terms

Basic business (p. 306) A business that sells its products or services primarily to consumers outside the settlement.

Business service (p. 292) A service that primarily meets the needs of other businesses, including professional, financial, and transportation services.

Central place (p. 294) A market center for the exchange of services by people attracted from the surrounding area.

Central place theory (p. 294) A theory that explains the distribution of services based on the fact that settlements serve as centers of market areas for services; larger settlements are fewer and farther apart than smaller settlements and provide services for a larger number of people who are willing to travel farther.

Clustered rural settlement (p. 308) A rural settlement in which the houses and farm buildings of each family are situated close to each other, with fields surrounding the settlement.

Consumer service (p. 292) A business that provides services primarily to individual consumers, including retail services and education, health, and leisure services.

Dispersed rural settlement (p. 308) A rural settlement pattern characterized by isolated farms rather than clustered villages.

Economic base (p. 306) A community's collection of basic businesses.

Enclosure movement (p. 309) The process of consolidating small landholdings into a smaller number of larger farms in England during the eighteenth century.

Food desert (p. 298) An area that has a substantial amount of low-income residents and has poor access to a grocery store.

Global city (p. 302) A major center for the provision of services in the global economy.

Gravity model (p. 298) A model which holds that the potential use of a service at a particular location is directly related to the number of people in a location and inversely related to the distance people must travel to reach the service.

Market area (or **hinterland**) (p. 294) The area surrounding a central place from which people are attracted to use the place's goods and services.

Nonbasic business (p. 306) A business that sells its products primarily to consumers in the community.

Periodic market (p. 300) A collection of individual vendors who come together to offer goods and services in a location on specified days.

Primate city (p. 296) The largest settlement in a country, if it has more than twice as many people as the second-ranking settlement.

Primate city rule (p. 296) A pattern of settlements in a country such that the largest settlement has more than twice as many people as the second-ranking settlement.

Public service (p. 292) A service offered by the government to provide security and protection for citizens and businesses.

Range (of a service) (p. 295) The maximum distance people are willing to travel to use a service.

Rank-size rule (p. 296) A pattern of settlements in a country such that the nth largest settlement is 1/n the population of the largest settlement.

Service (p. 292) Any activity that fulfills a human want or need and returns money to those who provide it.

Settlement (p. 293) A permanent collection of buildings and inhabitants.

Threshold (p. 295) The minimum number of people needed to support a service.

Urbanization (p. 312) An increase in the percentage of the number of people living in urban settlements.

Geospatial Analysis

Log in to the Mastering Geography Study Area to access MapMaster 2.0.

Urbanization and environment in China

China's cities are not distributed uniformly across the country. How are China's cities related to environmental features?

Add the *Cities* layer. ***Select*** the *Settings* icon from the *Legend* and ***select*** *Show Physical Labels*. ***Zoom*** to East Asia.

1. Are China's cities more likely to be located near water or far away from water? What might account for this distribution?
2. ***Add*** the *World Elevations* layer. Are China's cities more likely to be located in regions of high elevation or low elevation? What might account for this distribution?
3. ***Add*** the *Areas Affected by Acid Rain* layer and ***replace*** the *World Elevations* layer. Are China's cities more likely to be located in regions adversely affected by acid rain? What might account for this distribution?

▲ 12.CR.6 CITIES ENVIRONMENTS IN CHINA

Explore

New England clustered settlement

Most U.S. rural settlements are dispersed. Newfane, Vermont, is an example of a clustered rural settlement.

In Google Earth, ***search*** for *Newfane, Vermont*. ***Zoom*** in to around 500 meters.

Clustered rural settlements in New England were typically arranged around a central common or public open space. Newfane's common is divided by roads into three sections —a small triangular section to the west, a larger triangular section in the middle, and a semicircular section to the east.

1. Describe the uses and the building materials of the structures that surround the common in Newfane. Some are labeled. You will have to enter *Street View* to check out most of them.
2. Why do you think these structures were placed at the most prominent location in the rural village?

▲ 12.CR.7 NEWFANE

Mastering Geography

Looking for additional review and test prep materials? Visit the Study Area in Mastering Geography to enhance your geographic literacy, spatial reasoning skills, and understanding of this chapter's content. Access MapMaster™ interactive maps, video case studies, *In the News* current articles, flashcards, self-study quizzes, an eText of *Contemporary Human Geography*, and more. **pearson.com/mastering/geography**

CHAPTER

13 Urban Patterns

When you are staring at a skyscraper, you know you are in a city. When you are standing in a cornfield, you have no doubt that you are in the country. Geographers help explain why urban and rural settlements are different. The previous chapter examined the distribution of urban settlements at national and global scales. This chapter looks at where people and activities are distributed within urban areas.

◀ Map of Underground City, Montréal, Canada.

KEY ISSUES

1 How Are Cities Defined?

Services, especially business and public services, cluster downtown. The growth of cities surrounding downtown has resulted in the need to construct various definitions of their extent.

2 Where Are People Distributed Within an Urban Area?

Several models have been created to describe where different people tend to cluster within U.S. urban areas, depending on their age, income, and ethnicity, among other factors.

3 How Are Cities Outside North America Structured?

The models of urban structure developed in the United States can also describe—with modifications—urban areas elsewhere in the world.

4 How Do Cities Become More Sustainable?

The rapid growth of cities has resulted in development of extensive suburbs where residents depend exclusively on motor vehicles for transportation. Meanwhile, the central areas of many cities have become more animated.

LOCATIONS IN THIS CHAPTER

Chicago, *pp. 322, 323*
Cleveland, *p. 333*
New York City, *pp. 334, 337*
London, *p. 335*
Rotterdam, *p. 335*
St. Louis, *pp. 319, 332*
Mobile, *pp. 320, 321*
Portland, *p. 333*
Fès, *p. 329*
Beijing, *p. 328*
Los Angeles, *p. 336*
Orlando, *p. 332*
San Antonio, *pp. 324, 325*
New Orleans, *p. 337*
Paris, *pp. 326, 327*
Medellín, *p. 330*
Mexico City, *pp. 328, 329, 331*
Johannesburg, *p. 331*

micropolitan statistical area
sector model
central business district
annexation
rush hour
multiple nuclei model
concentric zone model
edge city
gentrification
downtown
market segmentation
central city
social area analysis
sprawl
megalopolis
public transport
galactic model
smart growth
homeless
density gradient
urbanized area
metropolitan statistical area
urban cluster
informal settlement

Defining Urban Settlements

- **Outline the various definitions of urban settlements.**

Historically, urban settlements were very small and compact. As these settlements have rapidly grown, however, definitions have been created to characterize their different parts: the metropolitan area, the central city, and the urban area.

Metropolitan Area

The economic and cultural area of influence of a settlement extends over a wide area. The U.S. Bureau of the Census has created a method of measuring the larger functional area of a settlement, known as the **metropolitan statistical area (MSA)**. An MSA includes the following (Figure 13.1.1):

- An urbanized area with a population of at least 50,000.
- The county within which the city is located.
- Adjacent counties with a high population density and a large percentage of residents working in the central city's county (specifically, a county with a density of 25 persons per square mile and at least 50 percent working in the central city's county).

Studies of metropolitan areas in the United States are usually based on information about MSAs. MSAs are widely used because many statistics are published for counties, the basic MSA building block. The Census Bureau had designated 389 MSAs as of 2015, encompassing 84 percent of the U.S. population (including Puerto Rico).

The census has also designated smaller urban areas as **micropolitan statistical areas (μSAs)** A μSA includes an urbanized area of between 10,000 and 50,000 inhabitants, the county in which it is found, and adjacent counties tied to the city. The United States had 556 micropolitan statistical areas as of 2015, for the most part found around southern and western communities previously considered rural in character. About 10 percent of Americans live in micropolitan statistical areas.

The census combines MSAs and μSAs in several other ways:

- A **core based statistical area (CBSA)** is any one MSA or μSAs (945 as of 2015, including the 389 MSAs and the 556 μSAs).
- A **combined statistical area (CSA)** is two or more contiguous CBSAs tied together by commuting patterns (174 as of 2015).

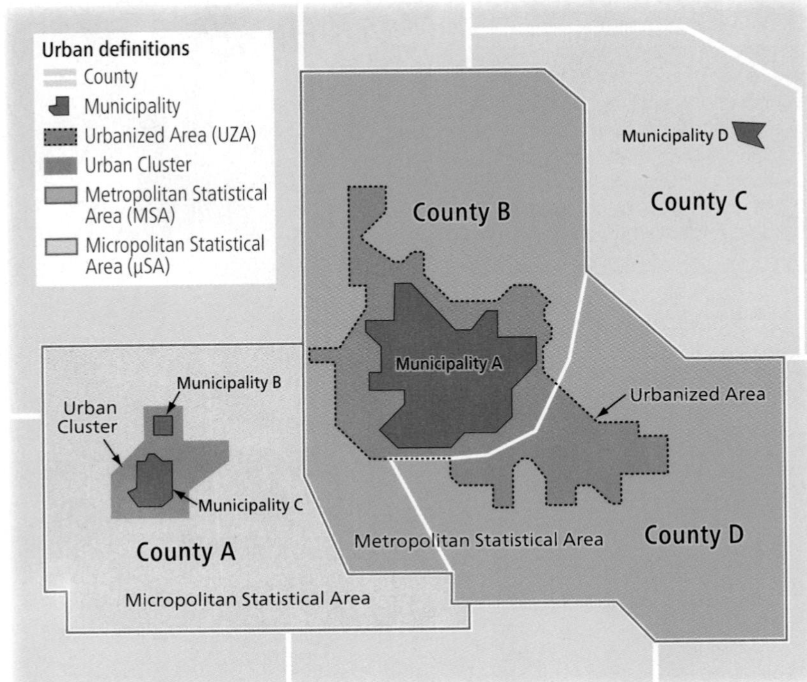

◀ **13.1.1 DEFINITIONS OF URBAN SETTLEMENTS**
The census definitions can be applied to this illustration:

- MSA: Counties B and D.
- μSA: County A.
- CBSAs: The illustration has two (the MSA consisting of Counties B and D and the μSA consisting of County A).
- CSA: A CSA comprising Counties A, B, and D would be designated if the Census Bureau determined that the adjacent MSA and μSA are closely linked.

Central City

The term **central city**, or simply city, defines an urban settlement that has been legally incorporated into an independent, self-governing unit. A city has locally elected officials, the ability to raise taxes, and responsibility for providing essential services. The boundaries of the city define the geographic area within which the local government has legal authority.

Urban Area

An **urban area** consists of a central city and its surrounding built-up suburbs. The U.S. census recognizes two types of urban areas:

- The **urbanized area** is an urban area with at least 50,000 inhabitants.
- **An urban cluster** is an urban area with between 2,500 and 50,000 inhabitants.

The census identified 486 urbanized areas and 3,087 urban clusters in the United States in 2010. Approximately 70 percent of the U.S. population lived in one of the 486 urbanized areas, including about 30 percent in central cities and 40 percent in surrounding jurisdictions. Approximately 10 percent of the U.S. population lived in one of the 3,087 urban clusters (Figure 13.1.2).

▲ 13.1.2 **DEFINITIONS OF URBAN SETTLEMENTS APPLIED TO ST LOUIS**
The City of St Louis comprises only 6 percent of the land area and 11 percent of the population of the MSA.

Overlapping Metropolitan Areas

MSAs overlap in northeastern United States and form one continuous urban complex, extending from north of Boston to south of Washington, D.C. Geographer Jean Gottmann named this region **Megalopolis**, a Greek word meaning "great city" (Figure 13.1.3). Other urban complexes exist in the United States, including the southern Great Lakes between Milwaukee and Pittsburgh, and southern California, between Los Angeles and Tijuana. Among important examples in other developed regions are the German Ruhr (including the cities of Dortmund, Düsseldorf, and Essen), Randstad in the Netherlands (including the cities of Amsterdam, The Hague, and Rotterdam), and Japan's Tokaido (including the cities of Tokyo and Yokohama).

Within Megalopolis, the downtown areas of individual cities such as Baltimore, New York, and Philadelphia retain distinctive identities, and the urban areas are visibly separated from each other by open space used as parks, military bases, and farms. But at the periphery of the urban areas, the boundaries overlap.

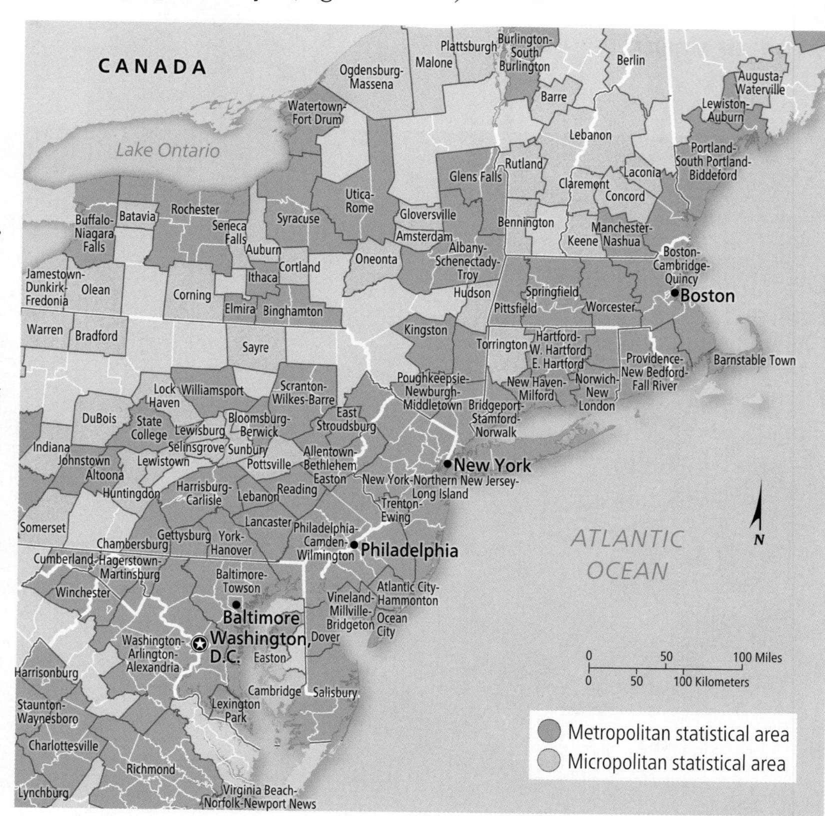

▶ 13.1.3 **MEGALOPOLIS**
Also known as the Boswash corridor, Megalopolis extends more than 700 kilometers (440 miles) between north of Boston and south of Washington. Megalopolis contains one-fourth of the U.S. population on only 2 percent of the country's total land area.

The Central Business District

- **Describe distinctive features of the central business district.**

The best-known and most visually distinctive area of most cities is downtown, which is known to geographers by the more precise term **central business district (CBD)** (Figure 13.2.1). The CBD is compact—less than 1 percent of the urban land area—but contains a large percentage of the region's services, especially business and public services. (Figures 13.2.2, 13.2.3, and 13.2.4).

Services are attracted to the CBD because of its accessibility. The center is the easiest part of the city to reach from the rest of the region and is the focal point of the region's transportation network.

The CBD is one of the oldest districts in a city, usually at or near the original site of the settlement. The CBDs of cities are often situated along a body of water, which served as a principal transportation route for passengers in the past and for freight today.

◀ 13.2.2 **PUBLIC SERVICES**
The CBD typically includes such public services as city hall, convention center, court house, library, and museums. Examples include buildings 1 and 2 in Figure 13.2.1 and the Mobile Museum of History (the image on the left). Semipublic services, such as places of worship, also cluster downtown, often in handsome historic structures. A central location facilitates access for people living in all parts of the settlement.

▼ 13.2.1 **MOBILE, ALABAMA, CBD**

1. COURT HOUSE
2. U.S. ARMY CORPS
3. WELLS FARGO BANK
4. REGIONS BANK
5. TRUSTMARK BANK
6. RSA BATTLE HOUSE TOWER
7. DAUPHIN STREET BARS AND RESTAURANTS
8. BATTLE HOUSE RENAISSANCE MOBILE HOTEL
9. HAMPTON INN
10. PORT OF MOBILE

▼ **13.2.3 BUSINESS SERVICES**
Offices cluster in a CBD for accessibility, including Mobile's tallest, the RSA Battle House Tower shown below, as well as buildings 3, 4, 5, and 6 in Figure 13.2.1. People in business services such as advertising, banking, finance, journalism, and law particularly depend on proximity to professional colleagues. Offices are centrally located to facilitate rapid communication of fast-breaking news through spatial proximity. Even with the diffusion of modern telecommunications, many professionals still exchange information with colleagues primarily through face-to-face contact.

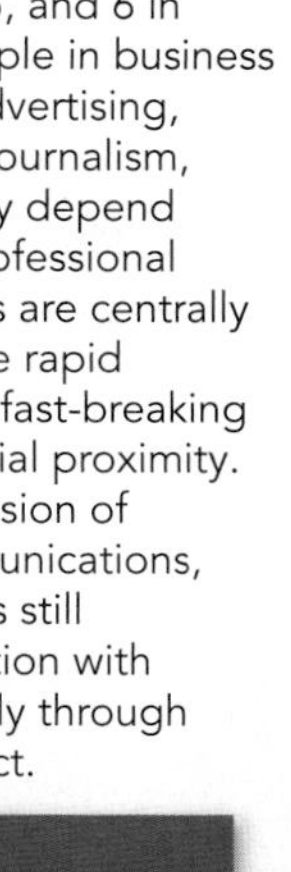

◀ **13.2.4 CONSUMER SERVICES**
The CBD attracts consumer services to serve the many people who work in the center and shop during lunch or working hours. These businesses provide such services as office supplies, clothing, and lunch. Hotels also cluster downtown (numbers 8 and 9 in Figure 13.2.1). Entertainment districts downtown, such as Mobile's Dauphin Street (the image to the left and building 7 in Figure 13.2.1), attract visitors as well as local residents.

Other Land Uses

Factories once clustered downtown, but few remain. The waterfronts of many CBDs were once lined with factories and piers to unload raw materials. Modern factories now locate in suburbs or rural areas (refer to Chapter 11). Most of the derelict warehouses and piers have been replaced with consumer services, but some may still be in use (number 10 in Figure 13.2.1).

Many people used to live in or near the CBD. In the twentieth century, downtown housing was abandoned. People were pushed from CBDs by congestion and crime and pulled to suburbs by large homes and modern schools.

In the twenty-first century, the population of many U.S. CBDs has increased. New apartment buildings and townhouses have been constructed, and abandoned warehouses and outdated office buildings have been converted into residential lofts. Downtown living is especially attractive to people without school-age children, either "empty nesters" whose children have left home or young professionals who have not yet had children.

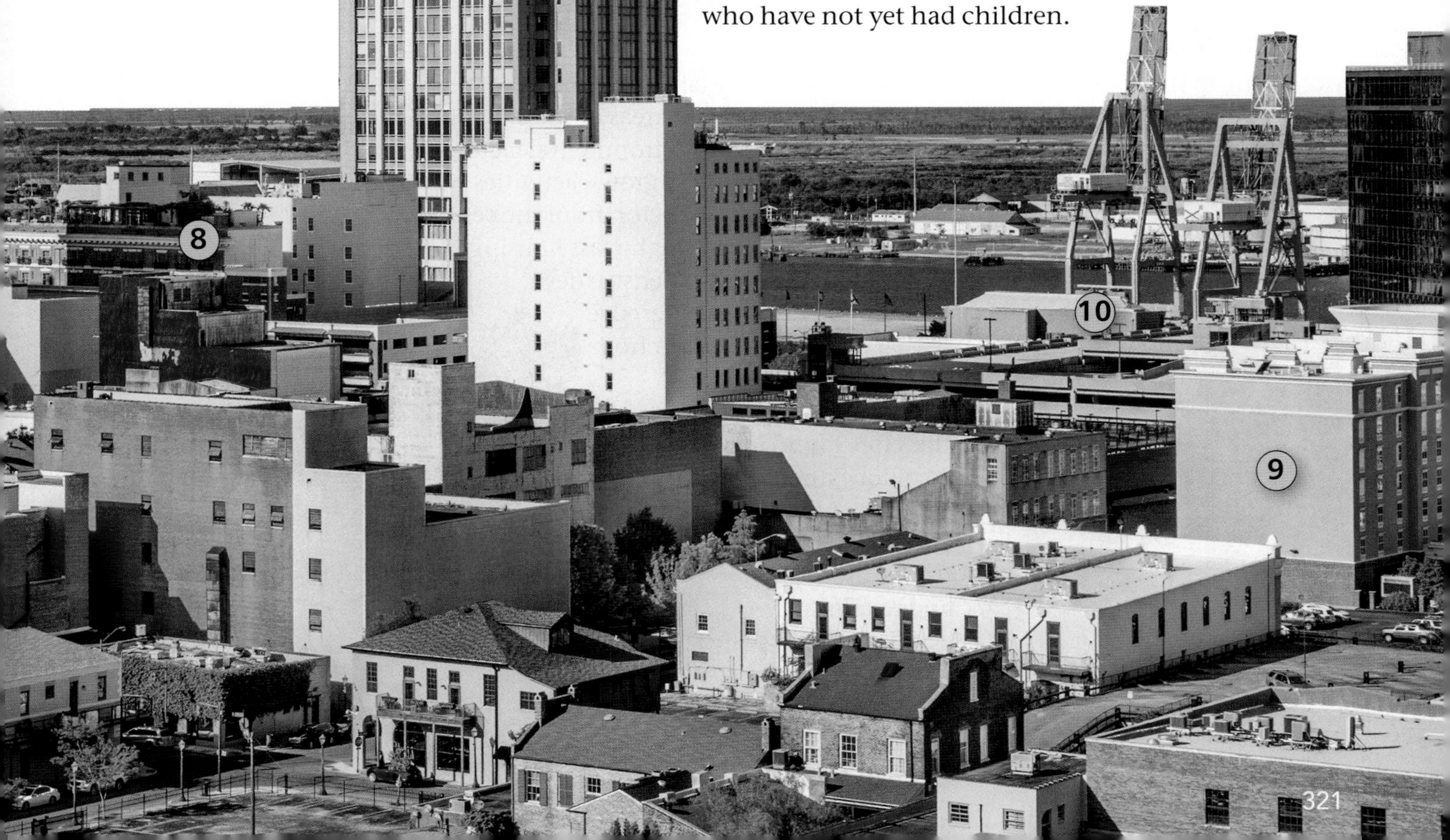

6

8

10

9

Models of Urban Structure

- **Describe three models of internal structure of urban areas.**

People are not distributed randomly within an urban area. They concentrate in particular neighborhoods, depending on their social characteristics. Sociologists, economists, and geographers have developed three models to help explain where different types of people tend to live in an urban area—the concentric zone, sector, and multiple nuclei models. In addition, the galactic (or peripheral) model is a variation of the multiple nuclei model.

Concentric Zone Model

According to the **concentric zone model**, created in 1923 by sociologist Ernest Burgess, a city grows outward from a central area in a series of concentric rings, like the growth rings of a tree. The precise size and width of the rings vary from one city to another, but the same basic types of rings appear in all cities in the same order. Back in the 1920s, Burgess identified five rings (Figures 13.3.1 and 13.3.2).

▶ 13.3.2 WORKING-CLASS HOMES, CHICAGO

▼ 13.3.1 CONCENTRIC ZONE MODEL

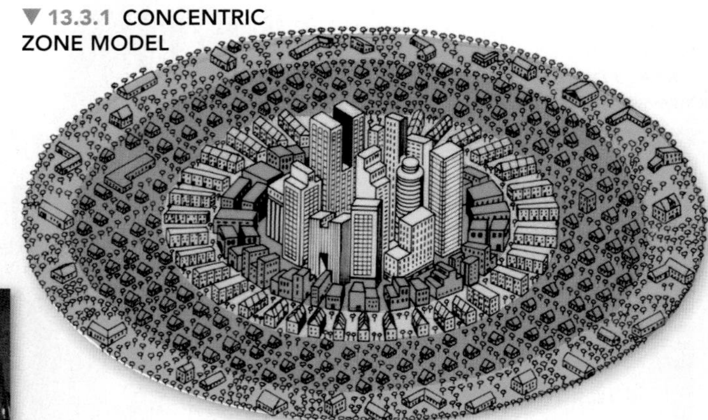

1 Central business district
2 Zone of transition
3 Zone of independent workers' homes
4 Zone of better residences
5 Commuter's zone

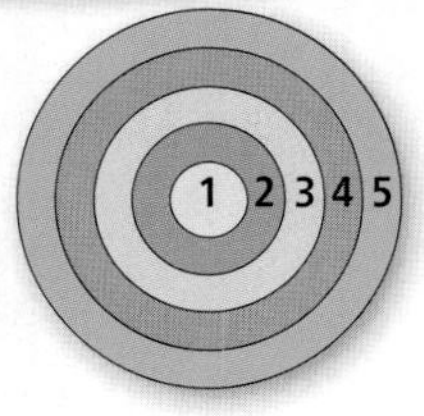

Sector Model

According to the **sector model**, developed in 1939 by land economist Homer Hoyt, a city develops in a series of sectors (Figure 13.3.3). Certain areas of the city are more attractive for various activities, originally because of an environmental factor or even by mere chance. As a city grows, activities expand outward in a wedge, or sector, from the center.

Once a district with high-class housing is established, the most expensive new housing is built on the outer edge of that district, farther out from the center (Figure 13.3.4). The best housing is therefore found in a corridor extending from downtown to the outer edge of the city. Industrial and retailing activities develop in other sectors, usually along good transportation lines.

▲ 13.3.4 HIGH-INCOME SECTOR
Chicago's North Side.

▼ 13.3.3 SECTOR MODEL

1 Central business district
2 Transportation and industry
3 Low-class residential
4 Middle-class residential
5 High-class residential

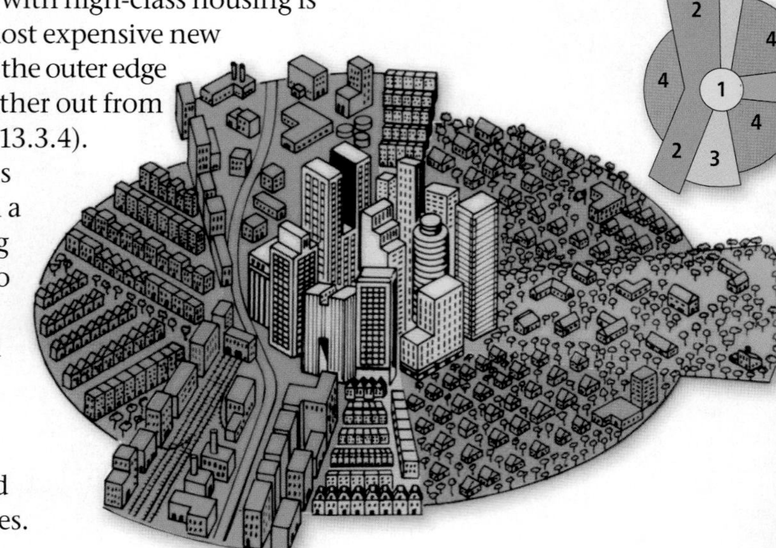

Multiple Nuclei and Galactic Models

According to the **multiple nuclei model**, developed by geographers Chauncey Harris and Edward Ullman in 1945, a city is a complex structure that includes more than one center around which activities occur (Figure 13.3.5). Examples of these nodes include a port, a neighborhood business center, a university, an airport, and a park.

The multiple nuclei theory states that some activities are attracted to particular nodes, whereas others try to avoid them. For example, a university node may attract well-educated residents, pizzerias, and bookstores (Figure 13.3.6), whereas an airport may attract hotels and warehouses. On the other hand, incompatible land-use activities avoid clustering in the same locations. Heavy industry and high-class housing, for example, rarely exist in the same neighborhood.

According to the **galactic (or peripheral) model**, developed by Harris in 1960, an urban area consists of an inner city surrounded by large suburban residential and service nodes or nuclei tied together by a beltway or ring road (Figure 13.3.7). Rather than an entirely new model, Harris considered the peripheral model to be a modification of the multiple nuclei model (which he co-authored), reflecting the growth of suburbs (see section 13.8). The nodes of consumer and business services around the beltway are called **edge cities** (Figure 13.3.8).

▲ 13.3.6 **UNIVERSITY NODE**
Bookstore near the University of Chicago.

▼ 13.3.5 **MULTIPLE NUCLEI MODEL**

1 Central business district
2 Wholesale, light manufacturing
3 Low-class residential
4 Medium-class residential
5 High-class residential
6 Heavy manufacturing
7 Outlying business district
8 Residential suburb
9 Industrial suburb

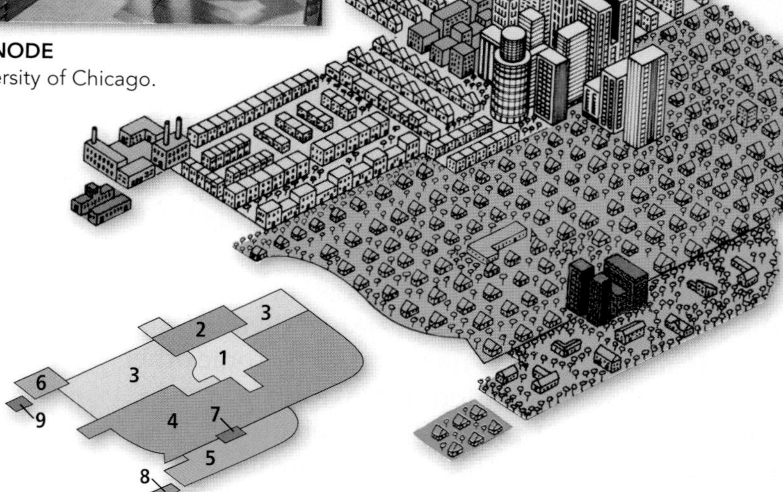

▲ 13.3.8 **EDGE CITY NEAR CHICAGO**
Schaumburg, Illinois.

► 13.3.7 **GALACTIC (OR PERIPHERAL) MODEL**

1 Central City
2 Suburban Residential Area
3 Shopping Mall
4 Industrial District
5 Office Park
6 Service Center
7 Airport Complex
8 Combined Employment & Shopping Center

Applying the Models

- Analyze how the models help to explain where people live within an urban area.

The models of internal structure help us understand where people with different social characteristics tend to live within an urban area. They can also help explain why certain types of people tend to live in particular places.

Social Area Analysis

The study of where people of varying living standards, ethnic background, and lifestyle live within an urban area is **social area analysis**. Social area analysis helps to create an overall picture of where various types of people tend to live, depending on their particular personal characteristics.

Effective application of the models depends on the availability of data at the scale of individual neighborhoods. In the United States and some other countries, that information comes from the census. Urban areas in the United States are divided into **census tracts** that each contain approximately 5,000 residents and correspond, where possible, to neighborhood boundaries.

Social Area Analysis: Concentric Zones

Consider two households with the same income and ethnic background. One household lives in a newly constructed home, whereas the other lives in an older one. The concentric zone model suggests (Figure 13.4.1) that the household in the older house is much more likely to live in an inner ring (Figure 13.4.2) and the household in the newer house in an outer ring (Figure 13.4.3).

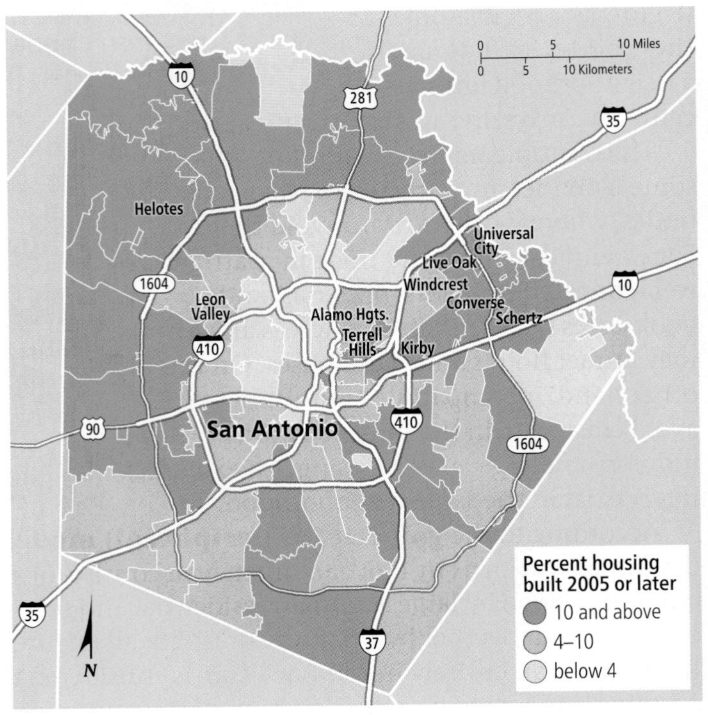

▲ 13.4.1 CONCENTRIC ZONES IN SAN ANTONIO: AGE OF HOUSING
The outer ring has a higher percentage of recently built housing.

▲ 13.4.2 SAN ANTONIO CONCENTRIC ZONE: OLDER HOUSING
Older housing is found in an inner ring of San Antonio.

◀ 13.4.3 SAN ANTONIO CONCENTRIC ZONE: NEWER HOUSING
Newer housing is found in an outer ring of San Antonio.

Social Area Analysis: Sectors

Given two households who own their homes, the sector model suggests (Figure 3.4.4) that the household with a more modest income (Figure 3.4.5) is unlikely to live in the same sector of the city as the household with the higher income (compare Figure 3.4.5 with Figure 3.4.3).

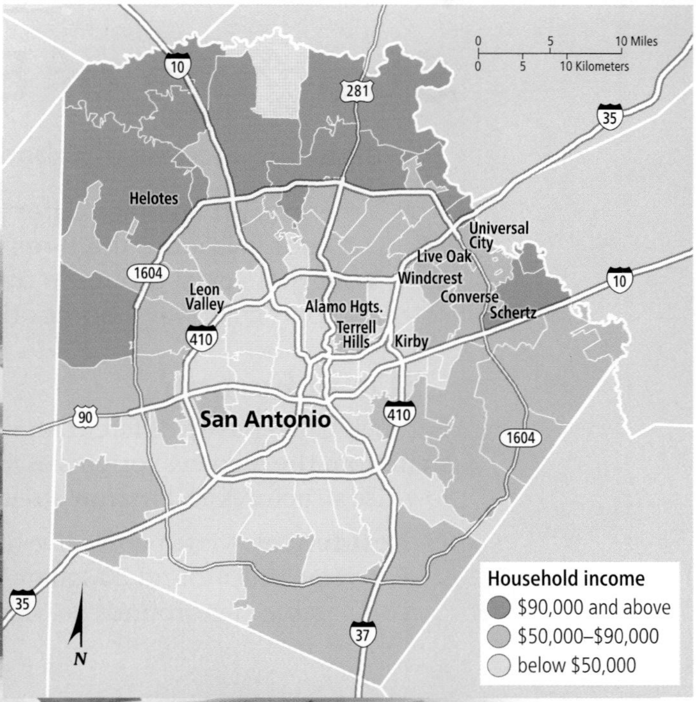

▲ **13.4.4 SECTORS IN SAN ANTONIO: INCOME**
Higher-income people tend to live in the northern sector.

◀ **13.4.5 SAN ANTONIO SECTOR: MIDDLE-CLASS HOUSING**
Compare with high-income housing in Figure 3.4.3.

Social Area Analysis: Nuclei

People with the same ethnic or racial background are likely to live near each other (Figure 13.4.6).

Limitations of the Models

None of the three models taken individually completely explains why different types of people live in distinctive parts of a city. If the models are combined rather than considered independently, they help geographers explain where different types of people live in a city. Putting the three models together, we can identify, for example, the neighborhood in which a high-income, Asian American owner-occupant is most likely to live.

Still, critics point out that the models are too simple and fail to consider the variety of reasons that lead people to select particular residential locations. Because the three models are all based on conditions that existed in U.S. cities during mid-twentieth century, critics also question their relevance to contemporary urban patterns in the United States or in other countries.

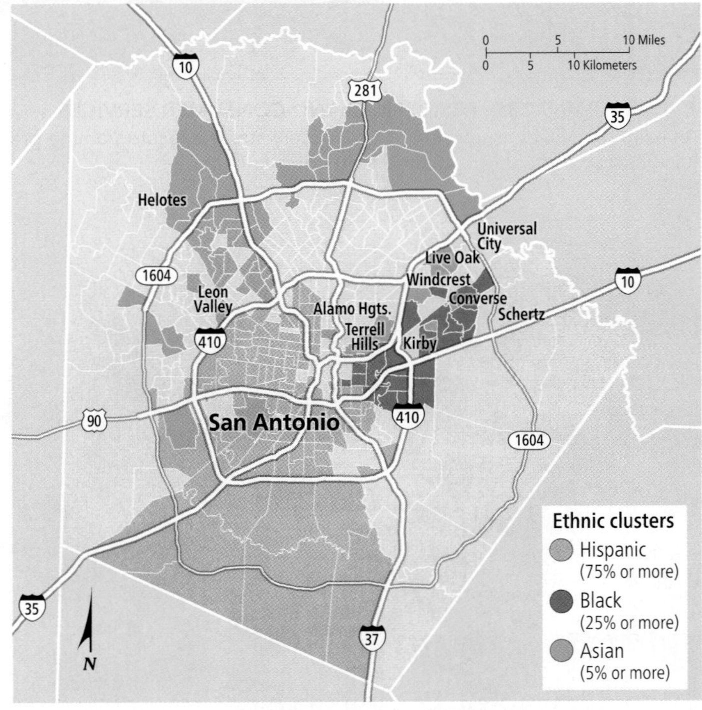

▲ **13.4.6 MULTIPLE NUCLEI IN SAN ANTONIO: ETHNICITIES**
African Americans, Asian Americans, and Hispanics cluster in different nodes.

Structure of Europe's Cities

- Relate the models of urban structure to European urban areas.

American urban areas differ from those elsewhere in the world. These differences do not invalidate the three models of internal urban structure, but they do point out that social groups in other countries may not have the same reasons for selecting particular neighborhoods within their cities.

CBDs in Europe

Europe's CBDs have a different mix of land uses than those in North America. Differences stem from the medieval origins of many of Europe's CBDs. European cities display a legacy of low-rise structures and narrow streets, built as long ago as medieval times.

- **Residences.** More people live downtown in cities outside North America. The CBD of Paris covering around 20 square kilometers (8 square miles) has about 400,000 residents. A comparable area around the CBD of Detroit has around 25,000 residents.
- **Consumer services.** More people live in Europe's CBDs in part because they are attracted to the concentration of consumer services, such as cultural activities and animated nightlife. And with more people living there, Europe's CBDs in turn contain more day-to-day consumer services, such as groceries, bakeries, and butchers (Figure 13.5.1).
- **Public services.** The most prominent structures in Europe's CBDs are often public and semipublic services, such as churches and former royal palaces, situated on the most important public squares (Figure 13.5.2). Parks in Europe's CBDs were often first laid out as private gardens for aristocratic families and later were opened to the public.
- **Business services.** Europe's CBDs contain professional and financial services. However, business services in Europe's CBDs are less likely to be housed in skyscrapers than those in North America. Some European cities try to preserve their historic CBDs by limiting high-rise buildings.

▲ 13.5.1 PARIS CBD: RESIDENCES AND CONSUMER SERVICES
An example of a consumer service, a grocery store, is located on the ground floor, and apartments are located on the upper floors.

Many service providers wish to be in the center of European cities, but constructing new buildings is difficult. The alternative is renovation of older buildings. However, renovation is more expensive and may not produce enough space to meet the demand. As a result, rents are much higher in the center of European cities than in U.S. cities of comparable size.

◀ 13.5.2 PARIS CBD: PUBLIC SERVICES AND BUSINESS SERVICES
An example of a public service, the Panthéon (foreground) houses the remains of distinguished French citizens. An example of a business service, the Montparnasse Tower (background) is the tallest office building inside the City of Paris.

Concentric Zones in Europe

The urban structure within Paris can be used to illustrate similarities and differences in the distribution of people within U.S. and European cities. As in U.S. urban areas, the newer housing in the Paris region is in outer rings and the older housing is closer to the center (Figure 13.5.3). Unlike U.S. urban areas, though, much of the newer suburban housing is in high-rise apartments rather than single-family homes (Figure 13.5.4).

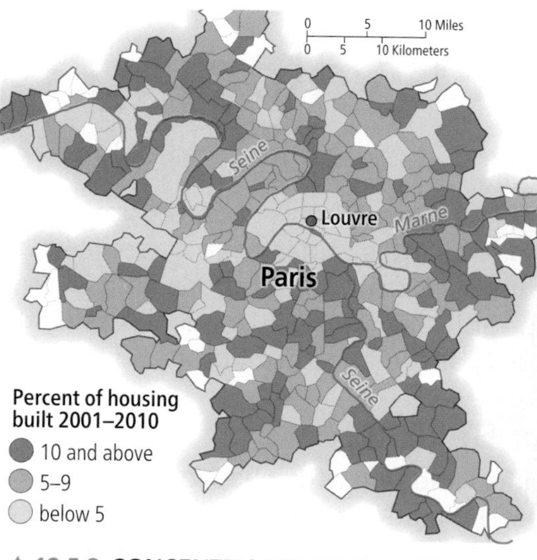

▲ 13.5.3 CONCENTRIC ZONES IN PARIS
The oldest housing is in the inner ring.

▲ 13.5.4 PARIS CONCENTRIC ZONE: NEWER LOWER-INCOME HOUSING
Compare with Figure 13.5.1, which shows older housing in the center of Paris.

Sectors in Europe

Similar to U.S. urban areas, higher income people cluster in a sector in the Paris region (Figure 13.5.5). Middle-class people are more likely to live in south and west sectors (Figure 13.5.6). The preference of Paris's wealthy to cluster in a southwest sector was reinforced during the Industrial Revolution in the nineteenth century, when factories were built to the south, east, and north along the Seine and Marne River valleys.

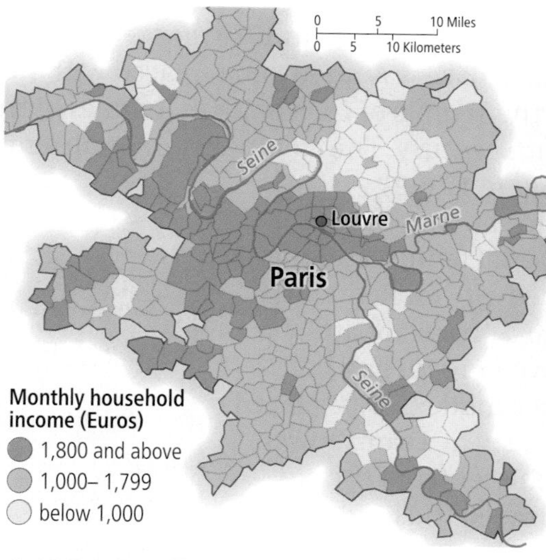

▲ 13.5.5 SECTORS IN PARIS
The southwest is the highest-income sector, and the northeast is the lowest-income sector.

▲ 13.5.6 PARIS SECTOR: MIDDLE-CLASS HOUSING
In Paris, even newer outer ring housing for middle-class people is likely to be in apartment buildings. Compare this recently built apartment in a higher-income sector with the apartment building in Figure 13.5.4, which is in a lower-income sector.

Multiple Nuclei in Europe

European urban areas, including Paris, have experienced a large increase in immigration from other regions of the world (see Chapter 3). In contrast to U.S. urban areas, most ethnic and racial minorities reside in the suburbs of Paris (Figures 13.5.7 and 13.5.8).

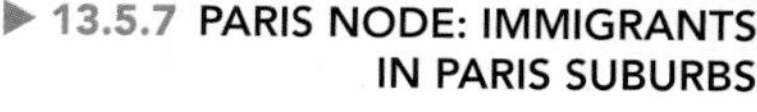

▶ 13.5.7 PARIS NODE: IMMIGRANTS IN PARIS SUBURBS

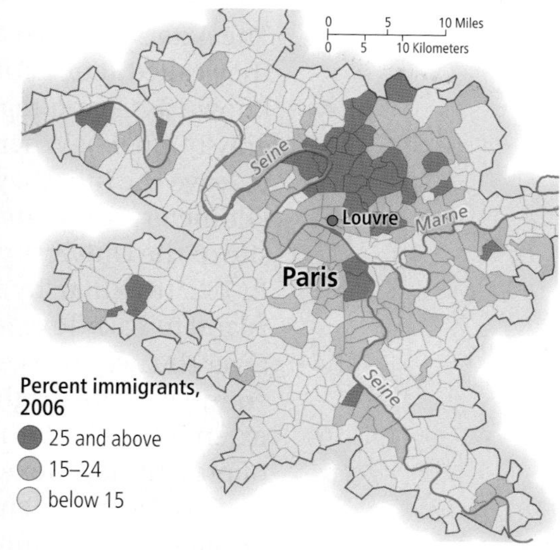

▲ 13.5.8 MULTIPLE NUCLEI IN PARIS
The highest percentage of immigrants is in a node in the northern suburbs.

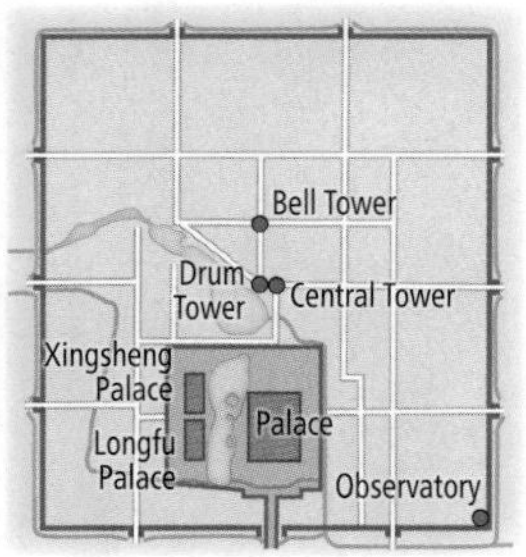

▲ 13.6.1 BEIJING (DADU) DURING THE YUAN DYNASTY

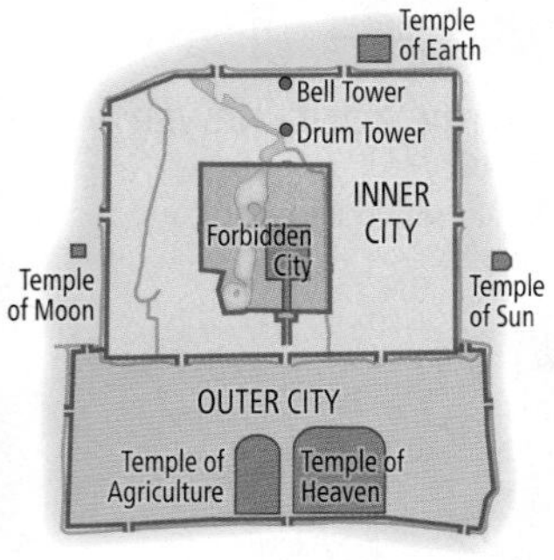

▲ 13.6.2 BEIJING DURING THE MING DYNASTY

Imperial City
Important building
Place of interest
Wall
Gate
Street
Canal

Cities in Developing Countries

- Compare patterns in precolonial and colonial cities in developing countries.

Some cities in developing countries date from ancient times. For most of recorded history, the world's largest cities have been in Asia (refer to section 12.10). The ancient and medieval structure of these cities was influenced by the cultural values of the indigenous peoples living there. In some cases, these cities passed through a period of restructuring at the hands of European colonial rulers.

Medieval City: Beijing

A succession of invaders and dynasties shaped what is now the central area of Beijing. The Yuan and Ming dynasties made an especially strong impact on the early structure of Beijing.

The Yuan dynasty's founder Kubla Khan constructed a new city called Dadu beginning in 1267. The heart of the Dadu was three palaces built on Qionghua Island in the middle of Taiye Lake (Figure 13.6.1).

The Ming dynasty captured Dadu in 1368 and reconstructed it over the next several decades. The imperial palace was razed and replaced with new structures, including the Forbidden City and the Temple of Heaven. The Temples of the Sun, Earth, and Moon were added in the sixteenth century. The city took on the current name Beijing ("Northern Capital") in 1403 (Figure 13.6.2).

The two palaces to the west of the lake housed the imperial family, and the eastern one contained offices. Residential areas were laid out in a checkerboard pattern divided by wider roads and narrower alleys. Three markets were placed in the residential areas. The Drum Tower was constructed at the center of the city. An outer wall surrounded the residential areas, and an inner wall surrounded the palaces.

▲ 13.6.3 PRECOLONIAL MEXICO CITY: TENOCHTITLÁN

Precolonial City: Mexico City

The Aztecs founded Mexico City—which they called Tenochtitlán—on a hill known as Chapultepec ("the hill of the grasshopper"). When forced by others to leave the hill, they migrated a few kilometers south, near the present-day site of the University of Mexico, and then in 1325 to a marshy 10-square-kilometer island in Lake Texcoco (Figure 13.6.3). Over the next two centuries, the Aztecs conquered the neighboring peoples and extended their control through much of present-day Mexico. As their wealth and power grew, Tenochtitlán grew to a population of a half-million. The node of religious life was the Great Temple (Figure 13.6.4).

▲ 13.6.4 PRECOLONIAL MEXICO CITY: THE GREAT TEMPLE

◀ **13.6.5 COLONIAL MEXICO CITY**
A Roman Catholic cathedral was built on the north side of the Zócalo, near the site of the demolished Great Temple, (under the green rectangles in the lower left), and the National Palace was erected on the east side, on the site of the Aztec emperor Moctezuma's destroyed palace. The Spanish reconstructed the streets in a grid pattern extending from the Zócalo.

Colonial Cities

When Europeans gained control of Africa, Asia, and Latin America, their colonial cities followed standardized plans. Spanish colonial cities in Latin America, for example, were built according to the Laws of the Indies, drafted in 1573.

After the Spanish conquered Tenochtitlán in 1521, following a two-year siege, they destroyed the city and dispersed or killed most of the inhabitants. The city, renamed Mexico City, was rebuilt around a main square, called the Zócalo, in the center of the island, on the site of the Aztecs' sacred precinct (Figure 13.6.5).

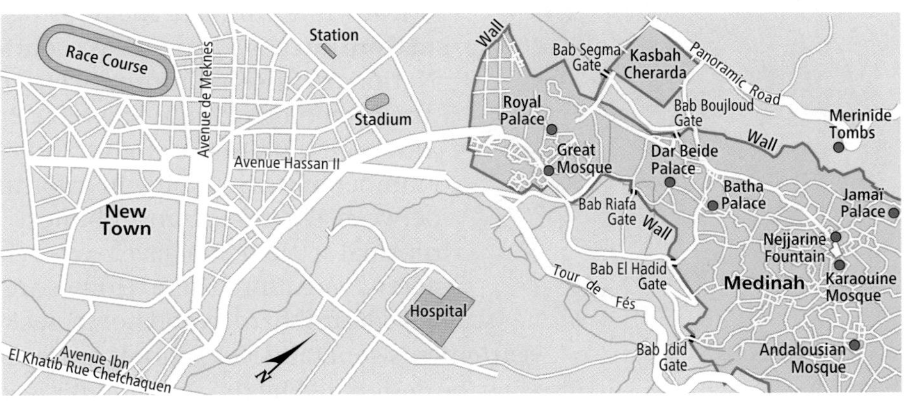

▲ **13.6.6 PRECOLONIAL AND COLONIAL FÈS (FEZ): STREET PATTERNS**
The precolonial town to the east had narrow irregularly arranged streets and numerous mosques. The French new town to the west had wide geometrically arranged streets.

In some places, European colonial powers built a new city next to the existing one. Fès (Fez), Morocco, is an example of a city that consists of two separate and distinct nodes: a precolonial city that existed before the French gained control and one built by the French colonialists (Figure 13.6.6). The center of the precolonial city included a mosque, a bazaar (marketplace), and narrow winding streets. The new city had large public buildings and larger streets (Figure 13.6.7).

▼ **13.6.7 PRECOLONIAL AND COLONIAL FÈS (FEZ): AERIAL VIEW**
The precolonial city is in the foreground and the colonial city is in the left rear.

Applying the Models to Developing Countries

- **Relate the models of urban structure to urban areas in developing countries.**

The three models of urban structure help to explain contemporary patterns within the urban areas in developing countries. Rapid growth of population and land area has strengthened the applicability of the models in some cities though reducing their usefulness in other cases.

Concentric Zones in Developing Countries

The concentric zone model has been applied most frequently to cities in developing countries (Figure 13.7.1). As cities grow rapidly in developing countries, rings are constantly being added on the periphery to accommodate immigrants from rural areas attracted by job opportunities. The inner rings house higher-income people. Inner rings have the most attractive residential areas, because they are near business and consumer services, and they offer such vital public services as water, electricity, paved roads, and garbage pickup.

▼ 13.7.1 CONCENTRIC ZONE MODEL: DEVELOPING CITIES

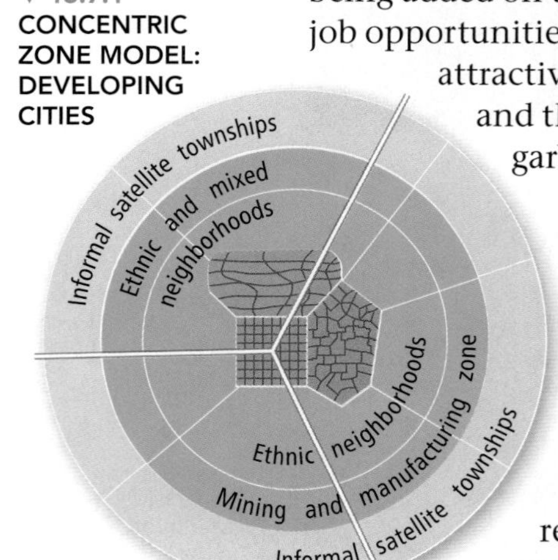

Colonial CBD
Traditional CBD
Market zone
Major road
Local street

Meanwhile, much of the housing in the outer rings is in **informal settlements**, also known as squatter settlements (Figure 13.7.2). The United Nations defines an informal settlement as a residential area where housing has been built on land to which the occupants have no legal claim, or has not been built to the city's standards for legal buildings. Estimates of the number of people living in informal settlements worldwide vary widely, between 175 million and 1 billion.

Informal settlements have few services because neither the city nor the residents can afford them. Homes are in primitive shelters made with scavenged cardboard, wood boxes, sackcloth, and crushed beverage cans. The settlements generally lack schools, paved roads, and sanitation (Figure 13.7.3). Latrines may be designated by the settlement's leaders, and water is carried from a central well or dispensed from a truck. Electricity service may be stolen by running a wire from the nearest power line. In the absence of bus service or available private cars, a resident may have to walk two hours to reach a place of employment.

▲ 13.7.2 CONCENTRIC ZONE MODEL: MEDELLÍN, COLOMBIA
Informal settlements, shown in purple, are in the outer ring.

▲ 13.7.3 CONCENTRIC ZONE: INFORMAL SETTLEMENT
Low-income people live in poor quality housing in the outer ring of Medellín, Colombia.

Sectors in Developing Countries

Geographers Ernest Griffin and Larry Ford show that in Latin American cities, wealthy people push out from the center in a well-defined elite residential sector. The elite sector forms on either side of a narrow spine that contains offices, shops, and amenities attractive to wealthy people, such as restaurants, theaters, parks, and zoos (Figure 13.7.4). The wealthy are also attracted to the center and spine because services such as water and electricity are more readily available and reliable there than elsewhere. Wealthy and middle-class residents avoid living near sectors of "disamenity," which are land uses that may be noisy or polluting or that cater to low-income residents.

In Mexico City, Emperor Maximilian (1864–1867) designed a 14-lane, tree-lined boulevard patterned after the Champs-Elysées in Paris. The boulevard (now known as the Paseo de la Reforma) extended 3 kilometers southwest from the center to Chapultepec (Figure 13.7.5). The Reforma between downtown and Chapultepec became the spine of an elite sector. During the late nineteenth century, the wealthy built pretentious palacios (palaces) along it.

Industrial park
Disamenity
Disamenity
Periférico
Periférico
Market
CBD
Spine
Mall

▲ **13.7.4 SECTOR MODEL: DEVELOPING CITIES**
Griffin-Ford model of a Latin America city.

Commercial
Market
Industrial
Elite residential sector
Zone of maturity
Zone of in situ accretion
Zone of peripheral squatter settlements
Gentrification
Middle-class residential

▶ **13.7.5 SECTOR MODEL IN A DEVELOPING CITY**
Mexico City's high-income sector grew along a major boulevard called Paseo de la Reforma.

Multiple Nuclei in Developing Countries

Cities in developing countries containing a complex mix of ethnic groups show evidence of the multiple nuclei model. During the apartheid era (see Chapter 7), South Africa's cities showed especially clear evidence of the multiple nuclei model, because each race was segregated into distinct neighborhoods (Figure 13.7.6).

T. G. McGee's model of a Southeast Asia city superimposes on concentric zones several nodes of squatter settlements and what he called "alien" zones where foreigners, usually Chinese, live and work (Figure 13.7.7). McGee found that Southeast Asia cities do not typically have a strong CBD. Instead, the various functions of the CBD are dispersed to several nodes.

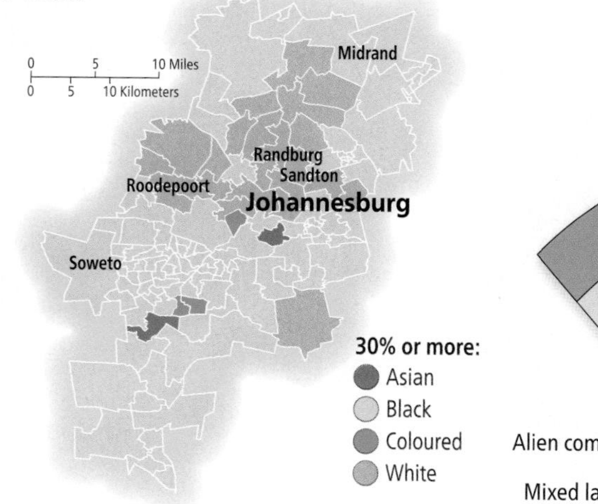

▲ **13.7.6 MULTIPLE-NUCLEI MODEL IN A DEVELOPING CITY**
Distribution of races in Johannesburg, South Africa.

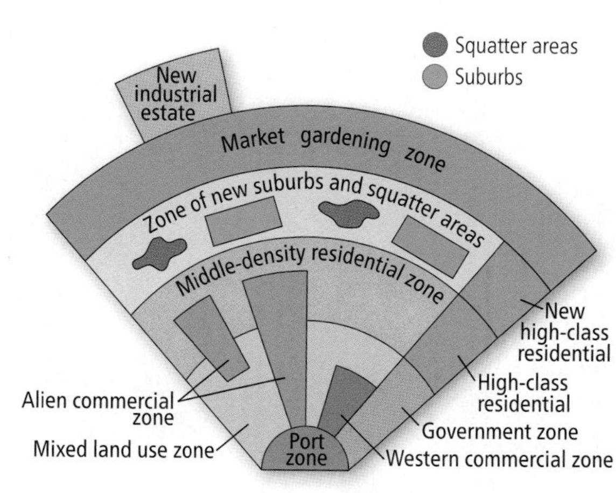

▲ **13.7.7 MULTIPLE-NUCLEI MODEL: DEVELOPING CITIES**
Griffin-Ford model of Southeast Asia city.

▲ 13.8.1 **U.S. SUBURB** Near Orlando, Florida.

Suburbs

- **Explain the process of suburban growth.**

A residential or commercial area situated within an urban area but outside the central city is a **suburb**. In 1950, only 20 percent of Americans lived in suburbs compared to 40 percent in cities and 40 percent in small towns and rural areas. In 2000, after a half-century of rapid suburban growth, 50 percent of Americans lived in suburbs compared to only 30 percent in cities and 20 percent in small towns and rural areas (Figure 13.8.1).

Annexation and Fragmentation

Until recently in the United States, as cities grew, they expanded by adding peripheral land (Figure 13.8.2). The process of legally adding land area to a city is **annexation**.

Now cities are surrounded by a collection of suburban jurisdictions whose residents prefer to remain legally independent of the large city. Given the difficulty in annexing suburbs, local government in the United States is extremely fragmented (Figure 13.8.3). According to the 2012 Census of Governments, the United States had 89,004 local governments, including 3,031 counties, 19,522 municipalities, 16,364 townships, 12,884 school districts, and 37,203 special districts (which provide such services as fire protection, water supply, libraries, and public transportation).

Sprawl

The term **sprawl** describes the development of suburbs at relatively low density and at locations that are not contiguous to the existing built-up area. Sprawl is fostered in the United States by the desire of many families to own large tracts of land and by private developers who recognize that land for new housing sites is cheaper if not contiguous to the existing built-up area. As a result of sprawl, roads and utilities must be extended to connect isolated new developments, motorists must drive longer distances and consume more fuel, agricultural land is lost to residential developments, and local governments must spend more to provide services to the sprawling areas than they are able collect in taxes.

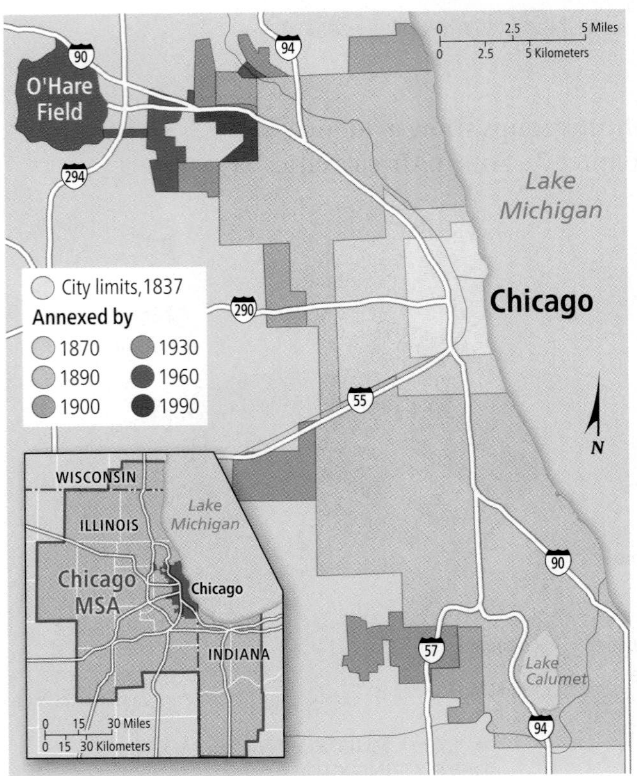

▲ 13.8.2 **ANNEXATION IN CHICAGO**

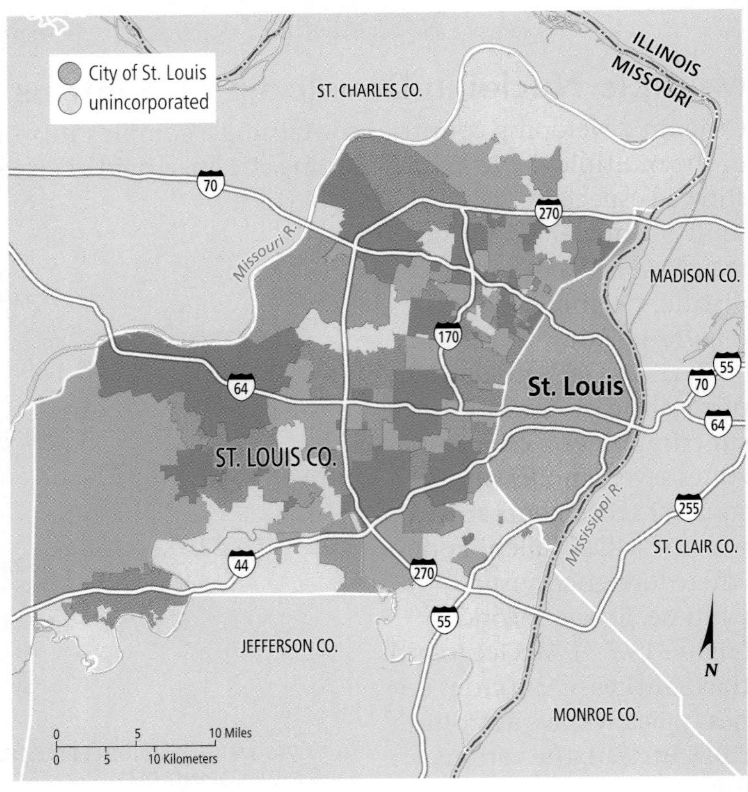

▲ 13.8.3 **MUNICIPALITIES IN ST. LOUIS COUNTY**

Smart Growth

Several U.S. states have taken steps to curb suburban growth. The goal is to produce a pattern of compact and contiguous development and protect rural land for agriculture, recreation, and wildlife. Legislation and regulations to limit suburban growth and preserve farmland has been called **smart growth**. Oregon and Tennessee have defined growth boundaries within which new development must occur (Figure 13.8.4). Cities can annex only lands that have been included in the urban growth areas.

The supply of land for the construction of new housing is more severely restricted in European urban areas than in the United States (Figure 13.8.5). Officials try to limit sprawl by designating areas of mandatory open space. Several British cities are surrounded by greenbelts, or rings of open space. New housing is built either in older suburbs inside the greenbelts or in planned extensions to small towns and new towns beyond the greenbelts (Figure 13.8.6).

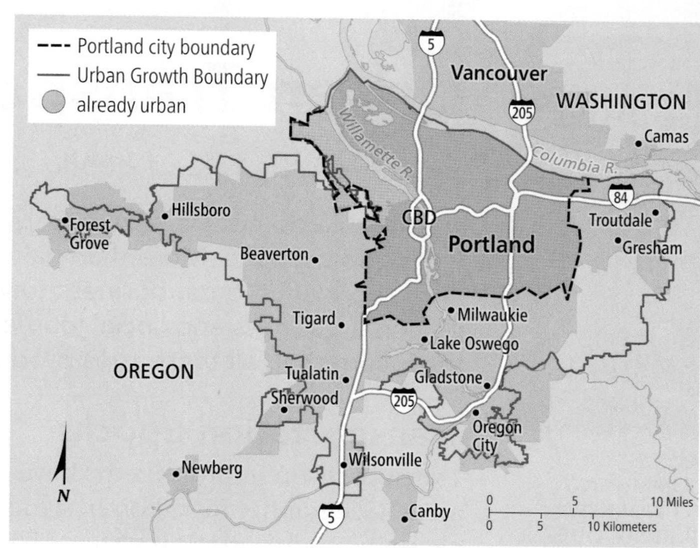

▲ 13.8.4 PORTLAND, OREGON, URBAN GROWTH BOUNDARY

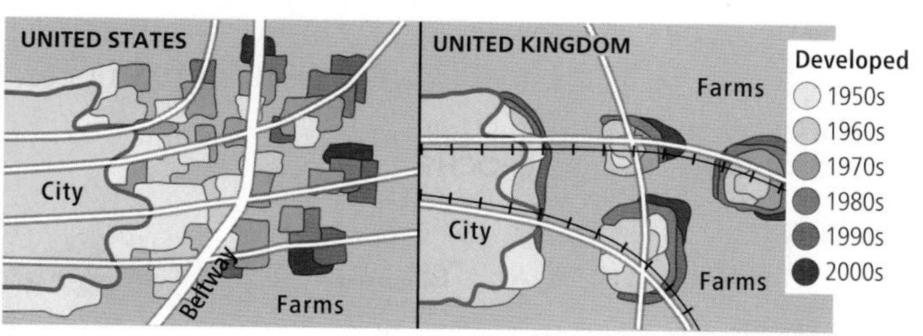

▲ 13.8.5 SUBURBAN DEVELOPMENT PATTERNS IN THE U.K. AND U.S.

The United States has much more sprawl than the United Kingdom where new housing is more likely to be concentrated in new towns or planned extentions of existing small towns.

▲ 13.8.6 U.K. SUBURB

A planned high-density residential area ends abruptly at a greenbelt.

Density Gradient

Traveling outward from the center of a city, the density at which people lived traditionally declined. This density change in an urban area is called the **density gradient**. According to the density gradient, the number of houses per unit of land diminished as distance from the center city increased.

The number of people living on a hectare of land decreased in the central residential areas during the first half of the twentieth century through population decline and abandonment of old housing. During the second half of the twentieth century, density increased on the periphery through construction of apartment and town-house projects and diffusion of suburbs across a larger area. These two changes flattened the density gradient and reduced the extremes of density between inner and outer areas traditionally found within cities (Figure 13.8.7).

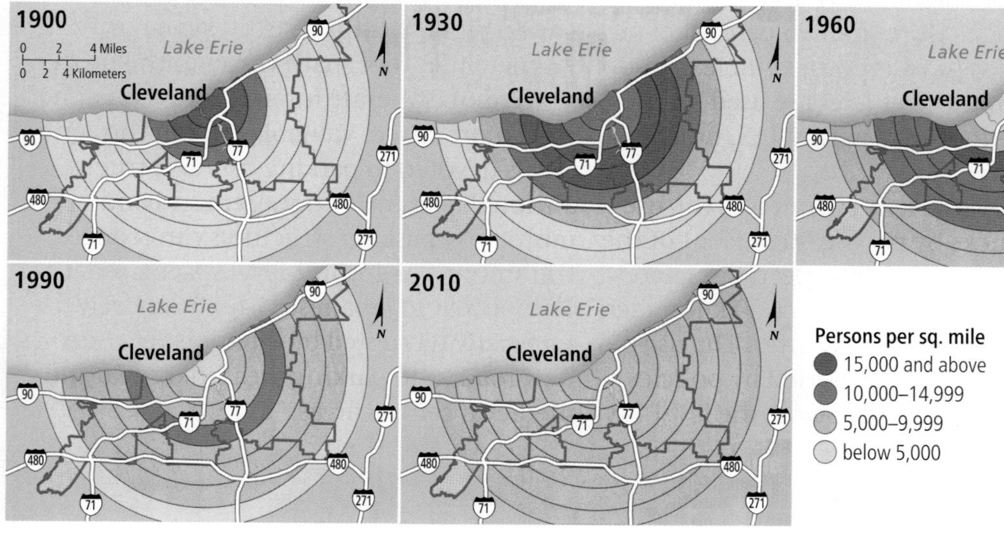

◀ 13.8.7 DENSITY GRADIENT IN CLEVELAND, 1900–2010

▲ 13.9.1 COMMUTING TO WORK BY SUBWAY, QUEENS, NEW YORK

Urban Transportation

- Explain the role of public and private transportation in cities.

People do not travel aimlessly; their trips have a precise point of origin, destination, and purpose. More than half of all trips are work related—commuting between work and home, business travel, or deliveries (Figure 13.9.1). Shopping or other personal business and social journeys each account for approximately one-fourth of all trips. Together, all these trips produce congestion in urban areas.

Transportation Epochs

Transportation improvements have played a key role in the changing structure of urban areas. Geographer John Borchert identified five eras of U.S. urban areas resulting from changing transportation systems (Figure 13.9.2).

Cities have prospered or suffered during the various epochs, depending on their proximity to economically important resources and migration patterns. At the same time, cities retain physical features from the earlier eras that may be assets or liabilities in subsequent eras.

▼ 13.9.2 TRANSPORTATION EPOCHS

1800

SAIL-WAGON EPOCH (1790–1830)

Urban areas were clustered along the Atlantic Coast. Communication was primarily by wind-powered ships plying up and down the Atlantic Coast.

1850

IRON HORSE EPOCH (1830–1870)

Steam-powered railroads provided transport from outlying areas into cities. Canals connected newly founded inland cities with existing urban centers on the East Coast.

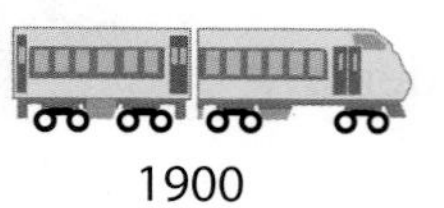

1900

STEEL RAIL EPOCH (1870–1920)

Long-haul rail lines connected urban areas around the country. Travel time between cities was greatly reduced.

1950

AUTO-AIR-AMENITY EPOCH (1920–1970)

The gasoline engine made it possible for motor vehicles to become the dominant transport within and between urban areas. Gasoline-powered airplanes facilitated travel between distant urban centers.

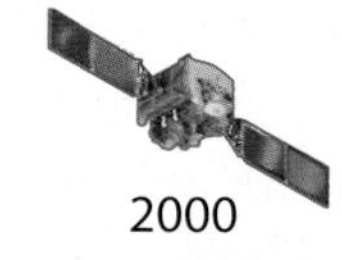

2000

SATELLITE-ELECTRONIC-JET PROPULSION (1970–?)

The current era is characterized by the ability to communicate electronically, as well as to control transport systems electronically.

Motor Vehicles

The United States has more motor vehicles than licensed drivers (approximately 270 million vehicles for only 220 million licensed drivers). More than 95 percent of all U.S. households have a motor vehicle. Not by coincidence, motor vehicles are used for more than 95 percent of trips within U.S. urban areas.

The U.S. government encourages the use of cars and trucks by paying 90 percent of the cost of limited-access, high-speed interstate highways, which stretch for 77,000 kilometers (48,000 miles) across the country. The use of motor vehicles is also supported by policies that keep the price of fuel below the level found in Europe.

The motor vehicle is an important user of land in the city. An average city allocates about one-fourth of its land to roads and parking lots. Multilane freeways cut a 23-meter (75-foot) path through the heart of a city, and elaborate interchanges consume even more space. Valuable land in the central city is devoted to parking cars and trucks, although expensive underground and multistory parking structures can reduce the amount of ground-level space needed. European and Japanese cities have been especially disrupted by attempts to insert new roads and parking areas in or near the medieval central areas.

Public Transport

Historically, people lived in crowded cities because they had to be within walking distance of shops and places of employment. The invention of the railroad in the nineteenth century enabled people to live in suburbs and work in the central city. To accommodate commuters, cities built railroads at street level (called trolleys, streetcars, or trams) and underground (subways). Gasoline-powered buses joined the public transportation fleet in the twentieth century, often replacing the street-level railroads.

The intense concentration of people in the CBD during working hours strains transportation systems because a large number of people must reach a small area of land at the same time in the morning and disperse at the same time in the afternoon. As much as 40 percent of all trips made into or out of a CBD occur during four hours of the day—two in the morning and two in the afternoon. **Rush hour** is the four consecutive 15-minute periods that have the heaviest traffic.

New subway and light rail lines have been constructed in recent years in a number of U.S. cities. But public transit ridership in the United States has declined from 23 billion per year in the 1940s to 10 billion in 2016, and service is minimal or non-existent outside the CBDs of larger cities (Figure 13.9.3).

Entirely new subway systems were opened between 1972 and 1993 in six U.S. cities: Atlanta, Baltimore, Los Angeles, Miami, San Francisco, and Washington. Cities with century-old systems such as Boston, Chicago, and New York have attracted new passengers through construction of new lines and modernization of existing ones. Since 1980, 30 new light-rail systems have been opened in the United States.

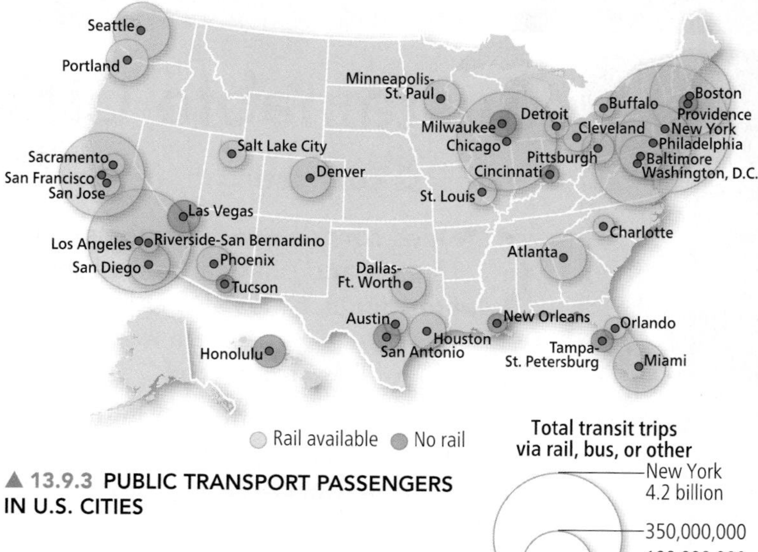

▲ 13.9.3 PUBLIC TRANSPORT PASSENGERS IN U.S. CITIES

By sitting in traffic jams over the course of a year, the average American wastes 19 gallons of gasoline, loses 42 hours, and is responsible for emitting 380 pounds of carbon dioxide, according to the Urban Mobility Report prepared by the Texas Transportation Institute. The total cost of congestion is valued at $160 billion per year in the United States. But most Americans still prefer to commute by vehicle. Most people overlook these costs because they place higher value on the privacy and flexibility of schedule offered by a car (see Debate It!).

In hundreds of cities around the world, extensive networks of bus, tram, and subway lines have been maintained, and funds for new construction have been provided in recent years.

DEBATE IT!
Should some urban streets be reserved for bicycles?

Bike-sharing programs have proliferated in urban areas, as well as on college campuses. Where should the bikes be ridden (Figures 13.9.4 and 13.9.5)?

STREETS SHOULD HAVE SEPARATE BIKE LANES

- Bikes use less energy than vehicles.
- Bikes help people stay fit.
- Bikes have more flexible origins and destinations than vehicles.

STREETS SHOULD NOT HAVE SEPARATE BIKE LANES

- Separate bike lanes cause more vehicle congestion in the remaining lanes.
- Bikes are dangerous to ride on busy urban streets.
- Bikes are easy to steal.

▶ 13.9.4 DEDICATED BIKE LANE, ROTTERDAM, THE NETHERLANDS

◀ 13.9.5 SHARING THE STREET, LONDON

▲ 13.10.1 FEEDING HOMELESS PEOPLE, LOS ANGELES

Sustainable Cities

- Assess contrasting trends in U.S. cities.

Cities contain concentrations of low income people who face a variety of economic, social, and physical challenges very different from those faced by suburban residents. Cities also contain neighborhoods that attract higher-income people.

The City Challenged

The low-income residents of inner-city neighborhoods are frequently referred to as a permanent **underclass** because they face an unending cycle of hardships:

- **Inadequate job Skills.** Inner city residents are increasingly disadvantaged in competing for jobs. They lack technical skills needed for most jobs because fewer than half complete high school.
- **Culture of Poverty.** Unwed mothers give birth to two-thirds of the babies in U.S. inner-city neighborhoods, and 80 percent of children in the inner city live with only one parent. Because of inadequate child-care services, single mothers may be forced to choose between working to generate income and staying at home to take care of children.
- **Crime.** Inner-city neighborhoods have a relatively high share of a metropolitan area's serious crimes, such as murder.
- **Drugs.** Trapped in a hopeless environment, some inner-city residents turn to drugs. Although drug use is a problem in suburbs as well, rates of use have been higher in inner cities. Some drug users obtain money through criminal activities.
- **Homelessness.** Several million people are homeless in the United States. Most people are homeless because they cannot afford housing and have no regular income. Homelessness may have been sparked by family problems or job loss (see Research & Analyze and Figure 13.10.1).
- **Municipal Finances.** Low-income residents in inner-city neighborhoods require public services, but they can pay very little of the taxes to support the services. Central cities face a growing gap between the cost of needed services in inner-city neighborhoods and the availability of funds to pay for them.
- **Inadequate Services.** Food deserts, discussed in Chapter 12, which are areas where healthy food is difficult to obtain, are especially common in low-income inner-city areas (refer to What's Your Services Geography? feature and Figure 12.4.2 on page 292).
- **Deteriorated Housing.** Inner-city housing is subdivided by absentee landlords into apartments for low-income families, a process known as **filtering**. Landlords stop maintaining houses when the rent they collect becomes less than the maintenance cost. In such a case, the building soon deteriorates and grows unfit for occupancy.

Market segmentation: You are where you live.

Marketing geographers apply sectors, rings, and nodes to match people with particular neighborhoods and retailers. A prominent example is My Best Segments, created by Nielsen Claritas.

1. Use your search engine to find *Claritas My Best Segments* website and ***select*** *ZIP Code look up.* Enter your 5-digit zip code and ***click*** *Submit.* What are the five clusters for your zip code?
2. ***Click*** on the names of the clusters to learn more about each of them. Do these five clusters accurately represent your expectations for your zip code? Why or why not?
3. Look up the segments for two San Antonio zip codes: 78257 and 78226 (Figure 13.10.2). What are the five clusters for each? Refer to pages 324–325. Do the segment clusters appear consistent with the ring, sector, and node of each of these two zip codes? Why or why not?

▶ 13.10.2 ZIP CODES 78226 AND 78257, SAN ANTONIO

Gentrification

Gentrification is the process by which higher-income people move into deteriorated inner-city neighborhoods and renovate the housing. Most cities have at least one substantially renovated inner-city neighborhood that has attracted higher-income residents, especially single people and couples without children who are not concerned with the quality of inner-city schools.

A deteriorated inner-city neighborhood is attractive for several reasons:

- The houses may be larger and more substantially constructed yet less expensive than houses in the suburbs.
- Houses may possess attractive architectural details associated with historical decor, such as ornate fireplaces, cornices, high ceilings, and wood trim.
- For people who work downtown, inner-city living eliminates the strain of commuting on crowded freeways or public transit.
- The neighborhoods are near theaters, bars, restaurants, stadiums, and other cultural and recreational facilities (Figure 13.10.3).

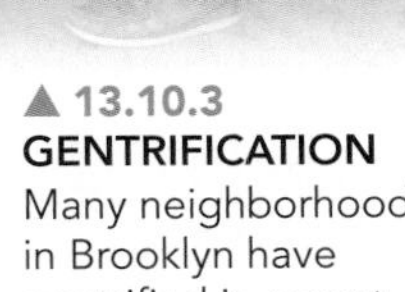

▲ 13.10.3
GENTRIFICATION
Many neighborhoods in Brooklyn have gentrified in recent years.

Some consumer services are returning to the inner-city, in part to meet day-to-day needs of residents of gentrified neighborhoods. Inner-city consumer services are also attracting people looking for leisure activities, such as unusual shops in a dramatic downtown setting or view of a harbor. Several North American CBDs now offer new consumer services that combine retailing services with leisure and recreation.

Gentrification has been controversial in some cities, where low-income residents have been forced to move out of the neighborhood. Newcomers may buy rental housing, displace the tenants, renovate the structure, and convert it to a single-family dwelling.

RESEARCH & ANALYZE
Your community's homeless population

Approximately half a million Americans are homeless. The number of homeless people varies by state and locality. Learn about the homeless population in your community. Open the web site **Homelessdata.com**. ***Select*** *Dashboard*. ***Select*** your home state. In *select your CoC* from the dropdown below, ***select*** *(all)*. ***Select*** the summary tab at the top of the page and scroll down.

1. Is the number of homeless people increasing or decreasing in your state?
2. ***Scroll down the page.*** Is the percentage of homeless people in your state increasing or decreasing? The national percentage of homeless is approximately 0.15 percent. Is the percentage of homeless in your state higher or lower than the national average? What might account for that difference?
3. ***Scroll down the page*** to the Homeless Population boxes. In what communities are they distributed? What might account for the distinctive distribution within your state?
4. ***Scroll down the page*** to Trends for All. Is the number of homeless changing at the same rate in your state's various communities? What might account for variations?
5. ***Scroll down the page*** to the Families & Individuals graph. Are most homeless in your state single individuals or part of families?

Homeless Data

https://goo.gl/T22J14

▶ 13.10.4 **HOMELESS PEOPLE, NEW ORLEANS**

CHAPTER 13 Review, Analyze, & Apply

KEY ISSUE 1 How Are Cities Defined?

Urban settlements can be defined as cities, urban areas, and metropolitan areas. The central business district contains a large share of the urban settlement's business and public services.

THINKING GEOGRAPHICALLY

1. Some professional sports arenas and stadiums are located in the CBD, and some are located in suburbs. What are the advantages and drawbacks for the fans of each location?

◀ 13.CR.1 ORIOLE PARK AT CAMDEN YARDS IN BALTIMORE'S CBD

KEY ISSUE 2 Where Are People Distributed Within an Urban Area?

Three models help to explain where different groups of people live in an urban area. According to the concentric zone model, a city grows outward in rings. According to the sector model, a city grows along transportation corridors. According to the multiple nuclei model, a city grows around several nodes. The galactic or peripheral model is a variation of the multiple nuclei model to account for suburban nodes. The models can be used to describe where people of varying characteristics tend to cluster within an urban area.

THINKING GEOGRAPHICALLY

2. Identify the ring, sector, and node in which you (or a friend or relation) live within an urban area. Do conditions in your place fit the overall patterns expected of the models? Why or why not?

◀ 13.CR.2 LAS VEGAS (Background) CBD ("the Strip"), (foreground) north sector outer ring residential area.

KEY ISSUE 3 How Are Cities Outside North America Structured?

The models of urban structure can also be used to describe where people and activities are located within urban areas in Europe and developing countries. As in North America, high-income people in other regions of the world tend to cluster in particular sectors of cities. Unlike North America, low-income people are more likely to locate in the outer ring of cities elsewhere in the world.

THINKING GEOGRAPHICALLY

3. Efforts are underway to improve the condition of peripheral informal settlements, such as the free Medellín Metrocable, which connects informal settlements with Medellín's CBD. Why might the gondola be useful to residents of informal settlements?

◀ 13.CR.3 MEDELLÍN, COLOMBIA, METROCABLE

KEY ISSUE 4 How Do Cities Become More Sustainable?

Cities have grown rapidly in land area, especially in North America, where sprawling suburbs are the norm. North American urban areas provide public transport, but the share of trips undertaken by private car is relatively high. Cities face contradictory trends: an increase in the underclass in proximity to an increase in gentrification.

THINKING GEOGRAPHICALLY

4. Some gentrifying neighborhoods, such as Cincinnati's Over-the-Rhine, are attempting to create a mix of low-income and upper-income residents. What are some of the benefits and challenges of providing housing and services for low-income residents in a gentrifying neighborhood?

▲ 13.CR.4 HOMELESS PEOPLE, CINCINNATI

Geospatial Analysis

Log in to the Mastering Geography Study Area to access MapMaster 2.0.

Urban air quality

Air quality varies among U.S. cities.

Add the *Urban Population (U.S.)* layer and ***deselect*** all classes below *61% urban*. ***Add*** the *Poor Urban Air Quality* layer and *join* the data. In *Settings*, ***click*** *Show City Labels.*

1. Are cities with poor air quality distributed uniformly across the United States? What might account for the distribution?

▶ 13.CR.5 URBAN AREAS WITH POOR AIR QUALITY

Key Terms

Annexation (p. 332) Legally adding land area to a city in the United States.

Census tract (p. 324) An area delineated by the U.S. Bureau of the Census for which statistics are published; in urban areas, census tracts correspond roughly to neighborhoods.

Central business district (CBD) (p. 320) The area of a city where retail and office activities are clustered.

Central city (p. 319) An urban settlement that has been legally incorporated into an independent, self-governing unit.

Combined statistical area (CSA) (p. 318) In the United States, two or more contiguous core based statistical areas tied together by commuting patterns.

Concentric zone model (p. 322) A model of the internal structure of cities in which social groups are spatially arranged in a series of rings.

Core based statistical area (CBSA) (p. 318) In the United States, the collection of all metropolitan statistical areas and micropolitan statistical areas.

Density gradient (p. 333) The change in density in an urban area from the center to the periphery.

Edge city (p. 323) A node of office and retail activities on the edge of an urban area.

Filtering (p. 336) A process of change in the use of a house, from single-family owner occupancy to abandonment.

Galactic (or **peripheral) model** (p. 323) A model of North American urban areas consisting of an inner city surrounded by large suburban residential and business areas tied together by a beltway or ring road.

Gentrification (p. 337) A process of converting an urban neighborhood from a predominantly low-income, renter-occupied area to a predominantly middle-class, owner-occupied area.

Informal settlement (p. 330) An area within a city in a less developed country in which people illegally establish residences on land they do not own or rent and erect homemade structures.

Megalopolis (p. 319) A continuous urban complex in the northeastern United States.

Metropolitan statistical area (MSA) (p. 318) In the United States, an urbanized area of at least 50,000 population, the county within which the city is located, and adjacent counties meeting one of several tests indicating a functional connection to the central city.

Micropolitan statistical area (μSA) (p. 318) An urbanized area of between 10,000 and 50,000 inhabitants, the county in which it is located, and adjacent counties tied to the city.

Multiple nuclei model (p. 323) A model of the internal structure of cities in which social groups are arranged around a collection of nodes of activities.

Rush hour (p. 335) The four consecutive 15-minute periods in the morning and evening with the heaviest volumes of traffic.

Sector model (p. 322) A model of the internal structure of cities in which social groups are arranged around a series of sectors, or wedges, radiating out from the central business district.

Smart growth (p. 325) Legislation and regulations to limit suburban sprawl and preserve farmland.

Social area analysis (p. 324) Statistical analysis used to identify where people of similar living standards, ethnic background, and lifestyle live within an urban area.

Sprawl (p. 332) Development of new housing sites at relatively low density and at locations that are not contiguous to the existing built-up area.

Suburb (p. 332) A residential or commercial area situated within an urban area but outside the central city.

Underclass (p. 336) A group in society prevented from participating in the material benefits of a more developed society because of a variety of social and economic disadvantages.

Urban area (p. 319) A dense core of census tracts, densely settled suburbs, and low-density land that links the dense suburbs with the core.

Urban cluster (p. 319) In the United States, an urban area with between 2,500 and 50,000 inhabitants.

Urbanized area (p. 319) In the United States, an urban area with at least 50,000 inhabitants.

GeoVideo

Log in to the Mastering Geography™ Study Area to view this video.

Brasília

A planned city completed in 1960, Brazil's capital, Brasília, provides an opportunity to compare a utopian dream with present-day social reality.

1. What values and aspirations motivated the creation of Brasília and shaped its design?
2. How does the form of Brasília reflect the different functions of a city and national capital?
3. Does Brasília today realize its founders' vision of society? Give examples from the video to support your answer.

Explore

London's congestion charge

To try to reduce congestion, London charges vehicles to enter the CBD during weekdays.

In Google Earth, ***search*** for *1 Marble Arch, London*. ***Zoom*** in to around 100 meters. Note the white C in a red circle. Motorists must pay a charge to drive across the red and white C into the CBD.

1. Use Street View to see street conditions in front of #1 Marble Arch. Do you see evidence that the charge is reducing congestion? What might be done to further address congestion?
2. There are no toll booths at the entrance to the congestion charge zone. How do you think the toll is being collected?

▲ 13.CR.1 **ENTERING LONDON'S CENTRAL ZONE**

Mastering Geography

Looking for additional review and test prep materials? Visit the Study Area in Mastering Geography to enhance your geographic literacy, spatial reasoning skills, and understanding of this chapter's content. Access MapMaster™ interactive maps, video case studies, *In the News* current articles, flashcards, self-study quizzes, an eText of *Contemporary Human Geography*, and more. **pearson.com/mastering/geography**

CHAPTER

14 Resource Issues

People have always transformed Earth's land, water, and air for their benefit. Humans once believed Earth's resources to be infinite, or at least so vast that human actions could never harm or deplete them. But human actions in recent years have consumed and polluted more of Earth's resources. Future generations will pay the price if we continue to rapidly consume and mismanage Earth's resources.

◀ The Compost Cats, a University of Arizona student organization, composts food waste from the city of Tucson, diverting it from landfills. Local farmers and landscapers use the compost to enrich the soil.

KEY ISSUES

1 What Are Earth's Principal Energy Resources?

Energy is derived primarily from three fossil fuels: coal, natural gas, and petroleum. Neither the supply nor the demand for these resources is uniformly distributed.

2 What Is the Future For Energy Resources?

Energy resources can be divided between renewable and nonrenewable sources. The three fossil fuels are nonrenewable, whereas other increasingly important energy resources are renewable.

3 How Are Resources Polluted?

Human actions pollute Earth's air, water, and land. Pollution occurs when more waste is added than a resource can accommodate.

4 How Are Resources Protected?

Sustainable development can be achieved through preservation and conservation of resources. Humans can reduce the amount of pollution by either consuming less of a product that causes pollution or by recycling more of the products that are used.

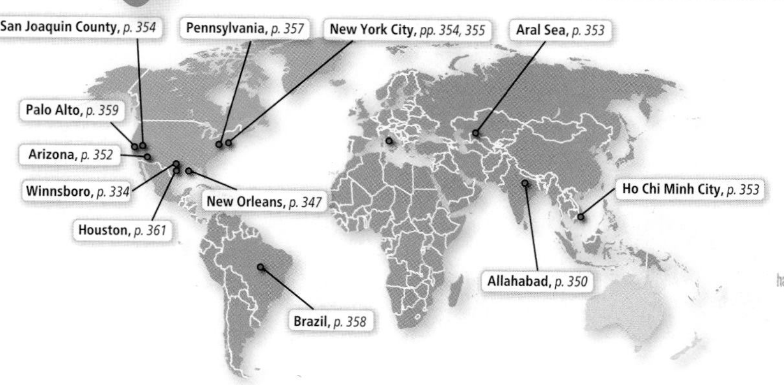

wind
recycling conservation
natural gas fossil fuel
nuclear energy
pollution petroleum
coal
renewable resource
biodiversity
geothermal
potential reserve
solar
sanitary landfill sustainable development
fracking
nonrenewable resource
hazardous waste
climate change remanufacturing
proven reserve
preservation

▲ 14.1.1 **ENERGY DEMAND**
Transportation is a major user of energy resources.

Energy Sources

- Identify the principal sources of energy supply used globally today.

Earth offers a large array of resources for people to use. A resource was defined in Chapter 1 as a substance in the environment that is useful to people, is economically and technologically feasible to access, and is socially acceptable to use. Resources include food, water, soil, plants, animals, air, and minerals.

Energy resources are especially valuable. We depend on abundant, low-cost energy and minerals to run our industries, transport ourselves, and keep our homes comfortable (Figure 14.1.1). But we are depleting the supply of some current energy resources.

Three Fossil Fuels

A **fossil fuel** is an energy source formed from the residue of plants and animals buried millions of years ago. As sediment accumulated over these remains, intense pressure and chemical reactions slowly converted them into the fossil fuels that are currently used. When the carbon in these substances is burned, energy that was stored in plants and animals millions of years ago is released.

Five-sixths of the world's energy needs are currently supplied by three fossil fuels (Figure 14.1.2).

16% Other
33% Petroleum
28% Coal
23% Natural gas

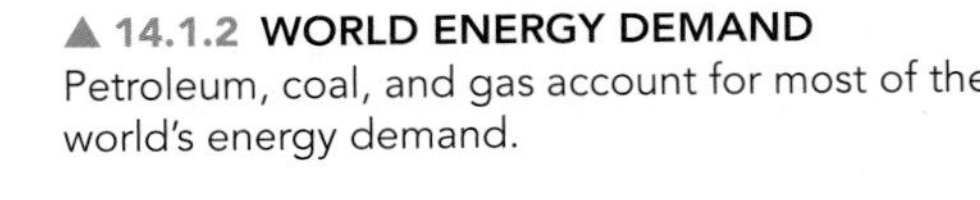

▲ 14.1.2 **WORLD ENERGY DEMAND**
Petroleum, coal, and gas account for most of the world's energy demand.

- **Coal.** Supplanted wood as the leading energy source in North America and Europe in the late 1800s, as these regions developed rapidly.
- **Petroleum.** First pumped in 1859 but did not become an important source of energy until the diffusion of motor vehicles in the twentieth century.
- **Natural gas.** Originally burned off as a waste product of petroleum drilling, but it is now used to heat homes and to produce electricity.

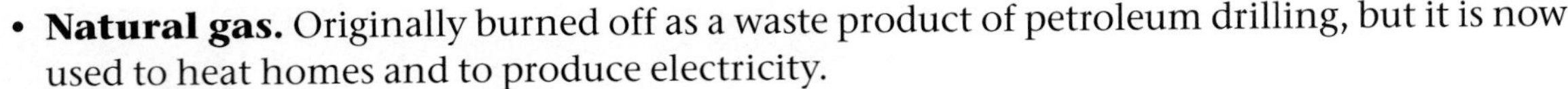

Historically, people relied primarily on **animate power**, which is power supplied by animals or by people themselves. Because animate power was limited and taxing to humans, it was eventually supplemented by **biomass fuel** (such as wood, plant material, and animal waste) which is burned directly or converted to charcoal, alcohol, or methane gas. Biomass remains the most important source of fuel in some developing countries, but during the past 200 years developed countries have converted primarily to energy from fossil fuels (Figure 14.1.3).

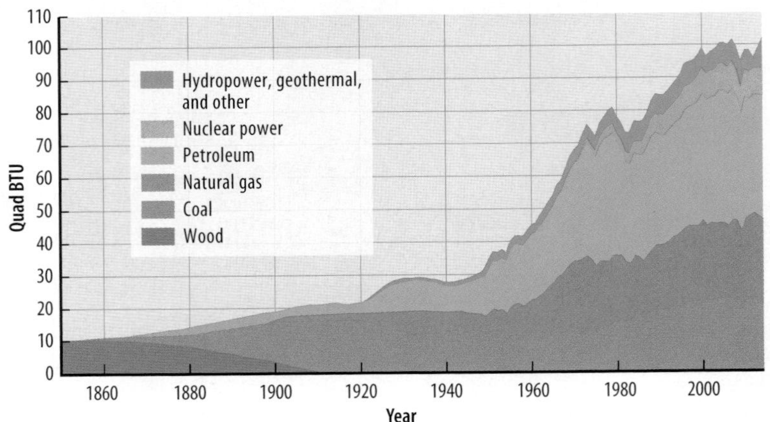

◀ 14.1.3 **CHANGING U.S. ENERGY DEMAND**
Coal was the principal energy source in 1900, and petroleum in 2000. What will be most important in 2100?

Distribution of Demand and Supply

Supply is the quantity of something that producers have available for sale. **Demand** is the quantity that people wish to consume and are able to buy. Geographers observe two important inequalities in the distribution of demand and supply for fossil fuels:

- **Demand.** The heaviest consumers of fossil fuel are in developed countries, whereas most of the reserves are in developing countries.
- **Supply.** Some developing regions have abundant reserves, whereas others have little.

Given the centrality of fossil fuels in contemporary economy and culture, the unequal distribution in the demand and supply of fossil fuels has been major a source of instability between developed and developing countries.

Demand for the world's energy is currently divided about equally between developed and developing countries (Figure 14.1.4). However, consumption of fossil fuels has been increasing at a much faster rate in developing countries. As a result, developing countries are expected to demand 60 percent of the world's energy in 2040 (Figure 14.1.5). China has surpassed the United States as the country that uses the most energy. Still, the highest per capita consumption of energy remains in North America; the region contains one-twentieth of the world's people but consumes one-fourth of the world's energy (Figure 14.1.6).

Demand for energy comes from three principal types of consumption in the United States:

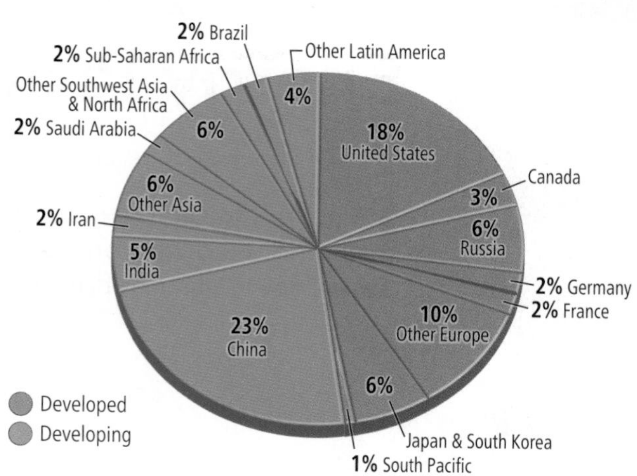

▲ 14.1.4 SHARE OF WORLD ENERGY DEMAND BY COUNTRY

Developed and developing countries each consume around one-half of the world's energy.

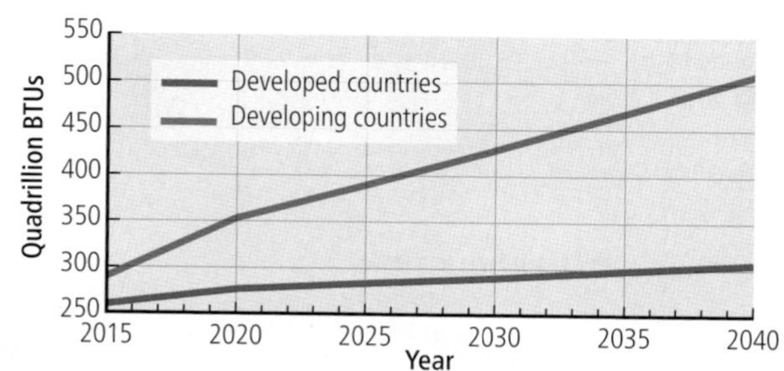

▲ 14.1.5 FUTURE ENERGY DEMAND

- **Businesses.** The main energy demand is for coal, followed by natural gas and petroleum. Some businesses directly burn coal in their own furnaces. Others rely on electricity, mostly generated at coal-burning power plants.
- **Homes.** Energy is demanded primarily for the heating of living spaces and water. Natural gas is the most common source, followed by petroleum (heating oil and kerosene).
- **Transportation.** Almost all transportation systems demand petroleum products, including cars, trucks, buses, airplanes, and most railroads. Only subways, streetcars, and some trains run on coal-generated electricity.

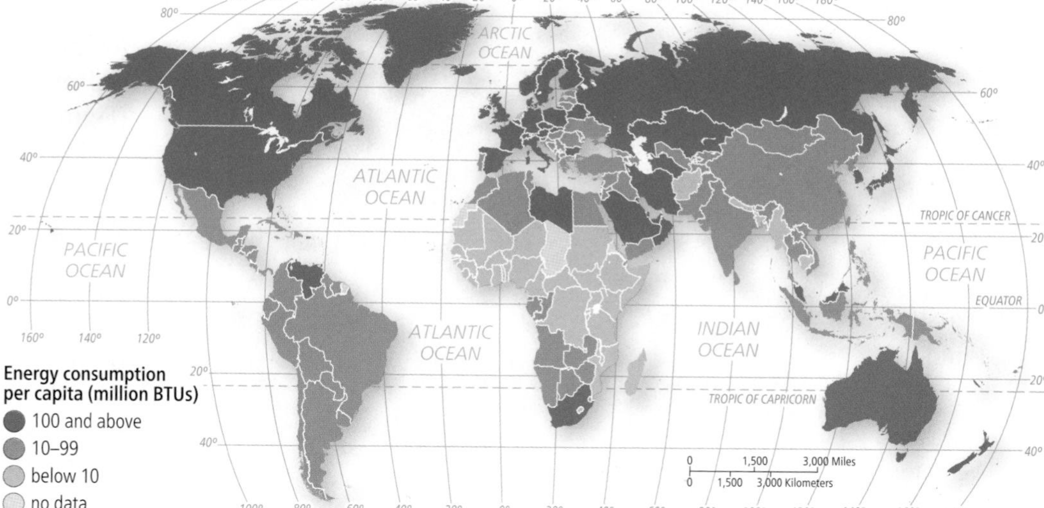

▶ 14.1.6 ENERGY DEMAND BY PER CAPITA

The highest per capita consumption is in North America, and the lowest is in sub-Saharan Africa.

Energy Production

- Summarize the distribution of fossil fuel production.

Earth's fossil fuel resources are not distributed evenly. Some regions are well-endowed with one or more fossil fuels, whereas other regions have little. The uneven distribution of fossil fuels partly reflects how fossil fuels form.

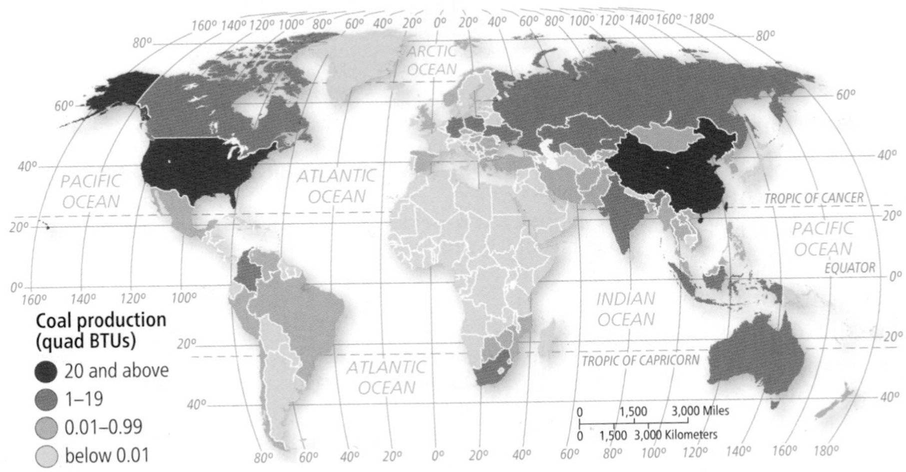

▲ 14.2.1 COAL PRODUCTION

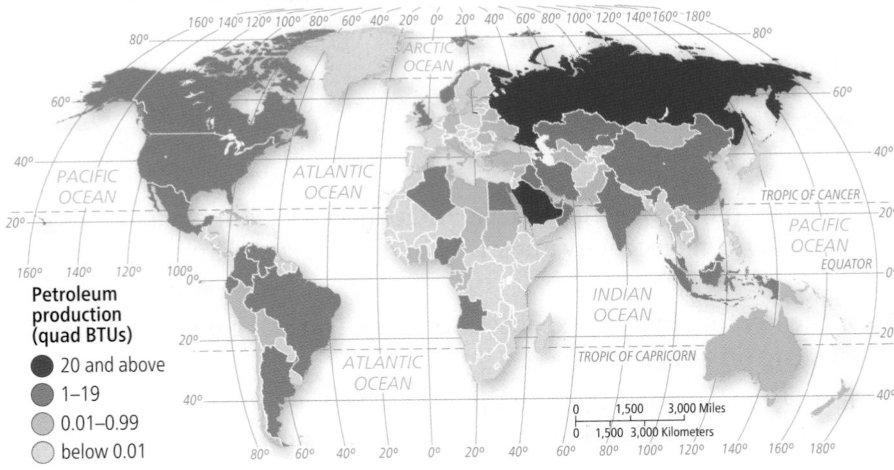

▲ 14.2.2 PETROLEUM PRODUCTION

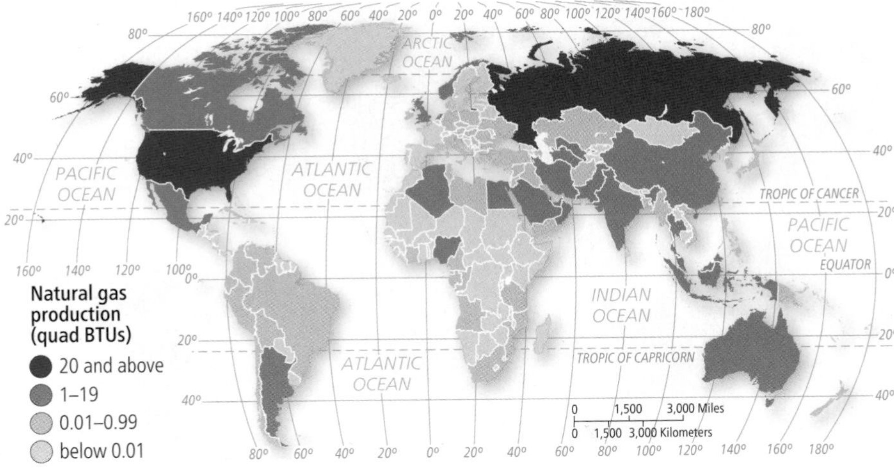

▲ 14.2.3 NATURAL GAS PRODUCTION

Distribution of Coal

China produces nearly one-half of the world's coal (Figure 14.2.1). Coal formed in tropical locations that were lush, swampy areas rich in plants. With the slow movement of Earth's drifting continents, the fossilized tropical swamps of 250 million years ago relocated to the mid-latitudes. As a result, today's main reserves of coal are in mid-latitude countries rather than in the tropics.

Distribution of Petroleum

Russia and Saudi Arabia together supply one-fourth of the world's petroleum (Figure 14.2.2). Petroleum formed millions of years ago from residue deposited on the seafloor. Some still lies beneath such seas as the Persian Gulf and the North Sea, but other reserves are located beneath land that was under water millions of years ago.

Distribution of Natural Gas

One-third of natural gas production is supplied by Russia and the United States. Natural gas, like petroleum, formed millions of years ago from sediment deposited on the seafloor (Figure 14.2.3).

Figures 14.2.1, 14.2.2, and 14.2.3 use the same units (quad BTU), as well as the same classes. "Quad" is short for quadrillion (1 quadrillion = 1,000,000,000,000,000), and BTU is short for British thermal unit. One quad BTU equals approximately 8 million U.S. gallons of gasoline, which would fill the tanks of approximately one-half million cars.

Control of Petroleum Supply

World supply of petroleum has been especially challenging in recent years. Most of the world's petroleum is produced in Southwest Asia & North Africa and Central Asia, two regions strongly impacted by religious, ethnic, and political conflicts discussed in Chapters 6 through 8.

The United States produced more petroleum than it consumed during the first half of the twentieth century. Beginning in the 1950s, the handful of large transnational companies then in control of international petroleum distribution determined that extracting petroleum in the United States was more expensive than importing it from Southwest and Central Asia.

Several developing countries possessing substantial petroleum reserves, primarily in Southwest Asia & North Africa, created the Organization of the Petroleum Exporting Countries (OPEC) in 1960. OPEC was originally formed to enable oil-rich countries to gain more control over their resource. U.S. and European transnational companies, which had originally explored and exploited the oil fields, were selling the petroleum at low prices to consumers in developed countries and keeping most of the profits. Countries possessing the oil reserves nationalized or more tightly controlled the fields, and prices were set by governments rather than by petroleum companies. Under OPEC control, world oil prices have increased sharply on several occasions, especially during the 1970s and 1980s and in the early twenty-first century.

The United States reduced import of oil from OPEC countries (Figure 14.2.4). Instead, U.S. imports have increased from neighboring countries, especially Canada. With U.S. oil consumption continuing to increase (Figure 14.2.5), imports from Canada are arriving through pipelines (Figure 14.2.6). Construction of the Keystone and Dakota Access pipelines have been controversial, especially because of fears of environmentally damaging leaks.

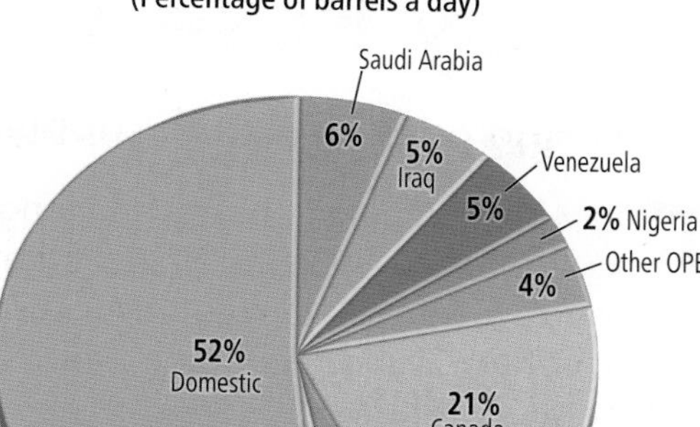

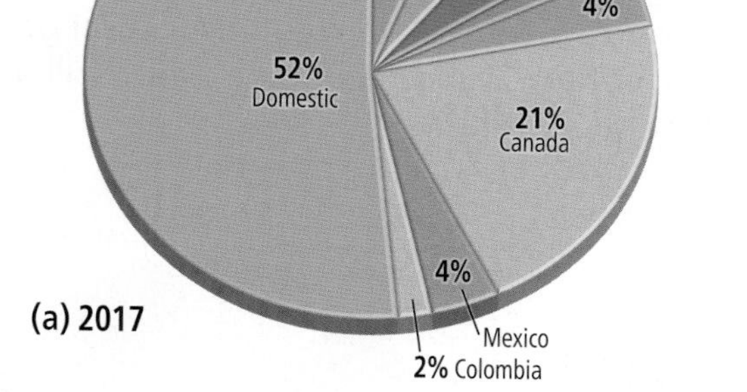

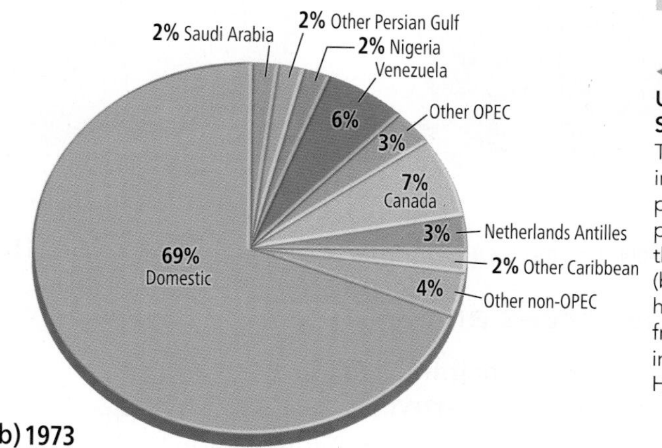

◀ **14.2.4 U.S. PETROLEUM SOURCES** The United States imports a higher percentage of petroleum now (a) than in the 1970s (b). The increase has come primarily from elsewhere in the Western Hemisphere.

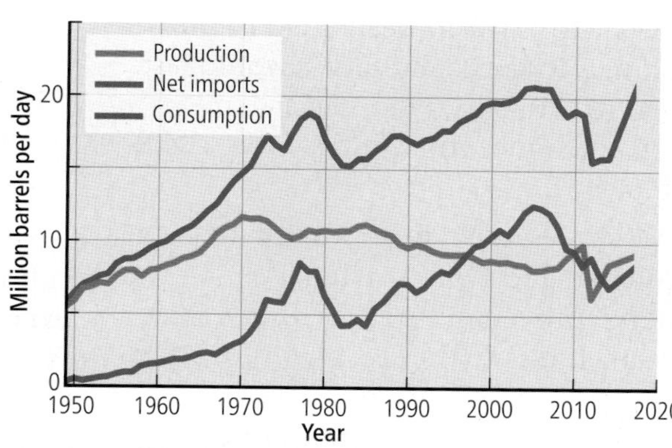

◀ **14.2.5 U.S. PETROLEUM CONSUMPTION, PRODUCTION, AND IMPORTS** U.S. production has remained relatively constant since the 1960s. Increasing consumption has been served by increasing imports.

▶ **14.2.6 KEYSTONE XL PIPELINE UNDER CONSTRUCTION, WINNSBORO, TEXAS**

Energy Reserves

- Describe possible future supply and demand for fossil fuels.

The world faces an energy challenge because of rapid depletion of the remaining supply of the three fossil fuels that currently meet most of the world's energy needs. Because petroleum, natural gas, and coal are deposited beneath Earth's surface, considerable technology and skill are required to locate these substances and estimate their volume.

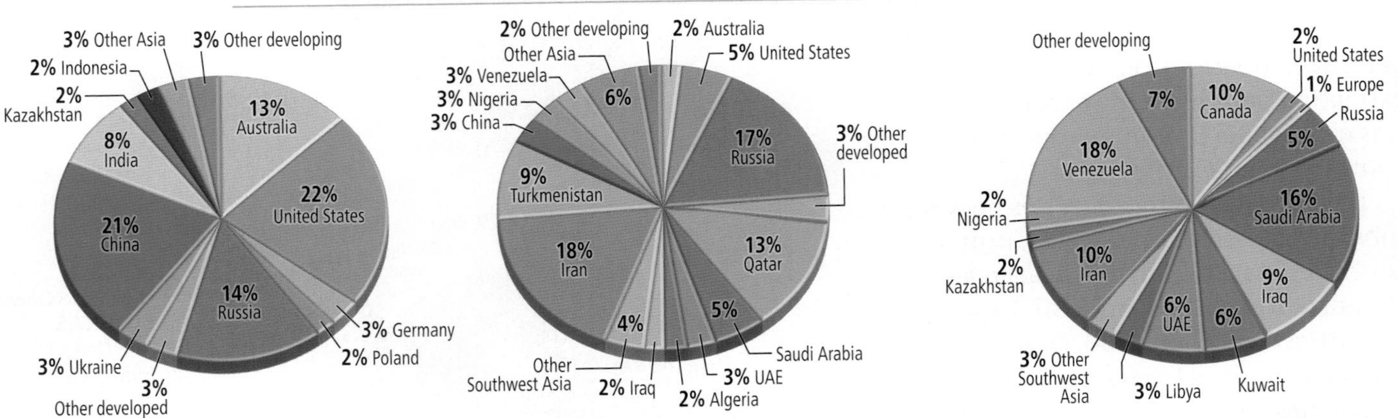

▲ 14.3.1 PROVEN RESERVES OF COAL ▲ 14.3.2 PROVEN RESERVES OF NATURAL GAS ▲ 14.3.3 PROVEN RESERVES OF PETROLEUM

Proven Reserves and Potential Reserves

The supply of energy remaining in deposits that have been discovered is called a **proven reserve**. Proven reserves can be measured with reasonable accuracy:

- **Coal.** World reserves are approximately 1 quadrillion metric tons (23 million quad BTUs). At current demand, proven coal reserves would last 110 years. The United States, Russia, China, and Australia have 70 percent of the world's proven coal reserves (Figure 14.3.1).
- **Natural gas.** World reserves are approximately 7,000 trillion cubic meters (7,200 quad BTUs). At current demand, proven natural gas reserves would last 54 years. Iran, Russia, and Qatar together have one-half of the world's proven reserves (Figure 14.3.2).
- **Petroleum.** World reserves are approximately 1.7 trillion barrels (9,000 quad BTUs). At current demand, proven petroleum reserves would last 43 years. Venezuela and Saudi Arabia are the two leading locations of proven petroleum reserves (Figure 14.3.3).

Some fossil fuel deposits have not yet been discovered. The supply in deposits that are undiscovered but thought to exist is a **potential reserve**. When a potential reserve is actually discovered, it is reclassified as a proven reserve.

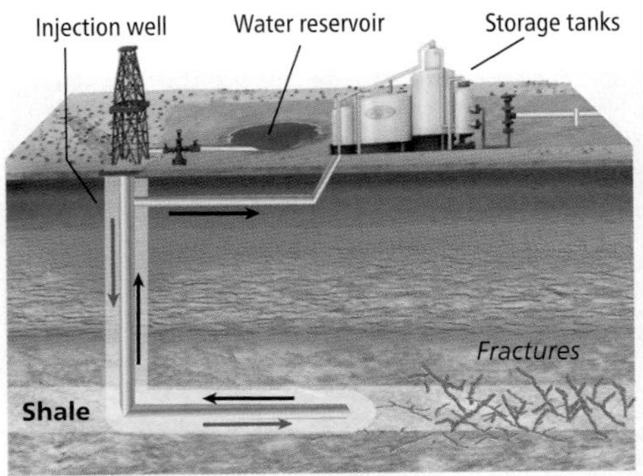

▲ 14.3.4 HYDRAULIC FRACKING

Unconventional Resources

Resources are considered unconventional if we lack economically feasible or environmentally sound technology with which to extract them. As demand increases for a resource, and prices rise, an unconventional source can become profitable to exploit. Here are two current examples:

- **Oil sands.** Abundant oil sands are found in Alberta, Canada, as well as in Venezuela and Russia. Oil sands are saturated with thick petroleum commonly called tar because of its dark color and strong odor.
- **Hydraulic fracturing.** Rocks break apart naturally, and gas can fill the space between the rocks. **Hydraulic fracturing**, commonly called fracking, involves pumping water at high pressure to further break apart rocks and thereby release more gas that can be extracted (Figure 14.3.4).

Reducing Demand

The world will not literally "run out" of petroleum during the twenty-first century. However, at some point, extracting the remaining petroleum reserves will prove so expensive and environmentally damaging that use of alternative energy sources will accelerate, and dependency on petroleum will diminish.

Demand for petroleum has been dampened in developed countries in two principal ways:

- **High price.** The average price paid for a gallon of petroleum exceeds $8 in most developed countries. When adjusted for inflation, prices are not high by historical standards in the United States (Figure 14.3.5), and they are lower than in other developed countries.
- **Conservation.** The average vehicle driven in the United States got 14 miles per gallon in 1975, 22 miles per gallon in 1985, and an anticipated 54 miles per gallon in 2025. A government mandate, known as Corporate Average Fuel Efficiency (CAFE), has been responsible for the higher standard. Other countries also mandate more fuel efficient vehicles.

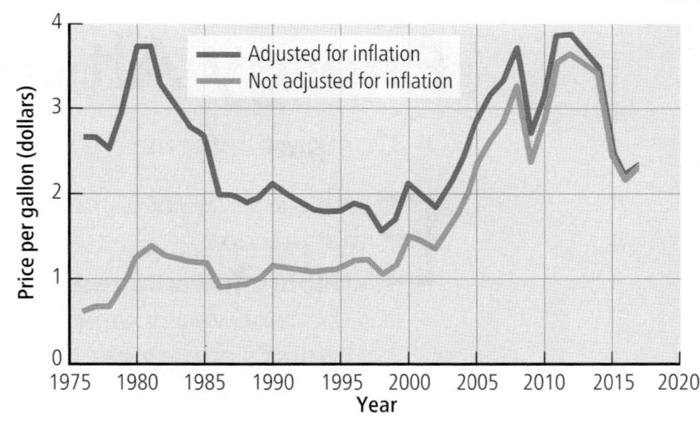

▲ 14.3.5 **U.S. GASOLINE PRICES**
The line adjusted for inflation is in 2017 dollars.

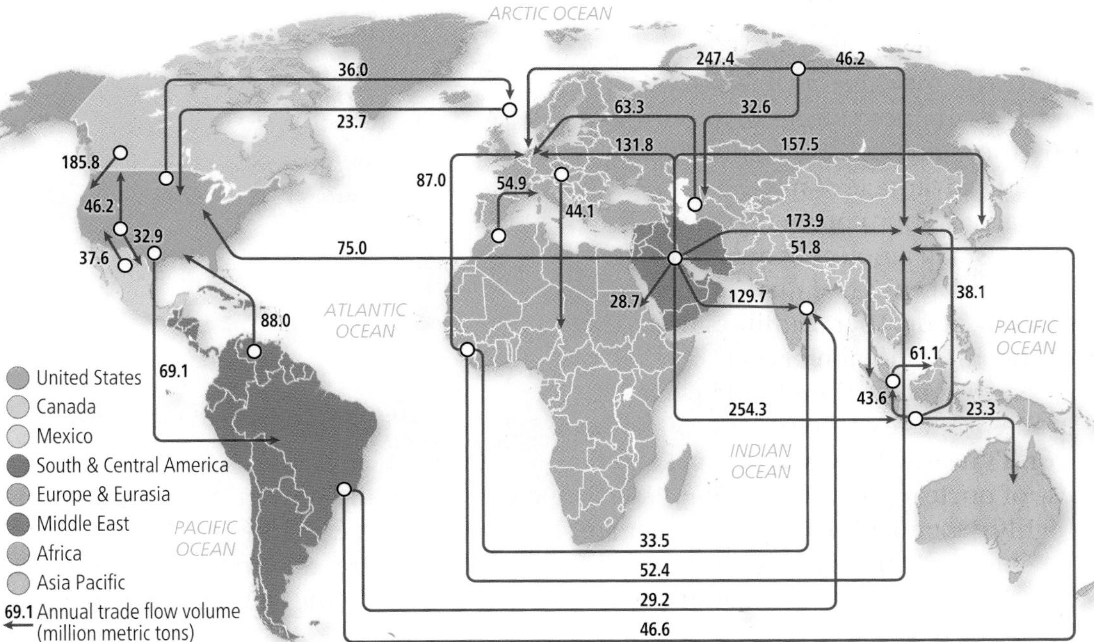

▶ 14.3.6 **PETROLEUM TRADE**

World Oil Trade

Developed countries supply a large share of the world's fossil fuels, but they demand more energy than they produce, so they must import fossil fuels, especially petroleum, from developing countries (Figure 14.3.6). The United States and Europe import more than half their petroleum, and Japan imports more than 90 percent (Figure 14.3.7).

The issues for the world are whether dwindling petroleum reserves are handled wisely and other energy sources are substituted peacefully. Given the massive growth in petroleum consumption expected in developing countries such as China and India, the United States and other developed countries may have little influence over when prices rise and supplies decline. In this challenging environment, all countries will need to pursue sustainable development strategies based on increased reliance on renewable energy sources.

▼ 14.3.7 **IMPORTING OIL**
Port of New Orleans.

Energy Alternatives

- Compare alternative sources of energy.

Earth's energy resources are divided between those that are renewable and those that are not:

- **Nonrenewable resources** form so slowly that for practical purposes, they cannot be renewed. Examples are the three fossil fuels that currently supply most of the world's energy needs.
- **Renewable resources** have an essentially unlimited supply and are not depleted when used by people. Water, wind, and the Sun provide sources of renewable energy. Nuclear power, though not renewable, is an important alternative to fossil fuels.

Nuclear Energy

A nuclear power plant produces electricity from energy released by splitting uranium atoms in a controlled environment, a process called fission. The big advantage of nuclear power is the large amount of energy released from a small amount of material. One kilogram of enriched nuclear fuel contains more than 2 million times the energy in 1 kilogram of coal.

Percent of electricity from nuclear power
40 and above
1–39
none

▲ 14.4.1 ELECTRICITY FROM NUCLEAR POWER
The size of the country reflects the proportion of the world's nuclear power generated there.

Nuclear power supplies 14 percent of the world's electricity. Only 30 of the world's nearly 200 countries make some use of nuclear power, including 19 developed countries and only 11 developing countries. The countries most highly dependent on nuclear power are clustered in Europe (Figure 14.4.1).

One product of all nuclear reactions is radioactive waste, certain types of which are lethal to people exposed to it. Elaborate safety precautions must be taken to prevent the leaking of nuclear fuel from a power plant, but accidents have happened.

Some nuclear power issues might be addressed through nuclear **fusion**, which is the fusing of hydrogen atoms to form helium. Fusion can occur only at very high temperatures (millions of degrees). Scientists have not yet discovered how to manage this process on a sustained basis for energy production.

Hydroelectric Power

Generating electricity from the movement of water is called **hydroelectric power**. Hydroelectric is now the world's second-most-popular source of electricity, after coal. Two-thirds of the world's hydroelectric power is generated in developing countries and one-third in developed countries. A number of developing countries depend on hydroelectric power for most of their electricity (Figure 14.4.2).

◀ 14.4.2 ELECTRICITY FROM HYDROELECTRIC POWER
The size of the country reflects the proportion of the world's hydroelectric power generated there.

Wind Power

Wind power is being utilized on a large scale in only a few places. China, North America, and Western Europe account for around one-fourth each of total world production (Figure 14.4.3).

Wind power has divided the environmental community. On the one hand, construction of a wind turbine modifies the environment much less severely than construction of a dam across a river. And wind power has potential for increased use, because only a small portion of the potential resource has been harnessed thus far. On the other hand, wind turbines can be noisy and lethal for birds and bats.

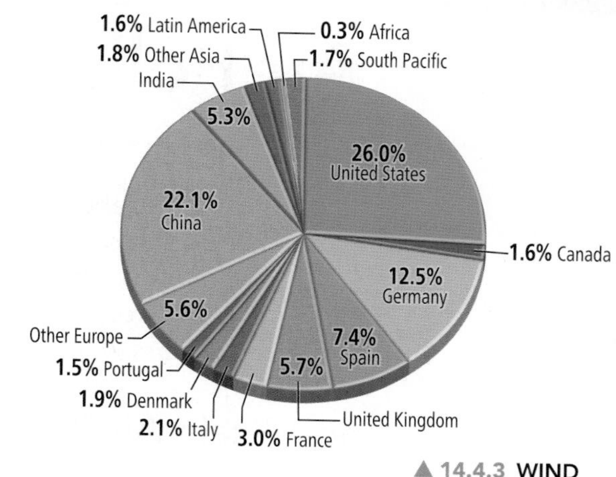

▲ 14.4.3 WIND POWER

Geothermal Energy

Heat released by radioactive elements makes Earth's interior hot. Toward the surface, in volcanic areas, this heat is especially pronounced. The hot rocks can encounter groundwater, producing heated water or steam that can be tapped by wells. Energy from this hot water or steam is called **geothermal energy**.

Harnessing geothermal energy is most feasible at sites along Earth's surface where crustal plates meet, which are also the sites of many earthquakes and volcanoes. The United States and the Philippines are the leading producers of geothermal power (Figure 14.4.4). In Iceland, an island named for its glaciers, nearly all homes and businesses in the capital of Reykjavik are heated with geothermal steam.

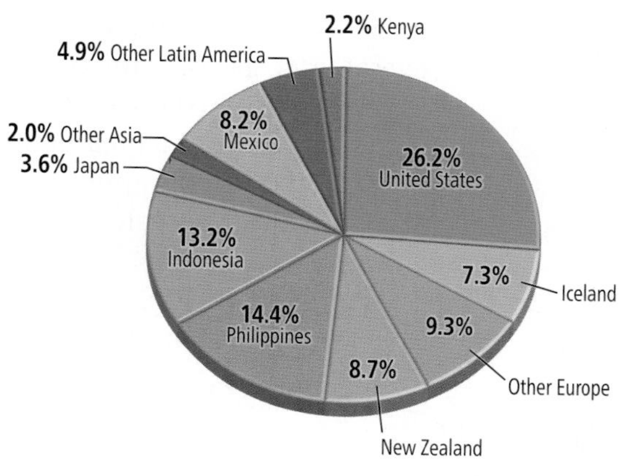

▲ 14.4.4 GEOTHERMAL POWER

Solar

The ultimate renewable resource for sustainable development is solar energy supplied by the Sun. Solar sources currently supply only 1 percent of electricity, but the potential for growth is limitless. Solar energy is harnessed through either **passive solar energy systems** or **active solar energy systems**:

- **Passive solar.** Energy is captured without using special devices. South-facing windows and dark surfaces heat and light buildings on sunny days. The Sun's rays penetrate the windows and are converted to heat (Figure 14.4.5).
- **Direct active solar.** Solar radiation is captured with **photovoltaic cells**, which convert light energy to electrical energy. These cells are made primarily of silicon (also used in computers), the second most abundant element in Earth's crust. When the silicon is combined with one or more other materials, it exhibits distinctive electrical properties in the presence of sunlight, known as the photovoltaic effect.
- **Indirect active solar.** Solar radiation is first converted to heat and then to electricity. The Sun's rays are concentrated by reflectors onto a pipe filled with synthetic oil. The heat from the oil-filled pipe generates steam to run turbines.

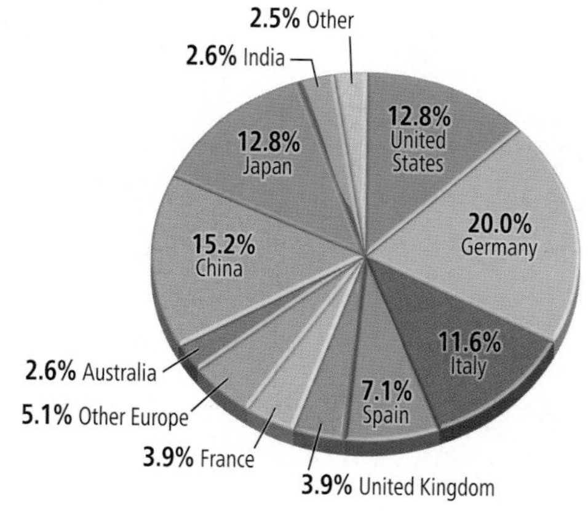

▲ 14.4.5 SOLAR POWER

Air Pollution

- **Explain sources of air pollution at global, regional, and local scales.**

In our consideration of resources, consumption is half of the equation—waste disposal is the other half. All of the resources we use are eventually returned to the atmosphere, bodies of water, or the land surface through burning, rinsing, or discarding. We rely on air, water, and land to remove and disperse (or bury) our waste. **Pollution** occurs when more waste is added than a resource can accommodate.

Local-Scale Air Pollution

At ground level, Earth's average atmosphere is made up of about 78 percent nitrogen, 21 percent oxygen, and less than 1 percent argon. The remaining 0.04 percent includes several trace gases, some of which are critical.

Air pollution is a concentration of trace substances at a greater level than occurs in average air. Geographers examine air pollution at three scales: local, regional, and global.

At the local scale, air pollution is especially severe in places where emission sources are concentrated, such as in urban areas. The air above urban areas may be polluted because a large number of factories, motor vehicles, and other polluters emit residuals in a concentrated area. Most of the cities with the worst air pollution are in Asia (Figure 14.5.1). The World Health Organization considers Zabol, Iran, to have the world's most polluted air (measured as the highest level of airborne particulates), followed by Gwalior, India, and Allahabad, India (Figure 14.5.2).

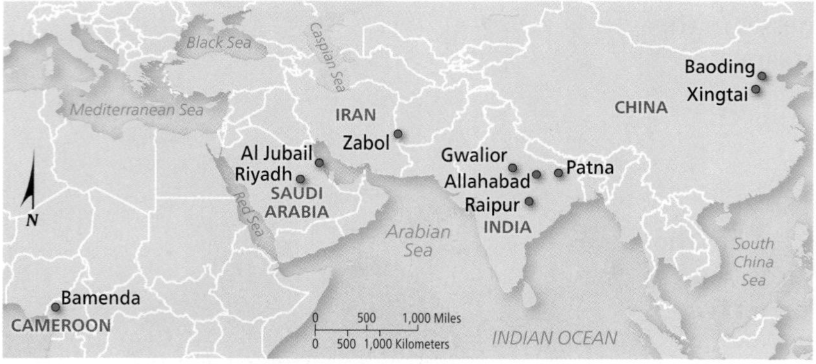

Urban air pollution has three basic components:

- **Carbon monoxide.** Breathing carbon monoxide reduces the oxygen level in blood, impairs vision and alertness, and threatens those with breathing problems.
- **Hydrocarbons.** In the presence of sunlight, hydrocarbons, as well as nitrogen oxides, form **photochemical smog**, which causes respiratory problems, stinging in the eyes, and an ugly haze over cities.
- **Particulates.** They include dust and smoke particles. The dark plume of smoke from a factory stack and the exhaust of a diesel truck are examples of particulate emission.

The worst urban air pollution occurs when winds are slight, skies are clear, and a temperature inversion exists. When the wind blows, it disperses pollutants; when it is calm, pollutants build. Sunlight provides the energy for the formation of smog. Air is normally cooler at higher elevations, but during temperature inversions—in which air is warmer at higher elevations—pollutants are trapped near the ground.

▲ 14.5.1 CITIES WITH THE MOST POLLUTED AIR
Most are in Asia.

◀ 14.5.2 AIR POLLUTION, ALLAHABAD, INDIA

Regional-Scale Air Pollution

At the regional scale, air pollution may damage a region's vegetation and water supply through **acid deposition**, which is the accumulation of acids, including sulfuric acid and nitric acid, on Earth's surface. Especially affected by acid deposition are the world's principal industrial regions (see Chapter 11).

Sulfur oxides and nitrogen oxides, emitted by burning fossil fuels, enter the atmosphere, where they combine with oxygen and water. When dissolved in water, the acids may fall as **acid precipitation**—rain, snow, or fog. The acids can also be deposited in dust. Before they reach the surface, these acidic droplets might be carried hundreds of kilometers.

▲ 14.5.3 ACID PRECIPITATION

Acid precipitation damages lakes, killing fish and plants. On land, concentrations of acid in the soil can injure plants by depriving them of nutrients and can harm worms and insects. Buildings and monuments made of marble and limestone have suffered corrosion from acid rain.

Geographers are particularly interested in the effects of acid precipitation because the worst damage is not experienced at the same location as the emission of the pollutants. Within the United States the major generators of acid deposition are in industrial states along the southern Great Lakes (Figure 14.5.3). However, the severest effects of acid rain are felt in several areas farther east. The United States reduced sulfur dioxide emissions significantly during the late twentieth century.

Global-Scale Air Pollution

At the global scale, the average temperature of Earth's surface has increased by 1°C (2°F) since 1880 (Figure 14.5.4). This temperature increase is directly linked to human actions, especially the burning of fossil fuels in factories and vehicles, according to an international team of UN scientists.

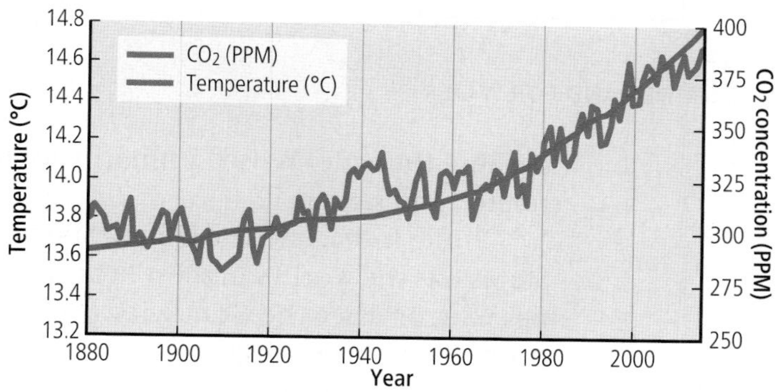

▲ 14.5.4 GLOBAL-SCALE AIR POLLUTION: GLOBAL WARMING AND CARBON DIOXIDE CONCENTRATIONS

Since 1880, carbon dioxide concentration has increased by more than one-third, and Earth has warmed by about 1°C (2°F).

When fossil fuels are burned, a trace gas called carbon dioxide is discharged into the atmosphere. Plants and oceans absorb much of the discharge, but increased fossil fuel burning during the past 200 years has caused the level of carbon dioxide in the atmosphere to rise by more than one-fourth, according to the UN Intergovernmental Panel on Climate Change (refer to Figure 14.5.4). The concentration of trace gases in the atmosphere can delay the return of some of the heat leaving Earth's surface heading for space, thereby raising Earth's temperatures. The increase in Earth's temperature, caused by carbon dioxide trapping some of the radiation emitted by the surface, is called the **greenhouse effect**.

Higher in the atmosphere, **ozone** is a gas that absorbs ultraviolet radiation in the stratosphere, a zone between 15 and 50 kilometers (9 to 30 miles) above Earth's surface. Were it not for the ozone in the stratosphere, UV rays would damage plants, cause skin cancer, and disrupt food chains.

Earth's protective ozone layer is threatened by pollutants called **chlorofluorocarbons (CFCs)**. CFCs such as Freon were once widely used as coolants in refrigerators and air conditioners. When they leak from these appliances, the CFCs are carried into the stratosphere, where they break down Earth's protective layer of ozone gas. In 2007, virtually all countries of the world agreed to cease using CFCs by 2020 in developed countries and by 2030 in developing countries.

Water Pollution

- List the principal sources of water pollution.

Water serves many human purposes. We use it for cooking and bathing, and we must drink it to survive. Water provides a location for boating, swimming, fishing, and other recreational activities. It is home to fish and other aquatic life. Water is essential for economic activities, including agriculture, manufacturing, and services discussed in previous chapters.

These uses depend on fresh, clean, unpolluted water. But that is not always available, because people also use water for purposes that pollute it. Pollution is widespread, because it is easy to dump waste into a river and let the water carry it downstream where it becomes someone else's problem. Water can decompose some waste without adversely impacting other activities, but the volume exceeds the capacity of many rivers and lakes to accommodate it.

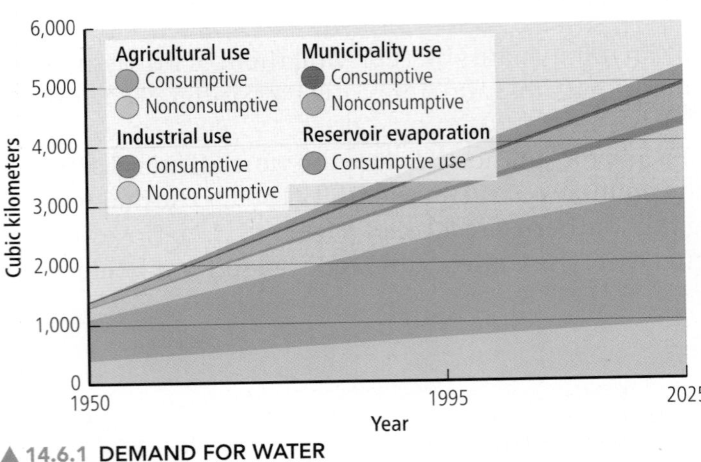

▲ 14.6.1 DEMAND FOR WATER

Demand for Water

Humans use around 9 billion cubic meters of water per year, or around 1,400 cubic meters per capita. The heaviest demand is for agriculture, followed by industry, and municipal sewage systems (Figure 14.6.1).

Water usage is either nonconsumptive or consumptive. Water usage is considered nonconsumptive if the water is returned to nature as a liquid and **consumptive** if the water is evaporated. Most industrial and municipal uses of water are **nonconsumptive,** because the wastewater is primarily discharged into lakes and streams. Most agricultural uses are consumptive, because the water is used primarily to supply plants that transpire it, and therefore cannot be treated and reused.

China, India, and the United States use more than 1 billion cubic meters each. The United States has the world's highest per capita consumption of water, at 2,800 cubic meters per person per year, or twice the worldwide average. Water usage is extremely high in the United States primarily because of agriculture. U.S. farmers raise a large number of animals to meet the high demand for meat that the average American consumes, as discussed in Chapter 9. These animals drink a lot of water in their lifetimes. A large amount of water is also needed in U.S. agriculture to irrigate fields of crops (Figure 14.6.2).

▼ 14.6.2 IRRIGATING CROPS, ARIZONA

Impact on Aquatic Life

Polluted water can harm aquatic life. Aquatic plants and animals consume oxygen, and so does the decomposing organic waste that humans dump in the water. The oxygen consumed by the decomposing organic waste constitutes the **biochemical oxygen demand (BOD)**. If too much waste is discharged into water, the water becomes oxygen starved and fish die.

This can occur when bodies of water become loaded with municipal sewage or industrial waste. The sewage and industrial pollutants consume so much oxygen that the water can become unlivable for normal plants and animals, creating a "dead" stream or lake. Similarly, when runoff carries fertilizer from farm fields into streams or lakes, the fertilizer nourishes excessive aquatic plant production—a "pond scum" of algae—that consumes too much oxygen. Either type of pollution reduces the normal oxygen level, threatening aquatic plants and animals.

Point-Source Pollution

The sources of pollution can be divided into point sources and nonpoint sources. **Point-source pollution** enters a body of water at a specific location, whereas **nonpoint-source pollution** comes from a large, diffuse area. Point-source pollutants are usually smaller in quantity and much easier to control than nonpoint-source pollutants.

Point-source water pollution originates from a specific point, such as a pipe from a wastewater treatment plant. The two main point sources of water pollution are manufacturers and municipal treatment plants.

Many factories use water for cooling and then discharge the warm water back into the river or lake. Fish adapted to cold water, such as salmon and trout, might not be able to survive in the warmer water. Steel, chemicals, paper products, and food processing are major industrial polluters of water.

In developed countries, sewers carry wastewater from sinks, bathtubs, and toilets to a municipal treatment plant, where most—but not all—of the pollutants are removed. The treated wastewater is then typically dumped back into a river or lake. Since passage of the U.S. Clean Water Act and equivalent laws in other developed countries, most treatment plants meet high water-quality standards.

In developing countries, sewer systems are rare, and wastewater usually drains, untreated, into rivers and lakes. The drinking water, usually removed from the same rivers, may be inadequately treated as well. The combination of untreated water and poor sanitation makes drinking water deadly in developing countries. Waterborne diseases such as cholera, typhoid, and dysentery are major causes of death (Figure 14.6.3).

▲ 14.6.3 **WATER POLLUTION: DEVELOPING COUNTRY**
In the absence of sewers, waste in Ho Chi Minh City, Vietnam, is dumped into the Saigon River. Sanitation workers on boats try to remove the trash from the river.

Nonpoint-Source Pollution

Nonpoint sources usually pollute in greater quantities and are much harder to control than point sources of pollution. The principal nonpoint source is agriculture. Fertilizers and pesticides spread on fields to increase agricultural productivity are carried into rivers and lakes by irrigation systems or natural runoff. Expanded use of these products may help to avoid a global food crisis in the short term, but they destroy aquatic life by polluting rivers and lakes. One of the world's most extreme instances of nonpoint water pollution is the Aral Sea in the former Soviet Union, now divided between the countries of Kazakhstan and Uzbekistan (see Research & Analyze feature and Figure 14.6.4).

RESEARCH & ANALYZE
The Shrinking Aral Sea

The Aral Sea, located in Kazakhstan and Uzbekistan, was once the world's fourth-largest lake. Use your search engine to see what has happened to the Aral Sea, and why it has happened.

Shrinking Aral Sea
https://goo.gl/8XQcM1

1. *Search* for *NASA World of Change: Shrinking Aral Sea*. Or go to the home page of **earthobservatory .nasa.gov** and *search* for *Shrinking Aral Sea*.
2. According to NASA, what was the cause of the shrinking of the Aral Sea beginning in the 1960s?
3. What was the reason that the government made changes to the Aral Sea?
4. What has happened to the Aral Sea as a result of the changes?
5. What is the government trying to do the counteract the changes?
6. In Figure 14.6.4, why has the color of much of the land near the lake changed from brown to white?

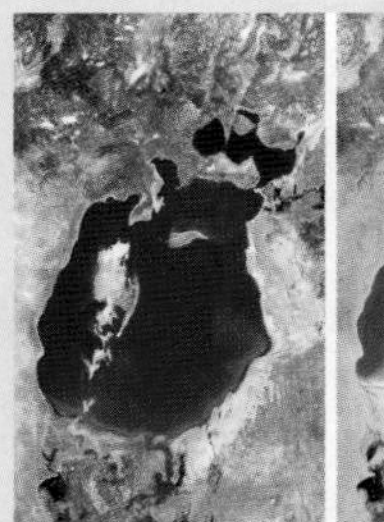
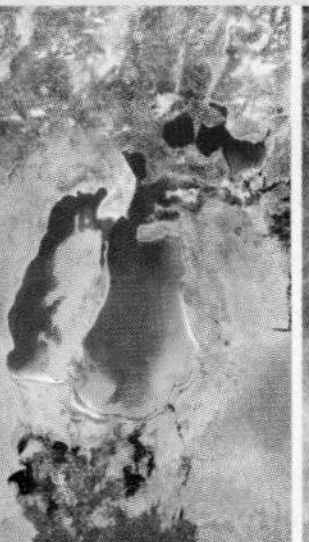
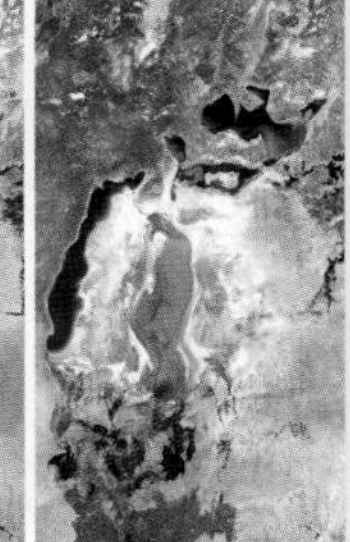

▲ 14.6.4 **ARAL SEA**
(a) 1990, (b) 2000, (c) 2010

Solid Waste Pollution

- Explain the principal sources of solid waste pollution.

The average American generates about 2 kilograms (4 pounds) of solid waste per day (see What's Your Resources Geography). Overall, residences generate around 60 percent of the solid waste and businesses 40 percent. Paper products, such as corrugated cardboard and newspapers, account for the largest share of solid waste in the United States, especially among residences and retailers (Figure 14.7.1). Manufacturers discard large quantities of metals as well as paper.

▲ 14.7.1 **SOLID WASTE**
New York City.

Sanitary Landfill

The **sanitary landfill** is by far the most common strategy for disposal of solid waste in the United States. More than one-half of the country's waste is trucked to landfills and buried under soil (Figure 14.7.2).

This strategy is the opposite of our disposal of gaseous and liquid wastes: We disperse air and water pollutants into the atmosphere, rivers, and eventually the ocean, but we concentrate solid waste in thousands of landfills. Concentration would seem to eliminate solid-waste pollution, but it may only hide it—temporarily. Chemicals released by the decomposing solid waste can leak from the landfill into groundwater. This can contaminate water wells, soil, and nearby streams.

The number of landfills in the United States has declined by three-fourths since 1990. Thousands of small-town "dumps" have been closed and replaced by a small number of large regional ones (Figure 14.7.3). Better compaction methods, combined with expansion in the land area of some of the large regional dumps, have resulted in expanded landfill capacity.

Some communities now pay to use landfills elsewhere. New Jersey and New York are two states that regularly dispose of their solid waste by transporting it out of state. New York City exports 25,000 tons of trash a day to other communities. Passaic County, New Jersey, hauls waste 400 kilometers (250 miles) west to Johnstown, Pennsylvania. San Francisco trucks solid waste to Altamont, California, 100 kilometers (60 miles) away.

▼ 14.7.2 **U.S. SANITARY LANDFILLS**
The United States has nearly 2,000 sites.

Landfill carbon footprints (CO_2 equivalent, metric tons)
- above 300,000
- 100,000–300,000
- below 100,000

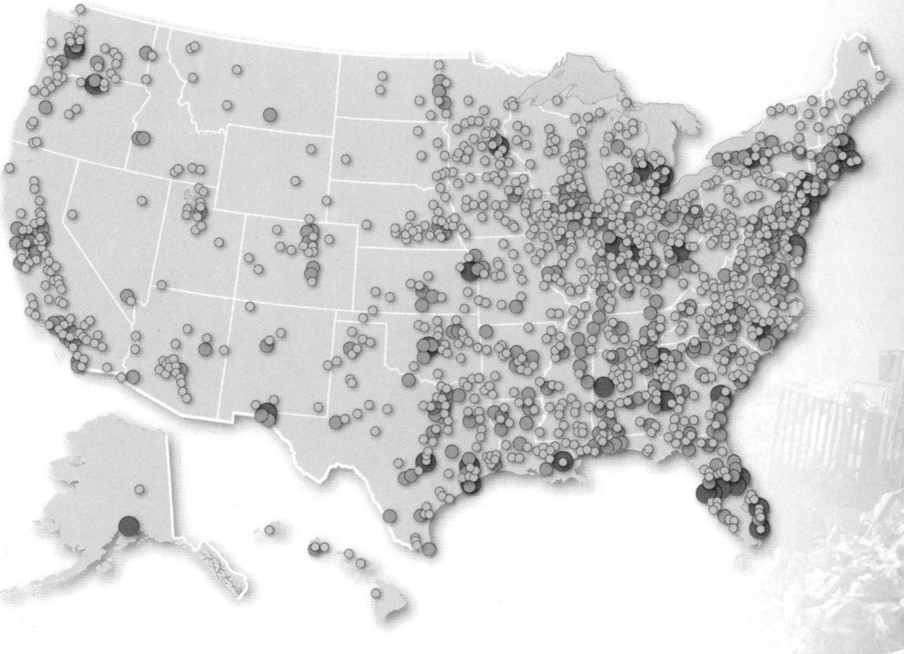

▼ 14.7.3 **SANITARY LANDFILL**
San Joaquin County, California.

Hazardous Waste

Disposing of hazardous waste is especially difficult. Hazardous wastes include heavy metals (including mercury, cadmium, and zinc), PCB oils from electrical equipment, cyanides, strong solvents, acids, and caustics. These may be unwanted by-products generated in manufacturing or waste to be discarded after usage.

According to the toxics release inventory published by the U.S. Environmental Protection Agency (EPA), 2 billion pounds of toxic chemicals were released into the land in 2015. Mining operations were the largest polluters. The four largest polluters were Red Dog zinc mine in Kotzebue, Alaska; Twin Creeks gold and copper mine in Golconda, Nevada; San Manuel copper mine in San Manuel, Arizona; and Kennecott copper mine in Copperton, Utah (Figure 14.7.4).

If poisonous industrial residuals are not carefully placed in protective containers (Figure 14.7.5), the chemicals may leak into the soil and contaminate groundwater or escape into the atmosphere. Breathing air or consuming water contaminated with toxic wastes can cause cancer, mutations, and chronic ailments.

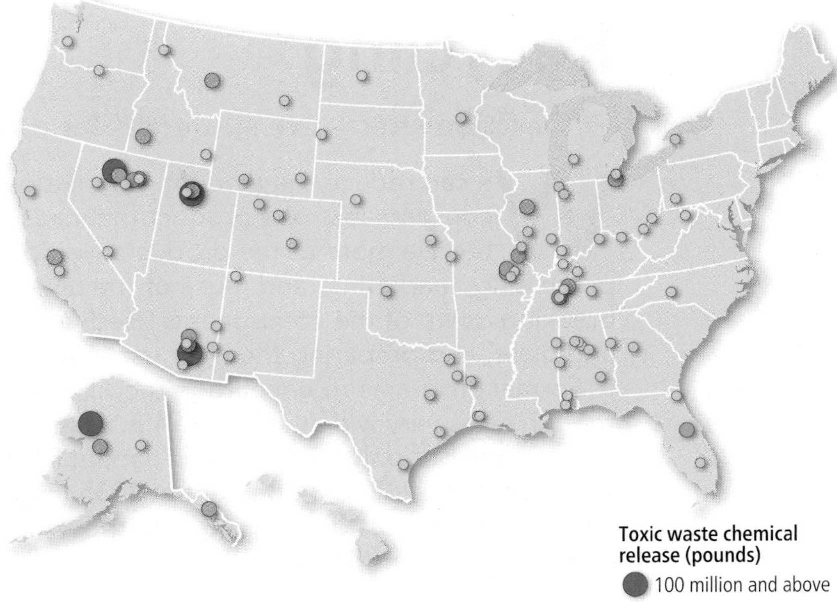

▲ 14.7.4 TOXIC CHEMICAL RELEASE SITES
Ohio has the most sites, although the largest sites are in the West.

WHAT'S YOUR RESOURCES GEOGRAPHY?

Plastic Water Bottles

Humans need to consume water to survive. Americans get their water either from a faucet or a bottle. What's your source of water?

1. The average American consumes around 100 plastic water bottles per year (2 per week). Do you consume more or less than the average number of plastic water bottles? Why do you use so few or so many bottles?
2. It takes around 2.5 gallons of petroleum to produce the 100 plastic bottles consumed by a typical American. That translates into around 65 miles of driving the typical American car. The average American drives around 25 miles per day. Do you (or a friend or family member) drive more or less than the average? What accounts for driving more or less than the average?
3. The average American recycles only 1 out of 6 water bottles. The rest are "thrown away" into landfills or into rivers, lakes, and oceans, where they take hundreds of years to disintegrate. What percentage of plastic bottles do you recycle? Why is your percentage higher or lower than the average?

▲ 14.7.6 DISCARDED WATER BOTTLE POLLUTING RIVER

▼ 14.7.5 HAZARDOUS WASTE DROP OFF
Brooklyn, New York.

Recycling

- Describe alternative strategies for recycling.

We can reduce the amount of pollution we generate in two basic ways: we can consume less of a product that causes pollution (such as petroleum), or we can recycle more of the products we do use. **Recycling** is the separation, collection, processing, marketing, and reuse of the unwanted material. Recycling involves the breaking down of the components used in the creation of plastics, papers, aluminum, and glass, and preparing them for use in a future application.

Formal programs to encourage recycling are common in developed countries, though rates vary widely (Figure 14.8.1). Around 65 percent of solid waste is recycled in Germany but only 19 percent in Japan. Recycling in the United States increased from 10 percent in 1985 to 34 percent in 2015 (Figure 14.8.2). Formal recycling programs are not in place in most developing countries, though informal recycling is common. Pickers comb through landfills and resell what they find.

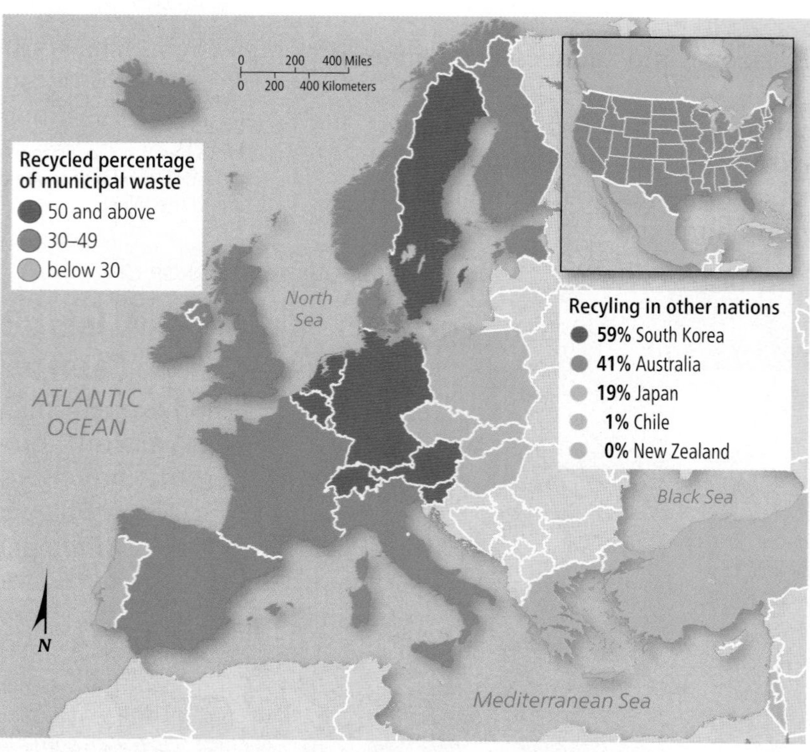

▲ 14.8.1 RECYCLING IN EUROPE AND OTHER DEVELOPED COUNTRIES

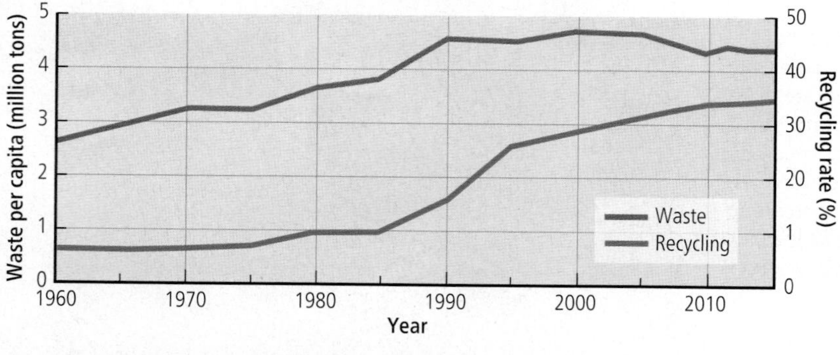

▲ 14.8.2 RECYCLING IN THE UNITED STATES

Pick-Up and Processing

Materials that would otherwise be "thrown away" are collected and sorted, in four principal ways:

- **Curbside programs.** Recyclables can often be placed at the curb in a container separate from the non-recyclable trash at a specified time each week, either at the same or different time as the other trash. The trash collector usually supplies homes with specially marked containers for the recyclable items.
- **Drop-off centers.** Drop-off centers are sites, typically with several large containers placed at a central location, for individuals to leave recyclable materials. A separate container is designated for each type of recyclable material, and the containers are periodically emptied by a processor or recycler but are otherwise left unattended.
- **Buy-back centers.** Commercial operations sometimes pay consumers for recyclable materials, especially aluminum cans, but also sometimes plastic containers and glass bottles. These materials are usually not processed at the buy-back center.
- **Deposit programs.** Glass and aluminum containers can sometimes be returned to retailers. The price a consumer pays for a beverage may include a deposit fee of 5¢ or 10¢ that the retailer refunds when the container is returned.

Remanufacturing

The percentage of materials recovered by recycling varies widely by product (Figure 14.8.3). Materials are manufactured into new products for which a market exists. Four major manufacturing sectors account for more than half of the recycling activity—paper mills, steel mills, plastic converters, and iron and steel foundries. Common household items that contain recycled materials include newspapers and paper towels; aluminum, plastic, and glass soft-drink containers; steel cans; and plastic laundry detergent bottles. Recycled materials are also used in such industrial applications as recovered glass in roadway asphalt ("glassphalt") and recovered plastic in carpet, park benches, and pedestrian bridges.

The principal inputs into manufacturing include recycled paper, plastic, glass, and aluminum:

- **Paper.** Most types of paper can be recycled. Newspapers have been recycled profitably for decades, and recycling of other paper, especially computer paper, is growing. Rapid increases in virgin paper pulp prices have stimulated construction of more plants capable of using waste paper. The key to recycling is collecting large quantities of clean, well-sorted, uncontaminated, and dry paper.
- **Plastic.** Different plastic types must not be mixed, as even a small amount of the wrong type of plastic can ruin the melt. Because it is impossible to tell one type from another by sight or touch, the plastic industry has developed a system of numbers marked inside triangles on the bottom of containers. Types 1 and 2 are commonly recycled, and the others generally less frequently.
- **Glass.** Glass can be used repeatedly with no loss in quality and is 100 percent recyclable. The process of creating new glass from old is extremely efficient, producing virtually no waste or unwanted by-products. Though unbroken clear glass is valuable, mixed-color glass is nearly worthless, and broken glass is hard to sort (Figure 14.8.4).
- **Aluminum.** The principal source of recycled aluminum is beverage containers. Aluminum cans began to replace glass bottles for beer during the 1950s and for soft drinks during the 1960s. Aluminum scrap is readily accepted for recycling, although other metals are rarely accepted.

▼ 14.8.3 **SOURCES OF SOLID WASTE BEFORE AND AFTER RECYCLING**
Around one-half of paper and one-fourth of yard waste are recycled, whereas 10 percent of other sources are recycled.

▶ 14.8.4 **RECYCLING GLASS, PENNSYLVANIA**

The Car of the Future

- **Describe alternative strategies for powering vehicles in the future.**

One of the greatest challenges to reducing pollution and conserving nonrenewable resources is reliance on petroleum as automotive fuel. Consumers in developed countries are reluctant to give up their motor vehicles, and demand for vehicles is soaring in developing countries.

Several alternatives to gas-powered vehicles are available, though together they accounted for only 3 percent of worldwide vehicle sales in 2017. However, several governments have taken steps to increase the share of alternative fuel vehicles. For example, the sale of gas-powered vehicles is banned in Norway as of 2025, in India as of 2030, and in France and the United Kingdom as of 2040. Several other countries have official targets for the sale of alternative fuel vehicles.

Ethanol

Ethanol is fuel made by distilling crops such as sugarcane, corn, and soybeans. Sugarcane is distilled for fuel in Brazil, where most vehicles run on ethanol (Figure 14.9.1). In the United States, corn has been the principal crop for ethanol, but this has proved controversial because the amount of fossil fuels needed to grow and distill the corn is comparable to—and possibly greater than—the amount saved in vehicle fuels. Furthermore, growing corn for ethanol diverts corn from the food chain, thereby allegedly causing higher food prices in the United States and globally. More promising is ethanol distilled from biomass containing cellulose, such as trees and grasses.

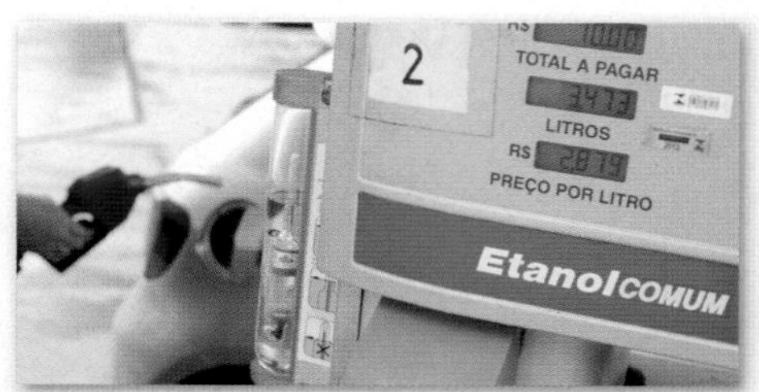

▲ 14.9.1 ETHANOL STATION, BRAZIL

Full Electric

A full electric vehicle has no gas engine. When the battery is discharged, the vehicle will not run until the battery is recharged by plugging it into an outlet. Electric vehicles have a range of 200+ miles (Figure 14.9.2).

▲ 14.9.2 FULL ELECTRIC: TESLA

Hybrid

A gasoline engine powers the vehicle at high speeds, and at low speeds, when the gas engine is at its least efficient, an electric motor takes over. Energy that would otherwise be wasted in coasting and braking is also captured as electricity and stored until needed (Figure 14.9.3).

▲ 14.9.3 HYBRID: TOYOTA PRIUS

Plug-In Hybrid

In a plug-in hybrid, the battery supplies the power at all speeds. Like a full electric, a plug-in hybrid is recharged by connecting it to an electrical outlet (Figure 14.9.4). When the electricity obtained from the outlet is fully discharged, gas takes over the job of powering the electric motor.

▲ 14.9.4 PLUG-IN HYBRID CHEVROLET VOLT

Hydrogen Fuel Cell

Hydrogen forced through a PEM (polymer electrolyte membrane or proton exchange membrane) combines with oxygen from the air, producing an electric charge. The electricity can then be used to power an electric motor. Fuel cell vehicles are being used in places where hydrogen fueling stations are available (Figure 14.9.5).

▲ 14.9.5 HYDROGEN FUELING STATION

Regional Variations in Electricity

Electricity is generated differently across the 50 U.S. states (Figure 14.9.6). Leading sources of electricity include coal in the Midwest, hydroelectric in the Northwest, natural gas in the Southwest and Florida, and nuclear in several Eastern states.

According to the U.S. Department of Energy, the average gas-powered car on the road today emits 11,435 pounds of carbon dioxide per year. The annual emissions are much lower for alternative fuel vehicles: 4,587 pounds for full electric vehicles, 6,192 pounds for plug-in hybrids, and 6,258 pounds for hybrids. Hybrid cars have lower emissions than full electrics in states most dependent on coal, whereas full electrics have lower emissions in states that generate electricity primarily through hydroelectricity, natural gas, and nuclear energy. (Figure 14.9.7). As alternative fuel vehicles increase in the years ahead, more stations will be needed to recharge them (Figure 14.9.8).

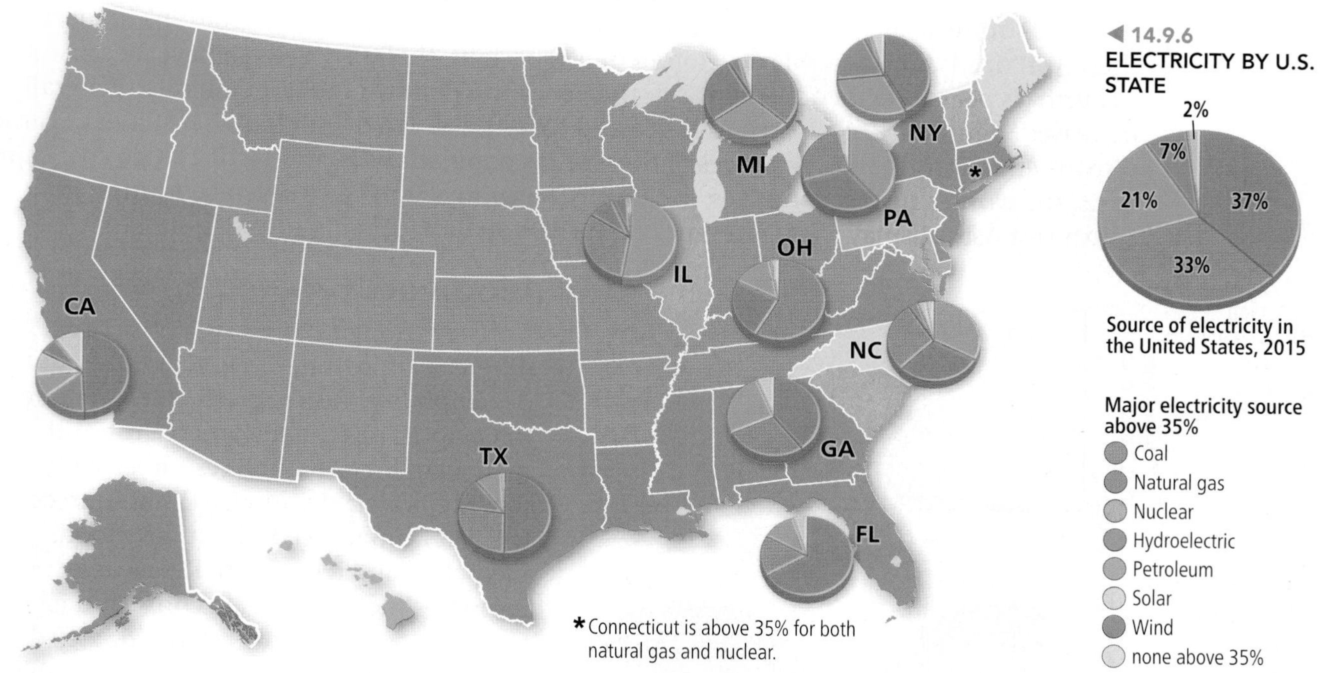

◀ 14.9.6 ELECTRICITY BY U.S. STATE

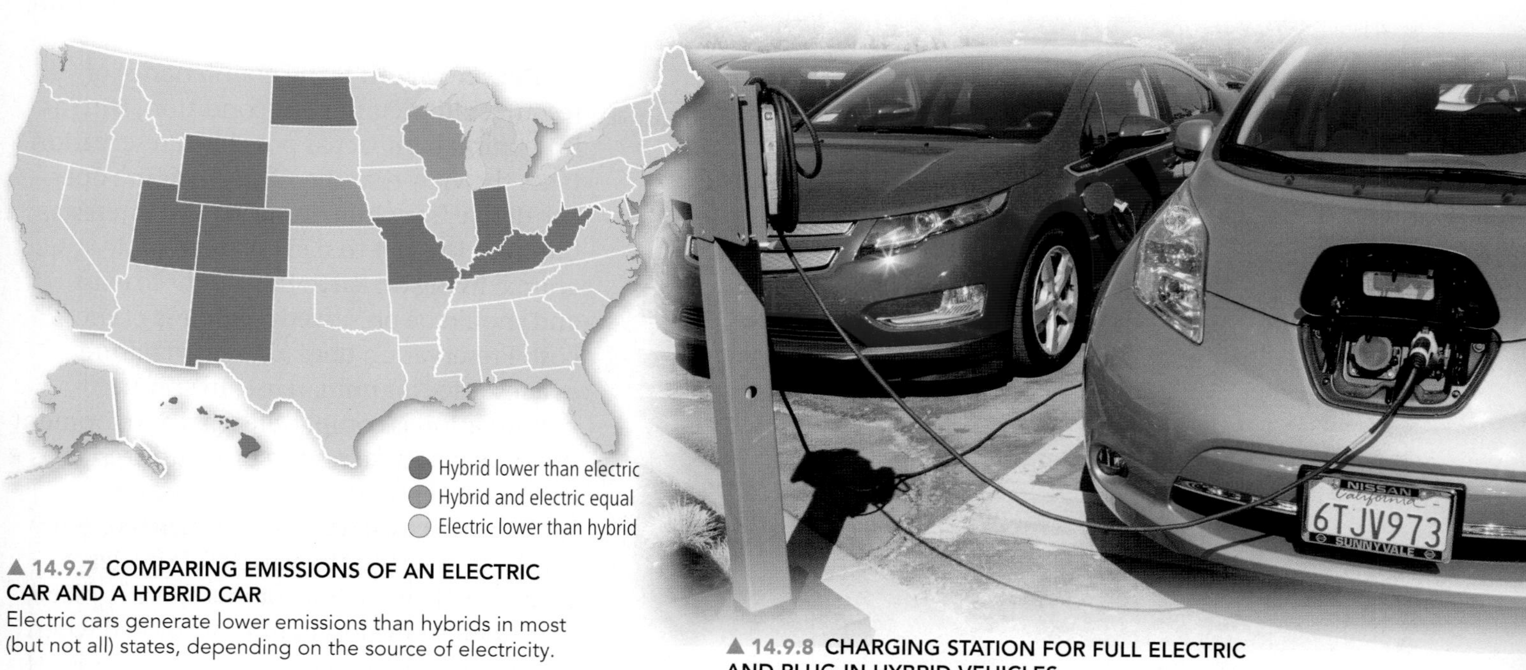

▲ 14.9.7 COMPARING EMISSIONS OF AN ELECTRIC CAR AND A HYBRID CAR

Electric cars generate lower emissions than hybrids in most (but not all) states, depending on the source of electricity.

▲ 14.9.8 CHARGING STATION FOR FULL ELECTRIC AND PLUG-IN HYBRID VEHICLES

Palo Alto, California.

A More Sustainable Future

- Assess prospects for sustainable development.

Sustainability was defined in Chapter 1 as the use of Earth's resources in ways that ensure their availability in the future. Sustainability was shown to rest on three pillars: environment, economy, and society.

Sustainable Development

According to the United Nations, **sustainable development** is "development that meets the needs of the present without compromising the ability of future generations to meet their own needs." Sustainable development is especially challenging to achieve, because as a country's per capita income increases, the per capita pollution that it emits also generally increases (Figure 14.10.1). North America and East Asia generate much higher shares of carbon dioxide emissions than their shares of the world's population (Figure 14.10.2). On a per capita basis, the world's richest countries, including the United States and several countries in Southwest Asia, display the highest per capita carbon dioxide emissions (Figure 14.10.3).

▶ **14.10.1 GNI AND POLLUTION** Carbon dioxide emissions generally increase with rising income.

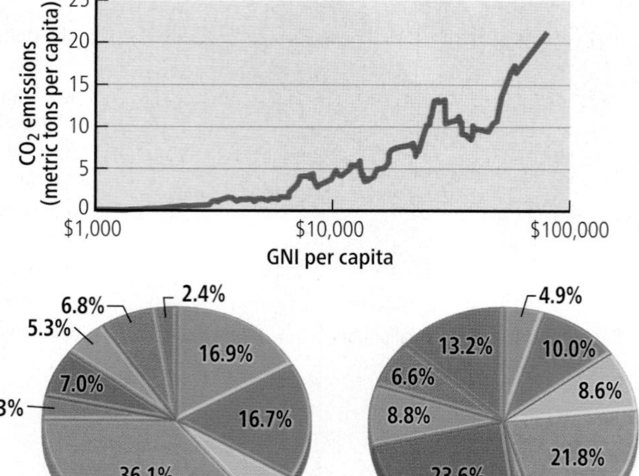

North America
Europe and Russia
Latin America
East Asia
Central Asia
South Asia
Southeast Asia and South Pacific
Southwest Asia and North Africa
Sub-Saharan Africa

▲ **14.10.2 CO_2 EMISSIONS AND POPULATION** (a) Share of CO_2 emissions by region (b) share of population by region.

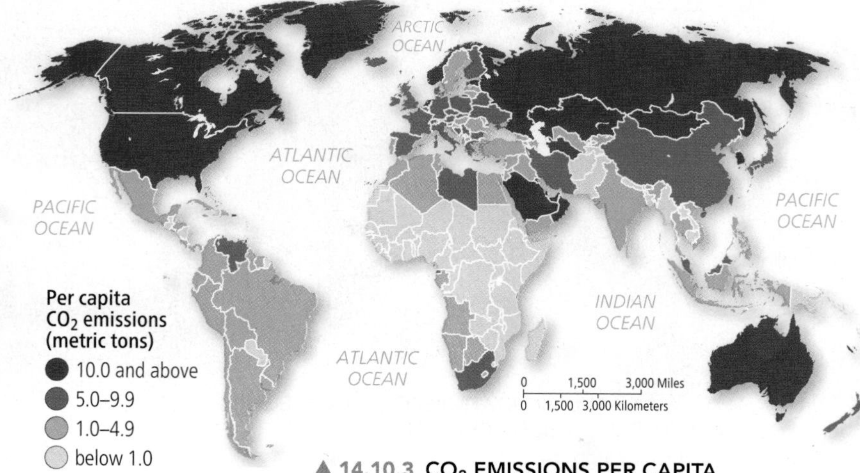

▲ **14.10.3 CO_2 EMISSIONS PER CAPITA**

Biodiversity

Conservation and preservation are two different approaches to sustainable development. **Conservation** was defined in Chapter 1 as the sustainable use and management of natural resources such as wildlife, water, air, and Earth's resources to meet human needs, including food, medicine, and recreation. Renewable resources such as trees are conserved if they are consumed at a less rapid rate than they can be replaced. Nonrenewable resources such as fossil fuels are conserved if remaining reserves are maintained for future generations.

Preservation is the maintenance of resources in their present condition, with as little human impact as possible. Preservation takes the view that the value of nature does not derive from human needs and interests, but from the fact that every plant and animal living on Earth has a right to exist and should be preserved regardless of the cost. Preservation does not regard nature as a resource for human use. In contrast, conservation is compatible with development but only if natural resources are utilized in a careful rather than a wasteful manner.

Biological diversity, or **biodiversity** for short, refers to the variety of species across Earth as a whole or in a specific place. Sustainable development is promoted when the biodiversity of a particular place or Earth as a whole is conserved or preserved.

Looking to the Future

The UN expects that strategies to achieve sustainable development will vary among countries. U.S. scientists working with the UN have offered a strategy with three key elements:

- Sharp decrease in the use of the three fossil fuels.
- Increase in the use of renewable energy sources, such as solar and wind, as well as biomass and nuclear.
- Use of **carbon capture and storage (CCS)** for large facilities, such as power plants, that burn coal and natural gas users. CCS is the capture of waste CO_2, transporting it to a storage site, and depositing it where it will not enter the atmosphere, normally underground.

Meeting targets in this threefold strategy would result in a 24 percent reduction in CO_2 emissions in the United States by 2050 (Figure 14.10.4). The principal impact on the average American would be reliance on electricity for nearly all household activities and transportation. This electricity would be generated almost exclusively through sources other than the three fossil fuels. Usage of fossil fuels would be restricted primarily to aviation, military equipment, and industrial activities that are difficult to electrify.

As hard as it will be for the United States to reduce its carbon footprint, the challenge is even greater for developing countries, especially China, which is now the world's leading manufacturing country. Many other developing countries lack the critical financial resources needed to transition to renewable energy alternatives. Critics charge that humans shouldn't bother with promoting sustainable development. They argue that sustainable development is either impossible to achieve or unnecessary (see Debate It! feature).

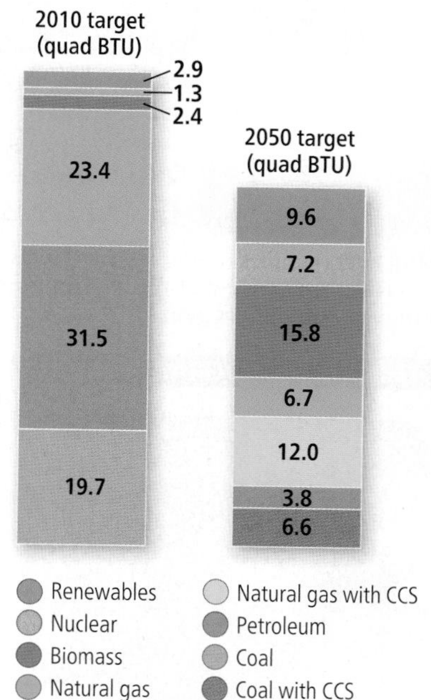

▲ **14.10.4 UN TARGET FOR CO_2 EMISSIONS REDUCTION IN THE UNITED STATES**

DEBATE IT!
Is sustainable development imperative or unnecessary?

Supporters maintain that sustainability is vital to humanity's future, whereas some critics argue that humans should not bother with making our daily lives more sustainable (Figures 14.10.5 and 14.10.6).

SUSTAINABLE ACTIONS ARE IMPORTANT

- Humans have an obligation as stewards of the Earth to conserve and preserve it for future generations.
- A disproportionately large share of Earth's resources is being used by a small percentage of people, who by reducing their use could have a large impact on the conservation of resources.
- Renewable substitutes for nonrenewable resources are available if people make an effort to choose them.

▲ **14.10.5 METRO TRAIN, HOUSTON**

SUSTAINABLE ACTIONS ARE IMPOSSIBLE OR UNNECESSARY

- It is too late to discuss sustainable development, because humans are currently using 13 billion hectares of Earth's land area, but Earth has only 11.4 billion hectares of biologically productive land, according to the World Wildlife Fund; so humans have none left to conserve for future growth.
- Future technologies will enable humans to survive by solving any problems resulting from today's unsustainable practices.
- Earth's resources have no absolute limit, because the definition of what is a resource changes dramatically and unpredictably over time.

▶ **14.10.6 HURRICANE HARVEY FLOODING, HOUSTON**

CHAPTER

14 Review, Analyze, & Apply

KEY ISSUE 1 Where Are Earth's Principal Energy Resources?

Most energy comes from three fossil fuels: petroleum, coal, and natural gas. Fossil fuels are not distributed uniformly, and demand for them varies among world regions.

THINKING GEOGRAPHICALLY

1. Much of the remaining petroleum is located either offshore or in shale or oil sands that need to be mined. What are some of the pollution challenges to increased use of these sources?

◀ 14.CR.1 **OIL SANDS MINING, ALBERTA**

KEY ISSUE 2 What Is The Future For Energy Resources?

The fossil fuels are nonrenewable. Other renewable energy sources are increasingly important, especially hydroelectric, wind, and solar.

THINKING GEOGRAPHICALLY

2. What initiatives have your community or state taken to promote alternative sources of energy? What have been some of the accomplishments and challenges in using alternative energy?

◀ 14.CR.2 **WIND TURBINES, PALM SPRINGS, CALIFORNIA**

KEY ISSUE 3 How Are Resources Polluted?

Waste—the unwanted byproducts of using resources—are discharged to air, water, and land. Pollution occurs when more waste is discharged than can be accommodated.

THINKING GEOGRAPHICALLY

3. When you throw something away in a trash can, where does it go? What challenges does your community face in hauling away your trash?

◀ 14.CR.3 **STREET TRASH, NEW YORK CITY**

KEY ISSUE 4 How Are Resources Protected?

Sustainable development conserves resources for future generations and preserves biodiversity. Sustainable development is promoted through consuming fewer resources and recycling more of those that are used.

THINKING GEOGRAPHICALLY

4. What initiatives have been undertaken at your university or school to encourage more sustainable development? In what ways might students, teachers, and staff be encouraged to adopt more sustainable practices?

◀ 14.CR.4 **CLEAN WATER FROM THE FAUCET**
A resource that most Americans take for granted.

Explore

Alternative fuel vehicles in Paris

Paris has one of the world's most extensive projects to support alternative vehicles.

In Google Earth, ***search*** for *3 rue de Suffren, Paris, France.* Use Street View to ***drop*** to 3 rue de Suffren. Look at the cars parked on the other side of the street from #3.

1. What famous structure is one block away?
2. What is distinctive about the cars across the street from #3?
3. What is written on the side of the cars parked there? Use a translation app if necessary.

▲ 14.CR.5 **PARIS EV STATION**

GeoVideo

Log in to the Mastering Geography™ Study Area to view this video.

Protecting The Amazon Rain Forest

The Amazon rain forest in Brazil shelters as much as 10 percent of Earth's biodiversity. However, deforestation threatens this vital resource, even as scientists and the government work to protect it.

1. What has been the principal cause of deforestation in the Amazon? How is the deforested land being used instead?
2. How is the Brazilian government using geospatial technology to monitor forest resources?
3. What efforts are underway to combine conservation with sustainable use of Amazon forest resources?

Key Terms

Acid deposition (p. 351) The accumulation of acids on Earth's surface.

Acid precipitation (p. 351) Conversion of sulfur oxides and nitrogen oxides to acids that return to Earth as rain, snow, or fog.

Active solar energy system (p. 349) A solar energy system that collects energy through the use of mechanical devices such as photovoltaic cells or flat-plate collectors.

Air pollution (p. 350) Concentration of trace substances, such as carbon monoxide, sulfur dioxide, nitrogen oxides, hydrocarbons, and solid particulates, at a greater level than occurs in average air.

Animate power (p. 342) Power supplied by animals or by people.

Biochemical oxygen demand (BOD) (p. 352) The amount of oxygen required by aquatic bacteria to decompose a given load of organic waste; a measure of water pollution.

Biological diversity (or **biodiversity**) (p. 360) The number of species within a specific habitat.

Biomass fuel (p. 342) Fuel derived from wood, plant material, or animal waste.

Carbon capture and storage (CCS) (p. 361) The process of capturing waste CO2, transporting it to a storage site, and depositing it where it will not enter the atmosphere, normally underground.

Chlorofluorocarbon (CFC) (p. 351) A gas used as a solvent, a propellant in aerosols, and a refrigerant, as well as in plastic foams and fire extinguishers.

Conservation (p. 360) The sustainable management of a natural resource.

Consumptive water usage (p. 352) The use of water that evaporates rather than being returned to nature as a liquid.

Demand (p. 343) The quantity of something that consumers are willing and able to buy.

Fossil fuel (p. 342) An energy source formed from the residue of plants and animals buried millions of years ago.

Fusion (p. 348) Creation of energy by joining the nuclei of two hydrogen atoms to form helium.

Geothermal energy (p. 349) Energy from steam or hot water produced from hot or molten underground rocks.

Greenhouse effect (p. 351) The anticipated increase in Earth's temperature caused by carbon dioxide (emitted by burning fossil fuels) trapping some of the radiation emitted by the surface.

Hydraulic fracturing (p. 346) Pumping water at high pressure to break apart rocks and thereby release natural gas.

Hydroelectric power (p. 348) Power generated from moving water.

Nonconsumptive water usage (p. 352) The use of water that is returned to nature as a liquid.

Nonpoint source pollution (p. 353) Pollution that originates from a large, diffuse area.

Nonrenewable resource (p. 348) Something produced in nature more slowly than it is consumed by humans.

Ozone (p. 351) A gas that absorbs ultraviolet solar radiation, found in the stratosphere, a zone between 15 to 50 kilometers (9 to 30 miles) above Earth's surface.

Passive solar energy systems (p. 349) Solar energy systems that collect energy without the use of mechanical devices.

Photochemical smog (p. 350) An atmospheric condition formed through a combination of weather conditions and pollution, especially from motor vehicle emissions.

Photovoltaic cell (p. 349) A solar energy cell, usually made from silicon, that collects solar rays to generate electricity.

Point source pollution (p. 353) Pollution that enters a body of water from a specific source.

Pollution (p. 350) Concentration of waste added to air, water, or land at a greater level than occurs in average air, water, or land.

Potential reserve (p. 346) The amount of energy in deposits not yet identified but thought to exist.

Preservation (p. 360) The maintenance of resources in their present condition, with as little human impact as possible.

Proven reserve (p. 346) The amount of a resource remaining in discovered deposits.

Recycling (p. 356) The separation, collection, processing, marketing, and reuse of unwanted material.

Renewable resource (p. 348) Something produced in nature more rapidly than it is consumed by humans.

Sanitary landfill (p. 354) A place to deposit solid waste, where a layer of earth is bulldozed over garbage each day to reduce emissions of gases and odors from the decaying trash, to minimize fires, and to discourage vermin.

Supply (p. 343) The quantity of something that producers have available for sale.

Sustainable development (p. 360) Development that meets the needs of the present without compromising the ability of future generations to meet their own needs.

Geospatial Analysis

Log in to the Mastering Geography Study Area to access MapMaster 2.0.

Emissions and energy consumption

Carbon dioxide emissions and energy consumption have both increased. At the national scale, are the two related?

Add the *Energy Consumption* layer.

1. What world regions have the highest energy consumption per capita?
2. ***Add*** the *Carbon Dioxide Emissions* layer and ***select*** *Join with data layer*. Probe the map. Are countries with high carbon dioxide emissions per capita those with relatively high energy consumption per capita or relatively low? What might account for this relationship?

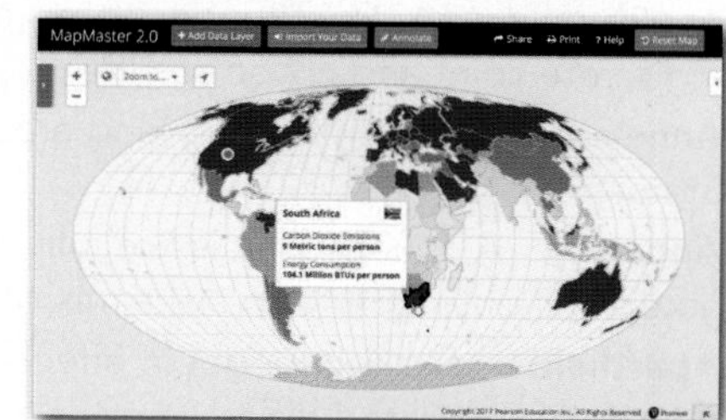

▲ **14.CR.7 ENERGY CONSUMPTION & CARBON DIOXIDE EMISSIONS**

Mastering Geography

Looking for additional review and test prep materials? Visit the Study Area in Mastering Geography to enhance your geographic literacy, spatial reasoning skills, and understanding of this chapter's content. Access MapMaster™ interactive maps, video case studies, *In the News* current articles, flashcards, self-study quizzes, an eText of *Contemporary Human Geography*, and more. **pearson.com/mastering/geography**

Glossary

A

Abiotic Composed of nonliving or inorganic matter.

Acculturation The process of changes in culture that result from the meeting of two groups, each of which retains distinct cultural features.

Acid deposition The accumulation of acids on Earth's surface.

Acid precipitation Conversion of sulfur oxides and nitrogen oxides to acids that return to Earth as rain, snow, or fog.

Active solar energy system A solar energy system that collects energy through the use of mechanical devices such as photovoltaic cells or flat-plate collectors.

Adolescent fertility rate The number of births per 1,000 women ages 15 to 19.

Agnosticism The belief that the existence of God can't be proven or disproven empirically.

Agribusiness Commercial agriculture characterized by the integration of different steps in the food-processing industry, usually through ownership by large corporations.

Agricultural density The ratio of the number of farmers to the total amount of arable land (land suitable for agriculture).

Agricultural revolution The time when human beings first domesticated plants and animals and no longer relied entirely on hunting and gathering.

Agriculture The deliberate effort to modify a portion of Earth's surface through the cultivation of crops and the raising of livestock for sustenance or economic gain.

Air pollution Concentration of trace substances, such as carbon monoxide, sulfur dioxide, nitrogen oxides, hydrocarbons, and solid particulates, at a greater level than occurs in average air.

Animate power Power supplied by animals or by people.

Animism The belief that objects, such as plants and stones, or natural events, like thunderstorms and earthquakes, have a discrete spirit and conscious life.

Annexation Legally adding land area to a city in the United States.

Anocracy A country that is not fully democratic or fully autocratic but rather displays a mix of the two types.

Apartheid Laws (no longer in effect) in South Africa that physically separated different races into different geographic areas.

Apparel An article of clothing.

Aquaculture The cultivation of seafood under controlled conditions.

Arable land Land suited for agriculture.

Arithmetic density The total number of people divided by the total land area.

Assimilation The process by which a group's cultural features are altered to resemble those of another group.

Asylum seeker Someone who has migrated to another country in the hope of being recognized as a refugee.

Atheism The belief that God does not exist.

Atmosphere The thin layer of gases surrounding Earth.

Autocracy A country that is run according to the interests of the ruler rather than the people.

Autonomous religion A religion that does not have a central authority but shares ideas and cooperates informally.

B

Balance of power A condition of roughly equal strength between opposing countries or alliances of countries.

Basic business A business that sells its products or services primarily to consumers outside the settlement.

Biochemical oxygen demand (BOD) The amount of oxygen required by aquatic bacteria to decompose a given load of organic waste; a measure of water pollution.

Biological diversity (or **biodiversity)** The number of species within a specific habitat.

Biomass fuel Fuel derived from wood, plant material, or animal waste.

Biosphere All living organisms on Earth, including plants and animals, as well as microorganisms.

Biotic Composed of living organisms.

Black Lives Matter Movement that campaigns against violence and perceived racism toward black people and educates others about the challenges that African Americans continue to face in the United States.

Blockbusting A process by which real estate agents convince white property owners to sell their houses at low prices because of fear that persons of color will soon move into the neighborhood.

Boundary An invisible line that marks the extent of a state's territory.

Brain drain Large-scale emigration by talented people.

Branch A large and fundamental division within a religion.

Break-of-bulk point A location where transfer is possible from one mode of transportation to another.

Bulk-gaining industry An industry in which the final product weighs more or comprises a greater volume than the inputs.

Bulk-reducing industry An industry in which the final product weighs less or comprises a lower volume than the inputs.

Business service A service that primarily meets the needs of other businesses, including professional, financial, and transportation services.

C

Carbon capture and storage (CCS) The process of capturing waste CO2, transporting it to a storage site, and depositing it where it will not enter the atmosphere, normally underground.

Cartography The science of making maps.

Caste The class or distinct hereditary order into which a Hindu is assigned, according to religious law.

Census A complete enumeration of a population.

Census tract An area delineated by the U.S. Bureau of the Census for which statistics are published; in urban areas, census tracts correspond roughly to neighborhoods.

Central business district (CBD) The area of a city where retail and office activities are clustered.

Central city An urban settlement that has been legally incorporated into an independent, self-governing unit.

Central place A market center for the exchange of services by people attracted from the surrounding area.

Central place theory A theory that explains the distribution of services based on the fact that settlements serve as centers of market areas for services; larger settlements are fewer and farther apart than smaller settlements and provide services for a larger number of people who are willing to travel farther.

Centripetal force An attitude that tends to unify people and enhance support for a state.

Cereal grain A grass that yields grain for food.

Chain migration Migration of people to a specific location because relatives or members of the same nationality previously migrated there.

Chlorofluorocarbon (CFC) A gas used as a solvent, a propellant in aerosols, and a refrigerant, as well as in plastic foams and fire extinguishers.

Citizen science Scientific research by amateur scientists.

City-state A sovereign state comprising a city and its immediately surrounding countryside.

Clustered rural settlement A rural settlement in which the houses and farm buildings of each family are situated close to each other, with fields surrounding the settlement.

Colonialism An attempt by one country to establish settlements and to impose its political, economic, and cultural principles in another territory.

Colony A territory that is legally tied to a sovereign state rather than completely independent.

Combined statistical area (CSA) In the United States, two or more contiguous core based statistical areas tied together by commuting patterns.

Commercial agriculture Agriculture undertaken primarily to generate products for sale off the farm.

Compact state A state in which the distance from the center to any boundary does not vary significantly.

Concentration The spread of something over a given area.

Concentric zone model A model of the internal structure of cities in which social groups are spatially arranged in a series of rings.

Congregation A local assembly of persons brought together for common religious worship.

Connection The relationships among people and objects across the barrier of space.

Conservation The sustainable management of a natural resource to meet human needs.

Conservation tillage A method of soil cultivation that reduces soil erosion and runoff.

Consumer service A business that provides services primarily to individual consumers, including retail services and education, health, and leisure services.

Consumptive water usage The use of water that evaporates rather than being returned to nature as a liquid.

Contagious diffusion The rapid, widespread diffusion of a feature or trend throughout a population.

Coordinated Universal Time (UTC) informally **Greenwich Mean Time, (GMT)** The time in the zone encompassing the prime meridian, or 0° longitude.

Core based statistical area (CBSA) In the United States, the collection of all metropolitan statistical areas and micropolitan statistical areas.

Cosmogony A set of beliefs concerning the origin of the universe.

Cottage industry Manufacturing based in homes rather than in factories, commonly found prior to the Industrial Revolution.

Counterurbanization Net migration from urban to rural areas in developed countries.

Creole (or **creolized) language** A language that results from the mixing of a colonizer's language with the indigenous language of the people being dominated.

Crop Any plant gathered from a field as a harvest during a particular season.

Crop rotation The practice of rotating use of different fields from crop to crop each year to avoid exhausting the soil.

Crude birth rate (CBR) The total number of live births in a year for every 1,000 people alive in the society.

Crude death rate (CDR) The total number of deaths in a year for every 1,000 people alive in the society.

Cultural ecology A geographic approach that emphasizes human-environment relationships.

Cultural homogenization The process of reduction in cultural diversity through the diffusion of popular culture.

Cultural landscape An approach to geography that emphasizes the relationships among social and physical phenomena in a particular study area.

Culture The body of customary beliefs, social forms, and material traits that together constitute a group's distinct tradition.

Custom The frequent repetition of an act, to the extent that it becomes characteristic of the group of people performing the act.

D

Dairy farm A form of commercial agriculture that specializes in the production of milk and other dairy products.

Demand The quantity of something that consumers are willing and able to buy.

Democracy A country in which citizens elect leaders and can run for office.

Demographic transition The process of change in a society's population from a condition of high crude birth and death rates and low rate of natural increase to a condition of low crude birth and death rates, low rate of natural increase, and higher total population.

Denglish A combination of Deutsch (the German word for German) and English.

Denomination A division of a branch that unites a number of local congregations into a single legal and administrative body.

Density The frequency with which something exists within a given unit of area.

Density gradient The change in density in an urban area from the center to the periphery.

Dependency ratio The number of people under age 15 and over age 64 compared to the number of people active in the labor force.

Desertification Degradation of land, especially in semiarid areas, primarily because of human actions such as excessive crop planting, animal grazing, and tree cutting. Also known as semiarid land degradation.

Developed country A country that has progressed relatively far along a continuum of development.

Developing country A country that is at a relatively early stage in the process of development.

Developing language A language spoken in daily use with a literary tradition that is not widely distributed.

Development A process of improvement in the conditions of people through diffusion of knowledge and technology.

Dialect A regional variety of a language distinguished by vocabulary, spelling, and pronunciation.

Dietary energy consumption The amount of food that an individual consumes, measured in kilocalories (calories in the United States).

Diffusion The process of spread of a feature or trend from one place to another over time.

Dispersed rural settlement A rural settlement pattern characterized by isolated farms rather than clustered villages.

Distance decay The diminished importance and eventual disappearance of a phenomenon with increasing distance from its origin.

Distribution The arrangement of something across Earth's surface.

Double cropping Harvesting twice a year from the same field.

Doubling time The number of years needed to double a population, assuming a constant rate of natural increase.

Dying language A language used by older people, but is not being transmitted to children.

E

Ebonics A dialect spoken by some African Americans.

Ecology The scientific study of ecosystems.

Economic base A community's collection of basic businesses.

Ecosystem A group of living organisms and the abiotic spheres with which they interact.

Ecumene The portion of Earth's surface occupied by permanent human settlement.

Edge city A node of office and retail activities on the edge of an urban area.

Elongated state A state with a long, narrow shape.

Emigration Migration from a location.

Enclosure movement The process of consolidating small landholdings into a smaller number of larger farms in England during the eighteenth century.

Endangered language A language at risk of extinction because it has few surviving speakers.

Environmental determinism A nineteenth- and early twentieth-century approach to the study of geography which argued that the general laws sought by human geographers could be found in the physical sciences. Geography was therefore the study of how the physical environment caused human activities.

Epidemiologic transition The process of change in the distinctive causes of death in each stage of the demographic transition.

Epidemiology The branch of medical science concerned with the incidence, distribution, and control of diseases that are prevalent among a population at a special time and are produced by some special causes not generally present in the affected locality.

Ethnic cleansing A purposeful policy designed by one ethnic or religious group to remove by violent and terror-inspiring means the civilian population of another ethnic or religious group from certain geographic areas.

Ethnic enclave A place with a high concentration of an ethnic group that is distinct from those in the surrounding area.

Ethnic religion A religion with a relatively concentrated spatial distribution whose principles are likely to be based on the physical characteristics of the particular location in which its adherents are concentrated.

Ethnicity Identity with a group of people who share the cultural traditions of a particular homeland or hearth.

Ethnoburb A suburban area with a cluster of a particular ethnic population.

Ethnophobia Fear of people of a particular ethnicity.

Expansion diffusion The spread of a feature or trend among people from one area to another in an additive process.

Extinct language A language that was once used by people in daily activities but is no longer used.

F

Fair trade A variation of international trade that provides greater equity to workers, small businesses, and consumers, focusing primarily on products exported from developing countries to developed countries.

Federal state An internal organization of a state that allocates most powers to units of local government.

Female labor force participation rate The percentage of women holding full-time jobs outside the home.

Filtering A process of change in the use of a house, from single-family owner occupancy to abandonment.

Fishing The capture of wild fish and other seafood living in the waters.

Floodplain The area subject to flooding during a given number of years, according to historical trends.

Folk culture Culture traditionally practiced by a small, homogeneous, rural group living in relative isolation from other groups.

Food desert An area that has a substantial amount of low-income residents and has poor access to a grocery store.

Food security Physical, social, and economic access at all times to safe and nutritious food sufficient to meet dietary needs and food preferences for an active and healthy life.

Fordist production A form of mass production in which each worker is assigned one specific task to perform repeatedly.

Foreign direct investment (FDI) Investment made by a foreign company in the economy of another country.

Formal region (or **uniform region**) An area in which most people share in one or more distinctive characteristics.

Fossil fuel An energy source formed from the residue of plants and animals buried millions of years ago.

Fragmented state A state that includes several discontinuous pieces of territory.

Franchise An agreement between a corporation and businesspeople to market that corporation's products in a local area.

Franglais A combination of français and anglais (the French words for French and English, respectively).

Frontier A zone separating two states in which neither state exercises political control.

Functional region (or **nodal region**) An area organized around a node or focal point.

Fundamentalism Literal interpretation and strict adherence to basic principles of a religion (or a religious branch, denomination, or congregation).

Fusion Creation of energy by joining the nuclei of two hydrogen atoms to form helium.

G

Galactic (or **peripheral) model** A model of North American urban areas consisting of an inner city surrounded by large suburban residential and business areas tied together by a beltway or ring road.

Gender Inequality Index (GII) An indicator constructed by the U.N. to measure the extent of each country's gender inequality in terms of reproductive health, empowerment, and the labor market.

Gender-related Development Index (GDI) An indicator constructed by the U.N. to measure the gender gap in the level of achievement in terms of income, education, and life expectancy.

Genetically modified organism (GMO) A living organism that possesses a novel combination of genetic material obtained through the use of modern biotechnology.

Genocide The mass killing of a group of people in an attempt to eliminate the entire group from existence.

Gentrification A process of converting an urban neighborhood from a predominantly low-income, renter-occupied area to a predominantly middle-class, owner-occupied area.

Geographic information science (GIScience) Analysis of data about Earth acquired through satellite and other electronic information technologies.

Geographic information system (GIS) A computer system that captures, stores, queries, and displays geographic data.

Geotagging Identification and storage of a piece of information by its precise latitude and longitude coordinates.

Geothermal energy Energy from steam or hot water produced from hot or molten underground rocks.

Gerrymandering The process of redrawing legislative boundaries for the purpose of benefiting the party in power.

Ghetto During the Middle Ages, a neighborhood in a city set up by law to be inhabited only by Jews; now used to denote a section of a city in which members of any minority group live because of social, legal, or economic pressure.

Global city A major center for the provision of services in the global economy.

Global Positioning System (GPS) A system that determines the precise position of something on Earth through a series of satellites, tracking stations, and receivers.

Globalization Actions or processes that involve entire world and result in making something worldwide in scope.

Grain Seed of a cereal grass.

Gravity model A model which holds that the potential use of a service at a particular location is directly related to the number of people in a location and inversely related to the distance people must travel to reach the service.

Green revolution Rapid diffusion of new agricultural technology, especially new high-yield seeds and fertilizers.

Greenhouse effect The anticipated increase in Earth's temperature caused by carbon dioxide (emitted by burning fossil fuels) trapping some of the radiation emitted by the surface.

Gross domestic product (GDP) The value of the total output of goods and services produced in a country in a year, not accounting for money that leaves and enters the country.

Gross national income (GNI) The value of the output of goods and services produced in a country in a year, including money that leaves and enters the country.

Guest worker A term once used for a worker who migrated to the developed countries of Northern and Western Europe, usually from Southern and Eastern Europe or from North Africa, in search of a higher-paying job.

H

Habit A repetitive act performed by a particular individual.

Hearth A center of innovation.

Hierarchical diffusion The spread of a feature or trend from one key person or node of authority or power to other persons or places.

Hierarchical religion A religion in which a central authority exercises a high degree of control.

Human Development Index (HDI) An indicator constructed by the U.N. to measure the level of development for a country through a combination of income, education, and life expectancy.

Hydraulic fracturing Pumping water at high pressure to break apart rocks and thereby release natural gas.

Hydroelectric power Power generated from moving water.

Hydrosphere All of the water on and near Earth's surface.

I

Immigration Migration to a new location.

Industrial Revolution A series of improvements in industrial technology that transformed the process of manufacturing goods.

Inequality-adjusted Human Development Index (IHDI) A modification of the HDI to account for inequality.

Infant mortality rate (IMR) The total number of deaths in a year among infants under 1 year of age for every 1,000 live births in a society.

Informal settlement An area within a city in a less developed country in which people illegally establish residences on land they do not own or rent and erect homemade structures.

Institutional language A language used in education, work, mass media, and government.

Intensive subsistence agriculture A form of subsistence agriculture characteristic of Asia's major population concentrations in which farmers must expend a relatively large amount of effort to produce the maximum feasible yield from a parcel of land.

Internal migration Permanent movement within a particular country.

Internally displaced person (IDP) Someone who has been forced to migrate for similar political reasons as a refugee but has not migrated across an international border.

International Date Line An arc that for the most part follows 180° longitude. When the International Date Line is crossed heading east (toward America), the clock moves back 24 hours, or one entire day. When it is crossed heading west (toward Asia), the calendar moves ahead one day.

International migration Permanent movement from one country to another.

Interregional migration Permanent movement from one region of a country to another.

Intervening obstacle An environmental or cultural feature of the landscape that hinders migration.

Intraregional migration Permanent movement within one region of a country.

Isogloss A boundary that separates regions in which different language usages predominate.

Isolated language A language that is unrelated to any other languages and therefore not attached to any language family.

J

Just-in-time delivery Shipment of parts and materials to arrive at a factory moments before they are needed.

L

Labor-intensive industry An industry for which labor costs comprise a high percentage of total expenses.

Landlocked state A state that does not have a direct outlet to the sea.

Language A system of communication through the use of speech, a collection of sounds understood by a group of people to have the same meaning.

Language branch A collection of languages related through a common ancestor that can be confirmed through archaeological evidence.

Language family A collection of languages related to each other through a common ancestor long before recorded history.

Language group A collection of languages within a branch that share a common origin in the relatively recent past and display relatively few differences in grammar and vocabulary.

Latitude The numbering system used to indicate the location of parallels drawn on a globe and measuring distance north and south of the equator (0°).

Life expectancy The average number of years an individual can be expected to live, given current social, economic, and medical conditions. Life expectancy at birth is the average number of years a newborn infant can expect to live.

Lingua franca A language mutually understood and commonly used in trade by people who have different native languages.

Literacy rate The percentage of a country's people who can read and write.

Literary tradition A language that is written as well as spoken.

Lithosphere Earth's crust and a portion of upper mantle directly below the crust.

Location The position of anything on Earth's surface.

Logogram A symbol that represents a word rather than a sound.

Longitude The numbering system used to indicate the location of meridians drawn on a globe and measuring distance east and west of the prime meridian (0°).

M

Map A two-dimensional, or flat, representation of Earth's surface or a portion of it.

Map scale The relationship between the size of an object on a map and the size of the actual feature on Earth's surface.

Maquiladora A factory built by a U.S. company in Mexico near the U.S. border, to take advantage of the much lower labor costs in Mexico.

Market area (or **hinterland)** The area surrounding a central place from which people are attracted to use the place's goods and services.

Mashup A map that overlays data from one source on top of a map provided by a mapping service.

Maternal mortality rate The annual number of female deaths per 100,000 live births from any cause related to or aggravated by pregnancy or its management (excluding accidental or incidental causes).

Medical revolution Medical technology invented in Europe and North America that has diffused to the poorer countries in Latin America, Asia, and Africa. Improved medical practices have eliminated many of the traditional causes of death in poorer countries and enabled more people to live longer and healthier lives.

Megalopolis A continuous urban complex in the northeastern United States.

Mental map A representation of a portion of Earth's surface based on what an individual knows about a place that contains personal impressions of what is in the place and where the place is located.

Meridian An arc drawn on a map between the North and South poles.

Metropolitan statistical area (MSA) In the United States, an urbanized area of at least 50,000 population, the county within which the city is located, and adjacent counties meeting one of several tests indicating a functional connection to the central city.

Microfinance Provision of small loans and financial services to individuals and small businesses in developing countries.

Micropolitan statistical area (μSA) An urbanized area of between 10,000 and 50,000 inhabitants, the county in which it is located, and adjacent counties tied to the city.

Microstate A state that encompasses a very small land area.

Migration A form of relocation diffusion involving a permanent move to a new location.

Migration transition A change in the migration pattern in a society that results from industrialization, population growth, and other social and economic changes that also produce the demographic transition.

Milkshed The area surrounding a city from which milk is supplied.

Millennium Development Goals Eight goals adopted by the U.N. in 2002 to reduce disparities between developed and developing countries by 2015.

Missionary An individual who helps to diffuse a universalizing religion.

Mixed crop and livestock farming Commercial farming characterized by integration of crops and livestock; most of the crops are fed to animals rather than consumed directly by humans.

Monotheism The doctrine of or belief in the existence of only one God.

Multinational state A state that contains two or more cultural groups with traditions of self-determination that agree to coexist peacefully by recognizing each other as distinct nationalities.

Multiple nuclei model A model of the internal structure of cities in which social groups are arranged around a collection of nodes of activities.

N

Nation A large group of people who are united by common cultural characteristics, such as language and ethnicity, or by shared history.

Nation-state A state whose territory corresponds to that occupied by a particular nation.

Nationalism Loyalty and devotion to a particular nationality.

Nationality Identity with a group of people who share legal attachment to a particular country.

Natural increase rate (NIR) The percentage growth of a population in a year, computed as the crude birth rate minus the crude death rate.

Net migration The difference between the level of immigration and the level of emigration.

Network A chain of communication that connects places.

New international division of labor Transfer of some types of jobs, especially those requiring low-paid, less-skilled workers, from developed to developing countries.

No tillage A farming practice that leaves all of the soil undisturbed and the entire residue of the previous year's harvest left untouched on the fields.

Nonbasic business A business that sells its products primarily to consumers in the community.

Nonconsumptive water usage The use of water that is returned to nature as a liquid.

Nonpoint source pollution Pollution that originates from a large, diffuse area.

Nonrenewable resource Something produced in nature more slowly than it is consumed by humans.

O

Official language The language adopted for use by a government for the conduct of business and publication of documents.

Outsourcing A decision by a corporation to turn over much of the responsibility for production to independent suppliers.

Overfishing Capturing fish faster than they can reproduce.

Overpopulation A situation in which the number of people in an area exceeds the capacity of the environment to support life at a decent standard of living.

Ozone A gas that absorbs ultraviolet solar radiation, found in the stratosphere, a zone between 15 to 50 kilometers (9 to 30 miles) above Earth's surface.

P

Paddy The Malay word for wet rice, increasingly used to describe a flooded field.

Pandemic Disease that occurs over a wide geographic area and affects a very high proportion of the population.

Parallel A circle drawn around the globe parallel to the equator and at right angles to the meridians.

Participatory GIS (PGIS) Community-based mapping, representing local knowledge and information.

Passive solar energy systems Solar energy systems that collect energy without the use of mechanical devices.

Pastoral nomadism A form of subsistence agriculture based on herding domesticated animals.

Pattern The geometric or regular arrangement of something in a particular area.

Perforated state A state that completely surrounds another one.

Periodic market A collection of individual vendors who come together to offer goods and services in a location on specified days.

Photochemical smog An atmospheric condition formed through a combination of weather conditions and pollution, especially from motor vehicle emissions.

Photogrammetry The science of taking measurements of Earth's surface from photographs.

Photovoltaic cell A solar energy cell, usually made from silicon, that collects solar rays to generate electricity.

Physiological density The number of people per unit area of arable land, which is land suitable for agriculture.

Pidgin language A form of speech that adopts a simplified grammar and limited vocabulary of a lingua franca; used for communications among speakers of two different languages.

Pilgrimage A journey to a place considered sacred for religious purposes.

Place A specific point on Earth, distinguished by a particular characteristic.

Plantation A large farm in tropical and subtropical climates that specializes in the production of one or two crops for sale, usually to a more developed country.

Point source pollution Pollution that enters a body of water from a specific source.

Polder Land that the Dutch have created by draining water from an area.

Pollution Concentration of waste added to air, water, or land at a greater level than occurs in average air, water, or land.

Polytheism Belief in or worship of more than one god.

Popular culture Culture found in a large, heterogeneous society that shares certain habits despite differences in other personal characteristics.

Population pyramid A bar graph that represents the distribution of population by age and sex.

Possibilism The theory that the physical environment may set limits on human actions, but people have the ability to adjust to the physical environment and choose a course of action from many alternatives.

Post-Fordist production Adoption by companies of flexible work rules, such as the allocation of workers to teams that perform a variety of tasks.

Potential reserve The amount of energy in deposits not yet identified but thought to exist.

Potential support ratio (or elderly support ratio) The number of working-age people (ages 15 to 64) divided by the number of persons 65 and older.

Preservation The maintenance of resources in their present condition, with as little human impact as possible.

Primary sector The portion of the economy concerned with the direct extraction of materials from Earth, generally through agriculture.

Primate city The largest settlement in a country, if it has more than twice as many people as the second-ranking settlement.

Primate city rule A pattern of settlements in a country such that the largest settlement has more than twice as many people as the second-ranking settlement.

Prime meridian The meridian, designated as 0° longitude, that passes through the Royal Observatory at Greenwich, England.

Productivity The value of a particular product compared to the amount of labor needed to make it.

Projection A system used to transfer locations from Earth's surface to a flat map.

Prorupted state An otherwise compact state with a large projecting extension.

Proven reserve The amount of a resource remaining in discovered deposits.

Public service A service offered by the government to provide security and protection for citizens and businesses.

Pull factor A factor that induces people to move to a new location.

Purchasing power parity (PPP) The amount of money needed in one country to purchase the same goods and services in another country.

Push factor A factor that induces people to leave old residences.

Q

Quota In reference to migration, a law that places maximum limits on the number of people who can immigrate to a country each year.

R

Race Identity with a group of people who are perceived to share a physiological trait, such as skin color.

Racism The belief that race is the primary determinant of human traits and capacities and that racial differences produce an inherent superiority of a particular race.

Racist A person who subscribes to the beliefs of racism.

Ranching A form of commercial agriculture in which livestock graze over an extensive area.

Range (of a service) The maximum distance people are willing to travel to use a service.

Rank-size rule A pattern of settlements in a country such that the nth largest settlement is 1/n the population of the largest settlement.

Recycling The separation, collection, processing, marketing, and reuse of unwanted material.

Redlining A process by which financial institutions draw red-colored lines on a map and refuse to lend money for people to purchase or improve property within the lines.

Refugees People who are forced to migrate from their home country and cannot return for fear of persecution because of their race, religion, nationality, membership in a social group, or political opinion.

Region An area distinguished by one or more distinctive characteristics.

Relocation diffusion The spread of a feature or trend through bodily movement of people from one place to another.

Remittance Transfer of money by workers to people in the country from which they emigrated.

Remote sensing The acquisition of data about Earth's surface from a satellite orbiting the planet or from other long-distance methods.

Renewable resource Something produced in nature more rapidly than it is consumed by humans.

Resource A substance in the environment that is useful to people, is economically and technologically feasible to access, and is socially acceptable to use.

Ridge tillage A system of planting crops on ridge tops in order to reduce farm production costs and promote greater soil conservation.

Right-to-work law A law in some U.S. states that prevents a union and a company from negotiating a contract that requires workers to join the union as a condition of employment.

Rush hour The four consecutive 15-minute periods in the morning and evening with the heaviest volumes of traffic.

S

Sanitary landfill A place to deposit solid waste, where a layer of earth is bulldozed over garbage each day to reduce emissions of gases and odors from the decaying trash, to minimize fires, and to discourage vermin.

Sawah A flooded field for growing rice.

Scale The relationship between the portion of Earth being studied and Earth as a whole.

Secondary sector The portion of the economy concerned with manufacturing useful products through processing, transforming, and assembling raw materials.

Sector model A model of the internal structure of cities in which social groups are arranged around a series of sectors, or wedges, radiating out from the central business district.

Self-determination The concept that ethnicities have the right to govern themselves.

Service Any activity that fulfills a human want or need and returns money to those who provide it.

Settlement A permanent collection of buildings and inhabitants.

Sex ratio The number of males per 100 females in the population.

Sharecropper A person who works fields rented from a landowner and pays the rent and repays loans by turning over to the landowner a share of the crops.

Shifting cultivation A form of subsistence agriculture in which people shift activity from one field to another; each field is used for crops for a relatively few years and left fallow for a relatively long period.

Site The physical character of a place.

Site factors Location factors related to the costs of factors of production inside a plant, such as land, labor, and capital.

Situation The location of a place relative to another place.

Situation factors Location factors related to the transportation of materials into and from a factory.

Smart growth Legislation and regulations to limit suburban sprawl and preserve farmland.

Social area analysis Statistical analysis used to identify where people of similar living standards, ethnic background, and lifestyle live within an urban area.

Social construction An idea or a meaning that is widely accepted as natural by a society but may not represent a reality shared by those outside the society.

Solstice An astronomical event that happens twice each year, when the tilt of Earth's axis is most inclined toward or away from the Sun, causing the Sun's apparent position in the sky to reach its northernmost or southernmost extreme, and resulting in the shortest and longest days of the year.

Sovereignty Ability of a state to govern its territory free from control of its internal affairs by other states.

Space The physical gap or interval between two objects.

Space-time compression The reduction in the time it takes to diffuse something to a distant place as a result of improved communications and transportation systems.

Spanglish A combination of Spanish and English spoken by Hispanic Americans.

Spatial association The relationship between the distribution of one feature and the distribution of another feature.

Sprawl Development of new housing sites at relatively low density and at locations that are not contiguous to the existing built-up area.

State An area organized into a political unit and ruled by an established government that has control over its internal and foreign affairs.

Stimulus diffusion The spread of an underlying principle.

Structural adjustment program Economic policies imposed on less developed countries by international agencies to create conditions that encourage international trade.

Subsistence agriculture Agriculture designed primarily to provide food for direct consumption by the farmer and the farmer's family.

Suburb A residential or commercial area situated within an urban area but outside the central city.

Supply The quantity of something that producers have available for sale.

Sustainability The use of Earth's renewable and nonrenewable natural resources in ways that do not constrain resource use in the future.

Sustainable development Development that meets the needs of the present without compromising the ability of future generations to meet their own needs.

Sustainable Development Goals Seventeen goals adopted by the U.N. in 2015 to reduce disparities between developed and developing countries by 2030.

Syncretic Combining several religious traditions.

Syncretism The combining of elements of two groups into a new cultural feature.

T

Taboo A restriction on behavior imposed by social custom.

Terroir The contribution of a location's distinctive physical features to the way food tastes.

Terrorism The systematic use of violence by a group calculated to create an atmosphere of fear and alarm among a population or to coerce a government into actions it would not otherwise undertake or refrain from actions it wants to take.

Tertiary sector The portion of the economy concerned with transportation, communications, and utilities, sometimes extended to the provision of all goods and services to people in exchange for payment.

Textile A fabric made by weaving, used in making clothing.

Threatened language A language used for face-to-face communication, but is losing users.

Threshold The minimum number of people needed to support a service.

Toponym The name given to a portion of Earth's surface.

Total fertility rate (TFR) The average number of children a woman will have throughout her childbearing years.

Transnational corporation A company that conducts research, operates factories, and sells products in many countries, not just where its headquarters or shareholders are located.

Triangular slave trade A practice, primarily during the eighteenth century, in which European ships transported slaves from Africa to Caribbean islands, molasses from the Caribbean to Europe, and trade goods from Europe to Africa.

Truck farming Commercial gardening and fruit farming, so named for the Middle English word truck, meaning "barter" or "exchange of commodities."

U

Unauthorized immigrant A person who enters a country without proper documents to do so.

Underclass A group in society prevented from participating in the material benefits of a more developed society because of a variety of social and economic disadvantages.

Undernourishment Dietary energy consumption that is continuously below the minimum requirement for maintaining a healthy life and carrying out light physical activity.

Uneven development The increasing gap in economic conditions between core and peripheral regions as a result of the globalization of the economy.

Unitary state An internal organization of a state that places most power in the hands of central government officials.

Universalizing religion A religion that attempts to appeal to all people, not just those living in a particular location.

Urban area A dense core of census tracts, densely settled suburbs, and low-density land that links the dense suburbs with the core.

Urban cluster In the United States, an urban area with between 2,500 and 50,000 inhabitants.

Urbanization An increase in the percentage of the number of people living in urban settlements.

Urbanized area In the United States, an urban area with at least 50,000 inhabitants.

Utopian settlement A community built around an ideal way of life, often based on a religion.

V

Value added The gross value of a product minus the costs of raw materials and energy.

Vernacular region (or **perceptual region**) An area that people believe exists as part of their cultural identity.

Vertical integration An approach typical of traditional mass production in which a company controls all phases of a highly complex production process.

Vigorous language A language that is spoken in daily use but that lacks a literary tradition.

Volunteered geographic information (VGI) Creation and dissemination of geographic data contributed voluntarily and for free by individuals.

W

Wet rice Rice planted on dry land in a nursery and then moved to a deliberately flooded field to promote growth.

X

Xenophobia Fear of people who are from other countries.

Z

Zero population growth (ZPG) A decline of the total fertility rate to the point where the natural increase rate equals zero.

Credits

Note: Uncredited maps and figures, International Mapping/Pearson Education, Inc.

Front Matter p. xxiv: Courtesy of Corey Brincks; p. xxv: Courtesy of Stuart Jackman; p. xxviii: Courtesy of James M. Rubenstein

Chapter 1 CO1.1: Byambasuren Byamba-Ochir/AFP/Getty Images; CO1.2: Aerial Archives/Alamy Stock Photo; CO1.3: Aleksey Boldin/Alamy Stock Photo; CO1.4: Art Collection 4/Alamy Stock Photo; CO1.5: V. Dorosz/Alamy Stock Photo; 1.1.1: Adek Berry/Getty Images; 1.1.2: AGF Srl/Alamy Stock Photo; 1.1.5: FLUEELER URS/Alamy Stock Photo; 1.1.6: Friedrich Stark/Alamy Stock Photo; 1.1.7: John Crux Photography/Getty Images; 1.2.1: Mauricio Abreu/Getty Images; 1.2.2: North Wind Picture Archives/Alamy Stock Photo; 1.2.3: Art Collection 4/Alamy Stock Photo; 1.2.4: Everett Collection, Inc./Alamy Stock Photo; 1.3.1: Bloomberg/Getty Images; 1.3.2: Timothy A. Clary/Getty Images; 1.3.3: Andrew Lloyd/Alamy Stock Photo; 1.3.4: Bruce D'Arcus, Chair, Dept. of Geography, Miami University; 1.4.1: Cameron Davidson/Getty Images; 1.4.2: Michael Spring/Alamy Stock Photo; 1.5.1: Gary Cook/Alamy Stock Photo; 1.5.4: Science History Images/Alamy Stock Photo; 1.6.1: David South/Alamy Stock Photo; 1.6.3a: Aerial Archives/Alamy Stock Photo; 1.6.3b: Ali Kabas/Alamy Stock Photo; 1.7.1: Saul Loeb/staff/Getty Images; 1.7.3: JeffG/Alamy Stock Photo; 1.7.6: Kevin Kipper/Alamy Stock Photo; 1.8.1: V. Dorosz/Alamy Stock Photo; 1.9.1: Jim Wark/Getty Images; 1.10.1: David R. Frazier Photolibrary, Inc./Alamy Stock Photo; 1.11.2: Thomas Koehler/Getty Images; 1.11.6: Aleksey Boldin/Alamy Stock Photo; 1.11.7: Pixellover RM 10/Alamy Stock Photo; 1.12.2: Dennis MacDonald/Alamy Stock Photo; 1.12.3: incamerastock/Alamy Stock Photo; 1.12.4: John Anderson/Alamy Stock Photo; 1.12.6: Rolf Nussbaumer Photography/Alamy Stock Photo; 1.13.1a: Colin Underhill/Alamy Stock Photo; 1.13.1b: Rosemarie Stennull/Alamy Stock Photo; 1.13.3: California DWR/Alamy Stock Photo; 1.13.4: Scott London/Alamy Stock Photo; 1.13.6: Source: Courtesy of Climate Central; 1.CR.1: Jeff Greenberg 6 of 6/Alamy Stock Photo; 1.CR.2: Jim West/Alamy Stock Photo; 1.CR.3: Kip Evans/Alamy Stock Photo; 1.CR.4: Louise Murray/Alamy Stock Photo; 1.CR.5: BBC Worldwide Americas, Inc.; 1.CR.7: Rhonda Gutenberg/Getty Images; 1.CR.8: robertharding/Alamy Stock Photo

Chapter 02 CO2.1: Ruby/Alamy Stock Photo; CO2.2: E.D. Torial/Alamy Stock Photo; CO2.3: Agencja Fotograficzna Caro/Alamy Stock Photo; CO2.4: Jake Lyell/Alamy Stock Photo; CO2.5: robertharding/Alamy Stock Photo; 2.1.1: Tomohiro Ohsumi/Getty Images; 2.1.5: Robert Harding/Alamy Stock Photo; 2.2.1: Frans Lemmens/Alamy Stock Photo; 2.3.6: E.D. Torial/Alamy Stock Photo; 2.4.2: Ian Dagnall/Alamy Stock Photo; 2.4.3: Liba Taylor/Getty Images; 2.4.4: Cultura Creative (RF)/Alamy Stock Photo; 2.4.5: Stock Connection Blue/Alamy Stock Photo; 2.5.1: Tom Salyer/Alamy Stock Photo; 2.5.4: Liba Taylor/Alamy Stock Photo; 2.7.3: Marmaduke St. John/Alamy Stock Photo; 2.7.6: Amelie Benoist/AGE Fotostock; 2.8.1: Prisma by Dukas Presseagentur GmbH/Alamy Stock Photo; 2.9.1: dbimages/Alamy Stock Photo; 2.9.3: Dinodia Photos/Alamy Stock Photo; 2.9.4: Alan Gignoux/Alamy Stock Photo; 2.10.3: Wilmar Photography/Alamy Stock Photo; 2.11.1: Ami Vitale/Alamy Stock Photo; 2.12.1: Jake Lyell/Alamy Stock Photo; 2.12.4: Brendan Donnelly/Alamy Stock Photo; 2.CR.1: Cultura-lEyes - AusGS2/Alamy Stock Photo; 2.CR.2: Hero Images Inc./Alamy Stock Photo; 2.CR.3: Sean Pavone/Alamy Stock Photo; 2.CR.4: Visions of America, LLC/Alamy Stock Photo; p. 60 (GeoVideo): BBC Worldwide Americas, Inc.; 2.CR.6: Image Source/Alamy Stock Photo

Chapter 03 CO3.1: Carl Court/Staff/Getty Images; CO3.2: 67photo/Alamy Stock Photo; CO3.3: Historical/Getty Images; CO3.4: PETER PARKS/Getty Images; CO3.5: ZUMA Press, Inc./Alamy Stock Photo; 3.1.1: John Moore/Getty Images; 3.1.3: Trinity Mirror/Mirrorpix/Alamy Stock Photo; 3.2.1: Historical/Getty Images; 3.2.2: The Protected Art Archive/Alamy Stock Photo; 3.2.5: Library of Congress/Handout/Getty Images; 3.3.1: Library of Congress/Contributor/Getty Images; 3.3.7: PETER PARKS/Getty Images; 3.4.1: Vince Bevan/Alamy Stock Photo; 3.4.4: cascoly/Alamy Stock Photo; 3.4.6: Mike Shipman/Alamy Stock Photo; 3.5.1: Andre Jenny/Alamy Stock Photo; 3.5.2: Terry Smith Images/Alamy Stock Photo; 3.5.6: imageBROKER/Alamy Stock Photo; 3.6.1: frans lemmens/Alamy Stock Photo; 3.6.3: ZUMA Press, Inc./Alamy Stock Photo; 3.7.1: Xinhua/Alamy Stock Photo; 3.7.2: ZUMA Press, Inc./Alamy Stock Photo; 3.7.5: Marmaduke St. John/Alamy Stock Photo; 3.8.1: image/Alamy Stock Photo; 3.8.3: Bettmann/Getty Images; 3.8.4: Norma Jean Gargasz/Alamy Stock Photo; 3.9.1: HERIKA MARTINEZ/AFP/Getty Images; 3.9.4: Julio Etchart/Alamy Stock Photo; 3.9.5: Mauro Ladu/Alamy Stock Photo; 3.9.6: Gary Moon/Alamy Stock Photo; 3.9.7: Sunpix Travel/Alamy Stock Photo; 3.10.2: 67photo/Alamy Stock Photo; 3.10.3: amer ghazzal/Alamy Stock Photo; 3.CR.1: Chuck Pefley/Alamy Stock Photo; 3.CR.2: Hero Images Inc./Alamy Stock Photo; 3.CR.3: Keith Dannemiller/Alamy Stock Photo; 3.CR.5: trekkerimages/Alamy Stock Photo; p. 85 (GeoVideo): BBC Worldwide Americas, Inc.

Chapter 04 CO4.1: NurPhoto/Contributor/Getty Images; CO4.2: Anjo Kan/Alamy Stock Photo; CO4.3: Joerg Boethling/Alamy Stock Photo; CO4.4: Thomas Cockrem/Alamy Stock Photo; CO4.5: Yawar Nazir/Getty Images; 4.1.1: Arterra Picture Library/Alamy Stock Photo; 4.1.2: MediaPunch Inc/Alamy Stock Photo; 4.1.3: Thomas Cockrem/Alamy Stock Photo; 4.1.5a: Dinodia Photos/Alamy Stock Photo; 4.1.5b: Michael Grant Travel/Alamy Stock Photo; 4.1.5c: Mpc92/Fotolia; 4.1.5d: pboehringer/Getty Images; 4.2.1: David Page/Alamy Stock Photo; p. 90 (text): From John Blacking and Joann W. Kealiinohomoku, eds., The Performing Arts: Music and Dance (The Hague: Mouton, 1979), 144.; 4.2.2: Hoang Dinh Nam/Getty Images; 4.2.4: Google - Map data, https://googledataorg.carto.com/u/googledata/viz/1500f20a-782f-11e5-8b78-42010a14800d/embed_map; 4.3.3: PCN Photography/Alamy Stock Photo; 4.3.5: ZUMA Press, Inc./Alamy Stock Photo; 4.4.1a: Anadolu Agency/Getty Images; 4.4.1b: Anjo Kan/Alamy Stock Photo; 4.4.2: Godong/AGE Fotostock; 4.4.5: Fairfax Media/Getty Images; 4.4.6: Marco Secchi/Alamy Stock Photo; 4.5.1a: Historic American Buildings Survey (Library of Congress); 4.5.1b: James M. Rubenstein; 4.5.1c: OlegAlbinsky/Getty Images; 4.5.2: GUY Christian/hemis.fr/Getty Images; 4.6.4: Joerg Boethling/Alamy Stock Photo; 4.7.1: JHPhoto/Alamy Stock Photo; 4.7.6: PhotoEdit/Alamy Stock Photo; 4.8.2: Entertainment Pictures/Alamy Stock Photo; 4.9.1: Barcroft Media/Contributor/Getty Images; 4.9.3: ALEX OGLE/Staff/Getty Images; 4.10.1: H. Mark Weidman Photography/Alamy Stock Photo; 4.10.3: Yawar Nazir/Getty Images; 4.10.4: Angry Brides is an Anti-dowry initiative by Shaadi.com, the World's No.1 Matchmaking Service; 4.11.1: F.Bettex - Mysterra.org/Alamy Stock Photo; 4.11.2: Willy Matheisl/Alamy Stock Photo; 4.11.3: Jim West/Alamy Stock Photo; 4.CR.1: Marc F. Henning/Alamy Stock Photo; 4.CR.2: Michael Kemp/Alamy Stock Photo; 4.CR.3: Robin Lund/Alamy Stock Photo; 4.CR.4: Vlincenzo Pinto/Staff/Getty Images; 4.CR.5: Dennis Cox/Alamy Stock Photo; p. 111 (GeoVideo): BBC Worldwide Americas, Inc.

Chapter 05 CO5.1: tunart/Getty Images; CO5.2: Andrey Kekyalyaynen/Alamy Stock Photo; CO5.4: Basque Country - Mark Baynes/Alamy Stock Photo; CO5.5: imageBROKER/Alamy Stock Photo;

5.1.1: LHB Photo/Alamy Stock Photo; 5.2.1: Andrey Kekyalyaynen/Alamy Stock Photo; 5.2.3: Israel by Blake-Ezra Cole/Alamy Stock Photo; 5.3.5: ITAR-TASS Photo Agency/Alamy Stock Photo; 5.5.1: Charles O. Cecil/Alamy Stock Photo; 5.6.1: Ian M Butterfield (Yorkshire)/Alamy Stock Photo; 5.7.1: imageBROKER/Alamy Stock Photo; 5.7.2: James Brunker/Alamy Stock Photo; 5.7.3: Christopher Canty Photography/Alamy Stock Photo; 5.8.4: imageBROKER/Alamy Stock Photo; 5.9.4: Basque Country - Mark Baynes/Alamy Stock Photo; 5.10.3: Alex Segre/Alamy Stock Photo; 5.10.4: Ira Berger/Alamy Stock Photo; 5.10.2: 5.CR.1: Elizabeth Leyden/Alamy Stock Photo; 5.CR.2: ITAR-TASS Photo Agency/Alamy Stock Photo; 5.CR.3: Jim West/Alamy Stock Photo; p. 134 (GeoVideo) BBC Worldwide Americas, Inc.; 5.CR.7: Skyfish/Alamy Stock Photo

Chapter 06 CO6.1: Lee Thomas/Alamy Stock Photo; CO6.2: Aerial Archives/Alamy Stock Photo; CO6.3: Arco Images GmbH/Alamy Stock Photo; CO6.4: Art Directors & TRIP/Alamy Stock Photo; CO6.5: P.Spiro/Alamy Stock Photo; 6.1.1: Lankowsky/Alamy Stock Photo; 6.2.1: Nico Stengert/AGE Fotostock; 6.2.3: Sean Pavone/Alamy Stock Photo; 6.2.1: Paul Springett D/Alamy Stock Photo; 6.3.3: Photosindia/Alamy Stock Photo; 6.4.1: Arco Images GmbH/Alamy Stock Photo; 6.5.1: Robert Preston/Alamy Stock Photo; 6.5.5: imageBROKER/Alamy Stock Photo; 6.6.1: Hakbong Kwon/Alamy Stock Photo; 6.6.2: Vladimir Gerasimov/Alamy Stock Photo; 6.6.3: Art Directors & TRIP/Alamy Stock Photo; 6.6.4: DANIEL GREENHOUSE/Alamy Stock Photo; 6.9.1: Jan Wlodarczyk/Alamy Stock Photo; 6.9.2: Randy Duchaine/Alamy Stock Photo; 6.9.3: Tom Hanslien Photography/Alamy Stock Photo; 6.10.1: Iain Masterton/Alamy Stock Photo; 6.10.3: Aerial Archives/Alamy Stock Photo; 6.11.1: roger askew/Alamy Stock Photo; 6.11.2: Tim Graham/Alamy Stock Photo; 6.11.3: Ira Berger/Alamy Stock Photo; 6.11.4: Sourabh Gandhi/Alamy Stock Photo; 6.12.1: DestinationImages/Alamy Stock Photo; 6.12.2: Raj Singh/Alamy Stock Photo; 6.12.3: Cícero Castro/Alamy Stock Photo; 6.12.4: Xinhua/Alamy Stock Photo; 6.13.1: P.Spiro/Alamy Stock Photo; 6.CR.1: Valentin Sama-Rojo/Alamy Stock Photo; 6.CR.2: Wai Kit Wong/Alamy Stock Photo; 6.CR.3: Xinhua/Alamy Stock Photo; p. 165 (GeoVideo): BBC Worldwide Americas, Inc.; 6.CR.5: Mawardi Bahar/Alamy Stock Photo

Chapter 07 CO7.1: Anadolu Agency/Contributor/Getty Images; CO7.2: FRANCK FIFE/Staff/Getty Images; CO7.3: North Wind Picture Archives/Alamy Stock Photo; CO7.4: Roger Hutchings/Alamy Stock Photo; CO7.5: Tony French/Alamy Stock Photo; 7.1.1: JAG IMAGES/Getty Images; 7.1.2: Jim West/Alamy Stock Photo; 7.1.5: Vibrant Pictures/Alamy Stock Photo; 7.2.4: dbimages/Alamy Stock Photo; 7.3.1: Patrick Ward/Alamy Stock Photo; 7.3.5: Tony French/Alamy Stock Photo; 7.4.3: North Wind Picture Archives/Alamy Stock Photo; 7.5.1: Elliott Erwitt/Magnum Photos; 7.5.2: National Archives/Handout/Getty Images; 7.5.4: Peter Jordan/Alamy Stock Photo; 7.6.1: Franck Fife/Staff/Getty Images; 7.6.2: Steve Liss/Getty Images; 7.6.4: Sebastian Meyer/Contributor/Getty Images; 7.6.5: David Grossman/Alamy Stock Photo; 7.7.1: Andy Bush/Alamy Stock Photo; 7.7.2: ITAR-TASS Photo Agency/Alamy Stock Photo; 7.7.3: PACIFIC PRESS/Alamy Stock Photo; 7.8.2: imageBROKER/Alamy Stock Photo; 7.8.3: J Marshall-Tribaleye Images/Alamy Stock Photo; 7.8.4: Julia Maudlin/Alamy Stock Photo; 7.9.2a: Agencja Fotograficzna Caro/Alamy Stock Photo; 7.9.2b: Aleksandar Todorovic/Shutterstock; 7.9.2c: Martin Mayer/Alamy Stock Photo; 7.9.3: Roger Hutchings/Alamy Stock Photo; 7.10.1: Azim Khan Ronnie/Alamy Stock Photo; 7.10.3: AfriPics.com/Alamy Stock Photo;7.CR.1: Brigette Supernova/Alamy Stock Photo; 7.CR.2: Diriye Amey/Alamy Stock Photo; 7.CR.3: Kaan Diskaya/Alamy Stock Photo; 7.CR.4: Waclaw Mostowski/EyeEm/Getty Images; 7.CR.6: age fotostock/Alamy Stock Photo; p. 189 (GeoVideo): BBC Worldwide Americas, Inc.

Chapter 08 CO8.1: Luis Tato/Contributor/Getty Images; CO8.2: David R. Frazier Photolibrary, Inc./Alamy Stock Photo; CO8.4: Henryk Sadura/Alamy Stock Photo; CO8.5: Mark Thomas/Alamy Stock Photo; 8.1.1: Mark Philips/Getty Images; 8.1.2: Henryk Sadura/Alamy Stock Photo; 8.1.4: Matthew Oldfield Editorial Photography/Alamy Stock Photo; 8.2.1: National Geographic Creative/Alamy Stock Photo; 8.2.2: PlanetObserver/Science Source; 8.3.2: Images & Stories/Alamy Stock Photo; 8.4.2: ZUMA Press, Inc./Alamy Stock Photo; 8.5.1: Jeff Morgan 12/Alamy Stock Photo; 8.6.1: David R. Frazier Photolibrary, Inc./Alamy Stock Photo; 8.6.3: Marcin Jamkowski/Adventure Pictures/Alamy Stock Photo; 8.6.6: Michael Wheatley/Alamy Stock Photo; 8.8.1: Julian Elliott/Alamy Stock Photo; 8.8.2: Rubens Alarcon/Alamy Stock Photo; 8.10.3: Mark Thomas/Alamy Stock Photo; 8.10.4: Martyn Evans/Alamy Stock Photo; 8.11.1: Bill Bachmann/Alamy Stock Photo; 8.11.2: Laperruque/Alamy Stock Photo; 8.11.5: Taylor Hill/Getty Images; 8.CR.1: Eike Leppert/Alamy Stock Photo; 8.CR.4: kpzfot/Alamy Stock Photo; Andia/Alamy Stock Photo; p. 214 (GeoVideo): BBC Worldwide Americas, Inc.

Chapter 09 CO9.1: Oleksandr Rupeta/Alamy Stock Photo; CO9.3: John Warburton-Lee Photography/Alamy Stock Photo; CO9.4: MBI/Alamy Stock Photo; CO9.5: Norma Jean Gargasz/Alamy Stock Photo; 9.9.1: John Warburton-Lee Photography/Alamy Stock Photo; 9.2.1: Neil Cooper/Alamy Stock Photo; 9.2.3: 9.2.4: FLPA/Alamy Stock Photo; 9.2.5: Jake Lyell/Alamy Stock Photo; 9.3.1: JeffG/Alamy Stock Photo; 9.3.5: { TWHPhotography }/Alamy Stock Photo; 9.4.3: B Christopher/Alamy Stock Photo; 9.4.4: Jake Lyell/Alamy Stock Photo; 9.4.5: 9.4.8: MBI/Alamy Stock Photo; 9.5.2: Design Pics Inc/Alamy Stock Photo; 9.6.1: Daniel J. Rao/Alamy Stock Photo; 9.6.3: Mostardi Photography/Alamy Stock Photo; 9.7.1: John Zada/Alamy Stock Photo; 9.7.6: Parawat Isarangura Na Ayudhaya/Alamy Stock Photo; 9.9.1: Sue Cunningham Photographic/Alamy Stock Photo; 9.10.1: Kevin Foy/Alamy Stock Photo; 9.10.5: Dairy Data, United States Department of Agriculture Economic Research Service, http://www.ers.usda.gov/data-products/dairy-data.aspx; 9.10.4: Joerg Boethling/Alamy Stock Photo; 238: Jim West/Alamy Stock Photo; 9.11.2: Jon Lovette/Alamy Stock Photo; 9.11.5: MediaWorldImages/Alamy Stock Photo; 9.CR.2: Justin Sullivan/Staff/Getty Images; 9.CR.3: robertharding/Alamy Stock Photo; 9.CR.4: Takahiro Yumada/Alamy Stock Photo; NA: ninetwobysix/Stockimo/Alamy Stock Photo; p. 240 (GeoVideo): BBC Worldwide Americas, Inc.

Chapter 10 CO10.1: jbdodane/Alamy Stock Photo; CO10.2: Friedrich Stark/Alamy Stock Photo; CO10.3: Joerg Boethling/Alamy Stock Photo; CO10.4: Mike Goldwater/Alamy Stock Photo; 10.1.1: Chris Pancewicz/Alamy Stock Photo; 10.1.3a: Boris Stroujko/Alamy Stock Photo; 10.1.3b: David Keith Brown/Alamy Stock Photo; 10.1.3c: dpa picture alliance/Alamy Stock Photo; 10.1.3d: Galit Seligmann/Alamy Stock Photo; 10.1.3e: Ian Dagnall/Alamy Stock Photo; 10.1.3f: PACIFIC PRESS/Alamy Stock Photo; 10.1.3g: philipus/Alamy Stock Photo; 10.1.3h: Sean Pavone/Alamy Stock Photo; 10.1.3i: Steve Taylor ARPS/Alamy Stock Photo; 10.2.6: Mike Goldwater/Alamy Stock Photo; 10.3.1: Jake Lyell/Alamy Stock Photo; 10.3.2: Media for Medical SARL/Alamy Stock Photo; 10.4.5: Mike Goldwater/Alamy Stock Photo; 10.5.1: Friedrich Stark/Alamy Stock Photo; 10.5.6: Kathy deWitt/Alamy Stock Photo; 10.7.1: dbimages/Alamy Stock Photo; 10.7.2: Pep Roig/Alamy Stock Photo; 10.7.3: dbimages/Alamy Stock Photo; 10.7.4: Ivan Batinic/Alamy Stock Photo; 10.7.5: Prasit Rodphan/Alamy Stock Photo; 10.8.2: Sergey Novikov/Alamy Stock Photo; 10.8.4: Ron Yue/Alamy Stock Photo; 10.9.3: Friedrich Stark/Alamy Stock Photo; 10.10.1: Jake Lyell/Alamy Stock Photo; 10.10.2: Rob Arnold/Alamy Stock Photo; 10.10.3: Chris Cooper-Smith/Alamy Stock Photo; 10.10.4: Joerg Boethling/Alamy Stock Photo; 10.CR.1: Duy Phuong Nguyen/Alamy Stock Photo; 10.CR.2: Novarc Images/Alamy Stock Photo; 10.CR.3: Paul Coleman/Alamy Stock Photo; 10.CR.4: Vibrant Pictures/Alamy Stock Photo; 10.CR.5: Zute Lightfoot/Alamy Stock Photo; p. 267 (GeoVideo): BBC Worldwide Americas, Inc.

Chapter 11 CO11.1: Jim West/AGE Fotostock; CO11.3: Archimage-Aerial/Alamy Stock Photo; CO11.4: The Photo Works/Alamy Stock Photo; CO11.5: ZUMA Press Inc/Alamy Stock Photo; 11.1.1: Pictorial Press Ltd/Alamy Stock Photo; 11.2.1: devi/Alamy Stock Photo; 11.2.2: dpa picture alliance/Alamy Stock Photo;

11.2.3: James M. Rubenstein; 11.2.4: Archimage-Aerial/Alamy Stock Photo; 11.3.1: Friedrich Stark/Alamy Stock Photo; 11.3.2b: Joerg Boethling/Alamy Stock Photo; 11.3.3: robertharding/Alamy Stock Photo; 11.3.5: James M. Rubenstein; 11.4.1: JG Photography/Alamy Stock Photo; 11.5.2: Aurora Photos/Alamy Stock Photo; 11.5.6: SQUIB/Alamy Stock Photo; 11.7.1: Steve Vidler/Alamy Stock Photo; 11.7.5: ZUMA Press Inc/Alamy Stock Photo; 11.8.6: The Photo Works/Alamy Stock Photo; 11.9.4: CREATIVE COLLECTION TOLBERT PHOTO/Alamy Stock Photo; 11.9.5: dpa picture alliance archive/Alamy Stock Photo; 11.CR.1: Blaize Pascall/Alamy Stock Photo; 11.CR.2: Carolyn Jenkins/Alamy Stock Photo; 11.CR.3: Graham Oliver/Alamy Stock Photo; 11.CR.4: Rolf Hicker Photography/Alamy Stock Photo; p. 289 (GeoVideo): BBC Worldwide Americas, Inc.; 11.CR.6: ZUMA Press, Inc./Alamy Stock Photo

Chapter 12 CO12.1: Roman Babakin/Alamy Stock Photo; CO12.3: David Pearson/Alamy Stock Photo; CO12.4: AfriPics.com/Alamy Stock Photo; CO12.5: Jonathan Weiss/Alamy Stock Photo; 12.2.1: Vespasian/Alamy Stock Photo; 12.2.3: William Mullins/Alamy Stock Photo; 12.3.2: age fotostock/Alamy Stock Photo; 12.2.3: robertharding/Alamy Stock Photo; 12.3.4: LOOK Die Bildagentur der Fotografen GmbH/Alamy Stock Photo; 12.3.6: Mira/Alamy Stock Photo; 12.4.1: StanRohrer/Getty Images; 12.4.2: Food Access Research Atlas, United States Department of Agriculture Economic Research Service, http://www.ers.usda.gov/data-products/food-access-research-atlas/go-to-the-atlas.aspx; 12.4.3: Food Access Research Atlas, United States Department of Agriculture Economic Research Service, http://www.ers.usda.gov/data-products/food-access-research-atlas/go-to-the-atlas.aspx; 12.4.5: Jonathan Weiss/Alamy Stock Photo; 12.5.1: Jake Lyell/Alamy Stock Photo; 12.5.2: Russell Hart/Alamy Stock Photo; 12.5.3: UrbanImages/Alamy Stock Photo; 12.5.4: VIEW Pictures Ltd/Alamy Stock Photo; 12.6.1: Steven Charles/Alamy Stock Photo; 12.6.4: Sean Pavone/Alamy Stock Photo; 12.7.2: David Pearson/Alamy Stock Photo; 12.9.1: AfriPics.com/Alamy Stock Photo; 12.9.2: All Canada Photos/Alamy Stock Photo; 12.9.3: Aerial Archives/Alamy Stock Photo; 12.9.4: Cotswolds Photo Library/Alamy Stock Photo; 12.10.1: Geof Kirby/Alamy Stock Photo; 12.10.4: arabianEye FZ LLC/Alamy Stock Photo; 12.10.7: Vichaya Kiatying-Angsulee/Alamy Stock Photo; 12.11.1: Aerial Archives/Alamy Stock Photo; 12.11.4: Xinhua/Alamy Stock Photo; 12.CR.2: Danita Delimont/Alamy Stock Photo; 12.CR.3: Kumar Sriskandan/Alamy Stock Photo; 12.CR.4: Paul Matzner/Alamy Stock Photo; p. 314 (GeoVideo): BBC Worldwide Americas, Inc.; 12.CR.7: Pegaz/Alamy Stock Photo

Chapter 13 CO13.1: Hemis/Alamy Stock Photo; CO13.2: Alex Segre/Alamy Stock Photo; CO13.3: Guillermo Montesinos/AGE Fotostock; CO13.4: Michael J. Kronmal/Alamy Stock Photo; CO13.5: Sean Pavone/Alamy Stock Photo; 13.2.1: Sean Pavone/Alamy Stock Photo; 13.2.2: Stephanie Sellers/Alamy Stock Photo; 13.2.3: Clarence Holmes Photography/Alamy Stock Photo; 13.2.4: Michael Snell/Alamy Stock Photo; 13.3.2: Danita Delimont/Alamy Stock Photo; 13.3.4: Patra Kongsirimongkolchai/Alamy Stock Photo; 13.3.6: Bruce Leibowitz/Alamy Stock Photo; 13.3.8: RosalreneBetancourt 9/Alamy Stock Photo; 13.4.2: Don Despain/Alamy Stock Photo; 13.4.3: picturelibrary/Alamy Stock Photo; 13.4.5: Michael J. Kronmal/Alamy Stock Photo; 13.5.1: edpics/Alamy Stock Photo; 13.5.2: Holger Burmeister/Alamy Stock Photo; 13.5.4: Agencja Fotograficzna Caro/Alamy Stock Photo; 13.5.6: Godong/Alamy Stock Photo; 13.5.8: Hemis/Alamy Stock Photo; 13.6.3: DEA PICTURE LIBRARY/Contributor/Getty Images; 13.6.4: DEA/G DAGLI ORTI/AGE Fotostock; 13.6.5: National Geographic Creative/Alamy Stock Photo; 13.6.7: robertharding/Alamy Stock Photo; 13.7.3: imageBROKER/Alamy Stock Photo; 13.7.5: Guillermo Montesinos/AGE Fotostock; 13.8.1: Matt May/Alamy Stock Photo; 13.8.6: A.P.S. (UK)/Alamy Stock Photo; 13.9.1: Ira Berger/Alamy Stock Photo; 13.9.3: Transit Trips By Mode: 2012, United States Department of Transportation, http://www.rita.dot.gov/bts/sites/rita.dot.gov.bts/files/PassengerTravelFactsFigures.pdf; 13.9.4: CAMimage/Alamy Stock Photo; 13.9.5: Juan Jimenez/Alamy Stock Photo; 13.10.1: Xinhua/Alamy Stock Photo; 13.10.3: Alex Segre/Alamy Stock Photo; 13.10.4: Images-USA/Alamy Stock Photo; 13.CR.1: Bella Falk/Alamy Stock Photo; 13.CR.2: Gijsbert Hanekroot/Alamy Stock Photo; 13.CR.3: Patrick Smith/Staff/Getty Images; 13.CR.4: Yvette Cardozo/Alamy Stock Photo; p. 339 (GeoVideo): BBC Worldwide Americas, Inc.; 13.CR.6: SUNG KUK KIM/Alamy Stock Photo

Chapter 14 CO14.1: Jim West/Alamy Stock Photo; CO14.2: DigitalVues/Alamy Stock Photo; CO14.3: Ellen Isaacs/Alamy Stock Photo; CO14.4: Jim West/Alamy Stock Photo; CO14.5: Stu/Alamy Stock Photo; 14.1.1: Peter W Titmuss/Alamy Stock Photo; 14.2.6: Jim West/Alamy Stock Photo; 14.3.7: DigitalVues/Alamy Stock Photo; 14.5.2: ZUMA Press, Inc./Alamy Stock Photo; 14.6.2: Jim Parkin/Alamy Stock Photo; 14.6.3: Hong Hanh Mac Thi/Alamy Stock Photo; 14.6.4: Universal Images Group North America LLC/Alamy Stock Photo; 14.7.1: David Grossman/Alamy Stock Photo; 14.7.3: Inga Spence/Alamy Stock Photo; 14.7.5 David Grossman/Alamy Stock Photo; 14.7.6: Stu/Alamy Stock Photo; 14.8.4: Philip Scalia/Alamy Stock Photo; 14.9.1: dpa picture alliance archive/Alamy Stock Photo; 14.9.2: Gavin Rodgers/Alamy Stock Photo; 14.9.3: MediaWorldImages/Alamy Stock Photo; 14.9.4: Michael Doolittle/Alamy Stock Photo; 14.9.5: MShieldsPhotos/Alamy Stock Photo; 14.9.8: Ellen Isaacs/Alamy Stock Photo; 14.10.5: Philipus/Alamy Stock Photo; 14.10.6: US Air Force Photo/Alamy Stock Photo; 14.CR.1: David Grossman/Alamy Stock Photo; 14.CR.2: Design Pics Inc/Alamy Stock Photo; 14.CR.3: Jochen Tack/Alamy Stock Photo; 14.CR.4: Ruth Grimes/Alamy Stock Photo; 14.CR.5: Sebastien Bonaime/Alamy Stock Photo; p. 362 (GeoVideo): BBC Worldwide Americas, Inc.

Front insert International Mapping, Inc.

Back insert Defense Meteorological Satellite Program (DMSP) NASA/GSFC.

Cover Chan Srithaweeporn/Getty Images

Index

Note: Page numbers followed by "f " indicate the entry is within a figure.

C

D

T

U

Earth at Night, City Lights

The Americas

These images of Earth at night from NASA's Suomi-NPP "Marble" series use a collection of satellite-based observations, stitched together in a seamless mosaic of our planet. This view is based on instrumentation that observes light emanating from the ground. Notice how strongly major population clusters show up in the image.

Africa, Europe, and the Middle East

Defense Meteorological Satellite Program (DMSP) NASA/GSFC